DATE DUE

SE 8 '97			
MR 12 '98			
FE 9 '99			
DE 19 '01			
AG 8 '02			
DE 21 '03			

DEMCO 38-296

The Life of Adam Smith

The Life of Adam Smith

Ian Simpson Ross

CLARENDON PRESS · OXFORD

1995

...ton Street, Oxford OX2 6DP

...ew York

...Bangkok Bombay

...Dar es Salaam Delhi

... Istanbul Karachi

...as Madrid Melbourne
Mexico City Nairobi Paris Singapore
Taipei Tokyo Toronto

and associated companies in
Berlin Ibadan

Oxford is a trade mark of Oxford University Press

Published in the United States
by Oxford University Press Inc., New York

British Library Cataloguing in Publication Data
Data available

Library of Congress Cataloging in Publication Data
Data available
ISBN 0–19–828821–2

1 3 5 7 9 10 8 6 4 2

Typeset by Hope Services (Abingdon) Ltd.
Printed and bound in Great Britain
by Bookcraft (Bath) Ltd.

In memory of
Carolyn and Ernest Mossner

Acknowledgements

My first acknowledgement is to my teacher at the University of Texas, Ernest Campbell Mossner, who asked me in 1964 to help with the preparation of an edition of the correspondence of Adam Smith commissioned by the Adam Smith Committee of the University of Glasgow. Ill health including eye problems forced him to give up this project in the early 1970s, and at his suggestion the Glasgow Committee asked me to complete the correspondence edition and write a biography of Smith. Professor Mossner took a lively interest in this work until his death in 1986, and helped me immensely by passing on his Smith notes and references. His wife Carolyn was also most supportive and encouraging about the Smith project, and I have dedicated my book to these never to be forgotten friends.

In writing this book I have called upon an enormous amount of help from colleagues, among whom I number many former students who worked with me to understand Smith's personality and thought, and friends from many walks of life. I wish to record with much affection and gratitude the readiness of the late Charles Finlayson of Edinburgh University Library, and the late Ian Rae of the National Library of Scotland, in answering queries and fulfilling requests for material. I have been similarly advantaged by their successors in their respective institutions, and by their counterparts in Aberdeen University Library; American Philosophical Society Library, Philadelphia; Andersonian Library, Strathclyde University; Archives Départementales de l'Hérault, Montpellier; Archives Départementales, Toulouse; Balliol College Library and the Bodleian, Oxford; Bibliothèque Nationale and Musée Carnavalet, Paris; Bibliothèque de l'Université de Genève; Boswell Office and Yale University Library; British Library; Dr Williams's Library, London; Edinburgh University Library; Glasgow University Library; House of Lords Record Office, Westminster; Huntington Library, Pasadena; Kent County Archives; Kirkcaldy District Council Administrative Office and Kirkcaldy Museum and Art Gallery; Public Record Office, Kew; Scottish Record Office, Edinburgh; Statni Oblastni Archiv, Klatovy, Czech Republic; and the University of British Columbia Library. I wish to thank warmly the librarians and keepers in these institutions for permission to consult and quote from material in their control. Quotations from SRO holdings appear with the approval of the Keeper of the Records of Scotland. Also, I wish to express my grateful appreciation to Col. A. E. Cameron, Aldourie Castle, Inverness, and Mr Keith Adam, Blair Adam, Kinross, for their willingness to let me quote from MSS they own.

Among many acts of kindness I wish to record the following. Beryl Skinner and Beth Buchanan gave invaluable help in producing texts and print-outs of drafts of chapters. May Brown of Burntisland sought out facts for me about the Kirkcaldy of Smith's time, and Customs officers in the 'lang toun' told me tales of Fife smugglers. Andrew Skinner walked with me through old Glasgow, from the cathedral to the Trongate and beyond, to view sites connected with Smith's student and professorial years. For almost thirty years he has provided a steady stream of advice about Smith's ideas generally, and his contributions in particular to the history of economic thought. Vincent Quinn helped me with Balliol College archives. Nicole Vallée was my guide in Paris exploring the haunts of the *philosophes*, where Smith encountered Quesnay and Turgot. Bernard Gagnebin advised me about sources dealing with Smith's contacts in Geneva. Peter Thal and Norbert Waszek provided key information about Smith's early impact on German thinkers.

In 1993, on a research visit to Germany, Hermann Real and Ulrich Horstmann invited me to present accounts of Smith's rhetoric and critical theory to their students at the Universities of Münster and Giessen. Hans G. Monissen and Rüdiger Ahrens invited me to lecture about Smith's ideas concerning language and economics at the University of Würzburg. Also, they organized a seminar on Adam Smith at Bildungszentrum Kloster Banz, at which I discussed my biographical approach to Smith with economics and English students and professors. This seminar was supported by a grant from the Hanns Martin Schleyer-Stiftung.

Over the years, Hiroshi Mizuta has responded promptly to many queries about Smith's Library, and he introduced me to courteous and obliging colleagues knowledgeable about Smith materials and scholarship in Japan: Yoshiaki Sudo, Toshihiro Tanaka, Hitoshi Hashimoto, and Hisashi Shinohara. During visits to Japan in 1985 and 1990, I had stimulating opportunities to discuss Smith's thought with Japanese faculty and students, also to examine Smith editions and documents much valued in their country.

John Dwyer awakened me to the social history connected with Smith's writings, and Michael Barfoot passed on his insights into Smith's medical history. Richard Sher generously made known to me important information about the Edinburgh literati, and Roger Emerson was never stumped when I called for some help about the Scottish Enlightenment.

I acknowledge gratefully that so much that is factually new in this book is due to the indefatigable researches of David Raynor on Hume and his circle. He has upheld, I believe, the highest ideals of scholarship in communicating his results to me and offering a commentary on them. I am equally indebted tō D. D. Raphael for his abiding interest in the writing of this biography. During the lengthy period of its composition, he has commented sympathetically and with judicious criticism on all problems and attempts at solutions that I have submitted to him.

I am also very grateful for the research awards and grants I have received from the Canada Council, the University of British Columbia, and the Killam Foundation in 1977–8, 1979, 1981, 1987–8, and 1989–92, which made possible work on specific aspects of Smith research and some of the writing of the book. In the summers of 1983–6 I was fortunate in securing BC Government Work Study grants for student assistants: Ted Alden, Alpha Demchuk, Elizabeth Hannon, and David Ransom, whose cheerful and efficient help I greatly appreciate. In 1992 John Marriott obtained another Work Study grant to help me with bibliographical references. I should also mention that in 1978, when acting as my research assistant, Alison Schwalm followed up some leads I had at the PRO, Kew, and recovered important Customs documents connected with Smith. Further, I take pleasure in recollecting that in January–February 1978 T. D. Campbell came to Vancouver on a British Academy award to work with me on aspects of Smith's moral philosophy illuminated by a biographical approach. As well, I wish to acknowledge the help and encouragement I received from the remarkable team of scholars who produced the six volumes of Smith's works published by the Clarendon Press between 1976 and 1983: J. C. Bryce, R. H. Campbell, A. L. Macfie, R. L. Meek, D. D. Raphael, A. S. Skinner, P. G. Stein, W. B. Todd, and W. P. D. Wightman.

Members of my family have provided solid support throughout this enterprise: my brother Angus; the young people—Isla, Bettina, Andrew, David, and Marion; and above all my dear wife, Ingrid, who has done so much to help me put my work in a form ready for publication. Somehow amid all pressures she has kept her equanimity, restored her husband's, and sustained happy companionship. Much of the book was written and rewritten at Bardscroft on Gambier Island, British Columbia, in the presence of our cat Fergus. In need of stimulation in daylight hours, I could always look out from my study window towards the rolling sea and the blue-green mountains of the north-west Pacific coastline: a far cry from Kirkcaldy and the Firth of Forth, but a setting I found conducive to evoking that Fife lad of genius who grew up two centuries ago by those distant waves and shore.

I.S.R.

Gambier Island, British Columbia
31 December 1994

Contents

List of Plates

References and Abbreviations

I. REFERENCES TO ADAM SMITH'S WORKS

Corr.   *Correspondence*, ed. E. C. Mossner and I. S. Ross (2nd edn., 1987).

EPS   *Essays on Philosophical Subjects*, ed. W. P. D. Wightman, J. C. Bryce, and I. S. Ross; general eds. D. D. Raphael and A. S. Skinner (1980).

ed. Wightman:
'Ancient Logics': 'The History of the Ancient Logics and Metaphysics'.
'Ancient Physics': 'The History of the Ancient Physics'.
'Astronomy': 'The History of Astronomy'.
'External Senses': 'Of the External Senses'.
'Imitative Arts': 'Of the Nature of that Imitation which takes place in what are called "The Imitative Arts"'.
'Music': 'Of the Affinity between Music, Dancing, and Poetry'.

ed. Bryce:
'English and Italian Verses': 'Of the Affinity between certain English and Italian Verses'.
Review of Johnson's *Dictionary*: 'A Dictionary of the English Language by Samuel Johnson' (*Edinburgh Review*, 1755).
'Letter': 'A Letter to the Authors of the *Edinburgh Review*' (1755–6).
Preface to Hamilton's *Poems*: Preface and Dedication to William Hamilton's *Poems on Several Occasions* (1748).

ed. Ross:
Stewart: Dugald Stewart, 'Account of the Life and Writings of Adam Smith, LL.D.'.

TMS   *The Theory of Moral Sentiments*, ed. D. D. Raphael and A. L. Macfie (1976).

WN   *An Inquiry into the Nature and Causes of the Wealth of Nations*, ed. R. H. Campbell and A. S. Skinner; textual editor W. B. Todd (1976).

LJ   *Lectures on Jurisprudence*, ed. R. L. Meek, D. D. Raphael, and P. G. Stein (1978).

(A) Report of 1762–3.
(B) Report of 1766.
ED: Early Draft of *WN*.
Fragment A (FA): First Fragment on the Division of Labour.
Fragment B (FB): Division of Labour Second Fragment on the Division of Labour.

LRBL   *Lectures on Rhetoric and Belles Lettres*, ed. J. C. Bryce (1983).
Languages: *Considerations Concerning the First Formation of Languages*.
'Smith Anecdotes': 'Anecdotes of the late Dr Smith' (*The Bee*, 3, 11 May 1791).

References to *Corr.* give letter numbers; for *LJ* and *LRBL* give volume and page number from the manuscripts as displayed in the cited editions; for *TMS* and *WN* give part
of book and section and paragraph numbers; and for *EPS* give section and paragraph
numbers. Italicized numbers direct readers to introductions of these editions.

2. OTHER FREQUENTLY CITED WORKS AND SOURCES:

AUL	Aberdeen University Library.
BL	British Library, London.
BLJ	*Boswell's Life of Johnson, Together with Boswell's Journal of a Tour to the Hebrides and Johnson's Diary of a Journey into North Wales*, ed. G. B. Hill, rev. L. F. Powell (6 vols., Oxford: Clarendon Press, 1934–50; v–vi rev. 1964).
BP	*Private Papers of James Boswell from Malahide Castle*, ed. G. Scott and F. A. Pottle (18 vols., New York: privately printed, 1928–34).
Corr.	Correspondence.
DSB	*Dictionary of Scientific Biography*, eds. in chief Charles Coulston Gillispie and Frederic L. Holmes (18 vols., New York: Scribner's, 1970–90).
EUL	Edinburgh University Library.
GUA	Glasgow University Archives.
GUL	Glasgow University Library.
HLRO	House of Lords Record Office, London.
HMSO	Her Majesty's Stationery Office.
HP	*The History of Parliament: The House of Commons 1754–1790*, ed. Sir Lewis Namier and John Brooke (3 vols., HMSO, 1964).
Hume,	
Essays	*Essays Moral, Political, and Literary*, ed. Eugene F. Miller (rev. edn., Indianapolis: Liberty Classics, 1987).
Dialogues	*Dialogues concerning Natural Religion*, ed. Norman Kemp Smith (Oxford: Clarendon Press, 1935).
Enquiries	*Enquiries concerning Human Understanding and concerning the Principles of Morals*, ed. L. A. Selby-Bigge (3rd edn., rev. P. H. Nidditch, Oxford: Clarendon Press, 1974).
History of England	*The History of England, from the Invasion of Julius Caesar to the Revolution in 1688*, with the Author's last corrections and improvements (8 vols., Edinburgh: G. Mudie *et al.*, 1792).
HL	*The Letters of David Hume*, ed. J. Y. T. Greig (2 vols., 1932, Oxford: Clarendon Press, repr. 1969).
Letters to Hume	*Letters of Eminent Persons addressed to David Hume*, ed. J. Hill Burton (Edinburgh: Blackwood, 1849).
NHL	*New Letters of David Hume*, ed. Raymond Klibansky and Ernest C. Mossner (1954, Oxford: Clarendon Press, repr. 1969).
Phil. Wks.	*The Philosophical Works*, ed. T. H. Green and T. H. Grose (4 vols., London: Longmans, Green, 1874–5).

Political Essays	*Hume: Political Essays*, ed. Knud Haakonssen (Cambridge University Press, 1994).
T	*A Treatise of Human Nature*, ed. L. A. Selby-Bigge (2nd edn., rev. P. H. Nidditch, Oxford: Clarendon Press, 1978).
Writings on Economics	*Writings on Economics*, ed. Eugene Rotwein (Madison: University of Wisconsin Press, 1955).
JHI	*Journal of the History of Ideas.*
Mizuta	*Adam Smith's Library: A Catalogue*, ed. Hiroshi Mizuta (typescript, 1994).
NLS	National Library of Scotland, Edinburgh.
NRA(S)	National Register of Archives, Scotland, SRO, Edinburgh.
PRO	Public Record Office, Kew, London.
RSE	Royal Society of Edinburgh.
RSL	Royal Society of London.
SRO	Scottish Record Office, Edinburgh.
SVEC	*Studies on Voltaire and the Eighteenth Century.*

Introduction

The smallest circumstances, the most minute transactions of a great man are
sought after with eagerness.

Ever since the writings of Adam Smith about morals and economics reached the
reading public, over 200 years ago, they have excited controversy. The debate
about the meaning of the systems of ideas appearing under his name, and their
application to contemporary society, is as lively as ever. Is it not dangerous to
base judgements about good and bad on feelings rather than reason? How can
we arrive at moral standards that are higher than those commonly accepted? Is
everybody prepared to swap or sell or bargain to achieve material advantage?
Should citizens insist that governments free markets as an essential part of a civil
society? In Moscow and Manchester, Nagoya and Nantes, Toronto and Turin,
Düsseldorf and Detroit, certainly, access to the wealth of nations is sought
through understanding or refuting Smithian free-market economics. The individual liberty associated with this is prized, but, as Ernest Gellner (1994) has
reminded us, the conditions for civil society that incorporates a free or relatively
free market are not easily created. Also, proponents of communitarian interests
and needs, such as Amitai Etzioni (1994), argue that the pursuit of self-interest
appropriate for the market-place, as Smith recognized, should have its limits.
Above all, they should not determine the nature of the loving relationships and
dutiful obligations of family and civic life.

This biography of Smith, the first full-scale one to be attempted since John
Rae's was published exactly 100 years ago, is based on two considerations relevant to ongoing debates in which his name is invoked. The first is that we are
naturally curious about the life of a writer of such wide influence as Smith.
Second, examination of both the writing and reading of texts is necessary to clarify and particularize their range of meanings. Plausible reconstruction of the
meanings of Smith's discourses from a historical standpoint can be helpfully con-
textualized by the life story. Rational, intertextualized interpretations can be
offered in the light of available commentary from intellectual disciplines to which
Smith's work made a contribution. The aim here is not to foreclose meaning by
strictly delimiting an author's intentions, surely an impossible task. Rather, a
remarkable personality can be depicted in identifiable settings, at work as a writer
on an array of subjects that, surprisingly, goes well beyond morals and economics. Also, the biography can objectively record what contemporary readers and
first translators made of Smith and his discourses, and how he viewed their
responses.

The story told in the following chapters, then, concerns a fatherless and sickly

child born in 1723 into a relatively well-to-do family in Kirkcaldy, a seaport on
the Firth of Forth opposite Edinburgh, where his dead father had been a
Customs officer. His country had a recent bloody past of wars fought over political supremacy and religion, but his father's family had been on the winning side
of the Protestant Whigs. Smith summed up this struggle by saying: 'our forefathers kicked out the Pope and the Pretender [to] preserve the pretious right of
private judgment' (*Corr.* No. 50). Here was one historical source of Smith's feeling for the 'natural liberty' he thought everyone should enjoy. This 'liberty' was
to be exercised responsibly, however, through self-command, a lesson Smith
probably learned first from his mother, Margaret Douglas. She was a remarkable
woman with firm religious values, who brought him through an illness-ridden
childhood and encouraged him to become a scholar of distinction. Through her
long life she continued to provide domestic stability for him.

This book stresses Smith's good fortune in his early education, first, on the
formal side, in the Kirkcaldy burgh school, where he was given a strong foundation in English composition and classical studies introducing him to Roman
history. Second, informally, he learned much about practical affairs from observation of local industries and the improving state of agriculture in the Fife hin-
terland. His father's friends who acted as guardians participated in the early
stages of the Enlightenment in Scotland, a movement of cosmopolitan outlook
which tried to better human lives through achieving more effective communication, recognition of the emotional basis of personality, clarity about motives and
values, and development of scientific thought, as well as its application to social
and economic problems. Our discussion traces Smith's contribution in these
respects to the Enlightenment.

Smith encountered leading Scottish figures in this movement when he went
on to Glasgow University (1737–40), where he became vitally interested in
Newtonian physics and mathematics, and also in Stoic philosophy emphasizing
self-command as a cardinal virtue. His principal inspiration was the 'never to be
forgotten' Francis Hutheson, whose teaching became the basis for Smith's moral
philosophy, including his system of economics. Glasgow's setting was also
instructive to Smith in providing an example of a growing economy as contrasted
with the declining one of Kirkcaldy. On the west coast, he could see how wealth
was being created through the expanding market for cross-Atlantic trade with
North America and the Caribbean countries, while trade across the North Sea
had been diminishing. Economic protection favoured Glasgow merchants and
manufacturers, but free trade extended beyond the British empire was a vision
that attracted them.

Following his stimulating experiences in Glasgow, Smith's years as an Oxford
student (1740–6) were an intellectual anticlimax, since the well-endowed dons
had little interest in teaching. Nevertheless, wide and intensive reading on his
own, at the cost of what seems to have been a temporary nervous breakdown,
gave Smith further command of the classics and introduced him to literature in

modern languages. In time, he drew on this reading to illustrate his favourite study of the interaction of political and economic history. Our discussion brings out the fact that Smith was later to reason that the inefficiency of the Oxford system of education came from the lack of academic competition and incentive in rich colleges where the members had easy livings. This insight supplemented what he had to say about the energizing and regulatory role of competition in sustaining the maximum utility of the general market.

Beginning his career as a teacher, Smith spent three extraordinarily seminal years (1748–51) as a freelance lecturer in Edinburgh. In the Scottish capital he met and formed a lasting friendship with David Hume, according to Smith 'by far the most illustrious philosopher and historian of the present age' (*WN* v.i.g.3). At the risk of the charge of speculation, for hard details are few, the biography dwells on the importance of this creative period in Smith's life. It was one of reconstruction in Scotland after the failure of the Jacobite rising of 1745, when there was an attempt to put the Stuart Pretender, James III, back on the throne of Britain and, some believed, to restore the supremacy of the Pope. Smith was brought to Edinburgh by Scottish leaders to teach rhetoric and criticism, mainly focused on English literature. One intention was to give the young professionals who attended his classes sufficient command of received standard English to allow them to share in the economic and other opportunities afforded by a Hanoverian British state and an empire run from London. It was hoped this would keep the country united and free from political violence. Smith's lectures in this series also included a theory of communication, distinguishing between types of discourse, principally the didactic or scientific type meant to convince by reasoned argument, and the rhetorical, designed to persuade by moving the passions. For the most part, he practised what he taught in using plain language as the vehicle of his didactic writings, to communicate his ideas effectively. He also used figurative language and other rhetorical strategies to sway his readers' feelings, which gives his writings pace and variety, yielding considerable pleasure.

In addition at Edinburgh, Smith gave a course of lectures on the history of philosophy or science, represented by a history of astronomy. A key part is Smith's theory of theorizing, which has one source in Hume's philosophy. Smith's account is that theorizing arises from the interplay of our emotions of surprise, wonder, and admiration, and the creative role of the imagination in bestowing order on the succession of our ideas. This order is expressed in the form of a system, defined as an 'imaginary machine' invented to provide a coherent pattern of cause and effect in phenomena. Smith says systems are to be judged not on the basis of their predictive power, but as to their success in soothing the imagination, also in achieving coherence and enhancing our response to the objects they covered. This is the clue, he reckons, that guides us through the 'labyrinths of philosophical history'.

This type of historical inquiry became a favourite tool of the philosophical writers in eighteenth-century Scotland. A contemporary observed that something like it was to be found in all of Smith's works, 'moral, political, or literary' (Stewart ii.44). In these works, as this book discusses, systems are presented in which a connecting principle—in particular, sympathy in ethics and division of labour in economics—binds together discordant phenomena with explanatory force. As for 'philosophical history', it involved accounting for the development of beliefs, practices, theories, and institutions on the basis of natural causes or principles, when actual records and reports of witnesses were lacking.

Smith turned again to 'philosophical history' in the third private course he gave at Edinburgh on 'civil law' or, more broadly, jurisprudence, which seems to have dealt with the 'general principles which ought to be the foundation of the laws of nations'. Our discussion suggests that, in this course, Smith dealt with the emergence of the institutions of 'civil society' in humanity's 'progress' through the four socioeconomic stages of hunting and fishing, pastoralism, agriculture, and commerce. A major theme developed by Smith in this context was the value of economic liberty for civil society. He urged that little more was needed to bring a state from 'barbarism' to 'opulence' but 'peace, easy taxes, and a tolerable administration of justice'. Here, too, he denounced interventionist governments as 'unnatural' and forced to become 'oppressive and tyrannical' (Stewart iv.25). In this course, then, he foreshadowed the free-enterprise model of the market economy ultimately presented in *WN*. He also foreshadowed *WN*'s allotment of the role of provider of limited public goods to the state.

The Edinburgh law lectures were so successful that in 1751 Smith was elected a Professor at his old University in Glasgow. He occupied first the Chair of Logic, and delivered a course taught in English on rhetoric and criticism. This was perceived as the 'best method of explaining and illustrating the various powers of the human mind' (Stewart i.16). The biography records that Smith's innovative approach to a foundation university course had considerable impact, because it was imitated in Scotland and in North American colleges, such as Princeton, influenced by Scottish education.

Since the Moral Philosophy Professor was ill, Smith taught the jurisprudence and politics sections of his course, in which economics had a part, derived from Hutcheson's teaching on value and price. When his colleague died in 1752, Smith was translated to his Chair. His public course in moral philosophy was organized in four parts. The first dealt with natural religion, presenting Smith's system of deistic belief ultimately derived from Stoicism, distanced from the orthodox Calvinist Christianity of Scotland, and certainly reflected in his moral philosophy of a contemplative utilitarian cast, which has a place for divinely ordained and harmoniously operating natural laws. The second investigated ethics, in particular the doctrines later published in *TMS*, in which sympathy is depicted as the hinge of moral life. The third part took up Justice, through examining the development of legal institutions evolved in 'civil history', and tracing the interactions of economics and government. The last part focused on expediency, comprehending 'political regulations . . . calculated to increase the riches, the power, and the prosperity of the state', which gave rise to *WN* (Stewart i.18–19). The biography follows the development of Smith's ideas from the presentation in lectures to their published form in *TMS* and *WN*.

Smith's personality is also brought out from the reports of his thirteen years as a Professor (1751–64), which late in life he remembered as 'by far the most useful, and, therefore, as by far the happiest and most honourable' of his career (*Corr.* No. 274). The subjects he taught became fashionable in Glasgow, and his opinions were debated in clubs and societies, including Provost Cochrane's Political Economy Club, where he exchanged ideas with merchants and manufacturers knowledgeable about trade with the American colonies and contemporary economic issues such as banking problems. By repute an archetypal absent-minded professor, Smith was entrusted by the University with sensitive administrative duties which he discharged ably, though his 'warmth' could not always be cooled down by sympathy. His ethics lectures suggested this mechanism could operate through an agent's attunement to the more restrained feelings of others, as well as by arousing the feelings of a bystander witnessing another person's understandable anger or pleasure.

Smith had his first success as a man of letters, and became famous as a contributor to the European Enlightenment, with the publication of his ethics lectures, new-cast as *TMS*, in 1759. The biography explores first the making of this fascinating work, now favoured as 'dialogic' according to the distinctions pioneered by the modern critic Bakhtin (1975/1981), because of its interplay of different voices (Brown, 1994). Second, there is offered exploration of the immediate criticism of its first readers, Hume and other figures in the Scottish Enlightenment such as Thomas Reid and Adam Ferguson. This could be viewed as an opportunity to see reception theory (Iser, 1972/1974; Fish, 1980; 1989) contemporaneously in action.

Smith's book is a direct challenge to the theories of intrinsic human selfishness advanced by Hobbes and Mandeville and also, closer to the date of its publication, by Rousseau. In defining what virtue is, and why we should act virtuously, Smith offers a sophisticated extension of the arguments of Hume and Hutcheson to the effect that our moral and aesthetic judgements and imperatives are based on feelings. The chief component in the system which unfolds is the role of sympathy in human transactions, through which we naturally judge the conduct and character of others and then, according to Smith, ourselves. Readers saw that in developing a system according to the ideas of the lectures on rhetoric and on the history of astronomy, Smith was presenting a kind of 'moral Newtonianism'. As one of them wrote: '[*TMS* is] founded on Sympathy, a very ingenious attempt to account for the principal phaenomina in the moral world from this one general principle, like that of Gravity in the natural world' (James Wodrow, June 1808: Mitchell Lib., Glasgow, Buchan MSS, Baillie 32225, fos. 47–51). The biography also traces, through successive editions of *TMS*, Smith's development of another main component of his system, that of the impartial spectator, introduced to account for our normative judgements of ourselves. The impartial spectator also appears in the lectures on jurisprudence to explain how it is that claims to acquired rights can be defended on the basis that evidence of expectation reasonable to an observer can be furnished by a claimant *LJ*(A) i.16–17).

A further important issue addressed in the review of Smith's moral economy and microeconomy is his rejection of utility as an explanation of the origin of moral rules. Our account stresses the fact, however, that Smith does apply the criterion of utility, formulated by Hutcheson as procuring the 'greatest happiness for the greatest numbers' (*An Inquiry into the Original of our Ideas of Beauty and Virtue*, 1725, ii. 164, in Hutcheson, 1969: i) when evaluating practices, institutions, and system (including economic ones). Identifying this procedure leads to the biography's claim that Smith is a contemplative rather than an operational utilitarian. It is from this perspective that we can understand the reference to the 'invisible hand' in *TMS* (developed further with reference to economics in *WN*), meaning an aspect of the 'oeconomy of nature'. It is in contemplation that we understand how the selfish rich, pursuing their own ends, help to distribute the 'necessaries of life' and tend to promote human welfare (*TMS* iv.1.10). Smith is not endorsing or advocating selfishness; he is saying that if we stand back from some selfish behaviour, we can see some good coming from it.

The biography recounts how Hume actually read *TMS*, and was active both in criticizing it to stimulate Smith to refine his system of morals, and then in distributing copies to influential people who might help Smith in his career. One of the recipients was the brilliant but erratic politician Charles Townshend, who happened to be stepfather of the young 3rd Duke of Buccleuch. Townshend was so impressed by *TMS* that he prevailed on its author in 1764 to accompany the Duke on a tour abroad as his tutor. This assignment over the next two years took Smith to Toulouse, Geneva, and Paris. Our book brings out the benefits for Smith of this phase of his career. He saw a range of regional economies in operation, and two distinct political systems: autocracy in France and republican oligarchy in Switzerland. In the aftermath of the Seven Years War fought with Britain over colonies and the balance of power in Europe, France was going through a financial crisis, with great tension between the central government and the *parlements* of the provincial cities, including Toulouse, over tax measures. Smith distilled what he saw into *WN*.

Also, through Hume, who had served as Secretary to the British Embassy in Paris, Smith had introductions to the *philosophes*, the foremost men of letters in Europe, among them d'Alembert, Diderot, d'Holbach, and Helvétius, who welcomed him as the author of *TMS*, which had impressed them. Smith visited Paris salons conducted or frequented by some of the foremost women of France, who were not put off by his big teeth and his bad French, but admired his simplicity of heart and great learning, and were sure his philosophy of sympathy was meant for them. One of them, a marquise no less, was said to have fallen in love with Smith, and he to have fallen in love with an English lady, but alas! we have no details of developments, unlike the intriguing story of Hume's involvement with the comtesse de Boufflers.

Near Geneva, he met his 'hero', Voltaire, leading a fight for tolerance in religion, in the aftermath of the dreadful Calas affair in Toulouse, in which a Calvinist father was broken on the wheel and then burned in 1762, for the alleged murder of a son who had turned Catholic and had then taken his own life in a fit of remorse. Voltaire secured a retrial in 1765, and a declaration that Calas was innocent (Bejaoui, 1994). Smith was in Toulouse at this time, and makes use of the case in the sixth and last edition of *TMS* (1790: iii.2.11).

Smith did research on economics in France, and in Paris was welcomed by the Physiocrats, the chief 'sect' of French economists, who held that the land gave rise to wealth, and that agriculture alone could increase it. They considered that manufactures and commerce formed a sterile sector of the economy, and that economic improvement would come only from scientific agriculture and maintenance of fair prices for agricultural products. This 'sect', not Smith, insisted that *laissez-faire*, complete freedom of trade, was necessary to restore the economy to its natural course. Smith respected Quesnay, the leader of the 'sect', and also Turgot, one of his associates, and learned important lessons from them that went into *WN*, for the treatment of topics such as the circulation of capital, and the balance between the productive and unproductive sectors. However, he thought the 'sect' in general was doctrinaire in its bias towards agriculture and against industry and trade.

Quesnay was a court physician, and Smith needed his help when the younger brother of the Duke of Buccleuch became mortally ill in Paris. The young man's death hastened Smith's return to Britain in 1766, when he had the unhappy duty of escorting the body home. The biography recounts Smith's experiences when he remained in London for a year, engaged on research projects for the Government, including work on public finances for Townshend, who was Chancellor of the Exchequer. Smith then returned to Kirkcaldy to live with his mother, still the pole of his existence, until 1773, deeply involved in the perplexing task of composing *WN*. Its medley of many kinds of economic and historical information and currents of argument finally attained unity in the form of discourse that Bakhtinian criticism calls 'monologic'.

The biography offers a fresh account of Smith's activity in refining and adding illustrative material to the system of economics he had taught in his jurisprudence lectures in Glasgow, and making adjustments to free-enterprise theory, as required by his ongoing research and a banking crisis in Scotland. He had to acknowledge that the Government was justified in regulating the money market to control 'beggarly bankers' who were reckless in issuing small notes, and larger-scale bankers who neglected their self-interest in giving way to pressure from clients to get loans that were not properly secured (*WN* ii.ii.73, 90, 94).

The next phase of Smith's life saw him in London from 1773 until 1776, putting finishing touches to *WN* and seeing it through the press, when Parliament was increasingly preoccupied with tumult in the American colonies and measures to suppress their armed rebellion. Evidence is provided of Smith attending debates as a result of his friendship with MPs on both sides of the House. The idea is supported that the publication of *WN* was timed to seize Parliament's attention, and influence Members to support a peaceful resolution of the conflict. America offered a major point of application for free-market theory, and if Smith could win supporters, there was some hope of ending the cycle of violence induced by efforts to preserve the old colonial system involving economic restraints and probitions. Smith was later to give specific policy advice to the Government to disengage from America (*Corr.* app. B).

Hume wrote from Edinburgh in February 1776 that he had heard Smith was 'very zealous in American Affairs', and he expressed anxiety about Smith's delay in publishing his book (*Corr.* No. 149). This anxiety was relieved when *WN* reached him in March, and Hume gave it unstinted praise: 'it has Depth and Solidity and Acuteness, and is so much illustrated by curious Facts that it must at last take the public Attention' (*Corr.* No. 150).

Another early reader, the MP Thomas Pownall, who had served as Governor of Massachusetts Bay and who favoured peaceful reconciliation with the Americans, was highly critical of a number of features of Smith's book, including his theoretical opposition to the monopoly of the colony trade. However, Pownall was greatly impressed by the methodology and explanatory comprehensiveness of its system. He went so far as to suggest that it was comparable at the level of analysis of human society with Newton's *Principia Mathematica*, portraying the operation of celestial mechanics. Accordingly, Pownall judged *WN* might become (as indeed it has) a foundation work in political economy. Here is the entry point of *WN* into the canon of its discipline. To be sure, Foucault, in pursuing the Enlightenment's agenda of liberation by establishing an 'archaeology of the human sciences', has problematized the text, seeing it as taking a step towards a new vision of man as *homo oeconomicus*, 'who spends, wears out, and wastes his life in evading the imminence of death' (Foucault, 1966/1973; Gutting, 1991: 187–8).

Having attended to the matrix for Smith's theorizing constituted by his family background, experience and education, friendships and alliances, temperament and mentality, and intellectual style, the biography offers an account of the two-part structure of *WN*. Books I and II identify and illustrate the principles which lead naturally to economic growth where societies have reached the stage of commerce embodied in market transactions. Books III–V deal with what legislators should and should not do to promote growth.

Smith models the processes of a market society, on which he is one of the first writers to offer extended commentary (Swedberg, 1994), in the form of the 'obvious and simple system of natural liberty' (*WN* IV.ix.51). His exposition of this system has a central role in *WN*. The leading features of the model, with its concept of a freely competitive and self-regulating market, have proved highly attractive up to the present day. Thus, following the collapse of faith in the counter-model of the command economy in the Communist bloc countries after 1989, much advice from Western countries was directed to the new regimes to switch forthwith to the free-market model, and the authority of Adam Smith was invoked to support such a stand.

This situation is wittily evoked in *Adam Smith Goes to Moscow* (Adams and Brock, 1993), in which a sceptical prime minister of a 'newly independent country' confesses to his American adviser that he finds it improbable that independent agriculture producers would 'miraculously make the right decisions' to supply the food market. He is promptly told that he does not understand the 'fundamental principles according to which markets coordinate the decisions of free individuals—the process Adam Smith called the hidden hand [*sic*]' (p. 22). The adviser then provides a version of Smith's argument to the effect that the unintended outcome of the free but just application of the market mechanism is to channel self-interest (not greed) into consumer satisfaction and profit, hence incentive, for the producer. The biography provides a historical perspective on such invocations of Smith by indicating what the 'invisible hand' concept meant in his system (*WN* IV.ii.9).

The second part of *WN* (III–V) proceeds to evaluation of the alternatives to the free-market system, and of the degrees of the emergence of that system. This gives rise to Smith's 'very violent attack . . . upon the whole commercial system of Great Britain' (*Corr.* No. 208), that is, the panoply of government restrictions and trade monopolies intended to promote growth. Smith depicts these measures as thwarting economic activity, against the grain of the 'simple system'. Smith also criticizes the 'agricultural System' of the Physiocrats, whose capital error, he concludes, was making out that those involved in manufacturing and trading did not contribute to a country's economic growth. However, he finds merit in the Physiocrats' definition of the 'wealth of nations as consisting, not in the unconsumable riches of money, but in the consumable goods annually reproduced by the labour of society', and in their prescription of 'perfect [economic] liberty' for maximizing wealth in this sense, though he believes this is a Utopian condition (*WN* IV.ix.38). Smith himself settles for restrictions on individual economic freedom to provide resources for the essential needs of a commercial and truly civil society, which he identifies as defence, justice, public works, and education.

His last chapter deals with 'publick Debts', in his day as in ours a highly important and much debated topic. He ends his discussion with the cogent advice to Britain in 1776 that, if the country cannot make the American colonies contribute to the support of the empire, then she should withdraw and 'endeavour to accommodate her future views and designs to the real mediocrity of her circumstances'. This sentence remained in all the editions of *WN* published in

Smith's lifetime, even after the conclusion of the Peace of Paris in 1782–3, negotiated in part by his friends, Franklin on the American side and the merchant Richard Oswald on the British, and supported, at the cost of the little popularity he had, by the Prime Minister, Shelburne, who declared he was a convert to Smith's economic principles (*EPS* Stewart, n. 1). The retention of *WN*'s last sentence is best seen, perhaps, as the considered advice of the economist and moral philosopher about the requirement that countries and their rulers should awaken from their golden dreams of empire, or of any other 'project' that they cannot pay for, and continue with the pattern of civil history.

The biography discusses the response of leaders of the Scottish Enlightenment to *WN*, and passes to an account of Smith's attendance on Hume in his last months. In the course of this Smith caused his friend some pain through his unwillingness to see through the press Hume's *Dialogues concerning Natural Religion*. Smith stated that this prudential decision was meant to contribute to his 'quiet'. As things fell out, however, he was violently abused by Christians for describing Hume, in a published letter about his death, 'as approaching as nearly to the idea of a perfectly wise and virtuous man, as perhaps the nature of human frailty will permit' (*Corr.* No. 178).

Smith by this time was living in retirement in Kirkcaldy, and working on another book dealing with the 'Imitative Arts', among which he included painting, sculpture, dancing, poetry, and (with qualifications) music. But he was never to finish this. On his appointment as Commissioner of Customs in Scotland in 1778, he moved to Edinburgh to live in Panmure House with his mother, a cousin, Jane Douglas, who acted as housekeeper, and David Douglas, a nephew's son who became his heir. He never permitted himself the leisure away from his official duties to carry through the sustained composition necessary for a major new project. Strange as it may seem at first sight, this apostle of free trade ended his days as a reasonably zealous enforcer of the system of restraints and prohibitions he had attacked so vigorously in *WN*.

The biography offers a reminder, however, that being a customs officer was a family tradition, and that Smith took a keen intellectual interest in relevant issues of public policy. Further, he may have welcomed the structured life required by his post as an antidote to the hypochondriac tendency which intensified, it seems, in his retirement. Also, he was never an across-the-board promoter of *laissez-faire*, and held that there were reasons of state, such as defence, which required restrictions on trade (*WN* IV.ii.24). He also argued there were economic considerations which could justify limits being placed on the natural liberty of individuals to sell their labour, their produce, and their imported wares on the open market. His general position, however, was to advocate removal of all trade barriers, except for the imposition of 'moderate duties' on imports and exports to raise revenue for the valid purposes of ruling a country. 'High duties', he thought, made it scarcely possible to trade fairly in the goods on which they were imposed, and were 'equally favourable to smuggling, as absolute prohibitions'

(*Corr.* No. 203). The chapters on Smith in the custom-house deal with the practical efforts of his Board to combat the rampant smuggling in Scotland, the policy advice he gave governments about this activity, and his efforts to remove trade barriers or at least render them less irksome. New material is introduced here, derived from documents in the Public Record Office, Kew.

Smith declared that he regretted the interruptions of his literary pursuits made by the duties of his office, and the biography records that in 1785 he had two 'great works on the anvil' (*Corr.* No. 248). One was certainly connected with the book on the 'Imitative Arts', since he described it as a 'sort of Philosophical History of all the different branches of Literature, of Philosophy, Poetry and Eloquence'. The other 'great work', whose materials were largely collected and also in part put into 'tollerable good order', was a 'sort of theory and History of Law and Government', which can be connected with Smith's promise at the end of *TMS* to publish a book on the 'theory of jurisprudence'.

By 1785, however, Smith acknowledged that the 'indolence of old age' was settling fast on him, and he felt it was 'uncertain' that he could finish these two projects. The biography describes Smith's efforts, in the face of declining strength and the grievous loss of his mother and Jane Douglas, to leave the works he had already published, in the 'best and most perfect state', behind him (*Corr.* No. 276). Thus, he completed the additions and corrections that went into the standard third edition of *WN* (1784), prepared amid political turmoils. These were occasioned by the ending of the American War under Shelburne, the subsequent Fox–North coalition that came to grief over attempts to reform the East India Company (an organization severely criticized in the third edition of *WN*), and the beginning of the Administration of Pitt the Younger, who read *WN* with attention and heeded its policy advice.

Also, Smith prepared the final sixth edition of *TMS* (1790), containing important insertions such as a further development of the concept of the impartial spectator, and an entirely new Part VI, focused on moral theory applicable to such practical considerations as new-modelling a constitution. These were highly relevant to his time, as the biography indicates, in view of the recent creation of the federally governed United States of America, and the early stages of the French Revolution, of whose serious implications Smith was fully aware. Smith also added a chapter arguing that, while our disposition to admire the rich and powerful is necessary to maintain the 'order of society', it is the 'great and most universal cause of the corruption of our moral sentiments' (*TMS* edn. 6, I.iii.3.1). His Stoic outlook thus afforded him a standpoint for criticism of the mechanisms sustaining the acquisitive society analysed in *WN*.

Smith was highly critical of the slow pace of his writing, expressed disappointment at the end of his life that he had not achieved more, and insisted that his literary executors should burn his manuscripts, so we cannot judge very well what he might have achieved, even taking *EPS* into account. No great fuss was made over his reputation when he died, which was probably what he would have wished, since he was a most unpretentious man. A contributor to the *Edinburgh Review*, the periodical of the era immediately following Smith's death which did more than any other to disseminate critically his ideas on political economy, ventured to state that Smith's attempt to create a system in this field was premature (Fontana, 1985: 52).

Nevertheless, we still seem to find intellectually impressive and provocative Smith's mastery of a way of dealing with the interdependence of economic phenomena: one notable for the 'beauty of systematic arrangement of different observations connected by a few common principles' (*WN* v.i.f.25). The biography also suggests that we should find in Smith not only the economist capable of 'systematic arrangement' that has aesthetic as well as theoretical appeal, but also a theorist of marked ingenuity about the arts and sciences, and above all a realistic moral philosopher with some wisdom about human nature and civil society to impart to his readers.

Historically, biography has been seen as an instrument for helping to resolve debates about a writer's meaning. Evidence about family background, social circle, developing personality and achievement or frustration, personal relationships, education, intellectual context, career, mature disposition, attitudes, aims, beliefs, politics, compositions, publications, impact on others, contemporary criticism, and reactions has been thought to provide clues to an author's intentions and declarations, and hence to what texts mean, even as to how an author believed they might be implemented, if they apply to living styles or institutional arrangements.

To be sure, we live in the latter days of literary criticism and theorizing. Nietzsche's pronouncement (1882/1961) that 'God is dead' has been paralleled by the revelation that 'the Author is dead' (Barthes, 1968/1986; Foucault, 1969/1977). Belief in this dogma is said to lead to privileging the reader rather than the writer, to resistance to closure of texts discussed, and to exploration of the richness of open textual meaning rather than search for overarching authorial intention and hence ultimate meaning (Brown, 1993; 1994). Another view, however, is that the a priori assumptions of the criticism of our times which rejects the concept of authorship, and stresses the indeterminacy of the meaning of texts (Derrida, 1967a/1976; 1967b/1978), may well divert rather than instruct, by dancing on the grave of Adam Smith. The stand of this book is that interpretation linked to the biographical record is a verifiable guide to a significant body of thought, enabling Smith to live on in his writings as long as we are prepared to read and debate him:

> The words of a dead man
> Are modified in the guts of the living.
>
> W. H. Auden

I

Kirkcaldy

a small Town in Scotland the place of my nativity

The Fife seaport of Kirkcaldy, ten miles across the Firth of Forth from Edinburgh, was the scene of Adam Smith's baptism on 5 June 1723. Possibly this was his birth-date, though there is no annotation on the 'Register of Baptismes in the Kirk of Kirkcaldie' (Bonar, 1932: 208), stating 'born this day', as there is in the case of Smith's great friend David Hume (Mossner, 1980: 6). It is reported, however, that as an infant Smith was 'infirm and sickly' (Stewart i.2), and understandable anxieties of the time about infant mortality and salvation often hastened baptism (Flinn, 1977: 284).

Hume, already 12, had begun his studies at Edinburgh University and, continuing them with 'Success', was to become the leading man of English letters of his era. Smith's birth-date places him among a cluster of others who contributed markedly to an age of intellectual distinction in Scotland: Thomas Reid, philosopher, born 1710, already a student at Marischal College, Aberdeen; Hugh Blair, critic, born in 1718; William Robertson, historian, born 1721; Adam Ferguson, pioneer sociologist, born 1724; James Hutton, geologist, born 1726; Robert Adam, architect, Joseph Black, chemist, and John Hunter, anatomist, all born in 1728.

Outside Scotland, Newton was nearing the end of his life, dying in 1727. Swift was to become a national hero in Ireland in 1724 on publishing the *Drapier's Letters*, attacking English political and economic control. Pope in 1723, suspected by the Government of Jacobite sympathies, was translating Homer and editing Shakespeare. In that year, Berkeley and Francis Hutcheson were both teaching in Dublin. No philosophical work had been published by Berkeley since the *Three Dialogues* of 1713, but Hutcheson was working out the moral philosophy to be presented in his *Inquiry into the Original of Our Ideas of Beauty and Virtue* (1725), an inspiration for Hume and Smith. On the Continent, Leibniz had died in 1716, and Kant was born in 1724. Thomasius (d. 1728) was nearing the end of his career in 1723 at Halle, when Wolff was expelled and began teaching at Marburg. Voltaire in 1723 published his epic poem *La Henriade* in its first form, and Rousseau was still serving out his time as an engraver in Geneva. Not yet an economist, Quesnay received the title of Surgeon-Royal that year, and was in practice in Mantes, near Paris. The later *philosophes*, Diderot (b. 1713) and d'Alembert (b. 1717), were schoolboys. Another of the *philosophes*, d'Holbach, was born the same year as Smith, and the economist Turgot four years later. Bach in 1723 became cantor at the Thomaskirche in Leipzig, and composed the St John Passion, while Handel had been away from Halle for some time, and was composing Italian operas in London. In America that year, Franklin at 17 moved from Boston to Philadelphia, and found work as an already expert printer. Washington's father was managing an estate in Westmoreland County, Virginia, where George was born in 1732. Jefferson's father was training as a surveyor, and moved out to the edge of western settlement in Virginia, to Goochland County, where Thomas was born in 1743.

No doubt restricted by his time, but also, like his memorable contemporaries, afforded opportunities for achievement by it, Adam Smith lived through the last Jacobite rising in his twenties, when he was completing his education at Oxford. The Prince who led it, Charles Edward Stuart, was three years his senior. Smith published his greatest book on economics during the crisis of the American Revolution, and he was to put down his concluding thoughts about moral philosophy in his last year, as the French Revolution gathered momentum.

His start in life was not particularly fortunate, since his father, also Adam, had died by 9 January 1723 (GUL MS Gen. 1035/55). The infant's upbringing, however, was in the hands of a remarkable mother, Margaret Douglas, supported by 'tutors and curators' (guardians) appointed in the father's will. Two of them were witnesses to the baptism: James Oswald, leading figure in Kirkcaldy and good friend of the father, and Henry Miller of Pourin, thought to be an uncle on the mother's side (Scott, 1937: 132 n. 10). Guided by them, the young widow proved equal to her task. To be sure, she was a Douglas, descended from that powerful house whose Black and Red branches had contributed so markedly to the achievements and unrest of medieval and Reformation Scotland. A direct ancestor was Sir William Douglas (later 5th Earl of Morton), gaoler of Mary Queen of Scots at Lochleven Castle from 1567 to 1568. Partly through hope of marrying the Queen, a younger brother of Sir William, distinguished as 'pretty Geordie', contrived Mary's escape from her island prison, with the help of 'little Willy' Douglas, an orphan nephew (Fraser, 1970: 400–1, 423–4). Of this stripe were Margaret Douglas's forebears.

She was born in 1694 (baptized 17 September), the fifth child of Lt. Col. Robert Douglas of Strathenry and his second wife, Susan Balfour, daughter of the 3rd Lord Balfour of Burleigh. The Balfours formed another Fife family prominent in Scottish history, especially during the civil war of the seventeenth century, in which many men from East Fife were killed. Their loss together with war damage brought economic decay for a generation to such burghs as Kirkcaldy (Anderson, 1863: i.210; House, 1975: 19).

The estate of Strathenry came to Adam Smith's maternal grandfather through his childless first marriage to an heiress, Helen Forrester of Strathenry. In the contemporary history of Fife (1710: Mizuta) by Sir Robert Sibbald,[1] we find Robert Douglas listed as one of the principal 'heritors' (owners of landed property) in the county. He served as MP for Fife in the Scottish Parliament from 1703 until his death on 25 April 1706. Adam Smith's Douglas uncles and cousins continued his grandfather's way of life as country lairds with army connections, and it is likely that through his association with them he acquired some of the attitudes of the gentry, as well as an admiration for soldiers, reflected in his writings.[2] In his London Journal, James Boswell recorded on 25 April 1763 that 'Mr Smith at Glasgow once told me that his friends had cut his throat in not allowing him to be a soldier'. For his part, the journalist thought such an idea 'completely ridiculous' in Adam Smith, 'for he is quite a learned, accurate, absent man' (Boswell, 1950). We may believe that a discerning parent such as Margaret Douglas would have insight into her son's true nature, and steer him into the life of scholarship for which he was suited.

She had married the elder Adam Smith in 1720 (marriage contract dated 17 November), when he was a widower with an 11-year-old son named Hugh. Her husband was baptized on 6 May 1679, one of the younger sons of John Smith (died 4 April 1712: GUL MS Gen. 1035/23) who was tacksman or leaseholder of Seaton, a property on the loop of the Don near Old Aberdeen (Scott, 1937: 395–408). The family has been identified as that of a younger branch of the Smiths of Rothiebirsden and Inveramsay, estates which lie in the parish of the Chapel of Garioch, about twenty miles to the north-east of Aberdeen. In dealing with this patronymic, however, even the most devoted genealogist knows that he hunts needles in haystacks. If we have found the right haystack, nevertheless, it is to be noted that, whereas the Smiths of Inveramsay favoured the Jacobite cause in the troubles of eighteenth-century Scotland, the Smiths of Seaton cleaved to the Hanoverians. And this allegiance is apparent in the career of Adam Smith the elder.

After studies under a cousin, William Walker, who was sub-principal of King's College, Aberdeen, which then claimed the full title of University in rivalry with the newer Reformation foundation of Marischal University, the elder Adam Smith went to Edinburgh to acquire a qualification in law. When he finished his course, he embarked in October 1698 on a stormy voyage to Bordeaux which ended in shipwreck (GUL MS Gen. 1035/2). It is not known how long he remained in France, but the books he owned listed in a surviving inventory reflected some interest in French culture (GUL MS Gen. 1035/61, 20 Feb. 1723). They included a grammar, dictionary, and Bible in French, also historical and fictional works, a comedy by Molière, and Fénelon's artful blend of Homeric lore, neo-classical sensibility, and moral didacticism, focused on the issue of the ideal education of a son: *Les Aventures de Télémaque* (1699). From the time of his student days in Oxford, Adam Smith the younger was to show considerable receptivity to French ideas, eloquence, and experience.[3]

We pick up the trail of the father again in 1705, when he is identified as private secretary to Hugh Campbell, 3rd Earl of Loudoun, appointed on 5 June of that year as one of the two Secretaries of State for Scotland (Scott, 1937: 6–7). This was the turbulent era of the movement to achieve a consolidating Union of the Parliaments of England and Scotland, a measure strongly supported by Loudoun in political alliance with the chief of his house, John, 2nd Duke of Argyll. Argyll had recently been appointed Lord High Commissioner of the Scottish Parliament to push through the Union in return for the rewards of money and an English peerage (Ferguson, 1968: 46).

The elder Adam Smith may have owed his position to a brother, Alexander, who was a writer (solicitor) in Edinburgh, then held government posts as General Collector of Taxes in Scotland and, from 1699, as Postmaster General. As a private secretary, Smith's duties included dealing with Loudoun's correspondence, both of an official nature and connected with the management of his estates, also securing intelligence and arranging interviews and visits. He went back and forth to London on business, and travelled elsewhere in Loudoun's retinue, for example, to Glasgow in March 1707, when he headed the list of eleven of its members admitted burgesses of the city (Scott, 1937: 10). This would be a consideration when the family decided to send Adam Smith to Glasgow University, where it was likely that the strong Campbell interest would be exerted for his advancement.

Extant correspondence of father Smith reveals that he was trusted by friends and acquaintances, ranging from the Earl of Southesk and the Countess of Stair to Robert Arbuthnot, an auditor of the Scottish Exchequer, who gave him a variety of commissions financial and domestic (GUL MS Gen. 1035/21, 22, 31, 68). It would appear that he served in some way or had a special regard for James Douglas, 2nd Duke of Queensberry, and his Duchess, for their portraits were hung in the West and East rooms of Smith's Kirkcaldy house (GUL MS Gen. 1035/62). Queensberry was the magnate who headed the Scottish commission sent to Westminster in April 1706 to deliberate about the terms of the Treaty of Union.

Smith's reward for service to Loudoun and, no doubt, the unionist cause, was a commission from Queen Anne dated 18 April 1707 for the office of 'Clerk of the Court Martial or Councill of War of all our forces within our ancient Kingdom of Scotland' (Scott, 1937: 129). However, he was put on the 'Contingent Dormant List' when the Union of the Parliaments was accomplished. This happened following the dissolution of the last Scottish Parliament by proclamation on 28 April 1707, after it voted on the several articles of the Treaty of Union and ratified the whole. Lord Chancellor Seafield is said to have made the cynical comment that this was the 'end o' an auld sang' (Ferguson, 1968: 51–2).

About this time, the elder Smith was admitted as a Writer to the Signet, that is, a solicitor qualified to practise in the Court of Session and handle legal aspects of estate and financial management. Writers were the 'great money agents' in

Scotland and had a vital role in the emerging money market which provided the capital for the schemes of improvement in agriculture, manufacture, and commerce devised in this period (Haldane, 1970: 35–8; Durie, 1978: 21–2).

Records show that Smith was a prudent manager of money, a trait also evinced by his son. This enabled him to marry advantageously and make his home in Old Provost's Close in Edinburgh, where he remained until 1714. His first wife (marriage contract, post-nuptial, 13 November 1710: GUL MS Gen. 1035/51) was Lilias, eldest daughter of Sir George Drummond of Milnab, who was Lord Provost of Edinburgh in 1683 and served in the Scottish Parliament. A more famous kinsman of the same name was Provost of Edinburgh six times between 1725 and 1762, in the course of which he gave vigorous leadership for developing the University, in particular its medical school, and improving the city, also envisioning its New Town (Chitnis, 1982: 86–97).

There are letters from Smith to 'Lillie' Drummond reflecting interest in her domestic concerns and solicitude about her health and for their little son Hugh, baptized 2 September 1709 (Huntington Lib. Loudoun Papers LO 9412; GUL MS Gen. 1035/33). Lilias died between 1716 and 1718, and Hugh, like his half-brother Adam, did not enjoy good health as a youngster, though his master at a Perth boarding-school, John Martin, reported in 1724 that 'he profited right well at his books'. He was dead by 15 December 1750, when the younger Adam Smith was declared his heir (GUL MS Gen. 1035/69, 70; Scott, 1937: 135). His occupation is cited as that of custom-house clerk at Kirkcaldy, a post surely obtained through family influence, for as we shall see his father became Comptroller of Customs in that burgh in 1714, and thereafter his clerk was yet another Adam Smith, who was father Smith's nephew. This Adam Smith in time also became Comptroller and then Collector of Customs at Kirkcaldy.

When he became active as Clerk of the Court Martial of Scotland, the elder Adam Smith was expected to see to it that the proper procedures were followed at military trials, to advise about points of law that might arise or report subsequently on those to which due weight had not been attached, to assist prisoners in their defence, and to ensure that all evidence was taken down in writing. He had to protect his commission against threatened encroachment by the Judge Advocate General, who wished to appoint his own deputy in Scotland in 1709–10, and he was not really secure in exercising it until the time of the Jacobite rising of 1715. This was led by the Earl of Mar, who had formerly been Loudoun's fellow-Secretary of State for Scotland. He was nicknamed 'Bobbing John', because he switched his political allegiance. The Hanoverian forces in Scotland were commanded by the Duke of Argyll (*Iain Ruadh nan Cath*, Red John of the Battles). His steadiness in the field following the indecisive battle of Sheriffmuir in November 1715 brought victory to the cause of George I.

The elder Smith was much occupied in 1716 at the military camp in Stirling, dealing with summonses for courts martial issued by Argyll in the aftermath of Sheriffmuir. Many years later, the younger Smith jested to his printer and publisher, William Strahan, that their 'forefathers kicked out the Pope and the Pretender' for the sake of the 'pretious right of private judgement' (*Corr.* No. 50). In this struggle his own father's involvement had to do with the necessary element of maintaining military discipline among the troops of the winning side. Though we have an incomplete record of the elder Smith's activities as a Clerk of the Court Martial, we do know that he participated in the imposition of the death penalty (GUL MS Gen. 1035/115, 119, 120, 123). Again, many years later, the younger Smith engaged in historical analysis of the 'rigid penalties of martial law' in his lectures on jurisprudence, and presented views on the emotions aroused by the imposition of these penalties in lectures on morals.[4] We can conjecture that Smith's mother would pass on to him stories about exciting parts of his father's career to satisfy his natural curiosity.

A parallel between the lives of the father and the famous son he was never destined to see is that both ended their days as officials in the Customs service. The elder Smith's appointment as Comptroller of Customs at Kirkcaldy on 11 March 1714 was due to Loudoun's influence at a time when the inefficiency of revenue collection in Scotland and its complex problems forced the adoption of measures of Customs reorganization and reform. In pre-Union days, the Scottish Customs revenues consisted of three branches that had been comparatively simple to administer, and they had been farmed out at £34,000 in peace and £28,500 during war with France. The younger Smith commented adversely on the system of farming out taxes, mostly with respect to French experience, and he praised the English system of a salaried revenue service: 'Upon the whole we may observe that the English are the best financeers in Europe, and their taxes are levied with more propriety than those of any country whatsoever' (*LJ*(B) 318; cf. *WN* v.ii.k.73).

Following the Union, the English system of revenues collected in twenty-four branches was extended to Scotland, together with the complicated apparatus of bounties and drawbacks which was part of the prevailing mercantilism. In consequence, a new Scottish Customs establishment had to be created under Godolphin, the Lord Treasurer of the United Kingdom. A five-member Board of Commissioners of Customs was appointed, together with its staff, to superintend operations at each outport handled by a collector, comptroller, and surveyor, supported by a number of landwaiters (officers who superintended landing of goods and examined them) and boatmen. The collector was the senior officer at the port and kept the accounts, while the comptroller kept similar accounts as a check on the collector. Both officers faced extensive problems that had to be reported to the Board of Customs.

Because of the widespread resistance in Scotland to the new revenue system, and the lucrative nature of smuggling, also the nature of the rugged Scottish coastline with its many landing-places, as well as the inexperience, human failure, and corruption of some of the Customs officers, there was considerable leakage of revenue (Riley, 1964: chs. 3, 4, 9, 13). Our Adam Smith served on this same Board as a Commissioner, and heard about the same kind of problems from 1778 until his death.

Father Smith's assumption of the Kirkcaldy Comptrollership in 1714 was part of the reorganization of the Scottish Customs establishment. From a letter he wrote to Loudoun on 20 March 1714, it is clear that he had hoped for something better from the scramble for new posts, and that he believed that Mar's protégé on the Customs Board, William Cleland, had been successful in securing plums that were more desirable, such as the post of keeper of the register of ships and seizures. In another letter to Loudoun, dated 3 May 1717, he solicited the post of Secretary to the Commissioners of the Salt Duty in Scotland. The salary of £100 would not be much better than that of his Kirkcaldy post, but he reckoned that it would be to his advantage to move to Edinburgh (Huntington Lib. Loudoun Papers LO 9409–11). He also claimed that he would be in a better position to serve Loudoun, a claim he repeated in yet another letter of the same kind, dated 6 September 1720, in which he asked to be appointed Inspector of Securities at the Board of Customs in Edinburgh (NRA(S) 631, Bute (Loudoun Papers), Bundle A/1319). Nothing came of these appeals, and he remained in Kirkcaldy, where his posthumous son was born.

Kirkcaldy is a settlement of some antiquity. The name comes from the Welsh forms *caer caled din*, meaning 'fort on the hard hill', an acknowledgement of the importance of Ravenscraig as a defensive site overlooking Kirkcaldy bay (Dorward, 1979: 29; Walker and Ritchie, 1987: 100, 105). In 1334 it was made a burgh of regality, permitting the organization of markets and fairs and collection of dues, under royal protection—part of the long history of the market society. It then passed under the jurisdiction of the abbot of nearby Dunfermline. About 1450 it became a free royal burgh, but the earliest surviving charter was one issued by Charles I in 1644 which established the form of burgh government, including the provisions that the provost was to have the title of admiral, and that the council of twenty-one members was to include at least eight mariners, eight merchants, and three craftsmen from the incorporated trades: smiths, wrights and masons, weavers, shoemakers, tailors, bakers, and fleshers. No provost was elected until 1658, however, because the burgesses, known locally as Neighbours, had come to see the office as entailing 'ane perpetuall servitude and slauerie to this toun'. They expressed this concern in a resolution of 22 April 1588 (House, 1975: 41). Behind this resolution is the fear that the provostship would be controlled by magnates in the vicinity, drawing the burgh into power struggles that would damage its livelihood. The theme of securing and maintaining natural liberty, of course, is one that has a central place in the writings of Adam Smith the younger.

The livelihood of Kirkcaldy was based on its export of coal and salt, a thriving trade in the later sixteenth century which brought prosperity to the Fife coastal burghs. The contrast between them and the poorer inland region prompted a saying of James VI, quoted by Adam Smith in one of the early fragments dealing with economics, to the effect that Fife 'was like a coarse woollen coat edged with gold lace' (FB 2, *LJ* 585). The civil-war period of the seventeenth century occasioned considerable losses of Kirkcaldy ships, and the modest recovery following Charles II's restoration in 1660 ended in the reign of William and Mary, when the French wars damaged the shipping trade of east-coast Scotland. Nevertheless, Kirkcaldy had an appreciable population represented by the paid hearth-tax figure of 1,008 (town and parish) in 1691. By the end of the seventeenth century, Scotland's economic centre was shifting to the west, as Glasgow (3,885 paid hearths in the burgh itself, plus 524 in the four wards of the adjacent Barony) responded to the opportunities of the Atlantic trade, in particular that associated with tobacco. The immediate effect of the Union of 1707 seemed to be depression of trade to France, Holland, and the Baltic, where Kirkcaldy had its links for the export of linen, coal, and salt (Hamilton, 1963: 249–54; Devine, 1975; Flinn, 1977: 191, 197–200). Our Adam Smith noted these bad effects in a letter to his publisher, William Strahan, in 1760, claiming the first two branches were 'almost totally annihilated' (*Corr.* No. 50).

As a consequence, there was good reason for the elder Smith's anxieties about a Customs post in Kirkcaldy. His real income, as distinct from his salary as a Comptroller, depended on the port's volume of trade. Senior Customs officers collected unofficial fees on the issue of 'cockets' and 'transires', certificates relating to the duties on taxable goods. Not only was Kirkcaldy's trade falling off, there was also resistance to the attention of the Customs service to that trade. In 1708, John Bruce as Collector complained of the 'great oppugnancy and opposition that we frequently meet with in the discharge of our duty' (Riley, 1964: 135). Since Smith's friends mostly lived in Edinburgh, it was probably a wrench for him to leave there, and at first the company of Fife merchants may not have seemed all that desirable, to say nothing of Fife lairds. In proverb, they were characterized as possessing 'a puckle land, a lump of debt, a doocot, and a law plea', and satire painted them as 'aye daft and maistly drunk . . . what they want in sense they have in greed' (Mackay, 1896: 266–7).

The evidence of the two wills and of Smith's accounts, however, as well as that of the inventory of his household endorsed by his widow Margaret Douglas in 1723, is that he extended family connections in Kirkcaldy, added to his circle of friends there, prospered financially, and was settled in some comfort. His second marriage in 1720 to a Douglas of Strathenry, of course, was a sign of acceptance by a substantial landed family in Fife. His salary as a Comptroller began at £30 a year and increased to £40 by 1722. A relation, yet another Adam Smith, who was Collector of Customs and of the salt duty at Alloa (each post worth £30 a year), stated in 1754 that his collectorship was worth 'above 200 Pounds per ann.' (*Corr.* No. 16). This suggests that fees and premiums allowed to collectors and comptrollers would yield more than double their salaries, and we have Smith's own statement of 1717 that his post was worth almost £100 a year. This sum, together with his allowance as Clerk of the Court Martial, if it was paid, would give him a yearly income from the Government of £236 17s. 6d. He would have to pay his clerk out of this, but his allowances and perquisites probably brought him in about £275 a year. This amount of money had considerable purchasing power in his time, and was nearly on a par with the salary of a judge of the Court of Session at £300. In addition, Smith was able to lend out money at interest, and a statement of his affairs in 1722 reveals that he earned in the course of that year the sum of £137 19s. 5½d. in interest on bonds. All in all, Comptroller Smith had a large income at his disposal for someone of his age, as well as some property, so that his widow and heirs could be well looked after (MS GUL Gen. 1035/44, 48, 50, 124, 125; Scott, 1937: 17–19, 408).

Writing about 1724, Daniel Defoe made out a case for the attractions and advantages of the Kirkcaldy where our Adam Smith was born and his father died. In his 'Account and Description of Scotland', Defoe conceded that the Union he supported had caused 'decline and decay' in the east-coast seaports in general, but he noted Kirkcaldy was 'larger, more populous, and better built' than other towns along the Fife coast. He described the town as consisting of a mile-long street running from east to west hugging the shore. This and the adjacent by-streets and lanes seemed to him clean and well-paved. Always keen to find evidence of thriving economic activity—did this soothe his conscience over the bribery and skulduggery behind the Union?—he painted a picture of Kirkcaldy's 'considerable merchants' transporting 'great Qualities' of corn and linen to England and Holland in 'several good Ships', which returned with needed foreign goods. He reported seeing coal-pits in the neighbourhood, one of them at the west end of the town, so close to the shore, he thought, as to be endangered by the tide. At the east end he saw a shipyard, and beyond that pans for boiling and making salt (Defoe, 1927: ii.780–1).

The contemporary Swedish industrial spy, Henrik Kalmeter, had noted in 1719–20 that five salt-pans were in operation in Kirkcaldy. There was profit to be made by this industry in Fife and along the opposite shore of the Forth arising from the steady demand in Scotland for its product to cure fish and beef, especially for the long winter months, as well as to season oats eaten as a staple of diet. Fife saltmasters had an advantage over their counterparts in north-east England and Cheshire, whose product was of better quality, in that they had to pay lower taxes. This form of protection ended in 1823, when our Adam Smith's advocacy of free trade had won enough adherents to sweep away the duties on salt made in Scotland or coming in from England, and an unfettered market caused the demise of the local salt manufacture (Smout, 1978: 40–1; Whatley, 1984; 1986: 4–17).

In the 1720s, however, it does seem that Kirkcaldy had some measure of success meeting Scottish and overseas demand for its salt, and Defoe contrasted the burgh with nearby Dysart, which he found 'in the full perfection of Decay', though he did notice there the activity of 'Nailers and Hard-Ware Workers'

(Defoe, 1927: ii.781). Indeed, such trades and those of blacksmiths, carpenters, and masons were stimulated by the needs of collieries and salt-pans all along the Fife coast. One result of the mining, manufacturing, craft, and trading activity of this region was urban development linking communities in a fashion typical of the seaboards of modern industrial countries, as in the conurbations of the eastern United States. In *Rob Roy*, Walter Scott puts into the mouth of Andrew Fairservice a picturesque account of this aspect of Fife *c.*1715, noting Kirkcaldy's distinction as the 'lang toun', arising from the spread of its buildings along a raised beach site at the foot of a steep slope (ch. 14).

Kirkcaldy tolbooth, where market dues (tolls) were paid and the town's weights and measures were stored, as well as its archives and weapons for the town guard, and where the town council and burgh court assembled, has not survived, but good examples, with their forestairs, and distinctive red 'Dutch pantiles' introduced *c.*1714 by the architect William Adam, can be seen along the coast at Inverkeithing, West Wemyss, and Dysart. The Fife Folk Museum, in the seventeenth-century weigh-house at Ceres, near Cupar, and the Fisheries Museum in a medieval Anstruther building evoke most effectively the rural and seafaring activities and the crafts of the bygone Fife which was the setting for our Adam Smith's earliest days (Walker and Ritchie, 1987: 31–2, 62; Gifford, 1989: 73–4).

Local tradition asserts that he was born in a house at the corner of Rose Street and the High Street, and afterwards lived with his mother in the house on the High Street (demolished in 1834), whose site is marked by a plaque at No. 220, on the wall of the Clydesdale and North of Scotland Bank (Fay, 1956: 41–2). We have some idea of the contents of the first house and its layout from the inventory signed by Margaret Douglas, widow and mother-to-be, on 20 February 1723. In addition to a dining-room and a kitchen, there is mention of a west room, a west back room, and an east room. On the walls of the dining-room, containing a big oval wainscot table and fifteen rush chairs, there were pictures of religious subjects—the Virgin Mary and the Eastern Kings—and secular subjects—King James VI, Robert the Bruce, and the Duke of Argyll (presumably John, the 2nd Duke, then alive). The west room had a large bed with blue hangings and a blue cover—perhaps the couple's own bed, in which Adam Smith was begotten. The west back room contained the master's riding gear: two saddles, boots, and spurs, as well as his weapons, a gun and a pair of holster pistols, reminding us that a Customs officer's lot was not always a happy one.

The contents of the kitchen give an indication of the standard of living in the Smith household and reveal something of the daily activities of its members, and also of the domestic regime maintained in the homes Margaret Douglas Smith kept for her son until her death. Cooking was done at a large fireplace, whose chimney had racks at either end. Drink was measured into flagons and stoups holding pints, chopins, and mutchkins. Mention of a tea-kettle with its 'winter' or trivet suggests that the newer habit of tea-drinking had been taken up as an alternative to the more robust drams and draughts of older custom. Brewing was carried out using the 'wort stand', 'wort Kinnen' (*kinkin* or *kilderkin* from the Dutch word 'kinneken' meaning the fourth part of a tun), and 'workin fat' (fermenting vat). There was a considerable amount of silver among the cutlery and related items. The inclusion of two spinning wheels and a check-reel suggests that material for weaving was also prepared in the house. The one picture in the kitchen was that of 'Calvin the Reformer', perhaps as a Presbyterian antidote to the Popish Virgin and Kings in the dining-room.

The inventory gives a list of the elder Adam Smith's clothes, which included a blue cloth cloak, a scarlet cloak, a silk nightgown, and a suit of white clothes. His books are said to number 'about Eightie pieces'. The last items on the inventory consist of a 'Childs Silver whistle with Seven bells and three Silver Chains and a red Corall', relics perhaps of the dead man's own childhood or of that of his first-born Hugh, and perhaps the very first things given to the younger Adam Smith to amuse him as an infant (GUL MS Gen. 1035/62).

The inventory was compiled by the clerk Adam Smith, but he would be instructed by Margaret Douglas, and the considerable number of Scots words (and, possibly, spellings of Fife pronunciations, such as 'fat' for vat and 'kinnen' for kilderkin) represented the mother tongue Adam Smith heard first and incorporated in his own, though he was said to have acquired the English pronunciation, much desired by the Scottish literati, from his residence at Oxford as a Snell Exhibitioner (Rae, 1965: 28).

The two wills of the elder Adam Smith—that of 30 August 1718, which was revoked, and that of 13 November 1722, which was enforced—tell us a great deal about his family connections, friends, and creditors, some of whom would have been entertained in what its plenishings suggest was a liberal Kirkcaldy household (GUL MS Gen. 1035/43, 47; Scott, 1937: 129–33). With the exception of one nobleman, the people mentioned in the wills are drawn from the middling landed gentry, professional classes, and merchants. Early family links with such people, as well as observation and experience later in life, probably helped to develop the attitudes about them revealed by Adam Smith in his writings. The father's world, then, can be considered a source for the respect shown by the son for the spirit of improvement in contemporary merchants, acknowledgement of the generosity of country gentlemen and farmers in sharing new ideas and practices, and awareness that the desire for status rather than profit was the motivating force for professional men.[5]

Country gentlemen listed among the 'tutors and curators' of the second will included Adam Smith the younger's uncles, Robert and John Douglas of Strathenry; David Skene of Pitlour, who married into the Douglas family; and Henry Miller of Pourin, mentioned already as one of the witnesses to Smith's baptism, who was related to David Miller, his distinguished teacher at Kirkcaldy burgh school. Those men are likely channels for Smith's early knowledge of farming improvement, which had begun in the previous century.

A figure who fits Smith's picture of the improving merchant was also listed as one of the guardians and appears, too, as a baptism witness: Captain James Oswald of Dunnikier. He was a wealthy merchant who served (1702–7) as Kirkcaldy's Dean of Guild (magistrate responsible for supervising buildings within the burgh); as its MP both in the Scottish Parliament (1702–7), where he voted consistently against the Union, and in the British one (1710–15); and as its Provost (1713–15). He bought the estate of Dunnikier in 1702, and was one of the principal landowners in the district, also the owner of a nailery in the village of Pathhead on his estate, but he was also a creditor of the elder Adam Smith. His eldest son, James (1715–69), was the friend of the younger Adam Smith and is believed to have discussed economic issues with him. Another merchant among the guardians was William Walker, a nephew of the testator, identified as a 'Dyer in Aberdeen' and connected in that city with the families of provosts and university principals.

Among the professional men listed as guardians was William Smith, who succeeded his uncle, the testator, as secretary to Loudoun. He then became steward to the 2nd Duke of Argyll, whose estate at Adderbury, near Oxford, he superintended on occasion, enabling him to play host to the younger Adam Smith when he was a student at Balliol College. Other professional men included Hercules Smith, cousin of the testator and Collector of Customs at Kirkcaldy. A cousin, William Smith, was a Regent of Marischal College, Aberdeen, until 1717, when he was deposed because of his Jacobite leanings. William Caddell of Fossochee was a Writer to the Signet, and Archibald Arnot was a surgeon in Kirkcaldy. John Steill, minister of the parish of Camnoch, was the testator's brother-in-law by his first marriage. The list also included two members of the prolific and ingenious family of Clerk of Penicuik: the lawyer Sir John, who inherited the baronetcy, and his cousin, the physician John Clerk of Listonshiels, another guardian related to the testator by his first marriage (Scott, 1937: 131–2).

The presence of the two Clerks on the list of guardians is of particular interest. It suggests, in the first place, that the elder Smith had links with an early generation of proponents of Enlightenment in Scotland, that complex intellectual movement which transformed so many aspects of the country in the course of the eighteenth century, and to which the younger Adam Smith was so notable a contributor. In the second place, the Clerk family in rising to prominence exhibited those traits of behaviour which Smith instanced as explanatory principles in his system of social science: that spirit of improvement so noticeable among the merchant and entrepreneurial class; their frugality and willingness to forego immediate satisfaction in the interest of long-run gains; the driving desire for social status; and the view that increased productivity and moderate profit-seeking added to human welfare. Smith was to hold that high profits destroyed parsimony (*WN* I.ix.24; IV.vii.c.61).

The Clerk family's fortunes were founded by the grandfather John (1611–74), a Montrose merchant who ran a highly successful general store in Paris, from which he exported to Scotland rare books and paintings, including some by Rembrandt and one of the Brueghels. His gains enabled him to marry a laird's daughter and buy the estate of Penicuik, nine miles from Edinburgh. His heir, another John (1649–1722), added to the family property, was made a Knight Baronet by Charles II when he was 30, and conducted coalmining operations with great efficiency. An ardent Calvinist in personal life, who recorded 109 covenants with his God in Christ between 1692 and 1722, he strove with equal diligence to regenerate his workers and generate profit. If anyone exemplified the paradoxical compatibility Max Weber found between certain forms of Protestantism and what appears to be capitalism, it was this man (Weber, 1958; Wuthnow, 1994: 626). His son noted that his father 'managed his affaires with great Frugality . . . [and] had a very great turn for business' (Gray, 1892: 8; Marshall, 1980: 235–47).

This John Clerk (1676–1755), friend of the elder Smith, was educated in law at Glasgow and Leiden, where he became the friend of the immensely learned physician Hermann Boerhaave. Against his father's wishes, he travelled to Italy to enjoy its music and painting and to explore Roman antiquities. Returning to Scotland, he was admitted advocate in 1700. Political patronage brought him the sinecure of a judge's seat in the newly created Scottish Court of Exchequer, which took over some of the functions of the Scottish Privy Council abolished in 1708. In his ample leisure he wrote poetry and history, and engaged in a wide range of practical, scientific, and cultural pursuits, including farm improvement (through enclosures and crop rotation), mining engineering, architecture, and archaeology (Fleming, 1962: 14–44; Brown, 1987: 33–49). He became a freemason on admittance to the Edinburgh Lodge (Mary's Chapel) in 1710. Thus he was in a position as a non-operative brother to discuss Enlightenment ideas in masonic circles. Perhaps freemasonry linked him to Kirkcaldy, which had a Lodge from at least 1658 (Stevenson, 1988: 8, 199, 213; Jacob, 1991).

About the time of the elder Adam Smith's death, Sir John Clerk began building a Palladian villa, partly inspired by the Mauritshuis at The Hague, at Mavisbank, near Loanhead, Midlothian, with the help of the Kirkcaldy contractor and architect William Adam, who had served his time as a mason, and was a freeman of the masons' incorporation of Dunfermline, which had existed as a Lodge since 1601 (Gifford, 1989: 46, 73, 90–5). Other activities, such as excavating Roman villas in Midlothian, helped to give a classical tone to the activities of the circle Baron Clerk gathered for meetings in Penicuik House. His leadership in aesthetic and antiquarian matters encouraged the feeling of enlightened Scots that they were among the authentic heirs of Roman civilization, and this feeling entered into the kind of education that our Adam Smith received and bestowed, focused on the Roman moralists and their culture.

With a caution about the technicalities of guardianship, as befitted a lawyer, Sir John Clerk expressed willingness to 'joyn in assisting the Sone of my deceased friend', that is, Adam Smith the elder. He also wrote that he might find it inconvenient to act as Hugh Smith's guardian (GUL MS Gen. 1035/55). In a more forthright fashion his cousin, Dr John Clerk (1689–1757), declined to be guardian on the grounds that his business confined him to Edinburgh, and Hugh was to be educated on the other side of the Firth of Forth (GUL MS Gen. 1035/56). As matters turned out, however, young Hugh fell dangerously ill in 1724, and Dr Clerk gave him medical attention.

The career of this celebrated physician illustrates the scientific side of the Scottish Enlightenment, and themes in our Adam Smith's life and writings. The drive to better his condition was manifested in aiming at higher professional rank than his surgeon father, Robert. He sought advanced training in medicine at a Dutch university, encountering the tradition initiated by Boerhaave, which became a formative influence on the emerging Edinburgh medical school (GUL Cullen MSS III: 3). Clerk's MD was awarded by St Andrews University in 1711 without examination, an instance of the 'dirty practice', as our Adam Smith called it, of the sale of medical degrees in Scotland (*Corr.* No. 143). Launched on his career in Edinburgh, Clerk became a Fellow of the College of Physicians there, and in 1721 reported on behalf of the College to the town council about the sanitation of the city, which had a fearful mortality rate from the ravages of cholera, smallpox, typhoid, and typhus. Another College enterprise in which he took a leading part was preparing the second edition of the *Edinburgh Pharmacopoeia*, 1722 (Currie, 1932: i.282). He was also prominent in the founding and staffing of the city's Infirmary, an important adjunct to medical teaching at the University from 1729. Ability and inclination made him a member of various societies and circles formed in typical Enlightenment fashion to exchange ideas, stimulate research, and promote improvement (Roche, 1978), for example, the Philosophical Society of Edinburgh, dating from 1731 and refounded in 1752, of which David Hume became Secretary and Adam Smith was a member (Emerson, 1979a; 1981: 143, 168, n. 48). Dr Clerk's clubbable but austere nature is suggested by the custom he kept of supping on bread and whey once a week with the anatomist Alexander Monro I, the Court of Session's Lord President Duncan Forbes, and the outstanding mathematician and interpreter of Newton, Colin Maclaurin. It is reported that 'Most of the Sciences and Parts of Literature were, sometime or other, Subjects of their Conversation' (Saint Clair, 1964: 51). In this life, with interests extending from science to classical literature, can be seen the main lineaments of that of our Adam Smith when he took his place among the literati of Edinburgh and Glasgow. To be sure, Adam Smith was never attracted to the profession of medicine, and was highly sceptical about its prescriptions (*Corr.* No. 161). Still, he remained lifelong on terms of close friendship with his physician, William Cullen, and his literary executor, the medical scientist Joseph Black, both of whom were protégés of Dr John Clerk, his father's friend (Donovan, 1975: 47, 174).

So much for the circle of friends and acquaintances of the elder Adam Smith as indicated by his second will, and the stirring of mind among them that led in time to the transformation of Scotland from a poor and backward country to one where wealth was on the increase, and our Adam Smith's inquiry into the nature and origins of that entity was one of the intellectual triumphs of the Enlightenment.

Men are known by their books as well as their friends, so we turn now to the 'Inventar' of father Smith's library to learn something about his personal culture (GUL MS Gen. 1035/61). Of the eighty items listed, there are rather few law books for someone with a legal training and career behind him. To the six books of this kind another title can be added from the surviving correspondence: Sir Thomas Craig's *Jus Feudale* (written *c*.1603, published in 1655) was sent by Smith to his master Loudoun in 1714. This legal treatise, of considerable historical insight and comparative breadth, was the subject of lectures at Utrecht and Leiden at the end of the seventeenth century, and it would be of interest to the Loudoun circle as the product of a writer who supported the idea of union between Scotland and England, and who chose to minimize the differences between English and Scots law (Huntington Lib. Loudoun Papers LO 9047; MacKechnie, 1936: 62–3, 202–4, 234).

Religious books, as it happens, compose the biggest group in the 'Inventar', an indication perhaps of their owner's deepest concern. Among the thirty-two items in this category there is to be found a 'Lairge bible in English', possibly the noble folio bible printed at Edinburgh in 1722 by James Watson surviving in the son's library (Simpson, 1979: 187–99; ASL Mizuta). Another book that may have passed from father to son is Humphrey Prideaux's account of cosmic history, much favoured by the severer Protestants in the eighteenth century: *The Old and New Testament connected in the history of the Jews and neighbouring nations, 1716–18* (Mizuta; Bailyn, 1992: 33). Contemporaries reported that Margaret Douglas was a very religious woman, in the sense of a Christian believer, and this may have helped to form a bond with her husband (Rae, 1965: 427–30; Scott, 1937: 20; *TMS* app. ii). Her son, however, distanced himself from Christianity and, indeed, felt free to poke fun on one occasion at the 'Whining Christian [who] dyed with pretended resignation to the will of God'. To be sure, this was in a private letter (*Corr.* No. 163), and in others as well as in his published writings he displays a theistic cast of thought, perhaps the product of his early home circumstances.

The father did not confine himself to collecting books about sacred love or the 'true Christian love', but also owned some dealing with the profane variety: 'Letters of Love in French', 'the life of Donna Olimpia', and Ovid's 'de Arte Amandi'. In all, twenty-four books, including the amatory ones, come from the realm of *belles-lettres* or classics. As a help for reading some of these there was a French grammar, which might be the copy of Lancelot and Arnauld's *Grammaire générale et raisonné* (Amsterdam, 1703) later in the younger Adam Smith's library (EUL JA 1564; Mizuta). The father's taste was broad enough to include Addison and Steele's *Spectator* papers, so important for setting the moderate and improving tone of enlightened Scotland, as well as the works of the witty and scabrous satirist Tom Brown. Surprisingly, nothing by Swift or Pope is mentioned, but perhaps their Tory politics told against them. Ten books in all of a historical nature are listed, among them 'The History of England in 2 Voll.', which could be the work by White Kennett (1706) of the Adam Smith library (Mizuta). Another book cited as 'The Civill Wars of the Lacedemonians' in the 'Inventar' might be *De Republica Lacedaemoniorum* (1670) by Niels Krag (Cragius) owned by the younger Smith (Mizuta). Of the remaining eight books of a miscellaneous nature in the father's collection, two are scientific (on physics and geography); one is on the occult (palmistry); one is a procedural handbook, 'the Secretary in Fashion'; one is on economics, 'A Discourse about Trade', appropriate for a Customs official, and surely making one think about the son's career. Another book, on philosophy, does seem to have passed to the son: Du Hamel's *Philosophia vetus et nova* (1685, 1700: Mizuta); and two are medical reference works. Of this last pair, 'Culpepers Midwife Enlarged' could be a relic of the lying-in of Lilias Drummond Smith, or might suggest forethought about the delivery of the son father Smith was never to see. It was, however, a popular and much-reprinted work, listed by Addison, for example, in Leonora's library (*Spectator* No. 37) As a whole, the 'Inventar' adds evidence of intellectual cultivation to the account that has emerged of Adam Smith's father as a man of parts, who had travelled to Bordeaux and London, able to endow his son with impressive financial and mental resources if, perhaps, a somewhat frail body.

A final document connected with the father that requires some discussion is the account for the expenses of his funeral, receipted by Margaret Douglas for the sum of 'Eighty pund Sexteen Shilling Six penes Scots', which she accepted from James Oswald of Dunnikier on 24 April 1724 (GUL MS Gen. 1097/11; Rae, 1965: 3). The details tell of the 'mourning letters' being sent 'thoro the toun and Country', also of expresses to Edinburgh; they suggest a company assembling for the burial service and a simple meal of bread, biscuit, and seed cake accompanied by ale and wine. A touching note is struck by the reference to the purchase of a 'pair of murning Shous to Hugh'. We may imagine that there was talk when the 'pipes and Tobacco' were put to use of the sad ending at 43 of the promising life of the Comptroller of Customs at Kirkcaldy. There would be commiseration, surely, for the twice-orphaned Hugh, and sympathy for the young widow carrying a child who would never see his father.

2

Boyhood

the great school of self-command

Culpepers Midwife Enlarged from her husband's library would not have been an entirely reliable guide for Margaret Smith facing childbirth. The book presumably describes contemporary practice following delivery, so it can give us some idea of the treatment of her child:

let the Midwife handle it gently. Roul it up with soft cloathes, and lay it in a cradle, and wash it first with warm wine; give it a little honey before it sucks, or a little oil of Almonds newly drawn, that if there be any filth contracted in the stomach from the womb it may be cleansed. (Culpeper, 1671: ii.229)

As noted earlier, Adam Smith in infancy was troubled with much sickness and there may be an acknowledgement of this and his subsequent history of ill health in a remark in *TMS* about colic, that affliction of early years from which he suffered throughout his life: 'no pain is more exquisite' (I.ii.1.11). His condition required great solicitude from his mother, and she was apparently blamed for treating the child with 'unlimited indulgence' (Stewart i.2). Culpeper gave a list of children's diseases of horrendous extent, and if she continued to consult him, there would not be much comfort for Margaret Smith in his book about mothering. He reckoned that scarce one woman in twenty was fit to suckle her child, in London at least, and held that mothers tended to 'cocker' or spoil the children they nursed. Despite the high rate of infant mortality in the period, and the dubious quality of traditional medical advice, Adam Smith survived, in the face, apparently, of a dysentery epidemic in the Eastern Lowlands in 1723–4 (Flinn, 1977: 212). There is every indication that he responded to his mother's care by loving her deeply and seeking to please her, not least in achieving distinction in his career as a professor and man of letters.

His monetary affairs when he was a child were looked after by Captain Oswald and Archibald Arnot, who were made factors of his father's estate on 20 February 1723. Oswald did not himself survive long to discharge this duty, for he is believed to have died within two years. He was succeeded as factor by the Adam Smith who had been the father's clerk.[1] In 1740 this man, by then Collector of Customs at Kirkcaldy, was required to appear for the heir to wind up affairs between Hercules Smith and father Smith from the time of their joint Customs service in Kirkcaldy. The settlement provided for a payment of £7 to the heirs of Hercules Smith (Scott, 1937: 134). Also in 1740, Collector Adam Smith was promoted Inspector General of the Outports in Scotland. His life may have been less than regular, because in 1742 his servant Christian Skinner confessed to the Kirkcaldy Kirk Session that she had 'brought forth a Child in Fornication' to him. The Session Moderator wrote to Collector Smith about this accusation but got no reply, while in the following year the servant girl 'Satisfied her Scandal of Fornication and was absolvd' (NLS MS Acc. 4811, 26 Nov., 7 Dec., 21 Dec. 1742; 14 June 1743).

Though residence in Kirkcaldy was said in general to promote longevity, it had a reputation for being an unhealthy place for children and people subject to rheumatism and chest complaints. Hugh Smith's guardian, William Walker, wrote to Captain Oswald on 3 June 1724 that the town was 'not a fitt place for one of [his charge's] distemper being so much exposed to the sea aire', and he suggested that the boy should be sent to the country (Fleming, 1791: ix.741; GUL MS Gen. 1035/70).

Margaret Smith may have felt the same way about her child, for she took him on visits to her sisters who were married to Fife lairds, one we can identify being Jean, the wife of David Skene of Pitlour. She also visited her old home of Strathe007y, seven miles inland among the hills of West Fife, between Leslie and Loch Leven, where her brother John was the laird. On one visit to Strathenry, there occurred the excitement of the 3-year-old Adam Smith being carried away by gypsies or tinklers. There was a gypsy encampment near Kirkcaldy at a place called John Marshall's Loan, and a Gypsy Way ran from it to the north passing over a hill near Strathenry. Adam Smith is said to have been snatched by a tinkler woman at a large stone near the sixteenth-century castle. There are two local traditions about the site of the snatching. One is that it occurred at the back of Strathendry Castle itself. The other connects it with a large stone under a yew tree in the grounds of the present Strathenry House, which was largely rebuilt in 1824 but, again according to local tradition, replaced an earlier mansion house dating from the end of the seventeenth century.[2]

Traditions vary concerning the recovery of the child. One story has it that he was soon missed, and that his uncle, getting some information about passing vagrants, overtook them in Leslie Wood and rescued the child. Another version recounts that the tinklers had travelled a good distance along the Gypsy Way before little Adam was recovered (Stewart i.3; Scott, 1937: 22–5). John Rae, Smith's nineteenth-century biographer, tells the picturesque tale of a gentleman meeting a gypsy woman carrying a piteously crying child. When a search party set out and was seen by her, she threw the little boy down and fled through Leslie Wood. Because of the many reports of the notorious absent-mindedness of our subject, Rae feared Adam Smith 'would have made a poor gypsy' (pp. 22–5).

But he did make a good scholar, in part due to the efforts of an understanding mother who divined, amidst the cares of his childhood illnesses, that he had a retentive memory and was studious by nature. In part, also, his success as a scholar must be attributed to Kirkcaldy's share of the national system of education (Ross, 1984*c*; Houston, 1989: 43–61). According to Smith's own account in *WN*, this consisted in the first place of the establishment of 'little schools' which had succeeded in teaching 'almost the whole common people to read, and a very great proportion of them to write and account'. Smith thought that the books used to teach reading could be 'somewhat more instructive', and he was critical of the preference for a smattering of Latin over the 'elementary parts of geometry and mechanicks' (v.i.f.55).

Smith's school-days were spent in the sturdy, two-room building of the burgh school on Hill Street, which was built by Kirkcaldy town council in 1723 and used for teaching purposes until 1843. After passing through the 'little school', he seems to have gone through the grammar school education from 1731 to 1737 under the direction of David Miller. He was a schoolmaster of sufficient reputation to be paid expenses by the Town Council to move in 1724 from Cupar, and he made a considerable impact on education in Kirkcaldy (Kirkcaldy Town House, Council Records 1718–46, 1/1/3: 154, 158, 169).

There remain two burgh school textbooks with Smith's signature, and one of these, *Eutropii Historiae Romanae Breviarium* (Edinburgh, 1725), bears the date in his hand, 'May 4th 1733' (Kirkcaldy Museum; Mizuta). That same year, on 5 February, there was entered in the Kirkcaldy Council Records an account of 'The Method of Teaching and regulations thereannent to be observed in the toun'. Perhaps representing Miller's aspirations, rather than the realities of the two-room Kirkcaldy schoolhouse, this document provides details of his curriculum, which appears comparable, for example, with that of Edinburgh High School. The document also offers some insights into his methods of teaching. The four highest classes were devoted to learning to write Latin, the fifth to reading Latin by covering the 'rudiments' or grammar, and the sixth class, the Lectors, to reading and writing English and mastering arithmetic (Kirkcaldy Council Records, 1/1/3: 299–300; Law, 1965: 74–5). The antecedents of this scheme lie in the Scottish Education Act of 1696, and the adaptation by the sixteenth-century Protestant reformers of the programme of the Italian humanists for the teaching of rhetoric. Founded in 1582, Kirkcaldy's grammar school dated back to the Reformation era (Ross, 1984*b*; Gifford, 1989: 191).

Miller aimed at setting homework nightly for the pupils in the highest or first class, in the form of a passage of translation 'to Exercise their Judgements to teach them by degrees to spell rightly to wryte good wryte [handwriting, as opposed to printing] Good Sense and Good Languadge'. The translations were to be examined after the morning assembly, and the boys required to translate back into Latin from the English, sticking to the 'naturall and Constituted order of the [Latin] words'. Later in the morning, the first and second classes were to write a theme. Adam Smith retained a large, schoolboyish hand all his life, as if he found the manipulative side of writing difficult, and composition itself always seemed to be a problem for him (*Corr.* Nos. 136, 276). During the late morning period, Miller's pupils in the third and fourth classes were to learn Latin grammar, the fifth to read English, and the sixth class were to read or write English or be taught arithmetic. Also, in the course of the morning, the fifth and sixth classes were to be put through questions in the Catechism. The education system was meant to inculcate individualistic piety as well as literacy in English. The pressure felt in the sixteenth century to acquire a distinguished Latin style at school had lessened in Scotland, because it was no longer the language of affairs. The rhetorical training was directed at expressiveness in English, though some Latin was needed as a means of entry into the classics. Smith probably studied his *Eutropius* in the fifth and fourth classes, in which it was used to promote mastery of the rudiments of Latin, and to enlarge vocabulary, also to provide a conspectus of Roman history from the founding of the city to the death of the Emperor Jovian in AD 364.

The second textbook which survives from Smith's schooldays is one embracing universal history: Justinus' third-century AD epitome of the *De historiis Philippicis* by the Augustan writer Pompeius Trogus, which covers the Ancient Orient and Greece as well as Rome (Simpson, 1979: 191; Mizuta). These works constituted a storehouse of episodes and anecdotes to be turned to rhetorical use—'to point a moral, or adorn a tale'—and they were approached by schoolmasters in that spirit. Adam Smith may have obtained much more from them, a lifelong interest in history, for example, which added so much depth to his theoretical work in social science (Vicenza, 1984).

Modern scholarship finds the qualities of 'impartiality' and 'good judgment' in *Eutropius* (McDonald, 1978). A view of the book given wide currency in Smith's time was quite different:

[it offered] a very lifeless abridgment of the Roman history, generally full of a great number of proper names, and chronological dates, which are apt to discourage children upon their first entrance on the study of Latin. (Rollin, 1759: i.169)

Thus Charles Rollin, classicist and historian, who drew on his experience as a professor of rhetoric at the University of Paris and knowledge of the curriculum of French schools, in a series of treatises entitled *De la Manière d'Enseigner et d'Étudier les Belles Lettres par rapport à l'esprit et au cœur* (Paris, 1726–8; English trans. 1734, 5th edn. Edinburgh, 1759; Law, 1984: 56–71). Rollin lays out a curriculum for the 'attainment of the Latin tongue' much like that of Miller in Kirkcaldy, involving the 'explaining of authors, the making of exercises, and translation'. Justinus turns up in the list of authors for the fourth class, together with Caesar's commentaries, Terence's comedies, and some of the discourses and epistles of Cicero (Rollin, 1759: i.182). At Aberdeen Grammar School in the 1730s, the fourth and fifth classes were reading Virgil, Terence, Livy, Sallust, and Caesar, writing three translations a week, and memorizing long passages of Latin poetry (Scotland, 1969: i.82).

These authors in representative selections would be familiar to the schoolboy Smith, and the mention of Terence in this context brings to mind Miller's initiative in enlisting drama or at least oratory to enliven his teaching. The seventeenth-century education reformer Comenius had advocated this in his *Schola ludus* (1656). For presentation in 1734, Miller wrote a piece with the expansive title 'A Royal Council for Advice, or the Regular Education of Boys the Foundation of all other Improvements'. In this piece, which was said to have given high satisfaction to its audience, the 'council consisted of a preses and twelve members, decently and gravely seated round a table like senators; the other boys were posted at a distance in a crowd, representing people coming to attend this meeting for advice'. From the crowd there entered in turn, a 'tradesman, a farmer, a country gentleman, a nobleman, two schoolmasters, etc., and last of all a gentleman who congratulated the council on their noble design and worthy performance' (Grant, 1876: 414). One longs to know what role, if any, was assigned to the 11-year-old Smith, principal or sweller of the crowd; but these and other efforts by Miller gave his pupil a serviceable education, with its training in English expression, firm basis in Latin, and apparently a start in Greek (though we have no details) for acceleration in university studies at Glasgow.

Thomas Carlyle, classics master at Kirkcaldy from 1816 to 1818, painted a picture in *Sartor Resartus* (completed 1831; serially published 1833–4) of the inhuman treatment of the young in the traditional classroom: 'Innumerable dead Vocables they crammed into us, and called it fostering the growth of Mind' (ch. 3). Adam Smith seems to have had a very different experience, however, which led to his love for the classics, skill with figures, perhaps his abiding interest in history, and very likely his desire to express his ideas sensibly and with style, also awareness of the importance of competition and self-reliance.

Fortunate in his Kirkcaldy school-days, Smith was doubly so in the friends and acquaintances of that early period of his life. His idiosyncrasies of 'speaking to himself when alone, and of *absence* in company', noticeable to the end of his life, were the object of wondering attention rather than cause for teasing and cruelty. His passion for books was respected as well as his retentive memory, and his warm but friendly and generous temper aroused genuine affection (Stewart i.5).

In his maturity, Smith saw the school years as crucial for the formation of character. He painted a picture of early childhood as a time of overwhelming emotions, when an indulgent nurse or parent must pit one violent feeling in the child against another, for example, fear inspired by noise or threats against angry aggressiveness, to restore their charge's even temper. At school, Smith believed, there is no such 'indulgent partiality'. The boy wishes to be well regarded by his equals and not to be scorned or hated. The basic drive of self-protection teaches him to attain his wishes by controlling his anger and other passions, to the extent that this wins the approval of those equals. Thus, the boy enters the 'great school of self-command', and studies to attain that discipline over his feelings which, if fully attained, is the principal virtue, lending lustre to all the others (*TMS* III.3.22; VI.iii.11). To be sure, this is the outlook of the Stoic moralists.[3] It was the Latin and rudiments of Greek that he learned in a Kirkcaldy classroom that gave him a key to understanding their philosophy presented to him at Glasgow University which, in turn, ultimately made sense to him of the tumultuous feelings of the Kirkcaldy schoolyard. In addition to the moral lessons in self-command there, he was experiencing psychologically the working of the cooling-down mechanism of sympathy of which he was to make so much in his own account of the moral sentiments (*TMS* 1.i.4.7–10).

It is also clear that among Smith's Kirkcaldy friends and near-contemporaries at the burgh school there was real intellectual distinction that was displayed in time in a variety of walks of life. The younger James Oswald of Dunnikier, already mentioned, followed his father into Parliament and rose high in the Government, serving on the Board of Trade (1751–9) and Treasury Board (1759–63: *HP* ii.237–40). From the family of the minister of the burgh's second charge came an able son, John Drysdale, who assumed leadership in due course of the powerful Moderate party in the Church of Scotland (Dalzel, 1794). From the Adam family came four architect brothers, with Adam Smith's friend Robert as the most brilliant of them all.[4] Each interesting in himself, such friends opened up to Adam Smith connections with professional and commercial life of great significance for the keen student of society he became.

Beyond the school walls lay another kind of education which Smith could acquire from the local scene. Carlyle in a letter of 12 February 1817 described Kirkcaldy as 'this long and dirty town', perhaps during a dyspeptic moment, but in his *Reminiscences* (1866: i.101–2), he wrote appreciatively of a first impression of its seacoast setting: 'waves all dancing and glancing out of a window, and beautifully humming and lullabying on that fine long sandy beach'. Elsewhere in the same book he described that beach as he recalled it in summer twilights:

a mile of the smoothest sand, with one long wave coming on gently, steadily, and break-ing in gradual explosion into harmless melodious white, at your hand all the way; the break of it rushing along like a mane of foam, beautifully sounding and advancing . . . from the West Burn to Kirkcaldy harbour, through the whole mile's distance.

One can imagine that such immediate surroundings gave aesthetic pleasure to Smith in boyhood, pleasure enhanced by the views: up the coast to the Isle of May with its lighthouse to the north-east, and across the shining waters of the firth to the long line of the Lothian shore, with the outlines of the Bass Rock and North Berwick Law prominent to the east, and almost due south the unmis-takable smudge from coal-fires that gave Edinburgh its nickname of Auld Reekie.

With a family background of Customs service, Smith's visits to the harbour would have the added interest of estimating the value of the cargoes of coal, salt, corn, linen, nails, and scrap iron passing in and out. There was a chance, too, of having an insider's information about the rummaging of the Dutch 'doggers' and the 'Bremeners' and 'cat-built' vessels of the coastal trade for undeclared ankers of brandy and other contraband goods (Falconer, 1789; Beaglehole, 1974; Kemp, 1979). On Sailor's Walk ears were assailed by the clack of North Sea and Baltic tongues, and nostrils distended by the pungent smells of fish, pitch, wet wood, cordage and sailcloth, salt water, and seaweed. Something of the dangers of sea-faring and commercial life was to be learned in this setting, and of the turbulence never far from eighteenth-century society.

In January 1736 there was excitement over the apprehension of the 'free-trader' Andrew Wilson, who had attempted to recoup his smuggling losses by robbing an excise collector at nearby Pittenweem. Subsequently he failed in an attempt to escape from the Tolbooth in Edinburgh, and tried again to escape during morning service in the Tolbooth Kirk, a scene witnessed by Smith's friend, Alexander Carlyle. At Wilson's execution, Captain Porteous of the Edinburgh City Guard ordered his men to fire on the mob. When Porteous was pardoned by the Government for this crime, a disciplined mob, said to have included many men from Fife, seized him on the night of 7 September 1736 and hanged him at the scene of Wilson's death, showing their detestation of the revenue system Wilson fought, and their utter defiance of official authority (Carlyle, 1973: 18–20; Scott, *Heart of Midlothian* (1818), ch. vii; Roughead, 1909).

In *WN* Smith considers the lot of the smuggler with some sympathy and understanding, representing him as a

person who, though no doubt highly blameable for violating the laws of his country, is frequently incapable of violating those of natural justice, and would have been, in every respect, an excellent citizen had not the laws of his country made that a crime which nature never meant to be so.

We might think that the fate of Alexander Wilson fits precisely what Smith paints as typical of the smuggler: someone who 'from being at first, perhaps, rather imprudent than criminal . . . at last too often becomes one of the hardiest and most determined violators of the laws of society' (v.ii.k.64).

Former schoolmates reported that Smith's health did not permit him to join their more active amusements, such as carrock (shinty) on the streets, and moral objections may have ruled out others, such as the traditional cock-fighting of Fastern's E'en (Shrove Tuesday), for in *WN* he wrote: 'a passion for cock-fighting has ruined many' (v.iii.1). However, walks would be an agreeable diversion from study and would offer much for observation and comment. Accompanying James Oswald from the family house in the burgh to the estate at Dunnikier would take the boys through the village of Pathhead, birthplace of the smuggler Wilson, up a steep brae from the harbour. In the village could be seen those workmen under 20 capable of making more and better nails, because of their specialization in that task, than the blacksmith, who had to cope with a wide variety of iron-forging tasks (*WN* I.i.6). In Pathhead or nearby Sinclairtown on the Dysart estate, it seems that nails were accepted as a form of currency at the baker's shop and ale-house (I.iv.3). Walks to these places would offer Smith a lesson in scale of division of labour, and distinctions of rank and status. An example was the degradation of the Scottish colliers and salters, who were bondsmen with legal status little better than slaves, since they were sold along with their places of work (ED 44; *LJ*(A) iii.126–7, (B) 138). Perhaps the seeds were planted of his later thesis that slavery is not profitable, since at some point he would learn that employers had to pay more to keep workers in bondage, and colliers would still run away to Newcastle to enjoy freedom with lower wages (*WN* 121, n. 15; Viner, 1965: 103–16; Whatley, 1984: ch. 3).

At his friend's home, Smith would find 'Lady Dunnikier' in charge, apex of local society and focus of its jealousies and ambitions, illustrating the importance of 'place' which he was to analyse in *TMS* (I.iii.2.8). Not far from Dunnikier was Ravenscraig Castle on its commanding and exposed clifftop site overlooking Kirkcaldy bay, reduced to ruins in 1651 by Commonwealth troops under General Monk, a vestige of feudal politics very different from those practised in Kirkcaldy's Tolbooth, Parliament House in Edinburgh, and (ultimately) Westminster by the Oswalds who, with their like in Scotland, were the beneficiaries in the long run of the breakdown of the power of the feudal nobility through war, and the 'silent and insensible operation of foreign commerce and manufactures' (*WN* III.iv.10; cf. *LJ*(A) iv.157).

That same 'insensible operation' was changing the patterns of farming and the Fife landscape that Smith saw as a boy when he visited the Dunnikier estate or travelled to that of his Uncle John Douglas at Strathenry. He must have observed, or had described to him, the survivals of the old system of Scottish agriculture which, he indicated in *WN*, was generally practised in the Lowlands before the Union of 1707. This consisted of dividing the land into a relatively small infield, ringing the farm buildings, where most of the cattle were kept, and a large outfield. The infield was supplied with enough manure to keep it under constant if low-yielding tillage of oats, to provide the meal that was the food staple, bere, a kind of barley for brewing and whisky-making, and also some wheat, pease, and beans.

The mature Smith reserved his scorn for the outfield, 'producing scarce anything but some miserable pasture, just sufficient to keep alive a few struggling, half-starved cattle'. After six or seven years in pasture 'in this wretched manner', the 'waste land' would be ploughed up to 'yield, perhaps, a poor crop or two of bad oats, or of some other coarse grain, and then, being entirely exhausted, it must be rested and pastured again' before further ploughing (I.xi.1.3). The ploughing was done traditionally by peasants settled in joint-farms, producing runrigs, S-shaped ridge strips, 200–500 yards long, separated from each other by weedy baulks (hollows) sometimes used as pasture. The configuration of the ground left by the runrig system can still be seen in the vicinity of Lochore, about three miles south-west of Strathenry (Handley, 1953: 57–8; Dodgshon, 1980: 69–92; Walker and Ritchie, 1987: 22).

Also visible in Fife, however, were signs of the new system of improved agriculture. A start often came when a laird moved from the family castle to an unfortified mansion nearby, as Smith's grandfather did at Strathenry, according to Scott (1937: 23) and local tradition. The ground between the two buildings was planted with trees, and such plantations were usually extended to shelter the 'policies' comprised of ornamental and kitchen gardens and enclosed parks. Food for the mansion was supplied by the home farm or mains. Crops such as legumes and turnips tried out in the kitchen garden (John Reid, *The Scots Gard'ner*, 1683: June) were introduced into the rotation in the parks. Sir John Clerk, the friend of Smith's father, moved in this direction at Penicuik, and well before his time the Hopes of Craighall, near Ceres, about sixteen miles from Strathenry, had been laying out money on improved systems of farm management (Di Folco, 1978). By the 1760s the improvement in these directions assumed a momentum in Lowland Scotland which was subsequently named an agricultural revolution (Smout and Fenton, 1965; Murison, 1982: 79; Whyte and Whyte, 1991: 127–9, 132, 135–50).

Perhaps harking back to the days, including boyhood, when he knew people actively engaged in farming, Smith thought the best improver was the 'small proprietor . . . who knows every part of his little territory, who views it with all the affection which property, especially small property, naturally inspires'. Such a man takes pleasure not only in improving but also in adorning his property—aesthetic effect is never forgotten by Smith—and of all improvers is generally the 'most industrious, the most intelligent, and the most successful' (*WN* III.iv.19). Smith's feeling for country life is revealed most endearingly in the praise he gives to the 'common ploughman', whose dialect might be hard to understand, and who is often thought stupid and ignorant, but who is 'seldom defective in understanding', and is superior in 'discretion and judgment' to the town tradesman (I.x.c.24). We might picture a boy in the fields near Strathenry, marvelling at the dexterity of the ploughman managing his team of six to ten horses or oxen pulling a heavy plough along the corn rigs, and so helping to create the wealth of Fife.

Turning from the tending of the soil to that of the soul, we find that Smith would meet the tradition of service to the Kirk in the household of the Drysdale family. The father, John Drysdale, was minister of the second charge (district) of the parish of Kirkcaldy from 1712 to February 1726, when he was transferred to the first one, only to die suddenly in May of that year. The mother, Mary Ferguson, daughter of a Provost of Kirkcaldy, was strong enough in her widowhood to hold her family together, perhaps the source of a bond with Smith's mother. The third son, John (1718–88), became Smith's friend at school, where he proved a good classical scholar under Miller's tutelage. Also a friend of Smith was another son, George, who became a merchant and Provost of Kirkcaldy, also

Collector of Customs there (Dalzel, 1794: 53). John Drysdale shared Smith's interest in the foundation of morals, perhaps awakened by early study of Cicero. His sermons reflect that modified Calvinism which helped to nurture Smith's thought, and to which he and Smith were exposed in impressionable boyhood through the religious exercises of the school, as well as the diets of worship on the Sabbath. We can be sure that the mothers of Smith and Drysdale saw that they went to the parish kirk, and were prepared for the minister's visits to their homes, when he came to catechize the 'examinable persons' from 12 upwards (Graham, 1899: ii.17).

The ethical and social bias of the theology to which the boys were exposed is well represented by the account in the *Larger Catechism* of the duties required by the eighth Commandment:

truth, faithfulness and justice in contracts, and commerce between man and man; rendering to every one his due; restitution of goods unlawfully detained from the right owners thereof; giving and lending freely, according to our abilities, and the necessities of others; moderation of our judgements, wills, and affections, concerning worldly goods; a provident care and study to get, keep, use and dispose those things which are necessary and convenient for the sustenation of our nature, and suteable to our condition; a lawful calling; and diligence in it; frugality; avoiding unnecessary lawsuits; and suretyship, or other like engagements; and an endeavour by all just, and lawfull means, to procure, preferye and further the wealth and outward estate of others as wel as our own . . . (*Confession of Faith*, 1671: 16–18)

Smith avoided the calling of the ministry, which Drysdale prepared for by studying, like his father, at Edinburgh University, beginning there in 1732. He was ordained in 1740 and later married Mary Adam, linking him to the family of architects and, through them, to the historian William Robertson, another prominent member of the Moderate party in the Kirk. From the relative obscurity of the parish of Kirkliston, Drysdale was manœuvred by the Moderates in 1762 into an Edinburgh charge, that of Lady Yester's Chapel. This was accomplished in the face of vigorous opposition by the rival Popular party (Sher, 1982). Drysdale's home-town connections with James Oswald and the Adam family, also his friendship with Robertson, by then Principal of Edinburgh University, no doubt had a good deal to do with his preferment, but his sermons and pastoral care endeared him to his parishioners, and political ability brought him prominence in the Kirk as Clerk of the General Assembly (nominally from 1778, but really for ten years before that) and its Moderator (1773, 1784). To Smith's early friendship with Drysdale, and through him with other ministers of his persuasion, may be traced that favourable view of Moderate Presbyterianism expressed in *WN* (v.i.g.37).

Diligence in a lawful calling, but also endeavour by all just and lawful means to procure wealth, were traits strikingly displayed by the Adam family. The father, William (d. 1748), followed his father in becoming an architect, but was extremely active in many lines of business beyond those connected with building. In 1728 Sir John Clerk recorded his impressions of a visit to Kirkcaldy:

I took a little time to consider a brickwork belonging to Mr Adams, Architect. This I found as expensive a piece of work as the nature of it required and I could not enough admire the enterprising temper of the proprietor who had at that time under his own care near to twenty general projects—Barley Mills, Timber Mills, Coal Works, Salt Pans, Marble Works, Highways, Farms, houses of his own a-building and houses belonging to others not a few. (Fleming, 1962: 7)

By this time William Adam could see himself as *Vitruvius Scoticus*, and was gathering subscriptions for the publication of his architectural designs under that title (Adam, 1980). On the practical side, he built or contributed to the building of a string of country houses, where Adam Smith's contemporaries indulged their classical taste for the life of the villa. These included Mavisbank, Sir John Clerk's home; Arniston, Midlothian, home of the legal dynasty of Dundas, well known to Smith; and Hopetoun, near Queensferry, where Smith might have been a resident if its Earl had secured his services as tutor to his son, Lord Hope.

In 1728 Adam was appointed to the lucrative post of Clerk and Storekeeper of the King's Works in Scotland, and two years later to that of Mason to the Board of Ordnance in North Britain. The growth of his private fortune allowed him to purchase property in Edinburgh in 1728, and move his family there in that year, though he conceded in 1741 that the capital was 'not the place I have most pleasure in'. In the 1730s he began to acquire land in Kinross for the Blair Adam estate, and he secured employment from public bodies to build Dundee's town hall, Robert Gordon Hospital in Aberdeen, and the Library at Glasgow University which became so familiar to Adam Smith (Gifford, 1989).

In the family home in Kirkcaldy there was a lively domestic scene. William Adam's wife, Mary Robertson, sister of the minister of Old Greyfriars in Edinburgh and aunt of the historian William Robertson, bore a large family, of whom survived four sons and six daughters. The heir, John (b. 1721), was Adam Smith's nearest contemporary, and probably attended school with him in Kirkcaldy, though he afterwards went to Dalkeith Grammar School. The next son, Robert (b. 1728), was born in Kirkcaldy, but when an infant was taken with his family to Edinburgh, where he entered the High School in 1734 to learn Latin, and did so to such good effect that he constantly stood either first or second in his class. His classical grounding served him well for the careful study he made of Diocletian's palace at Spalatro (Split), which, along with other researches he made while on the Grand Tour 1754–7, helped to carry his architectural thought to a higher power than his father had achieved, and brought him a European reputation for a distinctive style in designing buildings and their interiors (Saunders, 1992). The young friends of John and Robert Adam, including Adam Smith, were welcomed in the family circle. This 'was long the resort of men of genius and literature, the Ornaments of the Age', according to a life of Robert Adam by a cousin (SRO Clerk of Penicuik MSS; Fleming, 1962: 5). Friendship with the Adam family and proximity to the heart of their enterprises in Kirkcaldy would bring to Adam Smith awareness of many strands of economic activity in the Scotland of his boyhood, and of that stirring spirit of improvement and intellectual adventure, as well as of the shaping forces of neo-Calvinism and classical influence noticeable in the activities of the middling classes.

Exploration of Adam Smith's family background and boyhood years and experiences, then, suggests that there were some compensations for the lack of his father's presence in his life. His mother's strength and close kinship and family friendship bonds gave him emotional security and stability in his boyhood. In addition, he was well prepared intellectually for his student years and finding a vocation as a moral philosopher and man of letters during a stimulating era in his country's history, marked by a determined drive for improved performance in agriculture and other economic sectors. Most important of all, his form of Presbyterian inheritance, together with the rudiments of training in the Latin classics, apparently instilled in him the values of a frugal style of life, self-discipline of a Stoic cast, diligence in his calling, and strict justice towards others tempered with benevolence which characterized his actions and his teaching. At the same time, it should be acknowledged that there were elements in the religious culture Smith encountered in Kirkcaldy that could be oppressive and restrictive, just as they were for Hume at Chirnside (Streminger, 1994: 71–80). In time, Smith like Hume rebelled against this and, rather than embracing the strict controls of the Calvinist Kirk to check the original depravity of man, set store by human goodness and the will to enjoy natural liberty.

3

Glasgow

I agree with you in preferring Glasgow to Edinburgh.

Glasgow does not seem an obvious choice by Adam Smith's family as the place to send him for his university education. Within the confines of Fife, the ancient foundation of St Andrews was only twenty miles away. However, it was in decay for much of the eighteenth century, as Dr Johnson found and lamented during his visit with Boswell, described two years later in his *Journey to the Western Islands of Scotland*, 1775 (Johnson, 1985). In Aberdeen there was a family link with both universities (or colleges), King's and Marischal, but the members in question seem to have incurred the taint of Jacobitism (Scott, 1937: 398), and there were family and political squabbles among the faculty even after the Jacobites were purged in the wake of the 1715 Rising (Emerson, 1992: 59–63). As for Edinburgh, father Smith had certainly struggled to return there from Kirkcaldy, and its university was growing in reputation for the training it offered in law, medicine, and the ministry following the usual arts course. But in the son's eyes, the capital seems to have been identified as a place of dissipation and crime, at least in contrast to the state of affairs prevailing in Glasgow, this being a theme both in his correspondence and carried on from *LJ* to *WN*.[1]

Late in life he sent his heir, David Douglas, to study at Glasgow and board with a former pupil, Professor John Millar, and he advised another pupil, Henry Herbert, Lord Porchester, to do likewise with his son, agreeing with Porchester that Glasgow was to be preferred to Edinburgh (*Corr.*, app. E, p). In his own case he may have had a relative, Aunt Jane, to board with in Glasgow (Scott, 1937: 235). Also, his father had been made a burgess of the city in 1707, which might be expected to win the son acceptance. And his father's patron, Lord Loudoun, had been a student at Glasgow himself. The Campbell interest was predominant there from 1725 to 1742 and from 1746 to 1765, offering many opportunities for the exercise of patronage (Emerson, 1992: 6).

In 1737 Adam Smith went to Glasgow University at 14, quite a normal practice in his time, and matriculated on 14 November of that year, in the 'third class' under Professor John Loudoun (Scott, 1937: 364; Addison, 1913: 18). But before the course of his education is traced, the nature of the city has to be explored, as the setting for his impressionable student years. Also, the institutional arrangements of the University should be discussed. Their settlement as a result of a Commission, deliberating ten years before Smith matriculated, helps to explain how it was that Glasgow became one of the powerhouses of the Scottish Enlightenment, and stimulated so markedly his intellectual growth.

The boy Smith was exposed in Glasgow to a scale of urban life far beyond that of Kirkcaldy, and no doubt a scene instructive to him about morals, local politics, and burgeoning economic activity. The place-name is formed from the Celtic elements *glas* and *cau*, meaning 'green hollow' (Nicolaisen, 1976: 172). This was appropriate for a city generally regarded in Smith's time as beautiful, situated on banks sloping southwards to the Clyde amid streams such as the Molindinar and Camlachie which fed this river. An ancient ecclesiastical centre claiming foundation by St Mungo or Kentigern in 560, it began to thrive in the seventeenth and eighteenth centuries through its market and distribution services to the Clydesdale region, and its trading ventures to Ireland and further westward across the Atlantic to the Caribbean and American colonies, as well as southward and northward to Europe. When Thomas Tucker surveyed the organization of the Scottish Customs and Excise in 1656, he noted that Glasgow was 'one of the most considerable burghs in Scotland, as well for the structure as trade of it. The inhabitants (all but the students of the Colledge which is here) are traders and dealers' (quoted Hamilton, 1963: 249). After his visit in 1725, Defoe commented that it was the only city in Scotland that was apparently increasing in both foreign and domestic trade, the reason being that the Union had opened the door for the Scots into the American colonies, and the Glasgow merchants had seized their opportunities. He also noted that the locally chartered vessels had an advantage over their English rivals in sailing time and freedom from enemy attacks:

the Glasgow vessels are no sooner out of the Firth of Clyde, but they stretch away to the north-west, are out of the road of privateers immediately, and are often at the capes of Virginia before the London ships get clear of the Channel (1927: ii.748–51).

Travelling from Kirkcaldy to Glasgow must have been an eye-opening experience for Smith. The first part was probably a boat journey to Edinburgh, followed by a horseback ride to Linlithgow. The striking royal palace there, built for the Stuarts over the period 1425–1620, was still habitable and complete, a state of affairs ended by the carelessness and fires of the Duke of Cumberland's troops in 1746 (McWilliam, 1978: 293). The road led to Falkirk, notable for the *trysts* held from April to November on nearby Stenhouse Muir, when great quantities of cattle, sheep, and ponies from all over Scotland, including the Highlands and Islands, were brought to market and after sale were directed south on the great drove roads (Haldane, 1952). After the Treaty of Union in 1707, English dealers had come to Falkirk in increasing numbers and, of course, there was free trade across the Border (Murray, 1993: 145). Smith came to believe that the profits of this trade underwrote farming improvement in the Lowlands (*WN* I.xi.3). Opponents of the Union had argued that the Scots profited little from the cattle trade compared to the English middlemen who fattened the bedraggled 'runts' on their arrival from the north, and that it would pay more to fatten them in Scotland and then export barrelled beef, as the Irish did (Lenman, 1977: 57).

A striking feature of the landscape near Falkirk and beyond, likely to be drawn to the attention of the classically trained Smith, was the trace of the Roman occupation beginning in the second century AD. A friend of a later period, Alexander Carlyle of Inveresk, rode with his father on this journey from Edinburgh in 1742, to obtain a bursary to study divinity at Glasgow, and he remembered staying at Castlecary on the Antonine Wall, where there was a Roman fort. A return ride 'by the nearest road' from Glasgow to Edinburgh took the Carlyles sixteen hours to accomplish, and we might think of Adam Smith together with a relative or a servant making the same rate of progress (Carlyle, 1973: 33). After the dreary moorland past Falkirk and views of the wild surges of the Kilsyth Hills and the Campsie Fells, Smith would find it agreeable to wind down into the valley of the Kelvin and pass to Glasgow, described in 1736 as 'surrounded with Cornfields, Kitchen and Flower gardens and beautiful Orchyards abounding with Fruits of all Sorts, which by Reason of the open and large Streets send forth a pleasant and odoriferous Smell' (M'Ure, 1736: 122).

Entry to the city from the east was through the old Toll Bar. Generally, travellers went along the Gallowgate, passing the unenclosed College grounds, the Molendinar Burn somewhat polluted by the discharges of the dyers, and the tenements of the weavers, on to the Cross, the hub of Glasgow life. This was formed in Smith's time by the convergence of the long Gallowgate, the short Trongate to the west, the Saltmarket leading south to the Clyde, and the High Street to the north, onto which abutted the College which was Smith's destination.

Up the Bell o' the Brae from the High Street was the cathedral, a noble building constructed mainly between the late thirteenth and fifteenth centuries, which was preserved from destruction during the Reformation by the action of the trade guilds. Medieval life had revolved round the cathedral, and when Pope Nicholas V issued a bull on 7 January 1451 for the foundation of a *Studium generale* at Glasgow, the first university teaching was conducted in the 'Auld Pedagogy', thought to have been a chapter school, in the nearby Rottenrow: Gaelic *rat-an-righ*, the King's Road (Hetherington, 1985: 9–10; House, 1964). This street and the Drygate opposite formed a fashionable residential quarter in Smith's day, but the onset of an age of commerce drew the life of the city to the West End, radiating out from the Trongate.

The politics and religious outlook of the city affected the tone of the University where Smith was a student, and later was to teach. Long a Protestant city, Glasgow rejoiced in 1688 at the declaration of William of Orange that he and his consort, Mary Stuart, daughter of James II, were to assume the throne of the United Kingdom. On 30 November of that year the young Earl of Loudoun and other Glasgow students burned effigies of the Pope of Rome and the Archbishops of St Andrews and Glasgow, leaders of the Episcopalians in Scotland, who adhered to James II and the Stuart succession. Two years after the Revolution, Glasgow passed from being a burgh of barony under the jurisdiction of its archbishops and became a royal burgh, whose Town Council was answerable only to King and Parliament.

In 1711, its 'sett' (constitution) prescribed that local government was to be administered by a provost, three bailies, thirteen councillors of the merchant rank, and twelve of the trades rank. Other office-bearers who were, or after election became, councillors included a dean of guild, a deacon-convener, a treasurer, and a master of works. The outgoing Council elected the incoming provost and bailies, and these men, together with the provosts and bailies of the two previous years and others making a group of twelve, elected the new councillors. Undoubtedly self-perpetuating and oligarchic, the system did, however, work: able outsiders could break into it, and guild restrictions were evaded before 1740 (Eyre-Todd, 1934: iii.1–9, 78–9).

The Council met in the Tolbooth at the north-west corner of the Cross. Its seven-storey steeple, built in 1625–7, still stands, and it would be a familiar sight to Adam Smith, as would two other nearby steeples still remaining, also Gothic in profile, but with Renaissance touches (Williamson *et al.*, 1990: 39, 158, 194–5). These were the Tron (*c.*1592, spire 1630–6) and that of the old Merchants' House (1665). Familiar, too, would be the airs played in the carillon under the imperial crown of the Tolbooth steeple. Some years before Smith's arrival, the greatest Gaelic poet of the eighteenth century, Alasdair Mac Mhaighstir Alasdair (Alexander MacDonald), enjoyed the airs so much as a student that he set poems to them, but considered the splash of whisky into the drinking-horn to be a sweeter sound than the pealing bells:

> 'S binne [na] cluig-chiuil ud Ghlascha
> T'fhuaim le bastal dol sa' chorn.

> (MacDonald, quoted Thomson,
> 1983: 184)

Town development along the main streets round the Cross was conducted sensibly, because the Council secured compliance with good building standards by providing tax relief for those who upheld them. A decade before Smith became a student, an English engineer officer wrote that Glasgow was the 'most uniform and prettiest' city he had ever seen, notable for well-sashed, ashlar-dressed houses 'all of one model', and for 'piazzas' rising round them on either side, 'which gives a good air to the buildings' (Burt, 1815: i.22). These were 'lands' or tenements, occupied storey by storey by separate families living in flats, or devoted to social or business purposes as in the case of the Tradesland at the corner of the Saltmarket and the Gallowgate. Its erection was subsidized by the

Council in 1695. On the opposite side of the Saltmarket, on the Trongate corner, was the Merchants' House, which contained a coffee-house seemingly operated as Glasgow's first Exchange. The newsletters made available were paid for by the Town Council, until the town hall and a coffee-house next to the Tolbooth were opened the year after Adam Smith came to Glasgow (Eyre-Todd, 1934: iii.51).

The spirit of town planning in the early eighteenth-century city was connected with the drive for success in trading. In the 1720s a completely new and handsome thoroughfare, King Street, was built to join the Trongate and Briggate and offer a prospect up to the new St David's Kirk (1719–24), replaced by the present Ramshorn Kirk (1824–6) at the head of the Candleriggs. King Street illustrated Smith's remark that the 'town is a continual fair or market, to which the inhabitants of the country resort, in order to exchange their rude for manufactured produce' (*WN* iii.i.4). Along it were built the covered markets intended to take over from the open huckstering of street exchange, with its confusion, dirt, and liability to escape from municipal control. On the east side of the street there were stalls for butcher meat, and on the west side those for fish, mutton, and cheese (Gibson, 1777: 149; Eyre-Todd, 1934: iii.1440).

In 1743–4, his first year at Glasgow, Carlyle of Inveresk lodged with Dr Robert Hamilton, Professor of Anatomy, in a house on King Street opposite the butcher's market. He noted that the professors with boarders kept menservants, but few Glasgow merchants' families had them. Taking a different line from Smith's, that the absence of many servants was conducive to order (*WN* 336, n. 18), Carlyle remarked that the 'Manner of Living too at this time was but Coarse and Vulgar', with little of the genteel entertainment of Edinburgh. He also noted, however, that benefit was obtained from conversation with the 'Principal Merchants', certainly a feature of Smith's experience when he was a professor at Glasgow. In addition, he stated that it was usual for the sons of merchants to attend the University (Carlyle, 1973: 39, 45, 51). This was a broadening experience for them. In Adam Smith's first period in Glasgow, students encountered at the University the 'new light' theology and moral philosophy taught by Francis Hutcheson which counteracted the 'old light' Calvinism of the bulk of local clergy, who could be narrow and bigoted.[2] The students were also introduced to mathematics and science taught by Robert Simson and Robert Dick, which became a preparation for the modern world of commerce and technology.

Further strides towards modernity were being taken to the south of King Street, where the Briggate joined Stockwell Street at the approach to Old Glasgow Bridge. Its eight-arched structure dated back to the time of Bishop Rae in 1345. Contemporary prints show that the Clyde was still fordable at this point, but by 1736 barges and lighters could come to the Broomielaw westward along the north bank, where a harbour had been constructed and the Custom-house stood. Through this entry, and through Port Glasgow further yet to the west and on the Clyde estuary, which afforded deeper berths for shipping, came sugar and tobacco from the New World. The market for these commodities, together with the outgoing hardware and textiles and allied ship-servicing facilities, made the bulk of the Glasgow fortunes of Smith's day.

    As a result of the entrepôt trading, principally in tobacco, and the buoyancy of the city's industries, summed up in the phrase: 'suggaries, roapary, soapary, and glassary', as well as successful organization of the food market represented by the King Street development, Glasgow's population by 1737 was at least ten times that of Kirkcaldy, and ever-greater expansion was likely (Eyre-Todd, 1934: iii.59; Hamilton, 1963: 18). Smith matured as this expansion was in progress, and in due course as a professor and man of letters he reflected on the changes, and behind them the historical revolution which had led to the magistrates of Glasgow, for example, buying Newark Castle and the surrounding land in 1668 to establish the harbour of New Glasgow for the merchants venturing into the Atlantic trade (Stevenson, 1985: 57). These recent developments illustrated a generalization made by Smith, perhaps based on the ancient history he began reading in Kirkcaldy and Glasgow, as well as on what he saw with his own eyes in these ports. This was the claim that the 'first improvements . . . in arts and industry are always made in those places where the conveniency of water carriage affords the most extensive market to the produce of every sort of labour' (*LJ*: 585).

    The foundation for Smith's rise to fame as professor and man of letters was laid in his student years in the 'Old College' of Glasgow, lying on the High Street below the cathedral. It occupied in all about twenty-six acres of ground, sloping gradually to the Molendinar Burn to the east and rising beyond that to the Dow Hill. Walks led to a Physic Garden and other cultivated parts, also to open land used for pasture (Hetherington, 1985: 13). The second Professor of Divinity kept a cow there in Smith's time as a student, and was allowed to build a byre beside his University house. This was John Simson, who had excited his students about new developments in theology counter to orthodox Calvinism, and was disciplined in 1729 by the General Assembly of the Kirk for teaching heresy. He was forbidden to teach or preach thereafter, but kept his professorship until he died in 1740, and Principal Neil Campbell had to instruct the divinity students himself (Coutts, 1909: 210–12; Murray, 1927: 376).

    John Slezer in his *Theatrum Scotiae* (1693) described the buildings of the College as the 'chief ornament of the City' (Pl. 1). They were erected principally between 1632 and 1661 from the proceeds of a public subscription, whose chief benefactor was Zachary Boyd, a minister of the Barony parish actively involved in University affairs as Rector, Dean of the Faculty, and Vice-Chancellor. When Adam Smith passed through the archway in the Inner Quadrangle, he would walk under a marble bust of Boyd, erected in 1658 to record his munificence. This is now on view in the Hunterian Museum at Glasgow University.

    The building programme of the seventeenth century was energetically maintained by a protégé of Cromwell, Principal Patrick Gillespie, who oversaw the

The COLLEDGE of GLASGOW

Pl. 1. Glasgow College, 1693. From John Slezer, *Theatrum Scotiae* (GUL).

completion of the south and west sides of the Inner Quadrangle in 1656, the Tower and north and south sides of the Front Quadrangle in 1658, and in 1661 most of the remainder, including the frontage on the High Street. This was pierced by a decorated gateway with massive oaken doors studded with nails, over which was set the royal coat of arms and the initials 'C.R.2' for Charles II. Principal Neil Campbell's house was on the south side of the gateway, and Professor John Simson's on the north. By 1736, two sides of a Professors' Court had been built to provide houses replacing the chambers formerly assigned to the regents within the College buildings (Hetherington, 1985: 14–27).

Students could take lodgings within the college for about £1 a year, but fewer and fewer did so. Bothered with a cough during his first winter in his King Street lodgings, Carlyle took a 'College Room' the next year, 'only Bare Walls, and 20 feet by 17', where he never had a cold. A college servant lighted his fire and made his bed, and a maid under the landlady who furnished the room came once a fortnight to change his linen. Two English theology students, presumably Dissenters, lived below him, but there was nobody above him. We do not know where Smith lived in Glasgow as a student, but his expenses would have been very modest. The poorest students could live on a basic diet of oat- or pease-meal for roughly £5 a year. Assuming the maximum number of classes were taken, the fees amounted to £3.10s. a year, so university education at Glasgow could be obtained for £10 a year. Smith's family was well-to-do, and could afford the £30 or £40 that would be needed for staying with a relative or in a 'common boarding-house' or in a professor's house, these being the usual options (Campbell and Skinner, 1982b: 16–17).

The institutional framework for Adam Smith and the professors who taught him was largely determined by a Commission of Visitation appointed on 31 August 1726 and reporting the next year on 19 September. It was created ostensibly to complete the work of the Revolution settlement of the University of Glasgow beginning in 1690, but there was also a shift in Scottish political power behind the Commission's intervention. John Stirling, a masterful personality, who was Principal at Glasgow from 1701 until 1727, was attached to the Squadrone party led by John Kerr, 1st Duke of Roxburghe. In June 1725 the latter had proved ineffective in dealing with riots at Glasgow over the Walpole Government's imposition of a malt tax, and he was dismissed as Secretary of State for Scotland. Walpole turned to the 2nd Duke of Argyll to control the country, and Argyll relied on his brother Archibald, Lord Ilay, who became the leading political figure in Scotland. He worked through a group of supporters known as the Argathelians, who set out to restore order and secure economic improvement in Scotland through displaying power and exercising patronage in the universities and other institutions. Reform at Glasgow was an instrument to this end.[3]

In the first instance, the Commission saw a need to correct problems caused by Stirling antagonizing some colleagues and the students through insisting on his own decisions and the advancement of adherents in defiance of what were claimed to be the normal procedures. A case in point was the election of the rector, in Scotland as in many European countries the titular head of a university. Principal Stirling excluded students from the electoral body, and his action became a focus for discontent. While Glasgow students were mostly boys in their early teens, there was a sizeable number of Irish Presbyterian undergraduates and graduates, who were older and ready to be more politically active because of their awareness of the struggles of Dissenters in their homeland to secure civil and religious liberties. Responding to encouragement by professors opposed to Stirling, they employed against him a rhetoric that painted him as a tyrant and their cause as the vindication of rights.[4] These efforts sustained a tradition of political discourse that was to influence Smith in his stand for natural liberty. Student history at Glasgow must have helped to form his outlook as well as instruction and reading.

In 1722 a group of Smith's predecessors among the student body lit a bonfire opposite the college gate to celebrate the results of the general election. The Senior Regent, Gershom Carmichael, sought to have the bonfire quenched and was assaulted by one of the student leaders, John Smith, an Irish divinity student. Smith was expelled but later in the year published in Dublin a pamphlet dealing with the affair: *A Short Account of the Late Treatment of the Students of the University of G——w* (Stewart, 1987*b*). The students raised an action in the Court of Session, and planned to petition the House of Commons for restoration of their right to a franchise in the rectorial election, counting on a champion in the person of Lord Molesworth, leader of the Old Whig party in Dublin, who had been the friend of John Locke and Anthony Ashley Cooper, 3rd Earl of Shaftesbury. Carmichael, who had a role in the development of Scottish philosophy as a teacher of the natural law tradition associated with Grotius and Pufendorf, had inflamed the students in 1717 with a 'noble Harrangue . . . in praise of Liberty' (Smith, 1722: 10), but he had abandoned the students' cause in return for a favour to his son by Principal Stirling. In 1725 rebellious students attacked the house of the Rector, Sir Hugh Montgomerie of Hartfield, manœuvred into office by Stirling. The Presbyterian historian Robert Wodrow noted the effect on enrolment: 'The Colledge of Glasgou is very thin this session, and the Masters may blame themselves; their divisions and breaches have lessened the reputation of the society, and multitudes nou go to Edinburgh' (Wodrow, 1843: iii.240; Mackie, 1954: 177). But the work of the Commissioners of 1726–7 and conciliatory efforts by the Professor of Humanity (Latin), Andrew Rosse, and others within the College changed matters.

The membership of the Commission reflected the importance attached by the Argathelians to settling matters at Glasgow. The Kirk and the legal establishment were well represented, and the ousted Squadrone party had a voice in James Erskine of Grange, the Lord Justice-Clerk. Ilay chose to serve, together with his deputy minister in Scotland, Andrew Fletcher of Milton. Ilay was a collector of books, and had pronounced interests in languages, mathematics, and science, including botany with applications to gardening and afforestation. He made himself well acquainted with university affairs and used his patronage to secure able men as professors, among them in time Adam Smith.[5] Milton was the nephew of Andrew Fletcher of Saltoun, the philosophical republican and articulate opponent of the Union, who was one source of the current of civic humanist thought found in Smith (Robertson, 1983). While he did not share his uncle's politics, Milton resembled him in cultivating a taste for literature and philosophy, and he was a staunch promoter of agricultural improvement, manufactures, and trade (Shaw, 1983: 7). With these men in charge, the Commission met in Glasgow and Edinburgh a number of times, was informed about the government and policy of the University, reviewed its charters and other relevant documents, inquired into old usage and current practice, and heard the evidence presented by the Principal and the professors. The body of statutes issued by the Commission in 1727 regulated the practice and constitution of the University of Glasgow until the passing of the Universities (Scotland) Act of 1858, and thus covered the period of Smith's student days and his professorship.

Tackling the issue of the office of the rector, the Commission laid down that the students were to take part in the elections voting in their 'nations'. A far cry from their turbulent originals in the nationalities represented in the medieval University of Paris, the Glasgow 'nations' were determined by the regions of birthplace: Clydesdale, those from Glasgow and surrounding parts; Rothesay, those from the west, including the Hebrides and Ireland; Albany, those from north of the Forth, also foreign lands; and Teviotdale, those from south of the Forth, also England and the British colonies. While provision was made for electing the rector annually on 15 November (or the 16th when the 15th fell on a Sunday), the matriculation register for 1737 gives the 14th as the day of elections. Thus it happened that Adam Smith on matriculating would be qualified to vote on 14 November with the Albany nation to elect as Rector John Orr of Barrowfield, a Glasgow merchant who was a generous benefactor of the Library (Durkan and Kirk, 1977: 42; Coutts, 1909: 204–9, 255; Addison, 1913: 17; Mackie, 1954: 178–81). Smith was himself proposed unsuccessfully as a rectorial candidate in 1768, and finally elected Rector fifty years after matriculating (Murray, 1927: 327).

On the academic side, the Commissioners chiefly sought to bring arrangements into line with contemporary thinking. From their foundation, the Scottish universities had followed the regenting system whereby students were taken through four years of an arts course under one master appointed for each year. Efforts had been made from the time of the Reformation to 'fix' the masters or regents to particular subjects, and Principal William Carstares carried through this change at Edinburgh in 1708 through assignments of professorial Chairs.

Glasgow had made a beginning with the creation of two Chairs in Divinity by 1642, and a Royal Commission recommended further Chairs in 1661: Humanity,

Medicine, Civil and Canon Law, and Mathematics; but there was not enough money for these ambitious plans. Following the 1688–9 Revolution, however, more resources were made available and enduring provision was made for the following Chairs in existence in Smith's time: Mathematics (1691), Greek (1704), Botany and Anatomy (1704), Humanity (1706), Oriental Languages (1709), Law (1713), Medicine (1713), and (1716) Ecclesiastical History (Mackie, 1954: 99, 122, 154, 165, 169, 170; Emerson, 1992: app. v).

In 1727 the three Philosophy Regents were required to select Chairs, in order of their seniority; Gershom Carmichael chose Ethics (later distinguished as the Chair of Moral Philosophy), John Loudoun chose Logic and Metaphysics, and Robert Dick chose Natural Philosophy, that is, Physics (Murray, 1927: 22). St Andrews followed the example of Edinburgh and Glasgow by abandoning the regent system completely in 1747, Marischal College in Aberdeen was next in 1753, and King's College came last in 1799 (Cant, 1992: 108–9, n. 1).

At Glasgow, the 1727 regulations further prescribed the sequence of 'gown' classes needed for the MA degree: Greek for the first year following achievement of competence in Latin; then Logic and Metaphysics; followed by Moral Philosophy and Natural Philosophy in the order chosen by the students themselves. Degree examinations had to be passed in the ancient languages and in the three philosophical subjects.

Ten days or so after these statutes were passed, Principal Stirling died and was succeeded by the Minister of Renfrew, Neil Campbell. The latter was neither very learned nor outstanding as an administrator, but he kept peace among the hitherto warring factions among the professors, allowing their abilities to shine forth, and he accepted with equanimity the students exercising their privilege of electing rectors. Robert Wodrow had gloomy thoughts about this matter: '[a] litle stigma is put upon the last Visitors in restoring the boyes to their sensles pretended priviledge, because in my opinion it's to their own hurt' (Wodrow, 1843: iii.333; Mackie, 1954: 183).

We may believe the reverse, however: that exercise of the privilege, or right, of electing the rector was a valuable part of the unique experience of being a student at Glasgow. Adam Smith would see that his University was not a closed corporation of the masters, such as he found at Oxford, where learning seemed stultified. Rather, in a city of diverse and burgeoning economic life, he became part of an academic body to which he could give his loyalty as a kind of citizen, and whose teachers opened to him exciting new scenes of thought.

4

The Never to be Forgotten Hutcheson

soberest and most judicious patron of the system which makes virtue consist in benevolence

In Glasgow, on the morning of 10 October 1737, it was Principal Neil Campbell's duty to greet the Professors of Humanity, Greek, Logic, Moral Philosophy, and Natural Philosophy at a quarter before eleven o'clock in the Faculty Room or Fore-Hall on the west side of the Outer Quadrangle. This was the traditional opening of Adam Smith's first session. At eleven, the Little or Class Bell rang in the 140-ft. tower in the Inner Quadrangle, and the five 'gown' classes went to the assigned rooms, where the Professors named a censor and stated the hours of teaching and the assigned books. At quarter past eleven the Great or College Bell rang, and the 400 to 500 red-gowned students and their black-gowned Professors went to the Common Hall on the east side of the Inner Quadrangle, where prayers were offered and points cleared about college discipline (Scott, 1937: 32–3; Murray, 1927: 58–60).

The 'gown' classes in the Scottish universities of this era were organized as follows. The fifth or lowest one concentrated on Latin, and completed a pre-university year. The fourth went through the *bajan* year, when students focused on Greek. The designation came from the French *béjaune*, *bec jaune*: a young bird, an inexperienced youth. Adam Smith became a *semi* (*semi-bachelor* or *semi-bajan*) in the third class in 1737, because the Latin he had acquired at Kirkcaldy burgh school made taking the 'fifth class' unnecessary, and apparently he had made sufficient progress in Greek to bypass the *bajan* year. Ahead of him was the *tertian*, or *bachelor*, year and that of the *magistrand*, candidate for mastership (Cant, 1992: 21–2).

A contemporary source informs us about the curriculum for the *semis*: 'they read two Hours each Day *Logicks*, *Metaphysicks*, and *Pneumaticks*, with the Professors of these Branches of *Philosophy*, and this Year begin the study of *Geometry*, being taught an Hour each Day by the Professor of *Mathematics*, and may attend also the *Greek* Lectures' (Chamberlayne, 1737: II.iii.12–13).

Smith seems to have attended the Greek lectures, for he retained his copy of the *Tabula*, a text in his day ascribed to Cebes, the friend of Socrates. This was used at Glasgow by Professor Alexander Dunlop as a legacy from the teaching practice of the Protestant Humanists (Bolgar, 1977: 354). Now thought to date from the first century AD, this compilation offers in a Pythagorean setting a blend of the teaching of Plato, Aristotle, and the Stoics. As was often the case, Smith's *Tabula* was bound with the far more significant *Encheiridion* of Epictetus, in a London and Cambridge edition dated 1670, which has the book-plate of the library of the mature man, but also Smith's signature in the same 'round school-boy hand' as that of the matriculation roll. The *Tabula* has red pencilled stars in the margin, possibly indicating readings assigned by Dunlop, and two words of the text are crossed out as if emendations are required, though these are not recorded (GUL; Scott, 1937: 33–4, 365; Mizuta). Some philosophical interest attached to the *Tabula*, however, since it was regarded as a source of Pythagorean thought, which Smith like his contemporaries held to be the forerunner of modern moral and scientific systems.[1]

As for the *Encheiridion*, its teaching and that of other Stoic texts had a powerful effect on the formation of Smith's own intellectual systems. The story of Epictetus, the emancipated slave who became Nero's secretary, and preserved his tranquillity of mind under threat of exile and death, fascinated Smith until the end of his life. Perhaps he was something of a role model for Smith, embodying in a secular form the teaching about self-command he would encounter in his Calvinist upbringing. Certainly, the 'independent and spirited, but often harsh, Epictetus' figured in Smith's own moral philosophy lectures, and in all the editions of *TMS* (VII.ii.1.35), as the compelling teacher of command of the passions.

Smith's Greek teacher, Alexander Dunlop, was well connected in the academic world, being the son of Principal William Dunlop of Glasgow and a relation of Principal William Carstares of Edinburgh. He had secured the Greek Chair in 1704 after a trial in which he had analysed eleven lines of Homer to the satisfaction of Principal Stirling and his colleagues (Coutts, 1909: 187; Stewart, 1990). His forty-two years' service was creditable. In 1736 he published a standard Greek grammar praised in the 1755 *Edinburgh Review* for its 'accuracy' and 'conciseness' (1: 47). Carlyle of Inveresk paid tribute to his wit and liveliness, noting too that Dunlop was 'Distinguish'd by his Strong Good Sense and Capacity for Business, and being a Man of a Leading Mind was suppos'd with the aid of [Francis] Hutcheson to direct and Manage all the affairs of the University'. Dunlop's translations and criticism of the Greek tragedies were a much appreciated feature of his teaching (Carlyle, 1973: 37). Smith valued classical drama, and seems to have caught from Dunlop a love for the niceties of Greek grammar as well as for the literature of that beautiful language. Andrew Dalzel, Professor of Greek at Edinburgh, who knew Smith as an old man, was impressed with the retentiveness of his memory of the minutiae of the subject (Stewart 1.10).

John Loudoun, who taught Smith logic in his *semi* year, was a university teacher of even longer standing than Dunlop. He had been an unsuccessful candidate for a vacant Glasgow regency in 1690, but secured a post at St Andrews (Coutts, 1909: 169, 173, 208). From that period of his career there survives a set of 'Dictata' on Logic (GUL MS Murray 225). These are similar to sets dated after 1699, when he became a Regent at Glasgow, thereafter assuming in 1727 a Chair in Philosophy as a result of the Commission's recommendations. These 'Dictata', notes in Latin on the subject in hand, represent the core of the older teaching method, for the master slowly read them to the students, who copied down what was dictated. This procedure was supplemented by disputations among the students, oral examinations, and comments and criticisms by the master. Loudoun followed the Aristotelian tradition in teaching logic, defining equivocal, concrete, and abstract terms, then simple and compound propositions, and next the various formulae for arguments, in particular those connected with the syllogism, concluding with treatment of the major fallacies. The main text was Antoine Arnauld and Pierre Nicole's *Art of Thinking* (1st edn. 1662; English translation approved by the Royal Society, 1674; John Ozell's translation, 1717—often reprinted).

Loudoun supplemented this with reference to Locke's *Essay concerning Human Understanding* (1690), and clearly had a coherent philosophical viewpoint underpinned by his Calvinist theology.[2] The novelist Tobias Smollett, who attended Glasgow University about Smith's time, saw Loudoun's teaching in a reductive way, commenting that the 'art of logic has been transformed into a kind of legerdemain, by which boys can syllogize' (Knapp, 1949: 16, n. 50). Smith retained a similarly negative view of Loudoun's approach, and when he himself became Professor of Logic at Glasgow in 1751 he adopted a new method.

It cannot be recorded, alas, that Loudoun excited his students when he passed to the teaching of metaphysics and, disdaining the welcome innovation of Hutcheson in lecturing in English at Glasgow, stuck resolutely to Latin. Late in life, Samuel Kenrick, a contemporary of Smith's, remembered how the 'formal and venerable . . . John Loudon used in solemn peripatetic step to illustrate his own mysterious Compend, and the still more metaphysical subtleties of De Vries' (Glasgow, Mitchell Lib., Baillie MSS 32225, fos. 53, 55; Sher, 1990: 97, n. 26). The reference here is to Gerard De Vries, Professor of Theology at Utrecht, author of a textbook entitled, *Determinationes pneumatologicae et ontologicae* (1687, 1690; Edinburgh reprint 1712). The third part, dealing with the nature of God, was considered unorthodox, and Loudoun probably bewildered or alienated his young auditors, such as Kenrick and Adam Smith, by supplementing De Vries' text with the scholastic arguments of Genevan theologians to prove in a manner acceptable to the Kirk that the deity had unique, 'incommunicable' attributes such as infinity and omnipotence and 'communicable' ones such as knowledge and will. These were held to be common to God and men, and were deemed 'communicable' to the extent that men accepted Christ's mediation to redeem them from their original sin. The mentality reflected in Loudoun's teaching of metaphysics has been identified as Augustinian, one that magnifies the yawning chasm between human passions and politics infected with sin and the divine order suffused with grace (Moore, 1990: 44–5). This was the essence of the 'old light' Calvinism. Hutcheson's moral philosophy and natural theology directed at a mature audience challenged it, though he was capable on occasion of echoing Calvinist disparagement of our mortal state (Sher, 1990: 96). Smith, too, could write in this strain as a moral philosopher, describing God as a 'being of infinite perfection', whose wrath is justly visited on 'so vile an insect' as man; but he finally abandoned this language (*TMS* II.ii.3.12, edns. 1–5, but not in edn. 6, 1790).

One feature of Loudoun's teaching, however, connecting in a positive way with Smith's intellectual formation at Glasgow, was his professional commitment to his discipline. This drove him to acknowledge the New Philosophy of the post-Cartesian era. We have some idea of what his students made of this from a publication of 1708, which lists philosophical theses disputed in public as part of the exercises for the MA degree.[3] These include references to the Cartesian principle, 'I think therefore I am', and the empirical one, 'whatever is in the understanding was first in one of the senses', which is ultimately derived from Aristotle (*De anima*, 3.8.432^a). To be sure, the second principle had a history in scholastic thought, but Loudoun would be aware of its place in Lockeian empiricism (*Essay*, ii). His interest in the New Science stressing observation and experiment, associated with Locke's outlook, is indicated by the fact that in 1711–12 'Instruments' were bought for him and the other philosophical regents, Gershom Carmichael and Robert Dick, so that they could each teach their students experimental philosophy. This arrangement was replaced by the course in natural philosophy offered by Dick as Professor in that subject after 1727 (Emerson, 1986: 256). When Smith became a freelance teacher at Edinburgh some ten years later, he gave a course on the 'history of philosophy', and for this he probably followed up lines of enquiry opened by the Glasgow lectures on Metaphysics, but the fragments we have in *EPS* have a fresh, modern ring and are freed from the constraints of religious dogma observable in Loudoun.

The viewpoint of Smith's lectures can be linked to the course in 'Pneumatics' given by a much more vibrant personality, Francis Hutcheson, who also taught Smith in his *semi* year at Glasgow. Sometimes referred to as Pneumatology, this subject was taken to be a department of special metaphysics, as distinct from general metaphysics or ontology. Its older meaning was the 'science, doctrine, or theory of spirits or spiritual beings' (*OED*).[4] There was another subject, however, distinguished as the 'new Pneumaticks', meaning the 'branch of physics which deals with the mechanical properties (as density, elasticity, pressure, etc.) of air, or other elastic fluids or gases' (*OED*). The older tradition of pneumatology was upheld at Glasgow by Gershom Carmichael, who taught it in the form of natural theology as part of his assignment as Professor of Moral Philosophy (Moore and Silverthorne, 1983: 76). He was followed in this practice by his successor, Hutcheson, who discussed the nature of the 'supreme Good' and the passions and will and understanding of man as part of his system of moral philosophy. As for his treatment of natural theology, we have the following statement of William Leechman, his pupil, friend, and memorialist:

[Hutcheson] was extremely doubtful of the justice and force of all the metaphysical arguments, by which many have endeavoured to demonstrate the existence, unity, and perfections of the Deity. . . . Such attempts instead of conducting us to the absolute certainty proposed, leave the mind in such a state of doubt and uncertainty as leads to absolute scepticism. (Leechman, 1755: pp. iv–v)

Accordingly, Hutcheson was content with theistic arguments attaining probability, chiefly that resting on evident design in the universe pointing to the existence of a benevolent creator.

We can trace in Smith's mature criticism of the 'universities of Europe' his response to Hutcheson's doubting attitude to the traditional content of the 'pneumatics' course. Smith took the Enlightenment position that it had been an intellectual error in university education to make philosophy subservient to theology, and to subdivide what was concluded or conjectured about the nature of God or the human mind to the point of absurdity. The result was that the 'doctrine of spirits, of which so little can be known, came to take up as much room as the doctrine of bodies, of which so much can be known'. Metaphysics or pneumatics had been placed in opposition to physics and cultivated as the more sublime and, for the purposes of the clergy, the more useful science. Physics, as the science of observation and experiment which could lead to 'so many useful discoveries', was neglected (*WN* v.i.f.28). But not at Glasgow, where the teachers had to modernize the curriculum. In consequence, Hutcheson in the pneumatics course demonstrated the 'very few simple and almost obvious truths' of natural theology, leaving Robert Dick to deal with the 'doctrine of bodies' in the natural philosophy (physics) course, and Robert Simson to prepare the way with the necessary mathematics, before he applied or represented himself as applying the method of observation and experiment to moral subjects.

Given the evidence about the approach of Loudoun and Hutcheson to teaching the *semis* at Glasgow, it is no surprise to have Dugald Stewart's information about Adam Smith's preferences:

Dr Maclaine of the Hague, who was a fellow-student of Mr Smith's at Glasgow, told me some years ago, that his favourite pursuits while at that university were mathematics and natural philosophy; and I remember to have heard my father remind him of a geometrical problem of considerable difficulty, about which he was occupied at the time when their acquaintance commenced, and which had been proposed to him as an exercise by the celebrated Dr Simpson. (I.7)

Stewart's informant was an Ulsterman, Archibald Maclaine, who matriculated in the *tertian* class under Francis Hutcheson in 1739 and took his MA in 1746 (DD 1767), thereafter becoming minister of the Scottish kirk at The Hague from 1747 to 1796, when the French invasion drove him back to Britain. His brother

James became notorious as the 'gentleman-highwayman' and was hanged in 1750 (Allen, 1750). Archibald gave good counsel to Adam Smith's former pupil James Boswell, when that erratic young man was in Holland, 1763–4, and he was made preceptor to the Prince of Orange. Something of a man of letters, he contributed to the *Monthly Review*, and achieved some fame by his translation of Mosheim's *Ecclesiastical History* (1765; *Supplement*, 1768; reprints until 1825). He and Matthew Stewart, Dugald's father, were probably fellow-students with Smith, of Robert Simson, the Professor of Mathematics, appointed to the Chair in that subject in 1711.

Robert was a nephew and, at one time, secretary of the Professor of Divinity, John Simson, silenced in 1729, as mentioned above, for practising the 'art of teaching heresy orthodoxly', as a contemporary judge, Lord Grange, put it (Coutts, 1909: 210–11). The uncle's interest in Arianism encouraged some Glasgow divinity students to question Calvinist dogmas, including that of original sin, and helped to direct them to 'new light' theology, which was influenced by the optimistic philosophy of Anthony Ashley Cooper, 3rd Earl of Shaftesbury (Stewart, 1992: 5). Robert Simson made a European reputation for himself as the restorer of ancient geometry. In this connection, he published a textbook on conic sections at Edinburgh in 1735. This work, *Sectionum conicarum libri quinque*, apart from the definitions of the three conics, was based on the expositions of Apollonius of Perga (*fl.* 250 BC), who had studied with the pupils of Euclid. Smith owned the second edition of this book, published in 1750 (Mizuta).

On 17 April 1738 Francis Hutcheson wrote of Simson that 'if he were not indolent beyond imagination, [he] could in a fortnight's application finish another book which would surprise the connoisseurs'. Simson did, in fact, arrange for the printing of a text of Apollonius Pergaeius in 1738, but he was not satisfied with it, and did not publish it until 1746. Still dissatisfied, he withdrew copies of this edition, and revised and corrected it for publication at Glasgow in 1749 by Robert and Andrew Foulis: *Apollonii Pergaei locorum planorum libri II, restituti a Roberto Simson*. Hutcheson commented on this work on 5 August 1743: 'We expect immediately from Robert Simson a piece of amazing Geometry, reinventing 2 Books of Appollonius, and he has a third almost ready. He is the best geometer in the world' (GUL MS Gen. 1018/5, 12). The third book, the *Porisms* of Euclid (posthumously published in 1777), like the edition of Apollonius Pergaeius, was based on hints in the *Collections* of Pappus of Alexandria (*fl.* AD 320), an important source for Newton. Simson had published a paper on Pappus and Euclid's Porisms in the *Philosophical Transactions* for 1723 (*Abstracts* vi.659).

Simson would introduce geometry to Adam Smith through Euclid, on whom he also did fundamental research to produce a text appearing simultaneously in Latin and English in 1756, also from the Foulis press: *The Elements of Euclid* (based on the Latin edition of Fredericus Commandinus, 1572). A modern authority on classical mathematics has claimed that the 'merits of Simson, both as interpreter and as critic of Euclid, are very great; and it was mainly due to the excellence of his edition that the words "Euclid" and "geometry" became almost synonymous terms' in Britain (Heath, 1955: pp. vi–vii).

Smith certainly retained great respect for Simson to the end of his life, for in the sixth edition of *TMS* he claimed that his old teacher and Matthew Stewart, who was a Professor at Edinburgh from 1747 to 1775, were the two greatest mathematicians of his time, and cited their attitudes to prove his thesis that scholars in their field are secure about the importance of their discoveries and do not care if the public is unaware of them (III.2.20). Since Smith also knew d'Alembert for many years, he certainly gave high praise to Simson and his fellow-student in Simson's class.

It is possible that Smith came to know Simson outside the classroom in the context of his Friday's Club, which Alexander Carlyle was invited to join, when he was a student at Glasgow. Carlyle describes Simson as 'extremely Courteous' and showing 'Civility to every student who fell in his way . . . tho' a Great Humourist'. This latter trait came out in his bachelor ways, his aversion to the company of ladies, for example, because he had been jilted, though he did make an exception one day a year when he dined at Principal Campbell's and made his daughter Mally 'his 1st Toast'. Simson almost never left the bounds of the college, except on Saturdays, when he walked a mile into the country to have dinner in the village of Anderston. Simson's company was agreeable, for according to Carlyle he was 'of a Mild Temper and of an Engaging Demeanour, and was Master of all Knowledge . . . which he Deliver'd in an Easy Colloquial Style, with the Simplicity of a Child, and without the Least Symptom of Self-Sufficiency or Arrogance'. His air of mild benevolence is conveyed in the portrait of 1746 by William Cochrane, after one by Peter de Nune (Pl. 2).

In Carlyle's time, Simson's club consisted chiefly of men later to be colleagues of Adam Smith when he returned to Glasgow: Hercules Lindesay, Professor of Law, 'who was Talkative and assuming'; James Moor (Dunlop's successor as Professor of Greek), 'a very Lively and Witty Man and a famous Grecian, but a More Famous Punster'; and Robert Dick, who taught Smith physics, 'a very worthy man, and of an agreeable Temper'. Another member of the club was James Purdie, Rector of the Grammar School; he did not have much in his head, apparently, except grammar, but this was a subject of considerable interest to Smith. The 'most constant attendant however and Greatest Favourite' of Professor Simson was Adam Smith's friend Matthew Stewart, at this period 'highly Valued in the Society of Glasgow University' (Carlyle, 1973: 41–2).[5] It is pleasant to think of Stewart and Smith enjoying the company of their celebrated teacher of mathematics, and perhaps at a meeting of his club hearing him sing Greek odes to modern tunes, or chant a Latin hymn to the 'Divine Geometer' (Graham, 1908: 156).

A more serious occasion for Smith must have been the final examination of

ROBERTUS
SIMSON

Prof. Matheseos
in Coll. Glasg.

Pl. 2. Robert Simson, 1746. By William Cochrane, from a portrait by Peter de Nune
(Hunterian Gallery, University of Glasgow).

the *semi* year. Custom required him to be conducted to the examination hall
off the archway connecting the Outer and Inner Quadrangles. This was known
as the Blackstone Room because it contained a highly decorated chair into which
was set a black marble slab. Surviving from the medieval days of the University,
this formed part of the seat for examination candidates. In turn, each was questioned by the Professor of the class they had taken, and of the class to which
they wished to proceed, on books selected by the student (Murray, 1927: 79–92).
In the scheme of things outlined here, Adam Smith would be questioned in June
1738 by John Loudoun, who had instructed him in logic and metaphysics, and

by Francis Hutcheson, who was to receive him in the moral philosophy class after lecturing to him on 'Pneumaticks'.

We might wonder what intellectual experience during his *semi* year made the greatest impression on Smith? One answer might be the Greek lectures, which aroused lifelong interest in the grammar and literature of that language and in the Stoic thought of Epictetus. But an alternative answer might be Simson's philosophical approach to teaching Euclid, which surely lies behind Stewart's perceptive remark: 'If I am not mistaken too, the influence of [Smith's] early taste for Greek geometry may be remarked in the elementary clearness and fulness, bordering sometimes upon prolixity, with which he frequently states his political reasonings' (1.8).

Smith was introduced to 'political reasonings' at Glasgow by the teacher whose influence far exceeded that of Robert Simson. He revealed this in the tribute he paid in accepting the office of Rector in 1787, when he referred to the Chair of Moral Philosophy: 'to which the abilities and Virtues of the never to be forgotten Dr Hutcheson had given a superior degree of illustration' (*Corr.* No. 274). Smith was subjected most powerfully to Hutcheson's influence through following the curriculum for the *tertians* of 1738–9. This prescribed they were to be 'taught two Hours each Day by the Professor of *Moral Philosophy*, who reads either in *Greek* or *Latin* some ancient or modern Book of *Ethicks* or *Politicks*; and this Year the Scholars continue to attend the Lessons of *Geometry*, and perhaps attend a Lecture of *Humanity*' (Chamberlayne, 1737: II.iii.13).

Alexander Carlyle found 'Great Satisfaction and Improvement' in attending Hutcheson's lectures of 1743–4, held in the moral philosophy classroom on the upper floor of the west side of the Inner Quadrangle. We can believe that his impressions would be similar to those of Adam Smith:

[Hutcheson] was a Good Looking Man of an Engaging Countenance. He Deliver'd his Lectures without Notes walking Backwards and forwards in the Area of his Room—as his Elocution was Good and his Voice and Manner pleasing, he rais'd the attention of Hearers at all times, and when the Subject Led him to Explain and Inforce the Moral Virtues and Duties, he Display'd a fervent and Persuasive Eloquence which was Irresistible. Besides the Lectures he Gave thro' the Week, he every Sunday at Six a clock, open'd his class Room to whoever chose to attend, when he Deliver'd a Set of Lectures on Grotius' De Veritate Religionis Christianae, which tho' Learned and Ingenious were adapted to every Capacity. For on that evening he expected to be attended not only by Students but by many of the People of the City, and he was not Dissappointed. For this Free Lecture always drew Crowds of Attendants. (Carlyle, 1973: 36–7)

Hutcheson's attractive personality and classical and philosophical interests are reflected in the striking portrait of him holding a copy of Cicero's *De Finibus*, painted after his death by Allan Ramsay (Pl. 3). In person and in his teaching, he exemplified the ideal of politeness which had great philosophical and cultural fascination and currency in the eighteenth century in the often-reprinted writings of Shaftesbury (Klein, 1994).

Pl. 3. Francis Hutcheson, *c.*1750. From a posthumous portrait by Allan Ramsay
(Hunterian Gallery, University of Glasgow).

Grandson of an Ayrshire minister, Hutcheson was born at Drumalig in Co.
Down, Ulster, and, like many of his Presbyterian countrymen, he came to
Glasgow University in 1710 to complete his education. He seems to have rejected
outright the Protestant scholasticism of Loudoun. More congenial to him was
Gershom Carmichael's theory of natural jurisprudence. In Smith's terms, this is
the 'theory of the general principles which ought to run through and be the
foundation of the laws of all nations' (*TMS* VII.iv.37). Carmichael developed his
views from reflection on Samuel Pufendorf's book *De Officio Hominis et Civis*

(1673), which is an abridgement of his more complex and encyclopaedic work *De Jure Naturae et Gentium* (1672), itself a response to the *De Jure Belli ac Pacis* (1625) of Hugo Grotius. Before beginning divinity in 1712 under John Simson, whose liberal theology also appealed to him, Hutcheson spent a year on much-enjoyed Latin and Greek studies, focused in particular on the classical poets and Cicero. He attributed the core of his later philosophy to what he learned at Glasgow, including his concept of natural theology, and the central idea to which Smith warmed, though he did not finally endorse it, that virtue was constituted by benevolence. Hutcheson also joined in the students' struggle at Glasgow to retain their rights against the encroachments of Principal Stirling.

Returning to Ireland in 1718, Hutcheson served briefly as a Presbyterian minister in Ulster, like his father before him, but he went against his father's allegiances in siding with moderate, independent-minded Presbyterian ministers in Ulster. This group came to be designated 'new light', because their theological outlook was liberal, and they favoured Shaftesbury's theory that human nature was essentially benevolent. On coming to Dublin about 1720 to be the head of a 'new light' academy for the sons of dissenters, Hutcheson was drawn into a circle of intellectuals round Lord Molesworth, who stressed the importance of religious toleration and encouraged study of the philosophy of benevolence devised by Shaftesbury (Moore, 1990: 43–5; Stewart, 1992: 4–6).

Hutcheson responded to this stimulation by publishing, at London in 1725, a work often said to be the first to appear in Britain specifically dealing with aesthetics: *An Inquiry into the Original of our Ideas of Beauty and Virtue; in Two Treatises. In Which the Principles of the late Earl of Shaftesbury are explain'd and defended, against the Author of the Fable of the Bees: And the Ideas of Moral Good and Evil are establish'd according to the Sentiments of the antient Moralists, With an Attempt to introduce a Mathematical Calculation in Subjects of Morality*. This fulsome title reveals the eclectic nature of his arguments directed against those of Thomas Hobbes (*Leviathan*, 1650) and Bernard Mandeville (*The Fable of the Bees*, 1714) urging that human nature is intrinsically selfish. Hutcheson based himself on a widely taught classical Stoic text, Cicero's *De Officiis*, which affirms that morality is beautiful. Another influence on Hutcheson was the empirical psychology of Locke's extremely influential book, *An Essay concerning Human Understanding* (1st edn. 1690, 4th edn. 1700). Hutcheson also incorporated in his book the theory of benevolence and pleasure-principle philosophy, or universalistic hedonism, of Shaftesbury. A further source for him was the 'polite moralizing' of Addison's *Spectator* papers on the 'Pleasures of the Imagination' (Nos. 411–21). Combining insights from these sources, Hutcheson claims we have an internal sense of beauty and an analogous moral sense, the first responsive to 'Regularity, Order, Harmony' in objects contemplated, the second activated by the 'Affections, Actions or Characters of rational Agents which we call virtuous'. A theistic component is added to the set of arguments to link aesthetics to morals, through specifying an 'Author of Nature' who 'has made Virtue a lovely

Form, to excite our pursuit of it; and has given us strong Affections to be the Springs of each virtuous Action' (Preface to the Inquiry). This concept of a benevolent 'Author of Nature', who gave humans strong positive feelings to motivate them to act virtuously, came to have considerable appeal for many writers in the eighteenth century. Henry Fielding spins his plot of Tom Jones pursuing the lovely and virtuous Sophia from this theory. And Hutcheson's most gifted pupil, Adam Smith, reveals in *TMS* how deeply influenced he is by it (cf. III.5.7).

Hutcheson's book provoked charges in Continental periodicals that the author had taken his leading aesthetic idea that beauty consists of *unity amidst variety*, and illustrations of this, from the *Traité du Beau* (1714) of the Swiss philosopher, Jean-Pierre de Crousaz (Raynor, 1987*b*; Moore, 1990: 50–1). In Britain, however, it was perceived that Hutcheson had made an original contribution to philosophy by turning Shaftesbury's hint concerning the existence of a moral sense into a genuine theory to explain our moral judgments as arising from natural feelings of approval and disapproval about motives and actions with respect to their tendency to promote well-being. The theory becomes a form of utilitarianism, summed up in the famous phrase: '*that Action is best*, which accomplishes the *greatest Happiness* for the *greatest Numbers*' (*Inquiry*, 1725: ii.164). So stirring a slogan gained wide currency from its presence in the revised fourth edition of the *Inquiry* of 1738 (Shackleton, 1972; Raphael, 1992*b*). This appeared in Smith's second year at Glasgow University, when he was Hutcheson's student and was inspired, as Dugald Stewart wrote, to direct his studies systematically from his youth to 'subjects of the last importance to human happiness' (III.20).

Hutcheson added to his reputation as a philosopher by publishing a second book entitled *An Essay on the Nature and Conduct of the Passions and Affections with Illustrations upon the Moral Sense* (1728). This contained two treatises, the first of which dealt with the emotional basis of our value judgements. It is of lesser importance than the second which, in countering the rationalists' theories concerning morality, displayed great originality. Here are to be found the main lines of argument concerning moral psychology to be taken up by Hume in his *Treatise of Human Nature* (1739–40) and *Enquiry Concerning the Principles of Morals* (1751), then by Smith in *TMS* (1759).

Because of the success of his publications and his standing as a classical scholar, and also because of his previous connection with Glasgow, Hutcheson was elected Gershom Carmichael's successor as Professor of Moral Philosophy in 1729, a post he held until his death in Dublin in 1746 at the early age of 52. Before assuming his Chair, he underwent trials in logic, ethics, and physics, presenting to the faculty discourses on a topic in each subject (Coutts, 1909: 218–19). This suggests that he was expected to be capable of teaching any one of the three departments of philosophy, but Loudoun and Dick retained those of Logic and Natural Philosophy. Hutcheson went on to teach moral philosophy, attracting many students to Glasgow to hear him, particularly from his native Ireland.

His inaugural address was entitled *De naturali hominum socialitate* (reprinted by the Foulis Press in Glasgow in 1755, indicating its continuing relevance during Smith's professorial period). In the address, Hutcheson made it clear that he wished to continue the tradition of his former teacher, Gershom Carmichael, in making the staple of his courses the classical Stoic tradition, revived in the seventeenth century by Grotius and Pufendorf, of analysis of the sociable nature of man and illustration of the theory of natural jurisprudence. Robert Wodrow recorded that it was delivered 'very fast and lou . . . and was not well understood' (1843: iv.98). This has been seen as a measure of prudence, since the lecture is among other things an attack on Pufendorf for his closeness to Hobbes in emphasizing that human nature displays a selfishness which only civil or political society can control. By extension, there is an attack on 'old light' Calvinism's stress on human depravity. Hutcheson aligned himself with Carmichael and other authors, above all Shaftesbury, who had refuted Hobbes and Pufendorf by arguing that humanity's natural state was one encouraging constructive use of physical, emotional, and mental power. The lecture ended with an appeal to youth to abandon monkish repression and despair and live joyously, seeking instruction in nature and providence. Hutcheson expressed the hope that he had demonstrated the human race was sociable in the state of nature, and said he left to another occasion his explanation of the rise of civil government.

Broadly speaking, Smith in his student days seems to have received this message from Hutcheson's courses and from the books he read then or subsequently. With refinements and additional insights gained from Hume's 'science of man' (*T*, intro.), Smith made it the foundation of his own thinking about human nature and his programme of writing. To be sure, Paul Wood (1993: 47–9) has argued that Hutcheson was not a unique figure, in the context of the Scottish universities of his time, in dispensing this philosophical brew derived from the natural-law thinkers and Shaftesbury, but undoubtedly he made a profound impact on his Glasgow students.

There is a problem, however, in that new publications, believed to be textbooks, appearing over Hutchesons's name during his time at Glasgow and posthumously, are not exactly in accord with the inaugural lecture and the previous treatises. They defer more to Calvinist presuppositions (Haakonssen, 1990; Moore, 1990). These textbooks consist of a compend (handbook) of Morals (1742, 2nd edn. 1745), a synopsis of Metaphysics (1742, 2nd edn. 1744), and a compend of Logic (1756), all in Latin. Hutcheson disparaged the Metaphysics synopsis in his private correspondence, and it may be that he considered these Latin writings as teaching manuals suitable for youth in the context of Presbyterian academic institutions, whereas his treatises of the 1720s were meant for mature readers. In the 1740s, he set out to integrate his two kinds of writing in *A System of Moral Philosophy*. This was published posthumously in 1755, in Glasgow by Robert and Andrew Foulis brothers, and in London by Andrew Millar, with a large list of subscribers including Adam Smith and Thomas Reid, the two most famous successors in his Glasgow Chair. Hutcheson's efforts in this book were unsuccessful, and he described it as a 'confused Book . . . a Farrago' (Moore, 1990: 55–9; Sher, 1990: 94–8).

Perhaps the best guide to what Smith heard in his professor's lectures is to be found in Hutcheson's translation of the compend of Morals, which appeared posthumously in 1747 (further edns. 1753, 1764, 1772): *A Short Introduction to Moral Philosophy . . . containing the Elements of Ethics and the Law of Nature*. In the Preface, 'To the Students in Universities', Hutcheson indicated that he accepted the classical division of moral philosophy into two branches of ethics. The first aimed at 'teaching the nature of virtue and regulating the internal dispositions', and in his lectures on this branch Hutcheson would attack the human selfishness theory of Mandeville's *Fable of the Bees*. It is likely that this alerted Smith to the power of Mandeville's arguments, resulting in time in his own partial acceptance and qualification of them in *TMS* and *WN* (Macfie, 1967: 114–15).

The second branch of ethics taught by Hutcheson was 'knowledge of the law of nature'. This embraces three divisions:

1. the doctrine of *private rights*, or the laws obtaining in natural liberty;
2. *oeconomicks*, or the laws and rights of the several members of a family;
3. *politicks*, showing the various plans of civil government, and the rights of states with respect to each other.

Here, in the context of Hutcheson's teaching on the 'law of nature', we have the source of Smith's own lectures on jurisprudence, which gave rise in time to his system of economics, as will be discussed in connection with his Glasgow courses and the composition of *WN*.

Hutcheson saw *A Short Introduction to Moral Philosophy*, and no doubt the teaching practice on which it was based, as offering students an approach to the great authors who have handled the several topics: among the ancients Plato, Aristotle, Xenophon, Cicero, and among the moderns, Grotius, Richard Cumberland, Pufendorf, and James Harrington.

With the exception of Harrington, all these authors are represented in Adam Smith's Library (Mizuta), and are referred to in his writings. For Hutcheson, the political writings of Harrington (e.g. *Oceana*, 1656) were an important source of republican or 'Old Whig' theory, and in particular the theory that ownership of land was a precondition for civil liberty. Smith was to argue, however, following Hume, that participation in a commercial society—and Glasgow's trading community could be so regarded—afforded as many or more opportunities than landholding for a citizen to enjoy liberty (Moore and Silverthorne, 1983: 86). Connecting Harrington's ideas to the natural-jurisprudence tradition was a refinement of Hutcheson's, but he regarded the central formulation as the one provided by his old teacher:

The learned will at once discern how much of this compend is taken from the writings of others, from Cicero and Aristotle; and to name no other moderns, from Puffendorf's smaller work, *de officio hominis et civis*, which that worthy and ingenious man the late Professor Gerschom Carmichael of Glasgow, by far the best commentator on that book, has so supplied and corrected that the notes are of more value than the text. (Hutcheson, 1747: pp. i–ii).

From available information and traditions about the teaching of moral philosophy at Glasgow in the eighteenth century, it seems that Adam Smith heard Hutcheson lecture on ethics in English three days a week at the early morning hour, from 7.30 to 8.30, and was inspired by his enthusiasm for classical philosophy, particularly that of the Stoics, and by enquiries into human nature which demonstrated he sought truth with constancy and impartiality. At 11 a.m. Hutcheson conducted in Latin an examination session on the morning's lecture. In addition, Hutcheson taught a 'private' moral philosophy course twice a week, in which he is reported to have explained and illustrated the 'works of Arrian, Antoninus, and other Greek philosophers' (Richardson, 1803: 514). These references point to lectures on sources of Stoic philosophy, the *Discourses* of Epictetus preserved by his Roman soldier pupil, Arrian, and the *Meditations* of the Emperor Marcus Aurelius Antoninus. It is hard to believe that Smith would stay away from this course once his enthusiasm for Stoicism had been aroused. Certainly, from his reading of Stoics such as Marcus Aurelius, illuminated by Hutcheson's lectures at Glasgow, the mature Smith drew his understanding of the 'immense and connected system' of the universe operating harmoniously according to natural law (*TMS* vii.ii.1.37), and could envision within this framework the establishment of norms of human morality, and the operation of the 'invisible hand' of the market mechanism regulating economic activity (Macfie, 1967: 103–5, 1971; *TMS* 7).

Five days a week, in the afternoon, Smith would attend the 'prelection' of Hutcheson's main course covering jurisprudence and politics. A further inspiration here was the Professor's stress on the 'Old Whig' and civic humanist theme of the importance of civil and religious liberty for human happiness:

as a warm love of liberty, and manly zeal for promoting it, were ruling principles in his own breast, he always insisted upon it at great length, and with the greatest strength of argument and earnestness of persuasion: and he had such success on this important point, that few, if any, of his pupils, whatever contrary prejudices they might bring along with them, ever left him without favourable notions of that side of the question which he espoused and defended. (Leechman, 1755: pp. xxxv–xxxvi)

The pupil Smith absorbed the master's arguments for economic and political liberty, as we shall see, but he never pushed them as far as Hutcheson. Thus we do not find in Smith the emphasis on the contract origin of government notable in Hutcheson, responding to Grotius' natural-law theory, nor his appeal to the fundamental rights of self-defence and resistance to unjust government, which were accepted and acted upon by the revolutionary party among the American colonists (Norton, 1976: 1992).

If Smith's prudent temperament held him back from enthusiasm for Hutcheson's teaching about political resistance, it can be said that he made full use of his teacher's insights into moral psychology and the social interactions, which he regarded as following the patterns of natural law. He went beyond Hutcheson, however, in elaborating systems of ethics and political economy, which connected a comprehensive analysis of human nature with a persuasive explanation of the regularities in human behaviour manifested in social and economic institutions. Smith's drive to create such a system could well have been excited by his encounter with Newtonian physics in his third or *magistrand* year at Glasgow. The prescription for this period ran as follows:

[the scholars] are taught two Hours at least by the Professor of *Natural Philosophy*, as that science is improved by *Sir Isaac Newton*, and attend two Hours in the Week a Course of Experiments. Some continue to attend Lessons of *Mathematicks*, or of the Lessons of the *Law of Nature and Nations*, or of *Greek*, or *Latin*. (Chamberlayne, 1737: II.iii.13)

We recall that Smith's fellow-student, Archibald Maclaine, had said that his 'favourite pursuits while at [Glasgow] were mathematics and natural philosophy' (Stewart 1.7). The Professor of the second subject, Robert Dick, though not so distinguished as the mathematician Robert Simson, was a very able and genial teacher, whose classes on experimental philosophy, held twice a week, were much appreciated by his students. There was a tradition of experimental demonstration at Glasgow going back at least to the late seventeenth century, and there were regular expenditures for the necessary instruments and apparatus, such as the 'air pumps, barometers, Magdeburg hemispheres, and balances'. These instruments were used by Dr Robert Steuart at Edinburgh in 1711–12 for demonstrations of principles of hydrostatics and pneumatics (in the modern sense). At Glasgow students were charged three shillings per session 'to be a fund for the necessary expenses of the experiments' of the natural philosophy course (Emerson, 1986: 256).

The lectures and experiments in natural philosophy or physics were directed at elucidating the 'doctrine of bodies', as Smith called it, adding 'of which so much can be known', as contrasted with the 'doctrine of spirits, of which so little can be known', since it was made up of the 'subtleties and sophisms' composing the 'greater part of the Metaphysicks or Pneumaticks of the schools' and the 'whole of this cobweb science of Ontology' (*WN* v.i.f.28–9). The mature Smith noted that the improvements in philosophy, associated of course with the work of Newton, had been more readily introduced into the poorer universities, of which Glasgow would be an example, than into the 'richest and best endowed universities' such as Oxford, where he went as a Snell Exhibitioner in the next stage of his career. The reason was that at the poor universities the teachers' earnings depended on their reputation, and so they were required to 'pay more attention to the current opinions of the world' (*WN* v.i.f.34).

Current opinion in Smith's age was powerfully impressed with the outstanding success of Newton's method in accounting for the behaviour of bodies in the physical universe, and it was this method that Dick taught. Smith's later formulation of it in his rhetoric lectures, and distinction of it from that of Aristotle, were part of the Enlightenment movement, fed by such sources as the Glasgow natural philosophy course of his student days:

we may either like Aristotle go over the Different branches in that order they happen to cast up to us, giving a principle commonly a new one for every phaenomenon; or in the manner of . . . Newton we may lay down certain principles known or proved in the beginning, from when we account for the severall Phenomena, connecting all together by the same Chain.—This latter . . . is undoubtedly the most Philosophical, and in every scien[c]e w[h]ether of Moralls or Nat[ural] ph[ilosophy] etc., is vastly more ingenious and for that reason more engaging than the other. It gives us a pleasure to see the phaenomena which we reckoned the most unaccountable all deduced from some principle (commonly a well known one) and all united in one chain . . . (*LRBL* ii.133–4)

As to the details of Smith's early studies of mathematics and physics that led him to take such a view of Newton's method, we have no certain knowledge. However, we do have Patrick Murdoch's 1748 'Account of the Life and Writings' of Colin Maclaurin, Professor of Mathematics at Edinburgh from 1725 until his death in 1746. Maclaurin was the outstanding exponent of Newtonian science in his time, and his sequence of courses must have been approximated at Glasgow, though divided among the teaching of Simson and Dick. It must be emphasized, of course, that Maclaurin went far beyond his Glasgow colleagues in his comprehension of Newton.

Maclaurin taught his first class the first six books of Euclid's *Elements*, plain trigonometry, practical geometry, the elements of fortification (he put these to practical use in 1745 to help defend Edinburgh against the Jacobites), and an introduction to algebra. The second class studied algebra, the eleventh and twelfth books of Euclid, spherical trigonometry, conic sections (at Glasgow, Simson had a special interest in this subject), and the general principles of astronomy. The third class went on in astronomy and perspective, read a part of Newton's *Principia Mathematica*, and to illustrate this had a course of experiments performed and explained to them. Maclaurin afterwards lectured and demonstrated to his students the elements of fluxions, the Newtonian calculus. His students in the fourth class were required to study the system of fluxions he had devised to meet the metaphysical objections to Newton raised by Bishop Berkeley in *The Analyst* (1734), and they also studied the doctrine of chance and the rest of the *Principia* (Maclaurin, 1968—Murdoch's 1748 intro.: pp. v, vii; Barfoot, 1990). Maclaurin in his teaching about Newton drew attention not only to the master's use of observation and experiments informing the analysis and synthesis which traced causes from effects and effects, in turn, from causes, but also to the mathematical model, a 'sublime geometry', on which his system was built (Maclaurin, 1748: 8; Garrison, 1987).

Now Newton had added at the conclusion of his *Opticks* (3rd edn. 1730) his own account of his method of analysis and synthesis with respect to light, venturing to continue: 'And if natural Philosophy in all its Parts, by pursuing this Method, shall at length be perfected, the Bounds of Moral Philosophy will also be enlarged.' Hutcheson had taken up this challenge, with many other contemporaries, and Smith must have heard him discourse in the following vein:

there was ground to hope, that from a more strict philosophical enquiry into the various natural principles or natural dispositions of mankind, in the same way that we enquire into the structure of an animal body, of a plant, or of the solar system, a more exact theory of morals may be formed, than has yet appeared: and a theory too built upon such an obvious and firm foundation as would be satisfactory to every candid observer. (Leechman, 1755: pp. xiii–xv)

This passage reflects, perhaps, the enthusiasm for 'moral Newtonianism' of which Elie Halévy wrote (1955), rather than a sound grasp of Newtonian science. Nevertheless, the confidence it bred completed the intellectual formation Glasgow University could give Adam Smith. To add the knowledge of the Latin he had gained at Kirkcaldy burgh school, he had more exercise in that language as a result of the practices of John Loudoun and Francis Hutcheson in their teaching and examining of work in logic and metaphysics. Perhaps Loudoun administered a negative charge, most helpful to Smith later in his career when he replaced Aristotelian logic by rhetoric for the *semis* he taught. Alexander Dunlop brought him on in Greek to the point that he could read its greatest authors with appreciation, and apparently with attention to minute points of grammar. His Greek also provided an entry into the ancient geometry explored and restored by Robert Simson, which had its connection with the New Science of Newton, the most brilliant mind of the time, sympathetically taught by Robert Dick. Smith's 'juvenile' History of Astronomy, of course, reveals that he had been given and had absorbed an accurate understanding of Newton's mathematical and mechanical principles. Furthermore, his Greek allowed him to explore the authors so much loved by his more influential teacher, Francis Hutcheson. He was spurring Smith on by precept and example to systematize moral science by analysis of the springs of human nature and, through a resulting synthesis, to delineate the mechanics of society.

Can we see the boy Smith among the Glasgow student body of his time, the sons of merchants and professional men and the gentry, most from the west of Scotland, a good number from Ireland, a few from England and the American colonies? Some achieved a modest niche in history, for example, Clotworthy Upton from Co. Antrim in Ulster, who became Clerk Comptroller to the Dowager Princess of Wales. Others were more famous: Sir John Dalrymple of Cranstoun, a historian whose writings were influenced by Montesquieu, as were Smith's; Gavin Hamilton, the celebrated painter who pursued a career at Rome; and General Robert Melville of Monimail in Fife, who was governor-in-chief of the West Indies colonies captured from the French in the Seven Years War, played a role in the invention of the carronade, and became eminent as an antiquary (Addison, 1913: 17–25; Preble, 1859). Smith sat on the college benches with these peers, no doubt learned something of life from them, and possibly joined them in the student clubs of the day, which seem to have had wide interests and be stimulated by those of the professors.

Alexander Carlyle was a member of a group including Archibald Maclaine, Smith's friend, proposing to act Addison's tragedy *Cato*, and he also joined a Literary Society which 'took to Reviewing of Books as a proper Exercise'. William Thom, who became minister of Govan and had a career as a controversialist challenging the Glasgow professors including Smith, was a leader in this Society. Hearing Carlyle say that Hutcheson's book on the passions 'was not Intelligible', a criticism that has a grain of truth, he assigned it to him to criticize:

I accordingly Review'd it in a few pages, and took much Pains to unravel Certain Intricacies both of thought and expression that had ran thro' it; This I Did with much Freedom, tho' not without Respect to the Author. This Essay pleas'd my Friends—and one of them, by Thom's Instigation Carried a Copy of it to Hutcheson. He glanc'd it over, and Return'd it saying that the young Gentleman might be in the Right, But that he had long ago made up his Mind on those Subjects, and could not now take the Trouble to Revise them.

Not long after this, in 1744, Carlyle delivered a discourse in the Divinity Hall which was critical of Hutcheson's moral-sense theory. It was praised by William Leechman, Professor of Divinity and Hutcheson's friend and protégé, so Hutcheson asked to see a copy, and returned it to Carlyle 'with unqualified applause', which that young gentleman took to be 'certain proof of the Gentleness and Candour of this Eminent Professor' (Carlyle, 1973: 52). Since Smith developed pronounced interests in Hutcheson's subjects, it is not much of a conjecture to think that he came to this professor's attention like Carlyle and received encouragement from him.

Colin Maclaurin and Matthew Stewart seem to have been strongly encouraged in their mathematical and scientific interests at Glasgow, and there is every reason to believe that Smith received great intellectual stimulation there. His ability and promise were recognized with the award of a Snell Exhibition to take him to Balliol College, Oxford, for further education. Writing on 15 February 1739 to Charles Mackie, Professor of Universal History and Scottish History at Edinburgh and extremely successful teacher of his subject (Sharpe, 1962), his relative Alexander Dunlop had disappointing news about the progress of his son's studies, but provided the following information:

You may acquaint my Lady Sutty that so far as I can see, her son will certainly be nominated by us the next Vacancy for Oxford. There will two fall together next year, and I know no Candidates for them but Mr Sutty and another, one Smith, who is a very fine boy as any we have. (NLS MS 16577, fo. 221)

Just as the Professor of Greek predicted, Adam Smith and Charles Suttie, third son of Sir James Suttie of Balgonie and Marion, daughter of Sir Hew Dalrymple,

Lord President of the Court of Session, were nominated Snell Exhibitioners by Glasgow University on 4 March 1740 (Addison, 1901: 43–4).

The intent of the foundation was to support scholars preparing for ordination by the Church of England whose doctrine and discipline they were to propagate in Scotland, and Exhibitioners were required to give a bond for £500 that they would be ordained (Stones, 1984). If this very large sum of money was ever posted in Smith's name, it would signify that his guarantors believed he was prepared to become an Episcopalian minister (Scott, 1937: 42). After going to Oxford, however, Smith seems to have had no inclination for a career in the Church (Stewart 1.11). Whatever the effect on him of his life at Oxford and his reading there, to be explored in the next chapter, his ultimate aversion to the Church may have had its seed-bed in the state of religious feeling in Glasgow during his student days.

In philosophical and other studies at Glasgow University as we have described them, there were signs of the progress of the Scottish Enlightenment at Glasgow, of which in many ways Francis Hutcheson was the 'father' (Scott, 1900: 261–9). Nevertheless, the improving merchants and the tradesmen of the city, as well as the country people, had by and large not given up their Calvinist tradition in religion, and Hutcheson faced strong opposition among local ministers for his liberal views in theology.

William Leechman, whose election as Professor of Divinity Hutcheson had secured in 1743, faced a heresy trial within a few months of assuming his Chair, and wrote as follows to a dissenting minister who had been a fellow-student at Glasgow with Hutcheson:

I don't believe it is possible for one in your Situation to imagine to what hight bigottry and nonsense in Religion prevails in this Country, especially in this part of it: There is not one Man in the Presbytery of Glasgow, with whom I can use any freedom in discoursing on Religion, or from whom I can expect friendship in the present affair [the heresy trial], except one intimate Companion, who is quite disregarded by the Rest of them. From this view of my present Situation, you may easily perceive, how difficult a task it must be to teach pure and genuine Christianity, and at the same [time] not to expose myself to the fury of Bigots: There is the utmost care taken to watch every word pronounced by me. The Zealots have always some Secret Spies among the Students to give the proper Information, of what is taught on every Subject. (Manchester, John Rylands Lib., Benson Coll.)

Given this climate of opinion, in all likelihood painfully obvious to an intelligent youth like Smith, it is doubtful if the calling of the ministry would be appealing. Glasgow's University, however, had given Smith an inspiring revelation of the prevailing scientific and philosophical culture. There beckoned now the path of scholarship for Dunlop's 'very fine boy as any we have', also surely aspiration to a life of virtue as Hutcheson painted it. We can picture Smith returning to Kirkcaldy for the summer vacation in 1740, and making his preparations for the journey to Oxford.

5

Oxford

In the University of Oxford, the greater part of the publick professors have, for
these many years, given up altogether even the pretense of teaching.

Oxford was an appreciable distance to the south when Adam Smith rode there
on horseback in 1740, arriving on or before 6 June, when the first payment to
him as a Snell Exhibitioner was made at Balliol College (Battel Books, 23, 1).
The journey would take six to eight days from Edinburgh, Smith's route being
the one through the peat, bogs, and flow mosses of the Border country to Moffat,
then over the Esk at Gretna Green, and on to Carlisle, Lichfield, and Warwick
before arriving at the university city. The other route proceeded through the
eastern Border country near Berwick and on to Newcastle, then turned inland,
taking in Sheffield and Birmingham. These were two alternatives followed at different times by Smith's contemporary and friend, Alexander Carlyle.[1]

On approaching the town of Carlisle, Smith noticed a difference from the
extreme poverty of the Scottish Borders (Clayden, 1887: 92–3). Other travellers
were similarly impressed, and writing from Carlisle in 1744, the soldier James
Wolfe commented:

A mile on this side of the river that divided England from Scotland, one begins to perceive the difference that labour and industry can make on the face of the country. The
soil is much the same for some space either north or south, but the fences, enclosures,
and agriculture are not at all alike. The English are clean and laborious, and the Scotch
excessively lazy and dirty, though far short, indeed, of what we found at a greater distance from the borders. (Findlay, 1928: 299)

Smith was later to attribute the contrast to difference in diet: 'The common
people in Scotland, who are fed with oatmeal, are in general neither so strong,
nor so handsome as the same rank of people in England, who are fed with
wheaten bread. They neither work so well nor look so well' (*WN* I.xi.b.41). In
the same passage Smith also noted that the 'chairmen, porters, and coalheavers
in London, and those unfortunate women who live by prostitution, the strongest
men and the most beautiful women perhaps in the British dominions' were said
to be drawn from the 'lowest rank of people in Ireland', who lived chiefly on a
diet of potatoes. As it happened, 1740 was a year of famine in Scotland; the cultivation of the potato was being introduced into East Lothian, in the vicinity of

Edinburgh, and stores were brought from Kintyre that year to be sold in Glasgow, part of the transformation of Scottish agriculture mentioned as observable in the Fife of Smith's boyhood. Agricultural change was even further advanced in the England through which Smith was travelling for the first time, but strain in the agricultural economy may have been apparent in 1740–2, when grain prices were high, associated with an epidemic of typhus.[2]

Moreover, on his way to Oxford, he came to an 'inland country naturally fertile and easily cultivated', where land carriage was expensive and river navigation inconvenient, at least until a canal system was developed, but where manufactures and cultivation reciprocally stimulated progress in each sector. In the explanation Smith was to give about the rise of opulence, the north and midlands of England fitted in as places where manufacturers were able to make surplus produce into goods 'useful or agreeable' to cultivators, and were enabled by the sale of their surplus to improve their land. When their increased yield came to the local market, its cheapness allowed manufacturers to produce more goods cheaply enough to meet the transport charges of sending some of their product to more distant markets.

Travel through England beginning in 1740 must have added to Smith's reading and conversation with knowledgeable people, leading to his mature perception that the woollen manufacturers of Leeds and Halifax, as well as the metal-finishers of Sheffield, Birmingham, and Wolverhampton, represented the sophistication of domestic activity, and were the 'offspring of agriculture' (*WN* III.iii.20). Travel and observation, as well as reflection on memories of travel, would help in formulating such views as those suggesting that Birmingham specialized in manufactures meeting the demands of 'fancy and fashion', with its buttons and tinplate, while Sheffield met those of 'use and necessity' with its knives and scissors (*WN* I.x.b.42; Mathias, 1983: 114, 247–8; Wilson, 1971: 295, 302–3; Rule, 1992: 140–56). As in the Kirkcaldy of his boyhood and the Glasgow he had recently left, there was evident in the midlands of England through which he travelled in the summer of 1740 the spirit of competition among the nimble-fingered and quick-witted capable of producing a more rewarding standard of living. In the Oxford he approached, however, there predominated the uncritical self-regard and stagnation of social privilege.

When James Boswell taxed the people of Lichfield with idleness, Dr Johnson retaliated: 'Sir, we are a city of philosophers: we work with our heads, and make the boobies of Birmingham work for us with their hands' (*BLJ* ii.464). No doubt Smith expected to find Oxford a city of philosophers, in view of its tradition of learning reaching back to the times of Duns Scotus and William of Ockham, and in the recent past fostered by the scientific and linguistic work of the circle of John Wallis and Robert Boyle. From that group there lingered on Edmund Halley, who was appointed Savilian Professor of Geometry at Oxford in 1703, and had become Astronomer Royal in 1720. He was famous for calculating the return of comets, work that was certainly known to Adam Smith when he was completing his History of Astronomy, and it was Halley who had persuaded Newton to publish the *Principia Mathematica*. But he was a very old man, and died in 1742. Halley was succeeded as Astronomer Royal by James Bradley, who was admitted to Balliol as a Gentleman Commoner in 1711, and had become Savilian Professor of Astronomy in 1721. At first sight it appears that he fits into a group of men with scientific interests associated with Balliol (Jones, 1988: 148–50). Closer inspection, however, reveals that these men were not in residence at the College for any length of time, and did not contribute to education there. Three of them, in fact, take us back to the early stages of the Scottish Enlightenment as the formative influence on them, also to a political alignment on their part with a Jacobitism which might have been welcome, to some degree, at Balliol but which was not at all endorsed by Smith's family.

No Jacobite, Bradley received the impetus for his distinguished observational work in astronomy, done away from Oxford, and for his theoretical advances concerning aberration in light and parallactic displacement, not from his college, but from an uncle, the Revd James Pound, a friend of Halley and one of the foremost amateur astronomers in England. Bradley lectured from 1729 until 1760 on experimental philosophy at the Ashmolean Museum, but a register there reveals that only seventy-two Balliol men attended Bradley's lectures from 1746 to 1760 (*DSB* 1970, ii.387–9; Turner, 1986: 672–3). Smith probably did not attend during his years at Balliol, since he would have covered the material under Robert Dick at Glasgow. He does not mention knowing Bradley personally, but he was aware of his work. His assessment of this links up with his general criticism of the state of scholarship in the Oxford of his time. In the 1756 *Edinburgh Review* he wrote that Bradley and Thomas Smith, the Cambridge investigator of optics and harmonics, would have gone further in science if they had had 'more rivals and judges' ('Letter', para. 5).

Bradley did have a contemporary at Balliol who was an outstanding mathematician. This was James Stirling, who came to Oxford from Edinburgh University in 1711. Since he was awarded a Snell Exhibition, perhaps like Adam Smith he had a connection with Glasgow, though the founder seems to have intended that students from the other Scottish universities could be eligible for his benefaction. In 1715 it was reported to Newton that Stirling as an undergraduate had solved a complex problem sent by Leibniz to challenge the mathematicians of England. Stirling's career at Oxford ended in 1716 when he left Balliol for good, after refusing to take the oath of allegiance to George I necessary for the continuance of his scholarship and thus declaring his Jacobitism. He went to Venice, where he became the friend of the Paduan mathematician Nicholas Bernouilli. Thereafter he taught mathematics and physics in London, and was elected a Fellow of the Royal Society for continuing Newton's research on curves of the third degree. His chief contribution to mathematics was a study of infinite series: *Methodus differentialis* (1730). In the next stage of his career, from 1735 on, he became the successful manager of leadmining operations in

Lanarkshire, and Smith may have known him, or of him, during the 1750s, when Stirling taught French and practical subjects such as bookkeeping and navigation in Glasgow and Smith was a Professor at the University. Stirling's Jacobite background dogged him as late as 1746, excluding him from final consideration as successor to Colin Maclaurin, Professor of Mathematics at Edinburgh (*DSB* 1976, xiii.67–70; Tweedie, 1922; Dougall, 1937: 33).

The report of Stirling solving Leibniz's problem was made by John Keill, another Scot with Balliol connection (Hall and Trilling, 1976: vi.282; Hall, 1980). He had accompanied David Gregory to Oxford in 1692, when the latter gave up his Edinburgh Chair in Mathematics rather than subscribe to the Presbyterian Confession of Faith. Both were admitted to Balliol as senior Commoners, and Keill was awarded a Warner Exhibition, a scholarship also held by Smith during his period at Oxford. Gregory and Keill were probably accepted at Balliol more because of their Jacobite sympathies than for their scientific work. At Oxford, Gregory rehashed his Edinburgh lectures on Newtonian science, and remodelled astronomy in conformity with it in *Astronomiae Physicae et Geometricae Elementa* (1702). In addition, he completed an edition of Euclid for the Clarendon Press (1703) and planned with Halley an edition of Apollonius which was never completed (*DSB* 1972, v.520–2). These projects were taken up by Smith's teacher and later colleague at Glasgow, Robert Simson.

Keill became the first lecturer at Oxford on experimental philosophy, though this was at Hart Hall rather than Balliol, and he had an association from 1699 with Christ Church. In his publications, Keill refuted Descartes's theory of vortices, and he championed Newton's claims in the controversy with Leibniz over priority in discovering the infinitesimal calculus. He also wrote two widely used introductory textbooks, on physics (1701) and astronomy (1718) (*DSB* 1973, vii.275–7).

Like Halley, Smith was critical of Keill's first book ('Letter', para. 5), and the sketch of the history of astronomy in the second may have prompted him to adopt the very different approach of his own essay on that subject. In any event, Smith seems to have encountered at Balliol no scientific tradition whatever. If he read the works of Gregory, Keill, Stirling, or Bradley during his Oxford days, they would have had meaning because of his education under Simson and Dick at Glasgow. Alas for Smith, he seems to have experienced at Oxford more that suggested boobyishness than intellectual brilliance.

To be sure, we do not have a clear idea of the impression made on him by the physical appearance of Oxford, with its indication of a rich culture and the historical struggles to achieve it. We do not know if he came through the North Gate into St Michael's Street, past the prison known as *Bocardo*, where the Reformers Cranmer, Latimer, and Ridley were thrown before going to the stake in Broad Street during the Marian persecution. In Smith's time, prisoners let down their hats on cords from this prison to beg from passers-by (Godley, 1908: 24–5; Rowse, 1975: 67).

The scattered remarks on taste in ornament and architecture in Smith's essay on the 'Imitative Arts' (*EPS* i.3) indicate that he did not appreciate the variety in the features of Gothic buildings. It is entirely possible that Oxford glories such as Magdalen College and the university church of St Mary's had no appeal for him. He does comment favourably on the 'exact uniformity' of the columns in porticoes of the Corinthian and Ionic orders, and we may believe that Nicholas Hawksmoor's Clarendon Building off Broad Street, built for the Press which occupied it from 1713 until 1829, met his aesthetic standard. Smith would agree, surely, that the same architect's additions to the Queen's College made it worthy of Defoe's praise of 1726: 'without comparison the most Beautiful College in the University' (Royal Commission on Historical Monuments of England, 1939: 97; Woolley, 1972: 54).

If he took a stroll in St John's garden next to his own college, Smith would find what he came to describe as giving aesthetic pleasure: 'yew and holly trees, clipped into the artificial shapes of pyramids, and columns, and vases, and obelisks'. It grew fashionable to criticize these features, he noted, but he saw them as giving an 'air of neatness and correct culture . . . to the whole garden' ('Imitative Arts', i.14). Further afield, there was the Physic Garden on the banks of the Cherwell under Magdalen Bridge, founded in 1621 by Henry Danvers, later Earl of Danby, which is entered by a handsome portico built by Nicholas Stone to a design by Inigo Jones. This offered 'shady walks under the rare and feathery trees—ginko and pawlonia, arbutus and ailanthus, the service trees shedding their fruit, ruddy and gold, on the grass in autumns'. Here were to be found even more fantastic examples of the topiarist's art, trees and shrubs cut to represent flying birds and figures such as Hercules and Achilles (Godley, 1908: 31; Rowse, 1975: 84, 89).

Balliol College, standing on the corner of Broad Street and the street east of St Mary Magdalen Church, had mostly fifteenth-century buildings of local Oxfordshire stone with slate-covered roofs (Pl. 4). One of these buildings, on the north side of the Front Quadrangle, is the Old Library, whose collection was said by Anthony Wood to be among the best in Oxford. On the west side is the Old Hall, where Smith succumbed to a reverie over his first dinner. A servant disturbed him, and brought up the subject of the poverty of the Scots, encouraging him to fall to, for he could never have seen such a joint in Scotland. A writer in the *Monthly Review* stated that Smith was fond of relating this anecdote himself (Rae, 1965: 18). Next to the Old Hall to the right is the Chapel which Smith was made to attend. It was built between 1520 and 1530, and had stained glass windows from that period, also others from the next century known to be the work of Abraham van Linge (RCHM, 1939: 20–3; Davis, 1963: 304–12).

Contemporary opinion assigned Balliol an antiquity second to that of University College, considered to have been founded by King Alfred in 872 (Chamberlayne, 1741: II.iii.193). The founder of Smith's college was John de

Pl. 4. Balliol College, Oxford, 1707. From James Beeverell, *Les Délices de la Grand' Bretagne, et d'Irlande* (GUL).

Balliol (from the French *Bailleul*), an aggressive magnate who held land on either side of the Scottish border and married Devorguilla, descendant of the Kings of Scotland and St Margaret, heiress of the Saxon royal house founded by Alfred the Great. Balliol ran foul of the Bishop of Durham, and legend has it that in 1255 he was scourged for his sins at that city's cathedral door, also he was required to maintain sixteen poor scholars at the University of Oxford. Certainly, Balliol was induced to support scholars at Oxford, and a tenement was found for them outside the city's wall and ditch, on a site now occupied by the Master's lodgings. The College was in operation by the time of Balliol's death in 1269, its future thereafter secured by a charter still extant, issued by Devorguilla in 1282.

About the time of the St Scholastica's Day riots of 1355, which ended in the humiliation of what had been a merchants' city, and the assertion of the University's control over Oxford, Balliol elected its most famous medieval Master, John Wyclif. Two of his many works, one on ecclesiastical dominion and the other on civil dominion, articulated demands for reform in Church and State in the 1370s in England, and sowed the seeds of the Reformation movement in Bohemia and Germany. Wyclif had many adherents among the northern 'nation' in Oxford, the students born north of the Trent and the Scots. His followers in the next generation, known as Lollards, carried out the task he had projected of translating the Bible into English, thus providing a powerful weapon against Roman Catholic autocracy. Whatever the radical teaching or legacy of its former Master, and his place in the history of human freedom to which Smith was to contribute, the Balliol College of Smith's time was staunchly committed to the more extreme forms of upholding the authority of the Church and the monarchy.

In the fifteenth century the College was the home of leaders of the English Renaissance movement: George Neville, Archbishop of York, brother of Warwick 'the Kingmaker'; John Free, the first professional English humanist; and William Gray, Bishop of Ely (d. 1478), whose bequest of 200 manuscript volumes made a substantial addition to Balliol's Library, the great majority of the benefaction surviving to Smith's time and ours. The college statutes were recast in 1507 by Bishop Richard Fox of Winchester to provide for self-government, including election of the Visitor, to whom was submitted arbitration of disputes. In 1571 the tutorial method of teaching was institutionalized through a rule that commoners were to be assigned to tutors and made to do the same work as scholars on the foundation. And in 1610 fellow-commoners were admitted to provide more revenue.

The College had virtually no local connections until 1601, when it accepted the offer of an opulent London clothier, Peter Blundell, to endow one scholarship and one Fellowship, to be held only by claimants from the school he had founded at Tiverton in Devon. The Blundell scholar had the right to succeed to the Fellowship, which he could hold for ten years. In 1615 it was further arranged that, if the newly founded Fellowship was not available when a Blundell scholar took his BA, then he was to get the next old foundation vacancy. Moreover, in 1676 the College accepted £600 from the Blundell trustees on the condition that another Blundell scholarship and Fellowship would be instituted, and a Fellowship on the old foundation would be suppressed.

Balliol accepted in 1673 four Scots on the Warner foundation rejected by Magdalen, and in 1699 the first election of Snell Exhibitioners was made. These endowment schemes reinforced the mistaken idea that Balliol was a 'Scotch Foundation', but the primary intent of the benefactors, Bishop John Warner of Rochester (d. 1666) and John Snell (d. 1679), a minor civil servant educated at Glasgow University, was to strengthen episcopalianism in Scotland by making provision for educating Scottish clergymen of that denomination (Lee-Warner, 1901; Jones, 1988: 113, n. 3, 124-7).

Despite the broadening of the community that this development suggests, the grip of the Blundell connection was dominant, and eight years before Smith's arrival seven of the fourteen Fellows were from Blundell's school. The Visitor of this period did not mince his words about the evils of this system, and took the view that Tiverton men 'habitually voted for their compatriots without regard to the more important questions of good conduct and scholarship. Balliol . . . was fast degenerating into a country college' (Davis, 1963: 158).

The difficulties of the College were compounded by intense rivalries among the Fellows. When a new Master was to be elected in 1726, half of them supported a Senior Fellow, William Best, who had acted as Viceregent during the illness of the previous Master, while the other half wished to bring in Dr Theophilus Leigh, a young Fellow of Corpus Christi College, whose chief recommendation lay in being the nephew of the Visitor, Dr Henry Brydges, Canon of Rochester. He owed his Visitor's position to friendship with Bishop Atterbury, whose High Church principles and Jacobite leanings were admired in Oxford. Best's party included the Senior Fellow, William Lux, still on the establishment in Smith's time, though he was believed to be a lunatic. Leigh's party included a Junior Fellow, Humphrey Quick, who had never subscribed to the Act of Uniformity, that is, had not assented and consented to the contents of the Book of Common Prayer of the Church of England.

An extraordinary scene ensued in the Chapel on the day of the election, with efforts on the one hand to secure evidence of Mr Lux's lunacy and claims on the other that Mr Quick was a non-juror. Mr Best's party left the Chapel declaring their candidate elected, and the remaining party proclaimed the election was void and proceeded to elect Dr Leigh. Mr Best occupied the Master's lodging but was forced to evacuate it before 21 March 1727, when his rival, at the head of a great throng of sympathizers, took possession. When appealed to, the Visitor had decided in favour of his nephew, whom he correctly regarded as upholding the soundest of High Church views and Jacobite prejudices.

Leigh went on to reign as Master until 1785 over a College seemingly filled with discontent. He did try to reduce the absenteeism of Fellows, but he also protected the system of closed Fellowships and squelched competition for them on the basis of merit. He is said to have fomented prejudice against the Snell Exhibitioners because they were Scotsmen, who were thought to be Whigs and supporters of the Hanoverian succession, whereas he wished to inculcate in the next generation the Tory and Jacobite principles of Lord Bolingbroke and Bishop Atterbury. Best, who was a good tutor and scholar, quietly held onto his Fellowship until the next college living in the Church of England was open to him, that of St Lawrence Jewry in the City of London (Davis, 1963: 160–4).

This was the Oxford system of the day, essentially a holding operation for celibate clergymen, who regarded their Fellowships as forms of property, with the teaching role reduced to a minimum, to be enjoyed on the short term, either until Oxford plums fell to them, such as the headship of a College, or a well-endowed church place became available and they could marry. A lifetime as a Fellow could be a dispiriting experience. As Geoffrey Faber put it: 'A fellowship is an excellent breakfast, an indifferent dinner, and a most miserable supper.'[3]

Smith's analysis in his maturity was that in countries where church benefices are modest, the universities are likely to be able to select their professors from the churchmen who are 'men of letters', that is, scholars. Where church livings were rich, they would 'naturally' draw from the universities the 'greater part of their eminent men of letters'. The Church of England he considered the best endowed in Europe after that of Rome; in consequence, 'an old college tutor, who is known and distinguished in Europe as an eminent man of letters, is as rarely to be found [in England] as in any Roman catholick country'. By contrast, as Smith noted, in the Swiss Protestant cantons, also in the Protestant countries of Germany, Holland, Sweden, Denmark, and Scotland, 'by far the greater number of the eminent scholars have been professors of universities' (*WN* v.i.g.39).

Proof of Smith's contention is to be found in the surviving documents connected with his career at Oxford. He brought with him from Glasgow a certificate of his election as a Snell Exhibitioner dated 11 March 1740, which indicates that he did not take a degree at Glasgow. The certificate states that the Master and Fellows of Balliol intimated to Principal Neil Campbell that there were two Snell vacancies, and he notified the Glasgow professors and regents accordingly on 11 February. At a duly convened meeting on 4 March, the Principal and the professors and regents, as was their right, nominated and recommended

Adam Smith Son to the deceased Adam Smith at Kirkaldie bearer hereof for one of these Exhibitions Whom we Do hereby Certifie to be a Native of the Kingdom of Scotland and to have Studied three Years in the College of Glasgow without taking any Degree here or elsewhere and who we hope will be found [to] be of a good disposition and behaviour And, in regard of his Standing of good learning. (Balliol Coll. MS)

This is signed by Principal Campbell; by Charles Morthland, Professor of Oriental Languages, as Dean of Faculty; and by the professors, mostly of some distinction, who taught Smith as we have discussed in the previous chapter: George Rosse, Latin; Alexander Dunlop, Greek; John Loudoun, Logic; Robert Simson, Mathematics; Francis Hutcheson, Moral Philosophy; and Robert Dick, Natural Philosophy.

Consent at Oxford to Smith's admission to a Snell Exhibition, 'by virtue of a Decree made in the High Court of Chancery in 1693', was given on 4 July 1740 by the Master of Balliol and the heads of two other colleges: Joseph Smith, Provost of Queen's, and William Holmes, President of St John's (Balliol Coll. MS).

Dr Leigh at the time was Vice-Chancellor, but this was a concession to his Tory politics rather than his merits. Numbers at Balliol dwindled under his administration. The favourite amusements of the College were field sports and riding, and the Fellows were reported to have so little to do that they spent their time sitting in Broad Street to watch the passage of the London mail coach. When Balliol undergraduates threatened to thrash a canon of Windsor who reproved them for shouting Jacobite slogans, Dr Leigh endeavoured to have them excused as manifesting the normal behaviour of young men in drink. He was distinguished as the first clergyman to become a member of the High Borlace, a Tory wine club which met annually on 18 August to drink the health of the Stuart Pretender, James III, and confusion to the Constitution Club's Whigs (Davis, 1963: 165–6). Leigh's attitudes and actions as the Master of his College sustained the views of the Convocation of the University which met in July 1683, in the aftermath of the alleged Rye House Plot against Charles II's life. That august body demonstrated its loyalty to the Stuart dynasty by calling on Oxford teachers to instil into their students the doctrine of passive obedience, 'which in a manner is the badge and character of the Church of England'. Thereafter the Vice-Chancellor and the Bishop led a procession of the doctors and masters to a bonfire in the Schools Quadrangle where 'certain pernicious books . . . destructive to the sacred persons of princes', including works by John Knox, George Buchanan, and John Milton, were fed to the flames (Lenman, 1980: 204).

The second Oxford academic who signed the Snell document, Joseph Smith, was a chaplain to Queen Caroline, who served as Provost of Queen's for the last twenty-six years of a very long life (d. 1756). In the course of this, he secured endowments for his College and wrote against deists and non-jurors. Provost Smith interested himself in the teaching of philosophy and theology, and there survive questions he drew up for the formal disputations required for completing Oxford degrees, elements of his scheme persisting until 1823 (Queen's, MS 475, fos. 93 ff., MS 442 (1)).

This material offers some guide to the curriculum as envisioned by the head of an Oxford college. Of considerable interest is the reading linked to the questions for third-year students. Some of the questions reappear among those known to have been asked in 1774 at Oxford, and the suggested authors are found among those assigned to students at Christ Church during the eighteenth century. There is some similarity between the Oxford curriculum thus revealed and the Glasgow one Adam Smith followed. Among Provost Smith's examples for first-year students are to be found stock questions derived from scholastic logic about relations, universals, and the syllogism. Lockean influence is apparent, as in what is known of Professor Loudoun's teaching. For instance, a question by Aristotle is raised, fundamental to Locke's empiricism: can anything be in the mind which is not first in the senses? The second-year questions deal with topics in ethics such as free will, happiness as the goal of life, and the adequacy of conscience for guiding our actions. A scholastic approach is modified somewhat by awareness of contemporary moral philosophy, but no formative philosophical mind is reflected such as Adam Smith encountered at Glasgow in Francis Hutcheson. That philosopher's name does appear among authors listed in questions for third-year students, who continued with ethics and logic but were also taught physics, as we found was the practice at Glasgow. The unidentified writings by Hutcheson considered appropriate are likely to have been the eclectic university textbooks of his Glasgow period, thought to be safe from an orthodox theological standpoint, rather than the more philosophically original treatises, composed in Dublin, on virtue as benevolence and the arguments for a moral sense. Pufendorf is mentioned by Provost Smith, to shed light on the law of nature. The questions and readings on physics seem largely Cartesian with some awareness of Newton's contribution, represented in the work of his followers s'Gravesande and Keill (Quarrie, 1986: 493–506; Yolton, 1986: 566–91).

Here is a world of knowledge with which Adam Smith could connect if he found it in Oxford; but it would seem to him old-fashioned and unadventurous. No economic issues, for instance, seem to have been raised as they were in Hutcheson's moral philosophy teaching. The reports we have from Oxford students in this period, however, indicate that in general preparation for their examinations was a much more stultified procedure than Provost Smith's lists suggest, since they used 'strings' or rote questions, and most of their reading was done in summaries rather than original works. As we will find out, Adam Smith was to analyse the Oxford malaise of his time and offer some reasons why the teaching was so slack, and why research and productivity were at such a low ebb.

The career of the third signatory to Smith's Snell admission document does a little to redeem the dismal reputation of Oxford in this period. William Holmes was President of St John's from 1728 to 1748, after which he became Dean of Exeter. When he was Vice-Chancellor, he revived in 1733 what was termed the 'Act', the graduation exercises and ceremonies held in Wren's nobly proportioned Sheldonian Theatre. For this occasion he invited Handel to present his sacred oratorio, *Esther*, on the opening day. Tory Oxford, in the person of the antiquary Thomas Hearne, sneered at the foreigner who sold his book for an 'exorbitant sum'. As Regius Professor of History from 1736 until 1742, Holmes gave some lectures, but no publications arising from them seem to have appeared (Godley, 1908: 189; Sutherland and Mitchell, 1986: 474, 871).

Such were the heads of Oxford colleges when Adam Smith was admitted to Balliol, on 4 July 1740 in the Hilary Term.[4] On the 24th of August he wrote to his cousin, William Smith, who was one of his guardians and employed as secretary to the 2nd Duke of Argyll, to acknowledge receiving a bill for £16, 'but more for the good advice' that went with it. He goes on to say that his expenses 'must necessarily amount to a much greater sum this year than at any time hereafter, because of the extraordinary and most extravagant fees we are obligd to pay the College and University on our admittance'. Certainly, he would need funds from outside sources, since his Snell Exhibition paid him only £40 per year, but his 'Battels' (college accounts for board and provisions from the kitchen and buttery) seem to have amounted to between £22 and £32, and his tutors' fees would run to another £4 per year, which did not leave much for other required payments and extras such as books. Most Commoners reckoned on spending at least £60 a year. More galling, perhaps, than the expensiveness of Oxford was the indication that it was strenuous in piety and slack in learning. This drew from the 17-year-old Smith a remark characteristic of his dry humour: 'it will be his own fault if anyone should endanger his health at Oxford by excessive Study, our only business here being to go to prayers twice a day, and to lecture twice a week' (*Corr.* No. 1). These words came back to haunt him, however, when he suffered from a psychosomatic illness in 1743–4.

Regarding the dons at Balliol in Smith's time, we know their names in order of seniority as Fellows, and their functions in 1740, also in some cases the subjects they taught: Joseph Sanford, BA (elected 1714), Senior Bursar; William Lux, MA (elected 1716, non-resident, and regarded by some as a lunatic); Charles Godwyn, BA (elected 1722), lecturer in Hebrew; John Land, MA (elected 1728), Notary Public; William Fernyhaugh, MA (elected 1730); John Walker, MA (elected 1733); John Hunsdon, MA (elected 1736), Junior Bursar; George Drake, MA (elected 1736), Senior Dean, lecturer in Greek; Gerard Andrews, MA (elected 1737); William Parker, MA (elected 1737), Junior Dean, lecturer in Logic and Mathematics; and Dr Arthur Culme (elected 1738), lecturer in Rhetoric and Poetry. Three other Fellows were elected during Smith's time at Balliol: John Abbot (1740), John Foot (1744), and John Darch (1745).

The Senior Fellow, Sanford, was in residence from 1714 to 1774, a record still for the College. He earned a reputation as a serious scholar, and assisted Benjamin Kennicott with his Hebrew Bible, but he produced no major publications and was not active as a tutor. His friend Charles Godwyn (d. 1770) was more devoted to teaching, and was also a bibliophile and coin-collector. He left his collections to the University—his books are in the Bodleian—while Sanford left his books to Exeter College, which perhaps says something about their feelings concerning the Balliol they knew (College Lists, 1739–68; College Minutes; Jones, 1988: 168).

We do not know which of them was Smith's tutor, nor do we know anything of the circumstances of the claim that Smith was entered as 'studiosus' in civil law at Balliol (Scott, 1940: 267). This may point to further reading in the natural-law tradition of Grotius and Pufendorf, authors studied at Oxford during this period (Barton, 1986: 597–9). Such reading would have helped prepare Smith for giving lectures on jurisprudence at Edinburgh in the period 1748–51. Smith's friend John Douglas, a Warner Exhibitioner of this time and later on the Snell foundation from 1745 to 1748, had a good word to say about George Drake, 'whom I shall always have an affectionate Remembrance of, as I profitted much by his superintending my studies' (BL Egerton MS 2181, fo. 6).

It is to be feared, however, that Smith had the same disappointing experiences as Edward Gibbon, who was at Magdalen in 1752–3 for fourteen 'unprofitable months':

The fellows or monks of my time were decent easy men, who supinely enjoyed the gifts of the founder; their days were filled by a series of uniform employments; the chapel and the hall, the coffee-house and the common room, till they retired, weary and well satisfied to a long slumber. From the toil of reading, or thinking, or writing, they had absolved their conscience; and the first shoots of learning and ingenuity withered on the ground, without yielding any fruits to the owners or the public. As a gentleman-commoner, I was admitted to the society of the fellows, and fondly expected that some questions of literature would be the amusing and instructive topics of their discourse. Their conversation stagnated in a round of college business, Tory politics, personal anecdotes, and private scandal: their dull and deep potations excused the brisk intemperance of youth: and their constitutional toasts were not expressive of the most lively loyalty for the house of Hanover. (Gibbon, 1950: 40–2)

Some eight years later, Jeremy Bentham had an even more distressing time at Queen's, where his father pushed him to matriculate when he was 12, following the display of his powers as a prodigy at Westminster School. When other first-year students who were 18 or older got drunk and sang at midnight, he hid in his bed to escape from the ghosts of which he was terrified as the result of servants' tales. He met his pedantic tutor, the morose and hidebound Jacob Jewison, at eleven in the morning and at nine at night to go over lessons he had already covered at Westminster. This intellectual fare was supplemented by lectures on the Greek New Testament, oral disputations in Hall, and a course in physics which proved a fiasco when the instructor could not get his experiments to work. The one thing Queen's gave him that he prized was training in logic, perhaps Provost Smith's legacy to his college. What he hated most about Oxford was being made to subscribe to the Thirty-nine Articles of the Church of England. Some of them he found nonsense. Others he saw as conflicting with the Bible, and he believed that in subscribing he was forced to become a liar. This marked a stage in the growth of his hostility to the established institutions of his country, a prelude to the development of his radical views (Mack, 1962: 43–6; Bentham, 1968–89: i.49–50).

It seems likely that Smith was similarly offended by what he found taught at Balliol, and that Oxford became an example for him of one of the 'learned societies' that 'have chosen to remain, for a very long time, the sanctuaries in which exploded systems and obsolete prejudices found shelter and protection, after they had been hunted out of every other corner of the world' (*WN* v.i.f.34). His experiences as a student and, no doubt, the reflection of the mature man led him to offer some reasons for this state of affairs. He reckoned that it is each man's interest to live as much at ease as possible, and if someone's rewards are the same whether he performs or does not perform an onerous duty, he will either neglect it or perform it as slackly as his superiors permit. If the superior authority resides in a college of which he is a member, and the other members are teachers, they will all agree among themselves to overlook one man's neglect of duty, if each is allowed to neglect his own. Thus it came about, Smith argued, that the Oxford professors had given up even the pretence of teaching for many years (*WN* v.i.f.7–8).

Moreover, when colleges have rich endowments sufficient to attract students independent of the merit of the colleges, and charitable foundations (such as the Snell Exhibitions) do not permit students to choose the college they like best, there is no competition between the colleges. As well, when tutors are not chosen by the students on account of their teaching ability but are assigned by the head of the college, competition between tutors lapses, and when students cannot change their tutors without getting permission, tutors have no incentive to attend to their pupils.

Smith here explains the cause of the 'degradation and contempt' into which he believed by 1774 most contemporary universities and their teachers had fallen (*Corr.* No. 143). The root of this was an opulence enjoyed through privilege. Smith also traced to the same cause the unwillingness of Oxford and other wealthy universities to change their curricula to keep up with the times. He must have been struck at Balliol, for example, by the lack of commitment to providing instruction in the New Philosophy and Science of Locke and Newton taught at a poor university such as Glasgow, where attention had to be paid to the current interests and needs of society.

The practice at Oxford of teaching the 'exploded system' of Aristotle and his scholastic commentators seems to have struck him as an intellectual sham. It demeaned both those who taught in it and those obliged to submit to it as students by the necessity of obtaining a qualification to practise a profession:

If the teacher happens to be a man of sense, it must be an unpleasant thing to him to be conscious, while he is lecturing his students, that he is either speaking or reading nonsense, or what is little better than nonsense. It must too be unpleasant to him to observe that the greater part of his students desert his lectures; or perhaps attend upon them with plain enough marks of neglect, contempt, and derision.

To avoid that derision, Smith noted, the teacher falls back on the expedient of reading with the students a book in a 'foreign and dead language', and making them interpret it to him, 'by now and then making an occasional remark upon it, he may flatter himself that he is giving a lecture'. A very little effort and learning will allow him to do this without making himself ridiculous, and college discipline will force students to attend such a 'sham-lecture' regularly, and to 'maintain the most decent and respectful behaviour during the whole time of the performance' (*WN* v.i.f.13–14).

The system at Balliol along this line was kept up long enough, for we find another Snell Exhibitioner, Sir William Hamilton, writing to his mother on 15 November 1807:

I am so plagued by these foolish lectures of the College tutors that I have little time to do anything else—Aristotle to-day, ditto to-morrow; and I believe that if the ideas furnished by Aristotle to these numskulls were taken away, it would be doubtful whether there remained a single notion. I am quite tired of such uniformity of study. (Veitch, 1869: 29–36)

Very likely the Balliol dons were still relying on such textbooks as the *Artes Logicae Compendium* of Henry Aldrich, Dean of Christchurch, published in a long and short form in fourteen editions between 1691 and 1810, and reinforcing Aristotelianism against the tradition of scientific thought associated with Bacon, Boyle, and Locke, of such appeal to Adam Smith. Luckily for Hamilton, who wished at this time to study medicine, he could attend a 'very nice course of Anatomy' in Oxford, and he enjoyed physical exercise in the form of rowing and skating (letter of 27 November 1807). Later in his career, Hamilton returned to Smith's charge that the public professors did not teach, but he reported Balliol's striking success in the examination system of the nineteenth century, once Fellowships were made open and an able Master was elected (Hamilton, 1853: 363 n., 369–70, 401–18, 425–559, 742–832).

Smith also wrote to his mother about his activities and expectations. Like many a student, he was on the look out for money (*Corr.* No. 2). In October 1741 he spent fourteen days at Adderbury with his guardian, William Smith. This introduced Smith to the opulent circumstances of a great magnate in the English countryside. Adderbury House is situated on the east side of the main road to Banbury, within a mile of the Cherwell, about eighteen miles north of Oxford. It had been owned by the seventeenth-century poet Lord Rochester, but when it was filled with children he retreated from it to the old High Lodge at the west end of Woodstock Forest, where he died. It was leased by William Smith's employer, the 2nd Duke of Argyll, in 1717; according to Horace Walpole, he set about having it rebuilt in several stages, including the addition of arcaded wings designed by Roger Morris in 1731. Smith said of it: 'the Place is agreeable enough, and there is a great deal of good company in the town' (*Corr.* No. 3). The gardens and parkland of the house were extensive, and as the Duke was described as having a 'head admirably turned to mechanics', it is likely that Smith saw a well-managed estate where the building projects and the 'delightful art' of gardening (*WN* I.xi.b.25) received due attention. Adderbury House was later inherited by Duke John's grandson, the Duke of Buccleuch, who became Smith's pupil, and he continued to improve it before selling it in 1774, when it was reported to have fifty-six rooms, including a lofty entrance hall, three drawing-rooms, a library, and a billiard-room (Lobel and Crossley, 1969: 7–9).

After mentioning to his mother the visit to Adderbury, Smith goes on to say: 'In my last Letter I desir'd you to send me some Stocking's, the sooner you send 'em the better.' Hamilton also wrote to his mother about the need to have stockings at Balliol, providing a picture of the daily round of life in the College in May 1807, some part of which Smith must have experienced:

In the morning we wear white cotton stockings, go to chapel at seven o'clock, breakfast at nine, fag [study] all the forenoon, and dine at half-past three, and before dinner regularly dress in silk stockings, &c. After dinner we go to one another's rooms and drink some wine, then go to chapel at half-past five . . .

In a letter of 12 May 1742 to his mother, Smith informs her that a certificate of his age will not be needed as soon as he expected (*Corr.* No. 4). Perhaps this was required in connection with the award to him on 2 November of that year of a Warner Exhibition, worth £8. 5s. per year, by the patrons, the Archbishop of Canterbury and the Bishop of Rochester (Balliol MS). Smith also has the news that a Snell Exhibition will fall vacant soon, with the resignation of John Preston, younger son of Sir George Preston of Valleyfield, who was to take the letter to Edinburgh. Adam Smith wished his guardian William Smith to know of the vacancy, 'in case that he intends to make interest for any of his friends', which suggests that for career purposes the places at Oxford had value despite the disappointing nature of the education offered there.

Meantime, Smith's joke about injury to health at Oxford from 'excessive Study' being self-inflicted unfortunately rebounded on him. On 29 November 1743 he tells his mother: 'I am just recovered of a violent fit of laziness, which has confined me to my elbow chair these three months' (*Corr.* No. 5). In the next letter which has survived, dated 2 July 1744, he attributes to 'laziness' his inability to write more often to his mother, and he describes some physical symptoms: 'an inveterate scurvy and shaking of the head', which he claims have been cured by taking tar-water, a 'remedy very much in vogue here at present for almost all diseases' (*Corr.* No. 6). Later, he acknowledged that these disabilities continued as long as he could remember anything, and that in the end tar-water was not efficacious (Rae, 1965: 25).

The symptoms resemble those experienced by Adam Smith's great friend David Hume, when he had a kind of nervous breakdown in 1729, incurred as a result of prosecuting his philosophical enquiries with too much ardour (Hume,

HL i.13–17). It is entirely possible that at Balliol, led on by his desire for knowledge and neglecting the outdoor exercise that Sir William Hamilton enjoyed, Smith read himself into a lethargy of spirits, accompanied by involuntary shaking of the head and skin disease, or even the bodily debility, pains in the limbs, and skin eruptions usually associated with the heavily salted diet of sailors.

As his correspondence reveals, Smith struggled all his life with psychosomatic illness of this kind, which the medical profession came to denominate 'hypochondriasis'. Michael Barfoot has pointed out that this term in contemporary application went beyond the 'symptomatic hypochondria' of modern understanding. It covered primarily the 'vapours' or 'low spirits', and in some cases produced the symptoms of dyspepsia or, more alarmingly, hysterical states. Sometimes it was synonymous with 'spleen' and 'melancholy', but depression as we think of it was not always involved. The prevailing medical view was that the disease arose from the imagination affecting the body in a morbid fashion. A physician would attempt to change the state of mind exciting hypochondriasis by reaching it through the body, often prescribing diet, exercise, and avoidance of passion. Smith was later to receive advice along this line from his physician, Dr William Cullen (Barfoot, 1991: 209).

Smith's reliance on tar-water in Oxford to cure his disorder, however, was probably due to the sensational popularity of a pamphlet published by Bishop Berkeley in April 1744: *Philosophical Reflexions and Inquiries Concerning the Virtues of Tar-Water*. This was prefixed by the title *Siris* (Greek for 'chain') in the second edition which followed a few weeks after the first, and the short name has stuck for the publication. Pursuing his remarkable chain of thought linking medicine to metaphysics, Berkeley has a paragraph that seems to speak to Smith's condition:

Many (hysterical and hypochondriacal as well as) scorbutic ailments . . . might be safely removed or relieved by the sole use of tar-water; and those lives which seem hardly worth living for bad appetite, low spirits, restless nights, wasting pains and anxieties, be rendered easy and comfortable. (Berkeley, 1901: iii.179)

It is possible that Berkeley provided Smith with more than the tar-water remedy, since elsewhere he points out that the 'strength and numbers' of the people constitute the 'true wealth of a nation' (iii.181). This insight, whether derived from Berkeley or some other source, informs Smith's own appreciation of the worth of human capital in *WN*. To be sure, other sources of the phrase 'wealth of nations' have been pointed out in Dryden, Johnson, and the Physiocrats (Scott, 1937: 322–3, n. 2). Smith's favourable response to aspects of Berkeley's *Essay towards a New Theory of Vision* (1709), especially the idea that there is a 'language' of visual perception, is reflected in the essay on the 'External Senses' discussed in the next chapter. Berkeley's felicity as a writer (Walmsley, 1990) also commended itself to Smith. There must also have been some sharing of the viewpoint that led Berkeley to declare in his *Principles of Human Knowledge*

(1710) that philosophers cause difficulties for themselves: 'We have first raised a dust, and then complain we cannot see' (Berkeley, 1901: i.238).

We have some idea of the kinds of study which Adam Smith ardently prosecuted on his own at Oxford in default of instruction from the tutors and professors. Dugald Stewart tells us that Hutcheson's lectures directed Smith to the 'study of human nature in all its branches, more particularly of the political history of mankind', and that he devoted himself to this study 'almost entirely from the time of his removal to Oxford' (i.8). It is possible that Smith's private studies along this line brought him into conflict with the orthodox, not to say reactionary dons at Balliol. The nineteenth-century political economist John Ramsay McCulloch offered the following story as resting 'on the best authority':

Something had occurred, while Smith was at Oxford, to excite the suspicions of his superiors with respect to the nature of his private pursuits; and the heads of his college, having entered his apartment without his being aware, unluckily found him engaged reading Hume's *Treatise of Human Nature*. The objectionable work was, of course, seized; the young philosopher being at the same time severely reprimanded.[5]

Charles Godwyn had Hume's *Treatise* (1739–40) among his books, also his *Philosophical Essays concerning Human Understanding* (1748) and *Principles of Morals* (1751), and he saw fit to leave all these to the Bodleian in 1770 (Sutherland and Mitchell, 1986: 732). However, he and his fellow Balliol dons may not have favoured an undergraduate reading on his own a book by such a notorious sceptic.

Stewart also mentions that Smith 'diversified his leisure hours by the less severe occupations of polite literature', and that 'he employed himself frequently in the practice of translation, (particularly from the French), with a view to the improvement of his own style', for he believed such exercises were helpful to those who wished to improve their skill in composition. Further, Stewart considered it likely that Smith's cultivation of the study of languages was engaged in 'with the greatest care' at Oxford. His aim was not to be able to parade his learning, but to have a 'familiar acquaintance with everything that could illustrate the institutions, the manners, and the ideas of different ages and nations' (i.8–10). To acquire modern languages, Smith may have engaged the services of one of the freelance teachers available for this in Oxford. The Balliol Library was certainly to hand, with its shelves of works of the Greek, Latin, French, and Italian poets that he came to know so well, though in general access was reserved for senior members of the College. There was an Undergraduates' or Little Library, however, whose readers paid fees. Its holdings were said to be limited (Jones, 1988: 144–5, 147). If Smith was at all like Sir William Hamilton, he frequented the Oxford bookshops to pick up the bargains he could afford, possibly the first two parts of Antonini's *Dictionnaire italien, latin, et françois* (1735, 1743) remaining in his Library (Mizuta).

From and after the week ending 13 April 1744, he was styled 'Dominus' in the Balliol Buttery Books, this being the usual designation of someone with BA standing, to which he was entitled after sixteen weeks' residence. It is unlikely that he qualified for the degree by repeating the 'strings' of syllogisms memorized for examinations that by this time had become a farce (Sutherland and Mitchell, 1986: 471). We may ask if he would have made use of his BA standing by obtaining entry to the Bodleian Library, whose riches at this period were open to graduates only, and two years after their graduation at that. This would be April 1746, in Smith's case, four months before he left Oxford (Rae, 1965: 20, 23). Of course, he may have obtained special permission to become a reader, but his name does not appear on any of the Bodleian entry-books for the period 1740–6.

But whatever the stock of learning he was acquiring on his own, and perhaps in defiance of the Oxford guardians of orthodoxy, the great question before Smith was what career he was to adopt. The 'ecclesiastical profession', as Stewart called it, was not suitable to his taste (i.11), and though he could have held onto his Snell Exhibition for ten years, this was a bleak prospect. It may have been the case, too, that the Jacobite rising of 1745–6 deepened ill-feeling between the Snell Exhibitioners and the other members, senior and junior, of Balliol College, whose sentimental Jacobitism would be at variance with the alarm felt by Lowland Scots over the fate of their country then at the mercy of the Highland army of Prince Charles Edward Stuart.

In the context of a war between Britain and France, and French promises to invade Britain, the Prince had landed at Moidart on 25 July 1745 with his far-from-heroic Seven Men and a war-chest of only 4,000 *louis d'or*. He had opened *Bliadhna Thierlaich* (Charlie's Year) by winning over Highland chiefs through his charisma, and on 19 August he raised his standard at Glenfinnan in Clanranald country. Jacobite lairds swelled his army with their tenants, and he was joined by an experienced general of great strategic ability, Lord George Murray. In his way a man of the Enlightenment, Murray was interested in scientific farming and mine-development, and his favourite authors were Marcus Aurelius and Montaigne. But he was also 'convinced that the setting aside of the Royal [Stuart] line was an act of the highest injustice' (Tomasson, 1958: 2, 14, 253), and he knew how to lead Highlanders in battle.

News must have filtered through to Oxford of the Jacobite entry into Edinburgh in September, the subsequent rout of the Hanoverian Commander-in-Chief in Scotland, Sir John Cope, at Prestonpans, outside the city, then the rapid invasion of England beginning on 8 November, and the equally swift retreat to Scotland from the high point of reaching Derby on 4 December. This was 'Black Wednesday' to the Whigs, when their enemies were only 127 miles from London. Bitterly disappointed by the retreat—caused by the presence in the field of two menacing Hanoverian armies (Wade's and Cumberland's), also a report by an English spy (Dudley Bradstreet) of a phantom third army at Northampton—French inaction, and the failure of the Welsh and English

Jacobites to rise, the Prince never fully trusted Murray afterwards. Though a further battle was won at Falkirk in January 1746, the Jacobite command fell apart in the course of a further withdrawal to the Highlands. The nadir of the rising was the disastrous defeat at Culloden on 16 April, largely due to bad decisions by the Irish general, John William O'Sullivan, trusted by the Prince over Murray. Murray knew he could gather another Jacobite army to fight Cumberland again, but the Prince's nerve was gone. He gave a *sauve qui peut* order, and the rising collapsed: *Lochaber no more*. Smith would have appreciated the assessment of the Jacobite banker, Aeneas MacDonald, that the failure of English Jacobitism to help the Prince was due to a liquidity problem. His landed supporters did not have the ready cash to buy soldiers, and unlike the Scots they could not bring their dependents into a war, because they had no military training (Terry, 1922; McLynn, 1991; Lynch, 1994: 334–9).

Though there was no rush from Oxford to join Charles Edward Stuart, Jacobites there probably crowed at his victories. Political feeling over Jacobitism, before and during the rising, would exacerbate the sense of grievance of the Snell Exhibitioners about their treatment at Balliol. Their grievances had led them, including Adam Smith, to write to the Glasgow Senatus Academicus some time before 5 February 1745 about improving their situation, a move connected with a lawsuit in Chancery commenced in 1738 to compel the Exhibitioners to enter the Church of England. The Lord Chancellor struck down this appeal in 1744, and had called for a scheme or schemes to put the Snell charity on a better footing (EUL MS La. II.99[7]). When the Senatus took up with Balliol the complaints of the Exhibitioners about being treated uncivilly and habitually being assigned the worst rooms, Dr Leigh's answer was that since they had a 'total dislike of the college', they might with advantage be moved elsewhere (Addison, 1901: 19–22).

One of Smith's students, David Callander of Westertown, left a record that Smith acknowledged to him that he 'did not like Balliol and left in disgust' (EUL MS La. II.451/2, fos. 429–34; Raphael and Sakamoto, 1990; Raphael, 1992*b*). His departure from Balliol occurred during the third week of August 1746, when his last charge for 'Battels' was entered (Battel Books, 23, 2). The result of the Chancery suit had made it clear that Smith would not have to forfeit a bond of £500 for not taking Orders in the Church of England, as Snell's will had stipulated.

To be sure, of the surviving contemporaries of Smith on the Snell foundation, most did enter the Church. We do not know the fate of Charles Suttie and Thomas Crawford. John Stirling died within a year of going to Balliol. John Smith, who entered Balliol in 1744 and remained on friendly terms with Smith (*Corr.* No. 64), was the one Exhibitioner notable for success in a career at Oxford. He qualified as a medical doctor and then taught mathematics at Oxford, holding the Savilian Chair of Geometry from 1766 until 1797. Of the other Exhibitioners John Preston, who took a letter for Smith's mother to Edinburgh in 1742, became chaplain to the 26th Regiment of Foot. Smith's great friend into old age, James (Stuart by assumption) Menteath, became Rector of Barrowby in Lincolnshire. Andrew Wood served as chaplain to the King, 1760, and was Rector of Washington, Co. Durham, then of Gateshead on Tyne, before dying of a fever contracted after his exertions saving parishioners when the Newcastle bridge fell in 1772.

Another lifelong friend of Smith's, John Douglas, the son of a Pittenweem merchant, rose highest of all as a clergyman, becoming in turn Bishop of Carlisle, Dean of Windsor, and Bishop of Salisbury (Addison, 1901: 41–7). He was an example of Smith's observation that a well-endowed Church would draw men of letters away from a university: his preferments supported and rewarded a highly successful series of publications embracing literary detective work in the field of Milton scholarship, an attempted refutation of Hume on miracles, political tracts, exposure of religious fraud, and editions of the writings of the statesman and historian Clarendon and of Captain James Cook.

Adam Smith may or may not in time have developed some gratitude to Oxford for the opportunity it gave him of reading solidly for six years, and for taking away anxieties about his accent and his Scotticisms, which plagued David Hume. His letters from this period help us to form a picture of a young person of some self-confidence who is firmly committed to a life of scholarship, even to the point of endangering his health. There was a valuable lesson for him, of course, in seeing this ancient university in a state of 'degradation', an experience which contributed to his stress on the need for competition and opportunity for enterprise in human agencies. He went back to Kirkcaldy, as Stewart said, limiting his 'ambition to the uncertain prospect of obtaining, in time, some one of those modest preferments, to which literary attainments lead in Scotland' (i.11). But he also went off to do the work that led to his world fame as a man of letters.

6

A Respectable Auditory

innumerable witnesses . . . [of] lectures which I gave at Edinburgh

At Oxford, Adam Smith met dislike because the Scots at Balliol were thought to support the Hanoverian King. On his way north, we presume at the end of August 1746, it is entirely possible that he had to guard his identity because of hostility to the Scots as rebels. As a pamphlet entitled *Old England* appearing at the end of 1746 put the matter: 'A Scot is a natural hereditary Jacobite, and incurable by acts of lenity, generosity, and friendly dealing' (Lenman, 1980: 264).

Alexander Carlyle had been in London with the novelist, Tobias Smollett, the April night in 1746 when news arrived of the victory at Culloden of the Hanoverian troops under the Duke of Cumberland, George II's son, nicknamed 'the Butcher' because of his savagery in quelling the Jacobites. Carlyle remembered that he and Smollett were glad to go into a 'Narrow Entry' on their way home, to put their wigs in their pockets, and take their swords in their hands: 'The Mob were so Riotous, and the Squibs so Numerous and Incessant'. Smollett advised him not to say a word, 'Lest the Mob should discover my Country and become Insolent'. Carlyle thought John Bull that night was 'as Haughty and Valiant . . . as a few Months ago he was abject and cowardly, on the Black Wednesday [4 December 1745] when the highlanders were at Derby' (Carlyle, 1973: 98–9).

Smith would understand that the fury of the State directed at the unfortunate Jacobites by 'Butcher' Cumberland after Culloden, and the beheading of Lords Kilmarnock, Balmerino, and Lovat, also the hanging, drawing, and quartering of 116 unfortunates, as well as the transportation, death in prison, or disappearance of over 3,400 men, women, and children (Lenman, 1980: 271–5), was a similar sort of reaction after a severe fright. As for the initial success of the rising, he was to ascribe it to the 'bad effect of commerce' in sinking the courage of mankind:

In the year 1745 four or 5 thousand naked unarmed Highlanders took possession of the improved parts of this country without any opposition from the unwarlike inhabitants. They penetrated into England and alarmed the whole nation, and had they not been opposed by a standing army they would have seized the throne with little difficulty. (*LJ*(B) 331–2)

Even the Campbell militia, which should have formed the heart of the resistance to the Jacobite clans at the outset of the rising, had been seriously weakened through the scattering of the tacksmen, its officer corps, as a result of the improving policies of 'Red John of the Battles' himself, the 2nd Duke of Argyll. He seems to have been more interested latterly in developing Adderbury and his other English estates, as well as collecting higher rents in Scotland, than in the socioeconomic transformation he caused in the Campbell lands by wanting his clansmen to lust for profit, not blood and booty (Cregeen, 1970).

When Smith reached Kirkcaldy, where he spent the next two years with his mother, he no doubt found that it had been as alarmed by the Jacobites as any part of Lowland Scotland. In the '15 it had been raided and looted, but in the '45 it escaped with the levying of tributes of £20 and £35. No local figure seems to have been a leader in the rising, but up the coast at Anstruther, a laird named Charles Wightman hid survivors from Culloden until his smuggling connections could get them over to France (House, 1975: 21; Thirkell, n.d.: 24).

Smith continued his studies, and possibly tried to secure an appointment as a private tutor, to follow the example of a relative, William Smith, who had been 'Governor' to the future 12th Earl of Errol in 1704, before becoming a regent at Marischal College (Scott, 1937: 398). It is also conceivable that he had hopes of becoming Francis Hutcheson's successor after the latter's death on 8 August 1746; but on 1 October Glasgow University appointed as Professor of Moral Philosophy Thomas Craigie, Professor of Hebrew at the University of St Andrews (Coutts, 1909: 220). At this period Smith is reported to have taken up sea-bathing in the Firth of Forth, summer and winter, to avoid colds (EUL La. 451/2, fos. 429–30). However, immersion in salt water rather than imbibing tar-water could have been another way of fighting hypochondriasis.

Bliadhna Thierlaich (Charlie's Year) ended when the Stuart Prince, leaving his followers to their fate, escaped from his hiding-place in the heather and sailed for France on 20 September 1746. Once they were sure he was gone, the Hanoverian bluejackets and redcoats, with Scots among them, glutted themselves with killing, raping, pillaging, and burning in the Highlands and Hebrides. They then turned to longer-term measures to pacify the region by disarming the inhabitants, to the extent that this was possible, and making them give up their native dress. More military roads were built in the north and strong points constructed, such as Fort George near Inverness, where the masonry contract was held by the Adam family. A deadlier blow at the old order of things in Scotland was the passing of the Heritable Jurisdictions (Scotland) Act of 1747. This emphasized that the justice of the Hanoverian regime was to be centrally administered in Edinburgh, by taking away legal powers from the great landed families, a change which affected the magnates of the Lowlands more than the Highland chiefs, whose power was patriarchal rather than feudal (Lenman, 1980: 277–80).

Smith interested himself in such issues of legal reorganization, and was to fit them into lectures on jurisprudence, one course of which he gave in Edinburgh in 1750–1. From his later series delivered when he was a professor in Glasgow, we learn he adopted the framework of a four-stage theory of forms of society, to identify the nature of social institutions such as justice systems, and account for changes in them. Each stage was characterized by the chief mode of subsistence: hunting and fishing, pastoralism, agriculture, and commerce. Britain of the era of the '45 rising provided Smith with a contrast between the Highlands of Scotland at the pastoral stage with a warrior society and patriarchal leaders, and the unwarlike Lowlands, similar to England, organized for agriculture and commerce, and having to rely on a professional army for defence. In *LJ* and subsequently in *WN*, he commented on the successful exercise of patriarchal judicial functions by one of the leaders of the '45 rising, Donald Cameron of Lochiel, chief of the Clan Cameron (*LJ*(A) i.129; *WN* iii.iv.8). He also noted in *LJ* that the British Government was still so afraid of another rebellion in 1753 that Lochiel's brother, Dr Archibald Cameron, was put to death for alleged treason, when he probably would have been safe if he had kept out of the way for a few more years (*LJ*(A) ii.174, (B) 200).

Also in the aftermath of the '45 rising, leaders of Scottish society were stressing to the youth of the country the importance of that 'polite and useful learning' appropriate for gentlemen and necessary for the practice of their professions, also for attaching them to English culture. This was the theme of the discourse of Robert Dundas of Armiston on 1 November 1748, when he accepted in Edinburgh the congratulations of the Faculty of Advocates on his promotion as Lord President of the Court of Session, the supreme Bench in Scotland. He urged that, beyond learning thoroughly the principles of Roman law and the laws of nature and nations (an indication of his sense of the importance of the Grotius–Pufendorf tradition of natural law for Scottish lawyers), those wishing to become advocates, from whom in time sheriffs and judges would be drawn, 'should take pains to acquire other Sciences and accomplishments becoming the character of Gentlemen, particularly not to neglect Academical learning, before they should apply themselves to study the municipal Laws of their Country' (Macpherson, 1980: 225). In this connection, between 1748 and 1751, Adam Smith was invited to deliver public lectures in rhetoric, then the history of philosophy, and jurisprudence, in Edinburgh.

The Scottish capital derived its name from the mingling of Gaelic and Old English words which mean 'town by the fort on the hill slope'. This draws attention to features of the site which make it one of the most striking cities in Europe. Its castle is situated on a crag formed by an old volcanic core, and there is dense urban development on a tail of glacial debris descending to the Palace of Holyrood near another and higher old volcano, Arthur's Seat. Historically, Edinburgh's function was to defend the south-eastern approach to Scotland, and during the '45 Jacobite rising the castle had remained in Hanoverian hands, tying down insurgent forces and limiting their control of the country.

The Old Town straddles the Royal Mile running from the castle to the palace. An upper section has the Castlehill and Lawnmarket. Then comes the High Street, along which were to be found in Smith's time the burgh kirk of St Giles, with its graceful crown spire (*c*.1500); the mercat cross from which proclamations were read; the grim Old Tolbooth—jail and administrative centre; a huddle of shops and shops named the Luckenbooths; and the seventeenth-century Parliament House in which sat Scotland's supreme criminal and civil courts. The lower section, entered by the Netherbow Port, consisted of the separate burgh of the Canongate, where Smith lived from 1778, and where he is buried in the parish kirkyard, not far from Holyrood Palace.

The University, where Smith's friends James Oswald, Robert Adam, David Hume, William Robertson, Hugh Blair, Alexander Carlyle, and James Hutton had all been students, occupied undistinguished buildings, often contrasted unfavourably with the 'neat college' of Glasgow, on the Kirk o' Field site to the south of the High Street. The Royal Infirmary adjacent to the University was built by William Adam in Dutch Palladian style between 1738 and 1748. The friend of Smith's father, Dr John Clerk, practised there until 1757. Other notable public buildings that would be known to Smith from his teaching days in Edinburgh were, to the south, the Renaissance Heriot's School (1628–60); on or near the High Street, the guild halls of the Tailors (1621), Skinners (1643), and Candlemakers (1722), also the Surgeon's Hall (1697); and in the Canongate, the turreted Tolbooth from James VI's reign, and a pre-Reformation kirk.

The parish of Edinburgh together with those of St Cuthbert's and the Canongate had in 1755 an estimated population of 47,570 (Campbell, 1992: 11). The élite of the kirk, legal, academic, and medical establishment, and many families of the gentry when in town lived in the courts, closes, and wynds made up by the lofty tenements or flatted blocks of the Old Town. Like many Writers to the Signet, for example, Adam Smith's father had lived in a close off the High Street, Old Provost's, for about seven years after the Union (Scott, 1937: 13). From the 1770s on, more and more of the élite were to move to the New Town, created as a more wholesome environment when building land between the existing city and its port of Leith was made accessible by the draining of the Nor' Loch which began in 1759 (Horn, 1967: 18; Youngson, 1966: 227–8; Gifford *et al.*, 1988).

The prime mover in the scheme to bring Smith to Edinburgh as a lecturer in rhetoric was Henry Home of Kames, a leading advocate and keen agricultural improver, who was raised to the Bench in 1752 as Lord Kames. He had made a name for himself in his profession by collecting decisions of the Court of Session. Originally a supporter of the Stuart royal line, he switched to being a Whig in the 1730s, and attacked Jacobite political doctrines such as the theory of indefeasible right in *Essays on Several Subjects concerning British Antiquities* (1747). This was a pioneering attempt at the 'philosophical history' which Hume and Smith were to pursue. As Hume's neighbour and distant relation, he had given that young man advice and help as he struggled to make his way in the world. Kames had strong interests in literature and criticism. In fact, he was to write a treatise based on the aesthetics of Hume and Adam Smith, *Elements of Criticism* (1762), which became a foundation document in its field. It is entirely in keeping with Kames's notions of affirming good taste as a badge of social cohesion that, under his patronage, a lecture series on rhetoric and belles-lettres or criticism would be organized. Smith himself paid tribute later in his life to Kames's promotion of literary studies and the assistance he received, together with Hume and others who achieved fame. This came as a response to a remark about the number of outstanding writers that contemporary Scotland produced. Smith said: 'We must every one of us acknowledge Kames for our master' (Tytler, 1807: i.160; Ross, 1972: 31–3, 51–4, 90–1).

About 1748 Kames was taking over from Sir John Clerk of Penicuik, friend of Adam Smith's father, a leading role in the Philosophical Society of Edinburgh. Originally a medical research group, whose members included Dr John Clerk, it had expanded in 1737 at the prompting of Colin Maclaurin to deal with scientific knowledge generally and Scottish antiquities, also improvement in agriculture, manufactures, and technology (Emerson, 1979*a*). Dr Clerk became a Vice-President, as did his cousin, Sir John Clerk, who contributed papers on mining and his patriotic antiquarian pursuits. The Society languished during the '45, but three years later it was showing signs of life, and shortly after that Kames had replaced Sir John Clerk as Vice-President, and David Hume became one of the Secretaries (Emerson, 1981).

The suggestion has been made, with something of this background in mind, that the Philosophical Society sponsored Smith's rhetoric lectures (Scott, 1937: 49–50). Though no evidence has come to light about this, Kames would be a likely person to make this one of his new initiatives for the Society. Further, there was a precedent in that, from 1720 to 1758, John Ward lectured successfully on rhetoric at Gresham College (Howell, 1971: 87–120), long associated with the Royal Society of London, which the Philosophical Society of Edinburgh wished to emulate. It is well known that the Royal Society advocated a 'close, naked, natural way of speaking, positive expressions, clear senses, a native easiness, bringing all things as near the Mathematical plainness' as possible, and rejected 'all amplifications, digressions, and swellings of style' (Sprat, 1667/1958). Smith taught exactly a New Rhetoric of this kind, in keeping with New Science of Newton, which the Philosophical Society also wished to master and debate. His auditors could also find in Smith, from his years of being at Oxford, someone with a command of the received standard southern English. Scots were anxious to acquire this skill, to get on in an imperial world administered from London (*Edinburgh Review*, 1755: 1, p. iii; *Gentleman's Magazine*, 1790, lx. 762).

Concerning recommenders of Smith to Kames, or other patrons, two names have been suggested (Scott, 1937: 46). One was James Oswald of Dunnikier, already mentioned as Smith's boyhood friend in Kirkcaldy, and by 1748 an MP for Fife, with service as a Commissioner of the Navy behind him, and a ministerial career ahead of him as a lord of Trade and then of Treasury. Horace Walpole considered him one of the thirty best speakers in the House of Commons, where he made economic issues a specialty (*HP* iii.237–9). The other was Robert Craigie of Glendoick, who had been Lord Advocate during the '45 rising and was later to become Lord President of the Court of Session, 1754–60. His daughter Cecilia was married to Smith's cousin, Colonel Robert Douglas of Strathenry. Smith took their youngest son David (b. 1769) into his household as a young boy, and made him his heir.

No advertisement of Smith's series has been discovered in the Edinburgh newspapers for the period, but clearly there was a good deal of activity in the form of public lectures directly competing with those at Edinburgh University. This was a facet of life in the capital city of his country which must have pleased the young man disgusted with the lethargy of the Oxford professors and the lack of attention there to the needs of students. For example, the press advertised that Smith's friend, Professor Matthew Stuart, would begin his lectures on mathematics at the University on 25 November 1748. Meanwhile, Ebenezer Macfait, MD, proposed to give a course on the system of ancient and modern geometry at his own lodgings, commencing on 8 November. The public lectures were held in a variety of places in addition to a lecturer's lodgings: the Concert-Hall in the Canongate, the Society-Hall in Warriston's Close, Gibb's Meeting-House in Bristo-street, and so on. For a course on experimental philosophy, Dr Demainbury charged two guineas for the series of twelve lectures, or one shilling to be paid at the door of the 'Lecture Room at Mrs Baillie's lodgings . . . in the Flesh Market' (*Caledonian Mercury*, Oct., Nov. 1748).

We do not know where Smith's lectures were given, though one possibility is the Edinburgh masonic meeting-place, Mary's Chapel, off the High Street, which was demolished to make way for the South Bridge project in 1786. We hear of a lecture being given there on the 'Scottish language' on 15 March (1776), to counterbalance all the attention given in Edinburgh to the English language by Smith and his successors (Crawford, 1992: 24). We do know that Smith's lectures were a financial success, perhaps bringing in the customary guinea per person for the year's series (Rae, 1965: 32). David Hume wrote to Smith on 8 June 1758: 'You made above 100 Pound a Year by your Class when in this Place [Edinburgh], tho' you had not the character of a Professor. . . . John Stevenson . . . makes near 150' (*Corr.* No. 25). Hume is referring to the popular Professor of Logic at the University, who lectured on Aristotle's *Poetics* and the treatise *On the Sublime*, illustrating his remarks by readings from Dryden's criticism and the *Spectator* papers on taste (Mossner, 1980: 42).

Smith would welcome the spur of emulation to do well in the academic free market of Edinburgh, if we can take him at his own words: 'the rivalship of competitors, who are all endeavouring to justle one another out of employment, obliges every man to endeavour to execute his work with a certain degree of exactness' (*WN* v.i.f.4). His success, too, meant that he could resign his Snell Exhibition, which he did on 4 February 1749 (*Corr*. No. 7). An inheritance also made his situation easier. His half-brother Hugh died the next year intestate, and their father's will gave Adam Smith rights to some property in Aberdeen, the tenement of foreland, where there was a timber shop, on the west side of the Castlegate, opposite the Town House. Smith did not enjoy for very long the modest income from what became a valuable piece of land (site of the Athenaeum Hotel in the 1930s), because he sold it to a family member for £115 in 1757 (Aberdeen City Archives, Register of Sasines: B 1/1/62; GUL MS Gen. 1035/218; Scott, 1937: 135–6, 409).

Some details of attendance at Smith's course on rhetoric is provided by Kames's biographer. This was Alexander Fraser Tytler (later known as Lord Woodhouselee), who became Secretary of the Royal Society of Edinburgh. Woodhouselee wrote that the course was delivered at Edinburgh in 1748 and the following two years, 'to a respectable auditory, chiefly composed of students in law and theology'. He then listed auditors with a legal background. One was Smith's friend James Oswald, who was admitted advocate in 1738 and, as we have seen, was well on in his career as an MP. Yet another advocate was Alexander Wedderburn, who came to be on terms of warm friendship with Smith, Hume, and others of the literati, then qualified for the English Bar, and rose to be Lord Chancellor Loughborough. A third was William Johnstone, whom Smith described to Oswald in January 1752 as someone he had 'known intimately these four years' (*Corr*. No. 11). He married a rich heiress, took her name, and as Sir William Pulteney had a successful career in Parliament. A fourth was John Millar, who later studied under Smith at Glasgow, acted for two years as tutor to Kames's son, George Home Drummond, and became a noted Professor of Law at Glasgow. Millar's early years are not fully documented, but there is mention of him training as a Writer to Signet for a period; and possibly when he was in Edinburgh in this connection, he attended a first course by Smith (Craig, 1806: p. iv). Woodhouselee did mention one minister by name, Hugh Blair, who then supplied the second charge at the Canongate kirk. He had been a student at Edinburgh University, where Professor John Stevenson was greatly impressed by his youthful 'Essay on the Beautiful' (Tytler, 1807: i.190; Anderson, 1863: i.323).

It is much to be regretted that we do not have an auditor's report of Smith's rhetoric lectures at Edinburgh. There is one way round this difficulty. Smith went to Glasgow in October 1751 to assume his duties as Professor of Logic and take over some of those of Craigie, the Professor of Moral Philosophy. He apparently fell back on the rhetoric material presented at Edinburgh for his logic lectures, and he continued to teach this same rhetoric course, without much alteration, in his private class when he became Professor of Moral Philosophy in April 1752.

A set of these Glasgow rhetoric lectures was heard by James Wodrow, a former student of Francis Hutcheson, who was Library Keeper at Glasgow University until 1755, when he became the minister of Dunlop in Ayrshire. Wodrow's first assessment of Smith's rhetoric lectures in the 1750s was low, as will be discussed in Chapter 9. However, when Wodrow wrote again about the course late in life, in 1808, he summarized it in a much more favourable light, and he gives us an idea of what Smith presented to his Edinburgh auditors and did not have time, or perhaps inclination, to change when he moved to Glasgow:

Adam Smith delivered a set of admirable lectures on language (not as a grammarian but as a rhetorician) on the different kinds or characteristics of style suited to different subjects, simple, nervous, etc., the structure, the natural order, the proper arrangement of the different members of the sentence etc. He characterised the style and genius of some of the best of the ancient writers and poets, but especially historians, Thucydides, Polybius etc. translating long passages of them, also the style of the best English classics, Lord Clarendon, Addison, Swift, Pope, etc; . . . his remarks and rules given in the lectures I speak of, were the result of a fine taste and sound judgement, well calculated to be exceedingly useful to young composers, so that I have often regretted that some part of them has never been published. (GUL Murray Coll., Buchan Corr. ii.171)

In addition to what he heard in Edinburgh, John Millar apparently attended in 1751–2 the rhetoric course Smith gave as Professor of Logic at Glasgow. He wrote of his teacher delivering at Glasgow a 'system' of the subject organized in two divisions. The first examined the 'several ways of communicating our thoughts by speech'; and the second dealt with the 'principles of those literary compositions which contribute to persuasion or entertainment' (Stewart i.16). A student-reported version of the course given at Glasgow in 1762–3 lacks an opening lecture, but the remaining twenty-nine fall into the two divisions identified by Millar (*LRBL*).

We can conjecture that Smith opened his course by rejecting traditional rhetoric's piecemeal approach and complex analysis emphasizing figures of speech. Smith considered the old sources as 'generally a very silly set of books and not at all instructive' (*LRBL* i.v.59). Fitting in with the New Philosophy of Locke and the New Science of Newton, Smith offered a New Rhetoric that provides a general theory of the major kinds of expression: descriptive and narrative, as in history; poetical; didactic or scientific; and persuasive.[1] Going on the Glasgow model, it seems that approximately one-third of the course was devoted to language and style or, more broadly, aspects of communication (Lectures 2–11), and two-thirds to the several forms of expression with reference to their function (12–30).

The second lecture stresses the importance of perspicuity or transparency of style gained through adopting the standard, received English of the court, that is, the southern dialect as spoken and written by the gentlemen and ladies of the highest government circles. The goal of the effective communication of thought and sentiment in this variety of English is achieved, so Smith emphasizes in this second lecture (and later in Nos. 6, 7, 11 of this part of the course) by the plain style. This is created by adopting the 'naturall order of expression free of parentheses and superfluous words' (*LRBL* i.9–10). Jonathan Swift is presented as the best exponent of this style, and his success as a writer is attributed to mastery of his subjects, skill in arranging their parts, and vivacity of expression (i.106). Smith appreciated that Swift was widely read for his humour, but he reckoned that few in Scotland ('this country') understood his real worth. His Anglican religious sentiments were against him, also 'he never has such warm exclamations for civill or religious liberty as are now generally in fashion'. The attitudes of the plain man which Smith discerned in Swift led him to express himself in satire: 'ridiculing some prevailing vice or folly or exposing some particular character'. He did not value 'abstract and Speculative reasoning', which Smith says have recently been favoured by men of genius in Scotland (i.101–2).

Smith's case, however, is that the Scots should learn from Swift's command of the plain style. Most are aware, so Smith thinks, that the language they speak is far from 'perfection', that is, standard southern English. Accordingly, they value the style that is furthest away from what they commonly use. In consequence, Shaftesbury is universally admired because he 'keeps a vast distance' from everyday language. Smith considers this admiration completely misplaced, and proceeds to contrast Swift and Shaftesbury, indicating that the latter is the exponent of an outmoded style, relying too much on allegory and metaphor— the tropes and figures of speech of the Old Rhetoric. Smith thus insinuates that Swift provides the model to bc followed for the New Rhetoric, as the 'plainest, as well as the most proper and precise of all the English writers' (i.103–4).

Smith's Edinburgh auditors would understand that he was not hostile to Shaftesbury's project of overturning the 'Old Systems of Religion and Philosophy' and establishing something new in their place, a task Hobbes had failed to accomplish. Smith's mentor Hutcheson, who is not mentioned in the 1762–3 rhetoric lectures, had carried forward this task, but he too tended to write in a fulsome style, and Smith's strong attack on this must have caused some excitement among those taught to have a high regard for Shaftesbury and Hutcheson. Smith, to be sure, practised what he preached, and his compositions at their best are pithy and exact in language, matching Swift in epigrammatic force.

In exposing Shaftesbury's tendency to prolixity, Smith sees a defect that is incident to the historical development of English. He brings this out in the third lecture of the first part of the rhetoric course, which is devoted to the 'origin and progress of language'. His approach here became a favourite one, as Dugald Stewart pointed out in commenting on an expanded version of the lecture. This version was published first in *The Philological Miscellany* (1761), and later as an appendix to the third (1767) and subsequent editions of *TMS*, bearing the title, *Considerations concerning the first formation of Languages, and the different genius of original and compounded Languages*. Stewart names the kind of inquiry represented 'Theoretical or Conjectural History', a variant of Smith's own term 'philosophical history'.

Something similar, according to Stewart, is to be found in all Smith's various works, 'moral, political, or literary'. The procedure involved is a simple one:

In examining the history of mankind, as well as in examining the phenomena of the natural world, when we cannot trace the process by which an event has been produced, it is often of importance to be able to show how it may have been produced by natural causes. (Stewart ii.44–8)

Thus, the first part of Smith's third lecture (i.17–i.v.30) deals with conjecture or theory about the primitive formation of a jargon by savages. Ancient languages are depicted as emerging from the jargon stage with features such as word classes, inflection to indicate grammatical function, and parts of speech. This happened gradually and unintentionally by a process of comparison, abstraction, and 'love of analogy', limited by the capacity of the human memory. The brief second part of the lecture (i.v.31–4) has more to do with stylistics than the first. It deals with the historical mingling of peoples, and how grammatical structure changed, under compulsions to effect communication. Complex schemes of inflection were amended or dropped to produce compound or *analytic* languages, such as modern English, as contrasted with the original or *synthetic* languages such as Greek and the Old English tongue. Smith and one of his forerunners, Abbé Girard, seem to have been the first commentators on language development to make this important distinction in typology (Coseriu, 1970; Aarsleff, 1982: 349, n. 29).

Smith turns to the machine, as he often does seeking explanatory help when describing systems, to provide an analogy for the 'progress of language'. Original languages have the vast complexity of primitive machines, and both become simpler when gradually the 'different parts are more connected and supplied by one another'. But whereas simpler machines are better, this is not the case with languages. The simpler, compound languages have less variety and harmony of sound, according to Smith, and are less capable of various arrangements; also they are more prolix (i.v.34). Smith then fits this point into his general advocacy of the plain style as the best way to control the prolixity of English.

In one of his letters (No. 69, dated 7 February 1763), Smith relates that it was reading *Les vrais principes de la langue française* (1747) by the Abbé Gabriel Girard (Mizuta) 'which first set me thinking upon these subjects'. He means, presumably, that Girard's book set him theorizing about the deep past of languages in a naturalistic fashion, and linking his account of language typology to revolutions in cognition and society. The same conceptual themes are present in his writings about science, morals, and economics (Christie, 1987; Plank, 1992).

His first Edinburgh audience must have been greatly stimulated by the insights afforded by the methodology Smith adopted in the instance of the lecture on language, which was also to be found applied to law and government in

Montesquieu's *Considérations sur les causes de la grandeur des Romains et de leur décadence* (1734) as well as *L'Esprit des lois* (1748). Roger Emerson (1984) has pointed out that well-read auditors would recognize that Smith's approach can be linked to the history of language found in the Bible; to classical accounts of humanity's acquisition of arts and sciences, as in book v of *De natura rerum* by Lucretius; to Locke's 'plain historical method' of ascertaining the extent of human knowledge; and to comparative studies from the Renaissance onwards, associating travellers' discoveries about aboriginal cultures with phases of classical and modern history. As Stewart illustrates, some of Smith's auditors adopted this methodology of 'philosophical history' for their own enquiries into social and institutional change. For example, Kames used it in a developed fashion in his *Historical Law-Tracts* (1758), though he had anticipated elements of it in his *Essays on . . . British Antiquities* (1747). Millar takes it up in *The Origin and Distinction of Ranks* (1771) and *An Historical View of the English Government* (1787). There was also the example of Hume's *Natural History of Religion* (1757). In fact, 'philosophical' or 'natural' history became something of a staple of the contributors to the Scottish Enlightenment (Stewart ii.44–52). To be sure, David Raphael (1985: 105–7) has cautioned that Dugald Stewart's term 'conjectural history' is a misnomer, and does not describe the procedure of Smith's own History of Astronomy discussed below in Chapter 7.

Smith's Edinburgh auditors with their interests in history, 'philosophical' or actual, were well served by the second part of the rhetoric lectures dealing with composition. The evidence we have suggests that he gave prominence to historical writing when he discussed narrative, or relation of facts, as the first form of discourse worthy of attention. The other two forms he chose were didactic discourse, in his view required when a proposition had to be proved by putting forward two sides of a question for an audience to choose between on grounds of fact and logic; and rhetorical or oratorical discourse, required when proof is effected by praising one side and discrediting the other. Didactic discourse aims at conviction, while the rhetorical kind seeks to persuade (*LRBL* i.149).

In dealing with historical discourse, Smith offered a history of historians which gave him an opportunity to assess success or failure in achieving what he considered the 'design' of history:

It sets before us the more interesting and important events of human life, points out the causes by which these events were brought about and by this means points out to us by what manner and method we may produce similar good effects or avoid Similar bad ones. (ii.16–17)

Smith is innovative in drawing attention to Thucydides' outstanding command of this kind of design in history (ii.50). At least, Arnaldo Momigliano (1990: 49) states that the rise of the Greek historian's reputation did not begin until the second half of the eighteenth century, and he ascribes to the Abbé de Mably (*De la manière d'écrire l'histoire*, 1784: 125) and the writers of the Romantic movements the elevation of Thucydides to the position of 'model philosophic historian'. Equally perceptive and advanced, it seems, is Smith's praise of Tacitus for his psychological penetration (Phillips, 1993). Continuing his account of the field, Smith's finding is that 'of all Modern Historians [Machiavelli is] the only one who has contented himself with the chief purpose of History, to relate Events and connect them with their causes without becoming a party on either side' (ii.71). As for recent history, Smith comes down only as far as Rapin-Thoyras' *Histoire d'Angleterre* (1724), which suggests that the material in the 1762–3 rhetoric course, indeed, goes back to his Edinburgh period, since otherwise the omission of references to Voltaire, Hume, and Robertson is very strange (Mossner, 1965).

Smith is prescient in these lectures about what the Scots had to learn or were learning about the goal of design and impartiality in writing history, and the need to deal with psychology as well as causation, in a well-controlled style such as Livy exemplified. His teaching and advocacy of examples were persuasive. Gibbon, unrivalled historian of the fall of the Roman Empire, understood well the classical models his Scottish contemporaries aimed at, and he hailed Hume as *le Tacite et le Tite Live de l'Écosse* (1956, ii.107). Twenty years after Smith's lectures in Edinburgh, Hume joked about the widespread interest in his country in history-writing. In August 1770 he wrote to William Strahan, his publisher (and Smith's): 'this is the historical Age and this the historical Nation', since he knew of eight histories currently on the stocks in Scotland (*HL* ii.230).

Dealing further, in the second division of his course, with the principles of literary compositions, Smith passes in Lecture 17 to the 'Oratoricall' or 'Rhetoricall' style. The branches covered by Smith represent a creative adaptation of the three main genres of classical oratory as outlined, for example, in one of his major sources, Quintilian's *Institutio Oratoria* (Mizuta). These are judicial, deliberative (political), and epideictic oratory (panegyric). Smith begins with the last genre, whose real aim he thinks is to display the skill of the orator. We find here, perhaps, the seeds of *TMS* in that Smith discusses what is praiseworthy and blameworthy in conduct and motivation. He uses the Stoic scheme of virtues such as fortitude which commands respect, distinguished from amiable ones such as humanity, and likewise the vices we despise distinguished from those we detest (ii.102–3).

Historical considerations enter in, as Smith notes that poetic panegyric was 'very long in use' before prose examples appeared. Smith claims, indeed, that prose expression developed with the introduction of commerce or, at least opulence, whereas 'Poetry is cultivated in the most Rude and Barbarous nations' (ii.112–13). This argument is part of the primitivism of Smith's time, but it also reflects his interest in a stadial view of economic life and its links with culture, a feature of his thinking about jurisprudence.

Breaking off from persuasive expression at this point in the Glasgow course (we do not know if he followed the same sequence in Edinburgh), Smith turns in Lecture 24 to didactic composition, meant to win conviction for a philosophical proposition, or to 'Deliver a System of any Science e.g. Naturall Philosophy' (ii.130). An Edinburgh audience of young professional men would find Smith's thoughts here of practical account. They are also a guide to his own procedures as a teacher and a fashioner of systems. For once, he has a good word to say of Shaftesbury, observing that his *Inquiry concerning Virtue* (1699, 1711) adopts the perfect method of laying down the proposition to be proved, and then showing how its truth depends on several subordinate propositions, which are each proved in turn before the whole argument is summed up (ii.126).

Concerning the delivery of a system, Smith distinguishes between what he calls the Newtonian method and what he associates with Aristotle. The latter consists of going over the different branches of a science in the order in which they come, and establishing a new principle for every phenomenon. The first is 'undoubtedly' more philosophical, for it consists of laying down 'certain principles known or proved in the beginning, from when we account for the severall Phaenomena, connecting all together by the same Chain'. Smith continues that 'it gives us a pleasure to see the phenomena which we reckoned the most unaccountable all deduced from some principle (commonly a wellknown) and all united in one chain' (ii.133–4).

Smith in his rhetoric lectures had already demonstrated the efficacy of this so-called Newtonian method, which has an ancestry going back at least to Plato's time, in dealing with language. Its 'progress' he had ingeniously and convincingly attributed in the main to the operation of the commonly recognized principle of abstraction.

He tackled in another lecture series, which some evidence suggests was first given in Edinburgh, then repeated at Glasgow, the principles that 'lead and direct philosophical [or scientific] enquiries' (part of the full title of the History of Astronomy, *EPS*).

In due course he was to deliver at Glasgow a system of morals based on the operation of the principle of sympathy (*TMS*), then a system of economics hinging on the force of self-love promoting the division of labour to create wealth (*WN*). To be sure, he has been accused of moving from didactic to rhetorical composition in this second book when dealing with pressing political issues (Muller, 1993: 55).

Death overtook him before he could complete to his satisfaction 'two other great works', each involving theory and history, on which he was still working in 1785, but whose seeds seem to lie in the Edinburgh lectures courses. One of these works covered law and government, and the other 'all the different branches of Literature, of Philosophy, Poetry and Eloquence' (*Corr.* No. 248). Thus fruitful in his hands was the 'Newtonian method', which gave pleasure from yielding the opportunity to see phenomena deduced from a well-known principle and 'all united in one chain'.

The claim that Smith produced a New Rhetoric has been denounced as 'excessive' (Vickers, 1971). And his insistence on taking the master-works of English literature as guides to composition and style has been criticized for its 'anglo-centrism' (Crawford, 1992: 28–33). Further, his advocacy of Swift's plain style as a model to be followed for the clear communication of ideas has been questioned in the light of the notorious difficulties of Swift's critics in interpreting his irony. Also, a discrepancy has been detected between Smith's denunciation of figurative language and his own practice as a stylist in the rhetoric lectures themselves. The conclusion has been drawn that *LRBL* does not illustrate the theory Smith advances about effective communication of ideas through transparent, direct language (Brown, 1994: 15–18).

Some forcefulness should be allowed, however, in stating what Smith achieved as a teacher of rhetoric. He clearly made good use of his extensive reading at Oxford, and subsequently in Kirkcaldy, to offer a new and fruitful way of dealing with a subject that had become discredited but should be part of a liberal education. He allows a role for figures of speech when they are the 'just and naturall forms' of expression, and he created or revived memorable examples, such as the 'invisible hand' of *TMS* and *WN*. Whatever problems twentieth-century critics have with Swift's irony, Smith's advocacy of the Swiftian plain style for communicating meaning in pithy, idiomatic English was well directed. The new philosophical movement in Scotland had produced prolix writing inspired by Shaftesbury.[2] Also, he had true insight in suggesting that the mechanism of sympathy has a role in the natural use of figurative language to express feeling (*LRBL* i.v.56), an important anticipation of the role he allots the mechanism of sympathy in ethics. Besides renewing rhetoric in this way, he expanded its range to include poetics and dialectic (Lectures 21, 24).

The charge of betraying Scottish culture so that English political ends would be served seems wide of the mark. Smith's aim was that of the Enlightenment: to create a cosmopolitan culture, fed from the classics and the modern languages and literatures of Europe, and from what could be learned from the cultures, including aboriginal ones, of other continents. This is the real significance of the 'philosophical' histories, such as the one devoted to the 'origin and progress of language'. Something along these lines was surely enough of a lesson for the young lecturer to give to his auditors in Edinburgh and later to his Glasgow students.

Besides teaching students at Glasgow, Smith helped to found there a Literary Society, as we are told in the archives of the brothers Robert and Andrew Foulis, who enjoyed the patronage of the University in supervising a celebrated press and art academy when Smith was a Professor at Glasgow. We are also told that for this Society, Smith read 'papers . . . on Taste, Composition and the History of Philosophy which he had previously delivered while a lecturer on rhetoric at Edinburgh' (Duncan, 1831: 16). This suggests that, in addition to dealing with the principles of literary compositions, Smith expounded in some form at Edinburgh his theory of what constituted 'taste' or, in modern terms, aesthetics. We know that it was a psychological theory, focused on the wonder and admiration we feel at finding art forms imitating objects of very different kinds. He was still working on this theory in the 1785, for one of the 'great books', already mentioned, which his literary executors, Joseph Black and James Hutton, described in the Advertisement to *EPS* as a 'connected history of the liberal sciences and elegant arts'. Thus it fell out that, as late as 1788, he read a paper on the Imitative Arts to the Glasgow Literary Society (GUL MS Gen. 1035/178). In *EPS* we have materials for this piece, to be discussed in Chapter 22 below.

In connection with aesthetics, Smith conducted the kind of psychological analysis which is characteristic of his all system-building projects. More would be aimed at, however, in the Edinburgh course on rhetoric and belles-lettres than the formation in the auditors of correct English pronunciation and expression, and outlining for them a mimetic or representation theory of art. There was also the issue of the endowment of taste. The inspirer of Smith's procedure would appear to be Charles Rollin, the French rhetorician, whose approach to teaching literature can be linked to the way in which Smith was educated under David Miller at Kirkcaldy burgh school.[3]

Rollin's *Method of Teaching and Studying the Belles Lettres* stressed the value of translating the most beautiful passages as the 'surest way' of forming taste, a procedure Smith had followed at Oxford in self-directed translation exercises, particularly from French. Those following this practice, according to Rollin, 'become acquainted with their authors, and insensibly conceive their height of fancy, manner of writing, and way of thinking'. Rollin made a more general claim, of course, that taste 'is a kind of natural reason wrought up to perfection by study', and that though good taste may be formed by literary studies, most appropriately at the outset of life, 'it is not confined to literature; it takes in also . . . all arts and sciences, and branches of knowledge' (Rollin, 1759: i.61). Smith, of course, believed that taste was exercised in creating systems of politics and economics.

Secure in sharing such views, and pleased with Smith's success in advancing them in his lecture series at Edinburgh, when the latter departed for Glasgow Kames found a successor in a young minister Robert Watson, afterwards the historian of the reign of Philip II of Spain. When Watson in turn went on to become Professor of Logic at St Andrews in 1756, where he gave lectures on rhetoric, Hugh Blair was prevailed on by Kames to give lectures on belles-lettres at Edinburgh. Blair's ability as a preacher had brought him the position of first minister of the High Kirk of St Giles in 1758. The following year, on 11 December, he began a course on rhetoric and belles-lettres at Edinburgh University, receiving the title of Professor in 1760. Success in the subject Smith had pioneered led to Blair's appointment to a new Regius Chair on 7 April 1762, in effect the first professorship ever in English Literature, which was the staple of Blair's teaching. When he published his lectures in 1783, he acknowledged a debt of long standing to the work of his predecessor and friend:

of the General Characters of style, particularly, the Plain and the Simple, and the characters of the English authors who are classed under them, in this, and the following

Lecture, several ideas have been taken from a manuscript treatise on rhetoric, part of which was shown to me, many years ago by the learned and ingenious Author, Dr Adam Smith. (Blair, 1812: ii.22 n.)

As we shall see, Smith was concerned about theft from his jurisprudence lectures. However, he does not seem to have been concerned, or so it was alleged, about plagiarism of ideas in the rhetoric lectures by Blair. Henry Mackenzie, a member of Smith's circle later in his life, told him that Blair had made use of his ideas in sermons, but he replied: He is very welcome, there is enough left' (Clayden, 1887: 167; Hatch, 1994).

About the time of delivering his Edinburgh courses, Smith was drawn into his first publication enterprise, which indicates that he was relied on in his circle for the literary taste revealed to the public in his rhetoric lectures. He was asked to provide an unsigned preface for an octavo volume of pieces by the Jacobite poet William Hamilton, to be issued in his absence in exile. Hamilton became laird of Bangour, and is usually known by that title to distinguish him from another poet of the same name, William Hamilton of Gilbertfield. The work in question is *Poems on Several Occasions*, printed by Robert and Andrew Foulis at Glasgow, where the preface is dated 21 December 1748 (*EPS* 259–62).

Hamilton was pardoned for his part in the '45 rising in 1750, and returned to Scotland from his exile for two years before being forced back to the Continent by the onset of consumption. During this time he spent 'many happy and many flattering hours' with Smith and William Crawford, a Glasgow merchant to whom Hamilton entrusted MSS of his poems, and whose granddaughter, Elizabeth Dalrymple, he took as his second wife. We owe this piece of information to the lawyer and historian John Dalrymple, the poet's brother-in-law, who succeeded to the baronetcy of Cranstoun. He wrote to the printer Robert Foulis on 1 December 1757 about a second edition of Hamilton's poems, appearing in 1758, expressing the thought that none was so able as Smith to write its dedication to William Crawford. Dalrymple went on to say that Smith's association with Hamilton and Crawford made him think that '[Smith] will account his usual indolence a crime upon this occasion' (Duncan, 1831: 23–4). This 'usual indolence' ascribed to Smith is perhaps the 'laziness' he charged himself with in Oxford, to be linked to his hypochondriasis.

Hamilton's poetry reflected a broad range of literary culture, from an imitation ballad in Scots such as 'The Braes of Yarrow', which proved attractive to Wordsworth, to 'imitations' or free adaptations of Pindar, Anacreon, Sophocles, Virgil, Horace, Shakespeare, and Racine, and the first rendering into English blank verse of a passage from Homer, the Glaucus and Diomed episode from the sixth book of the *Iliad*. Kames, as an early and intimate friend of Hamilton, possibly suggested Smith should write the Preface. His interest and that of the Glasgow merchant, William Crawford, in such work suggests the taste of the society from which was drawn the 'respectable auditory' that heard Smith lecture on rhetoric and belles-lettres.

7

Lectures on the History of Philosophy and Law

'Tis evident, that all the sciences have a relation, greater or less, to human nature.

Lecturing on rhetoric, Smith certainly made evident that it had a powerful connection with sentient human nature. He also illustrated the claim Hume had made in the Introduction to the *Treatise of Human Nature* in two further series of lectures, on the history of philosophy and on law, which we have reason to believe he also gave in Edinburgh. In certain respects, our information about these series suggests that Smith was working on the programme for the 'science of man' which Hume had announced in the *Treatise*. We have first to follow up the clue in the Foulis Press papers that Smith also lectured on the history of philosophy in Edinburgh. Additional evidence comes from a biographical sketch by William Richardson, Professor of Humanity (Latin) at Glasgow (1773–1815). The subject is his friend Archibald Arthur, who matriculated there in 1757 or 1758, and became Thomas Reid's assistant, then his replacement in teaching moral philosophy (1780–96). Arthur finally occupied the Chair himself for the last year of his life (1796–7). Richardson, who like Arthur had been a student of Smith's at Glasgow, described the nature of the 'private' courses given by successive Professors of Moral Philosophy. Hutcheson lectured on 'Arrian, Antoninus, and other Greek philosophers', but Smith occupied the additional hours 'in delivering those lectures on taste, composition, and the history of philosophy, which, before his nomination to a professorship at Glasgow, he had delivered as a lecturer on rhetoric at Edinburgh'. Reid illustrated the doctrines presented later in his *Essays on the Intellectual Powers of Man* (1785) and *Essays on the Active Powers of Man* (1788).

In his turn Arthur gave 'private' lectures 'more agreeable to the method followed by Dr Smith', which dealt with 'fine-writing, the principles of criticism, and the "pleasures of the imagination" '. As reported by Richardson, Arthur's intention was 'to unfold and elucidate those processes of invention, that structure of language, and system of arrangement, which are the objects of genuine taste' (Richardson, 1803: 514).

Among the 'Literary Discourses' by Arthur to which Richardson's 'Account' is attached, we find one entitled, 'On the Importance of Natural Philosophy' (No. 11). It makes the following claim:

The study of natural philosophy may, in one light, be considered as the means of removing the astonishment occasioned by uncommon external objects, and their unexpected changes; and one of the principal inducements to rational inquiry, is the removal of that unsatisfied state of mind.[1]

This is strikingly reminiscent of Smith's teaching in the 'History of Astronomy' (*EPS*), which begins by distinguishing between our feelings of wonder, surprise, and admiration, and then explains their role in producing philosophical or, we would say, scientific theories. In brief, Smith's explanation is that we are surprised when we encounter objects appearing in unexpected sequences, and then we wonder how it is that we felt surprise at that point. We are disturbed by finding a gap between objects that imagination customarily joins, a point also made in the rhetoric lectures (*LRBL* ii.36). Smith argues that we seek to restore tranquillity of mind by deriving from the imagination something that bridges the gap, namely a hypothesis or theory. On this view, philosophy is defined as the 'science of the connecting principles of nature'. Smith goes so far as to state that 'philosophy, therefore, may be regarded as one of those arts which address themselves to the imagination', and he continues with the remark that philosophy's 'theory and history' are properly part of an essay on the influence of the sentiments of wonder, surprise, and admiration ('Astronomy' ii.12). Thereafter, Smith sketches out what his kind of 'theory and history' of philosophy will be like. It will trace 'philosophy' from its beginning to its supposed contemporary 'perfection', so the idea of progress is entailed. Its 'revolutions' have been the 'greatest, most frequent, and the most distinguished of all those that have happened in the literary world'; therefore, it will be entertaining and instructive.

Might it not be argued, therefore, that Smith's Edinburgh history of philosophy course is itself sketched out in the opening of the 'Astronomy' essay (ii.12)? Also, going a little further, might not the history of the hypotheses concerning 'Astronomy' which form the remaining part of this essay have been illustrative material for the course, perhaps together with some of the material in the essays on Ancient Physics, Ancient Logics and Metaphysics, and External Senses?

Now, as to Smith's concept of 'Philosophy', we find that in the History of Astronomy he defines this sceptically as 'that science which pretends to lay open the concealed connections that unite the various appearances of nature' (iii.3). It is reasonable to suppose, then, that the history of philosophy course at Edinburgh, like the lecture on 'origin and progress' of language, set out to account for successive scientific systems by explaining the 'connecting principles of nature' in terms of human propensities that gave rise to these systems, exploded them, and supplanted them as imaginative constructs, one after another, in the search that began with Greek thinkers for more satisfying ways of ordering appearances. To guide his thinking about the history of astronomy in this fashion, Smith would encounter the intellectual model of a combination of scepticism about 'concealed connections' behind appearances and a naturalistic explanation of theories about these 'connections', in Hume's *Treatise of Human Nature*, which he is said to have read at Oxford. Conceivably, the 'respectable auditory' of the Edinburgh rhetoric lectures, or the original sponsors, requested from Smith a course that would make comprehensible the systems of the ancients such as Aristotle and Ptolemy, and moderns such as Descartes and Newton.

Part of the context of the course could have been the Philosophical Society's interest in astronomy, specifically, an eclipse of the sun shortly before 16 July 1748 and a lunar eclipse on 28 July. The French academician Le Monnier was in Edinburgh in July 1748 to observe these eclipses (Emerson, 1981: 135–8). He was in a position to comment on French astronomical expeditions, one of them to Peru, 1735, and especially one to Lapland in 1736, in which he had taken part. Both are mentioned in Smith's text as furnishing observations that 'fully confirmed [Newton's] system' ('Astronomy' iv.72).

Looking back at his essay on the history of astronomy, when he was nearing 50 and had come to believe that Hume would survive him to become his literary executor, Smith described it as a 'fragment of an intended juvenile work'. He left the decision to publish it or not to his friend, stating candidly: 'I begin to suspect myself there is more refinement than solidity in some parts of it' (*Corr.* No. 137, 16 Apr. 1773). The application of the adjective 'juvenile' surely carries the essay back to Smith's twenties. Possibly he composed it in part in Kirkcaldy after returning from Oxford, and then made use of it in the history of philosophy course at Edinburgh.

Smith's originality lay, perhaps, in offering an estimate of the 'systems of nature' that set aside considerations of their 'absurdity or probability; their agreement or inconsistency with truth or reality'. He chose to judge the success of systems in soothing the imagination, also in achieving coherence, and enhancing our response to the objects they comprehend, as the 'clew that is most capable of conducting us through all the labyrinths of philosophical history' ('Astronomy' ii.12).

From this standpoint, Smith reviews with attention to accurate historical detail the four chief 'systems' elaborated to explain the movements of the sun, the moon, and the stars, regarded as the function of astronomy: those of Ptolemy, Copernicus, Descartes, and Newton. Acknowledging the place of beauty in early astronomy, Smith deals with an aspect of Greek thought that had appealed to his teachers Hutcheson and Simson. But he leaves this attractive theme to describe how actual observation of the night skies resulted in refinements to the beautiful early system, depicting the earth at the centre of the universe enclosed by eight crystalline concentric spheres, finally associated with the work of Ptolemy (*c*. AD 150). Ever more corrections, including hypotheses of eccentric spheres and epicycles, had to be made to the early system to bring it into correspondence with the phenomena, and the resulting 'complexity' and 'confusion' rendered it objectionable.

Building on his initial hypothesis that the task of science is to fill gaps in our assimilation of phenomena with imaginary entities, Smith defines a system as an 'imaginary machine invented to connect together in the fancy those different movements and effects which are already in reality effected' (iv.19). Recapitulating his analogy in the rhetoric lecture on language, he points out that, just as the first physical machines to be invented are complex and later ones are simplified, so the first systems are complex but subsequently fewer principles are needed to explain the same effects: ultimately, 'one great connecting principle is afterwards found to be sufficient to bind together all the discordant phaenomena that occur in a whole species of things' (iv.19). Smith illustrates his concept of a system as an 'imaginary machine' by citing the achievement of Copernicus, who was able to 'connect together celestial appearances, in a more simple as well as a more accurate manner, than that of Ptolemy' (iv.27). Smith's library included a prime source for understanding the new system: a copy of *De revolutionibus* (Nurnberg, 1543; Simpson, 1979: 190; Mizuta). Smith then continues his History of Astronomy by tracing the modification and improvements introduced into the Copernican system by Tycho Brahe, Galileo, Kepler, and Descartes, until he arrives at Newton, revealing his familiarity with the relevant scientific literature up to 1748, including Colin Maclaurin's *Account of Sir Isaac Newton's Discoveries* published that very year.

Smith takes an opportunity to refer to Newton's work on comets, noting that from the 'mechanical principle of gravity', and from observations, the 'nature and positions of their several orbits might be ascertained, and their periodic time determined'. Smith mentions, further, that followers of Newton from his principles had ventured to predict the return of comets, 'particularly of one which is to make its appearance in 1758' (iv.74). The remark indicates that the text of the History of Astronomy was completed before 1758, since the perihelion passage of Halley's Comet was observed on Christmas Day of that year. Smith does not refer to Edmund Halley by name, nor cite his *Astronomiae Cometicae Synopsis* (1705) as a source. This was reprinted in 1749, however, and published together with a posthumous edition of his lunar and mathematical tables by John Bevis (or Bevans), FRS, thus bringing Halley's work to the attention of the scientifically minded public at the time of the Edinburgh lectures.

It was not Smith's intention in the history of astronomy, which we are viewing as connected with the course on the history of philosophy, to dwell on the scientific contents of Newton's system, though he seems to have known it at first hand, certainly in the *Philosophiae naturalis principia mathematica*, of which he possessed the 1726 edition (Mizuta) and, as D. D. Raphael argues (1988), he did not depend on the vulgarizations of Voltaire and Maclaurin. Indeed, he left his account of Newton's system incomplete, as his literary executors Joseph Black and James Hutton pointed out in their edition (*EPS* 105). Smith's purpose as a historian of science was met, however, by recording that the parts of Newton's system 'are all more strictly connected together, than those of any other philosophical hypothesis', with the result that it 'now prevails over all opposition, and has advanced to the acquisition of the most universal empire that was ever established in philosophy' ('Astronomy' iv.76). There was a sceptical viewpoint concerning astronomy, however, which had emerged in the Renaissance (Jardine, 1987). From this source or, more generally perhaps, imbibed from Hume, scepticism appears in Smith's carefully flighted conclusion:

And even we, while we have been endeavouring to represent all philosophical systems as mere inventions of the imagination, to connect together the otherwise disjointed and discordant phenomena of nature, have insensibly been drawn in, to make use of language expressing the connecting principles of this one [Newton's], as if they were the real chains which Nature makes use of to bind together her several operations. ('Astronomy' iv.76)

David Hume, who became Smith's good friend about this time, struck the same note in an account in his *History of England*, vol. ii, published in 1757, of the progress of science in the later part of the Stuart era. He wrote that Robert Boyle was a 'great partizan of the mechanical philosophy; a theory, which by discovering some of the secrets of nature, and allowing us to imagine the rest, is so agreeable to the natural vanity and curiosity of men'. Hume went on to praise Newton as the 'greatest and rarest genius that ever arose for the ornament and instruction of the species'. He also stated:

While Newton seemed to draw off the veil from some of the mysteries of nature, he showed at the same time the imperfections of the mechanical philosophy, and thereby restored her ultimate secrets to that obscurity, in which they ever did and ever will remain. (Hume, 1792: viii.334)

As was noticed earlier, Smith in 1773 described the History of Astronomy as a 'fragment of an intended juvenile work'. The context was a request that Hume become Smith's literary executor, entrusted with the responsibility of judging whether or not to publish this 'fragment of a great work which contains a history of the Astronomical Systems that were successively in fashion down to the time of Des Cartes' (*Corr.* No. 137). The 'great work' itself must be the 'Philosophicall History of all the different branches of Literature, of Philosophy, Poetry, and Eloquence' which Smith acknowledged he had 'on the anvil' in 1785. In the event, the 'indolence of old age', as Smith put it, as well as ill health, prevented the completion of this project, and a complementary 'sort of theory and History of Law and Government' (*Corr.* No. 248).

Smith's literary executors, Black and Hutton, knew of the first of these 'great works', and presented *EPS* in connection with it, including the essays on the imitative arts, connected with Smith's theory of taste, as parts of a philosophical history of the 'liberal sciences and elegant arts' (*EPS*, Advertisement). Likely enough, Smith formed the plan at an early stage in life, and was able to give lectures in Edinburgh on the history of philosophy as a result of his reading. Certainly, the history of ancient physics and the history of ancient logics and metaphysics as discourses are connected by analogy to the history of astronomy, and illustrate similarly the 'principles which lead and direct philosophical enquiries', though in a more restricted form because limited to their 'Ancient' development. As Smith notes, to be sure, in its descent from 'arranging and methodizing the System of the Heavens', philosophy (or science) had a much more difficult task when confronted with the less beautiful and much more varied objects of the Earth, whose orders of succession seemed so intricate and irregular. Nevertheless, as Smith explains classical theorizing, the same psychological and aesthetic drive was manifested to make this 'lower part of the theatre of nature a coherent spectacle to the imagination' ('Ancient Physics' 1–2).

Smith's subsequent account of the Ancient Physics has been criticized for its neglect of the philosophy of causation introduced by the pre-Socratic thinkers and developed cogently by Aristotle (*EPS* 24). Nevertheless, in seizing on the four-element system of Empedocles (*c*.493–*c*.433) as a starting-point for the articulation of systems concerning matter, Smith makes a perceptive choice. Aristotle accepted the theory after criticism of it, and it had its place thereafter not only in the scholastic philosophy of nature, but also in atomism from which came the natural philosophy of the modern world.

Smith also offers two important points about the Ancient Physics highly relevant for his Edinburgh course on the history of philosophy. The first is that the 'principles of union' assigned to sublunary nature, though 'vague and undetermined in the highest degree', were 'such as, with all their imperfections, could enable mankind both to think and to talk, with more coherence, concerning those general subjects, than without them they would have been capable of doing'. The second point is that the system of the Ancient Physics was not 'entirely devoid of beauty or magnificence', and could be connected with the hypothesis of a world governed by uniform laws. Prior to this system's development, the 'seeming incoherence of the appearances of nature' had given rise to that 'pusillanimous superstition' of polytheism, 'which ascribes almost every unexpected event, to the arbitrary will of some designing, though invisible beings, who produced it for some private and particular purpose'.

When the philosophers 'discovered, or imagined they had discovered', the 'chain' which bound the parts of nature together, they conceived of the universe as a 'complete machine, as a coherent system, governed by general laws, and directed to general ends, viz. its own preservation and prosperity, and that of all the species that are in it'. In consequence, there arose the natural theology of Plato's World Soul, 'who formed the world, [and] endowed it with a principle of life and understanding'. Next came the formulation of Aristotle's First Cause, who effected the eternal world by 'exerting his divine energy from all eternity'. Thereafter, the Stoics posited a God who created a divine and harmonious universe to last its period and then return to the original 'aetherial and fiery nature' out of which a 'new Heaven and Earth' will come, in turn to be consumed and then re-created, again and again 'without end' ('Ancient Physics' 9–10). The Stoic concept of a harmonious universe operating according to natural law appealed to Smith, who made it part of the contemplative utilitarianism, together with a Newtonian concept of natural law, developed in *TMS*, and the free-market economics explored in *WN*.[2]

Smith's History of the Ancient Logics and Metaphysics surveys the teaching about the 'specific Essences of things' of four 'principal Sects of . . . Philosophers': the old Pythagoreans, the schools of Plato and Aristotle, and the Stoics. This teaching arose from the 'system of Natural Philosophy' which, for example, 'in considering the general nature of Water, takes no notice of those particularities which are peculiar to this Water, but confines itself to those things which are common to all water', and it comprised two 'sciences' which were 'apprehended to go before [Natural Philosophy], in the order in which the knowledge of Nature ought to be communicated'. The first 'science', known as Metaphysics, 'considered the general nature of Universals, and the different sorts or species into which they might be divided'. The second one, which Smith was grammatically consistent in naming 'Logics', is described as endeavouring 'to ascertain the general rules by which we might distribute all particular objects into general classes, and determine to which each individual object belonged'. Thus the ancients, according to Smith, 'justly enough apprehended . . . the whole art of philosophical reasoning' to consist of formal classification, and since 'Metaphysics is altogether subordinate to . . . Logic, they seem before the time of Aristotle, to have been regarded as one, and to have made up between them that ancient Dialectic of which we hear so much, and of which we understand so little' ('Ancient Logics' 1).

The essay entitled 'Of the External Senses' (*EPS*) cannot be placed exactly within the same framework of the history of philosophical enquiry as the pieces on astronomy, Ancient Physics, and Ancient Logics and Metaphysics. Nevertheless, it bears a relationship to the latter piece, in offering a complementary discussion of the epistemology derived from physical atomism of the modern variety. Further, in its own way, it illustrates the principles which Smith, at any rate, used to 'lead and direct philosophical enquiries'. Also, it has generally been regarded as an early composition, reflecting, for example, the stimulation of reading Berkeley's *Essay towards a New Theory of Vision* (1709), and making no overt reference to Hume's *Treatise of Human Nature*.

However, the theory of belief in the external world from the *Treatise* seems to be reflected in the History of Astronomy (Raphael, 1977). Also, the 'External Senses' essay does make use of the principle of the association of ideas (at 68 and 74), in a manner reminiscent of Hume's explanation of the associative origin in the imagination of causal belief (*Treatise* I.i.iv).

Still, Smith accepts the Lockean distinction between the primary and secondary qualities of bodies, without mention of Hume's sceptical rejection of this (*Treatise* I.iv.iv). Neither does he show awareness of Berkeley's objection to the doctrine of qualities in *Principles of Human Knowledge* (1710: i.9–15), which he does not seem to have read or chooses not to discuss. These two points suggest an early date for the piece. Nevertheless, an argument for a date of 1758 or after has been put forth by Kevin L. Brown (1992). He traces Smith's various references to Linnaeus in the essay to the tenth edition of the *Systema Natura* which was published in 1758. This has to be taken into consideration, but these references could have been added some time after the initial composition of the essay.

Perhaps Smith preserved the distinction between the primary and secondary qualities or 'Sensations', as he thought it more proper to call them ('External Senses' 25), because it had proved a useful part of the theory of physical atomism. This had two aspects that keenly interest him. The first was its acceptance of the conventional nature of the deliverances of the different 'Sensations', by analogy recognized as a kind of language. The second was the theory's reliance on empirical data. As far as Smith is concerned, Berkeley's most appealing insight in the *New Theory of Vision* is that the 'objects of sight . . . constitute a sort of language', constructed by convention whereby we apprehend tangible objects (61). To be sure, Smith claims that the 'language which nature addresses to our eyes' signifies the objects it denotes in a superior degree of precision to 'any of the artificial languages which human art and ingenuity have ever been able to invent' (62, 68). He also points out, however, that the 'affinity and correspondence' between visible and tangible objects is not alone sufficient for us to make rational inferences about which specific tangible object is represented by a visible one. We need the 'assistance of observation and experience' (63).

In making this point, Smith passes to his second chief interest in the philosophy, or perhaps we should say psychology, arising from the theory of physical atomism, its connection with empirical data. To illustrate this, he turns to a famous case history of the period, that of the 'young Gentleman, who was born blind, or lost his Sight so early, that he had no Remembrance of ever having seen, and who was cou'd [for cataracts] between 13 and 14 Years of Age'. The surgeon William Cheselden reported on this case (Cheselden, 1728).

The report satisfactorily answered the question William Molyneux asked Locke after reading the first edition of the *Essay concerning Human Understanding* (1690): could a person who was born blind and had his sight restored distinguish by seeing, and identify, those objects which touch had already made familiar? In brief, the answer was no, and Smith was clearly fascinated by Cheselden's account of the lengthy process required to correlate visible and tangible perceptions. Smith considers that in correlating visibles and tangibles young children possibly benefit from 'some instinctive perception', which might have atrophied in the formerly blind young man; and this thought leads him to present some empirical evidence he had collected himself about instinctive response to visual or other stimuli. He instances the ability of ground-nestlings such as chickens and the young of partridge and grouse to find their food on the ground almost as soon as they come from the shell, whereas the young from high-up nests, such as hawks, magpies, and sparrows, are born blind and have to be fed for some time by their parents ('External Senses' 70–1).

Arguing that appetites originating in certain states of the body 'seem to suggest the means of their own gratification', Smith reckons that there are anticipations of pleasure in gratifying an appetite before there is experience of it. The example he offers is that of the sexual appetite: 'which frequently, I am disposed to believe almost always, comes a long time before puberty' (79). From these details afforded by the essay 'Of the External Senses' we can think of Smith, the lecturer in Edinburgh or Glasgow on the history of philosophy, extending his reading from the ancient writers on astronomy, physics, and metaphysics, also the contributors to the scientific revolution of early modern times, to Locke, Hume, and now Berkeley, in whom there was considerable interest among Scottish readers (Davie, 1965; Stewart, 1985). We can also think of Smith reading the *Philosophical Transactions* produced by the Royal Society of London to inform himself of the latest developments in science, such as the case history presented by Cheselden. Another picture is also suggested, Smith observing instinctive sexual behaviour in children, as well as the feeding habits of barnyard fowl and game birds and those of the countryside, and connecting his observations of living creatures with the classification system of Linnaeus.

Though tantalizing in their incompleteness, suggestions that can be brought forward about Smith's Edinburgh lectures on rhetoric and the history of philosophy point to intellectual achievements of a high calibre by a young man still in his 20s. It was a third course, however, which brought about a decisive step in his career. Smith is said to have returned to Glasgow because the reputation earned by an Edinburgh course of lectures on law brought him a professorship. From the same source, anecdotes emanating from one of Smith's pupils, David Callander, and recorded by the antiquary George Chalmers, we also learn that Smith believed William Robertson had plagiarized from the law lectures in the first volume of his *History of the Reign of the Emperor Charles V* (1769). The report on these points runs as follows:

[Smith] went to Edinburgh about 1750 and privately taught the Civil Law to Students of Jurisprudence. It was the fame which he thus gained as a Teacher of Law, that Induced the patrons to invite him to the professorship in the College of Glasgow. Such were the Lectures, which he here gave, that he Used to appeal to [David] Callender That Dr Robertson had borrow'd the first vol. of his hist[or]y of Cha[rles] 5 from them; as Every Student Could testify. Of Robertson he liked to Say, That his judgement Enabled him to form a good Outline, but he wanted industry to fill up his plan; That Robertson inverted Morals, by blaming what he should have praised, and praised, what he should have blamed: That he liked Robertson better when at a distance than he did upon nearer inspection.[3]

Smith's estimate of Robertson, at this period already engaged in writing his *History of Scotland* (published in 1759), agreed pretty well with that of Carlyle of Inveresk, who knew him from 1737: '[he was] so much addicted to the Translation of other Peoples Thoughts, that he sometimes appear'd tedious to his Best Friends' (Carlyle, 1973: 144). For his part, Robertson valued Smith's work because of its historical dimension, and on the publication of *WN* he was forthright in acknowledging Smith as his 'Guide and instructor' in research on the American colonies (*Corr.* No. 153). Responding to news of the success of *TMS*, he expressed the hope that Smith's next book would be 'less abstruse', and he made this suggestion: 'I still wish you would think on the History of Philosophy' (*Corr.* No. 34). A possible explanation for this remark is that some years after Robertson heard Smith's lecture series at Edinburgh, or heard about them, he was sufficiently impressed to believe that the account of the history of philosophy or science would make a book that would add to Smith's reputation.

A more important relationship for Smith than that with Robertson is heralded in an insertion in Callander's note on Smith's civil law course in Edinburgh: 'It was then that he first became acquainted w[ith] D. Hume: The friendship between them continued thro' Life. Hume reviewed the Moral Sentiments [1759–1760]' (statement and dates: EUL La.II.451/2).

Hume had returned to London in January 1749 after serving as Secretary to General St Clair's diplomatic mission to the courts of Vienna and Turin. By the summer of that year he was back at his family home at Ninewells, Berwickshire, where he resided for most of the next two years, with visits at intervals to Edinburgh, during which he may have heard Adam Smith lecture. In April 1750 he was involved in the publication of a translation of two chapters of Montesquieu's *Esprit des lois*, a book of great interest to Smith as a lecturer on law. In October and November 1750 Hume was exchanging letters with Smith's friend Oswald of Dunnikier about economic topics in his forthcoming *Political Discourses* (1752). Smith later reported to the Glasgow Literary Society about Hume's book. Hume at this time was also preparing from book III of the *Treatise of Human Nature*, his *Enquiry concerning the Principles of Morals*, and collecting material for the *History of England* he had planned for some years (Mossner, 1980: 224, 232–3; Hume, *HL* i.142–4). Another of Hume's projects of this period was work on early drafts of the *Dialogues concerning Natural Religion*, a book that was to give Smith considerable intellectual difficulties (*HL* i.142–4; Mossner, 1968: 224, 232–3). There was much, then, in Hume's current activities that would stimulate and attract Smith but also disturb him, and the profound effect of Hume's thought and character on Smith will be traced in succeeding chapters.

Concerning Smith's preparations for lecturing on law, we have his admission of 5 March 1769 to a Scottish judge, Lord Hailes: 'I have read law entirely with a view to form some general notion of the great outlines of the plan according to which justice has [been] administered in different ages and nations' (*Corr.* No. 116). If the first volume of Robertson's book on Charles V (1769) is truly a guide to the scheme of the Edinburgh lectures, and thereafter to the Glasgow jurisprudence course which Callander attended as Smith's student, then they were similarly concerned with the 'Progress of Society in Europe', tracing the changing forms of legal institutions and government as responses to what Robertson was to call 'mode of subsistence' in another work, his *History of America*, 1777 (Meek, 1976: 138–45).

We have to understand that the 'Civil Law' taught by Smith, as reported by Callander, did not mean, as it often does, Roman law. This was already taught at Edinburgh University to prepare students for entry into the Faculty of Advocates. Rather it meant the Grotius–Pufendorf tradition of the 'Laws of Nature and Nations', which Lord President Dundas has referred to in 1748 as a necessary part of legal education in Scotland together with the principles of Roman law. As we have seen, Smith encountered this tradition in the moral philosophy class under Hutcheson, and he may have undertaken further study of it at Balliol when registered, according to W. R. Scott, as 'studiosus' in civil law. Smith's innovation at Edinburgh, however, seems to have been describing the dynamics of the emergence and development of law as civil society progressed through the four stages of food-gathering, pastoralism, agriculture, and commerce. Robertson could have heard Smith lecture on law at Edinburgh, when he was minister at Gladsmuir, thirteen and a half miles to the east of the city. It is unlikely he heard Smith teach at Glasgow. Possibly Smith thought that Robertson had borrowed elements of this four-stage theory from him, though in some respects there are other precursors, principally Grotius and Montesquieu (Meek, 1973: Intro., 5–6; 1976: 5–36).

Invoking the Grotius–Pufendorf tradition, Smith's Edinburgh lectures on law seem to have focused on jurisprudence, 'that science which inquires into the general principles which ought to be the foundation of the laws of all nations' (*LJ*(B) 1). The course must have been as extensive as that normally given in jurisprudence at Glasgow, because Smith was prepared at short notice in the autumn of 1751 to teach the subject for the Professor of Moral Philosophy there, Craigie, who was ill. Also, he was prepared to deal with Politics as well (*Corr.* No. 7). A major theme was the affirmation of the value of economic liberty, and it is the evidence on this point that indicates the treatment of law and government as subject to historical change arising, in part, from economic conditions.

It appears that Smith was concerned about plagiarism of his ideas on this topic also—at least so Dugald Stewart would have us believe in presenting two extracts from a 'paper' Smith drew up about 1755, and read to a Glasgow society of which he was a member. The first extract presented by Stewart anticipates the 'invisible hand' argument of *TMS* (IV.1.10) and *WN* (IV.ii.9), which reveals its origins in the Stoic doctrine of 'natural harmony':

projectors disturb nature in the course of her operations in human affairs; and it requires no more than to let her alone, and give her fair play in the pursuit of her ends, that she may establish her own designs.

The second extract contains the concept of the free market:

little else is requisite to carry a state to the highest degree of opulence from the lowest barbarism, but peace, easy taxes, and a tolerable administration of justice; all the rest being brought about by the natural course of things. All governments which thwart this natural course, which force things into another channel, or which endeavour to arrest the progress of society at a particular point are unnatural, and to support themselves are obliged to be oppressive and tyrannical.

Smith made it quite clear that he had arrived at these ideas in his Edinburgh lecturing period:

A great part of these opinions . . . enumerated in this paper is treated of at length in some lectures which I have still by me, and which were written in the hand of a clerk who left my service six years ago [i.e. in 1749]. They have all of them been the constant subject of my lectures since I first taught Mr Craigie's class [that of his predecessor as Professor of Moral Philosophy], the first winter I spent in Glasgow, down to this day, without any considerable variation. They had all of them been the subjects of lectures which I read at Edinburgh the winter before I left it [i.e. 1750–1], and I can adduce innumerable witnesses, both from that place and from this, who will ascertain them sufficiently to be mine. (Stewart, iv.25)

It is clear that the framework for this is an account of the history of civil society from 'barbarism' to the 'highest degree of opulence' in an age of commerce. Smith's thesis in his 1755 'paper' and, on his own account, in the Edinburgh lectures on law is that 'unnatural' government interventions thwart a country's economic growth. This had been argued before in Scotland, by Andrew Fletcher of Saltoun. In a piece entitled 'An Account of a Conversation &c' (1703), he had written: 'all governments which put discouragements on the industry of their subjects are not upon a right foot; but violent, and consequently unjust' (Fletcher, 1749: 298). Smith's audience may have appreciated his echo of Fletcher, since the latter's *Political Works* had recently been published in a Glasgow edition of 1749.

As for Smith's comment about the origin of his 'paper' in the form of an Edinburgh lecture course, he is drawing attention to the link between it and his thinking in the period of his Glasgow professorship. This thinking is the subject of the next chapter; in concluding the present one it will suffice to underscore the fertility in ideas of the youthful lecturer in Edinburgh. In ranging over aesthetic, scientific, philosophical, and jurisprudential topics in a penetrating way for the benefit of his 'respectable auditory', he reached a seminal understanding of the nature of intellectual systems, and thus laid the foundations for his mature work on social science.

8

Called to Glasgow University

It shall be my chief study to render myselfe a useful member of their Society.

Reward for his successful Edinburgh lectures came to Adam Smith in the welcome form of election to the Chair of Logic at Glasgow. His former teacher of that subject, John Loudoun, died on 1 November 1750, and the University meeting of 19 December decided to elect a successor on 9 January 1751. There were at least two 'able candidates' for the post, so John Anderson, future colleague of Smith's, reported to Gilbert Lang on 27 December 1750. These were George Muirhead, subsequently elected Professor of Oriental Languages in 1753, and Smith, who was the unanimous choice (Univ. of Strathclyde, Anderson Lib., Anderson/Lang; Meek, 1977: 74). The Clerk, Smith's former mathematics teacher, Robert Simson, was appointed to inform him of his election, to request him to come to Glasgow 'as soon as his affairs can allow him, in order to be admitted', and to require him to present a dissertation, 'De Origine Idearum', as a trial of his qualifications.

No text of the lecture seems to have survived, but it could have been drawn from his history of philosophy course at Edinburgh. Smith accepted his election on 10 January, presumably 'by first post', as he was asked, and went on to say that he would try to get to Glasgow 'on Tuesday night', but that he would have to return to Edinburgh within two days, also that he could not 'even be very certain if that absence will be consented to by my friends here' (*Corr.* No. 8). This is probably a reference to his commitment to Kames, William Johnstone (later Pulteney), possibly Oswald and Craigie of Glendoick, as well as others, to give his Edinburgh lecture courses during the winter months.

In the event, Smith attended a University meeting at Glasgow on 16 January, read the dissertation expected of him, to unanimous approval, and, having signed the Calvinist Confession of Faith before the Presbytery of Glasgow, he took the 'usual Oath de Fideli' to secure admission as a Professor of Glasgow University. Thereafter, he 'was solemnly received by all the members', and then permitted to return immediately to Edinburgh, since he had represented that his 'business' made this necessary. With the agreement of the University meeting, he appointed Dr Hercules Lindesay, Professor of Civil Law since 1750, to teach the 'Semi' class in his absence (GUA 26640; Scott, 1937: 137–9).

Despite the show of unanimity alluded to in the minutes of these University meetings, there seems to have been some feeling about Smith's election. This can be deduced from a draft letter to Smith in the hand of William Cullen, recently admitted Professor of Medicine, and believed to have been a friend of Smith's from his Edinburgh lecturing period, who became Smith's physician. This letter was written some time before Thomas Craigie, Professor of Moral Philosophy, was forced in April 1751 to cease teaching and retire to the country for health reasons. Cullen suggests that Smith has been troubled by divisions among the Glasgow faculty, and hopes this will end when Smith comes to Glasgow 'to live among us'. Craigie and six other professors apparently supported Smith 'without regard to any great man whatever', whereas William Ruat, the Professor of Oriental Languages, appointed on 31 October 1750, made out that Craigie's vote for Smith, also that of William Leechman, Professor of Divinity, was a 'compliment to Lord Hyndford and [the] Duke of Argyle'. Cullen also seems to suggest that Smith had written to London to the 3rd Duke of Argyll and to his cousin and guardian, William Smith, the 2nd Duke's secretary, about his election, and that this had been taken amiss in Glasgow.

Perhaps the best explanation that can be offered is that there were at least two factions among the professors: Craigie leading one determined to be seen as voting for a candidate on merit; and another, including Ruat, Lindesay, and possibly Leechman, who had their reasons for paying heed to the wishes of 'great men'. At the close of the letter, Cullen indicates that Smith still has the 'warm temper' which his Kirkcaldy companions noticed in him, and he begs Smith 'for the sake of your quiet and health you would not indulge in any anger or vexation till you are sure of your facts' (*Corr.* No. 304).

When Smith came to teach logic at Glasgow in October 1751, according to the account given by John Millar, already introduced as his student and later colleague and friend, he 'soon saw the necessity of departing widely from the plan that had been followed by his predecessors' (Stewart i.16). One of these was Loudoun, whose scholastic approach has already been described. In *WN*, Smith was to sum up logic on the ancient model as the 'science of the general principles of good and bad reasoning' (v.i.f.26). For his students, however, he was content to paint the syllogistic formulations of Aristotle as an 'artificial method of reasoning', about which curiosity should be gratified, since it had formerly taken up the attention of learned men. Apparently deciding that new times demanded a new approach, he proposed to turn to 'studies of a more interesting and useful nature', through presenting a 'system' of rhetoric and belles-lettres which we have suggested was worked out in his Edinburgh course.

Millar's defence of this procedure, which we must suppose was that of Smith himself, runs as follows:

The best method of explaining and illustrating the various powers of the human mind, the most useful part of metaphysics, arises from an examination of the several ways of communicating our thoughts by speech, and from an attention to the principles of those literary compositions which contribute to persuasion and entertainment. By these arts, every thing that we perceive or feel, every operation of our minds, is expressed and delineated in such a manner, that it may be clearly distinguished and remembered. There is, at the same time, no branch of literature more suited to youth at their first entrance upon philosophy than this, which lays hold of their taste and their feelings. (Stewart i.16)

Smith's innovative approach to teaching logic may have been partly determined by a critical view of Loudoun's achievement as a Professor, memories of the wearisome insistence at Oxford on Aristotelian logic, and demands on his time when he arrived in Glasgow. The consequences of the young Professor's innovations proved seminal and far-reaching, as we shall explain, but they did not please everyone within the University of Glasgow. A sour note is struck in the correspondence of James Wodrow, Library Keeper and ninth son of the Presbyterian historian Robert Wodrow. In a letter dated 20 December 1751, he turns down an invitation for the following Saturday because two friends who had planned to accompany him have made up their minds after some delay to attend Smith's rhetoric course, and a catch-up lecture has been arranged for them that very day. Wodrow describes the course to his correspondent, Samuel Kenrick, in these terms:

You must know that we have got a new sort of Lectures which by their novelty draw all men after them[.] I mean Lectures on Rhetoric by which Their heads are stuffed with the *Circumstantials[,] adjuncts[,] Heads and tails of Sentences, Nominatives[,] Accusatives* and I dont know how much more Grammatical Jargon which you may lay your account to be entertained with at meeting.

Wodrow resumes the topic of Smith's course in another letter to Kenrick dated 21 January 1752:

Smiths Reputation in his Rhetorical Lectures is sinking every day[.] As I am not a scholar of his I don't pretend to assign the cause. He begins next week to give lectures on Jurisprudentia which I design to attend. I hear he has thrown out some contemptuos Expressions of Mr Hutchison. Let the young man take care to guard his Censures by the Lines[,] Palisades and counterscarps of his science Rhetoric[.] For there are some of Mr H[utcheso]ns scholars still about the Coll[ege] who perhaps will try to turn the mouths of the Cannon against himself. (London, Dr Williams' Lib., MS 24.157, 14, 16)

We surmise the 'contemptuos [*sic*] Expressions' amounted to criticism by Smith of Hutcheson's style, which probably he connected to the florid manner of Shaftesbury and contrasted with the plain style of Swift which he admired. Late in life, Wodrow provided for Lord Buchan, one of Smith's students, the already quoted fuller and more favourable account of the rhetoric lectures; he also gave some details of Smith's lecturing style, which we shall draw on, as he sought briefly to measure up to that of his master (and Wodrow's), Francis Hutcheson.

As to Smith lecturing on jurisprudence in his first year at Glasgow, this came about because Craigie, Hutcheson's successor as Professor of Moral Philosophy, was too ill by April 1751, as we have mentioned, to continue teaching. On

3 September 1751 Smith wrote to Cullen from Edinburgh to say that, 'with great pleasure', he would do what he could to relieve Craigie: 'You mention Natural Jurisprudence and Politics as the parts of his lectures which it would be most agreeable for me to take upon me to teach. I shall willingly undertake both' (*Corr.* No. 9). This arrangement was confirmed at a University meeting on 11 September, when it was agreed that William Leechman, Professor of Divinity, would teach the 'Theologia Naturalis, and the first book of Mr Hutchesons Ethicks, and Mr Smith the other two books de Jurisprudentia Naturali et Politicis' (GU Meeting, Minutes 11 Sept. 1751; *LJ* 1–2).

The textbook alluded to here was Francis Hutcheson's *Philosophiae moralis institutio compendiaria, ethicis & jurisprudentiae naturalis elementa continuens*, published in three volumes at Glasgow in 1742. Even though Smith would be teaching from this source—and it is highly interesting he bound himself to do so—it is reasonable to suppose that he had little time to prepare new logic or jurisprudence lectures for his Glasgow post, but rather drew on the Edinburgh rhetoric and belles-lettres course, also the 'civil law' course he gave, with its historical dimension extending the teaching of Hutcheson about natural law as a major component of moral philosophy.

Smith planned to be in Glasgow by 1 October 1751, because he also told Cullen that if Craigie had not set out for Lisbon for the sake of his health by that date, he would meet with him to discuss his plan for teaching: 'I would pay great deference to it in every thing, and would follow it implicitly in this, as I shall consider myself as standing in his place and representing him' (*Corr.* No. 9). As matters turned out, Craigie, who had been given leave in September to travel to a warmer climate, died in Lisbon on 27 November. There must have been anticipation of this at the time, also of the eventuality of Smith succeeding him, with a consequent need to find another Professor of Logic. These points emerge in another letter to Cullen, written on a Tuesday that same November, when Smith was in Edinburgh.

It is of singular interest that Smith mentions Hume as a contender for a prospective vacant post at Glasgow, and he does so in terms that suggest he admired him as a man and as a philosopher. At the same time, Smith reveals the strong streak of prudence in his character, noting that public opinion did not favour Hume, no doubt because of his reputation as a sceptic, and that the 'interest' of the University in this respect had to be considered: 'I should prefer David Hume to any man for a colleague; but I am afraid the public would not be of my opinion; and the interest of the society will oblige us to have some regard to the opinion of the public' (*Corr.* No. 10). Perhaps Smith could not exactly see Hume signing the Confession of Faith before the Presbytery of Glasgow, as was required before admission to a professorship at the University (Stewart and Wright, 1995).

Both Hutcheson and William Leechman, the Divinity Professor (elected 1744), had been accused of heresy by members of the Presbytery, and they themselves had opposed Hume's candidacy for the professorship of Moral Philosophy at Edinburgh in 1744–5 (Scott, 1900: 84–5; Mackie, 1954: 202; Mossner, 1980: 157). Moreover, in his letter to Kenrick on 21 January 1751 already quoted, Wodrow mentions that the clergy of Glasgow went in a body to Principal Neil Campbell to say that they did not want Hume made a Professor. At the same time, Wodrow reports that he is reading Hume's *Political Discourses*, though he seems not to have understood the contents very well. However, the Literary Society of Glasgow was founded on 10 January of the same year, with Smith and other Professors as original members, and on 23 January Smith read an 'account of some of Mr David Hume's Essays on Commerce' (Duncan, 1831: 132). We may presume that Smith could offer some insights for a Glasgow audience into Hume's work, and these marked a stage in the development of the system of economics he was making part of his jurisprudence lectures (Skinner, 1990*a*).

Smith's letter to Cullen of November 1751 alludes to the manœuvring behind the scenes concerning the Glasgow appointments. He hints that his colleague, Hercules Lindesay, put forward Hume's name to his good friend Gilbert Elliot of Minto, Sheriff-depute of Roxburghshire and elected MP for Selkirkshire in 1753, a rising politician who had the ear of the 3rd Duke of Argyll. Hume was in the west of Scotland in the autumn of 1751 to visit friends including William Mure of Caldwell, like Elliot one of the managers of patronage in Scotland, mostly for the Argyll interest. The scheme to obtain a professorship for Hume, with Lindesay a party to it, may have been concocted on this occasion. Smith recalls a discussion with Cullen about the proposed resignation of Neil Campbell, who had served as Principal of Glasgow University since 1728. He asks Cullen to thank the Principal for mentioning his name to the Duke of Argyll, possibly in connection with transference to the Chair of Moral Philosophy. He had attended the Duke at his levee at Edinburgh, being introduced to him by Alexander Lind of Gorgie, Sheriff-depute of Midlothian and amateur chemist associated with Argyll in the operation of the Glasgow Delft Works. Perhaps conveniently, the great man had forgotten Principal Campbell's mention of Smith to him. It was apparently this Duke who squelched Hume's hopes of a Glasgow Chair, for Andrew Fletcher, son of Lord Milton, Argyll's chief agent in Scotland, reported to his father on 9 January 1752:

Yesterday I laid before His Grace the Letters &c concerning the Affair pendant at Glasgow: His Grace desires me to acquaint you that Mr David Hume cannot be recommended to a Proffesorship there and that for many reasons which must easily occur to you. (NLS Saltoun MSS; Mossner, 1980: 632)

Thwarted again in seeking to become a professor, David Hume secured in January 1752 election as Keeper of the Advocates' Library in Edinburgh, whose 30,000 volumes made it one of the best in Britain, especially for the historical research on which he was now embarked. His first surviving letter to Smith, dated 24 September 1752, alludes to a discussion between them about the appropriate place for beginning an 'English History' with the reign of Henry VII.

Hume acknowledges having received from Smith a letter, now missing, on this subject, also a request for a Latin book. He also gives his reasons for beginning his *History of England* with James I's reign, finding in it a great constitutional turning-point, whose outcome affected contemporary affairs:

Twas under James that the House of Commons began first to raise their Head, and then the Quarrel betwixt Privilege and Prerogative commenc'd. The Government, no longer opprest by the enormous Authority of the Crown, display'd its Genius; and the Factions, which then arose, having an Influence on our present Affairs, form the most curious, interesting, and instructive Part of our History. The preceding Events or Causes may be easily shown in a Reflection or Review, which may be artfully inserted in the Body of the Work and the whole, by that means, be render'd more compact and uniform.

Hume writes of entering on this work with 'great Ardour and Pleasure', and from this overview it can be seen how much thought he had given to historical composition, a subject of considerable interest to Smith. As discussed in Chapter 7, his lectures on rhetoric included a history of historians. Originally there was no mention of Hume, but a marginal note to a sentence in praise of Rapin-Thoyras for his candour (*LRBL* ii.73) adds, '10 years ago, a better now'. John M. Lothian, the first editor of Smith's rhetoric lectures (*LRBL*, 1963: 112 n. 2), took this to be a reference made on 12 January 1763 to Hume's *History of England*, published in six volumes 1754–62.

Also in his September 1752 letter, Hume asks Smith for any hint that might occur to him concerning insertions and retrenchments in his *Essays Moral and Political*, which Hume was then correcting for the first volume of *Essays and Treatises on Several Subjects* of 1753 (*Corr.* No. 12). Hume obviously recognized Smith as someone of intellectual distinction, whom he named as 'my Friend', in a letter dated from Edinburgh on 26 May 1753 (*Corr.* No. 13). He resumes there the topic of composing the *History of England*, noting the many volumes he peruses and the scrupulous method he has adopted, and he advises Smith to settle in Edinburgh for the vacation to regain his health affected by the 'Fatigues of your Class'. Hume writes, further, that he has 'many things to communicate' to Smith, and promises that Edinburgh always has 'some good Company', also that he can supply Smith with books, 'as much as you please'. Feeling the attraction of his personality reflected in Allan Ramsay's portrait of 1754 (Pl. 5), Smith returned Hume's friendship warmly, though he never fell in readily with Hume's schemes to gain his company. He did give him unfailing admiration, however, expressed in the accolade of *WN*, identifying Hume as 'by far the most illustrious philosopher and historian of the present age' (v.i.g.3).

Meantime, Smith's career at Glasgow University progressed. On 22 April 1752 he was unanimously elected to the vacant Chair of Moral Philosophy, on the express condition that he would content himself with the emoluments of the Logic Professorship until 10 October following (GUA 26640; Scott, 1937: 139–40). This measure was taken to cover payment for the distribution of

Pl. 5. David Hume, 1754. From a portrait by Allan Ramsay. Private Collection.

Craigie's teaching among a number of colleagues, including Smith. It seems that the stipend for both Chairs was about £50 a year. In addition, the Professors of Moral Philosophy and Natural Philosophy shared some income from payments made by students on taking the MA degree. Like all Scottish professors at this time, Smith earned fees paid directly to him by students attending his courses. A guinea was due for his private class, and another half-guinea for the public class, though these fees were no longer payable after two years in any one class. Some students attended the moral philosophy class for as many as five years. It is reported that Smith's friend Joseph Black, when a Professor at Edinburgh, resorted to weighing guineas on receipt from his students, since he had lost many pounds sterling from the light coins formerly tendered to him (Rae, 1965: 49).

Through seniority, Smith also enjoyed in time a rent-free house in Professors' Court, worth between £9 and £13 a year (Scott, 1937: 418; locations, p. 420). His income was further supplemented by taking in well-to-do students as boarders, for example, the Hon. Thomas Petty Fitzmarice, who lived with him from 1759 to 1761, on the recommendation of Gilbert Elliot of Minto, at a charge of £100 per year (*Corr.* No. 27). With 80–90 paying students in his moral philosophy class, and perhaps 20 in the private one, also taking into account the other perquisites, it may be computed for his best years as a Glasgow Professor that Smith earned something like £300 a year, with this income falling to £150 in a lean year such as 1753, when he and his successor as Professor of Logic, James Clow, reported that enrolment was so low that they wished to discontinue their classes (GUA 26649; Scott: 1937: 67).

The teaching of moral philosophy was at the core of the Scottish university education of Smith's time, and of the Scottish Enlightenment as a movement, as much recent scholarship has demonstrated (Stewart-Robertson, 1983; Emerson, Sher, and Wood, all 1990). The philosophical freedom and diversity within this academic development affords an instructive contrast to the monolithic tendencies in the state-administered universities of absolutist Protestant Germany, for example, Jena, Leipzig, Halle, and, from 1737, Göttingen (Nissen, 1989). Men of letters were certainly supported in these institutions, as *WN* notes (v.i.g.39), but they were constrained by political and religious controls, and also, for many decades, by the intellectual stranglehold of Christian Wolff (Boyle, 1992: 17–18). This was an experience remote from that of Adam Smith, with his abiding concern for 'natural liberty'.

The Glasgow tradition of a broad approach to moral philosophy went back to the sixteenth century, when in the early decades John Mair taught the *Ethics* of Aristotle, publishing an edition of this text in 1530, as well as taking up economic issues in lectures on the *Sentences* of Peter Lombard. In addition, Andrew Melville and his nephew James Melville in the 1570s taught the moral philosophy of Aristotle (Durkan and Kirk, 1977: 158, 279). Gershom Carmichael and Hutcheson had broken away from neo-Aristotelianism to introduce, between them, the natural-law tradition of Grotius and Pufendorf, Stoic ethics, and Shaftesbury's philosophy of benevolence and moral sense. The distribution of Craigie's duties, in which Smith participated, indicated the range—and liberal nature—of the public course in moral philosophy at Glasgow by 1751. It consisted of four parts: natural theology, ethics, jurisprudence, and politics. John Millar wrote that when Smith came to deal with the first part, he 'considered the proofs of the being and attributes of God, and those principles of the human mind upon which religion is founded' (Stewart i.18). These 'principles' are adduced by Smith in his essay on the History of Ancient Physics, which argues that 'ignorance, and confusion of thought' in the first ages of the world, 'necessarily gave birth to that pusillanimous superstition which ascribes almost every unexpected event, to the arbitrary will of some designing, though invisible beings, who produced it for some private and particular purpose'. In time, however, philosophers came to regard the universe as a 'complete system, governed by general laws, and directed to general ends, viz. its own preservation and prosperity, and that of all the species that are in it'. The unity of this system suggested the unity of the principle that created it and informed it. Thus, 'as ignorance begot superstition, science gave birth to the first theism that arose among those nations, who were not enlightened by divine Revelation' ('Ancient Physics' 9; cf. *WN* v.i.f.28).

Smith's emphasis on perception of a cosmic system accompanying enlightenment in theology is of a piece with his methodology in delivering systems of rhetoric, ethics, jurisprudence, and economics. Such a method gave coherence to the intellectual world he explored for the benefit of his students, and it had its counterpart in the teaching of colleagues, that of the medical scientists William Cullen and Joseph Black, for example. Once again, not everyone relished this approach. That persistent critic of the Glasgow professoriate William Thom, minister of Govan, made fun of them falling asleep in their rooms reading their own systems (Thom, 1764; Mackie, 1948: 49). Students were impressed, however, and then the readers of the books in which these systems were presented.

This intellectual tradition endured in the new industrial world that emerged in Britain in the late eighteenth century and prevailed in the nineteenth. Evidence of this is to be found in the currency of the phrase 'the system', meaning the mechanized production unit in which all the parts of the plant had to cooperate. Thus, in textile production, the spinning mill was organized to accommodate 'the system', so that preparatory machines and spinning frames did not outstrip or fall behind each other, but were balanced in an economic way to produce one weight of yarn or a limited range of weights (Watson, 1990: 28). In consequence, the architecture and layout of the mills was governed by 'the system', and hence the conditions faced by the textile workers.

Smith came to appreciate that the division of labour necessary to accommodate such manufacturing systems could produce mental mutilation of the workers (*WN* v.i.f.50), and he counselled that education would check the danger to the State resulting from its citizens being reduced to cogs in the machine of the workshop. He argued that education would increase the self-esteem of the common people and make them more esteemed by their superiors, and therefore more inclined to hold those superiors in esteem. Above all, education was an antidote, in his opinion, to the 'delusions of enthusiasm and superstition, which, among ignorant nations, frequently occasion the most dreadful disorders' (v.i.f.61).

As to his discussion of the 'proofs of the being and attributes of God' in the natural theology course, Smith most likely followed his former teacher

Hutcheson in criticizing Samuel Clarke's a priori reasoning (*A Demonstration of the Being and Attributes of God*, the Boyle Lectures, 1704), and in making use of the probabilistic argument from design of Bishop Butler (*The Analogy of Religion*, 1736). Smith conceived of the God of natural theology as 'that great, benevolent, and all-wise Being, who directs all the movements of nature; and who is determined, by his own unalterable perfections, to maintain in it, at all times, the greatest possible quantity of happiness' (*TMS* VI.ii.3.2). This concept is deeply influenced by Stoic doctrine, which was a staple of the 'private' class in moral philosophy taught by Hutcheson (Richardson, 1803: 514). Orthodox religious opinion was not impressed by Smith's handling of the first part of his course, a state of affairs reflected in the comments of the anecdotalist John Ramsay of Ochtertyre:

[Smith's] speculations upon natural religion, though not extended to any great length, were no less flattering to human pride than those of Hutcheson. From both the one and the other presumptuous striplings took upon themselves to draw an unwarranted conclusion—namely, that the great truths of theology, together with the duties which man owes of God and his neighbours, may be discovered by the light of nature without any special revelation.

Ramsay also mentioned that doubts were entertained about the soundness of Smith's principles, in view of the company he kept, an allusion to his friendship with Hume. Smith was also described as being 'very guarded in conversation', and Ramsay noted that he seemed to find it disagreeable to pray in public when opening his class, also that he petitioned unsuccessfully to be excused from this duty. The prayer he offered 'savoured strongly of natural religion', and it was further reported that Smith gave up Hutcheson's practice of convening the moral philosophy class on Sundays for an improving discourse (Ramsay, 1880: i.461–2).

We have a flash of Smith's distaste for the compulsory religious duties of his professorial days in a letter to his friend William Johnstone, advising him not to come to Glasgow during the 'sacrament week' at Easter, but to arrive at the end of his holiday: 'when you will find everything ten times more joyful on account of the melancholy of the foregoing week' (*Corr.* No. 297). Unlike Hume, however, Smith was not prepared to contemplate the notion of a world lacking a creator: 'the very suspicion of a fatherless world, must be the most melancholy of all reflections' (*TMS* VI.ii.3.2). Do we have in this statement, perhaps, a projection of his own feelings about his orphaned state?

Nothing of the natural theology part of Smith's course saw print as such, but that on ethics, according to John Millar, 'consisted chiefly of the doctrines . . . afterwards published in the Theory of Moral Sentiments'. When this book appeared the lectures were adjusted accordingly, with ethical doctrines occupying a smaller portion of the course and greater attention being directed to a fuller illustration of the principles of jurisprudence and political economy (Stewart i.18, iii.1). It has been plausibly argued that when lecturing on ethics, Smith began by posing two questions: what is virtue? and what prompts us to be virtuous? (*TMS* VII.I.2.) Thereafter, he would offer a historical survey of the answers to these questions provided by leading moral philosophers from Plato to Hume (cf. *TMS* VI, edns. 1–5; VII, edn. 6; Raphael, 1976: 4). We discuss the nature of Smith's survey and the formulation and development of his own theory of moral philosophy centring on the doctrine of sympathy in Chapter 11 below.

It will suffice here to say that a fragment of the ethics lectures has survived, reflecting a stage in his ethical thought before the preparation of his manuscript for his first book. The fragment is in the hand of an amanuensis, with two or three revisions in Smith's own writing, since it was his habit to dictate his compositions, including most revisions, and then to add only the last touches himself (GUL MS Gen. 1035/227; *TMS* 388–90).

The theme of the lecture from which the fragment came seems to have been justice in general. The Revd John Mitford reported in his notebooks that the fragment was found in 1831 in a volume of Aristotle. Smith possessed a four-volume set of the works of Aristotle in Greek and Latin, edited by Guillaume Du Val, Royal Professor of Greek and Latin at the University of Paris, and published at Paris in a second edition in 1629 (Mizuta). David Raphael has given reasons for conjecturing that the fragment was discovered in the third one, containing the *Nicomachean Ethics* (*TMS* 396–7). He suggests that, in composing *TMS* from his lectures, Smith would wish to check his statements against his sources such as Aristotle. The lecture fragment had indicated that 'doing good according to the most perfect propriety' is known 'in the Schools', i.e. in the medieval scholastic tradition thought of as descending from Aristotle, as 'distributive justice'. *TMS* at VII.ii.I.10 shows how Smith had qualified this bald view. He added a footnote, citing the *Nicomachean Ethics* (5.2), to make clear that the 'distributive justice of Aristotle is somewhat different . . . [consisting] of the distribution of rewards from the public stock of a community'. In the fragment, Smith expresses the view that commutative justice can 'alone properly be called Justice', by which he means the negative form of not harming a neighbour in person, estate, or reputation; and he holds to this position throughout his career.

The fragment deals with the concept of improper punishment, about which Smith comments as follows: 'punishment which is either not due at all or which exceeds the demerit of the Crime, is an injury to the Criminal.' He also takes up the case of the sentry who is executed for sleeping at his post. But he claims that the punishment is justified on the grounds of utility, 'meerly from a View to the general interest of Society'. At odds with his view that excessive punishment is an 'injury to the Criminal', and therefore unjust, he says with regard to the execution of the sentry: 'In our hearts we cannot blame this necessary Severity. Nothing can be more just, than that the one man should be sacrificed to the security of thousands.'

The sleeping sentry appears again both in the *Lectures on Jurisprudence* ((A) ii.92 and (B) 182) and *TMS* (II.ii.3.11). In his book, Smith omits the words about injury, perhaps indicating he sees a problem, but he has not found a solution to the conflict between our sense of injustice (a 'natural moral sentiment') and util-itarian considerations. Family memories of his father's role as Clerk of the Court Martial in Scotland, as mentioned in Chapter 1, may have aroused his interest in the case of the sleeping sentry. Also, family background may have its part to play as well as his reading, when he dealt with the 'Laws of War' and other legal topics covered in the third part of Smith's moral philosophy course heralded in the fragment from the ethics lectures:

The Rules by which it is most suitable to the natural principles of Justice, or to the Analogy of those Sentiments upon which our Sense of it is founded that such descisions should be regulated, constitute what is called Natural Jurisprudence, or the Theory of the general principles of Law. They make a very important part of the Theory of moral Sentiments. I shall not at present, however, stop to analyse them, as I intend hereafter to give a particular discourse upon that Subject. (*TMS* 389)

In Millar's account of the lectures that constituted this 'particular discourse', he draws attention to its debt to a new source of thought about natural jurispru-dence, adding the contribution of Montesquieu to the tradition familiar to Smith from his student days, represented by the writings of Grotius, Pufendorf, and Hutcheson:

Upon this subject [Smith] followed the plan that seems to be suggested by Montesquieu; endeavouring to trace the gradual progress of jurisprudence, both public and private, from the rudest to the most refined ages, and to point out the effects of those arts which con-tribute to subsistence, and to the accumulation of property, in producing correspondent improvements or alterations in law and government. (Stewart i.19)

In his own enquiry into the history of government in England, Millar developed further the approach taken by Smith, making clear its origin and the stimulus it gave him:

I am happy to acknowledge the obligations I feel myself under to this illustrious philoso-pher [Adam Smith], by having, at an early period of life, had the benefit of hearing his lectures on the History of Civil Society, and of enjoying his unreserved conversation on the same subject. The great Montesquieu pointed out the road. He was the Lord Bacon in this branch of philosophy. Dr Smith is the Newton. (Millar, 1803: ii.429–30 n.)

The reference here is to Montesquieu's *De l'esprit des lois*, which Hume was reading appreciatively in Turin shortly after it was first published in 1748. Montesquieu later sent Hume a copy of his book as a mark of his regard for the *Essays Moral and Political* (1748), in which Hume had offered insights into his-torical causation and the relationship between social circumstance and legal and other institutions. By 1749 Hume had helped to see through the press in Edinburgh excerpts in translation from *De l'esprit des lois* which had received its author's final corrections.

A direct link between the Scottish literati and Montesquieu was provided by

John Black, a wine merchant who was a member of Montesquieu's circle in Bordeaux and the father of Smith's friend and colleague at Glasgow, the medical scientist Joseph Black. Also interested in Montesquieu's work were Smith's patron Lord Kames and another Glasgow friend, Sir John Dalrymple of Cranstoun, who was involved with Smith in publishing the poetry of Hamilton of Bangour (Ross, 1972: 203–4). It is entirely possible that interest in Montesquieu's 'philosophical history' was reflected in Smith's Edinburgh lectures on 'civil law'. The primary insight of the French author to which Smith and his friends responded was that of the dynamism of law responding to human needs in varying and historically changing social and economic environments.[1]

Through good fortune, we have evidence about the presentation of Smith's Glasgow lectures on jurisprudence during three separate sessions. Probably between 1753 and 1755, John Anderson, a former student at Glasgow University who became Smith's colleague as Professor of Oriental Languages (1754–6) and then Natural Philosophy (from 1757), made in his Commonplace Book what seems to be selective extracts from a student's report of the jurisprudence part of Smith's moral philosophy course (Univ. of Strathclyde, Anderson Lib., Anderson Commonplace Book, MS 35.1: 292–368; Meek, 1977: 57–91). The order of the main topics appears to have been as follows: introductory; property (including testaments); contract; criminal law; husband and wife; parent and child; master and servant; government; and 'police' (a French term originally covering regulations about cleanliness, security, and cheapness of goods, but expanded by Smith in *LJ* to deal with regulations intended to promote 'opulence' or, as we would say, economic growth). This order is close to that observed in the textbook by Hutcheson, already mentioned, used at Glasgow: *Philosophiae moralis institutio compendiaria* (1742). A section title of this, 'De Rerum Pretium', is echoed in the heading for a discussion of prices in the Anderson extracts, 'De Pretio Rerum'. Also, there are two specific page references in the extracts to the English translation of this work, *A Short Introduction to Moral Philosophy* (1747), rather than to the final and expanded version of Hutcheson's thought, *A System of Moral Philosophy* (1755).

The extracts in Anderson's Commonplace Book reveal, however, that Smith had been stimulated to think in a fresh way about these topics as a result of reading Montesquieu, to whom there are a number of references, some admiring: '[his] division of the powers in a state very just' (p. [39]), and some critical: 'Fur manifestus and non manifestus [theft in the act and suspected]. Vide L'Esprit des Loix, an ingenious account but it seems not to be just' (p. [19]). Smith seems to have been led to think more deeply about one of the factors affecting a country's laws, namely, subsistence, and to have extended Montesquieu's idea that there were principally three such modes: those of huntsmen, shepherds, and farmers.

Ronald Meek believed that in the lectures reflected in the Anderson notes, Smith had not arrived at the fully fledged stadial theory of *LJ*(A) and (B). In particular, he had not separated unambiguously the economic base of each 'state of perfection in society' from the connected set of arrangements concerning property. The notes open, indeed, with comments derived from Montesquieu on the three states in relation to the issue of holding property, but a fourth state is described (p. [12]) as that of the 'establishment of commerce', when Smith considered the enclosure movement that began in England. Smith associated this state with manufacturing and trading, also with populousness of towns and villages, and demand-pull in agriculture which caused change to the common ownership of grazing land. Smith's thought about the four states of society is clear enough, though it is true that the notes are somewhat garbled.

It was from Hutcheson's concept of natural jurisprudence, however, that Smith's teaching about economics took its origin. In the *Short Introduction to Moral Philosophy*, also in the posthumous *System*, Hutcheson introduced chapters on prices, money, and interest as part of a general discussion of contract (in each work, bk. ii, chs. 12, 13). Hutcheson's general argument was that justice resided in the upholding of the individual's rights, both 'real' and 'personal'. He noted that the principal 'real' right was property, whose transference frequently required contracts. As a corollary, he pointed out that contracts often gave rise to 'personal' rights. In his view, contracts are the 'main engine of constituting either personal rights or real' (Hutcheson, 1969: v.358). Since he reckoned that property is freely transferred through gifts or for 'valuable consideration in commerce', Hutcheson is then led to deal with prices and money: 'to maintain any commerce among men in interchange of goods and services, the values of them must be in some way estimated.' If reported accurately in the Anderson extracts, Smith's early jurisprudence lectures also dealt with price and money under the heading of contract. The extracts suggest, however, that Smith went considerably beyond Hutcheson through including such matters as bills of exchange, stocks, and paper money. It can be suggested that, in the Anderson extracts, we see the birth of Smith's treatment of economics, perhaps resulting from his awareness that Glasgow had arrived at a relatively advanced stage of commerce, and students there would be naturally curious about a range of topics associated with contract. Further, a reference to Hume's essay 'Of Interest' (p. [12]), one of the seven economic pieces in the *Political Discourses* of 1752, reveals that Smith was keeping up with the developing relevant literature of economics (Meek, 1977: 73–4, 77–81, 85).

When we turn to firmer and fuller evidence about the contents of Smith's lectures on jurisprudence, in the form of reports of lectures delivered in two concurrent academic sessions: 1762–3 (*LJ*(A)) and 1763–4 (*LJ*(B)), we find that by this time the economic material had been transferred from the section on contract to that dealing with police. John Millar gave the following account of this division:

In the last part of his lectures, [Smith] examined those political regulations which are founded, not upon the principle of *justice*, but upon that of *expediency*, and which are calculated to increase the riches, the power, and the prosperity of a State. Under this view, he considered the political institutions relating to commerce, to finances, to ecclesiastical and military establishments. What he delivered on these subjects contained the substance of the work he afterwards published under the title of An Inquiry into the Nature and Causes of the Wealth of Nations. (Stewart i.20)

Accepting Millar's last remark as a guide, we shall deal with the lectures on police in Chapter 16, devoted to the scope of *WN*.

As to the origins and nature of the two reports themselves, (B) was discovered in manuscript in 1876, and on 21 April 1895 its survival was reported by an Edinburgh advocate, Charles C. Maconochie, to Edwin Cannan, a Professor at the London School of Economics, who edited it for publication by Oxford University Press in 1896. The octavo book containing the manuscript bears on its title-page the wording 'Jurisprudence or Notes from the Lectures on Justice, Police, Revenue, and Arms delivered in the University of Glasgow by Adam Smith Professor of Moral Philosophy'. To this information is added the date 'MDCCLXVI' which, together with internal evidence, has been taken to mean that the manuscript was produced in 1766 by a professional copyist working from a rewritten version compiled from notes actually taken in the moral philosophy classroom in 1763–4. Now, Smith left his Chair in January 1764, arranging that his course should be taught by a substitute, Thomas Young, who took his MA at Glasgow in 1763 and was therefore a former student. Since Young was enrolled as a divinity student at the time, it is probable that he dictated material Smith had left him, suggesting that *LJ*(B) is a better guide to what Smith wrote, just as *LJ*(A), based on a student's notes of 1762–3, is the better guide to Smith's delivery of the lectures. While (B) offers, in addition, a relatively reliable index, it has more of the character of a summary in places, and unlike (A) it does not give the dates of actual lectures (Raphael, 1976: 6–8; *LJ* intro.).

One other important difference between the two reports is found in the organization of the contents. In (B), Smith states his main thesis concerning the origin and nature of government:

Property and civil government very much depend on one another. The preservation of property and inequality of possession first formed it, and the state of property must always vary with the form of government.

He then offers a comment about the order of treatment of the main topics that arise from this approach:

The civilians [authorities on civil law originating in Rome] begin with considering government and then treat of property and other rights. Others who have written on this subject begin with the latter and then consider family and civil government. There are several advantages peculiar to each of these methods, tho' that of the civil law seems upon the whole preferable. (*LJ*(B) 11)

(B) adopts the procedure of the 'civilians' taking up government, domestic law, property, and other rights, and then 'police', chiefly in the sense of the 'most proper way of procuring wealth and abundance' (p. 205), which points us towards Smith's political economy.

An indication of the impact of Smith's legal thought, and that of jurists who contributed to the Scottish Enlightenment such as Lord Kames and John Millar, can be found in an outline of 1788 of the class of the Professor of Public Law and the Law of Nature and Nations at Edinburgh University. This gives the large picture of the kind of course that Smith delivered on in historical natural jurisprudence:

[The Professor] traces the rise of political institutions from the natural character and situation of the human species; follows their progress through the rude periods of society; and treats of their history and merits, as exhibited in the principal nations of ancients and modern times, which he examines separately, classing them according to those general causes to which he attributes the principal varieties in the forms, genius, and revolutions in government. In this manner, he endeavours to construct the science of the spirit of laws [*a revealing echo of Montesquieu*] on a connected view of what may be called the natural history of man as a political agent; and he accordingly concludes his course with treating of the general principles of municipal law, political oeconomy, and the law of nations. (Arnot, 1788: 398)

The teacher of this class was Allan Maconochie, later raised to the Bench as the 1st Lord Meadowbank. Presenting this passage in his account of Smith's influence on legal education in Scotland, John Cairns notes that this Professor was not a pupil of Smith's, but that he was the father of the first identified owner of *LJ*(B), James Allen Maconochie. Accordingly, there arises the intriguing possibility that the Professor may have obtained this text of Smith's lectures as an aid to preparing his own course (Cairns, 1992: 182–3).

As for *LJ*(A) (1762–3), like the Anderson extracts from the early 1750s, it follows the plan of 'others who have written on this subject', including Francis Hutcheson, as we have seen. Thus, it covers property and other rights, domestic law, government, and finally police. Unfortunately, report (A) is incomplete through stopping roughly two-thirds of the way through the police section of the course. Possibly a seventh volume of the manuscript is missing. The other six were discovered by Professor John M. Lothian in 1958, together with two other volumes containing the rhetoric lectures, among books and papers sold from the library of the Forbes-Leith family of Whitehaugh in Aberdeenshire. J. C. Bryce conjectured that they were brought to Whitehaugh by a tutor of members of the family, who was either a former student of Smith's or acquired the reports of the lectures directly or indirectly from someone who attended them. Another possibility is that Smith's successor in the Chair of Moral Philosophy, Thomas Reid, who came from Aberdeenshire and maintained links there, may have passed on the reports to a notably bookish family. He certainly made an appeal for such reports (*LRBL* intro. 1–2). In his inaugural lecture at Glasgow on 10 October 1764, Reid said that he would be 'much obliged to any of you Gentlemen or to any other, who can furnish me with Notes of [Smith's]

Prelections whether in Morals, Jurisprudence, Police, or in Rhetorick' (AUL Birkwood MS 2131/4/II).

To be sure, Smith did not encourage the taking down of notes in his classes, an attitude that was well known in his time and referred to in an obituary: 'the Doctor was in general extremely jealous of the property of his lectures . . . and, fearful lest they should be transcribed and published, used often to repeat, when he saw anyone taking notes, that "he hated scribblers" ' (*Gentleman's Magazine*, 60 (1790), 762). It is possible, however, that he would agree with a point made by Thomas Reid, that if students who wrote most in class understood least, 'those who write at home after carefull recollection, understand most, and write to the best Purpose' (AUL Birkwood MS 2131/8/III). This is precisely what is needed for thoughtful reconstruction of a philosophical discourse.

Smith's lecturing schedule was a demanding one, and Hume may well have been correct in fearing that the 'Fatigues of your Class' brought illness to his friend in the spring of 1753 (*Corr.* No. 13). From 10 October until 10 June, with only statutory holidays as relief, Smith lectured every week day for an hour to the full moral philosophy class from 7.30 a.m., and then at 11 a.m. he examined for another hour about a third of those who had attended the first lecture. These were the meetings of his 'public' class. On three days a week, Mondays, Wednesdays, and Fridays, he lectured from noon until 1 p.m. to his 'private' class.

From *LJ*(A) and *LRBL* we can reconstruct most fully the cycle of Smith's lectures for 1762–3. From October until Christmas Eve 1762, in his 'public' class he must have lectured on natural theology and ethics. He seems to have begun the rhetoric course on 17 November and to have completed it by 17 February 1763. Thereafter until the end of the session, we presume he taught the history of philosophy to his 'private' class. On 24 December he began the jurisprudence course, and after dealing with private and domestic law by mid-February, he opened the topic of justice with his 'public' class on Monday 21 February, and under that heading had completed by 24 March his account of the four-stage development of government institutions arising in turn from hunting and fishing, pastoralism, agriculture, and commerce as modes of subsistence. Next he discussed the rise and decay of feudalism, the growth of Tudor despotism in England, and then the ensuing restoration of civil liberty as a result of Parliament's opposition to James I and Charles I. In this section, Smith added his insights to those of Hume, Kames, and Dalrymple of Cranstoun, themselves stimulated by the inquiries of Montesquieu into the spirit of laws. Smith spoke of the power of the nobles declining in England as elsewhere because of the 'introduction of arts, commerce, and luxury' (*LJ*(A) iv.157), and he took up the theme of opulence created through commerce in the section of his course devoted to police, which began on 28 March and must have run through May at least, though we lack the report of the lectures after 13 April (*LJ* intro. 15–22).

According to James Wodrow's much later recollection, in teaching his 'public' class:

[Smith] made a laudable attempt at first to follow Hut[cheson]'s animated manner, lecturing on Ethics without Papers walking up and down his Class room: but not having the same facility in this that Hut[cheson] had, either naturally, or acquired by continued practise and habit in teaching his Academy at Dublin; Dr Smith soon relinquished the Attempt and read with propriety, all the rest of his valuable Lectures from the Desk. His Theory of Moral Sentiments founded on Sympathy, a very ingenious attempt to account for the principal phaenomena in the moral world from this one general principle, like that of Gravity in the natural World, did not please Hutcheson's Scholars, so well, as that to which they had been accustomed. The rest of his Lectures were admired by them, and by all, especially those on Money and commerce. (Mitchell Lib., Buchan MSS, Baillie 32225, fos. 47–51)

This picture of the young Professor Smith seeking to follow the practice of the ebullient Hutcheson, and then prudently retiring to the security of his desk to read his lectures, is complemented by a description of his handling of the opportunity for extempore teaching during the examination hour for the moral philosophy class. That other student of his, William Richardson, found great merit in the oral examination method:

Such examinations are reckoned of great utility to those who study, as tending to ensure their attention, to ascertain their proficiency, and give the teacher an opportunity of explaining more clearly any part of the lecture which may not have been fully understood. Those who received instruction from Dr Smith, will recollect, with much satisfaction, many of those incidental and digressive illustrations and even discussions, not only on morality, but in criticism, which were delivered by him with animated and extemporaneous eloquence, as they were suggested in the course of question and answer. They occurred likewise, with much display of learning and knowledge, in his occasional explanations of those philosophical works of Cicero, which are also a very useful and important subject of examination in the class of Moral Philosophy. (Richardson, 1803: 507–8)

Further evidence about Smith's 'animated and extemporaneous eloquence' comes from John Millar, who wrote that his former teacher in delivering his lectures 'trusted almost entirely to extemporary elocution'. Millar remembered a 'plain and unaffected' rather than 'graceful' manner, and another witness mentioned a 'harsh' voice and 'thick' enunciation, 'approaching to stammering' (Carlyle, 1973: 141).

Millar also noted in Smith that crucial interest in his subject which 'never failed to interest his hearers'. Very likely recalling the ethics or jurisprudence courses he attended, Millar described a characteristic pattern of organization which seems to reflect Smith's account of 'didactic eloquence' (*LRBL* ii.125–6), also a love of paradox which Smith claimed in his 'History of Astronomy' (iv.34) was 'so natural to the learned':

Each discourse commonly consisted of several distinct propositions, which [Smith] successively endeavoured to prove and illustrate. These propositions, when announced in general terms, had, from their extent, not infrequently something of the air of a paradox. In his attempts to explain them, he often appeared, at first, not to be sufficiently possessed of the subject, and spoke with some hesitation. As he advanced, however, the matter seemed to crowd upon him, his manner became warm and animated, and his expression easy and fluent. In points susceptible of controversy, you could easily discern that he secretly conceived an opposition to his opinions, and that he was led upon this account to support them with greater energy and vehemence. By the fulness and variety of his illustrations, the subject gradually swelled in his hands, and acquired a dimension which, without a tedious repetition of the same views, was calculated to seize the attention of his audience, and to afford them pleasure, as well as instruction, in following the same object, through all the diversity of shades and aspects in which it was presented, and afterwards in tracing it backwards to that original proposition or general truth from which this beautiful speculation had proceeded. (Stewart i.21)

We might think of Smith expounding his ethical doctrine concerning the objects of reward and punishment in this fashion, or the economic one of free trade (on 6 April 1763, for example, *LJ*(A) vi.87). There could be added to this picture in our mind's eye details of Smith's reliance on signs of the sympathy or lack of it of a selected hearer for gauging the effect of what he was saying. Smith described his practice thus to Archibald Alison the elder, an Edinburgh magistrate and Lord Provost:

During one whole session a certain student with a plain but expressive countenance was of great use to me in judging of my success. He sat conspicuously in front of a pillar: I had him constantly under my eye. If he leant forward to listen all was right, and I knew that I had the ear of my class; but if he leant back in an attitude of listlessness I felt at once that all was wrong, and that I must change either the subject or the style of my address.[2]

Thus, all the contemporary reports we have suggest that Adam Smith found the best situation for his abilities as a Professor at Glasgow. His years of study, and preliminary experience as a lecturer at Edinburgh, came to fruition in excellent and appreciated teaching of seminal ideas. Of particular significance was his growing sophistication of economic analysis in the jurisprudence lectures, as he extended the natural-law tradition of Grotius and Pufendorf, relayed through Carmichael and Hutcheson, in discussing value and exchange, and added his perspective to the comparative vision of Montesquieu and Hume concerning social and institutional transformation. It must indeed have been inspiring for his students to hear Smith expound his views on the dynamics of the creation of civil society and the alteration of values in its successive stages.

9

Teacher

by far the most useful, and, therefore, . . . by far the happiest and most honourable period of my life

Adam Smith's usefulness to the society of Glasgow University lay above all in his relationships with and impact on his students, those he dealt with generally in his classes and those he supervised personally. There is valuable evidence about the behaviour and responses of his students in the 'private' class, as well as of part of the instruction they received there, in the two slim volumes of the 'Notes of Dr Smith's Rhetorick Lectures', which Professor Lothian also turned up at the Whitehaugh library sale in 1958 (*LRBL* intro. 1).

John Bryce's assessment is that the 'Notes' appear to consist of transcriptions from jottings made in class rendered in two hands with a third hand, perhaps that of a later owner, chiefly represented touching up faded letters. The first writer seems to have worked from and revised full jottings made in class, recording such matters as that Lectures 21 and 24 were delivered by Smith without his 'Book', presumably the Professor's written-out version. The second writer filled in gaps in the transcriptions of the first one and made corrections in some places, but there was less need for this from Lecture 16 on, since the first writer got better at his job (*LRBL* 4–6). This person had a sense of humour, doodling a face which is perhaps that of Smith, and adding the remark: 'This is a picture of uncertainty' (ii.67). He also noted a joke made by Henry Herbert, an English aristocrat who was a boarder in Smith's house during the 1762–3 session. On Christmas Eve 1762, Smith discussed in the fifteenth rhetoric lecture La Bruyère's account of the absent-minded man, Menalcas. Herbert adapted a tag from Horace (*Satires* 1.1.69–70): *Mutato nomine de te fabula*, and wittily equated Menalcas and his Professor (*LRBL* i.196). Smith throughout his career, of course, was often painted at the epitome of absent-mindedness.

It cannot be claimed that Smith, after devising a system of rhetoric for his Edinburgh auditors, as we are led to believe, made great efforts to bring his lectures up to date for his Glasgow students. References to books or pieces published in or after 1751 are, therefore, few in number. In the extemporaneous Lecture 21 (*LRBL* ii.96), Thomas Gray's *Elegy in a Country Churchyard* (1751) is mentioned favourably, along with the *Ode on a Distant Prospect of Eton College*

(1747; Dodsley's 1748 *Collection*) and William Shenstone's *Pastoral Ballad* (anon. 1751; Dodsley's 1755 *Collection*). In Lecture 23, delivered on 21 January 1763, Smith refers to 'translations lately published' of 'Erse poetry' (ii.113), which could be James Macpherson's Ossianic *Fragments* (1760) or the 'epic' *Fingal* ([Dec. 1761], 1762). *Temora* (1763) was not published until March 1763. There is also the added marginal note referring to Hume's *History of England* (ii.73), which we have already discussed.

A further updating connects Lecture 3 on the 'origin and progress of language' with Rousseau's *Discours sur . . . l'inégalité*, published on 24 April 1755, which Smith had quoted from extensively within a few months to illustrate his comments on it in his letter to the *Edinburgh Review* (2 Mar. 1756). Smith points out that his lecture (i.v.19) offers an answer to a problem formulated by Rousseau: how could men create words without generalizing, and how could they generalize without words (i, ss. 23–31)? As mentioned earlier, however, Smith's declared starting-point for thinking philosophically about the history of language was Girard's *Les vrais principes de la langue françoise* (1747). We can go behind that even, for example, to find precursors for his account of cave-dwelling savages inventing, with ease, a jargon to refer to objects needed for food, drink, and shelter, then, with more difficulty, generalizing by abstraction to apply nouns to classes of nouns. This conjecture has an ancestry taking us back at least to Mandeville's *Fable of the Bees* (1729). There we read of a 'wild Pair' (a parody of Adam and Eve) who communicate first with 'Signs and Gestures' about basic necessities including sex, and we learn that speech only tentatively and slowly appeared, without forethought or plan, to help a speaker persuade others what he wanted them to believe, or to compel them to do what he wanted (pt. ii, Sixth Dialogue; Hudson, 1992). We find that Smith in his *Edinburgh Review* letter (11) states that part ii of the *Fable of the Bees* inspired Rousseau's 'system' of human nature and society.

Smith's conjectures about jargon-inventing savages also seem to be based on Condillac's account, in his *Essai sur l'origine des connoissances humaines* (1746), of the first speakers being 'two children' wandering in a desert, whose dialogue created a manner of thinking about themselves, their interests, and environment, representing a dawning of consciousness and reason (2.1.1). In putting his teaching about language into such a context, Smith was giving his students an idea of the ongoing European debate about linguistic origins and developments, in part begun by Locke's *Essay concerning Human Understanding*, and he provided an example of his own pioneering contributions such as the distinction between 'original' (synthetic) languages and 'compounded' ones. The intellectual confidence bred by his dissemination of his thought, including the separate publication of the language lecture as *Considerations concerning the first formation of Languages*, in the *Philological Miscellany* (1761), made its mark on his countrymen, and is reflected in such works as the first edition of the *Encyclopaedia Britannica*, an Edinburgh publication. Its article on Language (1771, vol. ii), anonymous but probably written by William Smellie, deals with typology in the Smithian manner (Plank, 1987: 1992).

Mercifully, Professor Smith did not forget the pleasure principle in his learned and innovative discourses to his 'private' class, and the young gentlemen on the benches in front of him must have heard with some relief, toward the conclusion of the lecture on Friday, 19 November 1762 that he would 'altogether pass over many other grammaticall parts as taedious and unentertaining' (i.16). Perhaps they also took comfort after the defects of English were exposed, from thinking that their Professor was reckoned to have a good English accent. The astute among them would certainly notice that the same methodology that accounted for the formation of languages on 22 November 1762 was adopted at the end of December of the same year, when Smith lectured on savages taming by natural contrivance the animals they hunted. In this way, hunters became shepherds who managed flocks and herds, representing a further stage in human development, complemented in turn by those of agriculture and commerce, which constituted the history of civil society (*LJ*(A) i.27).

As the rhetoric course progressed, students heard on Monday, 29 November 1762 that Smith's system for this subject was of a piece with the one he devised for ethics. He made this clear by challenging the standpoint of traditional rhetoric that the expressive *force* and *beauty* of language reside in figure of speech. Smith's claim is altogether different:

When the sentiment of the speaker is expressed in a neat, clear, plain and clever manner, and the passion or affection he is poss⟨ess⟩ed of and intends, *by sympathy* [reporter's italics], to communicate to his hearer, is plainly and cleverly hit off, then and then only the expression has all the force and beauty that language can give it. (*LRBL* i.v.56)

Thus, sympathy was presented as the 'Hinge' of Smith's system of Rhetoric, as Hume had noticed it performed the same function in the system of Ethics (*Corr.* No. 36).

In the second part of the course, dealing mainly with composition, Smith brought in the history of civil society, commenting on the fact that, as societies become commercial and opulent, prose is cultivated. It is 'naturally the Language of Business; as Poetry is of pleasure and amusement'. His general assessment was that 'Opulence and Commerce commonly precede the improvement of arts, and refinement of every Sort'. Lest the Glasgow students should congratulate themselves that their thriving city would inevitably witness artistic triumphs, however, he hastened to add: 'I do not mean that the improvement of arts and refinement of manners are the necessary consequence of Commerce, the Dutch and the Venetians bear testimony against me, but only that it is a necessary requisite' (ii.115–16). If some might think this statement showed blindness to the level of accomplishment in painting and architecture in Renaissance Venice and in seventeenth-century Amsterdam, at least Smith was on safer ground in taking up the theme of cultural relativism, and observing that Athenian oratory designed for a democracy would not have suited Rome with its patrician order of government (ii.162–3).

Smith could teach rhetoric as the staple of his 'private' moral philosophy class because his successor as Professor of Logic, James Clow, reverted to the traditional approach of Loudoun to the subject. In turn, however, Clow was succeeded by George Jardine (matriculated 1760), who was one of Smith's favourite pupils in the 1760s. Jardine shared Smith's view about reorganizing the logic course, and described his own scheme most fully in the second edition of *Outlines of Philosophical Education, illustrated by the Method of Teaching the Logic Class in the University of Glasgow* (1825). This book incorporates the legacy of Smith's reformulation of rhetoric and its integration into university studies, pedagogical practice maintained in higher education across North America from Smith's time until ours (Charvat, 1961: ch. 3; Corbett, 1965: 563–8; May, 1978: 346–50).

There were others besides Jardine and John Millar among Smith's students who went on to occupy university Chairs and spread their teacher's influence (Addison, 1913; Matthew, 1966; Webster, 1988). William Trail attended the moral philosophy class in 1763 after being a student at Marischal College, Aberdeen, and he returned there to become Professor of Mathematics (1766–79), a subject of great interest to Smith. From a slightly earlier time in the same class came William Richardson and Archibald Arthur, already cited for their evidence about Smith's teaching, both of whom matriculated in 1758. The first was retained as tutor to the sons of Lord Cathcart, and attended him as Secretary of his Embassy to St Petersburg (1768–72), thereafter assuming the Glasgow Chair of Humanity from 1773 until 1814. Responding, it seems, to Smith's handling of the rhetorical tradition of *ethologia* (Quintilian 1.9.3), in the form of the character sketches of the Plain Man (Swift) and Simple Man (Temple), Richardson produced *A philosophical analysis and illustration of some of Shakespeare's remarkable characters* (1774, 1784, 1788; Bryce, *LRBL* intro. 17). In some ways this marks the beginning of Shakespearean criticism focusing on character study.

As Keeper of the Library from 1774 until 1794, one focus of Smith's activities as an administrator at Glasgow, Arthur carried through the improvement of classifying the books according to the system of the Advocates' Library in Edinburgh. Then, as Thomas Reid's associate and successor, Arthur reverted to Smith's practice in delivering in the 'private' class of moral philosophy courses on rhetoric and the history of philosophy.

To be sure, Smith's teaching was taken further afield than Glasgow and Aberdeen. In 1761 the celebrated Genevan physician and contributor to the *Encyclopédie*, Théodore Tronchin, whose patients included members of the French royal family as well as Voltaire and who was the adversary of Rousseau, sent his son, François Louis, to Glasgow expressly to be educated by Smith before returning to his native Switzerland. That same year two Russian students, Semyon Efimovich Desnitsky and Ivan Andreyevich Tret'yakov, came to Glasgow and spent six years there, studying chiefly under Smith and John Millar as part of Catherine the Great's plan to send outstanding young Russians abroad to complete their education.

On returning home they both became Professors of Law at Moscow University, founded as recently as 1755, where they clashed with their mainly German colleagues over the issues of teaching in Russian instead of Latin, and passed on to their students the liberal jurisprudence to which they had been exposed at Glasgow (*Speeches at . . . Moscow University*, 1819; Penchko, 1962). Their published lectures reveal that they made use of Smith's four-stage analysis of the changing economic conditions of society as these affected the development of law, and Desnitsky in particular advocated legal and constitutional reform in line with Smith's principles (Alekseyev, 1937; Sacke, 1938). This advocacy is to be found in his 'Proposal concerning the Establishment of Legislative, Judicial and Executive Authorities in the Russian Empire', which he addressed to the Empress in February 1768. She responded in April of the same year by incorporating some of Desnitsky's formulations derived from Smith's lectures in the Second Supplement to her Nakaz (Edicts), noticeably in relation to ideas concerning the expenses of the sovereign, also the rules for taxation and the striking down of monopolies (Brown, 1974; 1975). Desnitsky made intelligent and critical use of Smith's ideas, so it appears, and adapted them to the Russian context of his day. Tret'yakov seems to have been less original in basing himself on Smith's lectures on jurisprudence, which are followed closely, for example, in a work meant to deal with the poverty of nations entitled 'A Discourse on the Causes of Public Opulence and the Slow Enrichment of Ancient and Modern Nations' (1772; Anikin, 1988: ch. 3).

The Russian students were sent to Glasgow on the recommendation of William Murray, Lord Mansfield, expert on commercial law and the first Lord Chief Justice of England to have a Scottish background, whose judicial eloquence Smith praised in *LRBL*. The University advanced them money in October 1762 through Adam Smith, when their Russian sources dried up. They applied for and ultimately obtained in 1767 doctorates in law as a result of 'attendance on Dr Smith's class of Ethicks and Jurisprudence and . . . attendance for three years on Mr Millar's class of civil law', and after submitting to 'Trials' and presenting theses on Justinian's *Pandects* found acceptable by Dean of Faculty George Muirhead and John Millar. Their time at Glasgow was not entirely smooth, for Desnitsky was disciplined by the Lord Rector for pulling off the wig of Professor John Anderson after a fracas about singing in the Chapel.

It appears that, through these former students, Smith's economic policy advice won a hearing in Russia eight years before the publication of *WN*.[1] Other Russians became enthusiastic about the book on its appearance, for example, the Vorontsov family; and when Princess Dashkova and her son Prince Pavel stayed in Edinburgh, 1776–9, they made a point of entertaining Smith in their home (Cross, 1980: 123–8, 131–3; Anikin, 1990: 81, 132, 307, 309, 311).

To be sure, Smith taught students who made their mark in law and government at home. One was Ilay Campbell of Succoth, a registrant in Professor Craigie's moral philosophy class in 1751 and therefore auditor of Smith's first courses on jurisprudence and politics, delivered when the ailing Craigie went to Lisbon that year. Campbell was described by Boswell in 1774 as the 'finest writing lawyer' in Scotland, where his talents earned him £1,600 a year. He was made Solicitor-General in 1783 and then Lord Advocate from that year until 1789, in the first administration of Pitt the Younger, ending his career as President of the Court of Session from 1789 until 1808. He retained his affection for Glasgow University and served as Lord Rector, 1799–1801. It was surely a tribute to Smith and his other teachers that a contemporary wrote of Ilay Campbell that he was 'greatly superior' to his brother judges 'in a genuine and liberal taste for the law's improvement, and the only one whose mind was thoroughly opened to the comprehension of modern mercantile jurisprudence' (Cockburn, 1856: 126).

Another judge, who sat as Lord Cullen from 1796 until his death in 1810, was Robert, son of Smith's friend and physician William Cullen. Smith described this young man, who matriculated in Professor George Rosse's humanity class in 1753, as the 'best Scholar he had ever had' (EUL La. II 451/2). He may well have recommended Cullen for his first post, succeeding John Millar as tutor to George Home Drummond, son of Smith's own patron, Lord Kames. Cullen's highly social disposition extended to entertainment of company with excellent mimicry, particularly of Principal Robertson of Edinburgh University. He was an active member of the Mirror Club and other literary societies in Edinburgh together with William Craig, matriculated 1758, who also became a Session Court judge. Both Cullen and Craig contributed to periodicals such as the *Mirror* and *Lounger* as proponents of Smith's ethical teaching (Dwyer, 1987: 29).

Destined for a career in law like his father, Lord Auchinleck, another judge of this period, but aspiring to distinction in politics, though authorship was his true vocation, was James Boswell, who matriculated at Glasgow on 17 November 1759 after six years at Edinburgh University. Besides taking the civil law course given by Hercules Lindesay, he attended lectures by Adam Smith, both the 'public' moral philosophy series and the 'private' rhetoric one. At this time, Boswell praised Smith highly for his accuracy and elegance of exposition, and he was greatly attracted by Smith's remark to the effect that even the smallest detail concerning a great man, such as Milton's reliance on latchets rather than buckles for his shoes, is of interest (*LRBL* 17–18). It is possible that this remark was an impetus to his own procedure as a writer of journals and biographer in building up scenes and portraits by accretion of factual details. Also, a case can be made for the role of Smith's notion of 'moral sentiments' in the creation of Boswellian biography (Turnbull, 1994).

Boswell noted Smith's benevolent disposition, as well as the pleasure he took in the company of his students, and he often referred to Smith's discerning judgement, expressed in a letter which unfortunately has not so far come to light, that Boswell had a 'happy facility of manners', certainly a trait to which figures as diverse as Hume, Dr Johnson, General Paoli, Rousseau, and Voltaire all paid their tribute. Flattering though Smith's approval was, it did not detain Boswell in Glasgow long, for he ran off to London in March 1760 to become a Roman Catholic convert, contemplate entering a monastery abroad, and settle for libertinism, all within three weeks (Pottle, 1965; 1966: 230–53).

A contemporary of Boswell's at Glasgow, matriculating on 8 January 1759, was the Hon. Thomas Petty Fitzmaurice, a gentleman boarder in Smith's house, whose student experiences are better documented in a series of letters than those of any other. He was introduced to Smith in a letter of 14 November 1758 by Gilbert Elliot of Minto, who wrote that he had described the nature of the Scottish universities to the young man's brother, Viscount Fitzmaurice (later Prime Minister under the title 2nd Earl of Shelburne), and had stated the advantages that might be derived from education under Smith. Lord Fitzmaurice was a former student at Oxford, and had no wish to send his brother there, so he had resolved to advise his father to follow Elliot's advice (*Corr.* No. 27).

Smith reported to the elder brother on 21 February 1759 that his pupil was 'perfectly tractable and docile in every respect', and far enough advanced in Greek to be likely to read it easily within a year, an attribute necessary for the moral philosophy class. Smith also promised to have the Professor of Mathematics, Robert Simson, begin teaching Petty Fitzmaurice both algebra and arithmetic 'in about a month hence' (No. 28). A further report of 10 March describes this student attending lectures on Greek, Latin, and philosophy (logic) for five hours a day, and then employed with Smith at home for two to three hours 'in going over the subjects of those different lectures' (No. 29).

The plan for Petty Fitzmaurice's further stay at Glasgow is sketched out in a letter dated 4 April 1759. He is to finish his philosophical studies, including Smith's moral philosophy class next winter, and will attend the civil law course, to teach him what a 'System of law is, what parts it consists of, and how these ought to be arranged'. Meantime, Smith will read with him an 'institute of the feudal law', possibly Craig's *Jus Feudale*, a copy of a textbook used in the Dutch universities, which had been among Smith's father's books, and of which Smith owned James Baillie's 1732 edition (Mizuta). During the forthcoming long vacation, Smith will read with his pupil the 'best greek, latin, and french Authors on Moral Philosophy'. Also, the Professor of Mathematics, 'who is now turned seventy, but preserves all the gaiety and vigour of youth', proposes to teach him Euclid 'as he was too late to learn it in the Class' (No. 30).

The father, who was descended from Sir William Petty, inventor of political arithmetic or statistics, was delighted with this news, since he regarded the 'Study of Euclid [as] . . . a far better teacher of Reasoning than Logic', and declared:

A knowledge in the Civil Law, is the best foundation he can have to introduce him to that of his own Country, the Study of it may make him Wise, but it is upon Your Precepts and Example in Morality, that I depend for making him Happy. (No. 32)

Smith certainly set an excellent example of solicitude for the young man in his care, making sure of the company he kept when he took Petty Fitzmaurice to Edinburgh, which Smith regarded as a 'very dissolute town' (No. 42, 29 Oct. 1759), and expressing concern about his unaccountable blunders in English grammar (No. 43, 3 Dec. 1759), also watching over him with anxious care when he ran a fever in March 1760 (Nos. 45, 46, 48, 49), and had eye trouble in November of that year (Nos. 52, 53).

On 15 July 1760 Smith wrote to Lord Shelburne that he had himself contracted a cold in March; it had hung about him until June, when he thought he had recovered completely, but after he had slept in a damp bed in the vicinity of Edinburgh at the beginning of July, the cold returned with great 'violence'. On 13 June Dr Cullen, his physician, 'took [him] aside on the street of Edinburgh, and told [him] that he thought it his duty to inform [Smith] plainly that if [he] had any hope of surviving next winter [he] must ride at least five hundred miles before the beginning of September'. Smith proposed to follow what seems strange advice for Cullen to give to a man in precarious health, but it was in line with contemporary ideas about treating hypochondriasis. Accordingly, Smith planned to ride to York and the west of England, a journey which took him to Shelburne's seat at High Wycombe. His pupil was to stay on at Smith's home in Glasgow, where he was reading the 'best English authors' and, after dinner, Montesquieu's *L'Esprit des lois* (No. 51). Smith noted that the young man's bent was towards the 'mathematical and mechanical learning', and observation borne out by Petty Fitzmaurice's later career when he managed a bleaching factory on his estate at Llewenny in Wales, and in 1785 astonished a visitor, Richard Twining, with the 'building he [had] erected, and the machines and apparatus he [had] placed in them'.

In 1762 Petty Fitzmaurice went from Glasgow to Oxford, where the legal studies he had begun under Smith and Lindesay were complemented by Blackstone's celebrated lectures on the law of England (No. 64, 26 Feb. 1762). Hume encountered him in Paris in 1763 in the circle of the *philosophe*, d'Holbach, taking an interest in a French translation of *TMS* (*Corr.* No. 77). He entered Parliament in 1762, as Member for Calne, on his brother's interest, and he retained this seat until 1774, then exchanged it for Chipping Wycombe; but financial difficulties and the demands of his linen-bleaching enterprise made him give up a parliamentary career in 1780 (*HP* ii.430).

Writing to Smith from Oxford on 26 February 1762, Petty Fitzmaurice expressed agreement with Smith about the expensiveness of the place, especially in the article of coal. At the end of the letter, which he signed 'your very Affectionate Thomas Fitzmaurice', he asked to be remembered to his 'old Friend' Robert Simson, also to Smith's mother and a cousin, Janet Douglas, who had joined the Professor's household by 1754, at least, as housekeeper (*Corr.* No. 18). He sent his compliments, in addition, to an Irish student, Luke Godfrey, one of a considerable number of young men of that nationality whom Smith taught, and who were a source, undoubtedly, for some of the opinions concerning Ireland he offered in *WN*. Petty Fitzmaurice himself ventured a favourable opinion of Smith's current students: 'Your young People are in general rather brighter than they were in my time I'm told at present' (*Corr.* No. 64).

One of these bright 'young People', who had studied under Smith along with Petty Fitzmaurice, was that striking personality David Steuart Erskine, Lord Cardross, later 11th Earl of Buchan in 1767. This title was one of the most ancient in Scotland, with a history running back to the twelfth century and an association with a territorial division of the kingdom of even greater antiquity. Awareness of his venerable and complex ancestry encouraged Cardross to be endlessly curious about historical and other matters. He was also fearless to a degree in thought and action, which gave him a reputation for eccentricity. His mother, Agnes Steuart, was the granddaughter of a Lord Advocate, Sir James Steuart of Goodtrees, and sister of the political economist of the same name. She had strong intellectual interests and is said to have studied mathematics at Edinburgh under Colin Maclaurin. The legal tradition of her family was upheld brilliantly by her younger sons. Henry became Lord Advocate in 1783 and condemned the Treason and Sedition Bills of 1795 as unconstitutional. Thomas, who helped to mould English commercial law, was the intimate friend of Richard Sheridan and Charles James Fox; became Lord Chancellor; and worked to ensure Greece's independence (Cant, 1981).

Cardross did his best to help his brothers in their careers, and in a letter of 6 June 1761 alludes to the financial strain of educating them since the family estates were entailed. He gives this as a reason for seeking Smith's support for nominating Henry for a Snell Exhibition. The letter also refers to the 'Multiplyed Civilities and Kindnesse's' that Cardross had received from Smith, and encloses a letter for Thomas Petty Fitzmaurice (*Corr.* No. 55). Cardross studied at St Andrews (1755–9) and Edinburgh (1760–1) before moving to Glasgow, where his name was inscribed in the matriculation album in 1762, and where he was twice awarded the LL D, first in 1763, in Smith's time, and again in 1766. He kept a letter-book and diary recording impressions of his early years and left anecdotes of Smith, his prevailing impression being summed up in a remark he published in *The Bee* (June, 1791):

I passed most of my time at Glasgow with those two first-rate men [Millar and Smith], and Smith read private lectures to me on jurisprudence, and accompanied them with his commentaries in conversation, exercises which I hope will give a colour and a substance to my sentiments and to my reason that will be eternal.

The Duchess of Gordon thought that the wit of Cardross's family came from his mother and was 'all settled on the younger branches', and Smith may himself not always have relished the older brother's airs and eccentricities. It is entirely possible that he figures in a story 'Jupiter' Carlyle reported after being in large company with Adam Smith in Glasgow in April 1763:

a Certain Young Peer was present, after a little while I whisper'd [to Smith], That I wonder'd they had set up this Man so high, as I thought him mighty Foolish. We know that perfectly said he, but he is the only Lord at our College. (Carlyle, 1973: 220)

Earlier that year, Cardross seems to have been called out to a duel by another of Smith's students of this period, Henry Herbert, author of the *bon mot* about Smith's absent-mindedness recorded in *LRBL*. We know this from a letter from his grandmother dated 8 March 1763, which mentions Cardross' application as a student, and his practical interest in drawing and engraving which was fostered by the Academy of Art set up by the printers Robert and Andrew Foulis in the Glasgow University precincts.

As early as 1761, on a visit to Old Aberdeen, Cardross manifested a strong interest in antiquities, an abiding concern of his later life culminating in the foundation in 1780 of the Society of Antiquaries of Scotland. It took as its subject-matter 'antiquities and natural and civil history in general', and thus affirmed a connection, about which Smith's former student was fully informed, with the work of the virtuosi such as Sir Robert Sibbald and Sir John Clerk of Penicuik whose work, mentioned in Chapter 1, on the early history of Scotland, its archaeology, and its natural life and setting had contributed to the first phases of the Scottish Enlightenment. Smith's deep feeling for civil liberty had some roots in the enterprises of these virtuosi, and his enthusiasm for this concept must have struck a chord in Cardross. When the latter became Earl of Buchan, he championed John Wilkes in his struggle for liberty in Britain and that of George Washington in America.

Late in life, Buchan annotated the letter from his grandmother about his duel with Henry Herbert with some circumstantial details:

the threatened Duel . . . was occasioned by Miss Somerville of Greenock a Beauty of the day at Glasgow having given me her hand to dance at a Ball after She had promised to dance with the present Earl of Caernarvon then Henry Herbert a pupil of Adam Smith and John Millar at Glasgow. The Duel was prevented by an arrest at the instance of the College. Herbert and I were immediately after the best friends in the World.

Lady Buchan had written of Herbert:

the young Gentleman you had the Quaril with is So unfortunate too be of a Mad Family[.] Scarce any of them passes through life with reason therefore when he is in heat tis less to be regarded than another. (GUL Buchan MSS, letter of 8 Mar. 1763)

Herbert was descended from the Earls of Pembroke, and was educated at Eton and Christ Church, Oxford, before matriculating at Glasgow in 1762. Smith described him to Hume as 'very well acquainted with your works, and upon that account extremely desirous of being introduced to the Author' (22 Feb. 1763, *Corr.* No. 70). Herbert duly went to Edinburgh, where he met and impressed Hume (28 March 1763, *Corr.* No. 71), who called him 'that severe Critic' (*Corr.* No. 75). He then travelled north to Aberdeen, where he encountered Thomas

Reid, at a time when his book *An Inquiry into the Human Mind, on the Principles of Common Sense* was in the press. He found Reid a 'very sensible man', and reckoned as 'agreeable' another adversary of Hume, George Campbell, who had sought to uphold the authenticity of Christian miracles. Herbert met members of the Scottish nobility of the region: the Earl Marischal, who was the friend of Rousseau, also Lords Panmure and Deskford, who were greatly interested in agricultural improvement. In addition, Herbert was in contact with the law lords Pitfour and Kames, who were on the northern circuit of the Justiciary Court (11 Sept. 1763, *Corr.* No. 74).

It is likely that Smith's teaching and conversation fitted Herbert for discussion with these men, all of them contributors to the Scottish Enlightenment. Herbert went on to be the MP for Wilton, 1768–80, and his parliamentary career was characterized by principled conduct, chiefly aimed at upholding civil and religious liberty. At first he supported the Court during early stages of the American war, but latterly he became critical of the Administration, a stand taken by Smith. He also shared Smith's views (and apparently those of Lord Kames) regarding the disadvantages of prohibitions on foreign trade, though he fell short of standing up for a 'free port' (*HP* ii.612; Ross, 1972: 194–6). He was created Baron Porchester in 1780 and then Earl of Carnarvon in 1793, ending his public career as a Privy Councillor, 1806, and Master of the Horse, 1806–7. In 1788 he proposed sending his son, the Hon. Henry George Herbert, to be educated at Glasgow, stating to Smith a preference for it over Edinburgh, and Smith agreed with this, declaring that the young man 'will be very happy and very well taken care of' in the house of another of his pupils, George Jardine, whom he described as 'after Millar *Longo sed proximus intervallo*' (*Corr.*, app. E, p).

Of lower rank in society were other students of Adam Smith's who advanced understanding of contemporary society. For example, James Gibson, who matriculated in the moral philosophy class on 14 November 1759, became a merchant, then an accountant, and wrote a *History of Glasgow* (1777), which made use of transcripts of early records provided by Father Thomas Innes from the archive holdings of the Scots College in Paris. Gibson was innovative in introducing extracts from the city's own records. He accounts for the economic progress of Glasgow, citing sugar and rum as the import commodities from which the first business fortunes were derived, and describing the management of the tobacco trade, also technological development such as the commencement of linen tape manufacture. Topics are treated analytically rather than in terms of chronology, and the argument is offered that 'our laws' are the 'greatest barrier to trade', a sentiment which Gibson must surely have heard Professor Smith express.

Directing his intellectual energies in an entirely different direction was John Stuart, who matriculated in Smith's moral philosophy class in 1761. He was the son of the Minister of Killin, when Perthshire was Gaelic-speaking, and he became a noted scholar in that language, seeing through the press in 1768, when he was 25, the poems of one of the great Gaelic poets of the century, Duncan Ban Macintyre (Donnchadh Ban Mac-an-t-Saoir), who, though he was not literate, had a profound knowledge of his native poetic tradition (Thomson, 1974: 181).

Smith seems to have had some interest himself in Gaelic poetry, and informed Hume some time before 16 August 1760 that he had heard the piper of the Argyleshire Militia repeat 'all those poems which Mr Macpherson has translated and many more of equal beauty' (*HL* i.329). Smith must be referring in the first instance to Macpherson's publication, *Fragments of Ancient Poetry collected in the Highlands of Scotland, and translated from the Gaelic or Erse* (1760). This was the first instalment of 'Ossian's' compositions, which caused so much dispute about their authenticity, provoking scorn at and exposure of Macpherson's literary frauds, but also alerting Europe to a Celtic past and present of rich intercultural significance (Weinbrot, 1993: 477–558). But what did Smith hear? Probably the Campbell piper's repertoire included some of the Gaelic ballads on which Macpherson based his prose versions in the *Fragments*, as well as the epics *Fingal* (1761) and (to a much lesser extent) *Temora* (1763). Scholars have pointed out that the 'Laoidh Dhiarmaid', for example, telling of the death of Diarmaid, was a favourite of Campbell reciters, who had a special interest in a hero regarded as one of their clan's ancestors (Thomson, 1952; 1963; 1979; Meek, 1990). Smith was at Inveraray with his student Thomas Petty Fitzmaurice to visit the 3rd Duke of Argyll in 1759 (*Corr.* No. 42), and it can be surmised that his Campbell friends explained to him what the piper recited on this or a similar occasion.

Smith continued his career as a man of letters in part through membership of the clubs and societies both in Glasgow and Edinburgh which advanced the Enlightenment. Soon after coming to Glasgow he helped to form the Literary Society of Glasgow, which met on Fridays during the University sessions and heard his paper on Hume's 'Essays on Commerce'. This Society included merchants among its members: Robert Bogle, William Crawfurd, and John Graham of Dougalston, and occasionally it heard discussions of commercial policy questions. Thomas Reid, Smith's successor as Professor of Moral Philosophy, read papers on paper credit (1767, during a banking crisis); warehousing foreign grain for re-exportation (1778); regulation of interest rates (1778); and Hume's views on contracts (1779). This indicates the level of town–gown sharing of concern for economic topics, from which Smith would benefit in an earlier phase (Murray, 1924: 445, n. 2). It is also believed that Smith attended Robert Simson's club, which dined at Anderston each Saturday; James Watt the inventor remembered having discussions with him, and the scientist Joseph Black was another member of the group.

On another weekday, Smith attended the Political Economy Club founded by Provost Andrew Cochrane, who presided when he was made an honorary burgess of Glasgow on 3 May 1762 (GUL MS Gen. 451). For Cochrane's club—

whose members included the wealthy tobacco merchant John Glassford and the future negotiator of the American peace treaty in 1783, Richard Oswald, also Carlyle of Inveresk's cousin, William Wight, a minister, and later Smith's colleague as Professor of Church History—it is claimed that Smith read his 1755 paper going back to the Edinburgh lectures on jurisprudence. This outlined the necessary conditions of a country's rise to opulence as 'peace, easy taxes, and a tolerable administration of justice' (Stewart iv.25). In addition to his extensive knowledge of the colonial trade and exports, Cochrane was an expert in the financial market, being one of the founders of the Glasgow Arms Bank in 1750 (Murray, 1924: 446, n. 2; Rae, 1965: 90–100; Scott, 1937: 82–3). According to Carlyle (1973: 38), Smith 'acknowledg'd his Obligations to [Cochrane's] Information when he was Collecting Materials' for *WN*.

Cochrane attributed the growth of Glasgow's economy in his lifetime mainly to four young men likely to have been members of his Club: William Cunninghame, Alexander Speirs, John Glassford, and James Ritchie. Glassford seems to have known Smith well and corresponded with him (*Corr.* No. 85). He and another merchant and financier, Archibald Ingram, helped Robert Foulis to establish his Academy of Fine Arts in Glasgow leading to the management of the Foulis Press, in which Smith was also warmly interested. In *LJ* Smith referred to economics classics being issued by this press: printed in 1750, John Law's *Money and Trade* and John Gee's *Trade and Navigation of Great Britain Considered*; in 1751, William Paterson's *Proposals and Reasons for Constituting a Council of Trade in Scotland* (wrongly attributed to Law), Sir William Petty's *Political Arithmetic*, Sir Joshua Child's *Discourse of Trade*, and Berkeley's *Querist*. Thomas Mun's England's *Benefit of Foreign Trade* was printed in 1755, and a further edition of Gee's book in 1760 (Murray, 1924: 442, 449). Robert Foulis attended the moral philosophy classes of Hutcheson, who is believed to have been his mentor in taking up the book trade (Sher, 1995: 325). The programme of publishing economics classics, which reflect deepening insights into the form of the interactions of the trading universe (Appleby, 1978), may well have stemmed from Hutcheson's arousal of his student's interest in political economy, and from Foulis's business sense that books connected with it would have appeal in a commercial city to groups such as Cochrane's club. One way or another, Smith had printed sources to feed his mind and men of experience with whom to discuss his liberal principles of market economics. This is part of the matrix of *WN*.

Travelling on the Glasgow–Edinburgh stagecoach, Smith could be in the capital before dinner, eaten at our lunchtime, spend the afternoon and evening in Edinburgh, and be back in Glasgow before dinner next day (Murray, 1927: 396). On such visits or during his vacations, Smith attended the clubs and societies of the literati in Edinburgh. The Philosophical Society, already mentioned in connection with possible sponsorship of Smith's rhetoric and history of science lectures, flourished from the 1750s. The painter Allan Ramsay, son of the poet of that name, was behind the formation of the Select Society in 1754, intended to promote literary and philosophical discussion. At the first meeting on 22 May of that year (in the Mason Lodge Mary's Chapel), Smith in his first and last speech, so it was said, presented the guiding proposals that members could suggest any topic for debate, 'except such as regard Revealed Religion, or . . . Principles of Jacobitism'. Leading members besides Ramsay and Smith were Hume, Kames, and young Alexander Wedderburn. An offshoot with some practical aims was formed in 1755, the Edinburgh Society for Encouraging Arts, Sciences, Manufactures, and Agriculture in Scotland. Smith and Hume were made members of Committee III, dealing with belles-lettres and criticism, together with the ministers Blair, William Wilkie (author of the *Epigoniad*), and George Wishart. Smith was less likely to be interested in the Select Society's drive to get Scots to speak like the southern English by sponsoring lessons from an Irish actor, Thomas Sheridan, father of the dramatist Richard Brinsley Sheridan, a scheme which aroused public mirth, and hastened the demise of the Society in 1763. It had almost ten years of vigorous intellectual life, however, and Carlyle of Inveresk wrote appreciatively of the Society's meetings, 'in particular [rubbing] off all Corners, as we call it, by Collision, and [making] the *Literati* of Edin[burgh] Less Captious and Pedantick than they were elsewhere' (1973: 150 n.; Emerson, 1973; Mossner, 1980: 281–4; Smart, 1992: 110–14).

Smith was among the original members, also, of the Poker Club, founded in 1762 to stir up the question of a Scotch militia denied Scotland after the '45 rising. Most members were drawn from the Select Society, and the meetings at first were held in Thomas Nicholson's tavern, near the Mercat cross, where over a shilling dinner and modest quantities of sherry and claret, lively discussions ensued on political topics and members were freely 'roasted' for their views (EUL MS Dc 5.126; Carlyle, 1973: 213–16; Mossner, 1980: 284–5). Hume had contributed to the debate over a Scotch militia, so David Raynor has argued, in an anonymously published pamphlet, *Sister Peg* (1760), which 'roasted' both the Elder Pitt ('Jowler') for expanding the national debt to maintain a large standing British army and Robert Dundas the Younger ('Bumbo'), the Lord Advocate, for speaking against the Scotch Militia Bill in Parliament. Hume probably disassociated himself from the pamphlet because the *Monthly Review* detected it was written by a 'North-Briton; not sufficiently acquainted with our language, to express himself decently in print' (24 (1761), 165). With his sensitivities over proneness to Scotticisms, he would be mortified to have his style so castigated (Raynor, 1982*b*).

Smith must have paid attention to the arguments of Hume and the others in the Poker Club favouring a militia over mercenary soldiers. However, his realism drove him to the conclusion that, though citizens would benefit from training in the martial arts, a professional corps would defeat militiamen. He did make an exception in *WN* in favour of the American militia engaged in a struggle for independence. Smith taught his Glasgow students that the rise of standing armies was connected with the commercial stage of society, and with the extension of the principle of the division of labour. Nevertheless, he did offer one argument in his lectures in line with the Poker Club political viewpoint: that standing armies could be a danger to the liberties of citizens (*LJ*(B) 334–8). It is doubtful, however, that he voiced this argument in Poker Club meetings, as Carlyle said he never 'heard Adam but once', at the opening meeting of the Select Society. Smith seems to have sunk into his own thoughts, perhaps already composing his lectures or passages of the books that he had 'upon the anvil'. According to Carlyle:

He was the most absent man in Company that I ever saw, Moving his Lips and talking to himself, and Smiling, in the midst of large Company's. If you awak'd him from his Reverie, and made him attend to the Subject of Conversation, he immediatly began a Harangue and never stop'd till he told you all he knew about it, with the utmost Philosophical Ingenuity.

Carlyle went on to say that Smith's travels abroad with the 3rd Duke of Buccleuch, which came at the end of his professorial stint, 'Cur'd him in Part of those Foibles' (Carlyle, 1973: 141–2).

10

Publishing Scholar and Administrator

That in every profession the fortune of the individual should depend as much as possible upon his merit, and as little as possible upon his privilege, is certainly for the interest of the public.

Smith understood well the requirement that a professor should address his peers and the public in print. The appearance in print of the essay on the first formation of languages has been mentioned, and will be discussed further; the composition, publication, and criticism of *TMS* and *WN* will be reviewed in separate chapters. Other publications were two contributions to the first *Edinburgh Review*, a periodical edited by Alexander Wedderburn, another offshoot of the Select Society, involving several members, principally the Moderate ministers Robertson, Blair, and John Jardine. One of its aims was to raise the standard of books written in Scotland by providing a vehicle for criticism of them, and another was to review books published in England likely to interest the Scots.

For the first issue (26 Aug. 1755, for 1 Jan.–1 July 1755), Smith assessed the merits and defects of Johnson's *Dictionary*, numbering among the latter the insufficiently grammatical nature of its plan (*EPS* 229–41). He later explained what he meant by 'Rational Grammar' in a letter addressed to George Baird on 7 February 1763 (*Corr.* No. 69). His brief account there of how he 'should have tried to investigate the origin and use of all the different parts of speech and of all their different modifications', together with the extended discussion of his essay on languages, suggests the principles he would have applied to dictionary-making. His *Review* article illustrates them by dealing with the words 'but' and 'humour'.

For the second issue of the *Review* (Mar. 1756, for July 1755–Jan. 1756), he wrote a letter proposing that the coverage of the periodical should become more cosmopolitan (*EPS* 242–56). He set an example by reviewing the state of learning in contemporary Italy, Spain, Germany (all dismissively), then England and France, dwelling on the recent achievements of the contributors to the *Encyclopédie* and French writers on natural history. He also gives particular attention to 'Mr Rousseau of Geneva', focusing on his *Discourse on Inequality* (1755), and supporting his favourable notice by presenting three passages in translation. Their burden is that the savage enjoys freedom and happiness in the simplicity of his individual wants, while civilized man is reduced to bondage and unhappiness through acquiring property and becoming dependent on others even if, ostensibly, they appear to serve him. Smith was to take up this argument both in *TMS* and in *WN*, especially with respect to the role of self-love as one driving force behind economic activity, identified by Rousseau, though he was following on from Machiavelli, Hobbes, and, as noted by Smith, Mandeville.

Though members of the Select Society, Lord Kames and Hume were kept out of the planning and execution of his *Edinburgh Review*. It is noticeable, too, that the first Stuart volume of Hume's *History of England* (published in London on 20 November 1754 and a little earlier in Edinburgh) is not discussed, presumably because it was regarded as too controversial. Hume afterwards wrote that he had 'presumed to shed a generous Tear for the fate of Charles I' (*My Own Life*), but this sentiment offended Whigs. The Moderates involved in producing the *Review* used it to advance their cause. For example, Blair praised the sermons of Thomas Sherlock, Bishop of London, notable for their vein of Anglican rationalism (*Edinburgh Review* 1: Appendix, Art. i; 2: Art. ix). Jardine had attacked enthusiasm in religion, represented by the sermons of Ebenezer Erskine, who was a High-flyer, a member of the rigidly orthodox Presbyterian party (1: Art. vi). The editors criticized attacks on Kames and Hume by the High-flyers (1: Arts. xiv, xv, xvi, xvii), but they did not wish to trail their coats by giving Hume any more attention. To be sure, Blair took on the responsibility of reviewing Hutcheson's posthumously published *System of Moral Philosophy* (1755), and praised Smith's teacher for 'having removed a great deal of rubbish from the science of morals', also for establishing 'as essentially connected with the foundations of morality . . . the great principles of natural religion' (1: Art. ii). These two claims were likely to arouse the ire of the High-flyers, who attacked the *Review* in the newspapers.[1]

Perhaps alarmed by the attacks of the High-flyers, and in any event drawn off to defend attacks on Hume, Kames, and John Home the poet in the General Assembly of the Church of Scotland, the Moderates abandoned the project of publishing the *Edinburgh Review*. The volatility of Wedderburn may also have been a factor in this decision, though he too was involved in the Assembly proceedings against the Humes as a lawyer and representative elder of the Kirk (Mossner, 1980: 337–48). Smith's wish to make the *Review* more cosmopolitan in future issues was thus frustrated; he may have concluded that Edinburgh was too much subject to literary factional fighting dictated by religious issues to be a setting for advance of the Enlightenment, a trace of this feeling surfacing in a letter he wrote to his publisher, Thomas Cadell, as late as 18 November 1789, stating he did not wish the sixth edition of *TMS* to be published in Edinburgh, because of the 'present state of Literary faction here' (Klemme, 1991: 280).

Meantime, Hume apparently responded to the invitation of the *Review* to contribute to their publication by writing out corrections to the text of seven of the articles in a copy that has recently been discovered of the second issue, including Smith's letter. For the most part the corrections are stylistic, as Hume seeks, perhaps, to refute the *Monthly Review* writer's opinion that, as a North Briton, Hume could not express himself decently in standard English. Among the marginalia for Smith's letter, however, are three substantive entries. First, Hume wished to delete mathematics from the list of 'sciences which require only plain judgment joined to labour and assiduity, without demanding a great deal of what is called either taste or genius', and substitute anatomy. He may also have intended to imply that the Germans were and continued to be successful in anatomy rather than mathematics. Second, Hume struck Spenser off Smith's list of English poets possessing a 'strength of imagination so vast, so gigantic and supernatural' as to astonish readers and make them despise criticism of 'inequalities in their writing' (p. 65). This would leave Shakespeare and Milton as sole possessors of such genius.

The third entry refers to a remark about a history of the War of Spanish Succession published over Voltaire's name but without his consent. Smith had written that this work contained 'very gross misrepresentations' about Britain's share. Hume noted that this was particularly true with regard to General St Clair's expedition (p. 79), namely, the descent on the French East India Company's base at Lorient in Brittany in 1746, in which he had himself served. The annotations indicate that Hume disagreed with Smith on two important points, or thought he knew better, and that he had inside information on one point supplementing Smith's.[2]

The phrasing of the letter itself and these points clinch the argument for Smith's authorship of the letter rather than Hume himself. Smith did not share Hume's anxieties over conformity to a southern English standard and, perhaps confident about his Oxford experience in acquiring it, he taught his Glasgow students and published his books without, so far as is known, consulting Hume or anyone else about his style. Hume did not give up fussing about Smith's style, however, and exhibited further concern about *WN*.

When he was not teaching, or composing his writings, or attending meetings of his clubs, a great deal of Smith's time was expended on administrative duties. Some of these no doubt helped or reinforced his intellectual formation, and provided useful experience for his writings, but other responsibilities must have vexed his spirit and drained his energies away from more rewarding work. While it is known that Smith's reputation for absent-mindedness grew at Glasgow, his colleagues recognized his sound practical bent, and entrusted him with the charge of legal and money matters, fabric and building supervision, the negotiation of University interests, chairing their official meetings, and various missions of diplomacy and governance requiring exceptional skill.

Securing and auditing University funds at Glasgow was a complicated affair because they were derived in large part from Crown allocations of former Church revenues, such as those connected until the Reformation with the Glasgow Archbishopric. In addition, University property was subject to Scottish feudal provisions. As the records indicate, Smith was fully involved in the handling of the accounting and endowments, introducing improved accounting methods, also in the feuing of land (GUA 26640; Scott, 1937 [henceforth S]: 96, 159, n. 3). Thus on 30 December 1755 it was reported officially that Smith, on undertaking a journey to Edinburgh, was required to deal with lawyers there about clearing the accounts going back to 1713 of an endowment by a Duchess of Hamilton, and about getting a Bill through Parliament to put this particular endowment on a better footing (GUA 26640; S 154).

Some six years later, when Smith planned to go to London during the long vacation, a visit that may have been connected with the publication of his essay 'On the First Formation of Languages', he was entrusted on 16 June 1761 with the mission of clearing with the Treasury the accounts of the University for the crop years 1755–8, also to meet with a Chancery lawyer to settle details connected with the Snell bequest and that of Dr Williams. He received the necessary accounts on 27 August and produced the required certificate from the Treasury at a University meeting held on 15 October (GUA 26642; S 156–7).

With respect to the administration of property, Smith was regularly called to inspect buildings and to offer advice about repairs and additions. In 1754–7 there was a lengthy series of meetings focusing on restoration of the principal's house, which on 26 March 1754 was said to be so ruinous as to be unsafe for occupancy. The Principal of the time was Neil Campbell, who had become paralysed in 1752 and unable thereafter to take part in official business. Since he had been offered £20 a year to move to a house in the town, some of the faculty were averse to expending funds on repairs to his house, but Smith and others battled away in this cause, and the work was finally agreed to on 10 May 1757, possibly because it was coupled with building the Observatory (GUA 26640; S 143).

Smith was also associated with improvements in 1757 to the Anatomy Room (GUA 26640; S 145) and with securing further apparatus and accommodation in 1755–7 for the Natural Philosophy Class (GUA 26640; S 146–7). As is often the case among academics, there was competition for the space available, and Smith played a role in the decisions in 1763 that left Robert Foulis in possession of certain rooms for his Academy of Arts sponsored by the University. He also found a classroom for the Mathematics Professor by deciding that the chemical laboratory should be converted for that purpose, and a new laboratory built (GUA 26642, 26643: S 147–8). Smith doubtless sustained his interest in mathematics and scientific subjects through these projects, as well as by his friendships with the medical scientists William Cullen and Joseph Black, Cullen's successor in the Anatomy Chair.

Serving on yet another committee dealing with space allocation, Smith in November 1762 had to approach Robert Foulis and James Watt to see if they could release rooms they had been given. From 1757 on, Watt had been given support by the University to do research on steam power as well as make and repair scientific instruments (GUA 26650; S 149). He worked under the supervision of Alexander Wilson, the type-founder for the Foulis Press, who was made Professor of Practical Astronomy and Observer in 1760.[3] Smith introduced Wilson to Hume in July 1759 as his 'Friend', and Hume tried to promote a scheme to have Wilson cast type-fount for a 'Set of the Classics' to be published by his own publisher, Andrew Millar (*Corr.* No. 36).

An area of administrative service of great professional interest to Smith was the development of the library. He served on its committees in his first year as a Professor, and had as a particular care its accounts, bringing into use the New Library designed by William Adam, which at first was affected by dampness, and stocking it with new books additional to those secured by the provisions of the Copyright Act of 1709, which enjoined Stationers' Hall in London to send up new books in an unbound state (GUA 26640, 26645; S 175–6).

Smith was largely responsible for the Quaestor's accounts from 1755 until he left the University in 1764, and had an influential voice in the ordering of books. The titles covered by his 'Quaestor Accounts' from 26 June 1758 to 26 June 1760 seem to connect with the legal and historical studies which underpinned his work on jurisprudence and political economy. The titles include, on the legal side, four volumes (1739–59) of Mathew Bacon's *New Abridgment of the [English] Law* (later to be completed in a fifth volume in 1766) and the third edition of Stair's *Institutions of the Laws of Scotland* (1759). On the historical side, we find listed Joseph de Guignes's *Histoire générale des Huns, Turcs, Mongols et autres Tartares occidentaux* (1756–8), a source of details concerning a shepherd society worked into the theory of the four stages of social organization. There are also histories of France (le père Daniel), Spain (Ferreras), Naples (Giannone), and Venice (its state historians); and Postlethwayt's *History of the Public Revenue*.

Another entry lists seven volumes of a set of seventeen comprising d'Alembert and Diderot's *Encyclopédie* (GUL MS Gen. 1035/219; S 178–9). The latter item was by far the largest expenditure for the period in question, accounting for 29 per cent of the total outlay on books including the cost of bindings. Obtaining books published in France at this period was difficult because of the Seven Years War, but the importance of such a work as the *Encyclopédie* was certainly appreciated in Glasgow. Its articles embraced Physiocratic thinking on economic issues, and may well have prepared Smith for his subsequent encounters in Paris with Quesnay and Turgot.

Smith's skill in composition was called upon on a number of occasions. These included a drafting for the University of a royal Address to King George III on his accession in 1760, which stresses a theme dear to the Professor of Moral Philosophy, 'that ardent spirit of Liberty which naturally animates the breast of every Briton' (GUA 26642; S 167–8). This responsibility of Smith's drew upon him a satirical attack from the Revd William Thom. This compulsive pamphleteer, already cited, had been worsted in a lawsuit with the University over his stipend, and thereafter seized every opportunity to blacken the name of his Alma Mater and its officers (S 75–6; Mackie, 1948: 46–52, 56–8).

Hitherto Smith has been represented as enlightened and disinterested in his administrative work, but his record is not entirely without blemish. He was willing to accept a commission to interest the Rector of 1761, Lord Erroll, in a scheme to found an 'Academy of dancing, fencing, and riding to be established at Glasgow under the direction of the University' (GUA 26650; S 149). However, he also served on a committee appointed on 25 November 1762 to pressure the magistrates of Glasgow not to allow a playhouse to be established in the city. This body prevailed with the magistrates, appealing to the 'Priviledges of the University of Oxford with regard to preventing any thing of that kind being established within their bounds'. Perhaps this was a touch which might have come from that former Oxford man, Adam Smith. In the event, the city and University jointly sent a memorial about the matter to the Lord Advocate of the day, Thomas Miller of Glenlee, a former student of Smith's. This law officer encouraged the memorialists to prosecute the players if they came to act in Glasgow (GUA 26642; S 164–6). There is no record of Smith protesting about this, though he expressed the view that the theatre was a valuable moral resource in a community (*WN* v.i.g.15). It seems a lame excuse to say that the University authorities were afraid of student disturbances connected with playacting (S 163, n. 3).

Smith appears in a better light getting back for students the duty on oatmeal that had been taken from them on their way into Glasgow in October 1757 (GUA 26640; S 163). Traditionally, Scots students brought this cereal from home for a term's consumption, and a tax on this would have been a real hardship for the poorer ones at Glasgow.

Smith also held out for principle in connection with the election of a difficult colleague, John Anderson, who apparently had a grudge against him. Anderson stated to a correspondent in a letter of 16 January 1755 that he had hoped to become Professor of Latin, but 'Doctor Cullen and Mr Smith, in a manner that I need not relate, jockied me out of [the Chair]' (Meek, 1977: 74, n. 44). In 1757 Anderson voted for himself to secure election as Professor of Natural Philosophy, holding to his right to vote as occupant of the Chair of Oriental Languages (GUA 26640; S 189–90). Smith opposed this, and was supported by Joseph Black and another difficult colleague, James Moor, the Professor of Greek.

Professor Leechman told his student, Samuel Kenrick, in 1760 that Smith was the principal object of Anderson's 'jealousies and enmities'. Kenrick remembered Smith being 'as fiery and choleric as Anderson himself', and was told by Professor William Leechman that their 'high words frequently brought them very near to blows at their Faculty meetings' (London, Dr Williams' Lib., MS 24.157 No. 92, letter of 22 Feb. 1785). This is a revelation of a side of Smith not much heard of except in relation to his 'warmth' as a schoolboy, and his 'anger and vexation' aroused by machinations surrounding his election as a Professor at Glasgow.

James Moor was an able classicist (Stewart, 1990a), and sufficiently skilled in mathematics to help edit Simson's works on geometry. He was said to have sustained himself in his meticulous work as corrector of proofs for the Greek editions of the Foulis Press, such as the magnificent Homer folios of 1756–8 and the ingenious Pindar of 1754–8, measuring 3 in. by 1.9 in., by taking copious drafts of tea and coffee and possibly stronger cordials. As a result, he could be alarmingly irritable, took inexplicable and extreme stands on issues, and was sometimes violent with students. After one such occasion in the spring of 1763, Smith as Vice-Rector had to chair eight extraordinary meetings to deal with Moor's complaints about the insolence of students and the feelings of colleagues that Moor had completely lost control of himself. In the end, he was 'rebuked and admonished in the strongest and most solemn manner', a record which was kept apart from the regular minutes and held 'in retentis'. In 1772 Moor again lost control of himself, this time striking a student, who had enraged him, on the head with a heavy wooden candlestick. The outcome was that the University forced Moor to resign in 1774 (GUA 26757; S 195–9).

Smith took up some of his responsibilities through seniority, such as holding the office of Quaestor of the Library, but it was the esteem in which his colleagues held him that was responsible for his unanimous election as Dean of Faculty in 1760–1 and the succeeding year. During this time there arose the complex constitutional issue at Glasgow of whose meetings were to conduct the more important business of the University: those chaired by the Rector (or his appointee the Vice-Rector, who was generally a Professor) or those chaired by the Principal. It would appear that the regulations devised by the Commission of 1727, building on the *Nova Erectio* of 1577 and subsequent practice, had in mind that the Rector's meeting was to deal with the election of faculty and the passing and approving of the University's final yearly budget; the Dean of Faculty's meeting was to deal with degrees and curriculum, also the Library and election of the King's bursars; and the Principal's meeting was to deal with all other matters, principally the application of the budget. Because of Principal Campbell's stroke in 1752 and his removal from business, the calling of University meetings devolved on James Moor as the Senior Professor among the incumbents of the Chairs created out of the Regents' positions. In 1755 Moor took offence at his colleagues, and no further University meetings were called until 6 November 1761. More and more business was transacted by the Rector's meeting, and since after 1754 the Rector himself rarely attended, a Professor presided as Vice-Rector. During the incapacity of Principal Campbell, 1756–61, the business of the University was largely in the hands of William Leechman, who served four years as Dean of Faculty and two years as Vice-Principal, without raising objections, it seems, to the prevailing system.

Campbell died on 22 June 1761, and a royal commission appointing Leechman as Principal was issued on 6 July. He set about restoring the position of Principal, planning to do so in part through meetings within that office's jurisdiction, raising the spectre of the dominance of what Sir William Hamilton called, following a lead given by Smith in *WN*, the 'worst and most corrupt depositories of academical patronage, namely a self-elective body of Professors' (S 91).

Meantime, Adam Smith as Dean of Faculty presided over a University meeting held on 15 July 1761, principally to admit John Millar to the Chair of Civil Law and to elect a Professor of Oriental Languages. Leechman wrote to Smith that day to stop the meeting since the Rector was not present, and he (Leechman) had resigned the office of Vice-Rector (*Corr.* No. 58). Smith went back and forth between the meeting and Leechman to get him to change his mind, and at one point Leechman agreed to come and preside as Vice-Principal if the election of a Professor of Oriental Language was held over. The meeting agreed to this, but in the end Leechman still would not appear. The meeting thereupon elected Smith to be its Preses (chairman) and, as Robert Simson would not appear either, elected Joseph Black to be its clerk. Thereafter, Millar was admitted to the Law Chair (GUA 26642; S 200–1).

There was some jockeying for the Chair of Oriental Languages, but it went to Robert Trail, who was translated within six weeks to Leechman's former Chair of Divinity. On 26 October 1761 the Professors elected in Trail's place Patrick Cumin, a candidate who had been recommended to Smith by William Cullen through his son, Robert (*Corr.* No. 56) and by Hume (No. 57). He remained as occupant of the Chair of Oriental Languages until his death fifty-nine years later, which remains a Glasgow record.

A meeting on 26 August 1761, presided over by the Earl of Errol as Rector, confirmed the proceedings of 15 July and upheld Smith's actions on that date (GUA 26642; S 201–2). Subsequently, a dispute arose between Leechman and his colleagues over the respective powers of Principal and Rector, and in the end a committee chaired by Adam Smith and consisting of Joseph Black, John Millar, and Alexander Wilson brought in a comprehensive report, dated 10 August 1762, which clarified the supervisory function of the Rector's meeting, the academic nature of the business of the Dean of Faculty's meeting, and the role of the Principal's meeting in connection with administrative routine (GUA 26642; S 202–15). Moor and Muirhead (Professor of Humanity) held out at this stage for the maximum powers for the Rector, but were overruled, and Leechman continued seeking to undermine the Rector's meeting chaired by a Vice-Rector, even when that officer was Adam Smith (GUA 26642, 26650; S 215–19).

One of the issues between Smith acting as Vice-Rector and Principal Leechman was financial provision for a chemical laboratory, and Smith signed a strong defence of this outlay:

It appeared to the Majority a step highly proper and becoming the present reputation of this University to further countenance the study and Teaching of a Science which is one of the most useful and solid, and which is dayly comeing into greater esteem. (GUA 26649; S 218)

In the essay on the history of astronomy, Smith had expressed no great esteem for the current state of Chemistry (ii.12), but perhaps the researches and teaching ability of Cullen and Black had brought him round to a more positive viewpoint.

As for Leechman's struggle to get the upper hand at Glasgow, this was resumed after Smith's resignation in 1764. Leechman finally took to court Professor Trail, and his supporters holding out for the Rector's power, essentially getting his way with respect to money matters in the decision of the Court of Session of 22 November 1770 (S 222–5). It would seem that once Smith's moderating influence was removed, only a court action could resolve the clash of conflicting viewpoints among the Glasgow faculty.

Their esteem for him was evinced by the citation for a Doctorate of Laws dated 21 October 1762. This degree supplemented the AM he apparently had by 28 April 1749 from Oxford, when his resignation from his Snell Exhibition was intimated at Glasgow (GUA 26649; S 137). The higher award was professed on the following terms of distinction:

The meeting considering Mr Adam Smith's universally acknowledged Reputation in letters and particularly that he has taught Jurisprudence these many years in this University with great applause and advantage to the Society do unanimously resolve to confer the Degree of Doctor of Laws upon him and appoint a Diploma to be accordingly expeded for that purpose. (GUA 26645; S 187)

In contemporary anecdotes, he was commonly referred to as 'Dr Smith', but as a man of letters he seems not to have set store by titles, as is indicated by his instructions to his publisher, William Strahan concerning the title-page of edn. 3 of *TMS* (1767): 'call me simply Adam Smith without any addition either before or behind' (*Corr*. No. 100).

One effort was made to translate Smith from Glasgow to the Chair of Public Law and the Law of Nature and Nations at Edinburgh. The instigators of this move in 1758 were Hume and William Johnstone. Their scheme was to have Smith buy out the old Professor, George Abercromby, and then settle Adam Ferguson in Smith's vacant Chair in Glasgow. They believed the purchase would be cheap, also that Smith would 'rate our Company as something' and wish to see Ferguson, who had no university appointment, settled (*Corr*. No. 25). There is no evidence Smith was tempted though, as we have seen, a later incumbent of the Chair, Allan Maconochie, gave a course that Smith might well have delivered.

A conclusion to Smith's career as a Professor at Glasgow was anticipated when Charles Townshend, stepfather of the 3rd Duke of Buccleuch, wrote to him on 24 October 1763 to say that the young man would be leaving Eton at Christmas, and to enquire if Smith was still disposed to travel abroad with Buccleuch as his tutor (*Corr*. No. 76). This subject had been broached by Townshend in the spring of 1759, arising from the reputation Smith had acquired as a man of letters on the publication of *TMS*. Hume had the idea of persuading Townshend to send Buccleuch to Glasgow (*Corr.* No. 31).

In July–August 1759 Townshend visited Scotland, hoping to make use of the connections of his wife, Lady Dalkeith, the daughter of the deceased 2nd Duke of Argyll, to become MP for Edinburgh and manage Scotland. This plan aroused the jealousy of the 3rd Duke of Argyll who checked it (Carlyle, 1973: 197–9). Townshend briefly dazzled the Scots in Edinburgh, and made some impression on Smith when he visited Glasgow. Indeed, Smith remained on good terms with Townshend until his death in 1767.

A somewhat hostile anecdotal obituary of Smith in the *Times* (6 Aug. 1790) recorded that he took Townshend on a tour of manufactures in Glasgow, and they visited a tannery, possibly one of those lying on the Molendinar Burn near the University. Smith fell into the pit—a noisome pool containing fat from hides, lime, and the gas generated by the mixture. He was dragged out, stripped, covered in blankets, placed in a sedan chair, and sent home, where he 'complained bitterly that he must leave life with all his affairs in the greatest disorder'. The anecdote alleges that he was 'talking warmly on his favourite subject, the division of labour', and forgot the dangerous nature of the ground on which he stood.

Smith does not allude to this incident in a letter of 17 September 1759 stating that Townshend's early departure from Scotland had prevented him from waiting on him at Dalkeith. Smith concludes with a reference to books Townshend had ordered from the Foulis Press, intended for the 13-year-old Buccleuch, who was to become Smith's pupil (*Corr.* Nos. 39, 41). These included the noble folio Homer, the pride of the Foulis brothers' printing endeavours, also editions of Epictetus and Marcus Aurelius, Smith's favourite Stoic authors, associated in his mind with development of self-command as part of a boy's education.

About this time the Earl of Hopetoun had attempted to secure Smith's services as tutor to his heir, Lord Hope, offering him £400 p.a. while he was attending the young man, and thereafter an annuity of £200 for life. This information, passed on by the publisher Andrew Millar, was mentioned in a letter dated 13 February 1759 from Robert Dundas the Younger to Lord Hopetoun (SRO Hope of Raehills-Johnstone papers, Bundle 269). The job went to Smith's colleague William Ruat, which led to legal action by the University in which Smith had a role (S 190–5).

Smith advised his colleagues on 8 November 1763 that he would probably be leaving Glasgow in the course of the winter, and he made two proposals. The first was that if he had not finished his course of lectures, he would pay back to his students the fees he had received from them, and if they would not accept them he would pay the University these fees. The second proposal was that his unfinished course would be completed by someone appointed by the University, whose salary would be determined by that body and paid by Smith. The Faculty accepted these terms and unanimously granted Smith leave for three months whenever he wished to take it (GUA 26645; S 220).

Smith's scrupulosity was part of his character, but his behaviour on this occasion and the generous terms of the Buccleuch family, of course, avoided the kind of scandal that attended William Ruat's self-regulated absence from his Chair of Ecclesiastical History in 1759–62 as travelling tutor to Lord Hope, ending in his demission. Ruat himself and Lord Hopetoun seemed to think that behind the manœuvring at Glasgow by Smith and other Professors was an attempt to obtain his chair for Adam Ferguson (SRO Hope of Raehills-Johnstone Papers, Bundle 269, letters of 17 May and 25 or 26 May 1759).

As mentioned already, Smith's substitute, who was paid the unexpended part of the Professor's salary, was his former student Thomas Young. Smith himself left Glasgow in mid-January 1764, leaving his mother and his cousin, Janet Douglas, to look after his house in Professors' Court, which was secured to them until June 1765, when the Faculty may have hoped that Smith would return (*Corr.* No. 79). The Professor may have had this in mind himself. At least, this is one reasonable assumption from a message sent to his friend Baron Mure of Caldwell on 2 February 1764: 'Mr Smith tells me that his recommendation of Mr Young was merely to teach his class this winter, and nothing more' (Mure, 1883: i. 232).

Following up the source of this message leads to the intriguing discovery of an economic text of 1763 whose ideas seem to emanate from Adam Smith, marking a stage in his thought between *LJ* and *WN*, in advance of what we find in the early draft of the latter book. The message was sent to Baron Mure by the Lord Privy Seal, at this time the Duke of Marlborough, serving in George Grenville's Administration (Watson, 1960: 575). As it happened, this officer and two good friends of Smith's, James Oswald and Gilbert Elliot of Minto, formed a Privy Council committee at that time dealing with a crisis in Scottish banking, on which Smith's economic teaching about market freedom and government regulation might be expected to shed some light (Checkland, 1975).

There was free entry into the banking business in Scotland, and the drive for economic growth coupled with a shortage of both capital and coin had resulted in excessive banknote issue. This activity was intensifying a Scottish balance of payments problem with England in the 1760s, and adding to economic stress in Scotland. The chartered or 'public' banks in Edinburgh, the Bank of Scotland (founded in 1695) and the Royal Bank of Scotland (founded in 1727), had sought legislation to give them a monopoly over banking in the country. They would thus control note issue by eliminating their provincial rivals, the 'private' banks in the major burghs, such as the Glasgow Arms Bank, co-founded by Smith's friend Andrew Cochrane, created by merchants seeking to provide local financial services. If they could not secure a monopoly, the 'public' banks wanted the notes issued by the 'private' banks, hitherto unrestricted, to be limited to £10 and upwards. The 'private' banks countered by proposing legislation to abolish the optional clause carried by the notes of the 'public' and 'private' banks. This allowed bank directors either to redeem notes on demand in gold or silver, or to postpone payment in coin up to six months at an interest rate of 5 per cent in the interval. Reviewing the optional clause device in *WN*, Smith wrote that it created uncertainty over payment and 'degraded' the notes below the value of gold or silver money (*WN* II.ii.98).

MPs were lobbied intensively about these matters, and pamphlets and memorials were written to influence them and the general public. Two of these papers in manuscript form were sent for comments to Sir James Steuart (later Steuart-Denham), former secretary to Prince Charles Edward Stuart, who had renounced his Jacobite principles and, though not pardoned, was allowed to live quietly in Scotland from 1763. He was then working on the fourth book of his *Inquiry into the Principles of Political Oeconomy* (1767). Steuart's interventionist economic principles provoked Smith to refute them in *WN* (*Corr.* No. 132). The fourth book of Steuart's *Inquiry* included an analysis of Scottish banking. He would accordingly be considered an appropriate critic of these papers on banking believed to have been written by two tobacco Glasgow merchants: Archibald Ingram, another Provost and partner in the Glasgow Arms Bank (1750), and John Glassford, also a partner in the Arms Bank and co-founder in 1761 of the Thistle Bank (Mure, 1883: i.220).

One paper, bearing the date 4 February 1763, was sent to the Lord Privy Seal in January 1764, presumably to influence any contemplated legislation. Dated February 1763 and in a slightly amended form, it was published as a pamphlet: *Memorial with Regard to the Paper Currency of Scotland* (1763). The other paper was revised considerably and, dated November 1763, was published independently in pamphlet form as *Thoughts Concerning Banks, and the Paper Currency of Scotland* (1763), also as an article with minor changes but the same title in the November 1763 issue of the *Scots Magazine* (25: 585–8).

Study of these texts has led James A. Gherity to conclude, first, that Steuart's criticisms did not lead to any revisions. Second, he is persuaded that the *Thoughts* manuscript text was written by a member or members of the Glasgow banking community, perhaps Ingram and Glassford, or one of them, familiar with Smith's views on money and banking. These are to be found in the jurisprudence lectures, and even in the material connected with the evolution of *WN*, such as the Early Draft. W. R. Scott found this document in the Buccleuch muniments at Dalkeith Palace among papers connected with Charles Townshend, and it has been dated prior to April 1763 (Meek and Skinner, 1973). Third, Gherity reasons that the pamphlet *Thoughts Concerning Banks* (1763), together with the counterpart article in the *Scots Magazine*, offers a text revised by Smith himself or by someone imbued with his ideas and even echoing his wording (Gherity, 1993).

This last notion is not so far-fetched as might appear, since Smith's former pupil and colleague, John Millar, testified as follows:

those branches of science which [Smith] taught became fashionable at [Glasgow], and his opinions were the chief topics of conversation in clubs and literary societies. Even the small peculiarities in his pronunciation or manner of speaking became frequently the objects of imitation. (Stewart i.22)

The content of the published *Thoughts Concerning Banking* is in line with the anti-monopolist stand on banks and banknotes of *LJ* (e.g. (B) 250) and ED (36). Accordingly, it contains a very strong statement against the idea of legislation aimed at granting a banking monopoly to the 'public' banks in Edinburgh. Its supporters 'did not foresee, that they were endeavouring to establish the most extensive, and the most dangerous, monopoly, that could have been contrived, no less than the monopoly of money' (Gherity, 1993: 277). The argument of *Thoughts* is that what Scotland needs is not the introduction of a banking monopoly, but a law to deal with the 'abuse' of paper credit that has crept in through the widespread adoption of the optional clause. Such a law would ensure that notes were equal to coin and at all times convertible into it. Strong banks would be able to comply with this law, and weak ones would give up business. In *WN* (II.ii.98), Smith described in similar terms the 'abuse' of the optional clause as taking place in 1763–4, and mentioned the act which ended it, 5 Geo. III, c. 49 (1765).

It should also be mentioned that *Thoughts* goes beyond *LJ* and ED in two significant places, and anticipates the thought and verbal texture of *WN*. First, the Bank of England is presented as a model in the extent of financial services it provides and in its promptness of payments, despite the fact that its parliamentary act of incorporation did not give it a monopoly in issuing bills and notes (Gherity, 1993: 275). This passage can be connected with one in *WN*, in which Smith depicts the strength and complex operations of the Bank of England, and uses this as a bridge to discussion of the advantages of circulation of paper money for enabling the capital of country to be 'active and productive' (II.ii.85–6). Second, unlike *LJ* (see (B) 246), *Thoughts* (Gherity, 1993: 274) draws the distinction between the limited yield from interest on loans and the profits that can be derived from employing capital in agriculture, manufactures, and trade. That order, as Smith finally saw things, represents a descending order of value added to the 'annual produce of the land and labour of the society' (cf. *WN* II.iv.17 and II.v.19).

Putting together the evidence we have and Gherity's analysis of *Thoughts Concerning Banks* (1763), it would appear that its author or authors, conceivably the Glasgow banking partners Glassford and Ingram, were familiar with ideas appearing in Smith's jurisprudence lectures and an early version of part of *WN*, not necessarily the extant ED, and perhaps one closer to the *WN* of 1776. They used these ideas in a political campaign for legislation to abolish the optional clause on Scottish banknotes. At an opportune time, when Smith was in London in mid-January 1764, on his way to France, he met with the Lord Privy Seal, charged with preparing such legislation, and possibly with his friends Oswald and Elliot, who were on the relevant committee with his Lordship. It is likely that Scottish banking would be discussed and Smith's ideas concerning it.

Certainly, writing to Smith in Toulouse on 5 November 1764, Glassford assumes Smith's interest in banking reform, and states that the one item of public business worth noting is that Scottish MPs 'seem resolved to carry the Bill for abolishing the optional clause in Bank and Bankers notes this ensuing Session which you know was drop'd in the Last'. Glassford also hopes that Smith is 'bringing forward at . . . Leisure Hours the usefull work that was so well advanced' in Glasgow (*Corr.* No. 85). This is an indication that he knew of stages of the composition of *WN*, which we must now see as contributing to *Thoughts Concerning Banks, and the Paper Currency of Scotland* (1763).

Whereas the banking crisis of 1762–4 arose in part from liquidity problems in Scotland, Smith had been given an ample allowance per year while travelling with the Duke, £500, and thereafter was granted an annuity of £300 (S 97). Possibly seeing his way to securing independence for study and writing, he resigned his Glasgow Chair, writing to this effect from Paris on 14 February 1764. In his letter he expressed his anxiety for the 'good of the College', and his sincere wish that his 'Successor may not only do Credit to the Office by his Abilities but be a comfort to the very excellent Men with whom he is likely to spend his life, by the Probity of his heart and the Goodness of his Temper' (*Corr.* No. 81). Perhaps these words are a veiled reference to what was needed to keep in check the stormy academic passions of the 'very excellent Men' revealed in the controversy over the powers of Principal and Rector. In the event, Thomas Young, who was supported for succession to Smith by Black and Millar, did not get the Chair of Moral Philosophy, for it went to the far more distinguished Thomas Reid, who was translated from King's College, Aberdeen (*Corr.* No. 80).

Before he left Glasgow, there was apparently an affecting scene in Smith's classroom, when he tried to pay back his students' fees and they tried to resist this through sheer affection for him.[4] As for his own feelings about his professorship, he described them on 16 November 1787, when he accepted election to the office of Lord Rector of Glasgow University: 'The period of thirteen years which I spent as a member of that society I remember as by far the most useful, and, therefore, as by far the happiest and most honourable period of my life; and now, after three and twenty years absence, to be remembered in so very agreeable a manner by my old friends and Protectors gives me a heartfelt joy which I cannot easily express. . .' (*Corr.* No. 274).

11

The Making of The Theory of Moral Sentiments

> I think, I have made it sufficiently plain that our judgments concerning the con-
> duct of others are founded on Sympathy.

Gilbert Elliot of Minto was active and influential in the world of London politics as an MP, and he maintained a strong interest in the flourishing intellectual
life in his homeland. Hume turned to him in the 1750s for help in composing
his *Dialogues concerning Natural Religion*, and their letters touch on many matters connected with philosophy and publication (*HL* i.153–7; NLS MS 11009,
Elliot/Hume corr.). Though unable to obtain a Glasgow Chair for Hume, Elliot
was successful, as we learned, in securing the Hon. Thomas Petty Fitzmaurice
as Smith's pupil at Glasgow University. This was part of a scheme to draw
well-born English youths there in preference to attending the stagnant English
universities, 'notwithstanding the distance and disadvantage of the dialect'. His
letter to Smith on this topic, dated 14 November 1758, ends with a query that
is the first extant reference to *TMS*: 'is your book in the press or will it be there
soon?' (*Corr.* No. 27).

No answer from Smith to this has come to light so far. In one of his most
delightful letters, however, reflecting cultivation of the arts of friendship and
irony, Hume acknowledged to Smith on 12 April following, that he had received
the 'agreeable Present' of his copy. He reported, further, that he and Alexander
Wedderburn, Smith's old 'disciple' from the time of the Edinburgh lecture series
(NLS MS 16696: 74) and now making his way at the English Bar, had sent other
copies to 'such of our Acquaintance as we thought good Judges, and proper to
spread the Reputation of the Book' (*Corr.* No. 31).

The list of these recipients, expanded by the names of those sent presentation
copies by Smith's publisher, Andrew Millar (*Corr.* No. 33), includes leading
politicians and men of letters of the time. These were Archibald, 3rd Duke of
Argyll, whom Smith had met in 1751 (*Corr.* No. 10), controller of patronage in
Scotland, and keenly interested in science and things of the mind generally; his
nephew, Lord Bute, soon to be Prime Minister as George III's favourite; Lord
Chancellor Hardwicke, who was well aware of the philosophical writings of

Hume and Kames (Ross, 1972: 156); Lord Lyttleton, a Chancellor of the Exchequer as well as an imaginative writer and a historian; the eminent authority on commercial law Lord Mansfield, who had sent the two Russian students to be Smith's pupils and had long been interested in literature from his days of friendship with Pope; Horace Walpole, following his Prime Minister father, Robert, as an MP, but far more involved with aesthetic matters; Soame Jenyns, MP and polemicist about the necessity of evil; Charles Townshend, brilliant and unpredictable as an MP, also stepfather to the Duke of Buccleuch, who became Smith's pupil as a result of the success of *TMS*; the Secretary of the Royal Society, Dr Thomas Birch; the Headmaster of Westminster School, Dr William Markham, later to be Archbishop of York; and a rising star in Parliament and philosophy: Edmund Burke, in Hume's description, 'an Irish Gentleman, who wrote lately a very pretty Treatise on the Sublime'.

By directing Smith's book to these influential people, Hume and Wedderburn no doubt hoped to secure favourable attention to it, stimulate critical evaluation of its teaching, and achieve career advancement for its author. Hume may have had rueful feelings promoting and contemplating the reception of *TMS*, in view of the fate of his own first book, the *Treatise of Human Nature*, launched with such high hopes twenty years before, only to see it fall 'dead-born from the press', as he admitted in *My Own Life*. Perhaps this is what lies behind the roasting he gives Smith in his letter, preparing his good friend for the 'melancholy News' that his book 'has been very unfortunate: For the Public seem disposed to applaud it extremely . . . and the Mob of Literati are beginning to be very loud in its Praises'.

Hume also mentions that, although *TMS* has been published 'only a few Weeks', Andrew Millar 'exults and brags that two thirds of the Edition are already sold'. Writing on 26 April, in addition to tallying the presentation copies and recording that one was to go to Hume's detractor, Bishop Warburton, Millar states that a new impression is to be published 'next Week', and declares that he has 'no Sort of doubt of this . . . being Soon gone'. He adds some business details about the book: he was to pay Smith two-thirds of the copyright money and the Edinburgh booksellers, Alexander Kincaid and John Bell, were to be responsible for one-third. With a sheet of errata sent by Smith for the new impression and a half-sheet for the contents, the whole was to consist of 34 sheets. The publisher reckons the book a 'Cheap 6s: volume bound especially considering the Matter which I am sure is excellent' (*Corr.* No. 33).

Millar obtained good advice about books to publish from his shop, the *Buchanan's Head* in the Strand opposite Catherine Street, and he paid his authors well. These included Fielding, Hume, and Johnson, who said of him: 'I respect Millar, Sir; he has raised the price of literature' (*BLJ* i.288). Printing was done for him by another Scot established in London, William Strahan, who prospered at his trade and entered Parliament in 1774 (Cochrane, 1964: 9, 23, 43–4, 162). He became Smith's friend from that time in 1759, when he put through his printing house at 10 Little New Street, off Shoe Lane, near Gough Square, the twelve prefatory pages and 552 succeeding ones of text in the single octavo volume of *TMS*.[1]

The plain title-page designates the author as Adam Smith, Professor of Moral Philosophy in the University of Glasgow and, as has been explained, its origin lies in the lectures in ethics given from that Chair. Yet the book has been carefully revised from the lecture format to bring out Smith's unique analysis of the nature of virtue, and what requires us to act virtuously. It is surely with this end in view that he placed at the end of his book the historical survey of systems of moral philosophy down to the moral-sense theory of Hutcheson (VII.ii.1.1–iii.2.9), from which in part his own system may be said to spring. While it is likely that Smith lectured to his students on the history of these systems as a convenient introduction to thinking about the problems of moral philosophy, he confronted his readers at the outset of the book with his doctrine of sympathy, to which he allots an organizing role in the formation of the moral sentiments (*TMS* intro. 3–5).

The title of the book occurs in the wording of the fragment which has survived from the lecture drafts. Its third paragraph illustrates Smith's naturalistic approach to the subject of morals and legal institutions. He traces criminal and civil jurisdiction to the natural feelings of resentment over injury and desire for revenge, arguing that magistrates in civil societies are empowered to deal with violators of justice and redress wrongs, thus avoiding the confusion and bloodshed caused by private acts of vengeance. This is basically the account that Kames gives in his article on 'Criminal Law' in his *Historical Law-Tracts* (1758), and it is difficult to say who had priority here. Each country, Smith observes, has its own criminal and civil jurisprudence made up of actual rules embodied in statutes, custom, and 'evident equity'. But in addition, there is a 'Natural Jurisprudence, or the Theory of the general principles of Law'. This is constituted by the 'Rules by which it is most suitable to the natural principles of Justice, or to the Analogy of those Sentiments upon which our sense of it is founded[,] that [the decisions of magistrates] should be regulated'. Smith further observes that these rules constituting 'Natural Jurisprudence' make a 'very important part of the Theory of moral Sentiments' (GUL MS Gen. 1035/227; *TMS* 388–90).

In turn, this last phrase echoes the title of a book by Lévesque de Pouilly, *Théorie des sentiments agréables*. Its first authorized edition appeared in Paris in 1747 (reprinted Paris 1749, London 1750), and it was published in English in 1749 as *The Theory of Agreeable Sensations*. This phrasing seems to have been modified by Smith to indicate his own 'contemplation' or 'spectatorship' or 'continuous exposition' or 'explanatory supposition'—the Greek word *theoria* covers these meanings, of morals understood as based on feeling. The use of the definite article indicates that the author is not emphasizing his own particular theory by the title of his book, but rather indicating treatment of his subject in the manner pursued by Hutcheson and Hume in their writings. Hume's statement makes this clear: 'This not solely in poetry and music, we must follow our taste and sentiment but likewise in philosophy' (*Treatise* I.iii.8). Pouilly was the foremost man of letters in Reims when Hume resided there, 1734–5, and they may have known each other personally. Hume certainly ordered the *Théorie des sentiments agréables* for the Advocates' Library when he was Keeper there in 1752 (Mossner, 1980: 97–8; Spink, 1982). Hume could well have drawn this book to Smith's attention.

In 1756 Smith referred to it with approval in the letter which Wedderburn accepted for the second issue of the *Edinburgh Review*. Essentially naming moralists writing in English to whom he responds in *TMS*, and whom he may have believed he was superseding, Smith cited as in some degree original thinkers 'Mr Hobbes, Mr Lock, and Dr Mandevil, Lord Shaftsbury, Dr Butler, Dr Clarke, and Mr Hutcheson'. Neglecting recent writers of the moral rationalist persuasion such as Richard Price, perhaps pointedly, Smith continues in the letter with the following claim:

This branch of the English philosophy, which seems now to be intirely neglected by the English themselves, has of late been transported into France. I observe some traces of it, not only in the Encyclopedia, but in the Theory of agreeable sentiments by Mr De Pouilly, a work that is in many respects original; and above all, in the late Discourse upon the origin and foundation of the inequality among mankind by Mr Rousseau of Geneva.

Whereas Pouilly's book suggested to Smith little more than a title for his own work on morals, and possibly some ideas concerning the psychology of pleasure, much from the *Discours sur l'origine de l'inégalité* seems to have remained on his mind. He connected its principles with those of the second volume of Mandeville's *Fable of the Bees*, in its sixth edition by 1729, a possible source of his theorizing about the beginnings of language. This book ascribes to selfishness the origins and slow development of human society. Smith wrote that, by a triumph of style, Rousseau 'softened, improved, and embellished' these principles, and 'stript [them] of all that tendency to corruption and licentiousness which has disgraced them in their original author'.

According to Smith, it is notable that Rousseau differed from Mandeville in representing the state of nature as a happy rather than a wretched one for man, but that both writers agreed in supposing 'there is in man no powerful instinct which necessarily determines him to seek society for its own sake'. Mandeville reckoned that man's misery drove him to take this step, by no means welcome in itself, while Rousseau asserted that misfortunes unleashed the 'unnatural passions of ambition and the vain desire of superiority' which brought about the establishment of society. On Smith's reading, again, both writers claim that 'those laws of justice, which maintain the present inequality among mankind, were originally the inventions of the cunning and powerful, in order to maintain or acquire an unnatural and unjust superiority over the rest of their fellow-creatures' (*EPS* Letter, paras. 10–11).

Smith offers in *TMS* a carefully considered and complex answer to the position he detects in Mandeville and Rousseau, which was also that of Hobbes. As the discourse of the fragment from the ethics lectures reveals, Smith is following the tradition of natural law upheld at Glasgow University, which emphasized man's intrinsically sociable nature and the fostering of morality in a social setting. Hobbes had long been the villain of the piece, for Gershom Carmichael had declared that in founding the discipline of natural law Hobbes had corrupted it by insisting on his theory of selfishness as the spring of human action (Pufendorf, 1724: p. vi; Forbes, 1982: 192).

Smith had surely been impressed with Hutcheson's teaching, following on from that of Carmichael, that the principle of our approval of moral acts is not based on self-love, and that 'it could not arise from any operation of reason' (*TMS* vii.iii.3.4). However, he jibs at Hutcheson's solution to the problem of the source of moral approval and disapproval through the theory of a special 'moral sense'. Rather, Smith builds on the new insights of his friend Hume, developed in the *Treatise* and the subsequent *Enquiry concerning the Principles of Morals* (1751), and certain suggestions of his patron Kames in *Essays on the Principles of Morality and Natural Religion* (1751).

Hutcheson recognized that Hume agreed with him in basing moral judgement on feelings, as we find in his letter to Hume dated 16 March 1740, in an exchange which Kames had brought about by sending Hutcheson a copy of the *Treatise* (Ross, 1964). Nevertheless, Hume had refused to stray after Hutcheson into teleological arguments: 'I wish from my Heart, I coud avoid concluding, that since Morality, according to your Opinion as well as mine, is determin'd merely by Sentiment, it regards only human Nature and human Life' (*HL* i.40). Further, according to Hume, the 'true origin of morals' is not Hutcheson's special 'moral sense', but something long familiar to us: the 'nature and force of sympathy'. The operation of this principle is then explained by Hume in a striking passage which must have remained in Smith's memory, for there are echoes of it in *TMS*. To be sure, Smith extends and sophisticates this principle of sympathy and makes it the 'hinge' of his whole system.

Hume's central account of sympathy in the *Treatise* is both descriptive and figurative. He writes of the similarity of all men in their 'feelings and operations', and of how, if one is aroused emotionally, others in some degree are subject to the same emotion. His point is reinforced with a musical simile: just as the movement of one string of an equally tautened set spreads to the others, so emotions are communicated among people and activate them. Hume then brings in his associationist cause-and-effect theory, also that of the double relationship obtaining between ideas and emotions. He claims that when he sees the effects of emotion in the gestures and sounds made by someone, he imagines the causes, and his mind forms so lively an idea of the emotion that this is soon transformed into the emotion itself. The reverse, he assures us, is also true:

Were I present at any of the more terrible operations of surgery, 'tis certain, that even before it begun, the preparation of the instruments, the laying of the bandages in order, the heating of the irons, with all the signs of anxiety and concern in the patient and assistants, wou'd have a very great effect upon my mind, and excite the strongest sentiments of pity and terror. No passion of another discovers itself immediately to the mind. We are only sensible of its causes or effects. From *these* we infer the passion: And consequently *these* give rise to our sympathy.

Having demonstrated the power of sympathy as a principle of human nature, Hume goes on to argue that 'it has a great influence on our taste of beauty, and that it produces our sentiments in all the artificial virtues', exemplified by 'justice, allegiance, the laws of nations, modesty, and good manners', which are represented as 'mere human contrivances for the interest of society' (*Treatise* III.iii.1). A manuscript note in Hume's hand added to a copy of volume III of the *Treatise* now in the British Library expanded the discussion of these 'mere human contrivances' to bring out a point that was also characteristic of Smith's thinking: that their inventors 'had chiefly in view their own Interest. But we carry our Approbation of them into the most distant Countreys and Ages, and much beyond our own Interest' (*Treatise*, p. 672; Connon, 1977; Raynor, 1978).

Kames responded to the *Treatise*, extending some of Hume's arguments and seeking to refute others, in the *Essays on . . . Morality and Natural Religion* (1751). This book begins with a consideration inspired by Hume of our problematic 'attachment to objects of distress'. This propensity is viewed as demonstrating that compassion is the 'great cement of human society' since, 'as no state is exempt from misfortune, mutual sympathy must greatly promote the security and happiness of mankind' (pp. 16–17). Kames parts company from Hume, however, in dealing with the 'foundation and principles of the law of nature', rejecting the argument that would 'resolve the moral sense into pure sympathy' (p. 57). Even more emphatically, Kames rejects Hume's viewpoint that justice is an artificial rather than a natural virtue (pp. 103–4). The case is made by Kames that we are endowed with a 'peculiar feeling' aroused when actions are directed against others 'by which they are hurt or prejudged in their persons, in their fame, or in their goods'. Such actions are 'perceived and felt not only as *unfit* to be done, but as absolutely *wrong* to be done, and what, at any rate, we *ought* not to do'. Benevolent and generous actions are 'more beautiful, and more attractive of love and esteem than justice', yet they are not mandatory for the survival of society. In consequence, 'they are left upon the general footing of approbatory pleasure; while justice, faith, truth, without which society could not at all survive, are the objects of the above peculiar feeling' (pp. 59–61). Kames thus places the 'foundation' of the law of nature in a special feeling which underpins justice, the virtue ensuring property rights and performance of promises (p. 104).

When Smith acknowledges the force of this distinction drawn between 'justice and all the other social virtues' as a point 'which has of late been particularly insisted upon by an author of very great and original genius' (*TMS* II.ii.1.5), this is more than a compliment to a former patron. Kames offers an insight which Smith accepts to articulate his own system of morals. In the *Treatise*, Hume had been led to base justice on the process of man's 'early education in society', whereby conventions are accepted 'by all members of the society' to secure and transfer property as a matter of common benefit (III.ii.2). Yet he conceded that concern for the common interest is a 'motive too remote and too sublime to affect the generality of mankind, and operate with any force in actions so contrary to private interest as are frequently those of justice and common honesty' (III.ii.1). In his *Enquiry concerning the Principles of Morals* (1751), Hume does not insist on the artificiality of justice, declaring that this provokes a verbal dispute, but he now plumps for the thesis that 'public utility is the *sole* origin of justice' (III.i.145; Raphael, 1972–3).

In a sense, there is something of a dialogue between these Scottish literati about the nature of morals, each representing a recognizable viewpoint. Hume is the free and inventive enquirer, while Kames the jurist seeks to defend existing social arrangements by framing them in an acceptable system of ethics. Smith, as the Professor of Moral Philosophy, must acknowledge the acuteness of Hume's perception of morality but also fill the role of public teacher of morals. He seems to have followed up Kames's appeal to common experience in dealing with the problem posed by Hume's swing towards utilitarianism, but also to have relied on the common terms of moral discourse rather than make use of Kames's device of 'special feelings'.

The achievement of Smith was to produce a definition of virtuous action comprehending what is truly lovable as benevolence, what must be present in the stern form of self-command, and what weight must be given to lesser principles such as prudence. We may reflect that prudence and self-command were instilled in Smith in the schoolyard, perhaps taking on neo-Calvinistic and Stoic overtones. Benevolence as a principle to live by was stressed by his teacher Hutcheson. Entertaining the further question in his book of the means by which judgements are to be made of what ought to be done and what avoided, Smith introduces new dimensions to the psychological mechanisms suggested by Hutcheson, Hume, and Kames, above all sympathy, imagination, and detached self-awareness and evaluation vested in a supposed impartial spectator of our motives and actions. It is also to be noted that an overriding aim of *TMS* concerns an issue prominent in Hume's treatment of justice: to show how the 'partial and contradictory motions of the passions' can be restrained (*Treatise* III.ii.2). A truly novel feature of Smith's argument in this connection, however, is that he wishes to demonstrate that this restraint comes about by natural rather than artificial means (Skinner, 1979: 48). The opening move of the book is to allow some force to the perception of human selfishness insisted on by Hobbes, Mandeville, and Rousseau, but to refute them by drawing attention to our feelings of concern for the welfare of others: 'How selfish soever man may be supposed, there are evidently some principles in his nature, which interest him in the fortunes of others, and render their happiness necessary to him, though he derives nothing from it except the pleasure of seeing it' (I.i.1.1). The intellectual significance of the moral psychology flowing from this opening sentence of *TMS* also illuminates Smith's economics in *WN* (Werhane, 1991).

In explaining the working of the 'principles' that interest us in the experiences and feelings of others, Smith turns, not to the scene of the surgical operation exploited by Hume, but to the torture chamber. He argues in the Humean fashion, however, that it is 'by our imagination only that we form any conception' of the sensations of 'our brother . . . upon the rack', since our senses never take us beyond ourselves, but the imagination allows us to switch roles with the victim, and 'thence form some idea of his sensations' (I.i.1.2).

Smith is extending the meaning of sympathy beyond the concept of sharing someone's feelings to that of an individual's *awareness* that he is sharing another person's feelings. This extension permits Smith to account for the different kinds of moral judgement: first, the 'propriety' of an action, that it is right or wrong; and second, that praise or blame is to be attached to it. For the first kind of judgement, Smith theorizes about sympathy with the motive of an agent, or antipathy: I switch roles with someone and consider such and such a thing to be the right thing to do, or the wrong thing. For the second kind of judgement, I imagine I share the feelings of someone acted upon, either those of gratitude or resentment, which leads me to consider an action praiseworthy or blameworthy. The concept of the sympathetic imagination was an attractive one to many of Smith's readers, and was part of the development of the literature of sensibility of the time. In book iv of *Tristram Shandy* (1761), Corporal Trim demonstrates the power of the sympathetic imagination in weeping over his recollection to Uncle Toby of the sufferings of his brother Tom—'tortured upon a rack for nothing' (ch. 4). Perhaps fortuitously, Sterne echoes Smith's own example of the working of this psychological mechanism.

To be sure, Smith maintains a distinction between imagination and reality. He notes that we desire others to sympathize with us, but we realize that they cannot experience the same feelings as we do, so we adjust the pitch of our feelings to the level 'spectators' can attain. Hume's simile of sympathetic communication resembling the resonance of equally wound up strings finds a counterpart in Smith's metaphoric use of musical pitch. Smith puts forward, also, the reverse argument: that 'spectators' will strive to identify themselves more closely with those gripped by feeling. These processes encourage social bonding through the toning down (cf. I.i.4.7: another musical metaphor) of emotional excess on the one hand and the deepening of emotional response on the other. At the stage of his book when he is examining kinds of ethical teaching, Smith points out that the first process leads to the virtue of self-command, and the second to that of benevolence (I.i.5.1). His own proclivity was more in the first direction, since beyond his experiences in the schoolyard and the teaching of the kirk, as a Glasgow student he had been much stimulated by his reading of Stoic philosophers, particularly Epictetus, the Greek slave who valued freedom of mind above all else and guided his actions by prudence and propriety.

Besides tracing the role of sympathy in moral judgements about others, Smith's second important contribution to ethics was developing the concept of the ideal or impartial spectator to account for the formation of our judgements of ourselves (Raphael, 1975; 1985: ch. 3; Hope, 1989). Elaborating the point of the admirable nature of self-command, Smith alludes to 'that noble and generous resentment which governs its pursuit of the greatest injuries, not by the rage which they are apt to excite in the breast of the sufferer, but by the indignation which they naturally call forth in the impartial spectator' (I.i.5.4). This seminal sentence generated further development of the concept of the impartial spectator in subsequent editions of *TMS*, as Smith sought to answer challenges to its teaching, both explicit, from his friends Hume and Elliot of Minto, and implicit, in the social changes he witnessed in his lifetime, and to make allowance for a more sceptical view of human nature that he adopted as he grew older (*TMS* intro. 16). In general, Scottish philosophy in the eighteenth century developed through creative tension between allegiance to Stoicism and scepticism (Stewart, 1991).

There are anticipations of the idea of the impartial spectator in the thinking of both Hutcheson and Hume, but it is possible that Smith may have drawn on the image created by Addison of Mr Spectator impartially assessing the human conduct he witnesses, though for Smith this role is internalized. A further, and highly important, theatrical dimension of the meaning of the spectator concept is emphasized by commentators who dwell on Smith's view of the moral instruction derived from observing the 'spectacle of human life' (*TMS* 59). This view extends to the analogy that the moral theorist is like a critic in a theatre, concerned to describe, analyse, synthesize, and assess the performance of actor. In the moral theatre, to be sure, the theorist and the ordinary man alike are actors as well as spectators, and their judgements of others, based on sympathy and imagination, are made part of their own ethical life (Marshall, 1984; Griswold, 1991).

On the score of internalization of moral judgements, another tradition available to Smith comes to mind, that of rigorous self-scrutiny advocated in Calvinism. In the *Institution of Christian Religion* (1634), Calvin emphasizes our need to examine ourselves rigorously: 'let it not grieve us to descend to look upon ourselves without flatterie or blind affection of love' (p. 364); again, 'let even the perfectest man descend into his own conscience, and call his doings to account' (p. 367). Also, as William J. Bouwsma explains, Calvin's vision depicted humans are both spectators and actors in the 'glorious theatre' of the world (1988: 177–80). Hume was brought up in this tradition (as Smith would be by a pious mother), and Boswell records Hume telling him that as a boy he tried to use a Calvinist manual, *The Whole Duty of Man* (1658 and many reprintings), as a guide to the vices he should look out for in his exercises in self-scrutiny

(Mossner, 1980: 34). Hume declared that he went on to take his 'Catalogue of Virtues' from the Stoic *Offices* of Cicero (*HL* i.34). Smith probably moved to a moral orientation based on Epictetus from his Calvinist upbringing. Still, it is likely to have retained some hold on him. This same Calvinist tradition certainly had the power to drive a contemporary author of considerable interest to Smith, as we have seen, to drive Rousseau to begin a last work entitled *Rousseau juge de Jean-Jacques*.

It is significant that Smith steers away from the term 'conscience' for his self-scrutinizing agency, though Bishop Butler and Kames had recently revived philosophical interest in it.[2] Presumably Smith wishes to avoid orthodox religious overtones here, though they are present elsewhere in his book, and concentrate on the social formation of our moral standards through the efficacy of the impartial spectator. Bereft of society, we could not think of our own character, or of the propriety of our conduct, any more than we could assess the ugliness or beauty of our own faces. Smith reckons that it is society that provides a mirror in which we can see these things. Aware of society's views about conduct and beauty, for example, we can become spectators of our own behaviour and appearance, and so make judgements. Of course, spectators are likely to have limited vision because they are misinformed or prejudiced. By the same token, Smith's realism makes him believe we are only too likely to be too partial towards our own conduct and features because we are dominated by self-interest or self-regard (Mitchell, 1987):

He is a bold surgeon, they say, whose hand does not tremble when he performs an operation upon his own person; and he is often equally bold who does not hesitate to pull of the mysterious veil of self-delusion, which covers from his own view the deformities of his own person. (*TMS* III.4.4)

Smith's answer to this problem is an intriguing one:

This self-deceit, this fatal weakness of mankind, is the source of half the disorders of mankind. If we saw ourselves in the light in which others see us, or in which they would see us if they knew all, a reformation would generally be unavoidable. We could not otherwise endure the sight. (III.4.6).

Robert Burns, who seems about 1783 to have been reading a copy of the first edition of Smith's book, possibly owned by his father (Burns, 1968: iii.1008–9, 1021, 1030), reflects awareness of the impartial spectator idea from the passage just quoted (Macfie, 1967: 66). The poet ruminates in the kirk on seeing a louse creep on a fine lady's balloon bonnet:

> O wad some Pow'er the giftie gie us
> To see oursels as others see us!
> It wad frae monie a blunder free us
>   An' foolish notion
>   ('To a Louse')

With respect to Smith's theory of ethics, his claim is that we guard ourselves against self-deceit by insensibly forming general rules about what is to be done and what avoided. These rules are based on our progressive observations of other people. In turn, a sense of duty is constituted by paying heed to these naturally derived general rules of morality.

To be sure, Smith is consistently hostile to utility as an explanation of the origin of moral rules, and as a principle to be applied routinely in day-to-day transactions. However, he does apply the criterion of utility—seeking the 'greatest happiness for the greatest numbers' in Hutcheson's stirring catchphrase—when evaluating practices, institutions, and systems (social, political, or economic) as a whole (Campbell and Ross, 1981). In consequence, he has to define his form of contemplative utilitarianism as being distinct from the operational variety upheld by Hume. The disagreement is couched in a marked tribute to Hume complementing that found in *WN*:

The same ingenious and agreeable author who first explained why utility pleases, has been so struck with this view of things, as to resolve our whole approbation of virtue into a perception of this species of beauty which results from the appearance of utility. . . . But I still affirm, that it is not the view of this utility or hurtfulness which is either the first or principal source of our approbation and disapprobation. (*TMS* iv.2.3)

Smith's procedure of limiting severely the role of utility in explaining and prescribing individual conduct, then returning to it for comprehensive evaluation (even for 'final' explanations in terms of the Creator's purposes, as at ii.iii.3.2–3), is consistent with the tenor of his thought. His whole approach to social philosophy is covered by the thesis that practices whose origins and supports lie in unreflective human sentiments, shaped by social experience, are beautifully adapted to the divinely planned end of human welfare. The ultimate source of Smith's thinking here is the Stoic doctrine of harmoniously unfolding nature, and this also lies behind the reference to the 'invisible hand' which leads the selfish rich in pursuing their own ends to cause a 'distribution of the necessaries of life' tending to promote human happiness (iv.1.10).

In a corresponding passage in *WN*, it is asserted that the individual employing capital in supporting domestic industry out of self-interest is led to promote the public interest, and unintentionally helps to maximize human happiness (*WN* iv.ii.9). In neither case is Smith implying that an anthropomorphic deity secretly intervenes in everyday affairs. His intention, surely, is that of making dramatic his conviction that there is an 'oeconomy of nature' (*TMS* ii.i.5.9), whose discovery is the object of philosophic or scientific enquiry (Macfie, 1967: ch. 6; Campbell, 1971: 60–1, 71–3). J. J. Spengler (1978) has drawn attention to the comparison made by Fontenelle (1728: 8–9) of what amounts to the 'invisible hand' to the 'Engineer in the Pit' at a French opera, who makes all the stage machinery work with 'Wheels and Movements' never seen on the stage. Smith owned Fontenelle's works in an edition of 1752, and refers to him in *TMS* (Mizuta).

While Smith dwells on the aesthetic pleasure afforded by well-functioning institutions or arrangements that have public utility, he sees a danger in confusing ends with means, and from the perspective of 1759 offers a prescient warning about those who would seek to create or restore ideal systems at the expense of real human feelings:

From a certain spirit of system, however, from a certain love of art and contrivance, we sometimes seem to value the means more than the end, and to be eager to promote the happiness of our fellow-creatures, rather from a view to perfect and improve a certain beautiful and orderly system, than from any immediate sense or feeling of what they either suffer or enjoy. (*TMS* IV.I.II)

Thus far described, Smith's 'science of morals' (pts. I–III) analyses the 'principles [of sympathy] by which men naturally judge concerning the conduct and character, first of their neighbours, and afterwards of themselves'. This was the subtitle added to the title-page for edition 4 of *TMS* in 1774. These judgements are made through the device of the impartial spectator. Smith then fits utility into his scheme (pt. IV), as we have seen, and next he takes up the problem of the 'many irregular and discordant opinions concerning what is blameable and praise-worthy' (v.i.1). One source of his answer must be another strand in the thought of Hutcheson, who suggested that fluctuations in aesthetic taste were due to the effects of custom, education, and example: *Inquiry into the Original of Our Ideas of Beauty and Virtue* (1725: I.viii.5; Ross, 1987). Smith, in turn, ascribes aesthetic and moral irregularities to the operation of the 'principles of custom and fashion' (pt. v). Documenting his contention that the 'influence of custom and fashion over dress and furniture, is not more absolute than over architecture, poetry, and music', he gives considerable attention to changing taste through force of artistic example in literature, culminating in the contemporary regard for Swift's plain style in short verses and Pope's 'nervous precision' in long (*TMS* v.1.4–7). He had championed Swift's plain style in prose, we remember, in *LRBL*. After entertaining to some degree the thesis of Claude Buffier that beauty's charm arises from 'its falling in with the habits which custom has impressed on the imagination', Smith stands on the bedrock of utilitarianism also found in Hume's aesthetics:

I cannot, however, be induced to believe that our sense even of external beauty is founded altogether on custom. The utility of any form, its fitness for the useful purposes for which it was intended, evidently recommends it, and renders it agreeable to use, independent of custom. (*TMS* v.1.9)

With regard to moral sentiments, Smith contends that, though the influence of custom and fashion is not so great as elsewhere, it is still 'perfectly similar', and when this influence coincides with the 'natural principles of right and wrong, they heighten the delicacy of our sentiments, and increase our abhorrence for everything which approaches to evil' (v.2.2). Nevertheless, he concedes that over time, up and down the social and occupational ranks, and from country to country and culture to culture, there is variety in degree and moral formation in what is either 'blamable' or 'praise-worthy'. Here Smith returns to the distinction he drew in dealing with propriety between the 'amiable' and the 'awful' or 'respectable' virtues (i.i.5.1), which has one source in Hume's *Treatise* (III.iii.4).

Like others of the literati in Scotland, Smith had been impressed with the comparative ethnographic data accumulating in his time through the efforts of European travellers to record their experience of the aboriginal people they met, especially in America and Africa. He responded to the tendency of reporters to assimilate what they encountered to what they had read of the values and manners of past societies, perhaps vestigially present in their own (Emerson, 1979*b*). Thus, Smith comments on the cultivation of the virtues 'founded on humanity' among the civilized nations, and their relative neglect in favour of virtues 'founded upon self-denial and the command of the passions', emphasized 'among the rude and barbarous nations' (*TMS* v.2.8).

In describing the 'savages' as submitting themselves to a 'sort of Spartan discipline', Smith shares the viewpoint of the Jesuit father Joseph-François Lafitau, in *Mœurs des sauvages ameriquains, comparées aux mœurs des premiers temps* (1724), and of Cadwallader Colden, who noted in his *History of the Five Nations of Canada* (1727, 1747) that the laws and customs of the Mohawks, for example, resembled those of the Lacedaemonians, 'being, in both, form'd to render the Minds and Bodies of the People fit for War' (p. 13). A work by another Jesuit, Pierre-François Xavier de Charlevoix, *Histoire et description générale de la Nouvelle France* (1744), which was in Smith's library (Mizuta), could have provided accounts of the 'magnanimity' and 'self-command' of the Amerindians, which he considered 'almost beyond the conception of Europeans', but comparable to the aspirations of Stoicism. Smith goes on to describe the practices of the 'savages in North America' in marriage and war, and becomes eloquent about their mental preparation for death by torture at the hands of their enemies, in particular by the composition of the 'song of death', consisting of 'insults about . . . tormentors' and expressions of the 'highest contempt of death and pain' (Pl. 6). In this passage, Smith is echoing Lafitau's *Mœurs des sauvages ameriquains*. Smith finds the same outlook in the negroes of the coast of Africa, and suggests that their magnanimity far exceeds any conception of their 'sordid' slave-masters. His indignation then flashes out against the enslavement of these people by the Europeans:

Fortune never exerted more cruelly her empire over mankind, than when she subjected those nations of heroes to the refuse of the jails of Europe, to wretches who possess the virtues neither of the countries which they came from, nor of those which they go to, and whose levity, brutality, and baseness, so justly expose them to the contempt of the vanquished. (*TMS* v.2.9)

It is to be hoped that the withers were wrung of readers in Glasgow and elsewhere engaged in business ventures profiting from slavery. There was, however,

Pl. 6. Amerindians' Song of Death, 1724. From Joseph-François Lafitau, *Mœurs des sauvages ameriquains* (GUL).

an adverse response from the Virginian Arthur Lee, who took his MD at Edinburgh in 1764 and once spent a day in Glasgow in the company of Smith (Brock, 1982: 122). He was moved to write a book rejecting the glorification in *TMS* of the Amerindians and Africans as noble savages, as well as exculpating the American slave-masters from the charge of cruelty, though also suggesting that Smith should have denounced in outright terms the institution of slavery: *An Essay in Vindication of the Continental Colonies of America* (London, 1764).

Writing in June 1808 to Lord Buchan about his memories of Smith's University (Glasgow, Mitchell Lib., Buchan MSS, Baillie 32225, fos. 47–51), James Wodrow drew attention to passages in Thomas Clarkson's *History of the Abolition of the Slave Trade* (1808) citing denunciations of slavery by Hutcheson, Smith, and Millar, and concluding:

It is a great honour to the University of Glasgow, that it should have produced, before any public agitation of this Question, three Professors all of whom bore their public testimony, against the continuance of this cruel trade. (i.87)

The issue of slavery was put to the test in the Scottish courts in the case of Joseph Knight, a black man kidnapped in Africa, against his master, John Wedderburn of Ballendean, who had bought him in Jamaica and taken him back to Perthshire. The case culminated in favour of Knight in a 9–4 decision in the Court of Session in 1778: 'the dominion assumed over this Negro, under the law of Jamaica, being unjust, could not be supported in this country to any extent'. Smith's old patron, Lord Kames, voted for freedom for the black man: '*We* cannot enforce [the laws of Jamaica], for we sit here to enforce right and not to enforce wrong.' Robert Cullen, the 'best Scholar Smith had ever had', appeared for Wedderburn, and sent some of his law papers on the case to Smith (Mizuta.) Another former pupil of Smith's in his moral philosophy class, Boswell, rejoiced in the decision because it went on a 'broader ground' than that in a similar case in England: 'being truly the general question, whether a perpetual obligation of service to any one master in any mode should be sanctified by the law of a free country'. The similar case was that of the black James Somerset who escaped from his master in England in 1772, was seized, and kept in irons in a ship in the Thames bound for Jamaica, where his master intended to sell him. Lord Mansfield in the Court of King's Bench discharged Somerset, stating in part that slavery was 'so odious, that nothing can be suffered to support it but positive law', and that an application to send Somerset into custody on a habeas corpus writ was not 'allowed or approved by the law of Enbgland' (*BLJ* iii: 87–8, n. 1). In the Scottish Court of Session, Boswell's father, Lord Auchinleck, spoke and voted from pressure of the moral sentiments about which Smith theorized: 'Is a man a slave because he is black? No. He is our brother, and he is a man, although not our colour; he is in a land of liberty, with his wife and child, let him remain there' (*BLJ* iii.212–14; Ross, 1972: 143–6).

Concluding the first edition of *TMS* with a sixth part (renumbered the seventh in 1790), Smith situates his own system of moral philosophy with respect to the others, taken in historical sequence, which have addressed the two fundamental questions likely to have been raised in his ethics class: 'wherein does virtue consist?' and 'by what power or faculty in the mind is it, that this character, whatever it be, is recommended to us?' (VII.i.2) His analysis of the nature of virtue is that it must be attributed to all our 'affections' when properly governed, thus making it consist in *propriety*; or in one or other of the chief divisions of these 'affections', the selfish or the benevolent, and thus consisting in either *prudence* or *benevolence* (VI.ii Intro., 4). In fitting an account of moral philosophy into this kind of framework, and treating his predecessors from a critical standpoint, he perhaps follows a procedure like that of Aristotle in book A of the *Metaphysics*. A historical perspective is adopted in considering whether previous philosophers have discovered causes other than the four specified in the *Physics*—material, formal, efficient, or final—and Aristotle finds that they did not. Smith is more generous, however, than Aristotle, who concludes that his forerunners dealt with these four causes in a 'vague' or 'stammering' way only (Ross, 1959: 153).

In *TMS*, the successive systems presented are discussed with some respect for their leading features, and with an approach that has been usefully described as that of a 'non-dogmatic sceptic', since it is not connected to any scheme of epistemology or metaphysics but appeals directly to our natural sentiments (Griswold, 1991: 225–8). First, we encounter the authors according to whom virtue consists in propriety, among the ancients, Plato, Aristotle, and the Stoics. The latter are treated in most detail, as might be expected from our knowledge of Smith's enthusiasm for this school. Among the moderns, the rationalist Deists Samuel Clarke and William Wollaston are cited, and, more dubiously, Shaftesbury, who seems to have defined virtue as an affection appropriate to the moral object (*TMS* 293, n. 30). Next comes Epicurus, representing the system which views virtue as residing in prudence. Finally, we read of the authors of systems making virtue consist in benevolence: the Eclectics in later classical times, certain fathers of the Christian Church, and in the seventeenth century the Cambridge Platonists. Smith reserves his highest praise in this category for his former moral philosophy teacher:

But of all the patrons of this system, ancient or modern, the late Dr Hutcheson was undoubtedly, beyond all comparison, the most acute, the most distinct, the most philosophical, and what is of the greatest consequence of all, the soberest and the most judicious. (VII.ii.3.3)

Smith is not effusive in praise, and the distinction he attributes to Kames (II.ii.1.5), in a higher degree to Hume (IV.1.2), and now in the highest terms to Hutcheson is carefully placed and deliberately weighted. He glances again at Hume in this chapter, arguing that his system, which defines virtue in terms of utility, 'coincides with that which makes it consist in propriety' (VII.ii.3.21). It is also noticeable that he does not go along with Hutcheson in ruling out self-love as a praiseworthy motive, and is prepared to recognize it as necessary and, on occasion, an admirable principle of action (VII.ii.3.16). Smith's own counsel is that society would benefit if people in general, or even those who claim to live 'according to any philosophical rule', would conduct themselves according to teaching of any one of these systems of propriety, benevolence, or prudence. He also points out how the strengths of any one are complemented by those of the others (VII.ii.4.5).

Smith has not finished with the topic of self-love, however, and resumes it when he turns to what he calls 'licentious systems', meaning those which seem to deny any distinction between virtue and vice and hence in his view are 'pernicious'. In the first edition of *TMS* Smith had in mind two books. The first was the *Maxims* (1st edn. 1665) of François VI, duc de La Rochefoucauld, which argued that the 'virtues join with self-interest as the rivers join with the sea' (p. 171). The second was Mandeville's *Enquiry into the Origin of Moral Virtue* (the first part of *The Fable of the Bees*), which argued that the 'Moral Virtues are the Political Offspring which Flattery begot upon Pride' (cf. *TMS* 309, n. 2).

Smith wrote that, though he considered the systems of these two authors 'almost in every respect erroneous', yet there are aspects of human nature which at first blush seem to support them. He then distinguished between the styles of the two authors: La Rochefoucauld's 'elegance and delicate precision' lightly sketching out these aspects, and Mandeville's 'lively and humorous, tho' coarse and rustic eloquence' more fully representing them (VII.ii.4.6). Smith never dealt with the content of La Rochefoucauld's *Maxims*, and when he came to know this author's great-grandson and was chided by him gently for lumping in his ancestor with Mandeville (*Corr.* No. 194), he decided to drop this reference, as will be mentioned in discussing the 1790 *TMS*. In 1759 Smith wished to show that Mandeville was wrong in proclaiming that vanity lay behind the wish to act honourably and nobly. Smith does think, however, that self-love may lie behind actions regarded as generous and public-spirited. Though he is not hesitant in condemning the self-deluding nature of vanity, he recognizes its force as a spur to ambition and to the maintenance of a rank-ordered society with solid benefits for its members. He then asks rhetorically: what are the advantages we propose 'by that great purpose of human life which we call bettering our condition?' His answer is that neither ease nor pleasure but vanity interests us (I.iii.2.1). At the same time, he is realistic about the destructive side of emulation with a root in vanity:

thus, place, that great object which divides the wives of aldermen, is the end of half the labours of human life; and is the cause of all the tumult and bustle, all the rapine and injustice, which avarice and ambition have introduced into this world. (I.iii.2.8)

This trenchant remark follows an apposite quotation of La Rochefoucauld's maxim number 490, to the effect that ambition usually follows love but the reverse is rarely true, as an indication of the strength of the ambitious drive in humanity.

Ending his survey of systems in terms of their definition of the nature of virtue with this rout of Mandeville, but recognition of the importance of the principle of self-love, Smith turns next to the second fundamental question addressed by moral philosophy: what is it that makes us approve of virtue and disapprove of vice? He concedes that, though this is an important question in a speculative sense, unlike the first question it has no practical application (VII.iii Intro., 3). Once again he attacks Hobbes and his followers, whom he cites as Pufendorf and Mandeville, for reducing the principle of approving virtue to self-love, claiming that this is a 'confused misapprehension of the system of sympathy'. His chief argument here is that sympathy cannot be viewed in any way as a selfish principle, and he states flatly, for example, that a 'man may sympathize with a woman in child-bed; though it is impossible that he should conceive himself as suffering her pains in her own proper person and character' (VII.iii.1.4). It is intriguing to think what Smith might have said about the *couvade*, the custom examined by nineteenth-century anthropologists but alluded to by Strabo and reported by Marco Polo (*OED*), of men in aboriginal societies feigning childbed pains when their wives give birth.

As to systems making reason the principle of moral approval, Smith accepts the thinking of Hutcheson and Hume that our 'first perceptions' of right and wrong and the 'experiments upon which any general rules are founded' are the object of 'immediate sense and feeling', and cannot be that of reason. Here he finds the explanations in the *Inquiry concerning Virtue* unanswerable, and imputes any controversy to 'inattention' to what Hutcheson wrote or 'superstitious attachment to certain forms of expression, a weakness not very uncommon in the learned' (VII.iii.2.9).

Nevertheless, he will not endorse Hutcheson's concept of a special moral sense, that is, a 'peculiar power of perception, somewhat analogous to the external senses' (VII.iii.3.5 and 8), or, taken another way, a reflex sense operating to perceive some species of an object after antecedent direct perception of another species, as the perception of the beauty of a colour might be held to follow upon perception of the colour itself (VII.iii.3.6). Smith simply puts Hutcheson's own argument (*TMS* 323) to demolish these contentions:

The qualities [Hutcheson] allows [*Illustrations upon the Moral Sense*, 3rd edn., 1742, s. 1, p. 237], which belong to the objects of any sense, cannot, without the greatest absurdity, be ascribed to the sense itself. Who ever thought of calling the sense of seeing black or white . . . ? And, according to [Hutcheson], it is equally absurd to call our moral faculties virtuous or vicious, morally good or evil. (VII.iii.3.8)

Having placed this check on Hutcheson's ingenuity, Smith can now draw together the main points of his own remarkably comprehensive system of moral philosophy. In so doing, he reveals how it carries forward the main thrust of the emotive theory through refinement of the concept of sympathy, without being weakened by Hume's over-reliance on the principle of utility:

When we approve of any character or action, the sentiments which we feel, are, according to the foregoing system, derived from four sources, which are in some respects different from one another. First, we sympathize with the motives of the agent; secondly, we enter into the gratitude of those who receive the benefit of his actions; thirdly, we observe that his conduct has been agreeable to the general rules by which those two sympathies generally act; and, last of all, when we consider such actions as making a part of a system of behaviour which tends to promote the happiness either of the individual or of the society, they appear to derive a beauty from this utility, not unlike that which we ascribe to any well-contrived machine. (VII.iii.16)

Smith devotes the closing pages of his book to reviewing the way in which different authors have dealt with the practical rules of morality. Only those of justice, he reckons, are 'precise and accurate' and can be compared to the rules of grammar. The other rules of morality are like those established by critics for achieving compositions that are elegant and sublime. The ancient moralists wrote like critics, contenting themselves with general descriptions of vices and virtues, the sentiments on which each virtue is based, and the general line of conduct to which these sentiments confine us. In the manner of grammarians, the casuists of the Christian Church and, to some extent, the seventeenth-century writers on jurisprudence have attempted to lay down exact rules for human behaviour, particularly with respect to justice. They clash, however, because jurisprudence aims at prescribing rules for judges and arbiters in making decisions, and casuistry prescribes rules for the conduct of the good man. There would appear to be a higher standard upheld by casuistry, for example, in the matter of performing promises extracted under duress. A difficulty has been the tendency of casuists to seek to be grammarians where the stance of critics is more appropriate:

they attempted, to no purpose, to direct by precise rules what it belongs to feeling and sentiment only to judge of. How is it possible to ascertain by rules the exact point at which, in every case, a delicate sense of justice begins to run into a frivolous and weak scrupulosity of conscience? (VII.iv.33)

Smith accordingly rejects casuistry as abstruse and conducive to moral error, and nominates 'Ethics and Jurisprudence' as the two useful parts of moral philosophy.

Since he has provided a system of ethics in the body of *TMS*, he finally takes stock of 'what might properly be called natural jurisprudence . . . a theory of the general principles which ought to run through and be the foundation of the laws of all nations' (VII.iv.37). The ancient moralists, specifically Plato, Aristotle, and Cicero, do not provide an 'enumeration of those rules of natural equity', and Grotius in his treatise *De jure belli ac pacis* (1st edn. 1625, definitive edn. 1631) is recognized as the first writer to do so. Smith makes clear that he considers this work, to which he was introduced no doubt by Hutcheson, and to which he had access in more than one copy in his library, had 'imperfections'. Perhaps this is the case because, as he claimed at the opening of *LJ*(B), it began as a 'sort of casuistical book for sovereigns and states determining in what cases war may justly be made'.

However, he concludes *TMS* in a vein that shows he understands the importance of Grotius' central thesis: that humanity has an impelling desire for peaceful and intelligently organized social life.[3] This thesis of human sociableness (a Stoic concept) was taken up constructively across Europe, leading to advances in thought about law, politics, history, and economics. Smith's last sentence in *TMS*, accordingly, furthers the agenda of Grotius, for he announces his intention of giving 'in another discourse . . . an account of the general principles of law and government, and of the different revolutions they have undergone in the different ages and periods of society'. While he was never able to complete to his satisfaction the promised work on 'what concerns justice', recent scholarship has established the leading principles of his thought about this subject and its relationship to his moral theory (Haakonssen, 1981; Brühlmeier, 1988). In *WN*, however, Smith produced the master-work that deals with 'what concerns police [detailed provisions for giving effect to justice, in order to promote economic growth], revenue, and arms'.

12

Criticism of The Theory of Moral Sentiments

> I am now about publishing a new edition of my Book, and would be greatly obliged for any criticisms.

The world has not generally agreed with Smith's reported verdict that he 'always considered [*TMS*] as a much superior work to [*WN*]' (Romilly, 1840: i.403). However, we should not let the earlier book stand in the shadow of the later one. Smith always regarded himself as a moralist, and for the seventeen years before the appearance of *WN* he had a solid reputation as a man of letters based on the circulation of *TMS*, to which book he returned when preparing five further editions, seeking to improve and correct it until the end of his life.

His friends, of course, encouraged him in this activity, and sent him reports of the acceptance of the book, advice for it or other projects, and such criticism as occurred to them that might lead to its further development. On 14 June 1759, for example, William Robertson wrote to Smith, mentioning that John Home, the dramatist, was just arrived in Edinburgh with the news that *TMS* 'is in the hands of all the persons of the best fashion' in London and much approved for its matter and style. The English are comforted that as Smith was 'bred at Oxford, they claim some part of you'. Home joins Robertson in insisting that Smith write next 'on some subject less abstruse', and Robertson's wish is that Smith should think about the 'History of Philosophy' (*Corr.* No. 34). Perhaps Robertson is harking back to what Smith broached in his lectures at Edinburgh on scientific theory and left to us in *EPS*, or he may wish to have an expansion of what is presented as a history of systems of moral philosophy in Part VI of the 1759 *TMS*.

A letter from Hume dated 28 July describes responses to his circulation of presentations copies of *TMS*. Charles Yorke, the second son of Lord Chancellor Hardwicke, who inherited the family talent for law, was 'much taken with it', as was Burke, thought to be on a visit to Ireland but intending to write to Smith himself. Soame Jenyns had 'spoken very highly of the Book' to James Oswald, Smith's friend from early Kirkcaldy days. The publisher Millar heard from Lord Fitzmaurice (later Shelburne the Prime Minister) that he had 'carryd over a few

Copies to the Hague for Presents', presumably to distribute among British expatriates and Dutch intellectuals. James Wodrow mentioned in a letter to Samuel Kenrick of 4 January 1761 that Smith had read an article on *TMS* in 'the Hague Review' (perhaps *Bibliothèque des sciences et des beaux arts*, La Haye, 1754–78). He also reported that Smith's fellow-student at Glasgow, now the Scots minister in The Hague, Archibald Maclaine, 'continues a warm Hutchesonian', and will 'exert himself to defend Benevolence & the Moral Sense against the beautiful & refined system of Hobbism' (London, Dr Williams's Lib., MSS 24.257 No. 42). Smith had failed to infect one reader, presumably, with his own rebelliousness against Hutcheson's complete rejection of self-love as a motive that in certain respects is praiseworthy.

Hume ends his letter by teasing his friend that he 'must not be much engross'd with your own Book, as never to mention mine', meaning the most recent two volumes of the *History of England: The Tudors*, published in March 1759. He reports being told the Whigs 'are anew in a Rage against me', and thinks Smith will have seen the abuse directed at him in *Moral and Political Dialogues* (1759) by Richard Hurd, one of the 'insolent' and 'scurrilous' Warburtonian school. This was composed of the followers of Bishop William Warburton, who had characterized Hume as an 'atheistical Jacobite' (Mossner, 1980: 309).

Hume is in doubt whether to stay in London or return to Scotland, which 'suits my Fortune best, and is the seat of my principal Friendships; but it is too narrow a Place for me, and it mortifies me that I sometimes hurt my Friends'. Presumably he means because of his reputation for scepticism if not atheism. He makes an appeal to Smith: 'Pray write me your Judgement soon', and continues by asking if the 'Bigots', the High-flying Calvinists in Scotland, are 'much in Arms' over his Tudor volumes, which of course dealt with the Reformation in Scotland. The final sentences refer, first, to Robertson's *History of Scotland* (1759), which also dealt with the Reformation, but from the perspective of a Protestant Christian believer. Second, Hume mentions *TMS*, which had criticized Hume's moral theory and which had religious overtones, though those of natural religion rather than Christianity except in a curious passage on the Atonement (II.ii.3.13—withdrawn in edn. 6). Hume acknowledges ruefully that his friends, more prudent than he in coming closer to contemporary opinion about religion and morals, had benefited by the furore stirred up by his works: 'Robertson's Book has great Merit; but it was visible that he profited here by the Animosity against me. I suppose the Case was the same with you.'

In the body of this letter, Hume's friendship for Smith goes beyond reporting good news of the response to *TMS*, for we find the fruits of critical examination of Smith's system of morals. Hume has learned that Smith is preparing a new edition, with 'Alterations and Additions, in order to obviate Objections'. Accordingly, he takes the freedom to offer one which, if it has 'any Weight', Smith can consider:

I wish you had more particularly and fully prov'd, that all kinds of Sympathy are necessarily Agreeable. This is the Hinge of your System, and yet you only mention the Matter cursorily in p. 20 [I.i.2.6]. Now it woud appear that there is a disagreeable Sympathy, as well as an agreeable: And indeed, as the Sympathetic Passion is a reflex Image of the principal, it must partake of its Qualities, and be painful where this is so. Indeed, *when we converse with a man with whom we can entirely sympathize*, that is, where there is a warm and intimate Friendship, the cordial openness of such a Commerce overpowers the Pain of a disagreeable Sympathy, and renders the whole Movement agreeable. But in ordinary Cases, this cannot have place. . . . It is always thought a difficult Problem to account for the Pleasure, received from the Tears and Grief and Sympathy of Tragedy; which woud not be the Case, if all Sympathy was agreeable. An Hospital woud be a more entertaining Place than a Ball. I am afraid that in p. 99 [I.ii.5.4] and 111 [I.iii.1.9] this Proposition has escapd you, or rather it is interwoven with your Reasonings in that place. You say expressly, *it is painful to go along with Grief and we always enter into it with Reluctance.* It will probably be requisite for you to modify or explain this Sentiment, and reconcile it to your System. (*Corr.* No. 36)

Smith took Hume's objection seriously, but it must also be recounted that, in addition to this private communication to Smith about his system, Hume in all likelihood published a favourable 'abstract' of his friend's book in the *Critical Review* for May 1759. We are put on the trail of this 'abstract', which Smith never mentioned as far as is known, by a statement in the collection of anecdotes believed to emanate from David Callander. This source affirms categorically: 'Hume reviewed the Moral Sentiments [1759–1760]' (EUL MSS Laing 451/2; Raphael and Sakamoto, 1990; Raphael, 1992*a*).

Well-grounded scholarship by David Raynor has revealed or strongly indicated that Hume, while in London in 1758–9 seeing his Tudor history volumes through the press, submitted to the *Critical Review*, a periodical edited by Tobias Smollett 1756–63, a series of pieces. These were an ironic notice of Helvétius' *De l'esprit* (Nov. 1758), an article on Robertson's *History of Scotland* (Feb. 1759), a letter to the 'Authors' (editors) puffing the second edition of William Wilkie's *Epigoniad* (April), and finally the *TMS* 'abstract' (Raynor, 1982*a*; 1984; 1987*a*; Hume, *Phil. Wks.* iv.425). Hume's good nature is behind these last three pieces, also his fellow-feeling for Scots authors, especially when publishing a first book, a tender issue for him in view of the fate of the *Treatise*.

There are some expected and some surprising points in the 'abstract'. As the preface to the *Treatise*, with its stress on proceeding by observation and experiment ('moral Newtonianism'), might lead us to expect, the author of *TMS* is praised for following the 'practice of our modern naturalists [Newtonians], and [making] an appeal every moment to fact and experiment' (Raynor's 1984 text, p. 66). Also, as might be expected from someone of Hume's philosophical acumen, the key arguments of Smith about the role of sympathy in forming moral judgements are elucidated carefully, with two caveats. The first is that the 'abstract' declares that Smith by means of sympathy '*hopes* [my italics] to explain all the species of approbation and disapprobation, which are excited by human action or behaviour'. The second caveat is expressed in this fashion: on finding 'we feel pleasure when any passion or emotion appears in another with which we can sympathize, and a pain whenever the contrary happens, [Smith] *thinks* [my italics again], that this pleasure or pain will account for all our approbation or disapprobation of human action or behaviour' (Raynor, 1984: 67). Hume's letter to Smith of 28 July 1759 shows that he believed Smith's system to have shortcomings here.

Unexpectedly and, at first sight, disingenuously, the 'abstract' asserts that Smith 'subjoins many irrefragable arguments, by which he refutes the sentiments of Mr Hume, who founded a great part of his moral system on the consideration of public utility' (p. 74). In a summation, after presenting extensive excerpts, the reviewer praises *TMS* for its 'lively, perspicuous, manly, unaffected stile', a tribute to Smith's success in practising what he taught about rhetoric. Again unexpectedly, the next point concerns the

strict regard which the writer every where preserves to the principles of religion: however some pretenders to science may endeavour to separate the philosopher from the lover of religion, it will always be found, that truth being everywhere uniform and consistent, it is impossible for a man to divest himself of the one character, without renouncing all just claim to the other. (pp. 78–9)

If this indeed came from Hume's pen, it is difficult to stomach in view of the words put in the mouth of his *alter ego*, Philo, in the *Dialogues concerning Natural Religion*, written about the same time: 'And when we have to do with a man, who makes a great profession of religion and devotion; has this any other effect upon several, who pass for prudent, than to put them on their guard, lest they be cheated and deceived by him?' (pt. xii) But in the end, what have we found in the 'abstract' but the same artful Hume who blandly assures us through Pamphilus that the principles of the theist Cleanthes 'approach still nearer the truth' than those of Philo, whose sceptical arguments have not been eluded? Setting aside an impartial spectator's reaction to Hume's strategy, surely we can sympathize with, and thus approve of, the action of the established but controversial, because 'infidel', author. Hume gives the kiss of life to a younger friend's first book by ironically declaring its success in upholding religion, and refuting *An Enquiry concerning the Principles of Morals*, which he regarded as 'incomparably the best' of his writings (*My Own Life*).

Dr Johnson once distinguished between the reviewers of his time: 'The Critical Reviewers, I believe, often review without reading the books through; but lay hold of a topick, and write chiefly from their own minds. The Monthly Reviewers are duller men, and glad to read the books through' (*BLJ* 10 Apr. 1776). In the case of *TMS*, however, it is more likely that Hume read the book through, and William Rose, the former Marischal College student, schoolmaster, and translator of Sallust, who founded the *Monthly Review* with Ralph Griffiths in 1749, and wrote a notice about Smith's work for the July 1759 issue

(21: 1–18), may not. He certainly echoes parts of the *Critical Review* abstract, praising Smith for his 'perspicuous' style and his use of 'fact and experience' in illustrating his system. Like Hume, he is prepared to endorse the view that sympathy is an 'unquestionable principle in human nature', without going along with the reasonings about it. He neatly applies to Smith the praise *TMS* bestows on Hume, that he is highly ingenious and deals with the 'most intricate subjects not only with perspicuity but with elegance' (cf. *TMS* IV.1.2). Also, he recognizes that Smith had Hume in mind when criticizing utilitarian theory. Again, like the *Critical Review* 'abstract', Rose's notice singles out for special mention Smith's survey of systems of moral theory and the 'strict regard preserved, throughout, to the principles of religion'. Smith declared himself 'greatly obliged' to Ralph Griffiths for the 'very handsom Character he gave of my book in his review', in a letter dated 4 April 1760 addressed to Strahan, co-publisher of the *Monthly Review* (*Corr.* No. 50).

Burke apologizes to Smith in a letter of 10 September 1759 for delay in acknowledging the gift of a copy of *TMS* passed on by Hume. He wished to do justice to it by reading it with 'proper care and attention', which he now believes to have been 'extremely well bestowed and abundantly repaid'. He is convinced of the 'solidity and Truth' of Smith's theory, because it is based on the 'whole of Human Nature', whereas the 'old Systems of morality were too contracted'. Calling on that 'store of imagery' Johnson said he possessed (*BLJ* 15 Aug. 1773), Burke finds in architecture a simile to identify Smith as a system-builder:

All the writers who have treated this Subject before you were like those Gothic Architects who were fond of turning great Vaults upon a single slender Pillar; There is art in this, and there is a degree of ingenuity without doubt; but it is not sensible, and cannot long be pleasing. A theory like yours founded on the Nature of man, which is always the same, will last . . .

Burke also describes Smith's style as 'well varied' and in some passages reaching the sublime, 'particularly in that fine Picture of the Stoic Philosophy . . . which is dressed out in all the grandeur and Pomp that becomes that magnificent delusion'. Smith may not have relished that barb, or the criticism that in certain places he was a 'little too diffuse'. The ensuing review Burke wrote for the *Annual Register* (1759: 484 ff.) is in the same strain, with an emphasis on Smith's originality of speculation, revealed in raising from a 'simple truth', that of the role of sympathy in forming our judgements, 'one of the most beautiful fabrics of moral theory, that has perhaps ever appeared'.

Far away from the 'Mob of Literati' in London, a severer view of *TMS* was taken in a Scottish country manse of the time, perhaps reflecting the outlook of middle-of-the-road clergy. This was entrusted to the diary kept by the Revd George Ridpath, minister of the parish of Stichel, near Kelso in the Border country. He attended to the sick in his parish, was not too hard on fornicators, liked gardening, was a friend of John Home the poet, could be found in the

company of Robertson and Carlyle of Inveresk at the meetings of the General
Assembly in Edinburgh, and loved books. He enjoyed the classics and some
modern authors such as Swift and Sterne. He did not think highly of Smollett's
Universal History, and Smith's first book did not come up to his standard for
style or content:

The work shows him to be a man of knowledge and of genius, too, but yet I can by no
means join in the applauses I have heard bestowed on it. What is new in it is perhaps of
no great moment in itself, and is neither distinctly nor clearly established. An extravagant
turn to declaim and embellish leads him quite astray from that study of accuracy, precision, and clearness that is so essentially necessary to the delivering of any theory, especially a new one; and his indulgence of this humour for playing everywhere the orator,
tho' his oratorical talents are far from being extraordinary, has made him spin out to the
tedious length of 400 pages what in my opinion might be delivered as fully and with far
more energy and perspicuity in 20. What can this arise from but the man's being used all
his life to declaim to boys and not attending to the distinction necessary to be made
betwixt a circle of *them* as auditors and a world of cool and reasonable men as readers?
The most valuable part of the work, tho' not altogether free from the fault taken notice
of, is the account given in the end of the different systems of Moral Philosophy, Ancient
and Modern. (Ridpath, 1922: 275)

Stylistic comparison of the 1759 text of *TMS* and material written specially
for the later editions suggests that Smith moved away from the declamation that
he had found successful in holding the attention of his large moral philosophy
classes of adolescents (*TMS* intro. 5). In Smith's good years, these would consist of eighty boys about 15 or 16, most of them destined to be ministers or
dominies, but some intended for careers as merchants and lawyers, and some taking the moral philosophy class for a second or third time.

Both a firming up of the style, then, and theoretical adjustment are found in
'Papers' which Smith sent to Gilbert Elliot on 10 October 1759 (*Corr.* No. 40).
These constitute draft amendments for the second edition of *TMS* in print by
30 December 1760 (*Corr.* No. 54). Included in the letter to Elliot is the following comment: 'You will find in the Papers I have sent you an answer to an objection of D. Humes. I think I have entirely discomfitted him.' Scholars have been
divided over whether Smith's claim here is justified. In a nutshell, Hume's view
is that Smith is inconsistent in arguing generally that pleasure is attached to our
sympathetic feelings, also that when we feel approval this is a specific kind of
pleasure we take in virtuous action. A further inconsistency, in Hume's view, is
Smith's claim that we sympathize with grief in appropriate circumstance thus
approving of it, and so experiencing pleasure. Yet, at the same time, Smith concedes that to sympathize with grief is painful (*Corr.* No. 36).

The answer, which went into edition 2 as a note to 1.iii.1.9, adds nothing new
to *TMS* but explains in more detail Smith's view that the nature of sympathy is
twofold: 'the Sympathetic passion of the Spectator; and, secondly, the emotion
that arises from his observing the perfect coincidence between this sympathetic

passion in himself and the original passion in the person principally concerned' (*Corr.* 51). The second kind is always delightful, but the first may be either agreeable or disagreeable.

The champion of Hume asks how the disagreeable can give rise to the agreeable, and detects Smith in a circular argument in accounting for moral judgements (Raynor, 1984: 58). A more finely drawn examination of the exchange, however, points out that Hume and Smith mean different things in using the word 'sympathy': Hume means the communication of feeling, and Smith means the psychological mechanism that provides an approach to mutuality of feeling. This insight leads to the assimilation of 'disagreeable Sympathy' into the operation of laws of sympathy yielding moral judgements (Campbell, 1971: 104–6).

The bulk of the draft amendments sent to Elliot, however, mark a theoretical advancement in Smith's system through further development of the concept of the impartial spectator. Commentators have been particularly interested in one outcome of this development. It is the parallel that can be drawn between moral forces achieving balance in society through the mechanism of sympathy in agent/impartial spectator interactions, on the one hand, and, on the other, the interplay of economic forces subjected to the market mechanism (as if led by an invisible hand) tending to establish the natural level of prices and wages and overall economic efficiency (Campbell, 1971: 138–9, n. 1; Skinner, 1979: 162, n. 11; Fleischacker, 1991: 258). Smith's sophistication in analysis of the interdependence of complex forces in each domain is clear, and no doubt the focus on moral psychology in *TMS* contributed to the later successful discussion of economics in *WN*.

We do not have information about the precise objection Elliot sent Smith, but David Raphael suggests that, judging from what Smith wrote in reply, it concerned the formation of moral judgements according to social attitudes of approval and disapproval. If our moral assessment of our own motives and actions depends on these attitudes, how can we uphold a different and higher standard of morality in the face of whatever society is prepared to accept? Smith reports to Elliot his difficulties in the composition of the alteration to his text: 'This cost me more time and thought than you can well imagine . . . for nothing is more difficult than to insert something into the middle of what is already composed and to connect it cleverly at both ends.'

Smith had other difficulties with composition: his penmanship was 'slow and laboured', as John Rae observed (1965: 261), and he resorted to dictating to an amanuensis, at least as early as the preparation of the Edinburgh lectures (Stewart iv.25). The 1759 *TMS* amendments are in the hand of the amanuensis who produced the early draft of *WN*, and this same hand is found extensively in the Glasgow University records of the period (*Corr.* 51, n. 9). Also, the watermark on the paper of the MS is the same as that of the fragment on justice (see *TMS* 388), but the hand in this case is different.

The manner of the amendment designed to obviate Elliot's objection mingles types of discourse associated with law, natural theology, and evolved Stoicism. It is not embellished with illustrations from literature or the contemporary social scene such as might have pleased Smith's student auditors, and which he provided liberally in edition 1 of *TMS*. Smith's argument is that the impartial spectator created by the imagination can attain an objectivity from which real spectators fall short because of ignorance and prejudice. One source of Smith's argument here could be Kames's 'Criminal Law' essay in *Historical Law-Tracts* (1758). In its opening pages the point is made that a delinquent who hurts others perceives, as do observers, that he is guilty, and feels remorse:

And which is extremely remarkable, his remorse is accompanied with an anxious dread that the punishment will be inflicted, unless it be prevented by reparation or atonement. Thus in the breast of man a tribunal is erected for conscience: sentence passeth against him for every delinquency; and he is delivered over to the hand of Providence to be punished in proportion to his guilt.

Smith maintains this terminology of the tribunal of conscience with its theological overtones, until he passes to the consideration that its authority comes from popular opinion with which it often clashes. The concept of the impartial spectator is then introduced through a legal metaphor:

We soon learn, therefore, to sett up in our minds a judge between ourselves and those we live with. We Conceive ourselves as acting in the presence of a person quite candid and equitable . . . meerly a man in general, an Impartial Spectator who considers our conduct with the same indifference with which we regard that of other people.

Stoic discourse comes in with the claim that the weak, vain, and frivolous never think of appealing to the superior court of the impartial spectator: when they are injured by the world, they cannot do themselves justice and are the 'Slaves of the world'. It is solely from the 'Station' of the impartial spectator that we see our 'real littleness . . . and learn the great lesson of Stoical magnanimity and firmness' (*Corr.* 54–6).

Smith notes, too, following Hume's second *Enquiry* (v.ii.185), that the exercise of the imagination to achieve moral objectivity resembles that attaining objective visual judgement, surely recalling his treatment of the latter subject in his essay on the external senses (*EPS* 152–3, n. 19). One difference between these texts, however, is that the essay refers to 'arms of the sea' (p. 54) in the view described by Smith, perhaps appropriate for a vantage-point in Edinburgh's Old Town, overlooking the Firth of Forth, whereas the phrase is dropped from Letter No. 40, as inappropriate for a view from a house in Glasgow.

Smith appeals in his letter to Elliot to comment on his arguments:

[to] confirm my Doctrine that our judgments concerning our own conduct have always a reference to the sentiments of some other being, and to show that, notwithstanding this, real magnanimity and conscious virtue can support itself under the disapprobation of all mankind.

He also calls for a comment on what he wrote concerning Mandeville's system, and asks Elliot to 'consider whether upon the whole I do not make Virtue sufficiently independent of popular opinion'. If Elliot is still not satisfied, Smith is prepared to make his teaching 'a great deal plainer, by a great number of new illustrations'. We do not have a reply from Elliot to this letter, but no further illustrations were added to the impartial spectator addition for the text of *TMS* edition 2.

Smith wrote to Strahan on 4 April 1760 that he had sent to Millar 'four of five Posts ago the same additions which I had formerly sent to you with a good many corrections and improvements which occurred to me since'. He then asks for a marked-up copy of his book containing all the corrections Strahan would wish him to make. He appreciates that it is troublesome, but it would oblige him greatly:

I know how much I shall be benefitted and I shall at the same time preserve the pretious right of private judgement for the sake of which our forefathers kicked out the Pope and the Pretender. I believe you to be much more infallible than the Pope, but as I am a Protestant my conscience makes me scruple to submit to any unscriptural authority. (*Corr.* No. 50)

Smith refers to the fact that as a printer Strahan exercised control over revisions of what are called 'accidentals' in a text, that is, punctuation, spelling, word division, and, of course, type-fount extending to the use of capitals, lower-case letters, and italic or romanic type. As an author, Smith would be responsible for changes in 'substantives', wording as expressive of meaning, but there might be issues connected with 'accidentals', punctuation and italicization, for instance, of importance to him and therefore to be introduced or rejected (*TMS* intro. 37–8).

In the event, Smith was not entirely pleased with Strahan's handling of the second edition, and wrote to him on 30 December 1760 enclosing an errata sheet with an admonition again in mock-religious terms also favoured by Hume in a jocular mood:

The opposite leaf will set before your eyes the manifold sins and iniquities you have been guilty of in printing my book. The first six, at least the first [approbation *to be changed to* disapprobation], third [utility *to* disutility] and fourth [pleased *to* displeased] and sixth [public or private *to* public to private] are what you call sins against the holy Ghost which cannot upon any account be pardoned. The Remainder are capable of remission in case of repentance, humiliation and contrition. (*Corr.* No. 54)

The sins against the Holy Ghost were expunged in edition 3 appearing in 1767, but of the twenty-five lesser errata only fifteen were corrected piecemeal up to the sixth edition of *TMS*, and others never were until the Glasgow edition of 1976. Smith wished to have the second edition as perfect as possible; he directed his amanuensis to make corrections in author's copies of it, and added some himself. Two such corrected copies of the edition have turned up, one of them a gift to Turgot (Jammes, 1976: item 765) and the other a recent saleroom item (Sotheby's Catalogue, 15 Dec. 1987: *English Literature and History*, item no. 312; Raphael, *TMS* repr. 1991: 402).

Smith may have transacted business concerning *TMS* in England in the summer of 1760. He had been ill off and on from March, then had gone to Edinburgh at the beginning of July and lay in a damp bed, provoking a violent recurrence of the illness. As mentioned already, Dr Cullen told him to save his life by riding 500 miles before September (*Corr.* No. 52). Smith's physician probably diagnosed his friend's illness as hypochondriasis, which seems to have afflicted Smith at Oxford. Writing about this condition, believed by contemporaries to arise from an excited imagination affecting the body in a morbid way, Cullen urged that the passions should be soothed, and that 'mechanical means of interrupting thought' should be tried as remedies. Horseback riding as part of a journey he reckoned to be best, since the sufferer would be removed from 'uneasiness and care' at home, engaged in 'more constant exercise' especially appropriate for the non-athletic, and afforded ever-changing objects of attention (Barfoot, 1991: 208–10).[1] Joseph Black's advice in 1789 to James Watt, another man of genius who suffered from anxiety and depression, was to buy a horse and ride as much as possible (Doig, 1982: 39).

Cullen was offering advice to Smith similar to what he had given in 1751, to alleviate anxiety over the Glasgow professorship (*Corr.* No. 304). In 1760 it is likely that he wished to help his friend recover from the prolonged nervous strain of composing *TMS*, and then putting fresh demands on himself to meet criticisms of his book while preparing a new edition. Hume was later to advise Smith to enjoy company and relaxation to cope with the hypochondriasis caused by work on *WN* (*Corr.* No. 129).

Smith accepted Cullen's advice on this occasion, and we know that he planned to go to York and the West of England, also that he visited Loakes House (now Wycombe Abbey), home of the 1st Earl of Shelburne, father of his pupil, the Hon. Thomas Petty Fitzmaurice (*Corr.* No. 52). This seat is about thirty miles from London, near a well-travelled road to Oxford. Smith's letter to Strahan of 30 December 1760 has a postscript asking that he be remembered to Dr Franklin and his son, who frequented the Strahan household, 1757–62 (Cochrane, 1964: 100–8). Smith also mentions Mrs Strahan. Since he had met the Franklins personally in Glasgow or Edinburgh in the early autumn of 1759, linking them with Strahan's wife may mean he has also met her in person in the Strahan home in London.

Further, Smith asks to be remembered to William Rose, whom we know to have been a reviewer of *TMS*: 'Tell him I have not forgot what I promised him. . . . My Delay, I hope, will occasion him no inconveniency: if it does I shall be excessively concerned and shall order some papers I left in England to be given to him.' Smith goes on to say that these 'Papers' are 'not what I would wish them, but I had rather lose a little reputation with the public as let him suffer by my negligence' (*Corr.* No. 54). Could it be the case that Smith met the

Strahans and Rose during this jaunt to regain his health, and could the 'Papers' be his essay on languages, published the next year in *The Philological Miscellany*, but later reprinted in edition 3 of *TMS* (1767)? David Raynor has traced in the Strahan Ledgers the transaction of 1,000 copies of the *Miscellany* being printed for Rose in April 1761, and he was also charged £3 11s. for extra corrections (BL Add. MS 48803A, fo. 57). About the same time, November or December 1760, Hume wrote to Strahan 'that it shoud be absolutely impossible for me, till my present Undertaking is finished [the *History of England*], to have any hand in what [Rose] proposes to me', and apologizes both on Strahan's 'Account' and that of Rose, so the printer must have been involved in this proposal too (*HL* i.336).

In the Advertisement to the *Miscellany*, the Editor, probably William Rose, states that its design is to publish the 'most useful and entertaining Essays in the *Memoirs of the Academy of Belles Lettres* at Paris', together with a 'variety of Articles from the French *Encyclopédie*', also 'Dissertations on Philological Subjects by foreign writers' unknown to English readers, and original essays by writers in Britain. Smith's essay seems to be the only one appearing for the first time, and the only one truly philological in nature. Some essays drawn from the *Memoirs of the Academy of Belles Lettres* deal with the problem of veracity in history, and are by authors of a sceptical tendency who contributed to the debate over miracles. One is Lévesque de Pouilly, represented by 'A Dissertation upon the Uncertainty of the History of the four first Ages of Rome' and 'New Critical Essays upon the Fidelity of History'. Another is Nicholas Fréret, represented by 'General Observations upon the study of the Ancient Philosophers'. Both writers contributed to contemporary historical Pyrrhonism, systematic and unresolvable doubt focused on truth claims in history, particularly in relation to miracles (Wootton, 1990).

Hume in a sense kept the debate over miracles going in 1760 with a 'new edition' of the *Essays and Treatises*, which contained the first *Enquiry* with its notorious essay 'Of Miracles', and he was to be answered in 1762 by the orthodox Aberdeen divine George Campbell in his *Dissertation on Miracles*. It is therefore understandable why he would be approached about appearing in such a publication as the *Miscellany*. As to Rose's involvement, he may well have been of a sceptical tendency himself. Certainly, Dr Johnson told George III 'that the authors of the Monthly Review were enemies to the Church' (*BLJ* Feb. 1767). Franklin seemed to think Strahan himself was an agnostic: 'If you had Christian Faith, quantum suff.', he once wrote to him (Cochrane, 1964: 155).

And what about Smith's role in the *Miscellany* beyond that of being one of its authors? Gilbert Elliot knew something about the matter, because he wrote in an undated letter to Hume about expected publications in the 1760s: 'Lord Littleton's history, Sir James Stuarts book, and Robertsons history and Fergusons Morals, will employ us for two years to come. Then your K[ing] Williams and Smiths Miscellany will succeed' (NLS MS 11009, fo. 125).[2] The

Advertisement to the *Miscellany* ends with the information that it has been printed solely at the 'Editor's' expense; if the first volume is well received, the 'second Volume will be published in January next, and afterwards a Volume every Six Months, till the whole design is compleated'.

The design itself seems to connect with Smith's appeal in his letter to the *Edinburgh Review* (1756) for attention to the products of European learning. Could Rose have taken Smith up on this idea? Perhaps Rose suggested that Smith and Hume contribute to a new periodical to be published by Strahan, through selection of French items and translations (both men had the necessary skills) and original contributions? Smith's essay responded to speculations by Mandeville, Condillac, and Rousseau about the 'origin and progress' of languages, expanding the third lecture of the rhetoric series. Smith's name continued to be associated with the intended periodical, and in an 1802 issue of *The European Magazine, and London Review* (41: 249), an anonymous letter dated 10 April of that year mentioned that 'in 1761 was published, I believe by Dr Smith, "The Philological Miscellany" ', in which appeared the essay on languages (*LRBL* 26). No further volume appeared after the first to shed more light on the *Miscellany*, and we must be content with the fact that in it Smith appeared in company with Lévesque de Pouilly, instigator of the title, at least, of *TMS*.

When Smith visited London in 1761, from late August to early October, on Glasgow University business, he apparently travelled south with the admirer of *TMS* who had distributed copies in The Hague, now the 2nd Earl of Shelburne, and made him a convert to his economic principles (Stewart, n. 1; *EPS* 347). He may well have hoped to enjoy recognition in London after the appearance earlier in the year of the new and, as he believed, improved version of his system of morals. One London Scots from whom he wished to have an opinion was Robert Clerk, advancing steadily in an army career, and Smith asked Gilbert Elliot to arrange this (*Corr.* No. 40). Clerk, who was a protégé in politics of Lord Shelburne, was described by Carlyle of Inveresk as a 'very Singular [Man] of a very Ingenious and Active Intellect'. Carlyle had to confess, however, that 'of all the Men who had so much understanding, he was the Most Disagreable person to Converse with whom I ever knew'. His style suited his profession: 'He applied his Warlike Ideas to Colloquial Intercourse, and attackd your Opinions as he would a Redoubt or a Castle, not by sap or mine, but by open Storm.' Carlyle once proposed to send Clerk to visit Adam Ferguson sick in bed with a fever: 'God forbid,' was the despairing rejoinder, '. . . as you Regard my Life!' (Carlyle, 1973: 231–2).

Writing some time after 1800, that being the date of the watermark on the manuscript, Adam Ferguson put down an account of a dialogue dealing with the principle of moral estimation. This is introduced with the words: 'When Mr Hume was at London to publish some volume of the *History of England*, General Clerk called in a morning and soon after Mr Smith came in also' (EUL MS Dc. I. 42, No. 25; Mossner, 1960). We know where such a meeting could have taken place. Hume had written to Smith on 29 June 1761, 'I am so far on my Road to London, where I hope to see you this Season. I shall lodge in Miss Elliots Lisle Street Leicester Fields; and I beg it of you to let me hear from you the Moment of your Arrival' (*Corr.* No. 57). Hume remained in London until December, staying in this boarding-house for Scots in London, kept by poor relations of Gilbert Elliot's family, and his business was indeed the publication of the final volumes (v and vi) of his *History*, dealing with the period from Julius Caesar to 1485, 'which I gave to the world in 1761 with tolerable, and but tolerable Success' (*My Own Life*). The 'new edition' of his *Essays and Treatises* of 1760 contained the second *Enquiry* dealing with morals, so that subject was on his mind as well. Clerk was also in London in the autumn of 1761, and Hume was on good terms with him, also with Shelburne, with whom Clerk was connected (*NHL* 64–5).

We have no evidence that Ferguson was himself in London during the period of Smith's stay, but the dialogue he composed could be a Boswellian report, that is, a conversation reconstructed from notes some time after it had taken place, to bring out nuances of character and the tenor of exchanges between individuals. The *Life of Johnson* reached a third edition in 1799 to growing acclaim, and could well have inspired Ferguson. More likely, he had the example of his close friend Alexander Carlyle of Inveresk who was writing down his *Anecdotes and Characters* between 1800 and 1804 dealing with the leading personalities of the Scottish Enlightenment, and basing himself on diary memoranda and journals, also on his prodigious memory, in presenting runs of conversation (Carlyle, 1973: pp. xix–xx).

Moreover, this dialogue on the principle of moral estimation goes together with another dialogue (watermarked 1799) extending discussion from ethics to aesthetics. The participants in this case are the architect Robert Adam; William Cleghorn, who secured the Edinburgh Chair in Moral Philosophy in preference to Hume in 1745, and who died in 1754; William Wilkie, the author of the *Epigoniad*; David Hume; and Ferguson himself, who is given the last word. In both dialogues, a focus for criticism is Smith's theory of sympathy. Taken together, the dialogues are more Platonic than Boswellian in that a specific philosophic doctrine is being pursued, though Ferguson is perhaps less interested in the possibilities of dialectic than his master Plato, and in the second case Ferguson allows himself an extended monologue to present his own views (EUL MS Dc. 1. 42, No. 5; Mossner, 1963).

The first dialogue begins with Clerk expressing pleasure that Hume has taken to writing history, after which these two fall to discussing moral theory. Clerk ends this part with the flat assertion: 'It is well known that there is a distinction of Good and Evil in human life and till we have ascertaind that distinction and made our Choice, all our Inquiries are nugatory and absurd' (Mossner, 1960: 227). Thereafter Smith is announced and enters the room, 'with a smile on his Countenance and muttering somewhat to himself' (p. 228). Carlyle of Inveresk described Adam Smith in precisely the same way: 'He was the most absent man in Company I ever saw, Moving his Lips and Talking to himself, and Smiling' (1973: 141).

Hume tells Smith they have been discussing the 'Theory of moral sentiment':

SMITH: My Book. I am sorry to have been away. I should willingly profit by your remarks. General, he said then, observing him for the first time, I have long wished to know your opinion. I think I have removed all difficulties and made the *Theory* Compleat.

To this the General made no answer tho Mr Smith made some pause as expecting to hear what he would say. But continued, People thought I should never be able to get over the difficulty of supposing a man to sympathize with himself or if he did not chance to take that trouble what means he had of being admonished of his Faults. I have removed both these difficulties and I should be glad to know your opinion.

CLERK: I don't much like to trouble authors with my opinion of their works.
SMITH: Ah, Do, you will oblige me!
CLERK: If you insist upon it. I must be plain and leave no doubts.
SMITH: Surely. Surely.
CLERK: Your Book is to me a Heap of absolute Nonsense. (p. 228)

Not surprisingly, Smith seems to be 'stunnd' by this response to his system. This is a dramatic turning-point in the dialogue similar to those of the numbing of Meno and then of his slave, when Plato has Socrates redirect the discussion of the nature of virtue. Ferguson has Smith explain his view of the twofold nature of sympathy and the role of the impartial spectator, along the lines of the 1759 draft amendments to *TMS*, but Clerk will have none of it:

You began with calling Sympathy to explain Moral Sentiment. You now call up moral sentiment to explain itself: what is a well informed and impartial observer, but a Virtuous Person whose Sympathy must be relied on as a Test of Virtue? . . . Such a person is not likely to misslead those who confide in him and such a Person every one is concerned to become in himself and instead of acquiesing in Sympathy as the Test of Virtue, appeals to Virtue as the test of Just Sympathy. (p. 229)

This same line of criticism of Smith's theory emerges in the *Lectures on Ethics* (1846: 147) of Thomas Brown, subsequent holder of Ferguson's Chair of Moral Philosophy in Edinburgh. In his day he was regarded as a brilliant teacher, though Principal J. C. Shairp of St Andrews University said he was a 'long-winded' one (Davie, 1961: 18, 147, 263). Brown wrote: '[Smith's error is] no less than the assumption, in every case, of those very moral feelings which are supposed to flow from sympathy, the assumption of them as necessarily existing before that very sympathy in which they are said to originate' (quoted in Campbell, 1971: 119).

In the second dialogue, Ferguson speaks in his own person in the discussion of beauty and happiness. He demonstrates his Platonism in expressing the desire to mount from apprehension of physical objects to those worthy of moral esteem and admiration, and in so doing to experience ecstasy in contemplating the

'Divine Artist'. Answering the question Smith posed in *TMS* as fundamental to ethics: 'On what Principle do men actually decide or entertain Sentiments of Praise or Blame?', Ferguson admits that self-interest plays a part in judging merit in others; then, responding to Smith and those of his persuasion, he states his own principles of moral realism, echoing some of the wording he had given Robert Clerk:

To others we may admit that what they are pleased to call sympathy or even coincidence of Sentiments or [the] reverse is the ordinary or frequent ground of Estimation of praise or Censure. But we cannot admit that either is a safe ground of Estimation, much less the only Ground which Nature has laid for the distinction of Right and Wrong. And every attempt to Instruct us on the Subject without distinguishing the Questions is not only Nugatory and Perplexing to the unwary but actually tending to explain away distinctions of the utmost importance to Mankind, turning Zeal for Morals into a mere selfish Interest or into a mere coincidence of sentiment which may take place among Knaves and Fools as well as among honest Men. (Mossner, 1963: 308)

The personal relationship between Smith and Ferguson, to be discussed more fully later, had its ups and downs. Carlyle of Inveresk alleged that Smith 'had been weak enough' to accuse Ferguson of plagiarism from him in his *History of Civil Society*. Carlyle also wrote that all of Ferguson's books met with undeserved disparagement, including his *Principles of Moral Philosophy* (1st edn. 1792). Certainly, Lord Kames wrote disparagingly to the Bern jurist, Daniel Fellenberg: 'Dr Ferguson's Institutes [of Morals] is a careless trifle intended for his scholars and never meant to wander out of that circle' (Bern, Bürgerbibliothek MS). It may be that tension between Smith and Ferguson over the relative success of their writings was reflected in these late dialogues, more notable for comic effect than serious philosophy.

Nevertheless Ferguson, in seeking to triumph in retrospect over Smith by demonstrating that his system of morals is refutable, points the way to later, more philosophically subtle, criticism of *TMS*. Ferguson's claim that Smith's system was actually pernicious paralleled that made by another important contemporary Scottish philosopher; but before dealing with that issue, one more confrontation involving Smith and plausibly dated 1761, like the one with Robert Clerk, must be recounted.

This concerns the Great Moralist himself, Dr Johnson. Robertson is the source of the story:

the first time I met [Johnson] was one evening at Strahan's, when he had just had an unlucky altercation with Adam Smith, to whom he had been so rough, that Strahan, after Smith was gone, had remonstrated with him, and told him that I was coming soon, and that he was uneasy to think that he might behave in the same manner to me. (*BLJ* iii.331–2)

Johnson himself acknowledged to Boswell on 14 July 1763 that he and Smith 'did not take to each other' at their first meeting (*BLJ* i.427), which suggests that the 'unhappy altercation' took place two years before, since Smith was not in London again until January 1764 *en route* to France. What did they quarrel about? One suggestion is that Smith was boasting about Glasgow, and Johnson offensively asked him if he had ever seen Brentford which had a reputation for being extraordinarily repulsive, the poet Thomson calling it a 'town of mud' (*Castle of Indolence*, lxxix: *BLJ* v.369; iv.186 and 513).

Another possibility is that on this occasion, as on others, Johnson was speaking of Hume 'in a very illiberal manner', which Boswell observed Johnson was 'often heard' to do (*BP* xii.227), and Smith took offence on behalf of his friend. Walter Scott had a garbled story to the effect that Johnson once attacked Smith for praising Hume and called him a liar, whereupon Smith retorted that Johnson was a son of a bitch. If this was the quarrel of 1761, it then has to be explained how Smith could accept in 1775 membership in The Club formed by Sir Joshua Reynolds to afford Johnson an opportunity for talking.[3]

At bottom, however, Johnson's antagonism to Smith and to his friend Hume is likely to have been on the score of religion. He clung to the revealed variety in the face of the scepticism his mind could not help revolving (cf. *BLJ* i.428). In 1761 Hume the avowed sceptic was one of Strahan's successful authors, and now his friend Smith had achieved two editions of a book whose naturalistic account of morals must have seemed dangerous in tendency to him, offering counsel for self-deceit leading to perdition. Boswell explains Johnson's stance succinctly: 'His profound adoration of the GREAT FIRST CAUSE was such as to set him above that "Philosophy and vain deceit" [Col. 2: 8] with which men of narrower conceptions had been infected' (*BLJ* iv.31, n. 1; Hudson, 1988: 75). Johnson would detect in Smith's viewpoint the 'infection of Hume's society', as Archbishop William Magee of Dublin called it (*TMS* 384). Though Smith was not a quarrelsome man, he had a 'warm' temper, and is not likely to have submitted in argument to Johnson. Hence, it may be supposed, the flare-up in Strahan's house.

At a philosophical level, the same distrust of Smith's teaching manifests itself in the response to *TMS* of that other Scottish moralist, whom we will now name as Thomas Reid. The turn of events here is that the acclaim given to Smith as the author of this book led to his removal from Glasgow to become the tutor of the 3rd Duke of Buccleuch. It was Reid who was elected Smith's successor in 1764, largely because of intervention by Kames (*Corr.* No. 80), and by February of the next year Reid was directing Glasgow students away from Smith's system of morals and towards a Common Sense formulation also favoured by Kames. Reid had begun making notes on *TMS* on its first publication, and as his moral philosophy course at Glasgow developed he arrived at the following critical views of his predecessor:

. . . it is obvious that according to [Smith's] System there is no fixed Standard of Virtue at all[;] it depends not upon our own Actions but upon the Tone of our Passions[,] which in different men is different from Constitution[.] Nor does it solely depend upon our own

Passions but also upon the Sympathetick passions of others[,] which may be different in different Persons or in the same Person at different Times. Nor is there any Standard according to which either the Emotions of the Actor or the Sympathy of the Spectator is to be measured[;] all that is required is that they be in Harmony or Concord. It is evident that the ultimate Measure and Standard of Right and Wrong in human Conduct according to this System of Sympathy, is not any fixed Judgment grounded upon Truth or upon the dictates of a well informed Conscience but the variable opinions and passions of Men. So that we may apply to this System, what Cicero says of the Epicurean[:] 'So your school undoubtedly preaches the pretence of justice instead of the real and genuine thing. Its lesson amounts to this—we are to despise the trustworthy voice of our own conscience, and to run after the fallible imaginations of other men.' (H. Rackham's Loeb Classical Library translation of *De Finibus* 2.22, quoted in Latin by Reid)[4]

If Smith was being supplanted by Reid on his native ground as a teacher of moral philosophy, *TMS* was making him famous in Europe. We trace the book's reception in France and something of its translation history there in the next chapter. The reception of Smith's moral thought in Germany is also a remarkable story. Lessing and Herder were reading *TMS* in English in the 1760s, as references to it in *Laokoon* (1766) and the *Kritischen Wälder* (1769) make clear. A letter to Kant dated 1771 from a friend named Markus Herz declares he has heard from David Friedländer that Smith is Kant's *Liebling* (favourite), suggesting a first flush of enthusiasm. The linkage in this letter of Smith's name to that of 'Home' (i.e. Kames) as author of the *Elements of Criticism* suggests the focus of attention was aesthetic theory. The concept of the sympathetic imagination, in particular, was highly attractive to German men of letters, and reflection on it probably helped to shape the new drama of the period, such as Lessing's *Nathan der Weise* (1779; English translation 1781). More generally, some prompting from *TMS*, as well as from Ferguson's *History of Civil Society*, may lie behind Kant's notion of the 'unsocial sociability' of man in the essay, 'Idee zu einer allgemeinen Geschichte in Weltbuergerlicher Absicht' (1784).

Of greater interest, however, is Kant's response to aspects of Smith's moral theory, such as the role of the impartial spectator, mentioned in the *Reflexionen* of various dates, but probably after 1771, also in the *Anthropologie in pragmatischer Hinsicht abgefasst* (1798). Further, Samuel Fleischacker has made out an interesting case for elucidating carefully references to the impartial spectator and Smithian moral rules and judgement, first pointed out by August Oncken (1877), in Kant's foremost writings, in particular the *Groundwork of the Metaphysics of Morals* (1785), *Critique of Practical Reason* (1788), and *Doctrine of Virtue* (*Metaphysik der Sitten*, pt. ii, 1797). To take up one strand of the argument, Smith had made an issue of humanity's capacity for self-deceit as the prime threat to our moral understanding and action (*TMS* III.4.4). Kant's categorical imperative, as portrayed by Fleischacker, functions above all as an antidote to self-deceit: 'act as if the maxim of your action were to become through your will a universal law of action' (Kant, *Groundwork*, trans. Paton, 1948: 89). The conclusion reached from this study of references to, or echoes of, *TMS* is that Kant 'shares the direction of his work, if not its destination, with the moral philosophy of Adam Smith' (Fleischacker, 1991).

There were two early translations of *TMS* into German. The first was by Christian Guenther Rautenberg, whose version of Kames's *Principles of Morality and Natural Religion* appeared in 1768, and his *Theorie der moralischen Empfindungen von Adam Smith*, based on edition 3 (1767), was published in 1770. Kant is not thought to have read English, and would have relied on the Rautenberg translation. The second translation was by Ludwig Theobul Kosegarten, and it came out in 1791: *Theorie der sittlichen Gefuehle*, based either on edition 4 of *TMS* (1774) or edition 5 (1781). This translator issued a supplementary volume in 1795 including the whole of part III as revised for edition 6 of 1790, and the chief additions to that text such as the new part VI, 'Of the Character of Virtue' (*TMS*, German trans., Eckstein, 1926). To his translation of Smith's account of systems of moral philosophy, which had successively pleased Hume, Reid, and Ferguson, despite their criticisms of Smith's own effort, Kosegarten added his own review of Kant's theory.[5] This is indication enough that, if not absolutely a landmark book, *TMS* was surely accepted into the mainstream of European thought. It made Kant ask the question: 'where in Germany is the man who can write so well about the moral character?'[6] In France, where we now follow Smith, he caused Voltaire to exclaim: 'We have nothing to compare with him, and I am embarrassed for my dear compatriots.'[7]

13

Travelling Tutor

I have had the honour of a letter from Charles Townshend renewing . . . his former proposal that I should travel with the Duke of Buccleugh.

David Hume is our source for the story behind Adam Smith's visit to France and Switzerland from 1764 to 1766. Of course, Smith had prepared himself for this visit with studies going back to his Oxford days. Also, he had reflected considerable knowledge of French literature and thought in *TMS*, and in the letter to the *Edinburgh Review* of 1755–6 he had expressed admiration for Diderot and d'Alembert, the editors of the *Encyclopédie*, who were to become his friends in Paris; for Rousseau, whose 'passionate esteem' for Geneva moved him; and, above all, for Voltaire, whom he was to meet several times at Ferney, in the vicinity of Geneva: 'the most universal genius perhaps which France has ever produced'. During the Seven Years War, when many of Smith's fellow-Britons were bent on killing Frenchmen, he was learning from them and seeking to make his students at Glasgow University learn from them. Hume's role in securing the opportunity for Smith to travel emerges in the letter, already quoted, which he wrote to his friend on 12 April 1759 to describe the success of *TMS*.

Hume reported as follows: 'Charles Towns[h]end, who passes for the cleverest Fellow in England, is so taken with the Performance, that he said . . . he wou'd put the Duke of Buccleugh under the Authors Care, and woud endeavour to make it worth his while to accept of that Charge' (*Corr.* No. 31). To advance this scheme, Hume called twice on Townshend, then MP for Saltash and, in the course of a mercurial career, enjoying the perquisites of the office of Treasurer of the Chamber (*HP* iii.539–48; Namier and Brooke, 1964). Hume thought the boy would have to go to Glasgow, because he could not believe that any terms offered Smith would tempt him to renounce his professorship to become a travelling tutor. However, Smith seems to have been ready enough to travel with Buccleuch, perhaps because at times he found Scotland 'barren of all sorts of transactions that can interest anybody that lives at a distance from it' (*Corr.* No. 28).

To be sure, there was criticism of the appointment of Smith as Buccleuch's travelling tutor. Sir David Dalrymple (later appointed to the Court of Session as Lord Hailes) wrote to Horace Walpole on 17 April 1764:

I am afraid Mr Charles Townshend will make a very indifferent *compagnon de voyage* out of a very able professor of ethics. Mr Smith has extensive knowledge and in particular has much of what may be termed constitutional knowledge, but he is awkward and has so bad an ear that he will never learn to express himself intelligibly in French. (Walpole, 1980: 40.321)

Smith ignored such views, if he knew of them. After giving notice of the resignation of his Chair on 8 November 1763, he wrote on 12 December to Hume, then in Paris as Secretary to the British Ambassador, that Buccleuch would leave Eton at Christmas and would go abroad soon afterwards.

Smith also expressed regret that the second edition of *TMS* (1761) was 'extremely incorrectly printed', and he wished he had a 'months leisure . . . to new cast both the second and third parts', whose form he described as 'by no means agreeable to me'. He reckoned it would be a year before he could attend to this matter, but he promised Hume that as soon as he did so, he would send the 'alterations' to the Baron d'Holbach, who was supervising a new translation into French. Perhaps anticipating meeting the *philosophes* during his coming travels with Buccleuch, he asked Hume to 'make my Compliments to all the men of Genius in France who do me the honour to know anything about me' (*Corr.* app. E, a; No. 77).

Smith travelled to London in January 1764 to meet his 18-year-old pupil, and they set out together for France, arriving at Paris (Pl. 7) on 13 February. The following day he wrote to Thomas Miller of Glenlee, Lord Rector of Glasgow University, to resign his Chair officially and to ask that his salary be reserved for Thomas Young, his former student, who was teaching the moral philosophy class as had been agreed with his colleagues (*Corr.* No. 81). Meantime, Joseph Black wrote to say that Smith's house in Professors' Court was secured for the time being for his mother and the niece, Janet Douglas, who was housekeeper, also that Young was performing 'admirably' (*Corr.* No. 79).

About a week later, John Millar reported that the Moral Philosophy Chair was likely to go to Thomas Reid, then Professor of Moral Philosophy at Aberdeen, a candidate pushed by Smith's former patron, Lord Kames (*Corr.* No. 80). Reid was the outstanding candidate and did become Smith's successor, as the result of an election on 22 May following (Scott, 1937: 221). He shared Kames's philosophical standpoint, emphasizing Common Sense as an antidote to the scepticism derived from Hume, and had a religious outlook similar to that of the 'new lights' of the Kirk. As noted in the last chapter, he was opposed to Smith's thought on morals. There is no evidence, however, that Smith's friends, such as Millar who endorsed Hume's viewpoint, sought to oppose Reid on intellectual grounds (Wood, 1984: 130–3).

Millar asked Smith to exert himself on Young's behalf, but there is no record of his doing so. Perhaps he was taken up during his stay in Paris of ten days or so with preparations for the further fifteen days' journey to Toulouse, and residence there that extended to eighteen months. During this first visit to Paris,

Pl. 7. Vue de Paris, prise en aval du Pont Royal, 1758, by Charles-Léopold Grevensbroeck.

Smith and Buccleuch were not in the company of French people, possibly because they could not yet speak the language, but they spent their time with Hume in the Hôtel de Grimberghen, rue St Dominique, in the fashionable Faubourg Saint-Germain, and thus near the British Embassy, occupying the Hôtel de Brancas on the rue de l'Université. They were joined by two of Buccleuch's friends from Eton: Lord Beauchamp, the son of the Ambassador, the Earl of Hertford; and Sir John Macdonald of Sleat, a descendant of the Lords of the Isles who had the Gaelic as well as the classical languages, and who charmed everyone with his quick mind and social disposition. He died two years later, greatly lamented, when completing his Grand Tour in Rome. Smith apparently obtained from him details of economic life in the Highlands and Islands (Smith/Henry Beaufoy, MP, 29 Jan. 1787, Piero Sraffa *Collection* B5/4, Trinity Coll., Cambridge).

Smith was no proponent of the scheme of sending young men abroad on a Grand Tour, and expressed himself sharply on that point in *WN*, also continuing his criticism of the 'greater part' of European universities whose decline, he thought, obliged families to send their sons abroad to complete their education. He conceded that a young man going abroad at 17 or 18 and returning home four years later is somewhat more mature, and he may even acquire a faint knowledge of foreign languages:

In other respects he commonly returns home more conceited, more unprincipled, more dissipated, and more incapable of any serious application either to study or business, than he could well have become in so short a time, had he lived at home. By travelling so very young, by spending in the most frivolous dissipation the most precious years of his life, at a distance from the inspection and controul of his parents and relations, every useful habit, which the earlier parts of his education might have had some tendency to form in him, instead of being rivetted and confirmed, is almost necessarily either weakened or effaced. Nothing but the discredit into which the universities are allowing themselves to fall, could ever have brought into repute so very absurd a practice as that of travelling at this early period of life. (v.i.f.36)

This must have made surprising reading for the Duke if he ever ploughed through the great work, but his stepfather, Charles Townshend, had written to him in a different strain in the course of the stay at Toulouse:

my own experience in business convinces me that, in this age, any Person of your rank and fortune may, with tolerable discretion, competent knowledge, and integrity be as great as even this Country can make Him, and therefore I wished to see you placed, with your own approbation, in a foreign Country, for some Time, where you might give to the necessary exercises of the body, to the improvement of your mind, and to the amusements of your youth, their proper and alternate influence.

Perhaps this was the exceptional case that proved Smith's rule about travelling abroad, and Smith as tutor might be reckoned to make all the difference. It was Townshend's hope that Smith's instruction would make Buccleuch 'a grounded politician in a short course of study', setting much store on the tutor being 'deeply read in the constitution and laws of your own Country'. Townshend also exhorted the Duke to give attention to composition, in particular the 'deliberative orations' of the English Civil War period (Ross, 1974). Smith was well equipped to supervise such studies, as we have seen, from giving his courses on rhetoric. Buccleuch's own inclination was against the career of the statesman that Townshend had mapped out for him, and after the latter's premature death on 4 September 1767, the Duke was heard to say that he regretted this event, 'yet to him it was attended with the Consalation that it left him at Liberty to chuse his own [Line] of Life, for had Mr T[ownshen]d Surviv'd, he might have been Drawn into the Vortex of Politicks much against his Will' (Carlyle, 1973: 249).

Various motives may be assigned to Smith for going to France with Buccleuch. There was the tie of hereditary duty to the young Duke's family, for he was the grandson of the 2nd Duke of Argyll, and Smith's father had been in the service of a Campbell Earl of Loudoun. Smith's guardian cousin was the grandfather's secretary; also Smith had received hospitality at Adderbury, the grandfather's seat which became Townshend's and then Buccleuch's, and at Inveraray, the home of Clan Campbell. The security provided by the handsome tutor's salary and the promised pension would be an important factor. Then, too, the attraction of France must have been considerable. There resided some of the foremost men of letters of Europe, in whom Smith was intensely interested as has been demonstrated. Also, the opportunity to study a country with a population three times that of Great Britain (cf. *TMS* VI.ii.2.4 and *WN* V.2.k.78), a contrasting political system resting on the principle of absolutism, and a range of regional economies was a lure in itself to the social scientist. Finally, France was beginning to appreciate *TMS*.

A laudatory notice of the book appeared in the October 1760 issue of the *Journal encyclopédique*, edited from Bouillon by the Toulousian journalist Pierre Rousseau. Bouillon (now in Belgium) was a duchy in the Ardennes detached from the Liégois by Louis XIV in 1678. The theoretical independence of this French protectorate and its close proximity to the French border permitted business deals which furthered the Enlightenment. In February 1760 its Duke, Charles-Godefroy de La Tour d'Auvergne, a leading Freemason sympathetic to the *philosophes*, granted Rousseau the privilege of publishing his *Journal* established in 1756 to circulate the modern, reforming ideas of the *encyclopédistes* led by Diderot and d'Alembert. French censorship had prevented the *Journal* from appearing in Paris, and it had been chased out of Liège and Brussels by clerical opposition. It flourished until the period of the Terror in 1793, after the revolutionaries' policy of freedom of the press had opened the market, ending the need for advanced periodicals to be published abroad and introduced in a clandestine fashion into France.

Rousseau (d. 1785) became director of the Société typographique de Bouillon, operating from 1767 to 1797, and responsible for the publication of many works prohibited by French censorship, as well as the prestigious *Encyclopédie économique* (16 vols., 1778–81), which made familiar to many Europeans the discourse of political economy into which Smith's *WN* was inserted. Rousseau's *Journal* became well known and was widely accepted in Europe as the leading rival to *L'Année littéraire*, favoured by the Roman Catholic Church and endorsed by the French government (Heirwegh and Mortier, 1983). A review of *TMS* in the *Journal Encyclopédique* meant that an account of Smith's moral thought became accessible to the European intelligentsia who read French, and it would be associated with the advanced ideas of the *philosophes*.

Further evidence of the effectiveness of the business system that spread Enlightenment books in France despite censorship (Darnton, 1979), and how far Smith's ideas were penetrating into France, heralded by clandestine circulation from Bouillon of the *Journal encyclopédique*, came in a letter Hume wrote to his good friend from Fontainebleau on 28 October 1763. He described to Smith how two of the greatest ladies in France, Mme de Pompadour, Louis XV's mistress, and the Duchess of Choiseul, seemed to have read with care in French almost all of his writings. These were, of course, officially subject to censorship, and from 1761 placed on the *Index Librorum Prohibitorum* (Bongie, 1958: 237; 1965: 65). Hume went on to tell Smith that d'Holbach was supervising a translation of *TMS* (*Corr.* No. 77). As mentioned above, Smith, on the eve of going to France, displayed interest in this project and offered to provide revisions in hand for a third edition (*Corr.* app. E, a.). To be sure, there were those in France who could, and did, read the work in English, such as the Abbé Morellet and Mme de Boufflers, who welcomed Smith to her salon in 1766 because of it, and because of their common friendship for Hume (Stewart, 1970). Smith might well have anticipated animated discussions with his French readers about his view of moral philosophy.

But why was Toulouse chosen as the residence of tutor and pupil during the greater part of their stay in France? Townshend probably had in mind the recommendations of a mild climate, a decorous provincial style of life, and the presence of the *Parlement* second in importance to that of Paris. A University was also to be found there, as well as four Academies: those of rhetoric and poetry; of science and belles-lettres; of painting, sculpture, and architecture; and of arms. In addition, Toulouse was the seat of an important archbishopric. Most of the citizens spoke the regional dialect, 'occitan', the *langue d'oc*, unfamiliar to those trained like Smith in metropolitan French, the *langue d'oil*; but upper-class people would be able to converse in the latter.

Commonly, the city was defined in terms of three Ss: 'sale, sainte, et savante'. The banks of the Garonne were, in fact, unhealthy and dangerous until the 1760s, when programmes of improvement began to open up promenades and construct quais, under the patronage of Archbishops Arthur Dillon (in office 1758–62) and Loménie de Brienne (1762–89). These great princes of the Church, however, were often absent from the city at the call of duty and pleasure. In addition, since the Intendant of Languedoc resided in Montpellier, the schemes for urban renewal did not come quickly to fruition, in marked contrast, for example, to the experience of Bordeaux under the leadership of Intendant Tourny.

The reputation of Toulouse for piety could not have been entirely welcome to Smith, for it involved intolerance and cruelty as witnessed by 'l'affaire Calas'. In 1761 the son of a Protestant merchant was found hanged. On the charge of murdering him to prevent conversion to Catholicism, the father was condemned by the *Parlement*, then broken on the wheel, strangled, then fed to the flames on 10 March 1762. Voltaire led a campaign to declare the innocence of Jean Calas, which was proclaimed by royal edict in 1765, during Smith's stay. There was a violent protest against this edict from the *Parlement* of Toulouse. Later in 1765, when he visited Ferney, Smith may have discussed the fate of Jean Calas with Voltaire, who had recounted this horrible story of fanaticism at the outset of his *Traité sur la tolérance* (1762). Smith introduced Calas's last words into the final edition of *TMS* to illustrate the indignation felt by an innocent man at the infamy which unjust punishment may attach to his memory (III.2.11).

As for 'savante Toulouse', there was a question mark over this ascription. The University was at a low ebb in Smith's time, except for the teaching of civil law, and the Academies were dominated by conservative *parlementaires*. Only gradually did the *lumières* penetrate them, though by 1768 Voltaire was able to comment to d'Alembert, 'Il s'est fait un prodigieux changement . . . dans le Parlement de Toulouse: la moitié est devenue philosophe et les vieilles têtes rongées de la teigne de la barbarie mourront bientôt' (quoted in Godechot and Tollon, 1974: 367). Younger men were active in masonic lodges, however, some of them following the 'rite écossais', and though not hostile to the Catholic Church they diffused the ideas of the Enlightenment. Smith owned a copy of Jean Raynal's *Histoire de la ville de Toulouse* (1759), which provided useful background information about the city (EUL MS JA 1390; Mizuta).

The *Parlement* dominated the social and economic life of the city in the eighteenth century, as well as that of the intellect, and by no means for the better. To a certain extent, Toulouse at this period lacked dynamism, a marked contrast to that other major inland city, Paris, with which Fernand Braudel usefully contrasts it (1988: 250; 1991: 175, 269). Its industries and commerce were far from any take-off point, with the energies and ambitions of the tiny proportion of the rich concentrated on ascent of the legal ranks, ennoblement, and the acquisition of land. Smith, now more the student of the 'dismal science' of economics than of the 'gay science' of rhetoric and poetry, kept his eyes on these aspects of Toulouse and generalized, apparently with justice, in *WN*: 'If you except Rouen and Bordeaux, there is little trade or industry in any of the parliamentary towns of France; and the inferior ranks of people, being chiefly maintained by the expense of the members of the courts of justice, and those who come to plead before them, are in general idle and poor'. He probably linked Toulouse to Edinburgh as cities where the revenue of courts of justice was spent and many servants were maintained; hence the common people were corrupted by idleness, and there was not enough incentive to employ 'capital' (II.iii.12).

The first news we have of Smith in Toulouse is contained in a letter of 4 March 1764 to Hume from his cousin, the Abbé Colbert du Seignelay de Castlehill, who was descended from the Cuthberts of Castlehill in Inverness. He had come to France in 1750, had entered the Gallican Church, and had recently been appointed Vicar-General of the city. Smith has just arrived and Colbert has met him only an instant, but he seems to be all that Hume said: 'un homme d'Esprit et un honnête homme'. Colbert regrets that the Archbishop, Loménie de Brienne, is not in residence but has been at Montpellier for about six weeks, and plans to go from there to Paris, where he longs to meet Hume. Colbert fears that his long black soutane will alarm Buccleuch, but despite this he will forget nothing to make the young man's stay as agreeable and useful as possible. Writing again on 22 April, Colbert praises Smith as 'un homme Sublime. Son cœur et son esprit sont également estimables.' His pupil, Buccleuch, is 'un fort joli Sujet' who does his exercises very well and is making progress in French. Colbert congratulates himself every day that Smith wanted to come to Toulouse, and he asks Hume to send more people like him, for the city is certainly to be recommended to English and Scottish visitors (NLS Hume MSS iv.34, 35 (old nos.)).

Smith's own report to Hume of 5 July was somewhat gloomier. Townshend had assured him that Choiseul, Prime Minister of France, would provide recommendations to 'all the people of fashion' in Toulouse and elsewhere in France, but these had not been forthcoming. Tutor and pupil had to fend for themselves, with the help of the Abbé Colbert, to be sure, but he was almost as much a stranger in Toulouse as they. The Duke knew no Frenchman, and Smith could not bring the few he knew to their house. We know of visitors to Toulouse at this period, however, who provided company for the Duke, namely two young Norwegians from a wealthy family, Peter and Karsten Anker, who with their tutor, Andreas Holt, had met Adam Smith in Glasgow on 28 May 1762, and who had in their diary a friendly greeting from Buccleuch dated 16 March 1764 (Banke, 1955: 172; Simpson, 1990: 125–6). Smith did not allude to this company, and his letter to Hume continued: 'The Life which I led at Glasgow was a pleasurable, dissipated life in comparison of that which I lead here at Present. I have begun to write a book in order to pass away the time. You may believe I have very little to do.' To provide diversion and instruction for Buccleuch, Smith planned an excursion to Bordeaux, and he asked Hume for introductions to its governor, the duc de Richelieu. Smith also asked if Sir James Macdonald of Sleat could be persuaded to spend a month with Buccleuch to encourage him by his 'influence and example' (*Corr.* No. 82).

Since the Glasgow merchant John Glassford wrote to Smith on 5 November following, expressing the hope that Smith was 'bringing forward at [his] Leisure hours the usefull work that was so well advanced here' (*Corr.* No. 85), there is something of a difficulty in identifying the book that Smith had 'begun to write' at Toulouse as *WN*. One possibility is that Smith was expanding on the Early Draft of *WN* ultimately deposited among the Townshend papers in the Buccleuch archives (SRO GD 224/33/4; *LJ* 562–81), and produced a text which was further expanded and revised in the course of the next twelve years to become the first edition of the work we know. Late in his life, W. R. Scott came to the opinion that Smith's new book in Toulouse was one dealing with taxation and linked to Townshend's project of writing a history of the Sinking Fund (*Corr.* No. 302; Scott, 1940: 269). The Abbé Colbert, in a letter to Hume of 28 February 1765, mentions that Smith and his pupils are well—the Duke had been joined by his brother, the Hon. Hew Campbell Scott—and tantalizingly adds that he has read Smith's book, and that he has enjoyed it very much (NLS Hume MSS iv.36 (old no.)). Unfortunately, Colbert gives no description of what he read, but he may have meant *TMS*.

The Early Draft makes the point that almost all the knowledge of the ordinary person is acquired at second hand, from books, and we certainly find armchair economics in the expanded *WN* itself. It can be argued, however, that for Smith residence in Toulouse yielded an important stock of facts, additional to those collected in Glasgow, about the economic issues that had seized his imagination. These included the division of labour, extent and fluctuation of market, agricultural and commercial systems, the role of transportation in creating wealth, and the struggle for natural liberty in the economic domain. Thus, a walk from the older part of the city to the *quartier parlementaire* to the south provided a lesson in economic history. It would take him, for instance, from the Hôtel d'Assézat, a beautiful Renaissance house built for a *capitoul* or local magistrate, whose fortune came from the pastel (woad) trade that flourished and declined between the fifteenth and the sixteenth centuries, to the contemporary Hôtel d'Espie (today Courtois de Viçose) in the rue Mage, an elegant building in the Louis XV style designed by the fashionable architect Hyacinthe Labat de Savignac. This was financed by the proceeds of the vineyards and wheatfields in the belt of the domains of the *parlementaires* extending some fifteen kilometres from the city and an hour's ride by carriage or on horseback. Near the Hôtel d'Assézat, in the rue de Nazareth and the rue de Perchepinte, were the more modest town houses of the *parlementaires*, but they reflected similarly the *douceur de vivre* of the period, with their chaste brickwork, iron-forged balconies and window agrafes, and inner courtyards flanked on the ground floor by salons, the dining-room, and often a library. Dugald Stewart says that Smith in the house of his stay in Toulouse lived in 'intimacy . . . with some of the principal persons of the Parliament' (iii.7), and we can imagine him being entertained in such surroundings.

To the north and east of the *Parlement* building itself ran the 'canal of Languedoc', as Smith called it, commenting on the 'very large estate' its tolls meant for the descendants of its engineer Riquet, who therefore had an interest in keeping the canal in constant repair (*WN* v.i.d.7). Canal traffic represented the potential for bringing opulence to Toulouse, but there were restrictions on the transport and export of grain, the great product of the region of the 'Midi-Pyrénées', which hampered economic growth. During Smith's time there, the combined pressures on royal authority by the chamber of commerce of Toulouse, the Estates of Languedoc, and the Physiocrats (the latter noted by Smith, *WN* IV.ix.38) resulted in an edict of July 1764 by Controller General L'Averdy granting, with certain exceptions meant to provide a buffer against dearths, a free export in grain; but ensuing bad harvests and the rise in prices brought about a return to protectionism (Frêche, 1974: 155, 212–17). As for the abundance of the product of the vineyards, Smith reckoned that it did not encourage drunkenness, instancing the behaviour of French regiments moving from the north to the south of the country, who were debauched at first by the availability of good, cheap wine, then became as sober for the most part as the local people (*WN* IV.iii.c.8).

Enough has been said, perhaps, to indicate how much there was of interest that lay under Smith's observant eye in Toulouse, ready for the application of his analytical mind. A final matter to be mentioned as one of fascination for the political economist was the stormy relationship between the Toulouse *Parlement* and the Crown. When Choiseul sought to reform French finances in 1763 at the close of the Seven Years War, the *Parlement* opposed the modifications in the 'vingtième', a tax on revenues, whereupon the commandant of Languedoc, the duc de Fitz-James, occupied the *Parlement* buildings and achieved the registration of the edicts creating the new taxes by military force. The *parlementaires* then interdicted the raising of these taxes, were arrested in their homes, and on being released decreed the seizure of the person of Fitz-James. Smith bought the pamphlets concerning this affair and had them shipped with his books to Scotland ((EUL MS JA 1429/1–1S; Mizuta). Reflecting on these writings and what he had learned on the spot, he acknowledged Choiseul's success in dealing peacefully with the *Parlement* of Paris in 1764, then he generalized as follows:

that experiment was not pursued. For though management and persuasion are always the easiest and safest instruments of government, as force and violence are the worst and most dangerous, yet such, it seems, is the natural insolence of man, that he almost always disdains to use the good instrument, except when he cannot or dare not use the bad one. The French government could and durst use force, and therefore disdained to use management and persuasion. (*WN* v.i.g.19)

It may have piqued Smith's interest in the Toulouse confrontation that Fitz-James, the employer of 'force and violence' on behalf of the French King, was a descendant of James II of Britain, who had lost his throne precisely for relying on the same instruments of government. At the end of his life, Smith's sense of the dangers of royal despotism was still so vivid that he brought this issue into an addition to the final version of *TMS* (VI.ii.2.18).

There were similar struggles in Bordeaux between Richelieu, Governor of

Guyenne, and the *Parlement*, also covered in pamphlets in Smith's Library (EUL MS JA 1423/1-8; Mizuta). He secured a letter of recommendation through Hume's agency for a visit to Bordeaux in July 1764, and expressed appreciation for the reception of his party by Richelieu, an entertaining old man famed for his prowess in love as well as in war (Porquerol, 1954; Lescure, 1869–71). He was said to detest the *philosophes*, but Smith encountered no animosity: 'We were all treated by the Marechal [Richelieu] with utmost Politeness and attention, particularly the Duke whom he distinguished in a very proper manner' (*Corr.* No. 83).

On this jaunt, Smith was in the company of the Abbé Colbert and the MP Isaac Barré. The latter wrote to Hume from Toulouse on 4 September, acknowledging a letter which he had received just as Smith, his pupil, and the Abbé were sitting down to dinner with him. Barré wrote that Colbert 'is a very honest fellow', and urged Hume to make him a bishop if he could, but the Abbé had to wait until 1781 to be advanced to the See of Rodez. Barré's letter continued with a snatch of his conversation with Smith:

[He] agrees with me in thinking that you are turnd soft by the delices of a French court, and that you don't write in that nervous manner you was remarkable for in the more Northern climates. Besides, what is still worse, you take your politicks from your Elliots, Rigbys and Selwyns . . . (NLS Hume MSS iii.35 (old no.))

The allusion here is to fellow-MPs Gilbert Elliot of Minto (*HP* ii.390–4), Richard Rigby (iii.355–60), and George Selwyn (iii.420–1), who were on comfortable terms with the Administrations of their day, unlike Barré (ii.50–4), who was frequently their critic, particularly with respect to America, about which he was knowledgeable as a result of his service there under Wolfe. His mentor in politics was Lord Shelburne, brother of Smith's former pupil, the Hon. Thomas Petty Fitzmaurice. A convert to Smith's views on political economy from 1761, Shelburne may have encouraged Barré to contact Smith in France.

Smith returned to Bordeaux in October 1764, to meet there Buccleuch's 17-year-old brother, the Hon. Hew Campbell Scott, and another journey about this time took him to Bagnères-de-Bigorre in the foothills of the Pyrenees, a spa whose mineral waters had been relished by Montaigne and Mme de Maintenon. Smith wrote to Hume that Buccleuch benefited a great deal from these journeys and had begun to 'familiarize himself to French company', also that he reckoned the rest of the time they lived together would be spent 'not only in Peace and contentment but in gayety and amusement' (*Corr.* No. 83). In the same letter, Smith asked Hume for more recommendations, to the Intendant of Languedoc, the Comte d'Eu, and the Archbishop of Narbonne, for he said he intended to take his pupils to Montpellier to attend a sitting of the Estates of Languedoc. This body was in session from 29 November 1764 to 7 January 1765, and their *procès-verbal* indicates that they sustained discussion at a high level of topics such as government finance, public works, and economic improvements of great interest to Smith and the young men in his charge who were owners of extensive estates.[1]

In April 1765 Townshend gave Buccleuch permission to leave Toulouse and settle in Paris, but this was not done immediately (Ross, 1974: 182). Colbert wrote to Hume on 10 April that it was hoped that Smith would remain in Toulouse for a month or two. He also suggested some reasons, perhaps, why the city was not so agreeable for 'Englishmen' at this time, though there were many of them there, and the place suited them. The local people displayed an astonishing fanaticism over the Calas case. In March, the *Parlement*'s conviction of Calas *père* had been condemned in Paris, and the 'capitoul', François-Raimond David de Beaudrigue, had been cited as the chief agent in a judicial murder. It was believed in Toulouse that the British Ambassador had instigated an attack on this man in Paris, because he had been the magistrate enforcing the legal disposal of the effects of two English officers who had died in the neighbourhood. While agreeing that David de Beaudrigue was culpable in the Calas case, Colbert believed he was only doing his duty in connection with the English officers, and he asked Hume to put this on the record for the sake of the family, also for the *capitoul* himself, who had been personally kind to English people (NLS Hume MSS iv.36, 37; BN Fond Français MS 6680; Bien, 1962). Smith and his charges left Toulouse about this time and toured more of the south of France, very likely the Gallo-Roman remains at places such as Nîmes, Arles, and the Pont du Gard and, one imagines, the Palace of the Popes at Avignon. They also visited a faience factory at Marseilles, where Buccleuch permitted himself the extravagance of buying a very expensive service. One wonders if the Duke obtained it from the establishment of La Veuve Perrin or that of Joseph-Gaspard Robert, notable, according to authorities on the subject, for their 'distinctive painted decorations in enamel colours—groups of juicy fish and crustaceans, freshly coloured and loosely-bunched sprigs of flowers (drawn from nature and not from prints), little landscapes, seascapes and rustic idylls, and frail spidery chinoiseries' (Fleming and Honour, 1977: 514).

Smith must also have ensured that the Duke stuck to his studies, for in a letter to Hume conjecturally dated August 1765 he writes that Buccleuch 'has read almost all your works several times over'. Smith continues: 'was it not for the more wholesome doctrine which I take care to instill into him, I am afraid he might be in danger of adopting some of your wicked Principles. You will find him very much improved' (*Corr.* No. 86). Jesting aside, Smith possibly took time to counter the religious scepticism in Hume's philosophical writings, at least to vindicate natural religion. It is also possible that in reading Hume's essays with his pupil, Smith went over the nine pieces on economic subjects in the *Political Discourses* (1752) and made clear his different stand on certain issues, such as accumulation of capital, perhaps to press home his advocacy of free-trade principles (Hume, *Writings on Economics*, 1955: pp. cvi–cix; Skinner, 1993: 118–19, 132–3).

A letter from Townshend to Buccleuch dated 10 June 1765 suggests that one of the works the Duke studied at this time was Hume's *History of England*, and he is urged 'to be very attentive to every event and every character in the reign of Charles the first, for, in those times, the rights of the people and the prescriptive claims of the Crown came to issue, and the contest called forth, created, and improved the Talents of men beyond any other period in any History ancient or modern'. Townshend gave high praise to Smith as a tutor dealing with these matters: 'He is ingenious, without being [over-re]fin'd; He is general, without being too systematical or singular in His notions of our Government.' Acquaintance with Smith must have put Townshend's mind at rest that Buccleuch would learn the 'wholesome doctrine' of Whiggism, and not become infected with the 'wicked' Tory principles often thought to lurk in Hume's *History of England*.

Another task given Buccleuch by his stepfather was that of anatomizing the monarchy of France, to discover what 'secret error in it's constitution' led to its failure by land and sea in the Seven Years War, despite its economic power (Ross, 1974: 183–4). This was a topic certainly congenial to Smith, and its pursuit is reflected in the pages devoted to the political and economic analysis of French absolutism in *WN*. Townshend would wish the Duke to learn from the analysis lessons useful for Britain in seeking to hold on to the colonial possessions in North America and India from which France had recently been expelled (Schroeder, 1994).

Smith's last recorded deed in Toulouse was that of acting as a commissioner on 4 October 1765 for taking evidence from the Abbé Colbert in connection with the Douglas Cause (Scott, 1937: 259–60). This intricate and prolonged legal process, involving actions in the Court of Session in Edinburgh, the Tournelle criminal court of the *Parlement* of Paris, and finally the House of Lords at Westminster, which lasted from 1763 to 1769, concerned the dispute over who was the rightful heir of the 1st and last Duke of Douglas. One claimant was Douglas's nephew, alleged to be the child of a French worker and passed off as her son by the Duke's sister. The other was the 7th Duke of Hamilton, the nearest male relative by another line of descent. Smith, like Hume and other Scottish literati favoured the Hamiltonian side, while the Douglasians were the popular party which ultimately prevailed. Scottish lawyers sent to France to assemble evidence for this Cause included Smith's friends Andrew Stuart of Torrance and Alexander Wedderburn, and Smith collected relevant French pamphlets. One of these turned on the issue of the relationship of the jurisdictions of the French and Scottish courts, a matter of significance to Smith as a student of jurisprudence: *Mémoire et consultation sur une question du droit des gens* (Paris: P. Simon, 1763; EUL MS JA 2976; Mizuta).

Some time in the autumn of 1765, Smith took his protégés to Geneva, a city attractive to British visitors because its citizens spoke good metropolitan French, there was a lively intellectual life, and above all it was Protestant. For Smith, there was the attraction of examining aspects of another economy and seeing a form of republican government in action. He does not feature Geneva in *WN*, but he did collect material in French on the dwindling economic life of the republic of Genoa for his great book (GUL MS Gen. 1035/231; *WN* IV. iii.b.2, v.iii.57).

Of the greatest interest, too, was the proximity of Voltaire at Ferney. We have a document addressed to Smith and dated 10–11 December from Voltaire's niece (and latterly mistress), Mme Denis, concerning the invasion of Ferney by a hunting party led by an Englishman, Charles Dillon, afterwards the 12th Viscount Dillon, who was the pupil of the scientist Joseph Turberville Needham, then on bad terms with Voltaire. There had been a fracas at Ferney, in which a gamekeeper was hurt and a hunting-dog killed. Mme Denis wished the English community to know about this affair, and she took the opportunity of informing Smith to send him Voltaire's respects (*Corr.* No. 89). Late in life, Smith told the English poet Samuel Rogers about several conversations he had with Voltaire, mentioning that among the topics discussed was the character of the duc de Richelieu, whom Smith had met at Bordeaux (Clayden, 1887: 95). He was something of a hero for Voltaire, who took the side of the exercise of royal prerogative by governors such as Richelieu against the claims of the provincial Estates. This was a viewpoint of the Physiocrats, the group of thinkers about economics led by François Quesnay, whom Smith was to encounter in Paris, both as economic theorist and in his professional role of physician. The Physiocratic argument was that the provincial assemblies, such as the one Smith had seen in session at Montpellier, were hotbeds of privilege and inimical to economic and other forms of social improvement, though this does not seem to have been true of the Estates of Languedoc.

Genevan society was opened to Smith through Dr Théodore Tronchin, whose son François had been his pupil in Glasgow. One of Tronchin's patients at this time was the comtesse Rohan-Chabot, who was accompanied in Geneva by her brother the duc de La Rochefoucauld and their mother, the duchesse d'Enville. This great lady of France was passionately interested in the newest advances in the sciences and humanities, and the range of possibilities for human improvement. The friend and confidante of Turgot, Intendant of Limoges from 1761, she encouraged him in his Physiocratic tendencies (Ruwet *et al.*, 1976). Thus she is a possible channel for Smith's awareness of the teaching and personalities of the Physiocrats, additional to what he may have learned from articles by Quesnay and Turgot in the *Encyclopédie*, such as those on *Épingle, Fermiers, Grain,* and *Foire* (Ross, 1984a: 178–9, 183).

It was in the circle of the duchesse d'Enville that Smith met the 2nd Earl Stanhope, one of the foremost mathematicians of the period. He came to be on such good terms with Stanhope that he acted as a go-between in 1774, when Stanhope secured the services of Adam Ferguson as travelling tutor to his ward, Lord Chesterfield (*Corr.* Nos. 138–42, also app. E, c–o; Raphael *et al.*, 1990; Raphael, 1994). Other literati whom Smith met in the d'Enville circle were Charles Bonnet, the natural philosopher, and Georges-Louis Le Sage, the physicist, both Professors at the University of Geneva, whose reputations supported Smith's thesis about 'universities . . . continually draining the church of all its most eminent men of letters' in Protestant countries where the church livings were modest (*WN* v.i.g.39). Devoted opponent of atheism and materialism (Marx, 1976), Bonnet did not comprehend Smith's friendship for Hume, since he believed himself to be on the same plane as Smith with respect to the doctrine of a Final Cause. This puzzlement comes out in a letter of 2 September 1785 from Bonnet to the Berlin Academician, H. B. Merian, stating that he did not know how Smith could have published an account of Hume's death mentioning that a few moments before his death he was reading the mordant satirist Lucian. Bonnet notes about Smith: 'Il étoit lié intimement avec ce Pyrrhon moderne' (Univ. de Genève bibliothèque, Bonnet MSS, Corr.).

It has been assumed that Smith and his pupils travelled to Paris from Geneva in December 1765, in time to see Hume and possibly Rousseau before they left the French capital for England on 4 January 1766 (cf. Rae, 1965: 194; West, 1976: 160). Extant correspondence suggests there was no such meeting. Hume began a letter to Smith at the end of January 1766: 'I can write as seldom and as Short as you—I am sorry I did not see you before I left Paris' (*Corr.* No. 90). Addressing Mme d'Enville from Geneva on 5 February, Le Sage writes as follows:

De toutes les personnes que je recontrois chez vous, Madame, c'est-à-dire de toute l'élite de notre bonne compagnie; je n'ai continué à voire que l'excellent mylord Stanhope, et quelque peu Mr Smith. Celui-ci vouloit me faire connoitre Myladi Conyers et le duc de Buckleugh [*sic*], mais je l'ai prié de me réserver ce bon office pour son retour. (Prevost, 1805: 226)

The first news from Paris of Smith being there comes from Horace Walpole, recipient of *TMS* in 1759, and in 1764 of Hailes's opinion that Townshend had made a bad choice for Buccleuch's tutor. Walpole recorded on 2 March that he had gone to an 'Italian play', possible Poinsinet's opera *Tom Jones*, with Buccleuch and Smith (Walpole, 1937–83: vii.305). Smith enjoyed the Paris opera season, and theorized about opera as an art form in the second of his pieces on the imitative arts. He recalled the 'deeply affecting' passages of serious pieces and the 'delicious pleasure' of the comic ones. However, he criticized the poor acting of the castrati, and the 'abuse of scenery' which aroused the applause of the 'ingenious' French ('Imitative Arts' ii.16, 27).

On 3 March Walpole wrote to the Duke's aunt, Lady Mary Coke, that her nephews and Smith 'are coming into the hotel I inhabit' (Walpole, 1937–83: xxxi.109). This was the Hotel du Parc Royal, rue Colombier, in the Faubourg Saint-Germain, very near the rue de Seine, and thus the town house of the La Rochefoucauld family, whose senior member was the duchesse d'Enville. On 15 March Smith accompanied Walpole to see James II's papers at the Catholic Scots College in Paris, and they exchanged stories about the impairment of the

2nd Duke of Argyll's mind towards the end of his life in 1743, when he feared being sent to the Tower for corresponding with Prince Charles Edward Stuart (Walpole, 1937–83: vii.360).

Smith attended the salons of the duchesse d'Enville in Paris, also those of Julie de L'Espinasse, a little further off, in rooms at No. 6 rue Saint Dominique, where d'Alembert was installed. The other members of the little flock of the *philosophes* were not far afield. Across the Seine on the right bank, at No. 8 rue des Moulins, was the home of the Baron d'Holbach, frequented by men of letters at dinners for which Morellet had high praise: 'Une grosse chère, mais bonne, d'excellent vin, d'excellent café, beaucoup de disputes, jamais de querelles.' Smith was invited to these meals, and later in life remembered the kindness d'Holbach had shown him (*Corr.* No. 259). Yet another house where Smith was entertained was that of the financier and *philosophe* Helvétius, one street over from d'Holbach's, at Nos. 16–18 rue Sainte-Anne. Morellet recollected that Turgot had a high estimation of Smith's talent, and that they saw him often after his presentation at Helvétius's home. Discussions covered commercial theory, banking, public credit, and many points taken up in *WN* which Smith's French friends appreciated he was then meditating (Morellet, 1821: i.237). There was the difficulty that Smith spoke French very badly, a point that Mme d'Enville corroborated, though she claimed that she had learned English before Smith left Paris (*Corr.* No. 142).

On first acquaintance, too, Smith's harsh voice and his big teeth were not prepossessing, according to the actress and novelist Mme Riccoboni, who met him in May 1766, and declared him as ugly as the devil; but the goodness of his heart won her over, and by October she was writing to David Garrick that she liked Smith very much, wishing the devil would carry off all the *gens de lettres* and bring back Smith. It is likely she read *TMS* in the interim and had been attracted, as many Frenchwomen were, to his teaching about sympathy (Nicholls, 1976). Deidre Dawson has suggested that Mme Riccoboni's fiction may have had a role in the formation of Smith's theory of sympathy, but the relationship between them is likely to have been not influence but affinity, based on their complementery insights into emotional relationships, and their contributions to the emerging 'culture of sensibility' (Dawson, 1991: 147–62; Barker-Benfield, 1992).

As for an emotional relationship that went awry, a common concern of the *philosophes* and Smith from April 1766 on was the quarrel that occurred between Rousseau and Hume, when the former's paranoia grew to such a pitch that he accused Hume of engaging in an international conspiracy to bury him in obscurity in England. This subject drew Smith and Turgot together, for at the first revelations of the quarrel they shared the viewpoint that Hume should not publish anything about it. Smith begins a letter to Hume, then in London, on 6 July by teasing him that he is as 'great a Rascal' as Rousseau, then continues with characteristically prudent advice not to 'unmask before the Public this hypocritical Pedant', because a publication of this kind would disturb the 'tranquillity of your whole life':

To write against [Rousseau], is, you may depend upon it, the very thing he wishes you to do. . . . He hopes to make himself considerable by provoking an illustrious adversary. . . . Your whole friends here wish you not to write, the Baron d'Holbach, D'Alembert, Madame Riccoboni, Mademoiselle Riancourt, Mr Turgot etc. etc. Mr Turgot, a friend every way worthy of you, desired me to recommend this advice to you in a Particular manner, as his most earnest entreaty and opinion. He and I are both afraid that you are surrounded by evil counsellours, and that the Advice of your English literati, who are themselves accustomed to publish all their little gossiping stories in Newspapers, may have too much influence upon you. (*Corr.* No. 93)

Smith in this letter asked to be remembered to Horace Walpole who, unbeknownst to Smith and Hume, had a role in mischievously fomenting Rousseau's paranoia at this time. Walpole had fabricated a letter, touched up by Helvétius, the duc de Nivernais, and Président Hénault, ostensibly addressed by Frederick of Prussia to Rousseau and making fun of his vanity over being persecuted. In due course this was printed and came to the attention of Rousseau. He suspected it was a part of a conspiracy to ridicule him, engineered by the *philosophes* and secretly aided by Hume (Mossner, 1980: 514, 524).

In the end, Turgot changed his mind and encouraged Hume to publish his account of the quarrel, an enterprise carried to completion in France the following October, when d'Alembert saw through the press the French text translated by Suard as *Exposé succinct de la contestation . . . entre M. Hume et M. Rousseau*. Smith continued to be interested in the outcome of the quarrel, together with literary Europe, and he wrote to Hume on 13 September 1767: 'I should be glad to have the true history of Rousseau before and since he left England. You may perfectly depend upon my never quoting you to any living soul upon that Subject' (*Corr.* No. 109). Hume replied on 8 October, correcting some details in a letter dated the 17th of the same month. He summed up Rousseau as a 'Composition of Whim, Affectation, Wickedness, Vanity, and Inquietude, with a small, if any Ingredient of Madness', adding to these 'ruling Qualities' some others listed at the end of the same paragraph: 'Ingratitude, Ferocity, and Lying, I need not mention, Eloquence and Invention' (*Corr.* No. 111). His anger clearly had not yet cooled, but he kept the quarrel out of his autobiography, *My Own Life* (1776), just as Rousseau does from the *Confessions*, but not from *Rousseau juge de Jean-Jacques*.

Smith kept on thinking about Rousseau, and it has been supposed that he had his teaching about inequality in mind in writing the sections in *WN* dealing with natural subordination and superiority (v.i.b.4–12; Bonar, 1932: 161; Dawson, 1991–2). When composing his essay on the imitative arts, Smith referred to Rousseau's *Dictionnaire de musique* (1768), and perhaps glanced at the personality of the author in describing him as 'more capable of feeling strongly than of analising accurately' ('Imitative Arts' ii.24). A last comment on Rousseau was made in conversation with a French visitor to Edinburgh in October–November 1782. Smith spoke of knowing Voltaire personally, but he made no such claim about Rousseau, whose writing and career he could now see in a certain perspective:

Voltaire set himself to correct the vices and follies of mankind by laughing at them, and sometimes even getting angry with them: Rousseau, by the attraction of sentiment, and the force of conviction, drew the reader into the heart of reason and truth. His Social Contract will in time avenge him for all the persecutions he suffered. (Faujas de Saint Fond, 1907: ii.245–6)

Another figure prominent in French society and greatly concerned about the outcome of the Hume–Rousseau quarrel in 1766 was the ever-fascinating comtesse de Boufflers. Patroness of Rousseau for many years, she had appealed to Hume in 1762 to find him an asylum in England, when the proscription of *Émile* by the *Parlement* of Paris forced him to leave France. She had watched Rousseau leave Paris on 4 January 1766 in Hume's company *en route* for England, her feelings a mixture of hope for Rousseau's safety and deep sadness at parting from Hume. In turn, she had been outraged to learn of Rousseau's subsequent ingratitude to Hume, and took the latter's side in the quarrel. Above all, she was a woman of complicated emotions, separated from her husband and mistress, though in the end in name only, of the third gentleman of France, the Prince du Conti, yet nourishing a romantic attachment to Hume, which he reciprocated, and which may have become intimacy in September–October 1764. Her vein of moralistic expression being at odds with her behaviour, she transcended the conflict by declaring, 'I wish to give back to virtue by my words what I take away by my actions.'

There was every reason for her to have a practical interest, as well as an intellectual one dictated by her literary tastes, in Smith's researches into morality and the emotions. Accordingly, we find *TMS* receiving attention in her correspondence. Writing to Hume on 6 May 1766, she declares that for love of him she gave Smith a warm welcome, adding: 'Je lis actuellement sa théorie des sentimens moraux: je n'en suis pas fort avancée, mais je crois que cela me plaira.' Another letter to Hume dated 25 July following recounts that Smith has just left after a visit paid at her request, possibly to the Temple, the Paris residence of the Prince du Conti, where tea was served in the English fashion in the evening and the servants were dismissed to permit freedom in conversation (Burton, 1849: 237–8; Mossner, 1980: 458–9). In 1770 Hugh Elliot, son of Sir Gilbert Elliot of Minto, the friend of Hume and Smith, reported being received by Mme de Boufflers in her bedchamber while she was at her studies. On this occasion, she claimed that if she had the time she would translate *TMS* into French, saying of its author: 'Il a des idées si juste de la sympathie'. Young Elliot noted that Smith's book was 'now in great vogue in Paris' (*Corr.* No. 130; Minto, 1868: 13).

Hume worried that Smith's worth might not be appreciated by the members of high French society, and he wrote to Mme de Boufflers on 15 July 1766: 'I am glad that you have taken my friend Smith under your protection: you will find him a man of true merit; though perhaps his sedentary recluse life may have hurt his air and appearance, as a man of the world' (*HL* ii.63). In fact, Smith seems to have been welcomed not only at the salon of Hume's special friend but also at that of Mme Geoffrin, and possibly that of Mme Necker, who had made Gibbon sigh 'as a lover' in her youth and went on to write about moral and literary topics. At this time, too, Smith attended many plays and concerts, as well as the operas already mentioned, providing aesthetic experience on which he comments in his discussion of the imitative arts. He took his protégés, Buccleuch and his brother, on excursions to places of interest such as Compiègne when the Court went there for the diversion of hunting. In his social activities, Smith must have presented a respectable and even, on some occasions, a splendid figure: his personal effects at this time included black suits, grey and red silk ones, and a coat of crimson velvet to go with gold breeches and waistcoat (Scott, 1937: 261–2).

On one jaunt to Abbeville from Paris, Smith was apparently smitten with love for an Englishwoman identified as a Mrs Nicol. There is mention of this in a rallying letter in French, dated 18 February 1766 and addressed to Smith and the Duke of Buccleuch by 'Le Gr[and] Vic[aire] Eccossois', a designation in all likelihood hiding the name of the Abbé Colbert. Though the date, 18 February 1766, is one early in Smith's stay in Paris, the writer seems to know about the impression he has made on the intellectual ladies there, and asks for news of Mmes d'Enville and de Boufflers. There is an allusion also to Mrs Nicol having a predecessor in Smith's affections, a Fife lady whom he had loved very much. Dugald Stewart, it is true, recorded meeting a Fife lady over 80 to whom Smith was attracted for several years early in his life. The letter of February 1766 closes with a reference to a member of Smith's party who was a piper and would be able to send to the writer something in Gaelic worthy of the Ossianic heroes then exciting the imagination of literary circles in Europe as a result of the effusions of James Macpherson (*Corr.* No. 91).

Further information about Smith's amorous propensities comes from a letter dated 14 July 1794, written by the Liverpool physician, James Currie, to Dugald Stewart in response to a present of the latter's 'Account of . . . Smith'. Currie passed on this anecdote, whose source was a Captain Lloyd, a scholarly retired soldier who was in the company of Smith and Buccleuch at Abbeville, when Smith 'was deeply in love with an English lady there':

What seems perhaps more singular, a French Marquise, a woman of talents and *esprit*, was smitten, or thought herself smitten, with [Smith], and made violent attempts to obtain his friendship. She was just come from Paris, where all the women were running after Mr Hume. She had heard that Mr Smith was Mr Hume's particular friend, and almost as great a philosopher as he. She was determined to obtain his friendship; but after various attempts was obliged to give the matter up. Dr Smith had not the easy and natural manner of Mr Hume, which accommodated itself to all circumstances. He was abstracted and inattentive. He could not endure this French woman, and was, besides, dying for another. The young noblemen of the party (of whom there were several) used to amuse themselves with seeing so great a philosopher under so cruel an embarrassment. (Currie, 1831: ii.318–19)

Henry Mackenzie, who was much in Smith's company when he lived in Edinburgh in the last twelve years of his life, recorded being aware his friend was 'seriously in love with a Miss Campbell of —— . . . a woman of as different dispositions and habits from his as possible'. Once more, nothing seems to have developed from this passion (Thompson, 1927: 176). It is to be feared that the biographer can do little more with the topic of Smith's sex life than contribute a footnote to the history of sublimation.

Bothered as he was at this time by what Dr Currie called the 'softer parts' of his nature, Smith gave his attention in 1766 to research on French taxes (London Univ., Goldsmiths' Lib. of Economic Literature, MS 'Etat actuel des finances', bearing Smith's bookplate), later incorporated in *WN* (v.ii.k.78), but possibly conducted first at the behest of Charles Townshend, who became Chancellor of the Exchequer in July 1766 and retained that office until his death the following year: *Corr.* No. 302 (Scott, 1935–6: 85–6).

Taxation was apparently one issue Smith discussed with members of the Physiocratic circle. A leading member of this group, Du Pont de Nemours, said they regarded Smith 'as a judicious and simple man, but one who had not yet proved his worth'. This informant also believed that because of a fear of vested interests there was a discrepancy between Smith's published views in *WN* and those he asserted in his own quarters, or in those of a friend, 'as I have seen him when we were fellow-disciples in the home of M. Quesnay' (Say, 1840: ii.562, n. 1). The point at issue, apparently, was the Physiocratic view that a direct tax on the wages of labour was inflationary, and that an indirect tax on commodities consumed by labourers had a similar effect. Smith expressed agreement with this view among the Quesnay circle, but in his book he denied that taxes on luxury goods were inflationary, since labourers would cut back on superfluities and would neither seek nor obtain a raise to offset such taxation (*WN* v.ii.k.1–9). Modern chancellors of the exchequer and ministers of finance, with their income tax depredations and steeper and steeper levies on 'booze' and 'baccy', would appear to have been entirely persuaded by Smith's side of the debate.

Regarding the issue of Smith's discipleship under Quesnay (Pl. 8), and by extension what he may have owed to Turgot, we have to see what they were doing in 1766. In the summer of that year, Quesnay was working on two articles: 'Analyse de la formule arithmétique du Tableau économique' and 'Problème économique', which were published in the June and August issues, respectively, of the *Journal de l'agriculture, du commerce, des arts, et des finances*, edited since the previous September by Du Pont. Smith collected the ten volumes of this periodical (July 1765–May–July 1767; Mizuta). With corrections and additional material, they were subsequently included in *Physiocratie*

Pl. 8. François Quesnay, 1769. From the bust by Louis-Claude Vassé
(Musée Royaux des Beaux-Arts de Belgique, Brussels).

(1767–8), the collection of Quesnay's writings edited by Du Pont whose title
identified thereafter the teaching of his school. Quesnay sent Smith a copy of
this book as an author's gift (Mizuta).

The first article offered the most accessible form of Quesnay's economic
model, with the qualitative and quantitative assumptions of the *Tableau*
expressed in non-technical terms, and the second article provided an important

application of the model to the problematic relationship of price and profit (Sauvy *et al.*, 1958). Cast in the plain style of expository writing that Smith championed in *LRBL* and was to exemplify himself in *WN*, these pieces are likely to have given him the clearest notion of Quesnay's system. Essentially, Smith encountered a macroeconomic model going well beyond his own thinking as expressed in *LJ* (B). He would recognize that, on the analogy of Harvey's principle of the circulation of the blood, the physician Quesnay had worked out comprehensively the details and interrelationships of that 'general system of expenditure, work, gain, and consumption' to which he had referred in his article on 'Grain' (*Encyclopédie* (1757), vii). The *Tableau* supplemented by the 'Analyse' provided a brilliant example of an 'imaginary machine', like those explored by Smith for languages and astronomy 'où tout se tient' (Meek and Kuczynski, 1972). As Hume had done in his *Political Discourses* (1752), Quesnay isolated two principal sectors of the economy, agriculture and manufacture. He further identified three chief socioeconomic groups associated with them: proprietors, farmers, and those involved in manufacturing. Then he added the concepts of investment in fixed and circulating capitals. With these tools, he could engage in period analysis of macroeconomic activity as a series of continuous withdrawals from and replacements for the market by capital users (Meek, 1962; Fox-Genovese, 1976; Blaug, 1991; Perrot, 1992).

A constraint on Physiocratic economics, however, was the doctrine that only agriculture was truly 'productive', i.e. capable of yielding a surplus over costs, which was defined at the 'net product' and said to be manifested in the form of land rent. Quesnay had outlined this viewpoint in 'Grain'. Smith came to see this approach as entirely speculative:

That system which represents the produce of land as the sole source of the revenue and wealth of every country, has, so far as I know, never been adopted by any nation, and it at present exists only in the speculations of a few men of great learning and ingenuity in France. (*WN* iv.ix.2)

He was struck, clearly, by the calibre of Quesnay's intellect as the 'very ingenious and very profound author of this system', but he also distanced himself from Quesnay, representing him in the final analysis not as a master to be followed, but as the doctrinaire head of a 'sect' or, in another figure of speech alluding to Quesnay's profession, 'a very speculative physician', who 'imagined that [the political body] would thrive and prosper only under a certain very precise regimen, the exact regimen of perfect liberty and perfect justice'. Smith himself was impressed with the empirical truth that some nations did prosper without enjoying 'perfect liberty and perfect justice'. The leading argument of *WN*, countering Quesnay, is that the 'natural effort which every man is continually making to better his own condition' prevents and corrects the bad effects of illiberal and unjust government interventions in economic activities (iv.ix.28).

Also, Smith refused to go along with Quesnay's 'capital error' in regarding 'artificers, manufacturers, and merchants, as altogether barren and unproductive' (*WN* IV.ix.29). Here, a line of thought entertained by the Abbé Baudeau and Turgot appealed to him, to the effect that manufacturing and commerce were sources of surplus that would accumulate. Turgot never regarded himself as a Physiocrat and had reservations about system-building (Laugier, 1979). In 1766, however, when he was meeting Smith, he seems to have been prompted by the incompleteness of Quesnay's economic model to elaborate his own system in the *Réflexions sur la formation et la distribution des richesses*, which he completed the following year. This treatise contained a model similar to Smith's in *LJ*(B), with division of labour and price mechanism features, but it included others such as circular flow and articulation of the factors of production—land, labour, and capital—which must have struck Smith as novel (Allais, 1992; Skinner, 1992*a*).

According to Ronald Meek, Turgot's thought marks an advance on that of the Physiocrats concerning capital, and his treatise paints a 'picture of society in which, behind the veil of money, we see the whole of agriculture, industry, and commerce depending on the continual advance and return of capitals owned by a great entrepreneurial class' (Meek, 1973: 22; see also Braudel, 1982: 232–43). Discussion of such topics must have fascinated Smith in the salon of Mme d'Enville, or round the hospitable tables of Helvétius or d'Holbach, or among the more earnest interlocutors in the apartment of Quesnay in the Palais de Luxembourg, where he had removed from the *entresol* at Versailles after the death of Mme de Pompadour, Louis XV's mistress, on 15 April 1764 (Weulersse, 1910; Craveri, 1987). Indeed, the encounters with the economic theorists of France can be considered the most exciting passage in Smith's intellectual development, second in importance only to his early contacts with Hume.[2]

In all likelihood Smith would have stayed in France until 1767, the year of the majority of the Duke of Buccleuch, but there was a dramatic change of plans occasioned by the fatal illness of the Hon. Hew Campbell Scott in October 1766. The previous August the Duke had himself been stricken by a fever after hunting with the French King and his courtiers at Compiègne. There survive two letters from Smith to Charles Townshend testifying to the anxiety of this occasion, and how Smith had turned to Quesnay for help as 'first ordinary physician to the King'. Also ill at this time, Quesnay told Smith 'he was an old infirm man, whose attendance could not be depended on, and advised [him], as his friend, to depend upon De La Saone, first physician to the Queen'. When the latter could not be reached, Quesnay did come to the Duke's bedside and prescribed a 'cooling ptisane drink', probably a concoction of barley-water. His illness then laid him low, and De La Saone took over the case. To Smith's great relief at the time of writing, 'Wednesday, 5 o'clock afternoon' on 26 August, this physician did not bleed Buccleuch. As Smith put it to Townshend: 'When a French physician judges bleeding unnecessary, you may be sure that the fever is not very violent' (*Corr.* No. 94). The next day, however, Smith reported to Townshend that De

La Saone had arrived just after the previous day's letter was sealed, found the
Duke's fever worse, and ordered 'three moderate cupfuls of blood to be taken
from him'. On Thursday the Duke's urine was found to have returned 'to its
old, bad colour but not so dark', and Senac, premier physician to the King, was
brought in for a long consultation, which impressed Smith with its thoroughness
in seeking to understand the history of the Duke's disease. The upshot was a
decision to take more blood (*Corr.* No. 95). The Duke recovered completely, but
Smith's worries at this period must have been compounded by news of the very
grave illness, then death at Rome, of Buccleuch's promising Eton friend, Sir
James Macdonald of Sleat. Hume wrote to Smith that same August: 'Were you
and I together Dear Smith we should shed Tears at present for the Death of
poor Sir James Macdonald. We coud not possibly have suffered a greater Loss
than in that valuable Young Man' (*Corr.* No. 96).

   Worse, however, was to come. On 15 October Smith wrote to Lady Frances
Scott that Hew, her brother, had succumbed to a fever, and was being attended
by Dr Gem, physician to the British Embassy, and by Quesnay, who prescribed
medicines, also purging and bleeding. Smith noticed alarming symptoms of
delirium in the patient, 'alterations in his speech, and an extraordinary hurry and
confusion in his Ideas'. Though he said he had 'entire confidence' in Gem and
Quesnay, he called in Théodore Tronchin, his 'particular and intimate friend'.
He devoted some sentences to praise of Gem and Quesnay:

one of the worthiest men in France and one of the best Physicians that is to be met with
in any country. He was not only the Physician but the friend and confident of Madame
de Pompadour a woman who was no contemptible Judge of merit.

Also, Smith wrote that both these physicians had 'good hopes' of the outcome
of the illness, but at the close of the letter he mentioned that the sound of the
patient's voice from the next room, 'makes me almost as delirious as he is', and
he prayed to God to preserve the mother and 'prepare her for whatever may be
the event of this terrible disorder' (*Corr.* No. 97).

   Four days later, Smith had the melancholy duty of informing Lady Frances
of the 'most terrible calamity that has befallen us'. He had gone to the British
Embassy to inform the Duke of Buccleuch that 'all hope was over', and that it
was not expected that his brother would outlive the following morning. Smith's
words are stark and poignant:

I returned in less than half an hour to do the last duty to my best friend. He had expired
about five minutes before I could get back and I had not the satisfaction of closing his
eyes with my own hands. I have no force to continue this letter. (*Corr.* No. 98)

Smith and his older pupil, whom he reported to Lady Frances, as being 'in very
great affliction', although otherwise 'in perfect health', made immediate plans for
returning to Britain, and landed at Dover on 1 November, accompanying the
body of the Hon. Hew Campbell Scott, subsequently interred at Dalkeith, where

there was a circumstantial story, put forth by the former rector of the grammar school, that the young man had been murdered on the streets of Paris (Steele, 1845: i.490).

Some time in October, before his pupil's death, Smith had manifested a strong desire to go home in a letter addressed from Paris to his publisher, Andrew Millar:

Tho I am very happy here, I long passionately to rejoin my old friends, and if I had once got fairly to your side of the water, I think I should never cross it again. Recommend the same sober way of thinking to Hume. He is light-headed, tell him, when he talks of coming to spend the remainder of his days here, or in France. Remember me to him most affectionately. (*Corr.* No. 99)

Hume had written to Smith the previous year about his indecision concerning his 'future Abode for Life', and had declared that 'Paris is the most agreeable Town in Europe, and suits me best', whereas, he went on, 'London . . . never pleased me much. Letters are there held in no honour: Scotsmen are hated: Superstition and Ignorance gain Ground daily.' Even Edinburgh, for Hume, had 'many Objections' as well as 'many Allurements', and it was his 'present Mind, this forenoon the fifth of September . . . to return to France' (*Corr.* No. 87). Smith never seems to have felt this way, and replied to Hume with a typically cool and shrewd piece of analysis:

A man is always displaced in a forreign Country, and notwithstanding the boasted humanity and politeness of this Nation, they appear to me to be, in general, more meanly interested, and that the cordiality of their friendship is much less to be depended on than that of our own countrymen. They live in such large societies and their affections are dissipated among so great a variety of objects, that they can bestow but a very small share of them upon any individual.

Smith reckoned that the 'hatred of Scotchmen' in London subsisted only among the 'stupidest of the People', and even they would give this up in a year, also the 'Clamour' against Hume because of 'Deism' would be dissipated in six months. In short, Smith argued that Hume's objections to London were 'without foundation', and then he confessed that he had a 'very great interest' in Hume settling there, because 'after many firm resolutions to return to Scotland', it was the place where he had decided to settle himself. He proposed that Hume should join him in 'short excursions' sometimes to see their friends in France and sometimes in Scotland: 'but let London be the place of our ordinary residence' (*Corr.* No. 88). Nothing came of Smith's plan in this direction, though it was to London that he first brought the rich memories and experiences of France and Geneva to share with friends, and there he entered briefly into government service as a prelude to the ten years of labour devoted to completion of *WN*.

14

Inquirer into the Wealth of Nations

My own schemes of Study . . . go forward like the web of Penelope, so that I
scarce see any Probability of their ending.

November 1766 found Smith in London, at first planning to travel soon to
Edinburgh, so the bookseller Andrew Millar reported to Hume on the 22nd of
that month. Millar was trying to get Hume to continue his *History of England*,
and as an inducement gave Smith's opinion shared by 'many more' of Hume's
'very good Sensible friends':

that the History of this country from the Revolution is not to be met with in books yet
printed[,] but from MSS in this country[,] to which [Smith] is sure you will have ready
access[,] from all accounts he hears from the great here[,] and therefor you should lay the
ground Work here after the Perusal of the MSS you may have access to. . . . I think it
my duty to inform you the opinion of your most judicious friends and I think that [Smith]
and Sir John Pringle [President of the Royal Society] may be reckoned among that number. (NLS Hume MSS vi.36 (old no.))

Hume did not succumb to Millar's blandishments on this occasion, nor to those
of William Strahan on a later one, and it is alleged that he gave the following
four reasons for declining Strahan's offer: 'I am too old, too fat, too lazy, and
too rich' (*New Evening Post*, 6 Dec. 1776; Mossner, 1980: 555–6).

Smith was still prosecuting his career as a man of letters, of course, and stayed
on in London through the winter, perhaps to see through the press the third
edition of *TMS*, printed by William Strahan, who had become Millar's partner
in publishing. Writing on a Friday during this winter, Smith asks Strahan not
to send him any more proof sheets for a few days because he is going off to the
country. He mentions that the essay on the first formation of languages is to be
printed at the end of *TMS*, and that the printed copy-text, presumably in *The
Philological Miscellany*, has some 'literal errors' which he wishes to have corrected. Despite his instructions that on the title-pages of *TMS* and the essay he
wished to be styled 'simply Adam Smith'(*Corr.* No. 100), when *TMS* appeared
in 1767 the author was designated 'Adam Smith, LL.D.'. This was repeated in
all his further publications, and probably gave rise to the habit some contemporaries had of referring to him as 'Dr Smith'.

Another reason for Smith staying on in London, however, may have been a requirement or an invitation to remain in Buccleuch's service. The Duke did not reach his majority until September 1767 (Pl. 9), and meantime his stepfather, Charles Townshend, apparently wished to keep him away from his great estates in Scotland, or so Carlyle of Inveresk informs us. Buccleuch as a minor had to put through a private Act to make a settlement for his forthcoming marriage (HLRO, Lords Journals, xxxi.535b, 23 Mar. 1767). Further, Townshend may have wished, against Buccleuch's own inclination, to draw him into the 'Vortex of Politicks'. One step in that direction was Buccleuch's presence with Townshend, now Chancellor of the Exchequer, at the Guildhall on Lord Mayor's Day,

Pl. 9. Henry Campbell Scott, 3rd Duke of Buccleuch. From a portrait by Thomas Gainsborough, by courtesy of His Grace the Duke of Buccleuch and Queensberry.

10 November 1766 (Rae, 1965: 232). A possible role for Smith would be that of mentor and friend to the young Buccleuch emerging in the public eye.

In his public career, Townshend was struggling with Britain's financial problems in the aftermath of the Seven Years War, and he certainly thought that Smith's talents lay in the direction of providing research assistance. Looking for measures to reduce the National Debt, he began to write a 'History of the Sinking Fund', that is, one that applied peacetime surplus revenue to pay off the Debt. The draft that survives in the Buccleuch papers has a covering note: 'Mr Townshend's History of the Funds and many calculations and other papers by Smith'. Unfortunately, the note goes on to record that 'Mr Smith's papers were taken out' (SRO Buccleuch Collection GD 224/47/2; Scott, 1935–6: 79–89). The writer and his brother, also involved in copying the 'History', are named in the margin as the 'Messrs Barrett', but are not otherwise identified, though we may conjecture they were Treasury clerks employed by Townshend. Accompanying the incomplete 'History' is an unaddressed letter which may have been directed at Smith. It states that the person addressed agrees with Townshend in regarding the reduction in 1717 of interest payable to creditors of the public as the start of the Sinking Fund, and Smith takes this position in *WN* (v.iii.27). He also makes use of much the same periods of Britain's financial history as Townshend for giving an account of the accumulation of the National Debt: 1688–97; 1697–1714; 1715–21; 1722–9; 1730–8 (*WN* v.iii.41–3). These dates refer to important phases of the development of public credit in England that has been viewed as a 'financial revolution' (Dickinson, 1967). Moreover, Townshend's letter refers to 'our difference over Totals', and the manuscript does have corrections of figures in Smith's hand. It seems that, in addition to the information that Smith had provided Townshend about French taxes, in this instance he was required to supply theoretical points and facts about the government funds, also to check and tabulate figures.

At the end of his letter Townshend threw out hints, perhaps expecting reactions from his correspondent, about measures he was contemplating for inclusion in next spring's budget:

Are we to hesitate upon every method and propose no other—victims of irresolution and decay. No! I will suggest another Plan: which is the simple one of ameliorating the branches of your Revenue, enriching the Sinking Fund, and appropriating the frequent and future Surplus in time of peace. The Branches I would ameliorate are your Customs, by a better method of preventing illicit trade, your Excise by better changes and regulations in the Soap and tea duty: by lessening the duties on Coffee, and by varying the duties on Spirits. I would enrich the Sinking Fund by new taxes *in themselves* proper, such as the late duty on French Cambricks, a tax on Servants, and other such wise regulations for the encouragement of labour and commerce. I would also fall upon plantations in the forests, and settlement of waste lands, which adding people and produce would of course encrease interior consumption, the only true source of solid Revenue. I will add to these a *real* American Revenue. (*Corr.* No. 302)

When Townshend brought his budget down on 15 April 1767, before Smith left for Scotland, he included some measures foreshadowed in his letter, including an increase in the Sinking Fund to £400,000. He had long been interested in the question of taxing Americans, and was always associated with plans for remodelling the colonial administration. In 1767 he inspired resolutions in the House of Commons that suspended the legislative functions of the New York Assembly, established Commissioners of Customs in America to supervise the trade laws, and proposed specific taxes. Among the latter was the celebrated imposition on tea (Financial Resolution of 2 June) which, with other incitements, provoked the Boston Tea Party of 16 December 1773 as one incident leading to the American Revolution. Though Smith certainly believed that Americans should contribute to the colonial administration, as did Franklin, there is no evidence that he favoured the specific duties imposed by Townshend, which seem to have been advised by his close associates outside the Cabinet such as Samuel Touchet and John Huske (Fay, 1956: 104–6; *HP* ii. 661, iii.535, 540, 542–3, 547). Smith's experience with the Chancellor's office in Downing Street, however, added to the knowledge he drew from printed sources in composing the second chapter of book v of *WN*, 'Of the sources of the general or publick Revenue of the Society'. Reflecting on the somewhat inchoate nature of Townshend's thoughts about his budget may have prompted Smith to formulate his canons of taxation: equality, certainty, conveniency, and economy. It should also be acknowledged, of course, that there was discussion of similar canons of taxation in the literature familiar to Smith. He cites the work of his former mentor, Lord Kames: *Sketches of the History of Man* (1774: 474 ff.). To this source can be added Hutcheson's *System of Moral Philosophy*, ii.340–1, and Sir James Steuart's *Principles of Political Economy* (1767/1966), v.iv–v (*WN* 827 n.). In the last phase of his career, Smith concerned himself with increasing government revenue as a Commissioner of Customs by controlling smuggling and promoting Customs and Excise reform.

Another of the 'great' with whom Smith renewed acquaintance in London was Lord Shelburne, now a colleague of Townshend's in the last Administration of the Elder William Pitt (created Earl of Chatham, 1766). He served as Secretary of State, Southern Department, which had responsibility for Home and Irish affairs, and dealt with correspondence relating to Western Europe, India, and the colonies. Shelburne was addressed on 24 November 1766 about the subject of South Pacific exploration, in a letter written by Alexander Dalrymple, younger brother of the Scottish judge and antiquary Lord Hailes. He described his brother Alexander to Boswell on 13 February 1763 as a 'more romantic person than our modern cold times have produced. Bred a merchant upon dry land, he has become an able navigator, and if he lives will be an author voluminous and vast' (Yale Univ. Lib., Boswell Papers; Fry, 1970: p. xviii). While in the service of the East India Company, Dalrymple became interested in the quest for *Terra Australis Incognita*, the unknown Southern Pacific continent which voyagers from

Quiros in the early seventeenth century to Roggeveen in 1722 had claimed to have sighted in the form of various 'promontories'. The Pacific quest theme had been taken up by Hume's correspondent, President de Brosses, in his *Histoire des Navigations aux Terres Australes* (1756), brazenly appropriated by John Callander of Craigforth in his *Terra Australis Cognita* (1766–8).

Dalrymple wrote to Shelburne that he wished to have official sanction for a collection of original accounts of Pacific voyagers, 'lest this general information should have any improper consequences to the Government'. He knew of the British probes into the Pacific by Anson (1744), Byron (1765), and Wallis and Carteret (then in progress), also of the rivalry with the French, represented at that moment by Bougainville, who set out to circumnavigate the globe in November 1766. The letter then brought up Dalrymple's real purpose:

Having had five years' experience in voyages of this kind, thro' seas unknown, and amongst people with whom we have no intercourse, I presume to think myself qualified to be usefully employed in such an undertaking. At the same time, I am not insensible, notwithstanding the instances of Dampier, Halley, etc, how foreign to rules of office it is, to form the most distant expectations, that a person may be employed in the publick Service by Sea, who has no rank in the Navy. (PRO Chatham Papers, 30/48, v.31, fo. 11; Fry, 1970: 113)

The letter attracted Shelburne's attention and he wished, apparently, to have more information about the writer. For this purpose he turned to Smith, who knew Dalrymple through his brother, Lord Hailes. Smith did some research on the originator of the idea of an unknown South Pacific continent, the Portuguese visionary and navigator Pedro Fernandez de Quiros, and sent to Shelburne on 12 February 1767 a translation of a memorial Quiros had addressed to Philip III of Spain, which had been published in Spanish in *Purchas His Pilgrimes* (1624–6). Smith stated further that he looked over Dalrymple's collection of voyages and imagined this memorial was what Shelburne would like to see. He added that Dalrymple was 'just finishing' a geographical account of South Pacific discoveries, and if permitted Dalrymple would read it to Shelburne, showing him on a map at the same time the situation of the islands mentioned. With consideration for the time available to a busy minister, Smith noted that this account was 'extremely short; not much longer than this memorial of Quiros'. He then came to the point and wrote that he thought that the existence of the unknown continent might be doubtful, but if it existed, 'I am very certain you will never find a man fitter for discovering it, or more determined to hazard everything in order to discover it'. Smith next relayed Dalrymple's terms for undertaking such a mission: absolute command of a single ship equipped with many boats, and the guarantee of a replacement if the ship should be lost before he got to the South Seas (*Corr.* No. 101). Shelburne is reported to have 'expressed a strong desire to employ Dalrymple on these discoveries', regretting that he had not known him when Wallis was sent out from England (*European Magazine* 42: 325; Fry, 1970: 114).

In the event, Dalrymple was chosen by the Royal Society, of which Smith became a Fellow on 21 May 1767 (though not admitted until 27 May 1773), to head the expedition intended to chart the transit of Venus in 1768, but with the ulterior purpose of Pacific discovery. The Admiralty would not agree to this, however, and the First Lord, Edward Hawke, chose James Cook to command the *Endeavour* on the voyage, 1768–71, which carried out the astronomical work, and discovered Tasmania and the outline of New Zealand as well as circumnavigating Australia. Cook's second voyage in the *Resolution*, 1772–5, disproved Dalrymple's theories about the unknown continent, but in a sense Dalrymple was the brains behind the North Pacific explorations of Cook and Vancouver as well as those of Cook in the South Pacific, because of his insistence that the North-West Passage controversy be settled in addition to that concerning the southern continent. Also, his later work as hydrographer for the East India Company and then the Admiralty was of the highest importance, so Smith's estimation of his character was entirely justified (Fry, 1970: p. xvi; Beaglehole, 1968: 191–3).

Smith's encounter with the history of Pacific exploration may not have excited his imagination; at least, there seems to be no indication of this in *WN*. Another subject, however, on which Shelburne called for research received in due course more of Smith's professional attention. This was the nature and conduct of colonies, perhaps investigated at this point in the recesses of the British Museum, which had opened on 15 January 1759 (Sherbo, 1972: 56). Smith reported that during the two days up to 12 February, he had 'looked over everything he could find relating to the Roman colonys'. It may be that the minister hoped to find enlightenment about handling the Americans in the history of classical colonization. Nothing much was forthcoming, according to Smith. Their constitutions were modelled on that of Rome, with counterparts of the two consuls and the senate. In respect of their citizens losing their rights of voting and election in the Roman comitia, they were inferior to many municipia. More ominously, Smith's conclusion was that the Roman colonies were 'very independent': twelve of the thirty colonies from whom the Romans demanded soldiers in the second Carthaginian war would not obey orders; also the colonies rebelled frequently and joined forces with the Republic's enemies. Smith's conclusion could have afforded little comfort to a politician concerned about historical patterns: 'Being in some measure little independent republics they naturally followed the interests which their peculiar Situation pointed to them' (*Corr.* No. 101).

For this report, Smith probably relied on the scattered references to the colonies of the Republic found in Livy, an author whom he regarded highly (*LRBL* ii.6, 27, 36; 'Amicus' interviews, *LRBL* 229). It is strange, however, that he does not reflect knowledge of the colonies established by the Caesars found in Pliny and Strabo, authors represented in his library (Mizuta).

Smith offers a rather different account of the Roman colonies in *WN*, no doubt after giving more time to the subject. He contrasts them in point of independence with the Greek colonies, whose advanced civilization he had acknowledged in the 'History of Astronomy' (iii.4) and *LRBL* (ii.117–19). He represents the Roman ones as garrison settlements whose economic growth was never rapid: 'The quantity of land assigned to each colonist was seldom very considerable, and as the colony was not independent, they were not always at liberty to manage their own affairs in the way that they judged was most suitable to their own interest' (*WN* iv.vii.b.5).

While in London, Smith moved in the same social circle that welcomed David Hume, though this good friend was in Scotland, in part recovering from the stress of the contestation with Rousseau. Hume came back to London on 20 February 1767 to assume office as Under-Secretary of State in the Northern Department. One of Hume's and Smith's hostesses of this period was Lady Mary Coke, daughter of the 2nd Duke of Argyll and thus Buccleuch's aunt. She kept a lively journal of her life, and her entry for Sunday 8 February 1767 paints Smith in a characteristic domestic scene:

While Lady George Lennox was with me Sir Gilbert Elliot came in: they talked of Mr Smith, the Gentleman that went abroad with the Duke of Buccleugh, I said many things in his praise, but added he was the most Absent Man that ever was. Lady George gave us an instance that made me laugh. Mr Damer [son of Lord Milton, who married the sculptress, Anne Conway, encouraged by Hume] She said, made him a visit the other morning as he was going to breakfast, and falling into discourse, Mr Smith took a piece of bread and butter, which, after he had rolled round and round, he put into the teapot and pour'd the water upon it; some time after he poured it into a cup, and when he had tasted it, he said it was the worst tea he had ever met with.

Lady Mary Coke was very fond of her nephews, the Duke of Buccleuch and his brother, Hew Campbell Scott. Horace Walpole wrote to her about the death of the younger one. Lady Mary thought the meeting between the Duke arriving with his brother's body and his mother would be 'terrible'. Lady Dalkeith bore up under the strain, however, and took comfort in receiving from Paris a painting of Hew Campbell Scott by Greuze (retained in Douglas Castle, Lanarkshire, in 1888). Lady Mary herself considered the portrait beautiful, making the young man bear a resemblance to the Argyll side of his family. Her journal records that Buccleuch had proposed to Lady Elizabeth, only daughter of the Duke of Montagu, and that they were privately married on 3 May 1767, no doubt because the family was still in mourning. She was offended at not being invited, but softened when she called on the bride three days after the wedding:

We found her dressing her head, and looking like a little Angel; her behaviour the prettiest in the World, cheerful, good humour'd, and proper in all respects. I believe her as sensible as She is handsome. The Duke of Buccleugh went to Court while we was there to be presented to the King: his Equipage was very genteel, and his Liveries extremely fine.

HRH Princess Amelia had already confided to Lady Mary on 23 February that 'She liked the Duke of Buccleugh, that he had the manner of a Man of Fashion'

(Coke, 1889: i.77, 79, 85–6, 112, 141, 153, 158, 231). As his mentor, Smith could take some credit for the young Duke's manners and appearance. Indeed, Buccleuch acknowledged 'every advantage that could be expected from the society of such a man [as Smith] . . . a friend whom I loved and respected, not only for his great talents, but for every private virtue' (Douglas, 1813: i.258).

The Duke's marriage is a sign of his maturity and independence by this time, and Smith could make his plans for returning to be with his mother and cousin in Kirkcaldy. Writing *WN* was on his mind as he did so. On 25 March 1767 we learn from a letter to Thomas Cadell, former apprentice to Andrew Millar as printer, and then taking over his publishing business this very year, that Smith wished to have four boxes of books shipped to Edinburgh, and insured for £200, a sizeable sum in those days (*Corr.* No. 102). The books were to include two that Cadell had obtained for Smith: Adam Anderson's *Historical and Chronological Deduction of the Origin of Commerce* (new edn. 1764), much drawn upon by Smith in *WN*; and another, designated 'Postlethwait', which could be either Malachi Postlethwayt's *Universal Dictionary of Trade and Commerce* (3rd edn. 1766), an expanded English version of the *Dictionnaire universel de commerce* (1723–30), by Jacques Savary des Brulons or, less likely, James Postlethwayt's *History of the Public Revenues from the Revolution to the Present Time* (1759). These three books have survived in Smith's library, of whose existence the Edinburgh shipment provides the first news (Mizuta, intro.). Smith was still consulting Anderson in 1780, perhaps in connection with his Customs work rather than *WN*, and on 25 October of that year he wrote to Cadell to say he had discovered an imperfection, in the book, and wished to have this remedied. He recalled that Cadell did not have the book in his shop and had to obtain it from a neighbour's, 'sometime in the month of [March] 1767, a few days before I left London' (*Corr.* No. 206).

Also in October 1780, Smith provided for a Danish friend, Andreas Holt, whom he had met in Toulouse, a general account of the next stage of his life:

Since I had the pleasure of seeing you, my own life has been extremely uniform. Upon my return to Britain I retired to a small Town in Scotland the place of my nativity, where I continued to live for six years in great tranquillity, and almost in complete retirement. During this time I amused myself principally with writing my Enquiry concerning the Wealth of Nations, in studying Botany (in which however I made no great progress) as well as some other sciences to which I had never given much attention before. (*Corr.* No. 208)

A trace of the interest in botany is the presence in the library of a book by the Hammersmith nurseryman James Lee, an *Introduction* to the subject, *containing an explanation of the theory of this science, and an interpretation of its technical terms; extracted from the works of Dr Linnaeus* (2nd edn. 1765; Mizuta), perhaps another book shipped to Edinburgh in the four boxes sent in the spring of 1767. Smith's library also contained four works by Linnaeus himself (Mizuta):

Philosophica botanica (1751), *Species plantarum* (2nd edn. 1762), *Genera plantarum* (new edn. 1767), and the *Systema naturae* (13th edn. 1767–70). Smith's reading of the last book listed is reflected in the essay on the external senses (71, 77, 83). As mentioned already, this has suggested a date after 1758 for the completion of this essay (Brown, 1992), since the references deal with a part of Linnaeus' classification of animals introduced into the tenth edition of that year, but perhaps his ownership of the thirteenth edition pushes the essay's completion even later.

Hume received a report from Smith of how things were proceeding in Kirkcaldy, in a letter written on 7 June 1767. The occasion was a request that Hume look after the Count de Sarsfield, whom Smith described as the 'best and most agreeable friend I had in france'. Smith wished to have him introduced in London to James Oswald of Dunnikier and Sir Gilbert Elliot. With Hume's letter was enclosed one for Dr Charles Morton, Secretary of the Royal Society, perhaps acknowledging Smith's election as Fellow and excusing his absence from admission. He asked Hume to remember him to 'Mr Adams's family', that of his boyhood friends, the brothers Robert and James Adam, who had returned from their Grand Tours in 1758 and 1763 respectively and were establishing brilliant reputations as architects and interior designers of Kedleston and Syon (Beard, 1981: 1–5). Smith also wished to be remembered to Mrs Elizabeth Montagu, the coalmine owner and bluestocking who, as an enthusiastic admirer of Ossian, had visited Scotland in 1766, in the van of tourists attracted to the Highlands by a combination of vestiges of a primitive society and picturesque and sublime scenery (Ross, 1965). Smith no doubt had been among the intellectuals invited to her London house, and Beattie and Blair kept her posted about their assessment of *WN* in due course. Smith explained his situation in Kirkcaldy thus to Hume:

My Business here is Study in which I have been very deeply engaged for about a month past. My Amusements are long, solitary walks by the Sea side. You may judge how I spend my time. I feel myself, however, extremely happy, comfortable and contented. I never was, perhaps, more so in all my life.

The letter ends with requests for information about Rousseau's activities: 'Has he gone abroad, because he cannot get himself sufficiently persecuted in Great Britain?' Also Smith asked about the 'Bargain' with the East India Company by the Administration in which Hume served (*Corr.* No. 103). The information he amassed about the East India Company was to swell into a history and indictment of it which he published as one of the Additions to the third edition of *WN* (1784). His interest in Indian affairs as well as his professional ability, no doubt, led his friend William Pulteney, now an MP, to suggest his name to the East India Company Directors as someone whose advice would be useful in connection with reform and possibly the technical matter of recoinage (*Corr.* No. 132).

Hume wrote back to Smith on 13 June agreeing that Sarsfield 'is really a Man of Merit', and that he was a 'good Acquaintance from the time I saw him at Paris'. There was a rumour that Sarsfield, who was of Irish extraction, would take over from de Guerchy as French ambassador to Britain in 1767, but this did not come about. Hume mentioned that he would like to have cultivated Sarsfield's friendship more but his official business prevented this. He had not introduced Sarsfield to Elliot because he judged that the latter's 'Reserve and Indolence wou'd make him neglect the Acquaintance'. As for Oswald of Dunnikier, Hume feared their friendship was broken for ever. He then told the 'strangest Story you ever heard of'. He had dined with Oswald two months ago, and in the company was Oswald's younger brother, John, who had pursued a career in the Church of Ireland and was Bishop of Raphoe. Hume made a joke of not being made a Bishop himself when his patron, Lord Hertford, became Lord Lieutenant of Ireland, after his Embassy to France:

The Right Reverend [Raphoe], without any further Provocation, burst out into the most furious, and indecent, and orthodox Rage, that was ever seen: Told me that I was most impertinent; that if he did not wear a Gown I durst not, no, I durst not have us'd him so; that none but a Coward woud treat a Clergyman in that manner; that henceforth he must either abstain from his Brother's House or I must; and that this was not the first time he had heard this stupid Joke from my Mouth.

Hume had begged his pardon with the 'utmost Tranquillity and Temper', but Raphoe was not to be appeased, and 'rav'd on in the same Style for a long time'. Hume finally got the conversation turned another way and then left the company. What distressed him more than Raphoe's rage and 'orthodox Zeal' was the fact that James Oswald kept silent and offered him no apology. Hume stayed away from his house, 'tho formerly I us'd to be three or four times a week with him'. Hume showed that he had regained his usual ironic composure in the subscription to the letter: 'If I were sure Dear Smith that you and I shoud not one day quarrel in some such manner, I shoud tell you, that I am Yours very affectionately and sincerely D.H.' (*Corr.* No. 104).

Hume received a reply to this from Smith written on 13 September:

I cannot easily express to you the indignation with which your last letter filled me. The Bishop is a brute and a beast and unmerited preferment has rendered him, it seems, still more so. I am very much ashamed that the very great affection which I owe to his Brother had ever imposed upon me as to give me a good opinion of him. He was at Kirkcaldy since I received your letter and I was obliged to see him, but I did not behave as I otherwise would have done.

Smith went to explain that James Oswald's conduct was occasioned by his 'most terrible distress', seemingly due to a terminal illness which ended his life within two years (*Corr.* No. 109).

Smith had an amiable letter from Sarsfield written on 23 June, expressing great regret at not finding him in London, and a wish to take walks by the seaside with him in Kirkcaldy. Much of the letter is taken up with comments on Ferguson's *Essay on the History of Civil Society*, which had appeared that year. Hume had read some chapters in draft when he returned from France, but his finding was unusually negative: 'I do not think them fit to be given to the Public, neither on account of the Style nor the Reasoning: the Form nor the Matter', and he thought publication would hurt Ferguson's reputation (*HL* ii.11–12). The book did receive acclaim on publication, however, and afterwards in Britain and on the Continent (Jogland, 1969; Waszec, 1985; 1988). Hume reported the early stages of this to Ferguson himself (*HL* ii.125–6), but even on rereading it he did not change his own adverse opinion (*HL* ii.133). Sarsfield wrote that the book gave him pleasure, but he did not agree with the praise Ferguson bestowed on the Spartans for their patriotism and love of liberty, and thought their institutions bizarre. He also thought Ferguson had been unfair to the medieval knights and their code of chivalry (*Corr.* No. 105).

Perhaps pointedly, and indicating that he did not think much of Ferguson's book, Smith did not refer to it in *WN*, though his position on the bad effects of the division of labour is close to that of the *History of Civil Society*, as the Glasgow editors indicate (*WN* ii.782, n. 48). Unaware of the contents of *LJ* which covered division of labour (e.g. (A) vi.28–57) and bad effects of this ((B) 329), and noting the priority in time of the *History of Civil Society* over *WN*, Marx concluded that Ferguson was Smith's teacher (Marx, 1954: i.123, n. 1). Perhaps Smith became sensitive about the delay in the publication of *WN* and anticipated such conclusions, occasioning the 'little Jealousy in his Temper' which Carlyle of Inveresk noted (1973: 142). On his side, Ferguson made a gesture to Smith of acknowledgement of the superior authority of his work on political economy, in an expanded sentence in the fourth edition of the *History of Civil Society* (1773, iii.4):

But I willingly quit a subject in which I am not much conversant, and still less engaged by the object for which I write. Speculations on commerce and wealth have been delivered by the ablest writers, *and the public will probably soon be furnished with a theory of national economy, equal to what has ever appeared on any subject of science whatever.**

*[Footnote] *By Mr Smith, author of the Theory of Moral Sentiments.*

This phrasing remained in the seventh edition of 1814, the last in Ferguson's lifetime, but a Basle edition of 1789 refers to *WN* rather than *TMS*, and adjusts the text to say *the public has lately been furnished* with this book (Mizuta).

Sarsfield ended his letter of 23 June by attributing to 'gens de paris' the rumour that Rousseau was at St Denis, though he could scarcely believe that the *Parlement* of Paris would leave him there long. This referred to another episode in the history of persecution endured by Rousseau, which Smith foretold Rousseau would avenge through the *Contrat social*. On 13 September Smith replied to Sarsfield, and he also wrote to Hume about other topics asking for a 'true history of Rousseau before and after he left England' (*Corr.* No. 109).

Hume obliged in a letter dated 8 October relating Rousseau's strange behaviour, which we now understand to have been caused by paranoia (*Corr.* No. 111).

Hume corrected some details of this account in another letter dated 17 October, and reported what Richard Davenport had seen at Wootton in Derbyshire, where Hume had found a refuge for Rousseau. It was nothing less than the 'memoirs' Rousseau was writing, which Davenport judged 'will be the most taking of all his Works' (*Corr.* No. 112). No doubt Hume had some apprehension about the manner in which Rousseau would handle the episode of the visit to England, and there were other famous people involved at one time with Rousseau, for example, Diderot and Madame d'Épinay, who wished to see the book suppressed. When the book was published in 1782–9 as the *Confessions*, as we have mentioned, it was found that Rousseau had not carried his story beyond 1765. For a time, Rousseau was given asylum at Trie-Château (Oise) by the Prince de Conti, Madame de Boufflers's lover. He finished work on the *Confessions* there, then resumed his wanderings, and was allowed to settle in Paris in 1770. He died eight years later on 3 July at Ermenonville, 86 kilometres from the capital. This became a Rousseau shrine, and the Isle of Poplars where his ashes rested was visited by throngs of devotees, including Franklin, Robespierre, Marie Antoinette, and Napoleon (Bonnefous, 1964; Schama, 1989: 156–60).

Among his last works was another autobiographical piece, a strange mutation of the impartial spectator idea, also published posthumously: *Dialogues de Rousseau juge de Jean-Jacques* (*Premier Dialogue*, 1780; *Trois Dialogues*, 1782). Rousseau revealed in the *Deuxième Dialogue* that he had brooded on the portrait Allan Ramsay had painted of him in 1766, dressed in Armenian costume, as a companion piece to one of Hume in the court dress of an Embassy Secretary. Hume declared in his *Exposé succinct* (1767) about the quarrel with Rousseau that it was Ramsay's idea to paint the portrait of Rousseau, and that he presented it as a gift to Hume. Rousseau wrote that Hume had desired this portrait as ardently as a lover desires that of a mistress. The portrait depicted him in a jet-black cap and dark brown robe, seated in shadow in an attitude requiring strained muscles which contorted his appearance. The point of all this, according to Rousseau, was to give him the 'face of a terrible Cyclops', and thus to degrade him in contrast to the elevated image of the handsome and generous Hume (Rousseau, 1959: 779–81). Unaware of such dark thoughts, Hume hung the two portraits side by side in his parlours, until 1771 in James's Court near the Castle, and thereafter in his house on 'St David's Street' in the New Town (Mossner, 1980: 537). Adam Smith must certainly have seen them there on his rare visits from Kirkcaldy, and perhaps wondered at the self-torment of the being who had written so eloquently about self-love and self-improvement, causal factors, as Smith saw things, in the generation of material wealth.[1]

Meantime, Smith's material needs were met by the Duke of Buccleuch's grant of an annuity of £300 per year, and we hear of a first payment of this on 26 June 1767 (*Corr.* No. 106). On 30 August he sent William Strahan a draft for

£12 11*s*., £10 of which he owed Strahan, presumably for books, the remaining sum being paid to Dr Morton for his Royal Society fees (*Corr.* No. 108). On 13 September he wrote to Hume from Dalkeith House, chief residence of the Buccleuch family on the North Esk near Edinburgh, and built by James Smith in 1702–11 for Duchess Anne, widow of the Duke of Monmouth (Marshall, 1973). With its warm sandstone appearance and Dutch Palladian courtyard organization, it has been described 'in its main aspect [as] the grandest of all early classical houses in Lothian and for that matter in Scotland' (McWilliam, 1978: 158–61). Smith's friend John Adam carried out repairs and refacing work in 1762–3, and the interior was well kept up, including Duchess Anne's Room, with its oak-panelled walls and red marble fireplace detailed in white, the overmantel containing a white marble panel by Grinling Gibbon depicting the story of Neptune and Galatea.

The newly married Duke and Duchess and Lady Frances Scott had come to this splendid home at the beginning of September, and were to celebrate the Duke's majority on the 13th, but the celebrations were put off because of the news of Charles Townshend's unexpected death on the 4th from a 'putrid fever'. Smith passed over all this in his report to Hume:

[The young couple] begin to open their house on Monday next and I flatter myself will both be very agreable to the People of this country. I am not sure that I have ever seen a more agreable woman than the Dutchess. I am sorry that you are not here because I am sure you would be perfectly in love with her. (*Corr.* No. 109)

Carlyle described the ensuing assembly of fifty ladies and gentlemen of the neighbourhood: 'The Fare was Sumptuous, but the Company was formal and Dull. Adam Smith their only Familiar at Table, was but ill qualifi'd to promote the Jollity of a Birthday, and Their Graces were quite unexperienc'd.' Fortunately, Carlyle and a convivial friend, Sandy McMillan, Keeper of Signet, were active in proposing toasts and 'we Got into Spirits that better Suited the Occasion'. Carlyle, like Smith, was struck by the beauty of the Duchess: 'Her Features were regular, her Complexion Good, her Black Eyes of an Impressive Lustre, and her Mouth when she Spoke uncommonly Gracefull.' Perhaps jealous of Smith's relationship with the Duke and Duchess, however, Carlyle ends his account of this occasion on a sour note:

Smith Remain'd with them for two months, and then Return's to Kirkcaldy to his Mother and his Studies. I have often thought Since that if they had brought Down a Man of more Address than he was, How much sooner their first appearance might have been; their own Good Sense and Discernment, enabled them sooner to Draw round them as familiars, a better Set of their own chusing, than Could have been pick'd out for them by the assistance of an Aid De Camp, or Led Captain [i.e. a hanger-on or parasite]. (Carlyle, 1973: 250)

Local authorities noted at this time that Smith's relationship with Buccleuch was a close one. We find that together with the Duke he was made a burgess of

Musselburgh on 26 September 1767 (Scott, 1937: 82, n. 1), and accorded the same honour at Edinburgh on 6 June 1770 (Town Council Minutes, City Chambers).

Smith's studies continued at Kirkcaldy, but the composition of *WN* did not proceed apace. He admitted as much in a letter to Lord Shelburne of 27 January 1768:

Since I came to this country I have employed myself pretty much in the manner that I proposed. I have not, however, made all the Progress that I expected; I have resolved, therefor, to prolong my stay here till November next, perhaps, till after the Christmass holidays next winter.

He also thanked Shelburne for his kindness to the Count de Sarsfield: 'There is nothing that your Lordship could Possibly have done that would have bound me more effectually to you'; and he asked his correspondent to pass on his thanks to Colonel Robert Clerk for unspecified but beneficial advice about his 'original contract' with Buccleuch, perhaps meaning his annuity (*Corr.* No. 113). If there had been the contretemps that Ferguson alleged in his dialogue, 'Of the Principle of Moral Estimation', both Clerk and Smith now overlooked it.

But Christmas 1768 came and went and Smith remained in Kirkcaldy. On 15 January following, he wrote the first of a series of six letters to Lord Hailes, which show Smith struggling in his workshop with the research material for *WN*, and helping another man of letters with his projects. In the first letter, he acknowledges an offer from Hailes to lend him a 'Collection of Papers concerning the Prices of Corn and other Provisions in Antient times'. He mentions that he has no 'papers upon this subject', presumably manuscripts, except a copy of a printed account of the 'fiars' of Midlothian from 1626. These were 'annual valuations made upon oath, according to the actual state of the market in every different county in Scotland' (*WN* I.xi.e.17). He hopes to get more information about provision prices from the Navy's Victualling Office, and he has by him a 'good number of remarks' on printed books on the subject, one of which he thinks Hailes has not seen, but which he considers the 'most judicious of them all'.

This is a comparative study obtained for Smith's Library (Mizuta) entitled, *Recherches sur la population des généralités d'Auvergne, de Lyon, de Rouen, et de quelques provinces et villes du royaume, avec des réflexions sur la valeur du bled tant en France qu'en Angleterre, depuis 1674 jusqu'en 1764*. The author was a tax-gatherer named Messance, identified as receiver of the 'tailles' (major French direct tax on persons and property: *WN* v.ii.g.6–7), in the election of Saint-Étienne. Smith must have acquired this book towards the end of his stay in France or have had it sent over recently, because the book was published in Paris in 1766. He also reports making use of Thomas Madox's 1711 *History of the Exchequer* (Mizuta), English Acts of Parliament, and 'Ordonnances of the french Kings'.

Then he comments on his present situation, which we may believe to be characteristic of a scholar who aims at exactness of coverage of his subject, as well as meticulous care in its organization: 'My own Papers are in very great disorder and I wait for some further information which I expect from different quarters before I attempt to give them the last Arrangement.' Next, he offers to send his 'Papers' to Hailes or to read them to him, when they are in a fit state. In his turn, he promises to read through the Scottish Acts of Parliament and 'compare them both with our own historians and with the laws of some other nations' that he has had occasion to examine, to help Hailes with a scheme to publish observations on the 'Scotch Acts', like Daines Barrington's recently published *Observations on the English Statues* (1766). He continues with a further admission about his plight. It is that of someone whose 'schemes of Study' leave him 'very little leisure', and resemble the web of Penelope, since he 'scarcely see[s] any Probability of their ending' (*Corr.* No. 115).

Hailes's 'Papers' had not reached Smith by 5 March, when he writes again, and he offers to send his servant to fetch them from the judge's house on New Street, Canongate, where he was a neighbour of Smith's former patron Lord Kames. Smith has been reading the Acts of the Parliaments of James I, and finding this instructive about the barbarous state of the Scotland of the time. He notes the provisions for hostelries for travellers and for control of 'numerous suite[s] of retainers' which made hospitality oppressive, but he regrets his remarks will be of less use to Hailes than the latter's to him. However, he expanded on the cause and effects of hospitality in feudal times in *WN* at III.iv.5, so his reading of the 'Scotch Acts' connected with his current project. In passing, he makes clear his own approach to legal studies:

I have read law entirely with a view to form some general notion of the great outlines of the plan according to which justice has [been] administered in different ages and nations: and I have entered very little into the detail of Particulars, of which, I see, your Lordship is very much master. Your Lordships particular facts will be of great use to correct my general views; but the latter, I fear, will always be too vague and superficial to be of much use to your Lordship.

The letter concludes with an expression of Smith's indignation at the outcome of the celebrated Douglas Cause. As an advocate Hailes had acted for the Hamilton family in claiming the estates of Archibald, 1st and last Duke of Douglas, for the 7th Duke of Hamilton, and in refuting the claim of the actual heir through an allegation that he was not the Duke of Douglas's grandson but a suppositious child. As we have seen, Smith was involved in the Cause as a Commissioner for collecting evidence in France in 1765, and like most of the literati he was a Hamiltonian, while Boswell, siding with the popular party, was a Douglasian. Boswell declared that in taking six years to go through the courts of Scotland, France, and England, the Douglas Cause 'shook the sacred security of *birth-right* in Scotland to its foundation' (*BLJ* v.28; *Corr.* No. 72).

Smith was indignant that the one-vote majority for the Duke of Hamilton in the Court of Session had been reversed by a decision of the House of Lords in London on 27 February 1769, and that, when the news reached Edinburgh, the Lord President of the Court of Session (Robert Dundas of Arniston the Younger) had been exposed to the 'insults of a brutal mob' (*Corr.* No. 116).

Without waiting for Smith's servant, Hailes sent the 'Papers' by post next day, 6 March. Headed 'Prices of Corn, Cattle &c in Scotland from the earliest accounts to the death of James V', the document presents extracts from the cartularies (registers of accounts) of the bishoprics of Moray and Aberdeen, and of the monasteries of Dryburgh, Arbroath, Kelso, Scone, Cambuskenneth, and Dunfermline, and makes reference to the Books of Sederunt of the Court of Session (GUL MS Gen. 1035/228; *Corr.* 145–50). The accompanying letter provides some details of the Edinburgh mob that threatened to pull the Lord President down from his sedan chair, and Hailes refers to the stoning of windows of judges who had voted for Hamilton (*Corr.* No. 117). Boswell is said to have been a ringleader of the stone-throwers, and to have announced as the glass shattered: 'These honest fellows in their turn are giving their *casting* votes' (Pottle, 1966: 399).

Replying on 12 March, Smith observes that he has read over the 'Prices of Corn' document 'with great pleasure and attention', and adds that it will be of 'very great use' to him. He notes that the 'estimated prices of grain among our ancestors seem to have been extremely Loose and inaccurate', and that the same 'nominal sum' was considered the average price of grain and other foodstuffs over years in which there were considerable changes in the intrinsic value of coin. Thus in 1523, so Smith writes in error for the document's 1525, and in 1540, the Court of Session estimated the boll of barley at 13*s*. 4*d*., though at the first date only £7 was coined out of a pound of silver, while at the second the sum coined was £9 12*s*. These amounts are expressed in pounds Scots, nominally one-twelfth of the value of the English pound sterling. He does not believe it 'conceivable' that during the sixteenth century, so long after the discovery of the Spanish West Indies, that grain could have sunk one-third its average price, or in the real amount of silver exchanged for it. He then goes into the matter of conversion prices, those sums of money accepted in Scotland in exchange for rents in kind (see *WN* I.xi.e.17). When landlords have the option, Smith remarks, and generally reside on their estates, they prefer for the convenience of their family to receive rents in kind, and do not much care how low the conversion price is, though it is to the tenants' benefit that it is low. The point here is that conversion prices are not good guides to average price of corn and other foodstuffs. Smith then adds a postscript about the rejoicing over the Douglas Cause verdict in Kirkcaldy, which he describes as 'four schoolboys [setting] up three candles on the tron' (*Corr.* No. 118).

Nothing came of Hailes's plan to publish observations on the 'Scotch Acts', other than the circulation in printed form of specimens, but he was able to send to Smith a copy of his *Examination of Some of the Arguments for the High*

Antiquity of the Regiam Majestatem; and an Inquiry into the Authenticity of the Leges Malcolmi (1769; Mizuta), receiving an acknowledgment on 16 May. Smith agrees with Hailes that the *Leges Malcolmi* 'are not the laws of any King Malcolm', but a description cast in historical rather than statutory terms of the 'great outlines of the Laws and customs' of Scotland, which the author supposed were made in times ancient in comparison with his own. Smith also observes that the discrepancies Hailes has discovered in the prices of different things resemble those which occur in the 'antient Coutumes' of many different French provinces. He jokes that one of the authorities he consulted on grain prices, Dupré de Saint-Maur, 'has tortured his brain to reconcile [those discrepancies] and make them all consistent' (cf. *WN* I.xi.e.24). For English prices, the French author relied, as did Smith himself, on Bishop Fleetwood's *Chronicon Preciosum* (1707), but had arrived at different conclusions. In Smith's opinion, discrepancies arose because authors of compilations of prices and courts alike followed ancient valuations or accommodated these to changes made afterwards in the standard of coin, 'pretty much as accidental circumstances had directed'. Having taken a copy of the document on prices, he promises to send it back by next week's carrier, and declares he will come to Edinburgh during the summer sitting of the Court of Session, 12 June–12 August, when he would 'beg [Hailes's] assistance to get access to the Cartularies' from which the corn prices were copied (*Corr.* No. 119). Hailes was not thought to be able to read charter-hand himself, but Smith could call on the help of his friend John Davidson, Clerk to the Signet, who had this skill (Innes, 1872: 8, n. 1, 11).

As promised, Smith sent the corn prices document off on 23 May, enclosing a letter which reflects further thought about Hailes's book on the *Regiam Majestatem*. He does not have the Latin text to hand, though a copy of the second edition of 1613 edited by Sir John Skene did come into his Library (Mizuta). Smith points out that in one passage (ch. 3, s. 5), Hailes has a different understanding from Skene in his translation of 1609: *Regiam Majestatem. The Auld Lawes and Constitutions of Scotland . . . from the Dayes of King Malcolme the Second untill the Time of King James the First*. The issue is what constitutes a reasonable day's subsistence for a Coroner and five assistants, including a clerk. Skene's punctuation and translation would make the clerk's fee 2s., but Smith points out that six people getting 4d. a day, splitting the 2s. evenly, would be in line with the 4d. daily wages of a master stonemason fixed by the Statute of Labourers of 1350 (see *WN* I.xi.e.2). Smith concludes his letter by offering to send legal papers dealing with the 'Antiquity of female honours and female fiefs' provided by friends in France, if this would help Hailes with the claim of his ward, Elizabeth Gordon, to be recognized as Countess of Sutherland (*Corr.* No. 120). Hailes's successful appeal in this case, which went to the House of Lords, is still regarded as an important source of peerage law, and Smith collected the printed pleadings (Mizuta).

In these letters to Hailes we find Smith receiving and commenting on information relevant to *WN*, as well as drawn in somewhat to further the projects of his correspondent as a legal antiquary. He scarcely sees the possibility of an end to his own enquiries and necessarily, then, the 'last Arrangement' is deferred. As this state of affairs was protracted his health seems to have suffered; he fought against this by taking long walks and, apparently, took up swimming again in the Firth of Forth. This pursuit very likely gave rise to the anecdote of his arriving in Dunfermline in his dressing gown, one Sunday morning as the bells were ringing and people were going to the kirk. He may have walked the fifteen miles from Kirkcaldy in a fit of abstraction, perhaps upon taking a wrong turning after a douse in the North Sea (Rae, 1965: 259–60; Scott, 1937: 325, n. 1).

But in his bouts of abstraction, no doubt, he was fitting his information into patterns and connecting the parts of political economy into a 'system'—a further example, after those he had constructed for rhetoric, languages, and astronomy, of an imaginary machine invented to connect together in the fancy those different movements and effects which are in reality performed' ('Astronomy' iv.19). In this instance, of course, he was emulating what Quesnay had achieved in the *Tableau économique*.

The comments on fluctuations in grain prices in the end formed part of the 'Digression concerning the Variation in the Value of Silver during the Course of the Four Last Centuries' (1.xi.e). Unlike Dupré de Saint-Maur, Smith did not 'torture his brain' to reconcile the difference in prices, but saw that commentators on the prices were misled about their levels, and had a mistaken belief that the value of silver diminished continually (para. 15). From the time of the Glasgow lectures on jurisprudence at least, he held to the point that the 'real price of everything, what every thing really cost to the man who wants to acquire it, is the toil and trouble of acquiring it' (*WN* I.v.2; cf. *LJ*(A) i.59). With commodities such as poultry, the 'spontaneous productions of nature', where supply usually exceeded demand, at different times different exertions of labour would buy them. The case is otherwise with corn. At any stage of development, raising this commodity in the same soil and climate will on average require appreciably the same exertion of labour or the price of this labour. As a result, a standard exists for measuring value:

Corn, accordingly . . . is, in all the different stages of wealth and improvement, a more accurate measure of value than any other commodity or sett of commodities. In all those different stages, therefore, we can judge better of the real value of silver, by comparing it with corn, than by comparing it with any other commodity, or sett of commodities. (*WN* I.xi.e.28)

Perhaps Smith found this idea in Locke's *Considerations of the lowering of Interest and raising of the Value of Money* (1691) as commented upon in Joseph Harris's two-part book of 1757–8: *An Essay upon Money and Coins* (*WN* i.54, n. 29). Though not mentioned in *WN*, Harris's book seems to lie behind a good deal of Smith's later thought about value (Mizuta). However, Smith connects this concept with an analysis of the components of price. In an MS once possessed by Dugald Stewart, Smith stated that this analysis was suggested to him by James Oswald of Dunnikier (Stewart, *Works*, 1856, ix.6). Smith's published account ran thus: 'In the price of corn . . . one part pays the rent of the landlord, another pays the wages of the maintenance of the labourers and the labouring cattle employed in producing it, and the third pays the profits of the farmer' (*WN* I.vi.11).

In turn, this insight leads to Smith's original formulation of the structure of 'every civilized society' and the wealth that it produces yearly, which comes in as the conclusion of the chapter containing the lengthy 'Digression' on silver values:

The whole annual produce of the land and labour of every country, or what comes to the same thing, the whole price of that annual produce, naturally divides itself . . . into three parts; the rent of land, the wages of labour, and the profits of stock; and constitutes a revenue to three different orders of people; to those who live by rent, to those who live by wages, and to those who live by profit. These are the three great, original and constituent orders of every civilized society, from whose revenue that of every other order is ultimately derived. (I.xi.p.7)

Ronald Meek has seen in this formulation evidence of a 'paradigm shift' for political economy.[2] Henceforth the profit-seeking drive of the third 'constituent order', animated by self-love, is regarded as creating economic growth, accelerated by the division of labour (I.i.1). To be sure, the operation of this principle has its grievously harmful effects on labourers (v.i.f.50). But through economic growth, the 'invisible hand', which we may equate with the operation of the market mechanism within the limits of commutative justice (*TMS* III.6.10; *WN* IV.ix.51), promotes human welfare as time elapses (*WN* IV.ii.9). At any given interval of time, free competition to secure maximum profit is held to ensure efficient allocation of resources among and within separate employments, also to serve the interests of consumers (I.xi.b.5; IV.ii.4; IV.v.7). Moreover, the 'general character' of modern commercial society is thus specified: 'every man . . . lives by exchanging, or becomes in some measure a merchant' (I.iv.1). Thus the commercial society is one characterized by the impersonal conditions of market exchange for commodities or labour. Recognizing that landlords may be indolent and neglect their own interest, that wage-earners may be ignorant of their own and the public interest, and that employers (or capitalists in later terminology) may understand their interest only too well and impose it as a false public interest on the other two constituent orders of the modern commercial society (I.xi.p.8–10), Smith nevertheless gives qualified approval to it, and advocates minimal government intervention in it: the 'obvious and simple system of natural liberty' (IV.ix.51).

At the same time, in so analysing the structure of a commercial society and delineating its operation, Smith draws attention to the central problems of classical and neo-classical economics: how value and price are to be determined; how income and benefits are to be distributed; and how the source and levels of profits are to be established. But he also offers a method for attacking these problems. If the economy is viewed as a machine governed by the price mechanism, involving a market for commodities and labour, then the outcomes though unintended will be amenable to law, and can be analysed by the tools successfully employed in the natural sciences, especially physics. Meek suggests that embedded thus in *WN* is a version of Schumpeter's 'universal interdependence of the magnitudes that constitute the economic cosmos' (Schumpeter, 1954: 308; Meek, 1973: p. xi; Skinner, 1979: 156–63).[3]

Meek further points out that, in the analytic part of *WN*, Smith develops his theory of value through bringing in the notion of equilibrium: subject to competition, prices of commodities move to 'natural' levels (equilibrium), which cover at their 'natural' rates the rents, wages, and profits of those involved in their production: (I.vii; Meek, 1973: p. xi; Myers, 1976). In terms of the organization and content of *WN*, Smith has given his economic doctrine more sophistication and more explanatory power than it attained in the Glasgow lectures on jurisprudence and the ED. Moreover, we find him always seeking the 'beauty of systematical arrangement of different observations connected by a few common principles' (v.i.f.25).

Understanding well the mental effort required for the highly abstract studies in which Smith was engaged, and with his own experience of the 'disease of the learned' in his youth, Hume on returning to Scotland in 1769 sought to draw his friend into some relaxation and refreshing companionship. On 20 August he wrote to Smith that he was 'glad to have come within sight' of him by having a view of Kirkcaldy from his window in James's Court, but he also wished to be on speaking terms, and since he declared himself to be as tired of travelling as Smith 'ought naturally to be, of staying at home', he suggested that Smith should come to join him in his 'Solitude' in Edinburgh:

I want to know what you have been doing, and propose to exact a rigorous Account of the method, in which you have employed yourself during your Retreat. I am positive you are in the wrong in many of your Speculations, especially where you have the Misfortune to differ from me. All these are Reasons for our meeting, and I wish you would make me some reasonable Proposal for the Purpose.

He then pointed out that there was the island of Inchkeith in the 'great Gulph' that lay between them, but it was uninhabited otherwise he would challenge Smith to meet him there, and 'neither [of] us ever to leave the Place, till we were fully agreed on all points of Controversy' (*Corr.* No. 121).

There is no record of Smith accepting Hume's teasing proposal, but on 6 February 1770 Hume wrote in mock-dudgeon about a report that Smith was to pass through Edinburgh on his way to have *WN* printed in London: 'What is the meaning of this, Dear Smith, which we hear, that you are not to be here above a day or two, in your Passage to London? How can you so much as entertain a thought of publishing a Book, full of Reason, Sense, and Learning, to these wicked, abandon'd Madmen?' The letter continued with news of the fall of the Duke of Grafton as head of the Government, and the firmness of the King and North, who became first minister. Hume's political experience in London had not endeared the English to him, apparently, and he expressed the sentiment that 'Nothing but a Rebellion and Bloodshed will open the Eyes of that deluded People, tho' were they alone concerned I think it is no matter what becomes of them' (*Corr.* No. 123). The letter closes with a request that Smith bring over with him two books we imagine Hume had lent him. One was Joseph Priestley's 'Grammar', perhaps the *Rudiments* (1769), or, perhaps, *A Course of Lectures on the Theory of Language, and Universal Grammar* (1762), which continued Smith's line of reasoning that inflections were replaced by prepositions and auxiliaries as more economy in expression was sought by speakers of languages. The other book was Thomas Percy's edition of the Northumberland Household Book (1770). Smith refers to this in his 'Digression concerning Variations in the Value of Silver', to which the correspondence with Hailes had contributed, and he gets from the Percy text some data about fluctuations in the price of wheat, but he is misled by a misprint (*WN* I.xi.e.9; i.197, n. 8).

Hume requested news of Smith's visit later that February, and asked him not to buy claret for him (*Corr.* No. 124), presumably from smugglers or their intermediaries on the Fife coast, whom Smith later had to control as a Commissioner of Customs. There is no further record of Smith visiting Edinburgh until early in 1771, and he was back in Kirkcaldy by 11 March, when he complained to John Davidson about an Edinburgh watchmaker: 'Your friend Cowan has not done justice to my Watch. Since I came to this side of the Water [Firth of Forth] she runs down as fast as I wind her up.' Smith thought the problem was that an apprentice had been given the repair job, and he 'begs' that Cowan should undertake it himself (*Corr.* No. 125). Another letter to John Davidson, written in the autumn of 1771, mentions a plan to see the Duke of Buccleuch at Dalkeith before he leaves for England. Smith states that he had intended to make a 'long visit' to his friends on the other side of the Firth of Forth. It seems that he had suffered from 'wind in [his] stomach', which he believed he would need a 'little dissipation' to dispel, but 'by taking three or four very laborious walks' he has got rid of it, and will not leave his retreat 'for above a day these six months [to come]' (*Corr.* No. 128). Writing on 28 January 1772, Hume mentions a promise from Smith to visit him at Christmas, whose performance he had not 'challenged' because his sister Katherine, who lived with him and of whom he was very fond, had fallen 'dangerously ill of a Fever'. She has now recovered and Hume looks for Smith's 'Company', teasing him about his pleas of ill health:

I shall not take any Excuse from your own State of Health, which I suppose only a Subterfuge invented by Indolence and Love of Solitude. Indeed, my Dear Smith, if you continue to hearken to Complaints of this Nature, you will cut Yourself out entirely from human Society, to the great Loss of both parties. (*Corr.* No. 129)

Hume's letter also gives Smith the address of Mme de Boufflers, to whom he wished to write about her concern to have a better French translation of *TMS* than that of Eidous, a project carried out by her protégé, the Abbé Blavet (*Corr.* No. 130). The postscript to this letter of 28 January suggests that in a previous letter Smith gave Hume advice about reading Boiardo's *Orlando innamorato* (1483–95), two copies of which were in his library in the tuscanized versions of Domenichi and Berni (editions of 1611 and 1768, respectively; Mizuta). Hume has been reading the 'Italian Historians', which confirms him in his opinion that no Italian author writes 'elegant correct Prose' though there are several 'excellent Poets'. Hume concludes: 'You say nothing to me of your own work.'

We hear of *WN* again in a letter from Smith to Sir William Pulteney dated 3 September 1772 which concludes:

My book would have been ready for the Press by the beginning of this winter; but the interruptions occasioned partly by bad health arising from want of amusement and from thinking too much upon one thing; and partly by the avocations above mentioned will oblige me to retard its publication for a few months longer. (*Corr.* No. 132)

Smith's hypochondriasis is a familiar enough theme in his life from his Oxford days, but what were these 'avocations' that consumed his time? The first paragraph mentions 'Public calamities' in which Smith himself has no concern, but it continues: 'some of my friends for whom I interest myself the most have been deeply concerned in them; and my attention has been a good deal occupied about the most proper method of extricating them.'

In a letter to Smith dated 27 June previously, Hume was more explicit about these 'calamities', describing 'Continual Bankruptcies, universal Loss of Credit, and endless Suspicion', in short, a financial crisis of the most aggravated sort in Scotland, connected with difficulties in the south, even extending to the Old Lady of Threadneedle Street, the Bank of England itself. Hume also appreciated the professional interest for Smith of the events he described, and he came to the same conclusion as is reached about them in *WN*, which presents a magisterial survey of 'Money considered as a Particular Branch of the general Stock of Society, or of the Expence of maintaining the National Capital' (II.ii). Hume put the question directly:

Do these Events any-wise affect your Theory? Or will it occasion the Revisal of any Chapters? . . . . On the whole, I believe, that the Check given to our exorbitant and ill grounded Credit will prove of Advantage in the long run, as it will reduce people to more solid and less sanguine Projects, and at the same time introduce Frugality among Merchants and Manufacturers: What say you? Here is Food for your Speculation. (*Corr.* No. 131)

In the 1760s, Scotland witnessed considerable economic development coupled with problems over the supply of sufficient capital and banking facilities. In response to this situation a new bank was formed, Douglas, Heron & Co., better known as the Ayr Bank, with landowners, including the Dukes of Buccleuch and Queensberry, prominent among the shareholders. The bank opened for business on 6 November 1769 and, chiefly to support land improvement schemes, it adopted policies that proved ruinous: 'This bank was more liberal than any other had ever been, both in granting cash accounts, and in discounting bills of exchange' (*WN* II.ii.73). As the bank got going, there was an economic crisis in Scotland, to which Hume alluded, arising from investments outrunning savings, a fall in the price of commodities such as linen, and a 'spirit of overtrading'. Also, in 1772–4 there was a movement towards a depression. On 8 June 1772, a London bank which had extensive dealings with the Ayr Bank collapsed. When the news reached Edinburgh four days later there was a financial panic, resulting in a run on the Ayr Bank for specie, and it was forced to suspend payments on 25 June.

Its note circulation was a profitable business, as Smith pointed out in *WN*, but in continually drawing bills of exchange on London, at interest and commission charges of more than 8 per cent, it was running deeper and deeper into debt. Hume continued the story of the fate of the Ayr Bank in a letter written in October of 1772, describing the reopening of the head office in Ayr on 28 September with a promise of exchanging notes for specie, and a consequent run on the Bank by rivals bent on forcing its closure. Hume further reported that the partners of the Bank had entered into an agreement to bear their share in raising money in London to satisfy the Bank's creditors by means of terminable annuities at a very high rate. Buccleuch was deeply involved in all this, to the point that he and Queensberry were sued for £300,000 by the Bank of England, and claims against them remained active for sixty years. There is no doubt that Buccleuch was among the 'friends' whom Smith endeavoured to extricate from the financial mess. In the end, all the creditors were paid off in full, though it was said that £750,000 worth of landed property had to be sold to achieve this (*Precipitation and Fall*, 1778; Hamilton, 1963: 317–25; Checkland, 1975; Fry, 1992: 45). Smith's part included more than giving advice, as Hume in the October 1772 letter mentions that he had applied to the Edinburgh banker, Sir William Forbes, to see if on Smith's account he would accept Ayr Bank notes. The answer was in the affirmative (*Corr.* No. 133).

Smith's conclusion about the spectacular failure of the Ayr Bank was that it helped to relieve the other Scottish banks from their difficulties over circulating bills of exchange: 'Those other banks, therefore, were enabled to get very easily out of that fatal circle, from which they could not otherwise have disengaged themselves without incurring a considerable loss, and perhaps too even some degree of discredit' (*WN* II.ii.74). Moreover, he argued that if the Ayr Bank had prospered as a 'mercantile company' acting as a 'general loan office for the whole country', its debtors would have been 'chimerical projectors, the drawers and redrawers of circulating bills of exchange, who would employ the money in extravagant undertaking'. Thus the capital of the country would have been transferred from 'prudent and profitable . . . undertaking' to the very reverse (para. 77).

In this fashion, the message of Hume's letter of 27 June 1772, written upon the very stroke of the Ayr Bank catastrophe, had its counterpart in *WN*; but dealing with the aftermath of this event as well as writing about it delayed further the completion of the book. Smith declared to Pulteney on 3 September that he had 'treated fully and distinctly of every part of the subject [presumably credit or paper-money] which you recommended', and that he had intended to send extracts, 'but they are too much interwoven with other parts of the work to be easily separated from it'. Smith also revealed to Pulteney another part of his agenda for *WN*:

I have the same opinion of Sir James Stewart's Book that you have. Without once mentioning it, I flatter myself, that every false principle in it, will meet with a clear and distinct confutation in mine. (*Corr.* No. 132)

Smith is referring to the *Inquiry into the Principles of Political Oeconomy* which Prince Charles Edward Stuart's former secretary, Sir James Steuart, later Steuart-Denham, had published in 1767. Hume is reported as being critical of the 'form and style' of this work (*HL* ii.158 n. 1), but 'exceedingly pleased' with it as an 'ingenious performance', when he looked it over in manuscript in 1766 (Steuart, 1767/1966: vol. i, p. xlv).

Recent commentary has emphasized continuity in Scottish economic thought from Hume to Steuart to Smith, with perhaps the criticism that Smith in certain ways sought for a 'theoretical elegance and precision', or at least suggested this to his followers, while the 'realism and relevance' of his predecessors suffered neglect (Skinner, 1993). The 'false principles' which Smith discerned in Steuart's book were probably the mercantilist ideas, arising from the refusal to credit the economy of a modern commercial society with a self-correcting capacity when supply and demand are not in balance, and the tendency to promote the intervention of the 'statesman' to deal with market failure, also the belief that time 'necessarily' puts a stop to economic growth in a 'trading and industrious nations'.[4] It is possible, also, that Smith is referring specifically to Steuart's 'principles' concerning banking in the fourth Book of his *Inquiry*, and if so he would have in mind the development of his own ideas from *LJ* to *WN*, possibly including the *Thoughts Concerning Banks, and the Paper Currency of Currency of Scotland* of 1763 discussed in Chapter 10.

Meantime, Hume continued to propose schemes for meetings and visits from Smith. He ended his 27 June 1772 letter with a point-blank question: 'Shall we see you again this Summer?' In a letter of 17 November that same year, he wrote that he had heard of an 'excellent House' for his friend in the New Town of Edinburgh, where he had removed from James's Court on Whitsunday 1771. The one he thought appropriate for his friend was the 'first Story of that Land at the Play-house' in which his brother John lived. Hume described it as having a 'Prospect of the Castle and Castle-hill, and all the Fields to the West; of the Calton Hill, the Sea, Arthur's Seat, and even, I believe Kirkaldy to the East'. He ended the letter by attempting to bolster Smith in breaking away from his solitude and self-absorption: 'Have you resolution enough to determine Yourself for your good?'

In a postscript, he responded to a request Smith had made for an 'account of the Money imported into Spain'. Presumably, Smith was seeking more data for his 'Digression on the Variations in the Value of Silver during the Course of the Four Last Centuries', which helped to make a 'very long chapter' (I.xi.p.1); and for his discussion of the effect on Spain of her proprietorship of the American mines (IV.v.a.18–20). This was a key to Smith's negative view of the theory that the wealth of nations consists of its holdings of gold and silver, which he had been attacking since the delivery of his lectures on jurisprudence (cf. *LJ*(A) vi.135–6 and (B) 251–3). Hume contributed a 'Scrawl' which has not survived, attributing the 'Account' it presented to the Spanish importation of money to an Austrian civil servant and expert on finance, Count Zinzendorf, whom he may have met either in Vienna or in London. Hume also stated that this 'Account' concurred 'very exactly' with one he had given in his own writings, though he could not recall the place' (*Corr.* app. E, b).

Smith's reply to this letter appears to have been lost, but another letter from Hume dated 23 November 1772 perhaps allows us to conjecture its contents. Hume wrote:

I shou'd agree to your Reasoning, if I coud trust your Resolution. Come hither for some weeks about Christmas; dissipate yourself a little; return to Kirkaldy; finish your Work before Autumn; go to London; print it; return and settle in this Town, which suits your studious, independant turn even better than London. Execute this plan faithfully; and I forgive you. (*Corr.* No. 134)

Smith must have alleged that he was by now nearing the completion of *WN* and within sight of going to London to have it published and could not, therefore, take a house in Edinburgh. As matters turned out, Smith was *en route* to London in April after receiving advice from Hume in February of the next year (*Corr.* No. 135) to get two recent books. The first was Andrew Stuart's attack on the Chief Justice of England for his partiality in the great Douglas Cause— *Letters to Lord Mansfield* (1773). The second was Lord Monboddo's highly original, comparative study, *Of the Origin and Progress of Language* (vol. i, 1773), marking an advance in empirical analysis over Smith's own enquiry into the formation of languages (Schreyer, 1993). Both books turn up in Smith's library (Mizuta). Hume knew of his plans on the 10th of April, but had no confidence in *WN* being finished: 'I expect to see you soon. Have you been busy, and whether in pulling down or building up?' (*Corr.* No. 136).

Hume alludes here to Smith's difficulties composing *WN* well known to his fellow-literati. Lord Kames wrote in this strain on 20 April 1773 to the Swiss jurist Daniel Fellenberg:

Dr Smiths friends are like you solicitous for a publication. For sometime past he has been employ'd in building and demolishing; and I am afraid the delicacy of his taste exceeds his powers of execution, so that the deliver of this Child may be yet at a distance, tho the time of reckoning is long past. (Berne, Bürgerbibliothek MS)

Besides his 'taste', another problem for Smith was the physical activity of writing. The evidence of his manuscript letters suggests that his penmanship was slow and laborious, the letters formed in a large, round manner like that of a child to whom the activity is not a comfortable or agreeable one. Smith characterized it as 'so very bad a hand' (*Corr.* No. 113). His procedure was to hire an amanuensis to write out his work, and the name of one transcriber of *WN* has survived: Alexander Gillies, who was employed as an Excise officer in Edinburgh in 1785 and rose to become in 1797 Supervisor of the Kilmarnock district. Smith's nephew and heir, David Douglas, supported Gillies for some time before his death (obituary notice, *Scots Magazine*, Mar. 1818; Scott, 1937: 360).

One anecdote has it that in his study in his mother's home in Kirkcaldy Smith dictated sections of *WN* to an amanuensis, perhaps Gillies. He did so standing and had the curious habit of rubbing his head against the wall above the chimney-piece. This is supposed to have left a mark on the wall from the pomatum of his wig, and the reporter of this anecdote, Robert Chambers, alleged in his *Picture of Scotland* (1827) that the traces remained until the wall was repainted. Lest devotees rush to the spot, it must be divulged that the house was pulled down in 1834. All that the visitor will find on the south side of the High Street of the Lang Toun is a plaque at No. 220, which depicts a traditional East Neuk of Fife three-storey dwelling with chimneys crowning the crow-stepped gables. The plaque is based on a water-colour now in the Department of Political Economy, University of Glasgow. This painting was derived from a lithograph published by John Jeffries Wilson in 1844, on which is also based an elevation and plan of the house and garden (Pl. 10).

Smith and Hume laboured the point of the solitude of Kirkcaldy, perhaps dwelling on a Rousseauistic theme, but Smith had the companionship of his cousin Janet Douglas and his mother, both women of character who were well connected with the Fife gentry, and there were neighbours such as Robert Beatson of Vicars Grange, who were certainly capable of instructive conversation about economics (*Corr.* No. 266). Also, there is a report that during his evening walks along the Kirkcaldy foreshore, Smith had the company of a blind boy from the neighbourhood, Henry Moyes, who displayed great intellectual ability. Smith adopted the role of teacher of this boy, and sent him on to Hume, who secured a bursary for him at Edinburgh University, thus paving the way for a notable career as a popular lecturer on chemistry and the philosophy of natural history (Viner's intro. to Rae, 1965: 74–7).

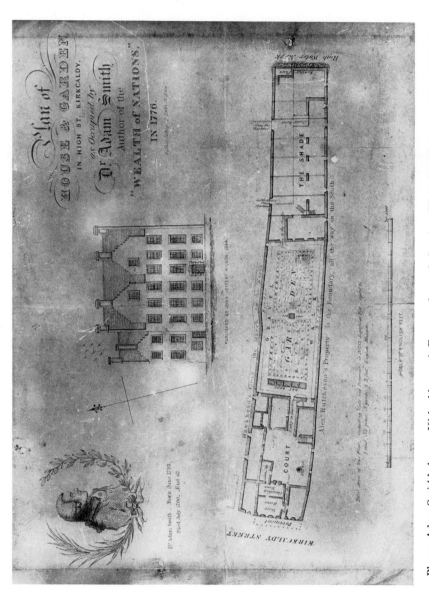

Pl. 10. Adam Smith's house, Kirkcaldy, 1776. From a plan and elevation (Kirkcaldy Museum and Art Gallery).

Though finally prepared to leave Kirkcaldy in the spring of 1773, and on his own admission (*Corr.* No. 208) drawn to London by the prospect of becoming tutor to that Duke of Hamilton whose family had not succeeded in acquiring the Douglas inheritance, Smith was concerned enough about the state of his health to make arrangement in the event of his death. On 16 April he made Hume his literary executor, with the care of all his papers, none of which he thought worth publishing except those connected with *WN*, and what has been mentioned already, a 'fragment of a great work which contains a history of . . . Astronomical systems'. He described it as being in a 'thin folio paper book in my writing desk', an article of furniture that was inherited by the Bannerman family, heirs of David Douglas (Scott, 1937: illustration facing p. 266). All the other loose papers in his bureau in his bedroom, and 'about eighteen thin paper folio books' behind the glass doors of the bureau, he desired Hume to destroy without examination if he die. Unless he died suddenly, the *WN* papers were to be sent to Hume for possible publication (*Corr.* No. 137). With these instructions passed on, Smith was ready for London again and the eventual publication of *WN* which, in the minds of his friends at least, was connected with giving advice to legislators as the American crisis became acute.

15

The American Crisis and The Wealth of Nations

[Your Book] has never yet been so much as advertised. What is the Reason? If you wait till the Fate of America be decided, you may wait long.

Hume wished Smith to publish his great book in London, and then return to Edinburgh to settle, so that he could enjoy his friend's company during his last years (*Corr.* No. 134). For his part, Smith, though apprehensive enough about his own health to declare Hume his literary executor and make provision for a sudden death (Pl. 11), was apparently thinking of going 'abroad' rather than settling down. He acknowledged that he was drawn to London in May 1773 by the prospect of becoming travelling tutor to the Duke of Hamilton, on terms his friends thought 'advantageous', but the Duke of Buccleuch dissuaded him (*Corr.* No. 208). Perhaps his former pupil thought that *WN* would never see print if its author went off again to the Continent. In any event, Smith stayed on in London for the next three years to see his book through the press, at a time when Parliament was increasingly involved in debates and measures connected with the disturbances in the American colonies, which ended in their armed rebellion and delaration of independence. At least one of his correspondents, Dr John Roebuck, the chemical engineer and entrepreneur who had helped to found the Carron Iron Company, went so far on 1 November 1775 as to hope that *WN* would change people's thinking about the outcome of the struggle:

I hoped by this time to have seen your Name in the Papers. The meeting of Parliament is a proper time for the Publication of such a works as yours. It might also have been of use in influencing the Opinion of many in this American contest. (*Corr.* No. 147)

It is certainly noticeable that, in the lectures on jurisprudence which incorporate Smith's thinking on political economy up to 1764, comparatively little attention is given to America, other than as a place where a small-scale slave economy is to be found, as contrasted with the extensive slave economies of ancient Greece and Rome. Mention is made of the Glasgow–Virginia tobacco trade connection (*LJ*(B) 198), however, and this clue is to be followed in tracing Smith's awareness of American issues and how they turned on economic

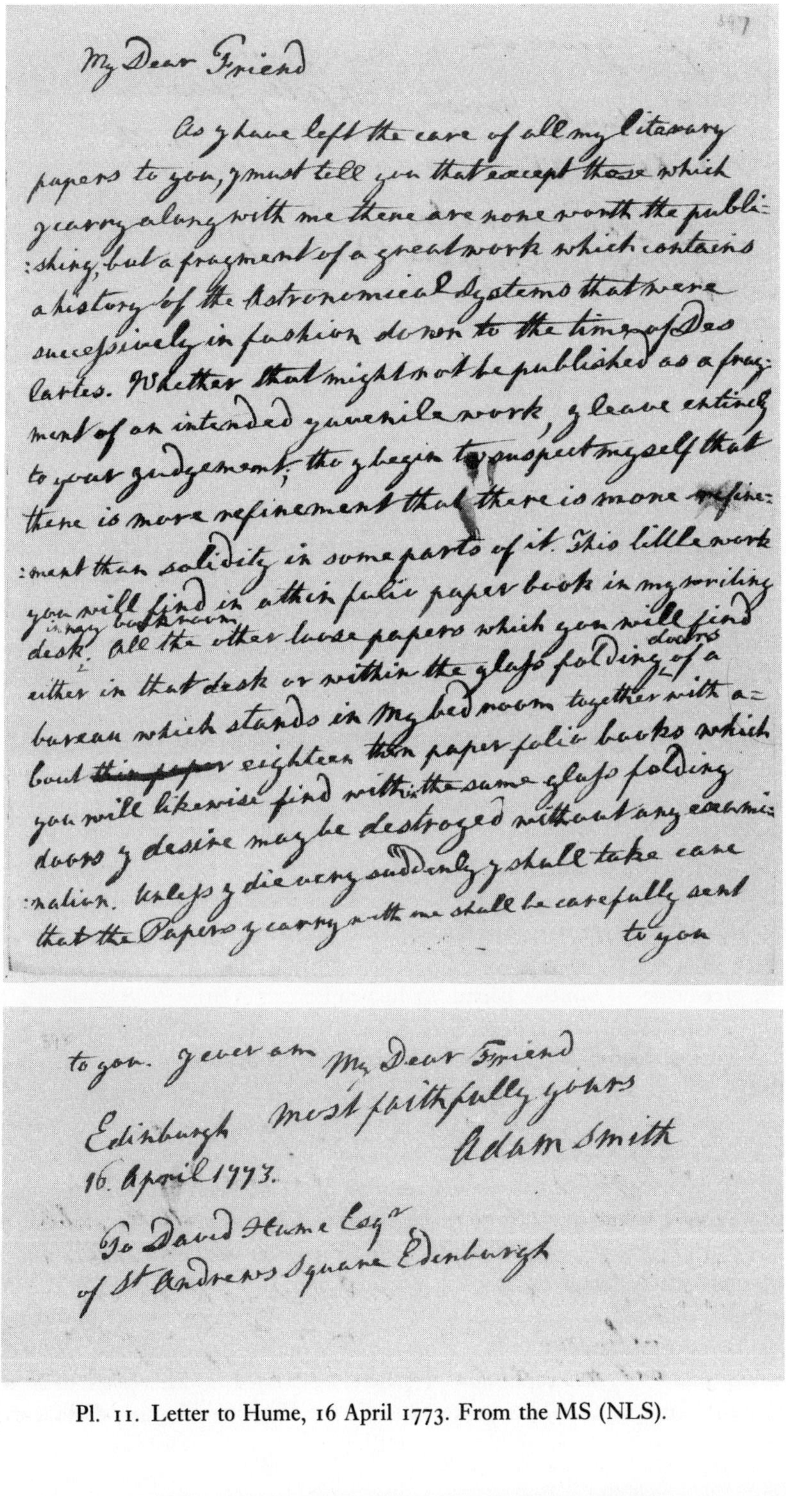

My Dear Friend

As I have left the care of all my literary papers to you, I must tell you that except those which I carry along with me there are none worth the publi:shing, but a fragment of a great work which contains a history of the Astronomical Systems that were successively in fashion down to the time of Des Cartes. Whether that might not be published as a frag:ment of an intended juvenile work, I leave entirely to your judgement; tho I begin to suspect myself that there is more refinement ~~that there is more refine~~:ment than solidity in some parts of it. This little work you will find in a thin folio paper book in my writing desk in my back room. All the other loose papers which you will find either in that desk or within the glass folding doors of a bureau which stands in my bed room together with a=bout ~~thin paper~~ eighteen thin paper folio books which you will likewise find within the same glass folding doors I desire may be destroyed without any exami:nation. Unless I die very suddenly I shall take care that the Papers I carry with me shall be carefully sent to you

to you. I ever am My Dear Friend
most faithfully yours
Adam Smith
Edinburgh
16. April 1773.

To David Hume Esqr
of St Andrews Square Edinburgh

Pl. 11. Letter to Hume, 16 April 1773. From the MS (NLS).

activity conducted within the imperial framework of laws and regulations imposed by the mother country.

During his professorial years Smith formed links with Glasgow merchants, such as John Glassford, George Kippen, and Andrew Cochrane, who were involved in the rapidly expanding and well-organized tobacco trade. Their information about America, we must suppose, taken together with his reading of classical and modern colonial history, also his brief association in 1766–7 with Charles Townshend at a crucial time of the formulation of imperial revenue policy, permitted Smith to theorize about the effects of the operation of a mercantile system finding expression in the form of the Navigation Acts controlling American trade. As he theorized on the basis of his researches, and developed some insights into the deepening American crisis, he was drawn into offering policy advice concerning American affairs. America thus became the major case study for the unfolding of Smith's theory of the free market, and the most urgent point for the application of the theory, to end the cycle of violence caused by attempts to maintain the old colonial system.

At the conclusion of *TMS*, he had promised 'in another discourse . . . to give an account of the general principles of law and government, and of the different revolutions they have undergone in the different ages and periods of society' (VII.iv.37). He did not live to deal with the 'revolutions . . . in what concerns justice', which was part of his promise, but *WN* was the 'discourse' that dealt with 'what concerns police [opulence of a state—*LJ*(B) 6], revenue, and arms' (Advertisement to *TMS* edn. 6). From 1773 to 1775, as *WN* went through the last stages of its creation, Smith's promise of 1759 must have been much on his mind.

As for outward events that took up his attention after his arrival in London, mention should be made of his admittance as a Fellow of the Royal Society on 27 May, in their premises in Crane Court, adjoining Fleet Street, the meeting-place since 1710. In 1780 the Royal Society moved to Somerset House during the presidency of Smith's friend Sir Jospeh Banks (O'Brian, 1988: 198–9). There were something like 160 foreign members, of whom Smith met Quesnay, d'Alembert, and Voltaire when he was on the Continent in 1766, and possibly Buffon, who was a correspondent of Hume's. He would certainly have been interested in any communications from them and others such as Euler and Linnaeus. There were about 360 ordinary members, a number of them antiquaries whose projects did not attract him, or so we must suppose from his declaration of total ignorance about the subject of vitrified forts in Scotland (*Corr.* No. 254). He would have affinities with representatives of the literary and artistic community, such as Horace Walpole and Joshua Reynolds. True to his waspish disposition and disdain for Scots men of letters, however, Walpole in his 'Book of Materials' (1787) castigated *WN* for its 'bad style, bad method, bad arrangement . . . and repetition'. Further, he classed Smith's book with Walter Harte's *Gustavus Adolphus* (1759) and Pierre François Hugues d'Hancarville's

'Progress of the Arts' (*Recherches sur l'origine . . . des arts de la Grèce*) (1785) as the 'three worst books, considering the quantity of valuable matter they contain' (Hazen, 1969: iii.45).

With the members of real scientific bent Smith would have much in common, and it was doubtless for the record of their work he collected the Transactions of the Royal Society so assiduously. In this regard, we might instance Nevil Maskelyne, the Astronomer Royal, the best lunarian of his time; Henry Cavendish, who made advances in the study of electricity and physics; Joseph Priestley, chemist as well as philosopher; the medical scientists known to Smith—Sir John Pringle (President), expert on military health, and John and William Hunter, whose special field, anatomy, interested Smith so much that he attended William's lectures during this period in London (Taylor, 1832: i.262); the naturalists—Sir Joseph Banks, botanist and explorer, who was polite and attentive to Smith in London (*Corr.* No. 275), Daines Barrington, whose legal scholarship was also known to Smith (*Corr.* No. 115), and Thomas Pennant, whose zoological studies were important, as well as his traveller's account of Scotland (1771), which focused attention on the Highlands and Islands as a distinctive region; the 2nd Earl Stanhope, an outstanding mathematician, and his son, Lord Mahon, deep student of electricity and calculating machines, with whom Smith had become acquainted in Geneva; and another, more famous experimenter with electricity, Benjamin Franklin. Smith would find intellectual stimulation in the company of these men, and perhaps guidance from their inquiries into the operation of natural law as he sought to perfect his own findings about patterns of social and economic functions and adaptation to change.

Another intellectual society in London to which Smith belonged was The Club, founded by Reynolds in 1764 for Dr Johnson's benefit (*BLJ* i.477). Smith was elected some time before 1 December 1775, when he attended a meeting for the first time. As mentioned earlier, Smith and Johnson were to some degree antipathetic, and this is reflected in gossip that has survived. Boswell on 17 March 1776 repeated to Bennet Langton that Johnson had told him Adam Smith was a 'most disagreeable fellow after he had drank some wine, which, he said, "bubbled in his mouth" '. In turn, Langton groaned over The Club's 'being overwhelmed with unsuitable members', and said he 'could perceive [Topham Beauclerk] had lost his relish for Adam Smith's conversation'. Goldsmith thought Smith's conversation 'flabby', and Johnson did not relish it, declaring on 13 April 1776 that Smith 'was as dull a dog as he had ever met with'. On hearing this last remark, Boswell said it was 'strange to me to find my old Professor in London, a professed Infidel with a bag wig'. Boswell did defend Smith from some attacks, to be sure, but his religious views were a subject of animosity, compounded by the strictures on Oxford University in *WN*, and then the published letter of 9 November 1776 about Hume's composure in facing death. On 14 September 1779 Boswell confided in his Journal: 'Since [Smith's] absurd eulogium on Hume, and his ignorant, ungrateful attack on the English University education, I have no desire to be much with him. Yet I do not forget that he was very civil to me at Glasgow' (Middendorf, 1961; Boswell, *Corr.*, ed. Fifer (1976), pp. xc–xcii).

However, Burke was one original member of The Club who remained for years on good terms with Smith. The latter thought well enough of Burke's treatise on the *Sublime and Beautiful* (1759) to form the opinion that the 'author of that book would be a great acquisition to [Glasgow University] if he would accept of a chair'. This information is reported to have come from Dugald Stewart (Prior, 1853: 47). Also, a recently admitted member, Edward Gibbon, elected 1774, proved warm in his friendship with Smith and highly receptive to his historical analysis, which he linked with that of Hume and Robertson:

On this interesting subject, the progress of society in Europe, a strong ray of philosophic light has broke from Scotland in our own times; and it is with private, as well as public regard, that I repeat the names of Hume, Robertson, and Adam Smith. (Gibbon, n.d.: ch. 61, n. 72)

Another member of The Club, elected in 1774, with whom Smith shared a common viewpoint was the politician Charles James Fox. At first a member of North's Administration as a Lord of Admiralty in 1770, he moved over between 1772 and 1774 to the Whigs opposed to coercion in America, joining in this stand Burke, his proposer for election to The Club. One fellow MP, Gibbon, was a bystander at debates in the House of Commons, and generally voted with the Administration, but others in The Club—Burke, Fox, and Lord Ossory—were all prominent in the debates on American issues which, during 1775–6, lasted until 3 and 4 o'clock in the morning (*London Chronicle*, 26–8 Oct., 16–18 Nov. 1775, xxxviii.415, 488), and 17–20, 20–22 Feb. 1776, xxxix.176, 184; Boswell, *Corr.* 66 n. 2). Smith must have followed these debates in the newspapers and had some personal exchanges with these participants, adding to the store of facts buttressing *WN*.

In a private capacity at this period in London, Smith engaged in the congenial activity of helping one of his former students. This was David Callander, whose anecdotes about Smith recorded by George Chalmers have been cited previously. He was the youngest son of Alexander Callander of Westertown, an estate near Stirling. Born in 1742, entering Glasgow University in 1756, and matriculating in Smith's ethics class the next year, then proceeding to Balliol College on a Snell Exhibition in 1760, which he vacated in 1771, this young man, according to his uncle Michael Ramsay of Mungale, both at Glasgow and Oxford 'not only had the approbation but the friendship of his Masters: indeed of them all particularly Dr Smith who was not only his kind and attentive Master when he was at Glasgow, but his warm and affectionate friend ever since'. David Callander's problem was the usual one of a talented younger son making a career for himself. His uncle's great friend Hume tried unsuccessfully to get him a position as tutor to the heir of the Duke of Dorset in 1760, and in 1768 Smith gave him advice about spending two years or so in France, possibly to learn the language and acquire a further qualification for becoming a tutor (Raphael and Sakamoto, 1990: 276).

We pick up his story on 7 July 1773, when his eldest brother John, later an army colonel who entered Parliament and was made a baronet, wrote to David that Smith had said he had received an 'offer of going abroad with Lord Clives Son', but he had refused this, again because this was the Duke of Buccleuch's wish. Smith had mentioned David Callander as an alternative, but Clive fixed on a Mr Frazer. Smith further told John Callander that ever since he came to London, he had had David 'constantly in his Eye' for a position, 'tho he says things of that kind [tutorships to aristocrats?] are very difficult to be had, especially good ones'. Smith had declared that he would use 'all his interest' for David Callander, and John promised to call on him the following night and to ask for his opinion and assistance about getting his brother into the service of the East India Company. He wished that Michael Ramsay would apply to his 'India Friends' for this purpose, in particular the Scottish MP George Dempster of Dunnichen, another friend of Smith's. On 16 September, John pushed the India scheme again and upbraided David for not writing to Smith.

In further undated letters, Smith is described as urging David to come to London to take advantage of opportunities there, as changing his lodgings to the house of Mr Mills, Wine Merchant, Dartmouth Street, Westminster, and as advising John that Louis Dutens, who had invited David to go to France, was back in London. This gentleman was a Huguenot scholar and clergyman who had been British *chargé d'affaires* in Turin but remained most of his life in England, benefiting from the patronage of Lord Bute. In yet another undated letter, John reported that Smith had said that he could recommend David to his cousin, Colonel Patrick Ross, Chief Engineer at Madras, whom the Callander brothers had met when staying with their uncle, Michael Ramsay. In this letter we read of Smith being confined to bed with a cold, but determined to be up in a few days and renew his efforts to get David Callander an appointment (Burn-Callander Papers, Preston Hall, Lothian, available in SRO). In the end, David had a career as a minor man of letters in the UK, and was awarded an LL D before his death in 1798. His second brother, Alexander, did go to India, where he made a fortune sufficient to purchase in 1789, three years after he returned to Scotland, the estate of Preston Hall near Dalkeith. Alexander put in hand there the building of a splendid new house designed by Robert Mitchell, and incorporating some of the principles of Robert Adam (McWilliam, 1978: 395–8).

Smith's good offices were further called upon and, it is to be feared, his patience and benevolence much stretched, in another instance of a travelling tutorship on offer in 1773. At some point after he got to London that year, Earl Stanhope applied to him to find a tutor for his near relative and ward, the 5th Earl of Chesterfield. Smith suggested Adam Ferguson, reported by Hume to be 'somewhat disgusted' in October 1772 by his Professorship of Moral Philosophy at Edinburgh. About that time his employers, the Town Council of Edinburgh, or their leader, wanted to be rid of him. On 18 February 1772 John Home the poet reported to Col. James Edmonstoune that Provost Dalrymple wished to replace Ferguson by a 'Mr Beattie, the Author of the most illiberal book written to abuse our friend David, and calculated if the times were violent to bring him to the stake' (NLS 1005, fos. 15–16). Also in 1772 Ferguson's name, like Smith's, had been suggested for membership of a committee of inquiry into the nearly bankrupt East India Company (*Corr.* Nos. 132, 133).

Ferguson wrote to Smith on 2 September 1773 with news of Hume's loss of weight, the first sign of what proved to be his terminal illness, and he indicated that he was prepared to negotiate with Lord Stanhope, bringing in Smith as the go-between (*Corr.* No. 138). Stanhope was anxious by 18 October 1773 to secure Ferguson's services for his ward, in view of the recommendations he had received from Smith and perhaps others:

I cannot help thinking that Dr Ferguson . . . would be an exceedingly fit Man, as not only his Writings discover in him a liberal and manly spirit, but I have heard such uncommon encomiums of his moral character, especially of his modesty, his sweetness of temper, & his engaging and endearing behaviour, that I should entertain the strongest hopes of his making himself both loved and respected by his Pupil. (quoted in Raphael, 1994)

There was a difficulty over suitable terms, however, since Ferguson did not think the initial offer of £400 p.a. as a tutor, followed by an annuity of £200 for life, sufficient. This certainly sounds less handsome than Smith's £500 p.a. as a tutor, but this included £200 travelling expenses. Dr John Moore also received £300 for acting as the Duke of Hamilton's tutor, and a pension of £100 after that, but Professor Ruat received £500 as his pension from Lord Hopetoun (Rae, 1965: 165–6). Ferguson held out for more to provide for his family in the event that he lost his Chair through going abroad with Lord Chesterfield (*Corr.* No. 139).

From the other side, Smith passed on the news that Chesterfield's guardians, who included the MPs Sir George Savile and John Hewett as well as Stanhope, did not have the legal control to attach the young man's estates to fund an annuity. Stanhope was willing to guarantee the annuity himself, so Smith also reported, though for this purpose he would encumber land he had inherited from the 4th Earl of Chesterfield, the famous letter-writer.

In these circumstances Ferguson accepted the initial terms, with the stipulation that the annuity was to commence when his pupil reached his majority or the tutorship ceased. Hume apparently felt excluded from Smith's activities at this time, and wrote to him on 13 February 1774: 'You are in the wrong for never informing me of your Intentions and Resolutions, if you have fix'd any.' He thought the proposed settlement for Ferguson, 'very narrow Compensation for his Class, if he must lose it'. Also, in his opinion Ferguson's scheme to retain his Chair and hire a deputy to teach for him, though common practice at the time, 'will appear invidious and is really scarce admissible'. Hume came up with another proposal, that Smith should teach in Ferguson's place, 'either as his Substitute or his Successor', and then resign when Ferguson returned. John Millar had hinted already in 1772 that Smith was to become Professor of Logic and Metaphysics at Edinburgh on John Stevenson's retirement (EUL, Corr. of Allan Maconochie, Lord Meadowbanks, A–C, Patrick Clason's letter, 29 Mar. 1772). Hume thought Smith could afford to be generous to Ferguson, because of his agreeableness about the income from the Chair of Natural Philosophy. While Ferguson occupied it from 1759 to 1764, he allowed the previous occupant part of the stipend as a pension.

Hume closed his letter by referring to a recent incident that had heated up the conflict between the British Government and the American colonists. In London for some years as agent for the Massachusetts House of Representatives, Franklin became convinced that exposing Thomas Hutchinson, Governor of that colony, as a determined enemy to its liberties would destroy him, and clear the air for creating better relationships with Britain (Becker, 1964: 12–13). To back up charges against the Governor, he secured some of Hutchinson's letters urging drastic measures against the Americans, but contrary to Franklin's wishes these were printed in Boston and circulated in London. On 29 January 1774 Franklin was examined before the Privy Council in the Cockpit, a government building opposite Whitehall, about his admission that he had procured the letters. Smith's friend and former 'disciple' in rhetoric studies, Alexander Wedderburn, conducted the examination as Solicitor General, and did so in a highly offensive manner.

Hume asked Smith for more news:

Pray, what strange Accounts were these we hear of Franklyn's Conduct? I am very slow in believing that he has been guilty in the extreme Degree that is pretended; tho' I always knew him to be a very factious man, and Faction, next to Fanaticism, is, of all passions, the most destructive of Morality. How is it suppos'd that he got Possession of these Letters? I hear that Wedderburn's Treatment of him before the Council, was most cruel, without being in the least blameable. What a Pity! (*Corr.* No. 140)

A contemporary squib was far more critical of Wedderburn:

> Sarcastic Sawney, swol'n with spite and prate
> On silent Franklin poured his venal hate.
> The calm philosopher, without reply,
> Withdrew and gave his country liberty.
> (Fay, 1956: 125)

On the evidence of *TMS* edn. 6 (III.3.43), Smith would have agreed with Hume's point about the destructive power of 'faction and fanaticism', but not necessarily the application of this sentiment to Franklin. There is circumstantial evidence that he was often in Franklin's company at this time, and even that he showed chapters of *WN* to him (see Viner, 1965: 44–7). This is not impossible. Hugh Blair recalled in 1776 that Smith had read parts of *WN* to him 'some years ago' (*Corr*. No. 151). Certainly, Smith and Franklin had views in common. The theory of free trade is to be found in an unsystematic way in the economic writings of Franklin, and Smith shared the American's vision of an incorporating political union to end the disputes between their respective countries. Franklin left London in March 1775 to begin his career as one of the founding fathers of revolutionary America. This included taking a hand in drafting the Declaration of Independence of 4 July 1776, four months after Smith had struck his blow for economic independence with the publication of *WN*.

Meantime nothing came of Hume's idea that Smith should teach moral philosophy at Edinburgh. Ferguson went abroad in 1774 to be with his pupil; the Town Council dismissed him from his Professorship, but had to reinstate him after legal action in 1775. Ferguson wrote to Smith from Geneva on 1 June 1774 to say that, in Paris while with Lord Stanhope, he had access to 'some very respectable and agreeable company, in which I was questioned concerning you, particularly by the Duchess D'Enville who complained of your French, as she did of mine'. Ferguson also reported that he was pleasantly surprised by young Chesterfield, whom he had expected to be difficult to handle: 'I have found not only vivacity and parts . . . but likewise good dispositions and attachments' (*Corr*. No. 142).

When Ferguson was back in London in June 1775, however, matters had deteriorated; also relationships between Chesterfield and his original guardians were strained, and they had resigned on 1 June. They were replaced by the Duke of Chandos and Lovell Stanhope, another MP, as well as being Chesterfield's uncle. They informed Ferguson that his position terminated on 24 June, and it was arranged that the young man was to return to the Continent with another tutor. Smith was told by Stanhope of the resignation of the original guardians, and he was dragged into Ferguson's attempts to get his annuity, either from Chesterfield or, if he would not accept liability, from Stanhope. Smith expressed his feelings about this situation in a letter to Stanhope dated 24 June 1775: 'I cannot express to your Lordship how much uneasiness it has given me that I ever had any concern in this very awkward affair' (*Corr*. app. E, c). Ferguson had already written to Smith's friend William Pulteney (formerly Johnstone) on 3 June, asking him to deal with the new guardians about the matter of the pension. He excluded Smith as a go-between at this point: 'Smith would occur to some of [the guardians] perhaps as the proper person to treat on this occasion but one Philosopher is enough in any one business' (New York: Pierpont Morgan Lib., Pulteney Corr. v.6).

In the event Chesterfield did not accept liability for Stanhope's arrangement about the annuity, professing to believe that two conditions had not been met: Ferguson had not stayed with him until his majority; and Ferguson had not lost his Chair. Smith left things at this impasse when he returned to Kirkcaldy to live with his mother, also to be close to the dying Hume in the period May to December 1776, and there was still no change when he came back to London in January 1777. Smith was much struck by the integrity displayed by Stanhope in promising to keep his side of the bargain about the annuity, and on 8 May 1777 asked for Stanhope's permission to keep the original copy of a letter expressing this commitment:

not only to shew it to some of my young friends in the mean time, but to leave it a legacy to my family and Posterity, if it should ever please God to grant me any, as an example of inflexible probity which they ought to follow on all occasions. (*Corr.* app. E, 1)

It is surely remarkable that Smith, still a bachelor in his 54th year, had not given up all hope of 'Posterity' in the form of children. If permission was given for Smith to keep the letter in question, its display to 'young friends' may have been unfortunate, since it seems to have gone astray.

The record is that Smith did everything in his power to relieve Stanhope of his liability. He asked Wedderburn to provide a legal opinion about the terms Ferguson had accepted from Stanhope about the annuity, and received this in a letter of 29 April 1777 to the effect that in common law and equity guardians can render their wards' estates liable for necessaries such as tuition. Apprised that Chesterfield might be prepared of his own free will to settle the annuity on Ferguson, he called on him on 1 May; but he was denied attendance on the score that the Earl was dressing, and the card he left went unacknowledged. Sir George Savile had the same experience with Chesterfield, so Smith advised that Wedderburn's legal opinion should be communicated to his Lordship, and that this be reinforced with a second opinion to be obtained from John Dunning, one of the best lawyers of the time. Dunning agreed with Wedderburn, and wrote that the best method to resolve the issue was to take Chesterfield to court.

Smith left for Scotland about mid-June; Stanhope's forceful son, Lord Mahon, took it upon himself to state the legal situation in blunt terms to Chesterfield and foretold he would lose to Ferguson in a Chancery suit. Chesterfield remained intractable, perhaps because at this time another former tutor, the Revd William Dodd, had been convicted of forging a bond for the huge sum of £4,200, and lay under sentence of death, carried out on 27 June. His Lordship refused to join the clamour for a reprieve, and gained some notoriety as the 'man who hung a parson'. More infamy might have attended him when Ferguson commenced a Chancery suit on 20 September directed against him and Stanhope, who assured Ferguson, however, that he regarded the legal action as 'entirely amicable'.

In pressing his legal threat, Ferguson did not display the 'sweetness of temper' of Smith's encomium, but more likely the personality that a later neighbour perceived was as 'fiery as gunpowder' (Cockburn, 1856: 57 n.; cf. Carlyle, 1973: 143–4). To be sure, Ferguson took the right tack with Chesterfield. When visiting York in October 1777, the latter made a dash to Edinburgh and capitulated to his former tutor. Ferguson finally got a first payment of the annuity in January 1778, a plum which must have cheered him until Chesterfield's death in 1815, realizing for two years' service the sum of £9,000. Smith, for his part, drew just over £8,000 for the three years he spent with Buccleuch.

Smith's marked sense of propriety and justice clearly motivated his actions in this affair. He felt responsibility for the bargain that was made between Stanhope and Ferguson since he was the go-between, explaining in turn each side to the other. It is clear that he could not accept Stanhope having to assume the unjust burden of the liability for the annuity (Raphael *et al.*, 1990; Raphael, 1994).

The political ramifications of the affair are also of significance. On returning to London in 1775, young Chesterfield aligned himself with members of the Court party, Chandos and Lovell Stanhope, and in time he became a favourite of George III. He thus distanced himself from Stanhope, Hewett, and Savile. Smith seems to have seen much of Savile, a descendant of Halifax, the great 'Trimmer', that consistent proponent of moderation in the political storms of the later seventeenth century (Kenyon, 1969: introd.). Savile was associated with Lord Rockingham in leadership of the Opposition Whigs but was always independent-minded in his approach to the business of Parliament, though coming out strongly from 1774 onwards against North's punitive policy towards the Americans, like Burke and Fox (*HP* iii.405–9). Savile's political discourse (e.g. 1762) was that of classical republicanism (Viroli, 1990), which had great appeal for Smith, and he represented the kind of virtuous legislator to whom Smith was addressing himself in *WN*. Smith's own political alignment remained with the Rockingham Whigs and their successors.

Ever a dilatory correspondent, Smith somehow kept in touch with his friends in Scotland and attended to their requests for help during these years in London working on *WN*. From August 1773 there survives a letter to his friend and physician, William Cullen, describing efforts to find a place aboard an East Indiaman for one of his correspondent's younger sons, with the assistance of various well-connected London Scots: Wedderburn, Pulteney, Dempster, and so on. Perhaps to cover a slow response, Smith ends his letter: 'I do not like to think that my friend should suspect, even for quarter of an hour that I neglect his business' (GUL Cullen MS 242).

Cullen involved Smith in more of his business the following year, though this time connected with his own profession. When the Duke of Buccleuch was elected an honorary Fellow of the Royal College of Physicians of Edinburgh in 1774, he offered to have the issue of examination for medical degrees brought up in Parliament. The College drafted a memorial urging that honorary medical degrees should not be awarded, and that regular ones should be granted by the Scottish universities only after personal examination of candidates and presentation of certificates guaranteeing that medical studies had been pursued for at least two years. If the Government would not intervene directly, a Royal Commission of Inquiry was advocated. This memorial was sent to Smith in London for his consideration. He replied to Cullen about this matter on 20 September 1774, apparently after some delay, stating that 'occurrences' in London which interested him greatly had made him forget a 'business which I do acknowledge interested me very little' (*Corr.* No. 143).

Nevertheless, Smith's letter reflects central concerns of *WN*: the bad effects of monopolies and the likely good effects of competition, here applied to medical education and the practice of medicine as a profession. Smith begins with a tribute to the Scottish universities, recognizing no doubt the quality of the education that he had received at Glasgow, his favourable experience (on the whole) teaching there, and the contribution of these institutions to the Enlightenment: 'In [their] present state . . . I do most sincerely look upon them as, in spite of all their faults, without exception the best seminaries of learning that are to be found any where in Europe.' He conceded, however, that, like all such 'public institutions', they contained 'in their very nature the seeds and causes of negligency and corruption', and that, despite their present state, they were capable of amendment, also that a 'Visitation' was the proper means for securing this. But who would be the Visitors, and on what plan would they act? Smith believed such uncertainties existed in this case that what was 'already . . . very *well*' should be left alone.

He then passed to the contents of the memorial, taking up, first, the requirement that candidates for medical degrees should earn certificates of undertaking university studies. But what about those who studied with private teachers, such as John and William Hunter, and what about the fact that at some universities medicine was not taught at all or taught superficially? In Smith's opinion, when something had been learned, it did not matter from whom the instruction had come. He then reveals that he is drawing on research into universities as publicly funded institutions he conducted for book v of *WN*, also that he had arrived at the conclusions he presented there (v.i.f). Thus, he writes to Cullen that he had 'thought a great deal upon this subject [university education], and [has] inquired very carefully into the constitution and history of several of the principal Universities of Europe'. In addition to his current research work, he is harking back to his memories of Oxford. As a result of his researches, he has satisfied himself that there are two chief reasons for the 'present state of degradation and contempt into which the greater part of those societies have fallen'. These are, first, the payment of large salaries by some universities to professors, without a requirement to be successful in their professions; and second, the enrolment of large numbers of students in certain universities for the sake of career qualifications or bursaries, whether the instruction was any good or not (cf. *WN* I.x.c.34 and v.i.f.1–35).

Smith considers that the Scottish universities enjoy 'present excellence' because these two cases do not apply in any large measure. He notes that medical professors at Edinburgh do not have large salaries and medical students have few if any bursaries, also that the University's 'monopoly of degrees is broken in upon by all other Universities, foreign and domestic'. It is his belief that this explains Edinburgh's superiority over similar societies in Europe.

Smith extends his principles of the beneficial effects of competition and the unfettered market, as well as the harmful effects of monopoly, when he turns to deal with the question of degrees. He is not impressed with high-minded claims for control of standards through examination for degrees. In this part of the letter he opens a vein of realism and scepticism that runs through *WN* and makes that work a joy to appreciative readers. To Cullen he is at pains to make clear the real meaning of the title 'Doctor':

[it] gives some credit and authority to the man upon whom it is bestowed; it extends his practice, and consequently his field for doing mischief; it is not improbable too that it may increase his presumption, and consequently his disposition to do mischief.

He is not prepared to defend the practice of awarding degrees to people the examiners scarcely know, but he does not think the practice does very much harm, since reputation and competition in the medical market-place are the factors that determine the choices of patients and thus the level of fees.

Smith thinks that behind the attempt to regulate degrees is the desire to raise fees and, of course, to protect entry to the market for those who have degrees. In fact, he sees an analogy between the status of apprenticeship and the conferment of degrees only on students of a certain academic standing: 'Bad work and high price have been the effects of the monopoly introduced by the former. Quackery, imposture, and exorbitant fees, have been the consequences of that established by the latter.'

A typical Smithian argument is then employed to deal with the case of the 'dirty practice' of selling degrees. Smith does not defend this either, but he points out that poor universities engage in it, endeavouring 'to turn the penny in the only way in which they could turn it'. If they do this carelessly, they bring 'ridicule and discredit upon themselves'. St Andrews University put itself in this position by conferring an MD on 'one Green, who happened to be a stage-doctor', that is, a quack who practiced medicine on a platform.[1]

The public is not hurt by this, so Smith reasons, for Green probably poisoned no more patients than he would have done without his degree. Moreover, the monopoly of the rich universities in awarding medical degrees is breached. In consequence, their graduates have to depend on their merit and skill for their fees and not their qualifications. Smith then pushes this point home vigorously to Cullen and his brethren: 'Not being able to derive much consequence from the character of Doctor, you are obliged, perhaps, to attend more to your characters as men, as gentlemen, and as men of letters.'

This is one of Smith's best letters, pithy, strongly argued, and drawing in humorous way on the tradition of satire on the medical profession as one embracing quacks, poisoners, and pulse-feelers more interested in fees than physique. Smith knew he was being outrageous in pushing his principles as far as he did here, and ended his letter by prophesying that he would get his ears boxed for what he had written (*Corr.* No. 143). He certainly seems to have extinguished the memorial, for nothing more is heard of it.

Cullen did offer counter-arguments to Smith's position on a free market for medical practitioners in a graduation address of 1776, and this was printed together with Smith's letter in John Thomson's *Life of Cullen* (1832: i.468–70). A Royal Commission did receive, in 1826, *Observations on the Preparatory Education of Candidates for the Degree of Doctor of Medicine*, as part of a wider inquiry into the functioning of the Scottish universities. The reforms proposed by Cullen and his backers had their place in the ensuing changes, but Thomson's publication of Smith's views together with those of Cullen helped to determine the nineteenth-century debate over the laws and economic arrangements deemed appropriate for medical qualification and practice. Modern historians of medicine have appreciated this, recognizing that Smith had valuable insights into the mentality of the doctors of his time, as well as a firm command of salient facts of the organization and economic activity of their profession (Guttmacher, 1930; Cowen, 1969).

We find this letter lively and amusing, representing the exercise of Smith's considerable power of argument on a subject of concern to him. What, then, could the 'occurrences' be in London that preoccupied Smith so much that he neglected his promise to give consideration to the memorial on medical education? In all likelihood, Smith was taken up with the business before Parliament in 1774 that pointed to bloody conflict in America. On 16 December 1773 there occurred the celebrated Boston Tea Party, when local men dressed as Red Indians dumped into the harbour the first batch of tea to be sold under a monopoly granted to the East India Company. Parliament had granted the monopoly to help save the East India Company from bankruptcy and, through making the tea low-priced but dutiable, to sweeten acceptance by Americans of Parliament's right to tax the colonies. The American 'patriots' denied this right as a matter of principle, and argued that it was to the interest of merchants to act to break a monopoly.

On 7 March 1774 George III asked Parliament to grant him power to take such necessary measures 'as would stop the violent and outrageous Proceedings at the Town and Port of Boston'. By June, four coercive bills had been passed: Marblehead, not Boston, was to be the site of the Custom-house; the Governor was to have crown appointees on his Council, and no town meetings could be held without his permission; capital offenders who had been engaged on official duties were to be tried in courts outside the province, at the Governor's discretion; and soldiers were to be quartered on the townspeople in the event of civil unrest.

Meantime a general, Thomas Gage, was appointed to replace Hutchinson as

Governor of Massachusetts Bay, and he arranged for a blockade of Boston in May. The Virginia House of Burgesses in Williamsburg, galvanized by Patrick Henry, called for a Continental Congress of delegates from the thirteen colonies to be assembled to demand an end to American grievances. It met in Philadelphia from 5 September to 26 October, and to support the Massachusetts Bay Colony it arrived at a formal agreement not to import or use British goods until the 'Intolerable Acts' were repealed. This Congress also rejected military preparations, and petitioned the King to restore the colonial arrangements in force at the end of the Seven Years War in 1763.

Burke wrote at this time the 'Popular current both within doors [of Parliament] and without, at present sets strangely against America' (Wallis *et al.*, 1975: 13–25). Indoors in Parliament, indeed, the Opposition was surprisingly inactive at first after the passage of the punitive measures directed at the colonies. The Boston port bill went unopposed, and neither Burke, nor Savile, nor Fox (who may have been attending the Newmarket races) voted on 6 May 1774 against the bill regulating justice in Massachusetts Bay. However, Burke made a notable pro-American speech on 19 April during the debate about repealing the tea duty, and Fox added his support, declaring: 'I think we should be content to tax [the Americans] virtually by regulating their trade.' He added, very sensibly, 'if soldiers are to collect the taxes in America, I doubt this country will be little benefited', and then he enunciated the principle controlling his responses to the several stages of the American crisis: 'Countries should always be guided by the will of the governed.'

Catching the Opposition in disarray, North had Parliament dissolved on 22 June, and in the ensuing general election it seems that the coercive acts did not receive a great deal of attention in the country, there being more resentment at the Quebec bill passed in May, which had granted toleration to Roman Catholics as well as fixing the boundaries of Canada (to the dudgeon of Americans). Still, there were more contested constituencies than at any time up to 1790, and considerable feeling was aroused over these. John Wilkes, now arrived at the dignity of being Lord Mayor of London, as well as being the darling of the Middlesex electors, espoused the cause of liberty in America as well as at home (Pl. 12). When he headed the poll yet again, the Ministry was too afraid to deny him the seat he took in the House of Commons on 2 December.[2]

Such 'occurrences' are likely to have riveted Smith's attention, for he would have the intelligence to see that North's American policy was putting the fate of the country and its empire in the balance. At the heart of the matter was the attempt to maintain a monopoly trade with the colonies through exercise of government power, an issue which was grist to his mill. We know that he attended the House of Commons during this period, for mention is made of this in the correspondence of William Adam, younger brother of the architects John, Robert, and James. Smith frequented the Adam family home in the Canongate with many of the Edinburgh literati; he knew this William Adam as a schoolboy,

Westminster Mag. Dec. 1774

Pl. 12. Cartoon of North bribing supporters and Wilkes pointing the accusing finger as America bursts into flames, 1774. From *Westminster Magazine*, 2 (BL).

and then would hear of him pursuing an erratic career as a merchant in the City of London (Fleming, 1962: 3).

In a letter of 23 January 1775 to his brother John, William Adam wrote thus:

Mr Adam Smith has been so obliging as to come from the house to inform me [of a speech by his nephew, yet another William Adam] . . . The Speaker introduced him to Lord North who paid him a very handsome compliment . . . but what pleases Willie most was his asking where he had left his Scotch language. (SRO, NRA(S) 1454, Section 4/ Bundle 3)

In vivid if unkind detail, Horace Walpole described Prime Minister North's unpromising exterior:

Nothing could be more coarse or clumsy or ungracious than his outside. Two large prominent eyes that rolled about to no purpose (for he was utterly short-sighted), a wide mouth, thick lips, and inflated visage, gave him the air of a blind trumpeter. A deep, untunable voice, which . . . he enforced with unnecessary pomp, a total neglect of his person, and ignorance of every civil attention, disgusted all who judge by appearance. (Walpole, 1963: 225)

But other contemporaries stressed his wit and good humour, also his serenity and courtesy (*HP* iii.204–5). His winning manner with a young Scottish MP was typical behaviour, which helped to secure support for him at first in the House of Commons. This was eroded, to be sure, after his war policy proved disastrous.

Smith must have heard from the gallery one of the forceful speeches which impressed the House in 'Willie' Adam's first session, and perhaps he was a witness to North exerting his considerable charm to secure the young man's allegiance. The business before the Commons in January 1775 can be gauged by a letter written by Gibbon on Tuesday the 31st. He wished to speak but could not pluck up the courage to do so, though he had been pumping Governor Hutchinson for information about America:

I am more and more convinced that we have both the right and the power on our side, and that though the effort may be accompanied with some melancholy circumstances we are now arrived at the decisive moment of preserving or losing forever our Trade and Empire. We expect next Thursday or Friday to be a very great day. Hitherto we have been chiefly employed in reading papers and rejecting petitions. Petitions were brought in from London, Bristol, Norwich etc etc, framed by party and designed to delay [Government action].

These petitions expressed merchants' concern about North's punitive policy causing the Americans to boycott British goods. On 8 February Gibbon reported on debates in which Fox and Wedderburn opposed each other over the declaration that Massachusetts Bay was in a state of rebellion, and authorizing the despatch of 10,000 troops under Generals Howe, Burgoyne, and Clinton. Gibbon feared these forces were insufficient to overawe the Americans, and expressed his doubts about Lord North as a leader (Gibbon, 1956: ii.58–9).

As an MP, 'Willie' Adam generally backed North, but was independent-minded enough to criticize him for 'indolence' (*HP* ii.8–9). Smith heard young Adam in action on another occasion later in 1775, as his proud uncle further reported to an unknown correspondent:

I am happy to inform you from every quarter the highest approbation of Willie's speech on Friday last[;] Adam Smith who was there supped with us last night. He says it was much superior to any of his Speeches last Session—That Lord Norths was the best Speech ever was made in that House and that Willies was the next best that was Spoke that day though many of the principal Speakers Spoke.

The older William added that Robert Adam had heard the same high opinion of this speech when he dined with Garrick and several MPs, also that it had such an effect on North that 'in finishing his vindication He actually cryed—as did many of his Audience' (SRO, NRA(S) 1454, Blair Adam papers, 4/3/20). There was nothing inhibited about eighteenth-century parliamentarians.

We can fix the date of this letter approximately, because there is a later reference in it to Lord Mountstuart being prepared to move for a Scottish militia 'in a few days'. He did so on 2 November 1775 (*HP* iii. 502).

Smith could not have shared 'Willie' Adam's negative attitude towards conciliation with the Americans, but they must have been closer on other issues because Adam became a member of Bentham's circle, and apparently in 1789 drew to Smith's attention that to be consistent he should not argue for tight control of interest rates, as Bentham pointed out in his *Defence of Usury* (BL, Bentham MSS, George Wilson's letter, 4 Dec. 1789).

Burke, who was so eloquent on the subject of conciliation with the Americans, wrote to Smith on 1 May 1775, but the subject was extending a patent for chinaware held by a friend in his constituency, the Bristol ceramist Richard Champion. Josiah Wedgwood was about to stir up the potters of Staffordshire against Champion's petition to Parliament, and Burke wished Smith to 'apply to Buccleugh that he may keep his mind open to the merits of this Cause', should it come before the House of Lords. Well knowing Smith's views, Burke mentions that Wedgwood 'pretends . . . that he is actuated . . . by nothing but a desire of the publick good'. Burke continues: 'I confess a declaration of the lowest species of any honest self Interest, would have much greater weight with me, from the mouth of a Tradesman' (*Corr*. No. 145). Smith expressed similar views in *WN* (iv.ii.9), and he also defended the 'temporary monopoly' of patents and copyright in books as forms of intellectual property (*LJ*(A) ii.31–3; *WN* v.i.e.30).

One of Smith's former students, Patrick Clason, now a travelling tutor in Geneva, forwarded from that city on 25 February 1775 two books by the scientist Charles Bonnet, to be presented to David Hume: *Recherches sur l'usage des feuilles dans les plantes* (1754) and *Palingénésie philosophique* (1769–70). The covering letter by Bonnet mentions Smith as the 'Sage of Glasgow' who is remembered in Geneva always with great pleasure (*Corr*. No. 144). Smith transmitted to Hume the letter from Bonnet on 9 May, describing this gentleman as 'one of the worthiest, and best hearted men in Geneva or indeed in the world', but adds, 'notwithstanding he is one of the most religious' (*Corr.* No. 145). In his letter, Bonnet claimed that he had never had a mania for conversion, but Smith may have feared the worst even for his sceptical friend in Edinburgh. Smith had a number of Bonnet's books in his library, including the one on the leaves of plants (Mizuta), but not the learned and original if somewhat eccentric work on palingenesis, which mingles religion and biology to build a theory of cosmic evolution. If they ever read it, both Hume and Smith would surely have found somewhat to their taste the picture of human nature swayed by self-love and the passions, but directed by a natural law of survival that develops through experience (Crocker, 1967: i.345–6).

In this letter of 9 May Smith has news about James Beattie, Professor of Moral Philosophy at Aberdeen, who had attempted to refute Hume's 'Sophistry and Scepticism' in his *Essay on the Nature and Immutability of Truth* (1773). This won Beattie admission to, and some cosseting by, the Johnson circle in 1773, also a pension from the King. The scurrilous personal attacks on Hume in the *Essay on Truth* for once got under his skin. In the Advertisement to the last edition of his *Essays and Treatises* (published 1777), which he corrected before his death, Hume reckoned that he gave a 'compleat Answer to Dr Reid and to that bigotted silly Fellow, Beattie' (*HL* ii.301).

Smith's Royal Society colleague Joseph Priestley sought to refute Beattie and the emerging Scottish Common Sense school of philosophy in a book entitled *An Examination of Reid's Inquiry, Beattie's Essay, and Oswald's Appeal to Common Sense* (1774). In London, as Smith reported to Hume, there was amusement at the tilting of the philosophers:

Your friends here have all been much diverted with Priestly's answer to Beatie. We were in great hopes that Beatie would have replyed, and we are assured he has a reply ready written; but your old friend Hurd [denouncer of Hume's *Natural History of Religion*], whom my Lord Mansfield has, with great judgement, made a Bishop, wrote to Beatie, I am assured, and advised him against answering; telling him that so excellent a work as the immutability of truth required no defence. We by this means have lost a most incomparable controversy. Priestly was perfectly prepared to carry it on thro' at least twenty rejoinders. I have some hopes still of getting somebody to provoke Beatie to draw his Pen again.

Then comes the announcement that Hume, ever concerned about the achievements of his friends, must have longed to read: 'I shall send my own Book to the Press in the end of this month or that of the beginning of the next' (*Corr.* No. 146). The Advertisement to the third edition of *WN* (1784) confirms this announcement, stating that the first edition 'was printed in the end of the year 1775, and in the beginning of the year 1776'.

When *WN* had still not appeared by November 1775, Dr Roebuck, as mentioned above, wrote to Smith about the opportunity to sway public opinion about the American contest when Parliament was in session. Roebuck sought to add to Smith's information about American affairs by enclosing an eyewitness account of the battle of Bunker Hill written on 23 June, six days after this first major armed encounter of the war. At the beginning of 1775 the British Government had determined to sever New England from the middle colonies, ruin and annihilate her trade and fisheries, and harry her by Canadian and Indian raiders until she sought protection from the British army.

The three generals and 10,000 troops that Gibbon heard about in Parliament were sent to Boston to carry out this plan. There were clashes between American militiamen and British regulars sent to destroy stores at Lexington and Concord on 19 April; and since the British were reported to have fired first, this produced, as Franklin foretold, a 'breach that can never afterwards be healed'.

The Americans invested Boston in late April and, forestalling Gage, they fortified Bunker Hill opposite the town. Howe, Clinton, and Burgoyne arrived on 12 May, martial law was declared on 12 June, and Gage agreed to clear the heights commanding Boston. Clinton advised an attack on the American rear to cut off retreat across the Charlestown peninsula, but Gage ordered a frontal assault on the trenches on Breeds Hill below Bunker Hill. It was ultimately successful but cost many more British casualties than American, losses that Gage could ill afford as a rebel build-up of troops continued, with George Washington taking command of an eventual siege of Boston that forced the British to retreat on 17 March 1776. Gage's official account of the Bunker Hill battle conceded that the American forces were formidable opponents, and 'not the despicable Rabble too many have supposed them to be' (Wallis *et al.*, 1975: 41–55).

The account of Bunker Hill sent to Smith by Roebuck was written by Captain Walter S. Laurie, who took part in the frontal assault and was the officer in charge of the detachment afterwards sent to bury the dead. He wrote of finding the slain Dr Joseph Warren, President of the Provincial Congress, who had sent Paul Revere and William Dawes on their famous ride to warn the men at Lexington on 18 April. Declining command, he fought as a volunteer in the American redoubt. Laurie did not mince words about Warren: '[I] stuffed the Scoundrel with another Rebel, into one hole, and there he, and his seditious principles may remain.' Laurie also wrote of the fury of the American resistance to the British soldiers, and their determination to fight on. He was pessimistic about the small British army being able to control the situation, and declared he had sent in his resignation some months before.

He supplemented his account of the battle with an annotated list entitled 'Characters of the Boston Patriots', which identified in scathing terms the leaders of the revolutionary party. These included John Hancock, the wealthy Boston merchant idolized by his fellow townsmen in 1768, when his sloop, symbolically called the *Liberty*, was the centre of a contraband dispute, which brought John Adams to his defence with the argument that Parliament was not competent to legislate for and tax the colonies, since they were not represented therein. This issue was the heart of the constitutional struggle as far as the Americans were concerned, exacerbated by their fears that a malignant, powerful, and highly corrupt central Government was seeking to deprive them of the liberties they already possessed through their own courts and legislatures (Bailyn, 1973; 1992: 144–75).

Hancock was described in Laurie's list as a man of 'irreproachable Honesty and benevolence, but of a weak ambition . . . a necessary and generous Dupe to another of deeper designs, to the utter ruin of his private Fortune'. The sinister figure behind Hancock was Samuel Adams:

A Maltster by profession, but of little reputation, untill he made himself conspicuous in political Disputes—a Man of superior cunning and Abilities, [who] was made a Collector of the Town Taxes for a Support, in which capacity, he in a most notorious manner, cheated the Town of a Sum not less than 2000 sterling, which after his Influence with the Community was established, he had the Audacity to get sponged off, in consideration of his secret Services. (GUL MS Gen. 1035/152 (y); Fay, 1956: 81–2)

Despoiler of the public funds or not, Samuel Adams exploited his position as Clerk to the Massachusetts House of Representatives to intensify radical opposition to Governor Hutchinson. His fiery oratory encouraged resistance to Charles Townshend's revenue acts, and to the garrisoning of British troops in Boston to enforce these acts. It seems clear that he wished to goad the British Government into punitive measures which, in turn, would inflame Americans to accomplish the violent overthrow of British rule (Brown: 1973).

Smith understood well the psychology at work in the case of revolutionary leaders such as this Adams. Accordingly, he argued in *WN* that the self-importance of the patriot colonists had risen to the point that force alone would not conquer them. Ingeniously, he suggested that perhaps within a federal union embracing the British Empire, a 'new method of acquiring importance, a new and more dazzling object of ambition would be presented to the leading men of each colony'. Careers in the Parliament of the Empire would be open to them:

Instead of piddling for the little prizes which are to be found in what may be called the paltry raffle of colony faction; they might hope, from the presumption which men naturally have in their own ability and good fortune, to draw some of the great prizes which sometimes come from the wheel of the great state lottery of British politics. (IV.vii.c.75)

Smith was even prepared to acknowledge that, such had been the 'rapid progress of [America] in wealth, population and improvement, that in the course of little more than a century, perhaps, the produce of American might exceed that of British taxation'. In which case, the 'seat of empire would then naturally remove itself to that part of the empire which contributed most to the general defence and support of the whole' (para. 79).

Smith is thinking his way past the 'hegemonic English myth', which J. C. D. Clark (1994) believes was dominant at this time, and attracting not only the English themselves, but also the Scots, Irish, and some American colonists. The concept of the Atlantic union suggests a willingness to embrace political change to accommodate economic dynamism, to develop new institutions to overcome old conflicts, and to allow a place for the revolutionary spirit to be exercised. Certainly, these new and positive ideas about America were being entertained by Smith and voiced among his friends, such as his former pupils Millar and Richardson in Glasgow, though such ideas, if tolerated, were not popular. Thus on 16 March 1778 James Wodrow wrote from Glasgow to Samuel Kenrick:

Your ingenious friend Dr Smith & his Companions may safely venture themselves amongst us & speak their Sentiments [about America] freely in every Company. I give you my word they may travel thro' the length and breadth of Scotland without the least hazard of being tarred & feathered. (London, Dr Williams's Lib., MSS 24.157, 60)

However salutary as well as novel, Smith's enlightened views about America were not to circulate in print in 1775. Hume was disturbed at the continuing delay in the publication of *WN*, and worry about his friend, as well as the pain of his illness, perhaps, made him upbraid Smith on 8 February 1776: 'I am as lazy a Correspondent as you; yet my Anxiety about you makes me write.' He had heard that the book was printed but had seen no advertisement, and he thought that if Smith was waiting until America's fate were decided, that might take a long time. From Buccleuch, he had learned that Smith was 'very zealous in American Affairs', but he advanced the 'Notion' that the matter was not so important as most people believed, though he conceded he might be wrong, and would change his view when he saw Smith or read him. In his opinion, Britain's 'Navigation and general Commerce may suffer more than our Manufactures'. Then he joked characteristically about the wasting effect of his illness: 'Shoud London fall as much in Size, as I have done, it will be the better. It is nothing but a Hulk of bad and unclean Humours.' Elsewhere in the letter, he mentioned to Smith 'his indifferent State of Health', and how when he weighed himself recently he found he had lost five stones: 'If you delay much longer, I shall probably disappear altogether' (*Corr.* No. 149).

Hume was not afraid of death, but he did not want to die disappointed in never seeing again his friend, or the great book to which Adam Smith had devoted so many years.

16

Euge! Belle! *Dear Mr Smith*

I am much pleas'd with your Performance, and the Perusal of it has taken me from a state of great Anxiety.

The Wealth of Nations was advertised in the *London Chronicle* number for 5–7 March 1776; it was published on 9 March, over 1,000 pages in two quarto volumes, between blue-grey or marbled boards. The title-page identified the author as Adam Smith, LL D. and FRS, despite his views on degrees and other honorifics (*Corr.* Nos. 100, 143). Following the *WN* title was an advertisement for the fourth edition of *TMS* (1774). Smith or his publisher Strahan, or both, did not wish readers to forget that the author of the new book was the moral philosopher who had written, as the expanded title of the previous book put it, *An Essay towards an Analysis of the Principles by which Men naturally judge concerning the Conduct and Character, first of their Neighbours, and afterwards of themselves.* The print-run was likely to have been 500 copies, at the very modest price of £1 16s., and Smith was paid £300 from copy money, that is, the price paid by the bookseller for the copyright of the book. In 1759 Millar had paid Robertson £600 for his first book, the *History of Scotland*, and with his partner, Thomas Cadell, is believed to have had a £6,000 turnover from this purchase. Robertson was paid 'no less than £4,000' as copy money for the *History of Charles V* (1769), and Strahan made money on this publication as well (Cochrane, 1964: 40). Perhaps Smith had good financial reasons for feeling aggrieved over Robertson borrowing his ideas about the history of civil society. Canny William Strahan would no doubt have been astonished to hear that after 200 years a copy of a first-edition *WN* was expected to reach between £20,000 and £30,000 in the auction room, though it did not sell at the expected figure, and was 'bought in' for £18,500 (Sotheby's Cat., 18 July 1991, *English Literature and History*; letter from Dr Peter Beal of Sotheby's, 28 Aug. 1991).

On the eve of the publication of Edward Gibbon's *The Decline and Fall of the Roman Empire*, another book issued in 1776 in partnership with Thomas Cadell, Strahan's 'prophetic taste', according to the author's *Memoirs*, led him to double the print-run from 500 copies to 1,000. Responding on 12 April to Hume's compliments on the joint appearance from his press of Gibbon's book and Smith's, Strahan gave his comparative estimate of the two works: 'The Former

is the more popular . . . but the Sale of the latter, tho' not near so rapid, has
been much more than I could have expected from a Work, that requires much
thought and Reflexion (Qualities that do not abound among modern Readers) to
peruse to any purpose' (NLS Hume MSS vii.67, old no.). Nevertheless, Smith's
book met growing reader demand. By November 1776 *WN* had been well
reviewed or, as Smith later drily commented, was 'less abused than I had reason
to expect' (*Corr.* No. 208).[1] Accordingly, he proposed that there should be a second edition 'in four vols. octavo', printed at Strahan's expense, and that he and
Strahan should divide the profits (*Corr.* 179). Though the second edition with a
print-run of 500 did not appear until 1778, Smith was achieving something of
the success for which he had hoped.

An Inquiry into the Nature and Causes of the Wealth of Nations is in many
respects a typical product of the Scottish Enlightenment. Thus, many of the
anthropological and sociological topics it covers, as well as some economic ones,
such as taxation, can be found in Lord Kames's far less rigorous and systematic
but equally comprehensive publication of 1774: *Sketches of the History of Man*.
To be sure, Kames had strong interests in economic thought and planning
expressed in a range of writings and activities, sometimes at odds with Smith's
principles (Ross, 1972: ch. 16; Tanaka, 1993).

Smith begins his book with a simple principle: that division of labour creates
wealth or economic prosperity; and he explains the operation of this principle in
terms of basic propensities he claims we share with everyone: our readiness to
'truck, barter, or exchange' our goods or services to satisfy our wants (I.ii.1), and
our drive to better ourselves (II.iii.31). Somewhat on the Newtonian model of
'statics', he offers an account of the operation of these psychological traits in the
economic sphere, and he adds to this a 'dynamics' accounting for an unfolding
'history of civil [or political] society', organized through response to four stages
of economic development: hunting and fishing, pastoralism, agriculture, and
commerce (see v.i.a.2–9, with respect to war; and v.i.b.2–24, with respect to justice). Throughout *WN*, of course, he chooses to dwell on the stage of commerce
at which his society had arrived, though he has the recent pastoralism of the
Highlands of Scotland to examine for comparative purposes, as well as a wide
range of historical and anthropological material about hunters, fishers, and farmers drawn from classical and modern literature, including the increasing number
of travel books. He thus offers the reader 'philosophical' history similar to his
pioneering attempt in his lecture and essay on the 'origin and progress of language', and to be found in the writings of his fellow Scots literati: Hume, Kames,
Steuart-Denham, Ferguson, Robertson, and Millar. There were also parallel historical studies by French writers of the 1750s period such as Turgot who, like
Smith, seems to have begun thinking about social and cultural evolution through
adaptation to economic base by reflecting on contexts of changes in language
(Meek, 1976: 69). But on this score, *WN* is notable for an assurance and global
range which is quite distinctive. 'The discovery of America, and that of a

passage to the East Indies', Smith relates, 'are the two greatest and most important events recorded in the history of mankind.' We are enabled to see the creation of a world market for European commercial cities, the spread and rivalry of their colonies, at least in the case of Britain, and the misfortunes of the aboriginal peoples disturbed by the discoveries and colonization. Smith also allows for the possibility that aboriginals will come into their own as Europeans or their descendants grow weaker, or the others establish equal or greater strength through 'mutual communication of knowledge and of all sorts of improvements which an extensive commerce from all countries to all countries naturally, or rather necessarily, carries along with it' (IV.vii.c.80).

Against this backdrop Smith builds an economic model, again on Newtonian lines, developing his theory of how wealth would naturally be created in an ideal society operating according to the 'obvious and simple system of natural liberty' (IV.ix.51).[2] The main features of such a system were already delineated in the 'paper' Smith delivered in 1755 in Glasgow, and, as we have traced, going back to the lectures on natural jurisprudence given at Edinburgh in 1750–1. As for the ideal society, it would be characterized by 'peace, easy taxes, and a tolerable administration of justice' (Stewart iv.25). In constructing his model, Smith drew on a wide array of sources, but in the opinion of Dugald Stewart there was a crucial concentration of ideas in Hume: 'The Political Discourses of Mr Hume were evidently of greater use to Mr Smith, than any other book that had appeared prior to his lectures' (iv.24). Specifically, Smith drew on the teaching of Hume about such matters as specie-flow adjustments, the basis for interest rates, and the claim that commerce flourishes where there is civil liberty. More broadly, Hume's influence, reinforced by Quesnay's thinking, was pervasive about the division of the economy into the sectors of agriculture and manufactures. Hume had also stressed the linkage of man's natural wants to the rise of arts and sciences.

It appears, also, that Edwin Cannan and W. R. Scott are well justified in drawing attention to the lead given Smith by Hutcheson's analytic treatment of economics through emphasizing the importance of the division of labour, involving interdependent functional support and accelerating production through specialization of function and increase in dexterity. Hutcheson also set Smith the example of insisting that enforcement of justice was the precondition for establishing a stable society conducive to economic growth. Moreover, Hutcheson had distinguished between value in use and value in exchange; between money as a medium of exchange and as a standard of value; and between supply and demand prices, with the former understood as comprehensive cost of labour, embracing cost of materials, the worker's skill, and the standing in society he expects to retain. Smith's 'never to be forgotten' teacher had also given a role to self-interest in the maintenance of the economic order, but Smith would not go along with a refusal to give moral approval to self-regarding actions, and on this point *TMS* adds a new perspective to economic activity: 'A person appears mean spirited, who does not pursue [the more extraordinary and important objects of self-interest] with some degree of earnestness for their own sake' (III.6.7). (Scott, 1900: 210, 231; *WN* ed. Cannan, 1950: vol. i, pp. xxxv–xliii; Skinner, 1979: 110).

To follow the progressive development of the economic model that is presented in *WN*, we have to begin with its formulation in the lectures on jurisprudence. Picking up the thread of the evidence of Smith's thought at Glasgow, we recall that the notes of the 1762–3 period (*LJ*(A)) treat topics more fully, but those of 1763–4 (*LJ*(B)) are more complete in the range of topics covered (Skinner, 1979: 11). Dwelling on *LJ*(B), then, we find there analysis of an economic system made up of agriculture, manufactures, and commerce. The chief feature of the analysis is an account of the division of labour, which is held to explain economic growth arising from perfection of skills answering 'natural wants'. Smith stresses the accompanying advance in dexterity, time-saving through specialization, and the role of technological change.

Taking up the homely example of the production of a labourer's woollen coat, Smith reveals the interdependence involved in the making of the necessary tools, also in the relevant processes: wool-gathering, spinning, dyeing, weaving, tailoring, and so on (*LJ*(B) 211–13). The significance of division of labour is further reinforced through discussion of the operations connected with making pins (Plate 13). Smith relates that eighteen workers combining their specialized tasks will each turn out 200 pins a day, whereas if each worked alone with ready-drawn wire, the output would scarcely be more than twenty pins in the same time (*LJ*(B) 213–14). Smith's source here is likely to have been the article 'Épingle' in the fifth volume of the *Encyclopédie* (1755), which cites the eighteen operations. Another source, Ephraim Chambers's *Cyclopaedia* (4th edn., 1741), lists 25 operations under 'Pin'. The lesson Smith draws is that in such division of labour there is considerable surplus above maintenance, thus creating opulence, though this is not determined by the price of labour, for labour becomes dearer as commodities become cheaper.

A further major point emphasized is that the worker can exchange his surplus for the goods he wants. This consideration permits Smith to go into the connected questions of price and allocation. The analysis is particularly acute with respect to the distinction between the *natural* price, that is, the comprehensive cost of supplying the commodity, and the *market* price, that prevailing at any distinct time, governed by the demand for the commodity. Smith examines the cases of market prices rising above and falling below the natural price, and he produces his argument that whatever policy has a tendency to hinder them from coinciding 'diminishes opulence'. With this form of equilibrium theory, Smith can and does criticize policies, such as taxes on manufactures, monopolies, and corporation privileges, which keep the market price above the natural one, as well as those, such as the corn bounty, which depress the market price. Hence Smith arrives at his conclusion: 'Upon the whole . . . it is by far the best police [way of procuring wealth and abundance—*LJ*(B) 205] to leave things to their natural

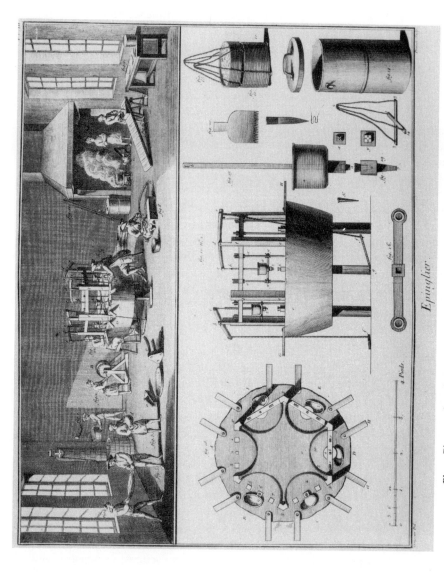

Epinglier

Pl.13. Pin-manufacturing, 1764. From the *Encyclopédie, Recueil des planches,* iv (GUL).

course' (*LJ*(B) 235). This is his own form of *laissez-faire*, a phrase which he never personally used, and is more appropriately associated with Quesnay and the Physiocrats (Viner, 1958: 213–45; Winch, 1978: 14–16; Skinner, 1979: 216–19; Teichgraeber, 1986: 4–6, 181, n. 2; Perrot, 1992: 91–2). Looking into the history of free enterprise economics before Smith, Dugald Stewart (*EPS* Stewart, n. 1) traced the ideas back to English and Dutch thinkers of the seventeenth century who influenced merchants in France. He identified the phrase *laissez nous faire* as one used by an old merchant, Le Gendre, in conversation with Colbert, the powerful statesman of Louis XIV's reign, devoted to framing mercantilist policies to make France a great nation.

Treatment of price leads naturally to a focus on money as a medium of exchange, the third major component of Smith's economic model. His standpoint allows him to attack the mercantile system for its false claim that natural wealth resides in money, and for enforcing such absurd policies as prohibiting free export of specie. He can thereupon return to the theme of allocation by demonstrating the bad effects of mercantilist attempts to control and divert resources. Thus free trade is presented as complimentary to the exercise of domestic economic freedom, and Smith's general argument culminates in advocacy of the unfettered international market:

From the above considerations it appears that Brittain should by all means be made a free port, that there should be no interruptions of any kind made to foreign trade, that if it were possible to defray the expences of government by any other method, all duties, customs, and excise should be abolished, and that free commerce and liberty of exchange should be allowed with all nations and for all things. (*LJ*(B) 269)

An additional important feature of Smith's thought even in this context is that he roots human economic activity in the delicacy of our bodies and minds, which determines the manifold exercises of our self-love. Thus, in the final economic analysis, he represents us as more significantly aesthetic than appetitive creatures (*LJ*(B) 208–9). Early in his career, of course, he had traced the significance of our aesthetic feelings, wonder, surprise, and admiration, in the building of scientific systems, discussed in his 'History of Astronomy'.

When *WN* was published, Glasgow merchants recognized Smith's doctrines about free trade and other subjects as views that had 'circulated with the punch' at their meetings (Sir Thomas Monro/Kirkman Finlay, 15 Aug. 1825, quoted in Hutchison, 1976: 510, n. 8). The view recently expressed that *WN*, though 'hailed by [Smith's] intellectual friends, found little favour among the Glasgow merchants faced by a collapse in the American tobacco trade' (Lynch, 1994: 348), seems to be speculation. Analysis of the Glasgow import–export trade up to and during the American war suggests that the firms involved for the most part were well equipped to handle the crisis, and all along had reason to deplore the instability of the colonial system and the sanctions that went with it (Devine, 1975: 103–50). In the light of this, merchants might well have discussed positively

freedom of trade and other leading policy ideas of *WN*. We have no information, alas, about their response to Smith's sallies against the 'mean rapacity, the
monopolising spirit of merchants and manufacturers' (IV.iii.c.9) and his countervailing praise of the 'generosity of the country gentlemen' (I.xi.10, IV.ii.21). This
may be explained by his Douglas family background connecting Smith with the
Fife gentry, also by his fondness for taking Swift as a model writer who used
city/country opposition as a satiric trope. As discussed, Smith disclosed at
Glasgow that he was turning his lectures into a book, and we know that the
tobacco merchant John Glassford believed that this 'usefull work' was 'well
advanced' in 1764 (*Corr.* No. 85). Also Glassford, or others in the Glasgow merchant community, were well aware of and sympathetic to Smith's economic
views in connection with proposed banking legislation in the 1760s, as reflected
in *Thoughts Concerning Banks* published in 1763 (Gherity, 1993).

In addition to this pamphlet, with its Smithian economic content but uncertain authorship, three manuscripts composed by Smith have survived which
appear to be connected with the early stages of the composition of *WN*. W. R.
Scott found the first one in papers associated with Charles Townshend in the
Buccleuch muniments at Dalkeith Palace, and entitled it Early Draft (ED) of
part of *WN*. It consists of an extensive chapter 2, over thirty pages in length,
devoted to the division of labour, under the heading, 'Of the nature and Causes
of public Opulence', and then eighteen pages of summaries of chapters 3, 4, and
5, dealing respectively with exchange or price, money, and the 'slow progress of
opulence' (SRO Buccleuch Muniments GD 224/33/4; Scott, 1937: 317–56; *LJ*
561–81).

After careful comparison of ED with *LJ*(A) and (B), Ronald Meek and
Andrew Skinner reached the conclusion that, though covering the major issues
addressed in the economic part of Smith's jurisprudence course, ED was composed at some stage prior to April 1763. It omits consideration of the important
point that the extent of the market determines the division of labour, which
seems to have been presented by Smith to his students on Tuesday 5 April 1763
as a kind of afterthought: *LJ*(A) vi.64 (Meek and Skinner, 1973: 1094–1116). In
addition, ED does not mention a law alleged to have been framed by Sesostris
(the conquering Pharaoh Senwosre I of the 12th Dynasty) that 'every one should
for ever adhere to his fathers [profession]' (*LJ*(A) iii.128 and vi.54). Neither is
there a reference to the 'naturall inclination every one has to persuade' as the
'principle of the human mind' on which is founded the 'disposition of trucking'
(p. 56).

Comparison of ED with *WN* itself uncovers a great deal of correspondence,
as well as transference of crucial points from the lectures: for instance, the argument that the division of labour is not the effect of human policy, but the necessary consequence of the natural inclination of men to truck, barter, and
exchange (*LJ*(A) vi.44; *LJ*(B) 219; ED 2.20–1; *WN* I.ii.1). It is in ED, however,
that we can see emerging the pithy turn of phrase exploited so cleverly in *WN*,

as in the example reinforcing the claim that humans are the only bartering animals: 'Nobody ever saw a dog make a fair and deliberate exchange of one bone for another with another dog' (ED 2.21; cf. *WN* I.ii.2). Yet it is noticeable that Smith exercises editorial control over the content of ED, rejecting for *WN* a striking passage on inequality in a 'civilized society' in the interest of keeping to a more direct line of argument about division of labour (ED 2.3–5). One passage at the conclusion of ED's chapter 2 expands on the topic of the social usefulness of porters and philosophers or men of letters in a fashion unique in Smith's writings, and making the point that so much of what we know comes at second hand from books, brought to the market like any other commodity (Skinner, 1979: 141, n. 15).

W. R. Scott was also responsible for securing the other two manuscripts connected with the composition of *WN*. They appeared among Smith's papers retained by the Bannerman branch of the descendants of Adam's heir, David Douglas. In 1935 Professor Scott supplied for Mrs Helen Bannerman, the acting executrix of the widow of David Douglas's grandson, a list of Smith documents he believed to have been in existence after Smith's death. In response he was sent four cardboard boxes of papers; in one of them, labelled 'iced almond cake', there were found a fragment of a lecture on justice, already discussed above, and two fragments relating to *WN*. Lord Hailes's compilation of 'Prices of Corn' was found at the same time (GUL MS Gen. 1035/227, 228, 229; Scott, 1940: 270–1).

Fragment A of these two consists of a folded, single folio sheet with writing covering almost all of the four pages it makes, and B has just over two and a half pages of writing on a similar, folded folio sheet. As in the case of ED, the writing is in the hand of an amanuensis, but there are traces of corrections and insertions in Smith's hand. The watermarks of ED and the fragments seem to be the same: an emblem presenting a lion rampant surmounted by a crown and bearing a motto, which Scott read as *Pro Patria eiusque Libertate*. Scott satisfied himself that the paper was of Dutch origin, and was of a type Smith used in Glasgow (Scott, 1937: 321–2; Skinner, 1979: 143–4; FA and FB—*LJ* 582–6).

As for content, Fragment A deals with division of labour in relation to extent of the market, illustrated by reference to the experience of Scottish Highlanders as well as that of remoter peoples: North American Indians, Tartars, Arabs, and Hottentots. Fragment B treats the same theme, but from the viewpoint afforded by considering ease of communication by sea. Here the experience of ancient Greece and Egypt is linked to that of the American colonies. The Fragments seem to be 'substitute' conclusions for those of ED's analysis of division of labour, and thus may be plausibly regarded as composed after it. Moreover, comparison of the Fragments with *WN* I.iii.1–2 bring out close parallels in argument and even in wording (Skinner, 1979: 146). We thus seem very close to the immediate antecedents of Smith's great book.

A working hypothesis is that, on publishing *TMS* in 1759, Smith would have been mindful of the concluding promise to write another book dealing with the 'general principles of law and government', including treatment of 'what concerns police, revenue, and arms' (VII.iv.37). He could not give his full attention to this project, however, until he had dealt with initial criticisms of *TMS* by Hume and Elliot of Minto in the second edition of 1761. In that year, too, he may have been involved in plans for issuing *The Philological Miscellany*. ED could well have been begun in the course of 1762–3, with the surviving text completed before April 1763, when Smith's 'afterthought' about the extent of the market limiting the division of labour came into his lectures. Moreover, this text has the confident assertion that 'Ossian plainly describes the exploits of a nation of hunters' (ED 2.27; cf. *LJ*(A) iv.101, dated 1 March 1763, assimilating Ossian's Picts and Scots to the American Indians). James Macpherson published his Ossianic *Fragments* in 1760, *Fingal* in 1762, and *Temora* in 1763 (Mizuta). Smith may have had special knowledge of these publications, because Macpherson's publishers were those of *The Philological Miscellany*: T. Beckett and P. A. Dehondt. Smith was aware of Ossian's poetry by 16 August 1760 (*HL* i.329). In 1763, however, there appeared Hugh Blair's *Critical Dissertation on the Poems of Ossian* founded on his rhetoric lectures (Sudo, 1995), which explicitly made the point that these poems were set in an age of hunters (p. 17; quoted in *LJ* 573, n. 2).

ED was discovered among Townshend's papers in the 'huge packing-case' which was sent to Dalkeith on the death of his widow, Buccleuch's mother (Scott, 1940: 269). Smith probably lent Townshend this document as a relatively complete version of his central ideas about division of labour and immediately related topics, possibly when he was in London in the winter of 1766–7 and working with Townshend. Fragments A and B fit in as substitutes for the conclusion of chapter 2 of ED, distinct from the lecture-note material. Since they are written on paper used by Smith in his Glasgow professorial period, they must date from the end of that period, or from some time afterwards when he still retained a stock of this kind of paper or had access to it. Their discovery among Smith's correspondence suggests that they were left behind in Kirkcaldy in 1773, together with Hailes's 'Prices of Corn' document, once Smith had incorporated the essence and the appropriate wording in the draft of *WN* that formed part of the 'literary papers' he took to London (*Corr.* No. 137).

At this stage Quesnay was still alive, and it was Smith's declared intention to dedicate *WN* to him, or so we are informed by Dugald Stewart (iii.12). The likely motive was to acknowledge Quesnay's achievement as leader of the outstanding school of French economists, and also the intellectual stimulation Smith received from meeting him in Paris and reading his work. Though Quesnay died in 1774 and Smith's gesture was never made, both Quesnay and the Physiocracy he advocated make their appearance in *WN*, adding a hitherto missing dimension through inspiring Smith's attention to macroeconomic issues and adoption of the principle of 'circular flow' as a guide to the working of the market economy. This is the most striking advance on the economic thought of the period of the jurisprudence lectures and ED, though we also have to find a place in the progress of Smith's ideas for the advanced economic insights appearing in *Thoughts Concerning Banks* (1763). As for Quesnay, *WN* reveals that Smith's admiration was judiciously qualified, and that with respect to his influence, as with that of all others who provided Smith with insights and theoretical guidance, Grotius and Pufendorf of the natural-law tradition, Gerschom Carmichael as a commentator on Pufendorf (Murray, 1924: 441), Hutcheson, Hume, and Steuart of the Scottish social philosophy school, as well as more technical writers such as Cantillon on trade and Harris on money, Smith kept a sense of his own position and could mount effective criticism.

The masterly treatise that came from Smith's extensive studies, his observation of human nature and economic activity in Britain, France, and briefly in Switzerland, his conversations with people in many walks of life, and with the writers of the time who shared his interests and could provide ideas and insights as well as hints about expression and composition, and the experience of writing *TMS*, unfolds in five books that make a two-part structure. The first two books present the principles which lead naturally to economic growth in commercial societies. In the last three books, Smith concentrates on what legislators have done and what they ought to do in the interest of achieving growth.

Book I, 'Of the Causes of Improvement in the productive Powers of Labour, and the Order according to which its Produce is naturally distributed among the different Ranks of People', introduces Smith's central idea that division of labour is the source of human improvement, and that behind this is self-love directed, within the limits of justice, at bettering one's condition, as well as the human propensity to truck, barter, and exchange. The universality of this drive, of course, has been challenged by Max Weber, Karl Polanyi, and others (Haskell and Teichgraeber, 1993: 5). Smith's book also deals with money, price, wages and profit, inequality, and value, to which topic is attached the long digression on silver. Smith makes no bones about the fact that he is prepared to be tedious to be 'perspicacious'. Book II is entitled 'Of the Nature, Accumulation, and Employment of Stock', and here Smith gives his capital theory and part of his monetary theory. He deals with the distinction between productive and unproductive labour, offering an alternative to Quesnay's account, countering the error that manufacturing is not productive. By following up Turgot's insight in his *Réflexions sur la formation et la distribution des richesses*, Smith focuses on the second major factor in growth after division of labour, namely, savings and investment, and gives an account of the use of capital in the wholesale and retail trades.[3] It is here that his vivid, aphoristic style expresses the idea, found also in Turgot, of fixed and circulating capitals, and we have Smith's sense of the interdependence of economic activity:

Land, mines, and fisheries, require both a fixed and a circulating capital to cultivate them; and their produce replaces with a profit, not only those capitals, but all the others in the society. Thus the farmer annually replaces to the manufacturer the provisions which he has consumed and the materials which he has wrought up the year before; and the manufacturer replaces to the farmer the finished work which he has wasted and worn out in the same time . . . Land even replaces, in part, at least, the capitals with which fisheries and mines are cultivated. It is the produce of land which draws the fish from the waters; and it is the produce of the surface of the earth which extracts the minerals from its bowels. (II.i.28)

Taken together, books I and II represent Smith's most profound achievement as an analytical economist, detailing a model that explained in an empirical and therefore refutable way the economic processes of a market society. Smith's own designation for the model was the 'obvious and simple system of natural liberty' (*WN* IV.ix.51). Its chief features of free competition and self-regulation through the market mechanism have continued to exert fascination ever since it was brought to the attention of the reading public.[4]

Of fundamental appeal is the basic idea that the exercise of freedom at the individual level is complemented by advance in welfare for the society. Smith's argument is that the unintended outcome of the free and fair operation of the market mechanism is to channel self-interest into positive benefits for consumers and producers. The profit motive drives producers to co-ordinate information about the supply-and-demand situation for commodities, and consumers seeking these commodities benefit from producers in competition moving towards 'natural' or equilibrium price. Accumulation of profit allows, among other benefits, for rising wages and enhancement of culture generally. This is Smith's rendering of the vision revealed by Mirabeau, one of Quesnay's disciples, in the *Philosophie rurale*, 1763 (Mizuta): 'the whole magic of a well-ordered society is that each man works for others, while believing that he is working for himself' (Meek, 1962: 70).

To be sure, Smith is well aware that there can also be negative consequences of the expression of self-interest by actors in the market-place whose poor judgement of ends and means exposes them to 'anxiety, to fear, and sorrow; to diseases, to danger, and to death' (*TMS* IV.1.8). Smith's answer to this condition, of course, is to hark back to the Stoic lesson of self-command begun, as he reckoned, in the schoolyard. Thereby, ambition for 'power and riches' can be turned to more positive account. Another idea is involved: that the jarring conditions faced by individuals with economic freedom can be related to the fundamentally harmonious universe of growing social good, operating according to natural law, which is another Stoic formulation. This whole complex set of ideas is ingeniously conveyed through the metaphor of the 'invisible hand' (*WN* IV.ii.9; cf. *TMS* IV.1.10).[5]

In books III, IV, and V of *WN* Smith turns from analysis to historical evaluation of the dynamic capacity of his model or 'system' in action. This gives him an opportunity to develop a polemic against mistaken and even mischievous attempts of governments, chiefly inspired by 'mercantilism', to reorganize, redirect, and thwart economic activity against the tendencies of his 'simple system'. As a conclusion, however, Smith offers constructive policy advice about necessary curtailment of individual economic freedom to provide resources for our chief social needs: justice, defence, public works, and education. In the interest of these considerations, book III, 'Of the different Progress of Opulence in different Nations', traces economic growth historically in terms of the 'natural' order of the employment of capital. Smith's argument, adumbrated in *Thoughts Concerning Banks* (1763), is that, without interference, capital will find its way to those employments which create for societies as a whole the greatest prosperity: first agriculture, then manufactures, and finally foreign trade. Picking up many insights from Hume's *History of England*, but expanding his account to cover the period in Europe from the fall of Rome and establishment of feudalism to the emergence and dominance of commercial society through the development of towns, Smith is concerned to show the major impact of foreign trade on socioeconomic change, in a phase when governments are not yet committed to restrictive ('mercantile') policies (see *WN* 381, n. 1).

Book IV, 'Of Systems of Political Economy', is the most vigorously polemical of them all, where Smith 'endeavours by all means to persuade us' (*LRBL* i.149). Among other topics, it castigates the mercantile policy of attempting to improve the balance of trade through restrictions and preferential trading policies; the general error of all restraints on freedom of trade, as well as on mobility of labour and capital; and the absurdity of monopolies and other conspiracies seeking to hinder free competition. Smith reserves his severest criticism for the extension by European merchants and manufacturers of the monopoly spirit to their colonies. In this connection, he deals with the issues of the American crisis and makes his 'very violent attack . . . upon the whole commercial system of Great Britain' (*Corr.* No. 208). Thus he denounces the shopkeeper mentality of the British Government, and comes down decisively on the side of the Americans in their conflict with the mother country:

To prohibit a great people, however, from making all that they can of every part of their own produce, or from employing their stock and industry in the way that they judge most advantageous to themselves, is a manifest violation of the most sacred rights of mankind. (IV.vii.b.44)

At the same time, however, Smith is not content to leave matters at level of polemic, but comes forward with a plan for an incorporating union of Britain and her American colonies (IV.vii.c.77), on which he expanded in his 'Thoughts on America' of 1778 (*Corr.* app. B).

In addition to its critique of mercantilism including the system of colonial monopoly, book IV deals with Physiocracy. Here Smith saluted Quesnay's ingenuity and profundity, recognizing that he had devised an economic system, presented in the 'arithmetical formularies' of the states of *Tableau économique*, which had important features in advance of the one outlined in *LJ*(B). Quesnay had written that his analysis was founded on nature, and Baudeau was specific that his master had calculated, for example, the proportion which holds between 'les avances primitives et les avances annuelles d'une bonne et grande culture de grains en Picardie, en Normandie, dans la Beauce, l'Île-de-France et la Brie'. But the other side of this coin highlighting agriculture was the portrayal of manufacturing and trading as unproductive. Smith could not accept this, very likely because of his knowledge of the vitality of the trading and manufacturing sector of the British economy. We can assume that he had a realistic grasp of the profit to be made, for example, in the 'suggaries, roapary, soapary, and glassary' of Glasgow, also in the city's tobacco and other colonial trading enterprises, and the role this played in the formation of capital laid out on investment in land, further manufacturing ventures, and financial services (Devine, 1975: 18–51).

Though Smith wrote that the sect of the 'French Oeconomists' followed 'implicitly, and without any sensible variation' the teaching of Quesnay, it was subjected to reform begun by Baudeau on the point of the productive capacity of the manufacturing side of the economy. Baudeau had made available for Physiocracy in 1766 his monthly journal *Les Éphémérides du citoyen*, and from November 1769 to January 1770 he published Turgot's *Réflexions sur la formation et la distribution des richesses*. Smith's set of this journal in his library includes the 1769 numbers (Mizuta), so he had access to two-thirds of Turgot's text. This would be sufficient to provide theoretical support for his intuitions or observations about the significance of the growth of capital invested in manufacturing as well as farming. Smith pushed these ideas further, and gave full value to the productions of manufacturers and the role of merchants in creating the demand-pull of the home market stimulated by middle-income growth and something of a consumer revolution. Thus was promoted the growth of capital (IV.ix.28–37; Meek, 1962: 309–10; Viner, 1965: 131–2; McKindrick *et al.*, 1982; Perrot, 1992: 220–1; Rule, 1992: 257–9; Brewer and Porter, 1993).

Having shown what the wealth of nations consists of and how growth may be encouraged, or at least not discouraged by governments, Smith discusses in book V their necessary expenses. In connection with defence, he can return to his theme of the division of labour in the stage of commercial society, and the requirement for security of funding a 'well-regulated standing army' (V.i.a.41). His was not a viewpoint endearing to contemporaries espousing civic humanism and maintaining the ancient fear of standing armies as threats to the liberties of citizens, thus favouring militia service (Robertson, 1985). Smith was flexible enough, however, to concede that a militia kept in the field for a few campaigns becomes in effect a standing army. He offered the opinion that if the American war dragged on, the militia there would become a match for the British regulars (V.i.a.27).[6]

Regarding justice, Smith assigns to the shepherd state the origins of sustained inequality of fortune entailing the enforcement of law. In consequence of this viewpoint, we are given an honest appraisal of institutions that maintain order and subordination among men: 'Civil government, so far as it is instituted for the security of property, is in reality instituted for the defence of the rich against the poor, or of those who have property against those who have none at all' (v.i.b.12).

Passing to the remaining public works and institutions, Smith covers, first, those designed to facilitate commerce, such as transport facilities, which he would prefer to see under local administration or even deregulated to put private interest to work to secure effective maintenance. Smith had emphasized in book I, of course, that good transport facilities (roads, canals, navigable rivers) broke down monopolies and encouraged 'free and universal competition' (I.xi.b.5). Again thinking of the adverse effects of monopolies, he added in 1784 for the third edition, his highly critical account of the regulated or joint stock companies (v.i.e).

Next, he deals with the education of youth and then of the people. These parts of book v have been drawn on as evidence about his responses to university education at Oxford. They also provide evidence about his sensitivity to the ill effects on working people of the division of labour, rendering them 'stupid and ignorant' (v.i.f.50), with a resulting obligation that government counter this affliction through some measure of universal education. There follows an entertaining 'article' about expenses devoted to the religious instruction of the people, in which Smith balances the gains of morality or at least docility against the dangers of faction and fanaticism, somewhat in the manner of Hume, whose *History of England* he quotes at some length (v.i.g.3–6). Reversing his stand against Dr Cullen, he comes out in favour of public examination and presumably certification of those wishing to practise the liberal professions, to maintain high standards of learning, since 'Science is the great antidote to the poison of enthusiasm and superstition; and where the superior ranks of people were secured from it, the inferior ranks could not be much exposed to it' (v.i.g.14).

The last chapters of book v deal, respectively, with taxation and public debt. Smith offers criticism of the existing revenue policy of Britain, and attends to the problem of smuggling. Also, he castigates Britain's incurrence of public debt to prosecute wars over colonies. For his peroration, Smith returns to the theme of the American crisis, building on the logic of his model of the freely competing, self-adjusting economic system, his historical surveys of growth, and the burden of his policy advice, to urge that legislators waken from the 'golden dream' of empire with which they have deluded themselves and the people, emancipate the colonies on the 'west side of the Atlantic', and 'endeavour to accommodate [Britain's] future views and designs to the real mediocrity of her circumstances' (v.iii.92).

Hume was entirely of Smith's opinion with respect to the American crisis, and he had written as follows to Strahan on 26 October 1775:

We hear that some of the Ministers have propos'd in Council, that both the Fleet and Army be withdrawn from America, and these Colonists be left entirely to themselves. I wish I had been a Member of His Majesty's Cabinet Council, that I might have seconded this Opinion. I shoud have said, that this Measure only anticipates the necessary Course of Events a few Years; that a forced and every day more precarious Monopoly of about 6 or 700,000 Pounds a year of Manufactures, was not worth contending for; that we shoud preserve the greater part of this Trade even if the ports of America were open to all Nations; that it is very likely, in our present method of proceeding, that we shoud be disappointed in our Scheme of conquering the Colonies; and that we ought to think beforehand how we are to govern them, after they were conquer'd. Arbitrary Power can extend its oppressive Arm to the Antipodes; but a limited Government can never long be upheld at a distance, even where no Disgusts have interven'd: Much less, where such violent Animosities have taken place.

Hume thought the necessary coercion would require an army of more than 30,000 men, and asked who would pay for this. The colonists could not at present after a devastating war, and Britain could not in the 'totally ruin'd State of our Finances'. The spirit of the Enlightenment breathes in Hume's conclusion: 'Let us, therefore, lay aside all Anger; shake hands, and part Friends. Of if we retain any anger, let it only be against ourselves for our past Folly.'

The spirit of the contemporary House of Commons breathed in one of its members, and Hume and Smith's own publisher, Strahan himself, who replied on 30 October:

I am entirely for coercive Methods with those obstinate madmen: and why should we despair of success? Why should we suffer the Empire to be so dismembered, without the utmost Exertions on our Part? I see nothing so very formidable in this Business, if we become a little more unanimous, and could stop the mouths of domestic Traitors, from whence all the Evil originated. Not that I wish to enslave the Colonists, or to make them one jot less happy than ourselves; but I am for keeping them subordinate to the British Legislature, and their Trade in a reasonable Degree, subservient to the Interest of the Mother Country; an advantage she well deserves, but which she must inevitably lose, if they are emancipated as you propose. (*HL* ii.300–1, and n. 1)

Hume in his private discourse and Smith in his public one had their work cut out to change minds so disposed. However, the march of events was on their side. North was depressed enough by the lack of success in America and the growing debt to tell the King in mid-1779 that the cost of the war exceeded its worth. Replying on 11 June, George III rejected this argument, stating it was 'only weighing such events in the scale of a tradesman behind his counter'. He countered with a version of the domino theory: loss of the American colonies would inevitably be followed by that of the remaining parts of the British Empire (quoted by Shy in Kurtz and Hutson, 1973: 140).

Hume's letter to Smith of 1 April 1776, congratulating him on the publication of *WN*, does not deal with its policy advice concerning American affairs. Perhaps he thought there was no need to declare in one way or another to Smith, as he had to Baron Mure of Caldwell on 27 October 1775: 'I am an American in my Principles, and wish we woud let them alone to govern or misgovern themselves as they think proper' (*HL* ii.303). Hume relates that the 'Perusal' of Smith's book has taken him from a 'State of great Anxiety'. He thinks the reading of it 'necessarily requires so much Attention, and the Public is disposed to give so little' that he will doubt for 'some time of its being at first very popular'. Then he gives his well-founded judgement about *WN*: 'But it has Depth and Solidity and Acuteness, and is so much illustrated by curious Facts, that it must at last take the public Attention.' Hume reckoned the book was 'probably much improved' by Smith's removal to London, but went on to mention some principles he would dispute with Smith if he had him at his fireside. One was the claim that the rent of farms made up part of the price of produce (see *WN* i.vi.8, qualified by i.xi.a.8). In Hume's opinion, the 'Price is determined altogether by the Quantity and Demand', a view that anticipates Ricardo's criticism of Smith in *The Principles of Political Economy and Taxation* (ch. 24). The other point Hume makes is that Smith must be wrong in alleging that the French king achieves a mark-up of 8 per cent in coining gold bullion. Smith was relying on a dictionary-type work of 1764—Bazinghen's *Traité des monnoies* (Mizuta), which cited an edict of 1726 (iv.vi.20)—but Garnier in his translation of *WN* (v.234) pointed out that this edict was in force a very short time, and the *seigneurage* had to come down. Hume hoped that such points could be discussed 'in Conversation' soon, 'For I am in a very bad State of Health and cannot afford a long Delay'.

His letter also mentions the publication of Gibbon's *Decline and Fall*. Hume wrote that he liked this book 'extremely', joked that, had he not been acquainted with Gibbon personally, he 'shoud never have expected such an excellent Work from the Pen of an Englishman'. Hume continued: 'It is lamentable to consider how much that Nation has declined in Literature during our time. I hope [Gibbon] did not take amiss the national Reflection' (*Corr.* No. 150). Smith was to give comparable praise to Gibbon, without innuendo, on the publication in 1788 of volumes iv, v, and vi of his elegiac epic: 'I cannot express to you the pleasure it gives me to find, that by the universal assent of every man of taste and learning, whom I either know or correspond with, it sets you at the very head of the whole literary tribe at present existing in Europe' (*Corr.* No. 283).

Writing to Smith on 3 April 1776, Hugh Blair expresses his sense of the magnitude of the achievement of *WN*. From what Smith had read to him 'some years ago', he had formed high expectations, but these had been exceeded: 'You have done great Service to the World by overturning all that interested Sophistry of Merchants, with which they had confounded the whole Subject of Commerce.' Blair considers that *WN* will become the 'Commercial Code of Nations', and that Europe has received no work since Montesquieu's *Esprit des lois* that 'tends so much to Enlarge and Rectify the ideas of mankind'. This statement leads to praise of the excellent arrangement of the book, with its chapters each paving the way for another, and the system gradually erecting itself. Since Blair was an expert on rhetoric and criticism, this is valuable comment, as is the commendation of the suitability of the style for the subject: 'clear and distinct to the last degree, full without being too much so, and as tercly as the Subject could admit', in short, the plain style Smith had long ago recommended to his countrymen. It carried Blair through some subjects that were certainly 'Dry', but he read the whole with 'avidity', and he took pleasure in the thought that he would give the book a 'Second and more deliberate perusal'.

As for the book's faults, Blair objects to the inclusion of the part about the 'measures we ought at present to take with respect to America', such as giving the colonists representation in Parliament (IV.vii.c.75–9). He wishes this had been omitted, because 'it is too much like a publication for the present moment', and he thinks that when the American crisis is over, these pages will be dropped or altered in 'Subsequent editions'; but meantime they will get into a French translation unless Smith writes to prevent this. Blair's concern is that Europe will read *WN* in French. He fears that Smith has 'raised up very formidable adversaries' by his chapters on the Universities and the Church (v.i.f and g), but he finds 'so much Sense and Truth' in Smith's doctrine, and it is so appropriate that this should be 'preached to the World', that he would have regretted the loss of this part of the book. It is not that he agrees entirely with Smith about the Church, for example, that 'Independency' is a viable alternative to a state religion. He reckons that the 'little Sects' of which Smith wrote would have 'Combined together into greater bodies, and done much Mischief to Society'. Rather curiously for a Church of Scotland minister, Blair expresses this criticism to Smith: 'you are, I think, too favourable by much to Presbytery. It connects the Teachers too closely with the People; and gives too much aid to that Austere System [of morality] you speak of, which is never favourable to the great improvements of mankind.' Behind this remark, however, is Blair's allegiance to the Moderate party of his Kirk rather than that of the High-flyers or evangelicals.

Smith had usefully distinguished between the 'austere system' of morality favoured by the 'common people' and the 'loose' or 'liberal' one adopted by people of fashion (v.i.g.10). Reviewing the history of various ecclesiastical orders, Smith judged that Episcopalian clergymen, including those in the Church of England, were respected by their superiors, but before their inferiors often could not defend 'their own sober and moderate doctrines' against the attacks of fanatics. Smith found more attractive the 'equality of authority' under Presbyterianism, and the 'independency of spirit' it bred, hence his conclusion: 'There is scarce perhaps to be found any where in Europe a more learned, decent, independent, and respectable set of men, than the greater part of the Presbyterian clergy of Holland, Geneva, Switzerland, and Scotland' (v.i.g.34, 37; Anderson, 1988).

Blair continues his letter by suggesting that Smith add an index to his book, and provide an overview at the beginning or end, expressing in 'short independent Propositions' what was 'handled and proved' in the order of treatment, 'like the Syllabus's we are in use to give of our College Lectures'. With appropriate page references, this feature would guide readers to what they wanted to find, and it would 'Exhibit a Scientifical View of the whole System; it would impress your Principles on our Memory'. After this suggestion, he has a comment on the good fortune of the season that has also brought Gibbon's 'Elegant and Masterly Book', though he adds: 'what the Deuce had he to do with Attacking Religion. It will both Clog his Work, and it is in itself Unhistorical and out of Place.' Clearly, he was bothered by the celebrated chapters 15 and 16 of *Decline and Fall*, whose handling of the progress of Christianity and the conduct of the Roman government towards the Christians aroused such heated controversy.

Finally, Blair passes to the melancholy subject of Hume's declining health: 'I dread, I dread—and I shudder at the prospect. We have suffered so much by the loss of Friends in our Circle here of late [Mure of Caldwell and Lord Alemore], that such a blow as that would be utterly overwhelming.' He expresses the hope, however, that Smith will settle in Edinburgh, a development that would clearly be of some consolation to the literati at this sad time for them (*Corr.* No. 151).

Another of the literati who congratulated Smith was Robertson the historian, writing on 8 April to give his views on *WN*. Like Blair, he commented on Smith's achievement in forming 'into a regular and complete system one of the most important and intricate parts of political science', and ventured the opinion that 'if the English be capable of extending their ideas beyond the narrow and illiberal arrangements introduced by the mercantile supporters of the Revolution, and countenanced by Locke and some of their favourite writers', then *WN* will bring about a 'total change' in economic policy and finance. Because he was at work on a *History of America*, he took a position quite different from that of Blair concerning book IV of *WN*:

I am happy to find my own ideas concerning the absurdity of the limitations upon Colony trade established much better than I could have done myself. I have now finished all my work, but what relates to the British Colonies, and in the present uncertain state into which they are thrown, I go on writing with hesitation.

If he did have some jealousy about Robertson's use of his ideas in the first volume of the *History of Charles V*, Smith may have read these words with a little heat. In the event, however, Robertson's publication of 1777 in eight volumes only dealt with the history of Spanish America, and his account of New England up to 1652 and of Virginia up to 1688 appeared in posthumous volumes ix and x, after their discovery by the author's son William in 1795. In his preface, he had promised that he would return to deal with the British colonies when the 'civil war with Great Britain terminated', and his failure to do so indicates an intellectual difficulty Smith was prepared to confront. Jeffery R. Smitten (1990) has argued that Robertson could not maintain the 'polite stance' of moderation and balance in dealing with the actual violent outcome of the American Revolution, and so he abandoned this project.

Reverting to Robertson's views on *WN*, we find that again like Blair he asked for an index, and also for 'what the Book-sellers call *Side-notes*, pointing out the progress of the subject in every paragraph' (*Corr.* No. 153). Edwin Cannan's edition of *WN* of 1904 finally provided this desirable second feature in the form of a 'marginal summary' of the text; in writing it Cannan professed that he 'felt like an architect commissioned to place a new building alongside some ancient masterpiece' (preface, p. vi).

Corresponding with Smith on 18 April, Adam Ferguson claimed that he had been so busy reading *WN*, and quoting and recommending it to students in his moral philosophy class, that he had no leisure to trouble his friend with letters. Like Blair, he referred to prior awareness of Smith's work, but his esteem has 'not a little increased' on further acquaintance: 'You are surely to reign alone on these subjects, to form the opinions, and I hope to govern at least the coming generations.' He warned Smith he need not expect the 'run of a novel, nor even of a true history', but prophesied that *WN* would have a 'steady and continuous sale, as long as people wish for information on these subjects'. He then teased Smith about his adversaries, among whom, on one issue at least, he had to include himself:

You have provoked, it is true, the church, the universities, and the merchants, against all of whom I am willing to take your part; but you have likewise provoked the militia, and there I must be against you. The gentlemen and peasants of this country do not need the authority of philosophers to make them supine and negligent of every resource they might have in themselves, in the case of certain extremities, of which the pressure, God knows, may be at no great distance. But of this more at Philippi.

Ferguson doubtless feared that the American conflict would widen into a European war, with a consequent need to defend Scotland's shores against a foreign invasion. Such an event almost came about when John Paul Jones, leading a Franco-American squadron in the *Bon homme Richard*, stood off Leith in September 1779, and Smith was on official duty as a Commissioner of Customs. Smith collected the mock-heroic poem of 1779, *Paul Jones: or the Fife Coast Garland* (Mizuta), which made fun of the sorry state of the home defences.

To conclude his letter, Ferguson got off his militia hobby-horse and touched on Hume's condition. He knew Smith had already heard from Black about this, and he reinforced the positive side of the physician's report: 'If anything in such a case could be agreeable, the easy and pleasant state of [Hume's] mind and spirits would be really so' (*Corr.* No. 154). But Smith must have appreciated that Hume was gravely ill and, despite his courage and steadiness of spirit, needed the solace of his friends' company.

17

Dialogue with a Dying Man

Since we must lose our friend [Hume] the most agreable thing that can happen is that he dyes [as] a man of sense ought to do.

At some time in April 1776, Joseph Black wrote congratulating Smith on the publication of *WN* but more particularly, as David Hume's physician, to acquaint Smith with the course of his friend's illness:

as I hear that you intend to Visit to this country, soon, I wish if possible to hasten your coming that he may have the Comfort of your Company so much the sooner. He has been declining several years and this in a Slow and gradual manner untill about a twelve month agoe Since which the progress of his Disorder has been more rapid. One of his Distresses has been a Sensation of excessive Heat cheifly in the nighttime . . . But there is another Disorder in his Constitution which is undermining him I am afraid in an irresistable manner. This is a Diarrhea with Colicy Pains attended with and I believe proceeding from an internal Haemorrage. . . . When the [diarrhoea] comes he passes a large quantity of blood which from its appearance and from the Seat of his Colicy pains must proceed from some of the higher parts of the intestines—he is greatly weakened and looks very ill after each discharge but recovers next day in some measure and enjoys upon the whole a Surprising degree of ease and good Spirits and takes a moderate quantity of food with appetite and relish. His mother he says had precisely the same constitution with himself and dyed of this very disorder, which has made him give up any hopes of his getting the better of it. (*Corr.* No. 152)

Black then asks Smith to acquaint their common friend, Sir John Pringle, with these details, to see if he had any advice to give. The consensus of modern medical opinion is that cancer of the large intestine was the likely cause of Hume's symptoms, with the further possibility that this was superimposed on chronic ulcerative colitis or regional enteritis (Doig, 1982; Wilkinson, 1988). Pringle meantime was urging Hume to come to London for further consultation and treatment. Hume added a codicil to his will on 15 April, in which he left bequests of £200 apiece to d'Alembert, Adam Ferguson, and Adam Smith—the original will of 4 January 1776 made Smith his literary executor. On 18 April Hume wrote his autobiographical testament, *My Own Life*, which declared: 'In spring 1775, I was struck with a Disorder in my Bowels, which at first gave me no Alarm, but has since, as I apprehend it, become mortal and incurable. I now reckon upon a speedy Dissolution.' Nevertheless, he set out for the south on 21 April, and two days afterwards, while he was resting in a Morpeth inn amid the ruined castles and attractive churches of Northumberland, a carriage drew up bringing the poet John Home and Adam Smith. They had set out together from London in response to Adam Ferguson's urgent message to John Home that David Hume was losing ground: 'I hope we shall see you *here soon*, and that your attentions will contribute to preserve what we can ill spare.'

After discussion among the friends, it was agreed that Smith would continue on to Kirkcaldy to be with his aged mother, and John Home would return with David to London. There Pringle decided that Hume suffered from a stricture in the colon, and that a course of Bath waters was likely to cure him. Another doctor at Bath, Dr John Gustard, decided Hume had a bilious complaint, then the anatomist John Hunter examined him and detected a 'Tumour or Swelling in my Liver', so the philosopher reported to his brother, diverted by the disagreement among the faculty about his illness (Pratt, 1777: 36–7). When the Bath waters proved harmful, Hume returned to Edinburgh via Buxton, and had a reunion dinner with his friends, in his home in St David's Street on 4 July, the momentous day on which the American Declaration of Independence was signed in Philadelphia.

Hume had written to Smith from London on 3 May to say he had found himself 'much recovered on the Road', and that he hoped the Bath waters and further journeys—Pringle was apparently suggesting that he go on to Buxton—might effect a cure. According to Hume, the 'Town [was] very full of [Smith's] Book, which [met] with general Approbation' (*Corr.* No. 156). The bluestocking Elizabeth Montagu received in London a letter written on 23 April by Hume's adversary, James Beattie. Though he had not yet read *WN*, he praised its author's capacity in dealing with politics and commerce. He said that he was once Smith's acquaintance, but since the publication of his *Essay on Truth* 'tout cela est changé', the implication being that Smith had cut Beattie dead because of his bias against Hume (San Marino, Calif., Huntington Lib., Montagu Corr., MO 480). Mrs Montagu had herself read *WN* and commented on it to Hugh Blair by 8 June, because he responded to her comments on that date: 'I heartily join in your wish, and would even convert it into a prayer, that the rulers of nations would listen to many of [Smith's] wise and salutary counsels' (MO 489).

The first paragraph of Hume's letter of 3 May referred to the charge he had given Smith to publish posthumously the *Dialogues concerning Natural Religion*. Hume wrote that he considered Smith's scruples groundless, and rather tactlessly invoked the example of Mallet publishing in 1754 the works of the deist Bolingbroke after his death, and still receiving patronage from George III and Bute. Smith may have been aware of the contemporary viewpoint, represented by Johnson's crushing denunciation of Bolingbroke: 'Sir, he was a scoundrel, and a coward: a scoundrel, for charging a blunderbuss against religion and morality;

a coward, because he had not resolution to fire it off himself, but left half a crown for a beggarly Scotchman, to draw the trigger after his death' (*BLJ* i.268, 269, n. 4). Hume's will of 4 January left Smith £200 as a 'small recompense of his pains in correcting and publishing the Dialogues', though Hume also said that he could 'trust to that intimate and sincere friendship, which has ever subsisted between us'. Enclosed with Hume's letter of 3 May was another ostensibly of the same date, leaving it to Smith's discretion when he would publish the *Dialogues*, or whether he would publish this work at all. Hume also mentioned that Smith would find among his papers a 'very inoffensive Piece, *My Own Life*', which he said he composed a few days before leaving Edinburgh, when he thought, as did all his friends, that his 'Life was despaired of' (*Corr.* No. 157, 156, n. 1). Hume reckoned there could be no objection to publishing this with any future edition of his works; but in adding to it his account of Hume's manner of dying, Smith was himself to create more controversy than anything caused by the *Dialogues*.

Though trusting in Smith's judgement as his literary executor, Hume was capable of finding and commenting on flaws in his friend's great book on the expressive side, apparently of a more serious nature than the relatively minor theoretical points he raised with Smith himself. This emerges in a letter to Hume from John Millar, undated but certainly written at this period. Millar begins: 'I am afraid your criticisms on Smith's Style are not altogether without foundation—tho' I think you rather severe.' On occasion, Hume would take refuge in commenting on an author's style when he did not wish to engage in controversy: this seems to have been the case when he was given an opportunity by Blair in 1763 to peruse the manuscript of Reid's *Inquiry into the Human Mind on the Principles of Common Sense*, which sought to refute his scepticism (*HL* i.375–6). At another time, in 1768, Hume can be found exercising a close watch over the style of a friend and rival for acclaim as a historian, Robertson, when he was given the sheets of the *History of Charles V* as they came off Strahan's press. Hume was to send them on to Suard to be translated into French, and his intent was to warn Robertson about bad writing habits so that his appeal to English readers would be greater, and there would be fewer problems for the French translator (*HL* ii.194). We may believe that Hume's concern for Smith's style was of a similar nature, and perhaps he hoped that Millar would pass on his hints to Smith.

Millar was himself not so concerned about Smith's style, which he considered as 'original' as the thought, with the one 'exceedingly well adapted to the other'. He was more exercised by Smith's 'positions'; he had difficulty in accepting many of them, and he was uncertain how far Smith wished to push some. One of these was Smith's 'great leading opinion—concerning the unbounded freedom of trade'. Millar expressed a desire to have Hume's viewpoint here, for he had only a vague notion of the truth of this 'opinion', and how far Smith meant that it ought to be carried. Millar conceded that rulers should be cautious about regulating trade, because they are usually bad judges of such matters; also trade regulations are not easily enforced, and the attempt to do so is expensive. Setting aside these considerations, he wondered if there were not some cases where control of trade might be proper. In his view, the point that had to be determined was where the interest of merchants and manufacturers might or might not coincide with that of the public. Millar had apparently not paid attention to Smith's 'invisible hand' argument. He then put the case of importation of wine being preferred by merchants over that of raw materials because of the profit factor. He thought that in this situation the government should certainly interfere. It had occurred to him, of course, that Smith made some exceptions himself when advocating generally the 'obvious and simple system of natural liberty', as in the case of 'infant manufactures' which needed some protection: *WN* i.457, n. 19 (NLS Hume MSS vi.38, old no.). Since Smith's advocacy of the principle that regulation distorted the 'natural balance of industry' went back to the time of the lectures on jurisprudence, when Millar was first his student at Glasgow and then his colleague, it is strange that he did not challenge Smith at first hand on this topic. It is clear, however, that he is raising with Hume some of the fundamental issues of Smith's system, especially to what extent questions of utility override the adherence to natural liberty in the economic sphere.

Having returned to his 'solitude' in Kirkcaldy, Smith was not apparently thinking about these issues, but continued to be preoccupied by the conflict in America, or so we apprehend from a letter to Strahan dated 6 June:

The American Campaign has begun awkwardly. I hope, I cannot say that I expect, it will end better. England, tho' in the present times it breeds men of great professional abilities in different ways, great Lawyers, great watch makers and Clockmakers, etc. etc., seems to breed neither Statesmen nor Generals. A letter from you, with your opinion upon the State of the times, will be a great comfort. (*Corr.* No. 158)

Smith's comparative estimate of ability is well directed. His English contemporaries included Blackstone, author of the celebrated *Commentaries on the Laws of England* (1765-9); Hardwicke, the Chancellor who did so much to make equity a scientific system; and Dunning, eloquent upholder of civil rights, whose help was secured in the affair of Ferguson's pension. Mansfield, the most effective advocate of his day, and builder as Lord Chief Justice of much of English commercial law, was a Scot by birth, and his decisions were seen by some as a threat to the English Constitution, because based on Scottish legal principles (Holdsworth, 1966: xii.237-95, 432-563, 705-24). The palm for making clocks and watches surely went to John Harrison, who died in 1776. With some help from a brother and then a son, he produced a series of chronometers and then a watch just over 5 in. in diameter, accurate enough to solve the outstanding problem of determining longitude at sea. It took personal intervention by the King and a petition to Parliament in 1773, supported by Burke and Fox among others, to obtain for Harrison the prize offered for this feat by the Board of

Longitude. Cook's explorations in the South Pacific from 1772 to 1775 were especially helped by Harrison's achievement, and a replica of his fourth chronometer was used to chart the coastlines of Australia and New Zealand with remarkable exactitude (Whitrow, 1988: 142–5).

As for the English statesmen and generals of the time, their sorry record in the American War of Independence speaks for itself. North may have had personal charm, but he was in a weak position as Government leader and was overawed by Lord George Germain (formerly Sackville), Secretary of State for America from 1775 to 1782, who drove on the war policy but had little control of the navy, and who quarrelled successively with the commanders-in-chief of the army, Carleton, Howe, and Burgoyne, and with most of his Cabinet colleagues (*HP* iii.395–6). Rockingham, the Opposition leader, aroused some admiration in Smith (*Corr.* No. 216), and he was notable for his political integrity and his moderation, which could restrain Fox's ardour and Burke's enthusiasm; but his health was poor, some alleged from venereal disease contracted in Italy in his youth, so there was never a great hope that he could form an effective alternative Administration (Wraxall, 1904: 472–4). The generals were no better than the statesmen. Carleton defended Quebec ably in the winter of 1775–6, but seemed incapable of taking the offensive, and had an unpleasant rigidity of manner which made co-operation with him difficult. In 1776 Burgoyne was put in command of the counter-offensive from Canada that was to link up with Howe's army advancing from New York, crush the American army in between, and shut off New England, regarded as the focus of the rebellion, from the other colonies. It is not certain what information Strahan or anyone in Parliament could have given Smith about this ambitious strategy. In the event, his pessimism about the 'American Campaign' proved well founded. Germain did not co-ordinate plans well with the separate commanders. Howe began his advance far too late, and Burgoyne, having miscalculated the strength of American resistance and of loyalist support, was trapped at Saratoga and surrendered there on 17 October 1777. This marked a turning-point in the war, for the Americans gained heart while the French, scenting an opportunity to get revenge for the defeat of the Seven Years War, contemplated entering this one in support of the Americans, and signed an alliance for this purpose on 1 May 1778. Meanwhile Tom Paine's pamphlet *Common Sense*, published in January 1776, won wide popular support for the cause of independence among the colonists; Jefferson expressed in memorable terms in the Declaration of Independence of 4 July the ideology of the Revolution and of republican government; and Washington in the course of 1776–8 made of the Continental army a formidable fighting force that checked and began gaining ascendancy over the British army under the dilatory Howe (Shy, 1973: 133–8; Wallis, 1975: 65–118).

Wedderburn wrote to Smith on 6 June, apparently responding to a letter from him the previous month consisting in part of 'Reflections . . . upon the bad advices from America'. A political ally of Germain's, and Solicitor-General still

under North, Wedderburn was in high feather because of the British successes
in Canada, and gave his own misreading of the American war, probably one that
was widespread in Britain:

I have a strong persuasion that in spite of our wretched Conduct, the mere force of government clumsily and unsteadily applied will beat down the more unsteady and unman-
ageable force of a democratical Rebellion. Fortune must be very adverse to us indeed, if
distraction, folly, Envy and Faction should not fight for, as well as against us. (*Corr.* No.
159)

Wedderburn went on to hint that he was considering taking an independent line
in Parliament, perhaps in concert with Smith's former student Henry Herbert,
whose wealth allowed him to remain free from party attachments and judge
issues on their merits. Like Herbert, Wedderburn became disenchanted with
North's conduct of the war. He intrigued against North and drafted proposals
for reconciliation with the Americans in 1776 and 1778. Perhaps his inclination
to seek peace was strengthened by the position paper on the American war which
he seems to have commissioned from Smith in the aftermath of the disaster at
Saratoga (*Corr.* app. B).

When news of Burgoyne's surrender eventually reached Britain, the Government felt the need to collect expert opinion. North wrote to the King on
4 December 1777:

[The] consequences of this most fatal event may be very important and serious and will
certainly require some material change of system. No time shall be lost, and no person
who can give good information left unconsulted in the present moment. (George III,
Corr., 1927, ii.504)

Wedderburn appears to have responded by securing 'Smiths Thoughts on the
State of the Contest with America, February 1778', a memorandum found
among his family papers so endorsed in his hand (Ann Arbor, Mich., William
L. Clements Lib., Rosslyn MSS). The document itself does not identify the
author by name, but he describes himself as a 'solitary philosopher', which was
certainly Smith's situation in late 1777, when he was living in Kirkcaldy, and
Hume's death in August, to anticipate that event, had left him no intimate friend
to tempt him to Edinburgh. Further, in vocabulary, phrasing, and sentence
structure, even to the characteristic placing of 'perhaps' to qualify cautiously
worded assertions, the document resembles *WN*, and it resumes the chief topics
of Smith's treatment in his book of American issues (parallels are extensively
reported in *WN*, e.g. at IV.vii.c.64 n. 52; cf. also the argument in *Corr.* No. 221).

The framework, however, is political advice rather than economic analysis.
Smith argues again that the best solution to the crisis would be a 'constitutional
union' of the mother country and the colonies, but realizes attitudes have hard-
ened so much that the time for this had passed. Franklin had raised this idea in
his Albany Plan of 1754, and as late as 1774 the first Continental Congress had

defeated Joseph Galloway's 'proposal for a grand legislative union' by only a very few votes (Skinner, 1990: 155–9). After Bunker Hill and the failed attempt to isolate New England ending in the Saratoga disaster, however, Smith holds that the 'ulcerated minds' of the Americans would likely prevent them from agreeing to any union, 'even upon the most advantageous terms'. He continues with the thought that one or two more successful British campaigns 'might perhaps bring [the Americans] to think more soberly upon the subject of their dispute with the mother country'. But this is no more likely than complete military victory for the British and the restoration of the old colonial system. Another possibility is granting the Americans their independence; but this would be too humiliating for the British people to swallow, though it would deliver their country from the enormous expense of maintaining authority by military force within America, and of defending the trade monopoly by naval strength.

The most likely outcome, in Smith's view, is also the worst: retention of part of America, and surrender of the other colonies, 'after a long, expensive and ruinous war'. Smith is not above a hint of *Realpolitik* in his advice, since he suggests that, to secure the independent Americans as allies, Britain should return Canada to the French and the Floridas to Spain. This plan is to be found in Johnson's pamphlet *Taxation No Tyranny* (1775), and a reporter of conversations with Smith in 1780 alleged that he spoke highly of Johnson's political pamphlets, though he was 'averse to the contest with America' (*LRBL* 228), which Johnson discusses with some truculence in the *Taxation* pamphlet. Boswell believed that Johnson was offended by Americans calling for liberty when they maintained the slavery of blacks (*BLJ* ii.312–13, 476–7).

We have no indication how Wedderburn received Smith's advice, but the Government in the main pursued the 'system' of military conquest until the surrender of Cornwallis at Yorktown in 1781, which was followed by the aftermath to the war predicted by Smith's memorandum. Wedderburn was not predisposed by the memorandum, apparently, to favour union with Ireland when rebellion was a possibility there in 1800, and he sought to prejudice George III against this measure, on the ground that it would lead to Catholic emancipation. Nevertheless, another scholar of Smith's, William Pitt the Younger, won the day for constitutional union with Ireland, and there is reason to think he had read *WN* with some care.

Wedderburn's letter of 6 June 1776 to Smith includes a discussion of a recent visit to Paris which had brought him into contact with some of Smith's 'French friends'. He named Suard, translator of Hume and Robertson, whom Smith probably met at d'Holbach's dinners, for he was one of the Baron's coterie. Wedderburn also met Necker, the Swiss banker who was to last as Louis XVI's finance minister from 1776 until 1781, and then to return for a tumultuous year on the eve of the French Revolution. Smith may have met Necker at the austere salon conducted by his wife with the help of Morellet. Sir James Mackintosh was later to claim that Smith came to be on intimate terms with Necker, but that he had a low opinion of the minister's talents. He did adopt from Necker's *Essai sur la législation et le commerce des grains* (1775) an estimate of the French population (*WN* v.ii.k.78), but he did not comment on its policy arguments aimed at refuting Turgot's advocacy of a free trade in grains. According to Mackintosh again, Smith predicted that Necker's political stock would fall as soon as he met a serious challenge, and he always ended discussion about him with the emphatic verdict: 'He is a mere man of detail' (Rae, 1965: 206). Modern assessment is not so dismissive (Egret, 1975; Harris, 1979—based on examination of the Necker papers, Château de Coppet, Switzerland; Schama, 1989: 88–95, 283–4, 372–7).

Showing his own familiarity with *WN*, Wedderburn was rather hard on Necker, and indicated that he was not likely to be converted to Smith's doctrines from his mercantilism:

Necker's conversation shows that he is very rich and accustomed to be heard with complaisance. I did not take him to be very profound even in the Subjects he has had the greatest opportunity of knowing. He seems to think that a Book of rates is a good method of augmenting the industry of a Country, a Great quantity of Coin the certain proof of Wealth, and that a nation is the poorer for all the manufactures bought of foreigners. He will not be a Convert to your System, for he is in possession of three or four terms that are too much use in all his arguments to be easily dropped and that you do not much employ. Corn is with him La Matiere premiere, Coin, Le Tresor Publique, and by a dextrous application of the various literal and figurative senses of these phrases, he is very successful in every argument.

Wedderburn declares himself unlucky in not meeting Mme Necker—Suzanne Curchod, who had captivated Gibbon. He then ends with a reference to a 'very chearfull Letter from D. Hume' (*Corr.* No. 159).

But the news about Hume sent to Smith by Strahan on 10 June was far from cheerful. The good symptoms that ensued after a first trial of the Bath waters had vanished, and his 'Distemper [had] returned with its usual Violence', so he now intended to go to Buxton, a spa in Derbyshire. Strahan expressed the great concern he felt for Hume, and how he was struck by his 'Magnanimity and Resignation'. Hume had given Strahan his instructions about the *Dialogues concerning Natural Religion* and the posthumous publication of an edition of his works. These appeared in 1777 as *Essays and Treatises on Several Subjects*, with an Advertisement disowning the *Treatise of Human Nature* (see *HL* ii.301). Strahan told Smith that Hume's instructions 'shall be duly attended to and religiously observed'. He also sought to counter his 'melancholy Account' of Hume with better news from America, somewhat in line with Wedderburn's, dealing with the repulse of the Americans besieging Quebec, and Burgoyne's arrival there, also the havoc the navy was wreaking on American merchant shipping. He thought, as did many MPs, that British military strength would wear out the Americans; he also hoped that Carleton would 'prove an Exception to [Smith's] general Maxim with regard to the Characters of the Age' (*Corr.* No. 160).

Next we have a letter from Smith to Hume dated 16 June, in which he expresses scepticism about the effects of mineral waters, either at Bath or Buxton. He thinks Hume has benefited from the medicine of 'travelling and change of air', and perhaps recalling the regimen that Dr Cullen prescribed for him in July 1760, the 500-mile horseback ride to preserve his life (*Corr.* No. 51), he gives his friend the following advice:

spend the summer in Sauntering thro all the different corners of England without halting above two or three nights in any one place. If before the month of October you do not find yourself thoroughly re'established, you may think of changing this cold climate for a better, and of visiting the venerable remains of ancient and modern arts that are to be seen about Rome and the Kingdom of Naples. A mineral water is as much a drug as any that comes out of the Apothecaries Shop. It produces the same violent effects upon the Body. It occasions a real disease, tho' but a transitory one, over and above that which nature occasions. If the new disease is not so hostile to the old one as to contribute to expell it, it necessarily weakens the Power which nature might otherwise have to expel it. Change of air and moderate exercise occasion no new disease: they only moderate the hurtful effects of any lingering disease which may be lurking in the constitution; and thereby preserve the body in as good order as it is capable of being during the continuance of that morbid state. They do not weaken, but invigorate the power of Nature to expel the disease.

Hume confessed to Strahan that he arrived back in Edinburgh in July, 'in a very shattered Condition: The Motion of the Chaise, especially during the last days, made me suffer very much, and my Physicians are now of Opinion (which was always my Sentiment) that all Exercise is hurtful to me' (*HL* ii.329). He had already informed Smith that he was 'mortally sick at Sea' (*Corr.* No. 121). It is likely, therefore, that he would be as sceptical about Smith's prescription as his correspondent was about those of the medical faculty. Hume might recognize in it, however, the kind of Stoic natural law thinking that Smith had applied in diagnosing the economic ills of the body politic, and suggesting a cure for them: avoid violent government interventions and let nature take its course. From wisdom of this sort, Smith passed to an assurance to Hume that, if he had the misfortune to survive him, he would take 'every possible measure' to preserve his literary remains according to his wishes, and he added a postscript that he was to go to Edinburgh for some weeks (*Corr.* No. 161).

But did Hume ever receive this letter? In another one to Strahan from Edinburgh dated 6 July, Smith says that Hume had not done so, also that he thought Hume was taking his 'supposed neglect unkindly'. He appears to have seen Hume recently, perhaps at the farewell dinner on 4 July, and conceded his 'strength . . . is a good deal wasted so that he cannot now bear the jolting of a Post chaise upon our rough roads'. Accordingly, we hear no more of sauntering over the country, or of a journey to Italy (*Corr.* No. 162). By 16 July Hume's physicians had agreed to his 'Suspension of Exercise', and Smith joked with him about the application of another favourite philosophical principle. The sick man could see from his windows in St David Street that it was 'fine dry airy weather' outside, suitable for haymaking, and he wrote to the poet John Home:

instead of grudging that I cannot partake, directly, of this great Pleasure; Mr Smith tells me, that I ought to enjoy [the weather] by Sympathy, which I endeavour to do. It is by Sympathy only I can partake of a Dinner which Ferguson gives to several of our friends to day . . . (EUL Dk 6.27/3; Streminger, 1994: 651)

On August 14, when Smith writes again to Wedderburn from Kirkcaldy, it seems that Hume got over his feelings about Smith's 'supposed neglect', and Smith had been staying with him in Edinburgh. In this text we get details that Smith was to expand on, and some remarks that he was to censor, in the letter of 9 November to Strahan which went over the same ground of Hume's final illness, and which was to be printed with *My Own Life* in 1777. One remark reveals unequivocally that there was to be no deathbed conversion or recantation by Hume of his philosophical principles, such as Boswell hoped for when he called to see Hume on 8 August and 'contrived to get the subject of Immortality introduced', to which Hume replied that, 'it was a most unreasonable fancy that we should exist for ever' (Boswell, *BP* xii.227–32). Smith's sentence to Wedderburn ran:

Poor David Hume is dying very fast, but with great chearfulness and good humour and with more real resignation to the necessary course of things, than any whining Christian ever dyed with pretended resignation to the will of God.

Perhaps this is Smith's retort to the anecdote recounted of Addison, that on his deathbed he thus addressed his dissolute young stepson, Lord Warwick: 'I have sent for you, that you may see how a Christian can die.'[1]

Smith told Wedderburn that he had been with Hume on Thursday 8 August, and he was shown a letter from an old friend, Col. Edmonstoune, bidding Hume an 'eternal adieu'. Smith had alleged to Hume that his spirits were so very good, that his disease might take a turn for the better. Hume countered:

Smith, your hopes are groundless. . . . When I rise in the morning I find myself weaker than when I went to bed at night, and when I go to bed at night weaker than when I rose in the morning, so that in a few days I trust the business will be over.

Smith said then that Hume had the comfort of thinking that he had left all his 'friends' (Scots for 'kin') prosperous, particularly his brother's family, who would benefit from his will. Hume replied that they were well off independent of him, and then continued:

I so far agree with you, that when I was lately reading the dialogues of Lucian [his favourite author, according to Morellet, *HL* ii.157, n. 1] in which he represents one Ghost as pleading for a short delay until he should marry a young daughter, another till he should finish a house he had begun, a third till he had provided a portion for two or three young Children, I began to think what Excuse I could alledge to Charon in order to procure a short delay, and as I have now done everything that I ever intended to do, I acknowledge that for some time no tolerable one occurred to me; at last I thought I might say, Good Charon, I have been endeavouring to open the eyes of the people; have a little patience only till I have the pleasure of seeing the churches shut up, and the Clergy sent about their business; but Charon would reply, O you loitering rogue; that wont happen these two hundred years; do you fancy I will give you a lease for so long a time? Get into the boat this instant.

For Wedderburn's benefit Smith added the thought that, since they had to lose their friend, 'the most agreable thing that can happen is that he dyes [as] a man of sense ought to do'. Smith then reported that he had left Edinburgh until Hume should recall him, since Hume was so weak that even Smith's company tired him, and he was in such good spirits that he could not help talking 'incessantly' with visitors. When he was alone, Hume diverted himself with correcting his works and 'all ordinary amusements' (*Corr.* No. 163). One of these was reading the recently published *Philosophy of Rhetoric* by George Campbell (Mossner, 1980: 597), in which Smith told Strahan he found 'good sense, and learning, and philosophy', but he thought it 'so unfashioned' that he did not believe the bookseller would be a great gainer by it (*Corr.* No. 162).

Smith had a letter from Joseph Black written on 15 August mentioning that Hume had been 'much shocked' with the appearance of his dissipated nephew Joseph Home, a lieutenant in the Dragoon Guards, and fatigued by the 'Stir and Noise' the young man caused living in his house for nine days. Hume's disease had become worse, but he was more at ease again (*Corr.* No. 164). Hume wrote himself the same day about the disposition of manuscripts of the *Dialogues concerning Natural Religion*, and he asked Smith to accept the property of the copy if the book was not published within five years of his death. Since he knew that his friend was concerned about the content of the *Dialogues*, he sought to remind Smith of their literary quality: 'On revising them (which I have not done these 15 Years) I find that nothing can be more cautiously and artfully written. You had certainly forgotten them.' Hume asked for an answer 'soon', well knowing his friend's dilatory habits: 'My State of Health does not permit me to wait Months for it' (*Corr.* No. 165).

By a 'strange blunder', as Hume called it (*Corr.* No. 168), the above letter was sent by carrier, and Smith did not receive it until 22 August, when he wrote immediately to Hume expressing willingness to receive and preserve carefully the manuscript of the *Dialogues*. He remained unwilling to commit himself to publishing the *Dialogues* if Strahan had not done so within five years. He reckoned there was no probability of Strahan delaying publication; but if anything would impel delay, it would be a clause threatening Strahan with loss of the property after five years, which would give him an 'honourable pretence' for not publishing the *Dialogues*. Smith then made out that he would be put in an invidious position: 'It would then be said that I had published, for the sake of an Emolument, not from respect to the memory of my friend, what even a printer for the sake of the same emolument had not published.' Seeking to reassure Hume of Strahan's intentions about acceding to Hume's wishes, Smith enclosed a copy of the publisher's letter of 10 June (*Corr.* No. 160).

Smith then offered to add a 'few lines' to Hume's *Life*—describing Hume's behaviour in his illness if, unhappily, it should prove his last. Smith mentioned that some account of Hume's last conversations with him, particularly the excuses given to Charon, would 'make no disagreeable part of the history'. Smith appreciated that the reading public would be extremely interested in the 'infidel' Hume's own statement about the course of his life, and the principles he had upheld in it; thus it would be fitting to have the close of that life treated in the same philosophical manner. Smith also offered to correct the sheets of the new edition of Hume's works, and to do so in London, where he expected to be 'this winter'. He said he wrote all this on the supposition that the outcome of Hume's disease would be different from his hopes, which were still sanguine. Even the 'cool and steady Dr Black' was not averse to these same hopes. Finally, Smith repeated his willingness to come over from Kirkcaldy whenever Hume wished to see him' (*Corr.* No. 166). There is no question of the deep affection and respect Smith felt for his 'dearest friend', but his unwillingness to oversee the publication of the *Dialogues* must have troubled Hume on his deathbed (Campbell and Ross, 1982).

Black wrote that same day, 22 August, with news of Hume's further decline (*Corr.* No. 167). He was seeing very few people, and amusing himself with reading, perhaps as on the last journey to England 'chiefly in the classics' (Mossner, 1980: 594). Hume's last letter to Smith, and the last he seems to have composed, was written on Friday 23 August; he was so weak by this time it had to be done by the hand of his nephew and heir, David Hume the Younger. He said that he had every confidence in Strahan, but he had decided to leave the property of the *Dialogues* to his nephew David, if Strahan did not publish them within three years of his death. He had accepted that Smith was not to take on this duty. Next, he gave Smith permission to make the additions he pleased to his *Life*, and then he wrote: 'I go very fast to decline, and last night had a small fever, which I hoped might put a quicker period to this tedious Illness, but unluckily it has in a great measure gone of.' Ever considerate, he did not ask Smith to come to Edinburgh, because he would be able to see him only a small part of the day, but he left it to Black to inform Smith about the degree of strength that might remain with him. With that message, he bade his friend 'adieu' (*Corr.* No. 168). The next news Smith had was in a letter from Black, written on Monday 26 August, to say that Hume had died the previous day about four o'clock in the afternoon:

He continued to the last perfectly sensible and free from much pain or feelings of distress. He never dropped the smallest expression of impatience but when he had occasion to speak to the people about him always did it with affection and tenderness. I thought it improper to bring you over, especially as I heard that he had dictated a letter to you

. . . desiring you not to come. When he became very weak it cost him an effort to speak and he died in such a happy composure of mind that nothing could have made it better. (*Corr.* No. 169)

The funeral of Hume took place in pouring rain on Thursday, 29 August when, in the presence of a large crowd, the coffin was conveyed from St David's Street to the Old Calton Burying Ground. We do not know if Smith attended, but it is likely enough, because he wrote a letter from Dalkeith House two days later, where he had accompanied the Duke of Buccleuch. In this letter, addressed to John Home of Ninewells, David's elder brother, Smith renounced his legacy of £200, no doubt in view of his desire not to be connected with the publication of the *Dialogues* (*Corr.* No. 170). Writing on 2 September, John Home would not accept this gesture, stating to Smith that it was a testimony of his brother's friendship. He mentioned that copies of the *Dialogues* were completed, also of his brother's autobiography, and he would make them available to Smith, to add to *My Own Life*, and to correct the *Dialogues* as he saw fit. In addition, Smith was to receive the copy of the new edition of Hume's works which he had volunteered to correct (*Corr.* No. 171).

Smith went over the ground of all this and his exchanges about the *Dialogues* with Hume in a letter to Strahan dated 5 September, emphasizing that *My Own Life* with the addition of his account of Hume's death should be published separately from the *Dialogues*, and prefixed to the next edition of Hume's former works, 'upon which he has made many very proper corrections, chiefly in what concerns language'. Smith then promised to be in London by the beginning of November, if his mother's health permitted, and to attend then to the revision of proofs of Hume's works, also to authenticate Hume's last corrections, if publication of the edition should be in progress (*Corr.* No. 172). Strahan acknowledged this letter on 16 September, and in his turn promised to do nothing about the *Dialogues* until he had given them a 'very attentive perusal'. He was clearly somewhat mystified by Smith's coyness about the *Dialogues*, and mentioned that Hume had written him to say, '*there is nothing in them worse than what I have already published*, or Words to that Effect' (*Corr.* No. 173).

Smith finally got to London in mid-January 1777 and remained there until June (*Corr.*, app. E, o). A first duty was to write to Governor Thomas Pownall to thank him for his published *Letter* of 25 September 1776, which expressed some highly interesting points of criticism of *WN* (*Corr.* app. A). Smith also became 'intangled' again, as has been related above, in the 'disagreeable affairs' of Ferguson concerning his annuity from Lord Chesterfield. This brought him into the company of the Stanhope family, the MPs Sir George Savile and John Hewett, and the Solicitor-General, Alexander Wedderburn. On 14 March we hear of Smith attending a meeting of The Club when Fox was in the chair, and the others attending included Burke, Dr George Fordyce, Garrick, Gibbon, Johnson, and Reynolds (Leslie and Taylor, 1865: ii.199). There seems to be no record of the conversation, but the old animosity between Smith and Johnson may have been under the surface, perhaps stirred up by the 'Letter to Strahan' ostensibly of 9 November 1776, about the death of Hume (*Corr.* No. 178), which was published in the *Scots Magazine* in January 1777 (39: 5–7), and with *My Own Life* in February (Todd, 1974: 202). At any rate, Johnson wrote to Boswell on 11 March:

It is proposed to augment our club from twenty to thirty, of which I am glad; for as we have several in it whom I do not much like to consort with, I am for reducing it to a mere miscellaneous collection of conspicuous men, without any determinate character. (*BLJ* iii.106)

As for other activities of Smith of this period in London, it is to be presumed that he carried out his promise to correct Hume's works for the 'New Edition' of 1777, and we can be sure he was at work on the correction for the second edition of *WN* which was published in 1778. This can be deduced from the concluding paragraph of his letter from Kirkcaldy of 27 October to Strahan, in which he writes of sending a week ago a 'very important cancel' to Andrew Strahan, dealing with a 'very great inconsistency between some of the new corrections and a part of the old text as it stood before'. Smith says that he will be anxious until he hears that Andrew, who worked in the printing-house, 'has received [the cancel] and has executed it with his usual attention', which makes it appear that printing the new edition had been in progress for some time before he had left for Scotland (*Corr.* No. 184).

In the course of 1777, the monument for which Hume left £100 in his will was built in the Old Calton Burying Ground to a design by Robert Adam. The preliminary sketches reveal that the conception began with Theodoric's tomb at Ravenna, and yielded a strong Roman tower of rough ashlar, with a fluted frieze on the lower stage, a Doric entablature on the upper, and a large urn over the door (Gifford *et al.*, 1988: 438). Later, Smith commented: 'I don't like that monument. It is the greatest piece of vanity I ever saw in my friend Hume' (Mossner, 1980: 591). His own monument in the Canongate kirkyard, also designed by Robert Adam, is much simpler: a wall-tablet set in a round-arched recess with fluted spandrels, and a keyblock carved with the bearded head of a classical philosopher (*Book of the Old Edinburgh Club: 1924*: 16–17; Gifford *et al.*, 1988: 150). The tablet bears the stark details of Smith's name, the titles of his two great books, and the dates of his birth and death.

For Hume, Smith composed a monument in words, taking the form of an account of his friend's last illness and, as we have mentioned, meant to be an addition to Hume's text, *My Own Life*. He completed this by 7 October 1776 and sent it to Hume's brother John for his remarks (*Corr.* No. 175), also to Black, who was expected to collect the further remarks of John Home the poet and other friends (*Corr.* No. 177B). Smith felt there was a 'propriety in addressing it as a letter to Mr Strahan', because Hume had left him the care of his works (*Corr.* No. 175). When he received it, Strahan liked it 'exceedingly', but thought it too short together with Hume's *Life* to 'make a Volume even of the *smallest Size*', and wished to annex some letters Hume had sent to him on political subjects (*Corr.* No. 180). Predictably, Smith scotched this scheme: 'Nothing has contributed so much to sink the value of Swifts works as the undistinguished publication of his letters; and be assured that your publication [of Hume's letters], however select, would soon be followed by an undistinguished one' (*Corr.* No. 181). He suggested that Hume's *Life* and his letter to Strahan, which he dated 9 November 1776, would make a small pamphlet, and this is how it was issued in 1777 (*Corr.* No. 178).

The letter takes up where *My Own Life* ends, with Hume's journey to England in quest of health. Smith sticks to his viewpoint that 'exercise and change of air' benefited Hume when travelling, and he gives an engaging picture of Hume back in Edinburgh following the journey, much weaker but cheerful, and diverting himself with correcting his works for a new edition, reading books of amusement, conversing with friends, and 'sometimes in the evening, with a party at his favourite game whist'. A doctor is so impressed with Hume's imperturbability that he offers to tell a friend the philosopher is recovering, and in reply we have a characteristic Humean flash of humour: 'as I believe you would not chuse to tell anything but the truth, you had better tell him, that I am dying as fast as my enemies, if I have any, could wish, and as easily and cheerfully as my best friends could desire.'

Adam Smith visits Hume as he is reading the letter from Col. Edmonstoune bidding him eternal adieu, and 'applying to him, as to a dying man, the beautiful French verses in which the Abbé Chaulieu, in expectation of his own death, laments his approaching separation, from his friend, the Marquis de la Fare'. It is a very nice touch of the cosmopolitan culture of the Scottish Enlightenment, and a reminder of Hume's own appreciation of France, where in youth he went to cultivate the art of living. Now, he practises the art of dying. Smith, too, hopes for recovery, but Hume provides the grim facts about the 'habitual diarrhoea of more than a year's standing' which progressively weakens him. There follows the amusing parody of Lucian's *Dialogues of the Dead*, applied to Hume's case, but lacking the phrase found in the letter to Wedderburn, about wishing to see the 'churches shut up, and the Clergy sent about their business'. For public inspection, Smith substitutes the generalized form, 'seeing the downfal of the prevailing systems of superstition'. Smith could have spared himself his modifications, for his letter as it stood stirred up the zealots from the Royal Chaplain George Horne, with his orthodox Christian animosity, to the minor poet William Julius Mickle, who bore several grudges against Smith as well the cross of his religious feelings (Viner, 1965: 70–4).

Smith's letter of 9 November continues with the account of his last parting from Hume, brought about because the exertion of talking wearied the dying man so much. We then have Black's letter of 22 August about his patient's further weakness and yet tranquillity; Hume's of 23 August: 'I go very fast to decline . . .'; and then Black's letter of 26 August, describing the actual death. Next comes the last paragraph, which is a beautifully flighted piece of prose, perhaps the best Smith ever wrote.

Various feelings have been detected behind the 'Letter to Strahan'. Ernest Mossner found anxiety over Hume's resolve to have the threatening *Dialogues* published, and guilt over denying a deathbed wish, but also courage in proclaiming what Hume meant to Smith and his friends (1980: 605). David Raphael has alerted us to phrasing that recalls the *Phaedo* (*TMS* 401), and the praise of Socrates in the last sentence of Plato's dialogue: 'that of all the men of his time whom I have known, he was the wisest and justest, and best' (Benjamin Jowett's translation). We may find in the deft word choice, the sure cadences, and the rounded periods the recognition that Smith met and rejoiced to know in Hume the fulfilment of the ideals of his moral philosophy:

His temper, indeed, seemed to be more happily balanced, if I may be allowed such an expression, than that perhaps of any other man I have ever known. Even in the lowest state of his fortune, his great and necessary frugality never hindered him from exercising, upon proper occasions, acts both of charity and generosity. It was a frugality founded, not upon avarice, but upon the love of independency. The extreme gentleness of his nature never weakened either the firmness of his mind, or the steadiness of his resolutions. His constant pleasantry was the genuine effusion of good-nature and good-humour, tempered with delicacy and modesty, and without even the slightest tincture of malignity, so frequently the disagreeable source of what is called wit in other men. It never was the meaning of his raillery to mortify; and therefore, far from offending, it seldom failed to please and delight, even those who were the objects of it. To his friends, who were frequently the objects of it, there was not perhaps any one of all his great and amiable qualities, which contributed more to endear his conversation. And that gaiety of temper, so agreeable in society, but which is so often accompanied with frivolous and superficial qualities, was in him certainly attended with the most severe application, the most extensive learning, the greatest depth of thought, and a capacity in every respect the most comprehensive. Upon the whole, I have always considered him, both in his lifetime and since his death, as approaching as nearly to the idea of a perfectly wise and virtuous man, as perhaps the nature of human frailty will permit.

18

Settlement in Edinburgh

I was informed that a place of Commissioner of Customs in Scotland had been
given to a Philosopher who for his own glory and for the benefit of mankind
had enlightened the world by the most profound and systematic treatise on the
great objects of trade and revenue which had ever been published in any age or
any Country.

Thus Gibbon greeted the news which reached him in London in November 1777
(*Corr.* No. 187). Smith's own account of his life in the aftermath of the publication of *WN*, and the turn of events that took him from solitude in Kirkcaldy
to a busy life in Edinburgh as a Customs Commissioner, runs as follows:

I had returned to my old retirement in Kirkcaldy and was employing in writing another
Work concerning the Imitative Arts, when by the interest of the Duke of Buccleuch, I
was appointed to my present Office; which though it requires a good deal of attendance
is both easy and honourable. (*Corr.* No. 208)

He had anticipated, apparently, concentrating on part of that 'Philosophical
History of all the different branches of Literature, of Philosophy, Poetry, and
Eloquence', one of the 'two great works' which he indicated in 1785 he still had
'upon the anvil' (*Corr.* No. 248). But the people above him had other views.

The family connection with the Custom-house may have suggested to members of Lord North's Administration, including Wedderburn, and Henry
Dundas, who had become Lord Advocate in 1775 and thus chief controller of
patronage in Scotland, that Smith could be provided for, and his bent for economic affairs utilized in the revenue service. Through these friends in high
places, he became one of the five 'Commissioners for Managing and Causing to
be Levied and Collected His Majesty's Customs, and Subsidies and other Duties
in that part of Great Britain called Scotland, and also the Duties of the Excise
upon all Salt and Rock Salt Imported . . . into . . . Scotland', as they were styled
in official documents.

Smith had proved himself an able administrator at Glasgow University, and
he had a strong sense of duty, so it is entirely understandable that he would
respond positively to an overture about such a position, especially if assured of
the backing of Buccleuch, his former pupil, who also exercised considerable
patronage in Scotland. It is possible, too, that structure in his life from official

routine appealed to Smith, helping him combat hypochondriasis (Barfoot, 1991: 211). Also, the prospect of removal to Edinburgh and nearness to his friends among the literati must have been attractive, however much he had resisted the blandishments of Hume on that score during the years of his intense involvement in composing *WN*. Hugh Blair hoped Smith would be appointed to one of the Edinburgh Boards after *WN* was published, and wrote that the literati there 'flattered our Selves with the prospect of your Settling among us' (*Corr.* No. 151).

Financial inducement could not have been a strong factor. Smith offered to give up the pension of £300 he held from Buccleuch on receiving the Customs appointment, a gesture which was not accepted:

his Grace sent me word by his Cashier, to whom I had offered to deliver up his bond, that though I had considered what was fit for my own honour, I had not consider'd what was fit for his; and that he would never suffer it to be suspected that he had procured an office for a friend, in order to relieve himself from the burden of such an annuity. (*Corr.* No. 208)

Thus Smith retained the pension of £300 and a salary amounting to £600, the Commissionership of Customs earning him £500 and that of Salt Duties £100; but he gave away a great deal of his money in friendly and, for the most part, secret help to others (Stewart v.4 n.).

Following the death in 1777 of Archibald Menzies, one of the Commissioners, Smith announced his candidacy to Strahan on 27 October 1777, and asked him to find out how matters stood at the Treasury Board, claiming, however: 'I am not apt to be over-sanguine in my expectations; and my mind has not upon the present occasion, lost its usual temper' (*Corr.* No. 184). The Duchess of Buccleuch took up his cause, writing a note which Wedderburn 'immediately conveyed to Lord North', reporting to Smith on 30 October he was convinced this 'had its full effect'. Wedderburn also commented on Smith and his servant warning off a highwayman (*Corr.* No. 185). The assistance of Sir Grey Cooper, Secretary to the Treasury, had also been secured, and he wrote a joshing letter on 7 November stating that Smith's merit was so well known to Lord North and to 'all the world' that the position he sought, apparently with some diffidence, would soon be his (*Corr.* No. 186). The required fees of £147 18s. were paid by Strahan or his agent in due course. The Letters Patent for Smith's Commission were granted on 24 January 1778, and the appointment was published in the *London Gazette* five days later. In the interim, Smith was guilty of an uncharacteristic 'sally of bad humour' directed at Strahan, which was forgiven him, but which suggests he was more anxious over the appointment than he led others to believe (*Corr.* No. 192).

In gratitude to the Administration, Smith caused to be sent to North and Cooper 'handsomely bound and guilt [*sic*]' copies of edition 2 (1778) of *WN*. Before receiving his gift, North may even have read *WN* or discussed it with those who had, since the 1777 budget measures included a tax on the rentable value of houses, imposed 'nearly upon the . . . principles' of *WN*, as a note to the second edition made clear (v.ii.e.8 n.) For his part, North acknowledged in his budget speech of 1777 that Smith provided support for the added impositions in *WN* (Cobbett and Hansard, 1814: xix.214–19; Ehrman, 1969: i.249). Smith kept track of what was happening in budget measures, and observed, elsewhere in the second edition, that a new tax on menservants fell heaviest on the middling rank (v.ii.g.12). On 28 November 1778 a correspondent described a conversation with the Prime Minister, and stated Smith had 'awaked some new Ideas about improving the Revenue. For [North] said the absurdity of enforcing the prevention of Contraband Trade in America was evinced from the Difficulties of it in the faithful Kingdom of Scotland, as appeared by late Representations' (*Corr.* No. 197). This could be an allusion to a passage in *WN* in which Smith assesses the problem of smuggling in the 'thinly populated countries', Scotland and America (v.iii.77). North also paid heed in his budget of 1778 to Smith's advice that the 'opportunities and the temptation to smuggle' might be reduced by raising the duties on malt and lowering those on the distillery. Smith, of course, had to face the practical problems of trying to control smuggling as a Commissioner of Customs, no small task when it was understood that even under his nose in Edinburgh there were eight licensed and 400 illicit whisky stills (Daiches, 1969: 33; Williams, 1959: chs. 4, 5).

On accepting his appointment, Smith moved his household to Panmure House, the town residence of a prominent Forfarshire landed family forced to lay out nearly £50,000 in 1764 to recover the estates forfeited after the 1715 Jacobite rising (*HP* iii.121). The building, which is still standing, is a plain, L-shaped rubble building, with a raised courtyard and the attractive crow-stepped gables of similar seventeenth-century houses nearby (Pl. 14). It is to be found in Little Lochend Close on the north side of the Canongate, formerly a separate burgh and essentially the suburb of the ancient Palace of Holyroodhouse (McKean and Walker, 1982: 27, no. 42).

Someone writing from Edinburgh about this time, possibly Henry Mackenzie, Smith's friend and colleague as Crown Attorney in Scotland, declared that where his correspondent would 'remember our Judges and People of the first rank lodged', that is, in the Old Town, 'now you would find Shopkeepers and Tradesmen'. He went on to extol the New Town—'built on the ground to the North side of the North Loch, which we used to walk over under the name of *Barefoot's Park*, Multreas Hill etc . . . covered with regular and splendid Buildings' (NLS MS 646 fo. 4). Hume had built a house there in 1770–1, on St David Street, perhaps a mischievous elevation of him to sainthood (Mossner, 1980: 566, 620). However, the New Town, commodious as it was, and pleasing to classical taste with its squares and rectilinear grid of streets, presenting ashlar and mouldings chiefly of creamy sandstone from the Craigleith Quarries, did not drain off all the people of quality from the Old Town.

Pl. 14. Panmure House. From a photograph in the collection of Professor Gerhart
Streminger.

In particular, the literati with whom Smith had both friendly and professional
dealings seemed to linger on in the older neighbourhoods, or escape the city altogether. His former Glasgow colleague and literary executor, Dr Black, lived in
term-time in Nicolson Street, near the University where he was Professor of
Chemistry and Medicine; in the vacations, for a change of air, he rented houses
at Leith Links and the Meadows (Anderson, 1986: 94). Black's expertise was
called upon by the Customs Board on 22 December 1778 (SRO, Minutes, vol.
16), in the matter of distinguishing coal from culm, a low-grade stony coal in
Scotland. Duty on this had long been a matter of grievance, and Smith's other
literary executor, James Hutton, had published his first book on this subject, to
persuade the Government to give up the imposition: *Considerations on the Nature,
Quality and Distinctions of Coal and Culm* (1777). In 1770 Hutton built a house
for himself and his three sisters on St John's Hill looking over to Salisbury
Crags, whose rock forms stimulated his growing interest in geology (Jones, 1986:
119). Smith's physician, Dr Cullen, occupied the upper floors over the old
Scottish Mint in the Cowgate which ran parallel to the High Street on the South
Side. Lord Kames, Smith's former patron, who was thanked in a letter co-signed

by Smith on 19 December 1780 for improving procedures before the justiciary involving revenue officers (*Corr.* 409), lived in New Street adjoining the Canongate, as did Lord Hailes. Monboddo lived in nearby St John Street, just a few closes up from Panmure House in the Horse Wynd. Dugald Stewart rented the Lothian Hut, town house of the Marquis of Lothian, delighting in his view, which was also that of Smith, of the green slopes of the Calton Hill, then outside the city's confines (Chambers, 1912/1967: 131, 261, 300, 303, 323). Robertson was further away from the Canongate in the Grange House during vacations, but occupied the principal's house in the Old College during the Winter. Adam Ferguson at Sciennes was so remote in the eyes of his contemporaries that they called his residence 'Kamtschatka' and pretended he was in Siberia (Graham, 1908: 101, 118).

At their pleasure, without an invitation, these and other friends of Smith came to Panmure House for plain suppers on Sundays that were a notable feature of Smith's years in Edinburgh. On these occasions he would sometimes entertain distinguished visitors, such as the poet Samuel Rogers, who recorded details of conversations, and the MP William Windham, who had studied at Glasgow under Millar. After one visit to see Smith on 13 September 1785, Windham wrote in his *Diary* (1866): 'Felt strongly the impression of a family completely Scotch.'

The senior member of the household, and first in Smith's affection, was his mother. We have a portrait of her dated 1778, painted by C. Metz, an artist whose studio was in Edinburgh at this time and who was given commissions by Smith's former pupil Lord Buchan, including that of producing from a pencil sketch and a death-mask a portrait of Colin Maclaurin which was engraved in John Pinkerton's *Iconographia Scotica* (1797).

As Metz represents her, perhaps recalling a tradition of paintings of older women which we associate with Rembrandt's study of his mother now in the British Royal Collection, Margaret Smith is an austere and dignified figure, swathed in a sombre cloak and hood, thrown back somewhat to reveal a white covering caught by a black ribbon framing white hair and the high forehead and face. She is painted half-length, turning to her right, and a gnarled right hand is partly exposed, thumb and forefinger holding a thin book, perhaps a Psalter. The face seems to be that of a woman of strong character, with dark, heavy-lidded eyes under dark eyebrows. The flesh drawn over high cheek-bones is that of someone in good health, and a straight and firmly chiselled nose over the lips drawn decisively together and slightly turned down above the well-rounded and dimpled chin all suggest the distinction of her Douglas family lineage (Pl. 15; also flattering engraving by Emory Walker in Bonar, 1932: p. xxii). When Smith writes in *WN* of the two systems of morality, on the one hand the *liberal* and on the other the *strict and austere* (v.i.g.10), it is perhaps appropriate to think of his mother as upholding the values of the second.

Also having authority in Panmure House was Janet Douglas, that cousin of

Pl. 15. Margaret Douglas Smith, 1778. From a portrait by C. Metz
(Kirkcaldy Museum and Art Gallery).

Smith who had been his housekeeper since his professorial days in Glasgow and who was always remembered affectionately by his former students (*Corr.* Nos. 55, 64, 245). Walter Scott, who was 17 when Janet Douglas died, and was apparently received in the household, recounts the following anecdote, no doubt highly coloured but based on fact, about his host and Miss Douglas:

we shall never forget one particular evening, when [Smith] put an elderly maiden lady, who presided at the tea-table, to sore confusion, by neglecting utterly her invitation to be seated, and walked round and round the circle, stopping ever and anon to steal a lump from the sugar basin, which the venerable spinster was at length constrained to place on her own knee, as the only method of securing it from his most uneconomical depredations. His appearance mumping the eternal sugar, was something indescribable. (Scott, n.d.: 388)

Smith certainly took an economist's interest in the price of sugar, and remembered in 1786 the high price of the time of the American war as compared with the current 'eight pence or nine pence a pound' he was paying for 'what good Housewives call breakfast Sugar'. He also remembered what was paid in Glasgow for a hogshead of 'Muscovado Sugar', but apparently he never required Janet Douglas to stock this for the family (*Corr.* No. 258).

Within a few months of Smith's removal to Edinburgh in 1778, he took into his care David Douglas, the 9-year-old youngest son of another cousin, Col. Robert Douglas of Strathenry (Rae, 1965: 326). Smith delighted in the company of this boy, occupied his leisure hours in helping to educate him (Stewart v.18), and secured the mathematician and natural philosopher John Leslie to be his tutor, 1785–7 (*Corr.* No. 275). David Douglas would be a blink of sunshine in that house of elderly people, and perhaps recreated for Smith what he seems to have enjoyed at Glasgow, contact with the expanding mind of youth.

It is from this period that we have some images of Smith and can visualize him in his Edinburgh surroundings (Pl. 16). In general terms, we are told by William Smellie the antiquarian printer and naturalist, who knew him well, that 'in stature he somewhat exceeded the ordinary size; and his countenance was manly and agreeable'. He was not an ostentatious man, and remarked once, 'I am a beau in nothing but my books' (Smellie, 1800: 297). Indeed his library, which was passed on to David Douglas, reveals that great care was given to its selection, and to the elegance of bindings.

We can think of him leaving his family and his books for the Custom-house, every weekday except Friday and during holiday times. Walking out from his close into the Canongate to pass the little Doric portico piercing the gracefully gabled south front of the burgh kirk, he would climb towards the High Street of Edinburgh between substantial buildings of seventeenth- and sixteenth-century origin, with some space around them, such as Acheson House, Huntly House, and the Canongate Tolbooth with its aura of a French château.

Edinburgh proper was entered from the Head of the Canongate, where the stately Netherbow Port had stood until 1764. The 'lands' or multiple-storeyed dwellings, such as Tweeddale House, towered over the High Street, and each at the back had a long, narrow 'tenement' for a garden and drying green. These 'lands' were organized somewhat like today's condominiums, and each floor could be owned separately. Until well on into the eighteenth century, the series of occupants who ranged through the ranks of Scottish society were able to practise that sociability about which Smith and other moralists of his day theorized. One such building of the first class about the time of Smith's Edinburgh Lectures sheltered on its first floor Mrs Stirling, a fishmonger; on the second Mrs Urquart, a lodging-house keeper; on the third the Countess Dowager of Balcarres; on the fourth Mrs Buchan of Kelloe; on the fifth the Misses Elliot, milliners and mantua-makers; and in the garrets, some tailors and other tradesmen (Chambers, 1914/1967: 4 n.). The buildings evoked striking events in

The Author of the Wealth of Nations

Pl. 16. Memorial print of Adam Smith, 1790. From John Kay, *Original Portraits*, 1842 (GUL).

Scotland's history. For example, the house at 45 High Street was popularly associated with the Reformer John Knox who upbraided Mary Queen of Scots, and it was certainly owned by her goldsmith. Its timber front extended into the street, and its outside stairs led to galleries from which the inhabitants could take the air well above the smelly pavement.

Just beyond Knox's Manse, the North Bridge, completed in 1772 as the result of a proposal by Lord Kames, led to the New Town (Ross, 1972: 329–31). It was not until 1788 that the South Bridge was built to make a connection with the southern districts and new developments such as George Square, where Smith told Samuel Rogers he would have preferred to live (Rae, 1965: 417; Youngson, 1966). Ahead of the North Bridge and the Tron Kirk, Smith would pass the Town Guard building, where the old Highlanders of the force with their fearsome Lochaber axes were stationed, and then he came to the site of the Mercat

Pl. 17. Adam Smith on the way to the Custom-house, 1787. From John Kay, *Original Portraits*, 1842 (GUL).

Pl. 18. View looking up the High Street, Edinburgh, from John Knox's house. From a painting by David Allan (1744–96) (National Gallery of Scotland).

Cross, a structure which had been taken down in 1756. This was a place of popular assembly in good weather at certain hours of the day, with nobles, lairds, merchants, professional men and others, among them, some said, men of genius and, Smith reckoned, madmen, emerging from the nearby coffee-houses and booksellers' shops to exchange news and gossip (Chambers, 1914/1967: 174–7; Mackenzie, 1927: 173).

Directly ahead again were situated the Luckenbooths, a shopping centre, then the grim Edinburgh Tolbooth, evincing the *squalor carcaris* designated by Scots law; further on was the open space of the Lawnmarket with its high 'lands', among them James Court and Riddle's Court where Hume, Blair, and Boswell had lived at one time (Mossner, 1980: 244, 409, 504, 533, 563). Beyond the Lawnmarket rose the Castle. Sir Adolphus Oughton, something of a Gaelic enthusiast, was installed there on 29 May 1778 as Commander-in-Chief of the Forces in North Britain, and in due course Smith was called upon to assist him in line of duty through the American war period.

Just beyond the Cross on the south side of the High Street was the High Kirk of St Giles (Pl. 18). In one of the four places available for worship, described in 1773 as 'shamefully dirty' (*BLJ* v.41), Hugh Blair preached so eloquently, according to Boswell, that he 'would stop hounds' (*BP* xiii.109). Under the crowned tower of St Giles lay Parliament Square, with a lead equestrian statue of Charles II, closed off by a free-standing L-shaped building constructed in 1632–9 to house the Scottish national assembly in two halls one above the other. Smith would have seen the original Parliament Square façade with its 'respectable turrets, some ornamental windows and doors, and a handsome balustrade' (Cockburn, 1856: 106–7), features well handled in the building renaissance of the sixteenth and seventeenth centuries represented elsewhere in Edinburgh (McKean and Walker, 1982: 19, No. 21), and familiar to him in the old College of Glasgow. Under the broad hammerbeam roof of the Upper Hall the Session Court Judges, including Kames, Hailes, Monboddo, and, in time, David Douglas, as well as Smith's favourite pupil Robert Cullen, gave their decisions individually in the Outer House. The Inner House of the 'haill fifteen' of the Judges met in the wing to the south-east to give final decisions and, in rare cases, to appeal to the House of Lords. Also in this wing were constituted the Commissary Court and the Exchequer Court, whose Barons had jurisdiction over the revenue collection which was Smith's concern (Ross, 1972: 17–19, 121–3).

Under Parliament Hall was the Laigh Hall, which contained the archives of Scotland until the completion in 1788 of the first stage of the Register House designed by Robert and James Adam (Youngson, 1966: 66–8). This Hall also held the Advocates' Library, and it is inconceivable that Smith at one time or another did not avail himself of the liberal borrowing privileges (Ross, 1972: 27–30; Cadell and Matheson, 1989; Brown, 1989).

Walking amid or towards these buildings and the legal and administrative heart of this city, Smith was seemingly a curious sight passing the throng of street messengers known as *caddies*; wives and servants on pattens going to the markets (poultry behind the Tron Kirk, flesh near the Head of the Canongate, and fish—very noisome in summer—near the Cross); law clerks and lawyers; douce citizens proceeding on business to shops and taverns; and folk of lesser pretensions, soldiers, whores, Macaronis, loungers, and riff-raff of all descriptions. John Kay, whose engraver's shop was at the corner of Parliament Close, and who must have seen Adam Smith many times going towards the Royal Exchange opposite, on whose upper floors was the Custom-house, issued a print dated 1787 showing him in a broad-brimmed hat, wearing a light linen coat and carrying in his left hand a bunch of flowers, perhaps to ward off the notorious Edinburgh effluvia (Pl. 17: Kay, 1842, i.72, 75; Evans and Evans, 1973). In his right hand he grasps his cane by the middle, sloping it against his shoulder, according to Smellie, 'as a soldier carries his musket'. He also described Smith's strange gait, his head moving in a gentle manner from side to side, and his body swaying 'vermicularly' (a nice touch from a naturalist) as if with each step 'he meant to alter his direction, or even to turn back'. Meantime, his lips would move and form smiles as if he were deep in conversation with persons unseen (Smellie, 1800: 293). Edinburgh anecdote had it that an old market-woman observing him in these oddities exclaimed: 'Hegh, sirs!' and shook her head, to which a companion answered by sighing compassionately, then observed: 'and he is well put on too', thus expressing surprise that an obviously well-to-do lunatic would be allowed to wander freely (W. Scott, n.d.: 388).

The building to which Smith directed his steps was based on a design by John Adam and adapted and supervised in construction, 1753–61, by John Fergus. Now expanded to serve as the City Chambers, and approached through a single-storey, rusticated screen on the High Street and across a courtyard, the central block with its pediments and pilasters is not considered architecturally impressive (Youngson, 1966: 55–9; McKean and Walker, 1982: 21, No. 23). When Smollett brings Matthew Bramble to Edinburgh in the late 1760s and has him acknowledge it is a 'hot bed of genius', alluding to Smith and the other literati, Bramble comments on the failure in purpose of the building:

All the people of business in Edinburgh, and even the genteel company, may be seen standing in crowds every day from one to two in the afternoon, in the open street, at a place where formerly stood a market-cross . . . from the force of custom, rather than move a few yards to an Exchange that stands empty on one side . . . (*Humphry Clinker*, 1776, vol. ii, 18 July letter)

At the entrance of the Exchange in Smith's time, to convey visitors on Custom-house business upstairs, was the doorkeeper, Adam Matheson. He appears in the official records, desiring on Christmas Eve 1778 more accommodation for his family in the garrets (SRO, Customs Board Minutes vol. 16), and getting a replacement for his scarlet gown bedecked with frogs of worsted lace.

He was armed with a seven-foot wooden staff; when the Board sat he saluted each Commissioner with the kind of drill infantry officers used to perform with their spontoons or halberds, and then conducted them to the meeting-hall. Walter Scott heard from one of the other Commissioners a tale of Smith being so mesmerized by the doorkeeper's salute that he returned it compulsively with his cane, to the servant's amazement (Scott, n.d.: 388–9).

A suggestion has been made that this happened because Smith had been subjected to drill routine after becoming an Honorary Captain of the Trained Bands of Edinburgh—the City Guard—on 4 June 1781 (Graham, 1908: 169; Rae, 1965: 374). It is more likely, however, that Smith was deep in thought coming up the High Street and simply entranced by a military manœuvre. The story is of a piece with another one Scott presents of Smith taking a long time to sign a Customs document, and being found to have imitated laboriously the signature of the colleague going before him.

The colleagues with whom Smith served on the Customs Board can be identified by their signatures in the Minutes and their appearance in contemporary accounts. The senior Commissioner was Mansfeldt de Cardonnel, who claimed descent on the wrong side of the blanket from the Duke of Monmouth and thus from Charles II. Carlyle of Inveresk knew him well as a neighbour, and recalled that he 'excell'd in Story telling like his Great Grand Father Charles the 2d.—But he Seldom or ever repeated them' (1973: 112). Next in seniority came George Clerk Maxwell. After him came Basil Cochrane, brother of the 8th Earl of Dundonald, a former soldier who was Boswell's great-uncle and advised that rascal against hard drinking (Boswell, 1963: 8). Cochrane was made Commissioner of Excise in 1761 and of Customs two years later. William Nelthorp followed in seniority, but his name disappears from the record by 19 December 1780, and we hear there were plans for him to be 'removed' on 26 November of that year (*Corr.* 254). This probably means he was bought out. Nelthorp's replacement was James Edgar, another old soldier who had been Collector at Leith, and who shared Smith's interest in the Greek classics. Other Commissioners who served with Smith in due course were David Reid, James Buchanan, John Henry Cochrane, and Robert Hepburn. The Solicitor to the Board and Inspector-General for most of Smith's time was a giant of a man, Alexander Osborne (Kay, 1842: i.343–4, 384–8). The Secretary was Richard Elliston Phillips, who lived to be 104 and who shares Adam Smith's grave in the Canongate kirkyard (Rae, 1965: 330).

Before his appointment as a Commissioner and reflecting family knowledge of the Customs service and his own reading and inquiries, Smith presents in the fifth book of *WN* a clear as well as extensive discussion of the function and organization of customs, as he puts it, 'taxes upon consumable commodities . . . either necessaries or luxuries' (v.ii.k.1–80). As Smith explains the fiscal system in Scotland obtaining in his day, the first charge on revenue from Customs and Excise was paying for the balance of the civil establishment in the country, including the maintenance of the Courts of Session, Justiciary, and Exchequer, the part not covered by Crown income, all of which was considered as the 'private estate of the king'. The remainder of the Scottish revenue was remitted to the Receivers General of the Customs and Excise in England. Smith asserts that the amount of the civil establishment in Scotland for 1782–3 was £66,879 10s. 8d. (*Corr.* 235). He does not reveal what proportion of this was met by Customs and Excise revenue, but since it has been estimated that the net produce of this in 1781 was approximately £186,000 in 1781, we can assume that a lesser sum than that went to England to be added to make the United Kingdom approximate revenue total of that year £3,019,000.

Scotland's contribution was thus rather small, but it required the full exertions of the Board to levy and collect the Customs and to control the officers responsible for this, from the Collectors and Comptrollers at the outports, such as Kirkcaldy where Smith's father was stationed, down to the tidewaiters and boatmen who brought incoming ships into the Customs net. Moreover, the Commissioners had legal powers to administer oaths, search ships, seize and destroy goods, authorize the sale and delivery of condemned goods from warehouses, initiate prosecutions for customs violation, and remit penalties for those convicted. Thus Smith and his colleagues acted as administrative judges and as the 'import police'. And they had further powers of supervising the proceeds of seizures to reward officers and of recommending promotions for them or incentives for the informers who assisted them. In addition, the Board had a 'coast guard command' role, to ensure the coasts of Scotland East and West were patrolled by seaworthy ships manned by capable officers and seamen.[1] The small fleet maintained for this purpose consisted in 1779 of three cutters: *Prince of Wales*, *Cumbraes Wherry*, and *Princess Royal*, and two smaller sloops: *Prince William* and *Princess Ann*. Two new cutters were being built in November 1779 as replacements, because even with crews of about 30, carrying about a dozen guns, and displacing over 120 tuns, these ships were often outsailed and outgunned by those of the smugglers. Smuggling, of course, was the greatest headache for the Board, compounded by the fact there was an 'agency problem' caused by collusion between certain Customs officers and the smugglers. Thus, under Smith's chairmanship on 23 June 1778, the Board registered horror that an officer named McPhie was 'in the pay of the smugglers' (Macfie, 1961: 151).

The question arises, however, whether Smith the Customs Commissioner is at odds with the author of *WN*? As the book is generally understood, its central message is to the effect that monopolies, restraints on trade, restrictions on the right of individuals to deploy their labour, stock, and land as they judge this to be of benefit to themselves, are all unnatural interventions in that they impede the instinctive propensity in people to truck, barter, and exchange, as well as their prudential desire to further their economic interests. In addition, the restrictions and impediments foster inefficiency because they remove the need for hard work and interfere with the mechanisms whereby competition produces an adequate supply of goods to the market at a price as low as the cost of production permits. Writing about *WN* in October 1780, Smith characterized it as the 'very violent attack I had made upon the whole commercial system of Britain' (*Corr.* No. 202).

At the time of expressing himself in this manner, he was demonstrating exemplary conscientiousness as an official regulating and enforcing this very 'commercial, or mercantile System' (*WN* IV.i.35–45). It must be pointed out, nevertheless, that Smith did not argue for economic freedom across the board. Not only did he declare that there were reasons of state, such as those connected with defence, which required restrictions on trade, he also pointed to purely economic considerations which justified limitations on the natural liberty of individuals to sell their labour and produce in the unfettered market. He did not indulge in high hopes concerning the triumph of the system of natural liberty in the economic affairs of his own country (*WN* IV.ii.43).

19

Economic Theorist as Commissioner of Customs

To expect, indeed, that the freedom of trade should ever be entirely restored in Great Britain, is as absurd as to expect that an Oceana or a Utopia should ever be established in it.

On the matter of trade policy, Smith's most characteristic position was to advocate removal of all trade barriers, qualified only by the need to raise revenue for the proper purposes of governing a country. Called upon to give advice, he recommended levying 'moderate duties' on imports and exports. These should not be so high as to make smuggling profitable, for in this case the revenue is sharply diminished. Moreover, such duties should be equal for different producers and importers, so that one group does not have an advantage over another.

These points are well taken in another letter of 1780, that directed on 3 January to William Eden, an MP who had married a daughter of Gilbert Elliot of Minto, was allied to Wedderburn, had worked for peace with the Americans, and served as a Lord of Trade 1776–82. Smith wrote to him:

The sole effect of a prohibition is to hinder the revenue from profiting by the importation. All those high duties, which make it scarce profitable to trade fairly in the goods upon which they are imposed, are equally hurtful to the revenue and equally favourable to smuggling, as absolute prohibitions.

The letter continues with a reference to the prohibition on the export of wool as essentially a tax laid on the grower to benefit the manufacturer (*Corr.* No. 203).

The implication is that raising a moderate revenue in a non-discriminatory way does not gravely affect the tendency towards price equilibrium on which economic efficiency depends. Also, certain political supports had to be provided. First, there was the necessity of providing for the administration of justice—for example, the maintenance of the three Courts in Scotland, as we have seen. Second came the need for the defence of person and property, all the more important in the time of war when Smith was writing. Next was the requirement to provide for some access to education—in Scotland, money from the Crown went into the school and university system. Last, there was the need to provide for the creation and repair of public works such as docks and roads, without which the economy could not run.

Awareness of the economic benefits of the political order suffices to explain Smith's willingness to regulate and enforce the mercantile system, even though he viewed some of its features as unwise and unjust, as in the case of prohibiting certain imports and punishing smugglers harshly. It was not his view that absolutely free trade was essential for economic progress, and he could accept rough justice and even some injustice as the price to be paid for the benefits of the imperfect but continuing and alterable system of law. There is no hint in his writings or behaviour as reported that he exculpated smugglers as the real 'free-traders' they sometimes claimed to be.

At the same time, it is clear that he did not regard smuggling as a natural crime like theft or murder, identified as such (we recall from *TMS*) through the arousal of spontaneous resentment in victims and spectators. On this view, smuggling is an artificial misdemeanour based on the arbitrary will of administrations: it is, in consequence, imprudent rather than immoral. Smith was led to oppose restrictions on trade in *WN* because they entailed punishment of smugglers, often perfectly moral people who, branded as criminals in this respect, went on to commit real crimes. A case in point here was that of Alexander Wilson, mentioned in our first chapter, the Fife smuggler who committed violence against a revenue official, and whose apprehension set in motion the chain of events leading to the Porteous riots. In *WN*, smuggling is analysed from the economic point of view, Smith noting that, though the profits of this activity are high, they do not outweigh the risks of being caught, so that in the end it is the 'infallible road to bankruptcy' (*WN* i.x.b.33).

This seemingly amoral approach to smuggling is not to be explained away on the grounds that *WN* is concerned with economics rather than morality. Smith is always as ready to address questions of injustice as those involving profit. It comes as a surprise, therefore, that there is no record of him entertaining qualms of conscience about his role as supervisor of those who brought smugglers to book. That he felt some degree of discomfort about his position, however, is indicated by a further, albeit whimsical passage in that same letter to Eden:

About a week after I was made a Commissioner of the Customs, upon looking over the list of prohibited goods, (which is hung up in every Customhouse and which is well worth your considering) and upon examining my own wearing apparel, I found, to my great astonishment, that I had scarce a stock, a cravat, a pair of ruffles, or a pocket handkerchief which was not prohibited to be worn or used in Great Britain. I wished to set an example and burnt them all. I will not advise you to examine either your own or Mrs Edens apparel or household furniture, least you be brought into a scrape of the same kind. (*Corr.* No. 203)

This is not, perhaps, a very considered piece of moral advice, but together with the stated wish 'to set an example', it indicates some ambivalence in Smith over his responsibility for the suppression of smuggling in the prevailing circumstances. His action of burning smuggled goods seems to have been motivated more by prudential considerations about protecting his reputation as a Commissioner of Customs than by his desire to observe a rule of conduct acceptable to an impartial spectator. Weight is lent to such a view by the consideration that Smith as a private citizen would not have disposed of his cravats and ruffles and so forth, since in *WN* he ridiculed those pretending to have a conscience about buying smuggled articles, as persons likely to be regarded as hypocrites and knaves (v.ii.k.64).

Such tension as exists in Smith's thought on the issue of smuggling can be located in the conflict between two utilitarian considerations. The first concerns the good or bad economic consequences of customs and excise laws. The second has to do with the serious long-term disutility of lack of respect for the law itself, setting aside disagreement over the content. In the event, Smith was prepared, in practice, to judge his conduct by utilitarian considerations of one kind or another, and to take action against smuggling regardless of the fact that he did not view it as a 'natural' crime.

On the issue of trade barriers in general, he was ready both to invoke justice and to appeal directly to the standard of utility. Thus, he frequently comments on restrictions of trade as being inequitable as well as hampering economic growth, and he objects vigorously to taxing the necessities of the poor, on the grounds of 'oppression', although this is a utilitarian objection in that oppressing the vast majority of a society reduces that majority's happiness. He also objects, however, on the grounds of 'equity', to taxing the products of one country more than those of another. Moreover, Smith denounces the inequity of exempting from excise duty the product of private brewing and distilling, and hence the alcoholic consumption of the rich, and leaving the poor man's drink to bear the burden of taxation (*WN* v.ii.k.45). He recognized the utility of saving the private family from the 'odious visit and examination of the tax-gatherer', but the exemption cannot meet the higher criterion of his first maxim of taxation: 'The subjects of every state ought to contribute towards the support of the government . . . in proportion to the revenue which they respectively enjoy under the protection of the state' (v.ii.b.3). The possibility that considerations of the justice and utility of taxation measures may conflict seems not to have been entertained seriously by Smith, and he states flatly after presenting his four maxims of taxation: '[their] evident justice and utility . . . have recommended them more or less to the attention of all nations' (v.ii.b.7).

On 1 November 1779 Smith wrote in the same strain in an exchange of letters with Henry Dundas on the subject of free trade for Ireland. Dundas had expressed himself on 30 October in favour of freeing restrictions on Irish trade on utilitarian grounds, with awareness of what is today called the theory of comparative advantage: 'it has long appeared to me that the bearing down of Ireland, was in truth bearing down a substantial part of the Naval and Military strength of our own Country' (*Corr.* No. 200).

Responding to a request for policy advice, Smith was 'happy' to go along with Dundas:

I perfectly agree . . . that to crush the Industry of so great and so fine a province of the empire, in order to favour the monopoly of some particular towns in Scotland or England, is equally unjust and impolitic. The general opulence and improvement of Ireland might certainly, under proper management, afford much greater resources to Government, than can ever be drawn from a few mercantile or manufacturing towns.

Smith judged that the action of freeing Irish trade was warranted because it would promote the greater happiness of the greater number: 'Nothing, in my opinion, would be more advantageous to both countries than this mutual freedom of trade. It would help to break down that absurd monopoly which we have most absurdly established against ourselves in favour of almost all the different classes of our manufacturers.' Characteristically, Smith ascribed resistance to the proposals to the 'group interest behaviour' of the manufacturers, and he claimed to be able to put the finger on 'some persons' who could deal successfully with the leaders among the manufacturers, and so avoid the 'madness' of rejecting 'in the present situation' what the Irish were demanding (*Corr*. No. 201).[1]

In a parallel letter to Lord Carlisle, Smith makes the point that Ireland is a long way from being in serious competition with Britain as a manufacturing country, since it lacked coal and wood necessary for 'Great Manufactures'. With considerable prescience, he adds:

[Ireland] wants order, police, and a regular administration of justice both to protect and restrain the inferior ranks of people, articles more essential to the progress of Industry than both coal and wood put together, and which Ireland must continue to want as long as it continues to be divided between two hostile nations, the oppressors and the oppressed, the protestants and the Papists. (*Corr*. No. 202)

Men of the stamp of Dundas, Eden, and Carlisle (President of the Board of Trade in 1779) were swayed by utilitarian arguments and, though Smith avoids discussion of possible conflicts of justice and utility in the justification of moderate trade restraints, it is the criterion of utility that preoccupies him both as an adviser to Government and in his action as a Commissioner of Customs (Campbell and Ross, 1981).

As to that action, we have an unusually complete record of this period of Smith's life, since he was a faithful attender of the meetings of the Customs Board, except for periods of absence in 1782 and 1787 when he visited London, and from 1787, when it appears that ill health began increasingly to interfere with attendance. Functioning as a well-organized bureaucracy, the Board conducted business during this period that fills almost nine massive Minute Books in the Scottish Record Office (CE1, vols. 15–23; cited below by vol. no. and date), and carried on extensive correspondence with the outports entered in Letter Books, of which that for Dunbar is perhaps the most complete (SRO CE56/2/5A–F). Recent research estimates that the Board issued 1,165 letters, including duplicates, from February 1778, when Smith qualified as a Commissioner, until April 1790, when his terminal illness forced absence. Smith seems to have signed about 90 per cent of these letters (Anderson *et al.*, 1985: 746, n. 7).

A point to be made about this, however, is that Smith was one member of a Board guided by government and office policy and tradition, and he would have limited room for swaying his colleagues in the direction of putting into practice his own ideas about revenue collection and economic policy. The letters to Dundas and Carlisle about free trade for Ireland (*Corr.* Nos. 201, 202), also to Eden about raising revenue and American commerce (Nos. 203, 233), and to Sinclair of Ulbster about the economic drain of empire and realistic duties (Nos. 221, 299) all indicate that Smith made no secret of his views to influential people asking for his comments and advice which, if taken, would affect practice in the Customs service.

He was invited to present his ideas about reducing smuggling to a House of Commons Committee dealing with this topic in 1783, and there is some evidence that Pitt's Commutation Act of 1784 did embody Smith's principles in part at least in connection with duty on tea, also that by 1789 the contraband trade in that commodity had been dealt a severe blow (*Corr.* app. D, p. 411). When Smith had a free hand to negotiate reformation of Customs duties, as we shall hear, he certainly did uphold his principles, but he also showed tenderness on the issue of the effect of such a reformation on the livelihood of the Customs officers in Scotland. Moreover, as a Commissioner he did hear representations from concerned bodies that reflected the ideas expressed in *WN*.

As sources of information and theorizing about revenue, Smith's library had the standard works of national reference by Henry Crouch, Henry Saxby, and Timothy Cunningham, also several copies of *Instructions* for the officers of the Customs in Scotland from the collectors and comptrollers on down (Mizuta). Smith also interested himself in comparative study of revenue, and as one source of this used J. L. Moreau de Beaumont, *Mémoires concernant les impositions et droits en Europe* (Paris, 1768–9). On one occasion, Sinclair of Ulbster wanted to borrow this book, perhaps in the course of preparing his first serious book, *A History of the Public Revenue of the British Empire* (1st edn. 1784). Writing in answer on 24 November 1778, Smith was a 'little uneasy' about sending it to Caithness, the north-east tip of Scotland, and stated: 'he has frequent occasion to consult the book himself both in the course of his private studies and in the business of his present employment; and is, therefore, not very willing to let it go out of Edinburgh.' He went on to say copies of the book were rare, and he had obtained his by the 'particular favour' of Turgot, then he offers to let Sinclair consult the book or anything else he has on finances, in print or in manuscript, in Edinburgh (*Corr.* No. 196). In *WN*, Smith claimed that the book was more accurate on French taxes than on those of other nations, but he appears to have relied on it for information about taxes in Hamburg, Holland, Switzerland,

Prussia, and Venice (v.ii.a.4; Bonar, 1932: 18–21; Mizuta). One wonders if *WN*'s success in employing Moreau de Beaumont's rare book, as well as other sources, did not promote that state of affairs eliciting Smith's dry comment: 'There is no art which one government sooner learns of another than that of draining money from the pockets of the people' (*WN* v.ii.h.12).

To illustrate Smith's participation in Custom-house routine, we turn now to Wednesday 4 February 1778, the day after Smith qualified as a Commissioner, when he attended a Board meeting. George Clerk Maxwell took the chair, and the other Commissioner present was Basil Cochrane. The acting Comptroller at Ayr was given leave to attend to his private business for three days provided he arranged for a substitute. Then come details of a successful detection in May 1771 of 'running a Quantity of Wine', a resulting prosecution of the parties involved, and the payment of £450 accepted by the Lords of Treasury as a 'Composition' for the penalties imposed. The costs of the prosecution were recorded as £320 4s. 4d., and this being deducted from the sum recovered, there remained £18 15s. 8d. to be distributed according to a Treasury Warrant. One-third was allocated to the informer, Patrick Sutherland, schoolmaster at Brora on the Sutherland coast, who was said to have gone abroad, no doubt to escape opprobrium; one-third went to the Receiver General as the King's Share; and Osborne, the Board's Solicitor, was to keep the other third pending instructions from the Treasury (Minutes vol. 15).

In the early years of Smith's Customs service, issues connected with the American war came before the Board. Maxwell chaired a meeting on 27 May 1779 with Smith attending, at which it was ordered a proclamation was to be printed and circulated relative to trade with the ports of New York and Newport, Rhode Island. The Treasury called for this action in response to a letter from Adam Ferguson, then serving as 'Secretary to the Commissioners appointed to treat of the Means of quieting the Disorders in America' (Minutes vol. 16). The Commissioners, in effect led by Eden, had left for America in April 1778, but their mission was undercut by the Franco-American alliance, and their proposals were dismissed with contempt by Congress (Dull, 1985: 100).

On 5 July 1779 the Board heard that Adam Smith had attended on the Lord Advocate, Henry Dundas, who approved 'very much' of directions given to the Customs officers to assist impressment for the Navy, and signified that they would be supported by the civil magistrates and the military. The Board learned, too, Dundas had held off from a proposal from Oughton, the Commander-in-Chief, regarding imprisonment of persons suspected of 'illicit designs against the state'. Perhaps Smith advised caution about measures affecting civil liberty (Minutes vol. 16).

The most exciting episode of Smith's wartime service was that concerning the appearance off the east coast of Scotland in September 1779 of enemy ships. Captain Brown was sent out to reconnoitre in the Customs cutter *Princess Royal* on 17 September, with orders to fire three guns when he had intelligence and fly a 'Jack or Flag at the Cutters Mast Head' if they were enemy ships. He returned at 11.30 a.m. and made this declaration in the presence of the naval Regulating Officer and the Customs Commissioners, Maxwell and Smith:

[He] found himself within Pistol Shot of a fifty Gun French Ship, upon which he tacked about and afterwards retook a prize they had taken in the Mouth of the Firth [of Forth] but a French twenty four Gun Frigate immediately made up, and obliged him to abandon the Prize[.] [T]hey brought on Shore a Boy from the Prize who says they put four Soldiers, four Men and two Officers on Board him. The French Squadron [is completed with] a Brig mounting ten Guns. The Ships sail ill, and they say they are determined to come up to Leith Road. The Commander of the fifty Gun Ship is said to be acquainted with the Coast. Both the fifty Gun Ship and Frigate are painted Black. The fifty Gun Ship has a White Bottom and very clumsy mast head. The Boy says seven Sail of them sailed in Company[.] [T]hey went north the length of Shetland, and returned Separated in a Gale of Wind some Days ago from the rest of Squadron.

Maxwell and Smith sent the declaration off by express to their masters, the Lords of Treasury in London, and ordered the commanders of the revenue sloops stationed on the east coast to place themselves under the direction of the Commander-in-Chief. The Board approved of these actions on 20 September, and continued with the usual business of granting leaves and dealing with fines and forfeitures incurred by the sloop *Betsey* of Philadelphia, also the recovery of money paid to tidesmen who had seized rum in this vessel (Minutes vol. 16).

Meantime, the French squadron, which was actually sailing under the American ensign and operating according to United States naval regulations, was engaged in carrying the American war home to Britain. The commander, John Paul Jones, knew something about the Scottish coast: he was born at Arbigland on the Solway Firth, and early in his career sailed in and out of Kirkcudbright. Jones's mission was to carry out a diversionary raid on Scotland or Northern England to mask an invasion of the south of England by French and Spanish forces. The main operation came to nothing in 1779 because of sickness in the fleet, but the French-American squadron successfully frightened the authorities and the people in Scotland. Already, American and French privateers had harried Glasgow shipping in the Clyde estuary bound for America and the Caribbean (Devine, 1975: 139–43).

Jones's plan in sailing into the Firth of Forth was to land at Leith and hold the town to ransom. On 17 September the squadron had sailed within a mile of Smith's home town, Kirkcaldy, then tacked across to Leith and was almost within cannon shot of it. The landing boats were about to be ordered into the water, but an offshore gale blew up and drove the ships to the entrance to the Firth. Thereafter, Jones sailed down the east coast and gained a famous victory on 23 September off Flamborough Head. His ship, the *Bonnhomme Richard* (named after Poor Richard, a character invented by Smith's friend Franklin), engaged the new British frigate *Serapis* on convoy duty with merchantmen returning from the Baltic, and struggled with her from sunset until she surrendered three hours later in moonlight, though at one point her captain was confident enough to call upon Jones to strike his flag, only to receive the celebrated retort: 'I have not yet begun to fight.' Jones and his men took over the *Serapis* on 24 September; leaving their burning ship to sink the next day, they sailed on to France and a welcome for heroes (Morison, 1964: 213–40).

Discomfited by these British reverses of the American war, in particular the surrender at Saratoga, Sinclair of Ulbster once lamented to Smith: 'If we go on at this rate, the nation *must be ruined.*' Smith replied with characteristic realism and pithy utterance: 'Be assured, my young friend, that there is a great deal of *ruin* in a nation' (Sinclair, 1831: i.390–1).

In fact, the merchantmen convoyed by the *Serapis* all reached their home ports safely, and Jones's success did not hold up the much-needed naval stores they brought from the Baltic. Smith maintained a focus on the economic consequences of war and peace with America, hoping that their outcome would be instructive for policy-makers in Britain. This is the burden of his letter of 15 December 1783 to Eden, suggesting that Britain should follow the declared American intention of subjecting the 'goods of all different nations to the same duties, and [of granting] them the same indulgences', and that the same 'commercial connection' that existed before the war between North America and the Caribbean colonies should be maintained after it. He declared that he was not anxious about the fate of the American commerce: 'By an equality of treatment of all nations, we might soon open a commerce with the neighbouring nations of Europe infinitely more advantageous than that of so distant a country as America.' Smith also noted that the Americans were attempting in practice, as opposed to their avowed intention, to discriminate against the products of British colonies and her ally, Portugal (*Corr.* No. 233). This movement to punish Britain and reduce economic dependence on the mother country and her connections did not last long, however, and Glasgow merchants, for example, resumed their close links with America soon after the signing of the Treaty of Paris in 1783 ended the war (Devine, 1975: 162–5).

France was the real loser in the American war, since her costly intervention hastened the bankruptcy of the *ancien régime* bringing on the Revolution (Dull, 1985: 161). Once she gave up the 'dream' of an American empire, as Smith called it, Britain under Pitt the Younger's Administration went on to increased economic strength. Despite Smith's cool view of the American market as opposed to the potential European one, the greater growth came through trade to the United States, in a phase that has been called the 'Americanization of British exports'. Protectionism in this trade still remained a British goal, of course. To the last, whether on grounds of utility or national self-interest, Smith was an enforcer of this policy. Thus he took the chair, for instance, at a Customs Board meeting on 7 April 1789 that received an Order in Council regulating trade with the United States, essentially maintaining the mercantilist Navigation Acts on the British side, and as routine business it was resolved to have this Order printed and transmitted to the ports, with directions that the officers there were to comply duly and strictly with the regulations (Minutes vol. 22).

With peace in 1783 and the growth of legitimate trade, requiring the due and strict attention of the Customs Commissioners and the officers in their service, came the intensification of the conflict with those lawless free-traders, the smugglers. A report to the Lords of Treasury from the Commissioners of Excise in Scotland dated 4 December 1783 assessed the problem (PRO, Kew, Treasury T 1/589, xiv/0173). Up to the time of the American war, the importation and landing of contraband goods was carried out by small, unarmed British sloops with few hands, seizing opportunities afforded by the absence of revenue cruisers, an extended coastline, and long and dark nights. If caught, the smugglers would attempt to escape, but if that was unsuccessful, they would normally submit to detention and forfeiture, or contest the seizure in the Court of Exchequer, rather than use force.

The situation grew worse through the war and particularly after the peace, with privateers turning to smuggling in large, swift, well-armed cutters, luggers, and other vessels, operating in pairs in daytime, 'with a determined Resolution of running their Cargoes, under force of arms, or of resisting to Blood and Death every Attempt by His Majesty's Officers to prevent them'. In one vessel, they could bring in 800 chests of tea and 1,000 ankers of brandy; goods were quickly landed ashore under her guns and then dispersed overland by large bands of horsemen. The price of the goods was paid in specie, draining the country of gold and silver, and to complete this mercantilist horror story, it was further alleged that the smugglers were thereafter 'employed in the very pernicious practice of Exporting Wool'.

The south-west coast from the Water of Orr to the Firth of Clyde was declared to be notorious for smuggling activity conducted by three companies made up of merchants and farmers: the first based at Cloan, or Port William, in Glenluce Bay, Wigtown; the second in the Mull of Galloway; and the third in Carrick, Ayrshire. Their network extended to Ulster and the Isle of Man, and their twelve large cutters and other vessels from 60 to 300 tons burthen carried from 10 to 24 guns, including 12-pounders. They shipped their cargoes of tea and spirits from Ostend, Flushing, Gothenburg, and even Copenhagen, and landed them at fortified farms before conveyance to those commissioning them. On 1 October 1783, Lt Gellie, commander of the *Prince of Wales* revenue yacht, attempted to intercept the *Thunderer*, a 24–gun cutter with a crew of 70 associated with the Carrick Company, but was raked by a broadside from the smugglers, and next day his men refused to resume the unequal engagement. On the east coast, smuggling was said to be conducted by individuals and generally in smaller ships, but it was described as extensive, and capable of stocking with tea and spirits the neighbouring towns, and above all Edinburgh, as a result of landings 'about Dunbar, Fifeness, St Andrew's, Lunan Bay, at, or near Aberdeen, Peterhead, and Frazerburgh, and all along the Murray Firth'.

Regarding answers to the evil of smuggling, the Excise Board, with tact but nevertheless at the outset of their recommendations, suggests that lowering duties would reduce the temptation to smuggle. Smith was thus not alone in thinking along these lines, and later on firm support for free trade even came from members of official bodies enforcing monopolies, the tariff system, and the Navigation Acts.[2]

The Customs Board effected some of these suggestions to control smuggling in the south-west of Scotland, as appears from a letter co-signed by Adam Smith on 7 April 1785. This bears on the assignment of a hulk to the east side of Glenluce Bay, where troops were stationed to assist the revenue officers, and a plan to bring another hulk to the west side for the same purpose, also to exchange troops between the hulks from time to time, 'to prevent intimacies being formed by the Smugglers with the Soldiers, which might defeat the Plan'. It was reported by the Collector of Wigtown that the smugglers had shown 'great despondency' ever since the arrival of the first hulk. Smith and his colleagues wished the Lords of Treasury to see to it that the Commander in Chief in Scotland had adequate numbers of troops at his disposal for such assignments (PRO, Kew, Treasury T/619, CAPS 29555).

Another letter of 6 August 1789 co-signed by Smith deals with further measures against the smuggling companies in the south-west. In this instance we learn of the success of a naval sloop in capturing a smuggler named Yawkins, the prototype of Dirk Hatteraick in Scott's novel *Guy Mannering*, before his lugger could land its cargo on the Galloway coast. The capture was due to the 'proper and efficient Water-guard', as the Excise Board called it, maintained by the local Tide Surveyor, the commander of one of the hulks, and the officers under them. A gratuity was requested for them, but Smith and his fellow-Commissioners are not giving anything away: 'tho' the Services stated are very commendable, and what we much approve of, they are only such as come within the Line of . . . duty' (*Corr.* app. D, p. 411).

In *WN*, Smith expressed the opinion that the 'excise laws . . . obstruct and embarrass the operations of the smuggler much more effectually than those of the customs'. He considered that the introduction into the customs of a system similar to that of the excise, where applicable, might cause difficulties for smugglers (v.ii.k.36). He also reported that many people supposed that this change might be easily made; but it was not carried through until the next century (Mathias, 1983: 274–5). Another proposal Smith made for reforming the customs, that of warehousing imports under close inspection, with duty to be paid on goods when drawn out for home consumption, and to be duty-free if exported, was an extension of the excise practice in levying duties on rum (v.ii.k.37). A memorial on this very subject was submitted by Patrick Colquhoun, Lord Provost of Glasgow,[3] and other merchants of that city concerned in the tobacco and sugar trade, asking that a change be made in the mode of levying duty on these commodities, and that both might be put under joint custody. The

Customs Board considered the memorial and forwarded it with an extensive and favourable report to the Lords of Treasury, dated 18 June 1783, and signed by every one of the Commissioners then in office: James Edgar, Basil Cochrane, Adam Smith, James Buchanan, and George Clerk [Maxwell] (PRO, Kew, Treasury T1/589, CAPS 29555). Glasgow might well be expected to espouse customs reforms suggested by Smith, especially as applied to the warehousing of sugar and tobacco, and could well have been the original source of such suggestions. In any event, the Commissioners' report clearly reflects Smith's thinking about the issue.

The report is written to safeguard the interests of the Crown, of course, rather than merchants. Thus the Commissioners recommend that there should be a differential between duties paid immediately on the importation of goods for home consumption and those levied on goods that have the benefit of being warehoused to suit the convenience of merchants. It is considered that this will prevent unnecessary delay in satisfying duties. The Commissioners also point out that, in allowing goods to be warehoused without the duties being satisfied, the Crown will incur a risk from accidents due to fire and so on. Further, the revenue officers will have more responsibilities such as care of warehouses, inspections, and delivery of goods. In view of this there should be a stipulation about the quantity of goods delivered from the warehouse, 'not less than two legal Packages'. Smith exhibits a similar caution in *WN* (v.ii.k.37), stating that public warehousing could not be extended to all sorts of goods, because suitable facilities could not be provided, and delicate or perishable goods requiring a great deal of care could be entrusted to a merchant's own warehouse. A nineteenth-century view was that warehousing, 'largely practised by the Dutch in the beginning of the seventeenth century, and . . . one of the happiest measures of [William] Huskisson in the nineteenth, had been part of the excise scheme of [Robert] Walpole' (Lecky, 1878: 362). The pamphlets and miscellaneous economic writings of Josiah Tucker in Smith's library (Mizuta) may have been one source for Smith's arguments about warehousing. Dean Tucker, to be sure, had personal links with Kames, Hume, and the French economists, among whom his ideas circulated, and from whom they could have been passed on to Smith (Shelton, 1981).

The Scottish Customs Board report is marked on the cover as having been read on 10 December 1783, and a further endorsement reads, 'Extract sent to Mr Colquhoun [i.e. the Glasgow Provost] 15 Decr. 1783'. This would demonstrate to the memorialists that they had the support of the Scottish Commissioners of Customs. A warehousing act was finally passed in 1799–1800, but full consolidation of the proposal came later with the passage of a statute, 59 Geo. III, c. 52 (1819), dealing with 'Goods which may be warehoused, or otherwise secured on Importation into Great Britain without Payment of Duty in the First Instance'. Three reigns afterwards came another statute which included details of the provision for warehousing tobacco: 16 and 17 Vict., c. 107, para. 10 (1853), but by this time Glasgow had long since 'become a manufacturing instead of a mercantile town' (*Glasgow Courier*, 8 Sept. 1791; Devine, 1975: 166).

In connection with the warehousing proposal, Smith acted in concert with his colleagues, though we may think the wording of their report has something of the flavour of his style, and may in part have been composed by him. On at least one occasion, however, he had a free hand in making recommendations about Custom-house practice in Scotland, and apparently altering policy in the direction of his reforming and even free-trade principles. This occurred in 1782, when Smith obtained leave from the Board from 19 March to 11 July. He went to London during this period on private business, attending meetings of The Club in the Turk's Head, not altogether to Johnson and Boswell's taste, but more to that of Burke and Gibbon (*Letters*, 1956: ii.291), who was President in February. Smith met with Whig politicians of the Rockingham circle, which included Burke (*Corr.* No. 217), and bought books and possibly did some research work in connection with edition 3 of *WN* (*Corr.* No. 222).

At a Customs Board meeting on 18 April, however, it was reported that the Treasury, on the advice of the Lord Advocate, Dundas, had asked Smith to deal with two proposals made by the Convention of Royal Burghs of Scotland: that there should be a uniform table of fees taken by the Customs officers; and that estuary rivers and firths should be put on the same footing as those of England. Smith reported on 24 May, and his report was considered by the Treasury Lords three days later. At first he did not have the relevant papers, but these were brought to him in London by the Secretary of the Board, R. E. Phillips. Smith learned that the Birmingham ironmaster, Samuel Garbett, one of the partners in the Carron Ironworks, had complained in 1766 that there was no precise table of fees in Scotland, and the Scottish Board of Customs was directed in 1767 to prepare a general table of fees. The Commissioners collected the appropriate information from their officers, but stated that they did not have grounds to introduce regularity, because where there were differences, these were believed necessary to supplement small salaries. This answer surprised the Treasury Lords, who commanded the Board to reconsider the matter and prepare a plan for regulating fees. The order was obeyed and a plan sent to the Treasury on 5 October 1767, but their Lordships never responded one way or another, so the matter was left in abeyance.

At first Smith thought he would recommend the general table of fees prepared by the Board in 1767, and he had a meeting with the Lord Provost of Edinburgh, the deputy of the Royal Burghs, with this in mind. The Provost proposed another list of fees, however, and after several conferences he and Smith reached agreement on the subject. Smith submitted a new list to the Treasury with 'great diffidence', because it was not the same as that proposed by the Customs Board in 1767, and the differences for the most part were to the disadvantage of the Customs officers, but he felt himself obliged to yield. Perhaps the Provost brought up the authority of *WN* in favour of disburdening trade as much as possible and equitable application of any restraints.

Smith asked that before the Lords of Treasury approved of the new list, it should be sent with his report to his colleagues in Edinburgh to correct his errors. He was concerned that instituting the new fees would mean loss of income:

Of many Officers the Income may even be so far reduced as to make it difficult for them to subsist suitably to that Rank in the Society which in reason ought to belong to them; The narrowness of their Circumstances may even force many of them into a dependancy upon the Merchants which must immediately prove hurtful to the Public Revenue and in the end probably ruinous to the unhappy Persons who may have thus endeavoured to relieve their necessities by accepting of improper Gratuities.

As for the second proposal, Smith had to confess that he did not know on what footing estuary rivers and firths were in England, but he had come on several Acts of Parliament in the Statute Book altering the footing, so he presumed there were differences even in that country. He believed that what the Royal Burghs wanted was freedom of trade in the inland waters from variable fees for certificates relating to taxable goods. Agreeable to his principles, he finds no difficulty with this:

I have always been of opinion that not only the Trade within such Rivers and Friths but the whole Coasting Trade of Great Britain so far as it is carried on in Goods [not prohibited to be exported, or not liable to any duty . . . upon exportation], may with great conveniency to the Merchants and with Security to the Revenue of the Customs be exempted from the formality of Bonds and Cockets.

He noted that a Bill to this end had been drafted for the Customs Board applicable to the Firth of Forth, and accordingly he argued that 'it would be not only much shorter, but much more just and equal, to extend this exemption at once to the whole Coasting Trade of Great Britain' (PRO, Kew, Treasury T1/570).

Predictably, the officers of the Customs service petitioned against the loss of income threatened by these proposals; but they did go into effect in large part, as appears by a printed letter issued by the Board on 2 September 1784, surviving with the cover addressed to the Collector and Comptroller of the Customs, Dundee. In view of the resulting loss of income from fees, the Board signified they would indemnify present officers from such losses, and the Collector and Comptroller were required to 'transmit quarterly, an Account on Oath, showing in a comparative View, the Fees received under these Regulations, and the Fees that would have been due according to the established Practice at your Port at the Date hereof' (EUL, Customs Board printed letter No. 66, signed by Commissioners Smith, Reid, and Edgar).

On 23 January 1781 the physician and merchant, also confidant of Lord Shelburne, Benjamin Vaughan, gave his Lordship an account of a visit to Edinburgh. He reported that he found Adam Smith 'more to his relish than I know some hold he ought to be in the South . . . he is among the best of them [the Edinburgh literati], though with peculiarities of manners well enough known here'. He continued: '[Smith] is very well provided for in the customs, where he does not innovate; but I believe he at times wishes he had kept in his college, where he had both more time and more respect and perhaps more company.' Next followed news about Smith's writings: 'He is ready with a history of Astronomy it seems, but I hear of nothing else that he is yet prepared to publish' (Philadelphia, American Philosophical Soc., Vaughan/Shelburne).

Despite the disclaimer about Smith as an innovator in the Customs service, we have some evidence that, in the course of his career as a Commissioner, his insights as an economic theorist, as well as his knowledge of practical affairs, led him to promote changes he viewed as both useful and just. As to the effect on his career as a writer, that is a question still to be pursued.

20

Literary Pursuits

> The only thing I regret is the interruption of my literary pursuits, which the duties of my office necessarily occasion.

Custom-house records of his attendance at Board meetings reveal the pattern of the remaining years of Adam Smith's life (SRO CE 1/15–23; Campbell and Skinner, 1982b: 200). He was never absent from entering office until 19 March 1782, when he began four months' leave, mostly spent in London in literary society and in giving attention to extensive revision of *WN* for a third edition, but broken in upon, as we have seen, to negotiate with the deputy of the Convention of Royal Burghs of Scotland about Customs fees. On resuming attendance on 11 July 1782, he was absent only twenty-four times until the beginning of 1787, six of these days falling when he was grieving for the death of his mother on 23 May 1784. On 1 November 1785 he wrote to the duc de La Rochefoucauld promising to finish the sixth edition of *TMS* 'before the end of the ensuing winter', and stating, as we have already mentioned, that he had 'two other great works upon the anvil' (*Corr.* No. 248). From 3 January until 30 July 1787 he took another leave to visit London in quest of health, also to meet members of the Younger Pitt's Administration, and to continue work revising *TMS* for the last time. When he returned to the Customs Board in July 1787, he had to struggle against failing health and old age which, he conceded to La Rochefoucauld, made it uncertain whether or not he could complete his 'great works'. In 1788 he suffered another emotional blow from the death of his cousin, Janet Douglas, who had become the centre of his domestic life. In 1789 there was some recovery, with 111 attendances recorded at the Board, and he wrote on 18 November that he had finished work on *TMS* 'to the very last sentence' (Klemme, 1991: 279).

Dugald Stewart, for one, lamented that the duties of Smith's Customs office wasted his spirits and dissipated his attention. He also went so far as to affirm that, after moving to Edinburgh, Smith gave up his studies for a time: 'his passion for letters served only to amuse his leisure, and to animate his conversation' (v.6). One record of his animated conversation about literary pursuits surfaced in the issue of *The Bee* dated 11 May 1791. The anonymous contributor, 'Amicus', wrote that as a young man in 1780 he had several interviews with Smith, who was 'extremely communicative, and delivered himself, on every subject, with a freedom, and even boldness, quite opposite to the apparent reserve of his appearance'.

The bold opinions delivered were about literature and literary personages (*LRBL* 32–3, 227–31). Smith described Dr Johnson's oddness:

I have seen that creature bolt up in the midst of mixed company; and, without any previous notice, fall upon his knees behind a chair, repeat the Lord's Prayer, and then resume his seat at table.—He has played this freak over and over, perhaps five or six times in the course of an evening. It is not hypocrisy, but madness.

Smith also considered Johnson was 'always patronizing scoundrels', citing as an example the poet and self-proclaimed 'bastard' Richard Savage, who spent his allowance on a scarlet cloak trimmed with gold lace, and wore this when his 'naked toes were sticking through his shoes'. Though he 'hinted' he had never been able to read the *The Rambler* and *The Idler*, Smith extolled the political pamphlets which included *Taxation no Tyranny* (1775) against the American patriots. His favourite in this group was the one on the *Transactions respecting Falkland's Islands* (1771), 'as it displayed, in such forcible language, the madness of modern wars'. To another acquaintance he declared that Johnson's *Preface to Shakespeare* was the 'most *manly* piece of criticism that was ever published in any country' (Seward, 1797: v.151). Smith retained his interest in Johnson as a writer late in life, acquiring his *Prayers and Meditations* (Mizuta), published in 1785 by George Strahan, whom Johnson befriended when he displeased his father William by objecting to the trade of printer, and exceeding his income as an Anglican clergyman (Cochrane, 1964: 153–7).

A lesser-known writer on whom Amicus elicited Smith's comments was Dr John Campbell, referred to anonymously by Boswell as a 'very respectable authour who had married a printer's devil' (*BLJ* iv.99). Johnson considered him a 'man of much knowledge . . . who has a good share of imagination', and praised his translation of J. H. Cohausen's *Hermippus Redivivus* (1744) for its account of the 'Hermetick philosophy'. Boswell used to attend his Sunday soirées in a large, newly built house on the north-west corner of Queen Street, off Bloomsbury Square, 'till I began to consider that the shoals of Scotchmen who flocked about him might probably say, when anything of mine was well done, "Ay, ay, he has learnt this of Cawmell." ' The quantity of Campbell's publications was prodigious, and Johnson quipped that he was the 'richest author that ever grazed the common of literature' (*BLJ* i.417–18). Smith said that he had been in Campbell's company once, and that he was the kind of writer who wrote from the beginning of the week to the end. A gentleman dining with him once dropped the hint that he would like a set of the Doctor's works. Next day a cart brought them round, and the cartage cost £70. These books would have included his part of the *Biographia Britannica* edited by Kippis and his very useful *Political Survey of Great Britain*, both works to be found in Smith's Library (Mizuta).

In keeping with the attention given to Swift in *LRBL*, Smith spoke very favourably of him to Amicus as a 'pattern of correctness in stile and sentiment'. He would not allow that the early Pindaric odes were Swift's, but said that he 'wanted nothing but inclination to have become one of the greatest of all poets'. He enjoyed the poems addressed to Stella, and thought Swift's masterpiece the verses on his own death. Other poems Smith regarded as gossip occasioned by Swift writing 'for the entertainment of a private circle'.

A surprise to Amicus was Smith's high estimate of Livy as a historian, but this is in keeping with the account given of him in *LRBL*. Amicus thought Smith would have preferred Polybius, who is praised in the *Lectures* for the instructive and agreeable views he provides of the civil constitution of the Romans, but Livy is presented as the superior in the *Lectures* for his narrative flow (ii.54–78). Smith was attracted to the epic quality of Livy's writings and, no doubt, to his stress on the attachment of the Roman republicans to moral integrity and freedom. Of modern historians, Hume, as we might expect, was Smith's candidate for rivalry with Livy.

Like many of the Scottish literati, except perhaps Lord Kames and his own pupil William Richardson, Smith was no devotee of Shakespeare, and reminded Amicus of Voltaire's remark that *Hamlet* was the 'dream of a drunken savage' (Dissertation preceding *Sémiramis*, 1748). When Amicus hinted disparagement of this play himself, to 'sound' Smith, 'he gave a smile, as if he thought I would detect him in a contradiction and replied, "Yes! but still Hamlet is full of fine passages." '

He had an 'invincible contempt and aversion for blank verse, Milton's excepted', and reckoned that, if Dryden had possessed a tenth part of the dramatic genius of Shakespeare, he would have brought rhyming tragedies into vogue in England as much as they were in France. Indeed, he held that the French theatre was the 'standard of dramatic excellence'. Voltaire, of course, as a dramatist and man had Smith's unbounded admiration, and his library contained a Dresden edition of the works (1748–50) and the Kehl one in 70 volumes (Mizuta).

On 14 July 1763 Boswell told Johnson in conversation of Smith's views on poetic measure, to which came the reply: 'Sir, I was once in company with Smith, and we did not take to each other; but had I known that he loved rhyme as much as you tell me he does, I should have hugged him' (*BLJ* i.427–8). Apart from *L'Allegro* and *Il Penseroso*, all the rest of Milton's short poems were trash as far as Smith was concerned, and he could not imagine why Johnson (in his Life of Dryden) found anything in Dryden's ode on Mrs Anne Killigrew comparable to *Alexander's Feast*. His view of Pope's translation of the *Iliad* was that people did well 'to call it *Pope's* Homer; for it is not Homer's Homer. It has no resemblance to the majesty and simplicity of the Greek.' Yet he liked Pope's poetry and had memorized many passages of which he was fond. He did not admire Pope's private character, which he thought 'all affectation', and described the *Epistle to Dr Arbuthnot* as a 'consummate piece of canting'. His opinion of

Dryden was high, and he 'loudly extolled' his *Fables*. Amicus brought up the criticisms expressed by Hume:

[Dryden's] plays, excepting a few scenes, are utterly disfigured by vice, or folly, or both. His translations appear too much the offspring of haste and hunger; even his fables are ill-chosen tales, conveyed in an incorrect, though spirited versification. (*History of England* viii.336)

Smith gave the unanswerable retort: 'You will learn more as to poetry by reading one good poem, than by a thousand volumes of criticism.' His review of what might be called Augustan poetry was completed by reading some passages from Defoe, 'which breathed, as he thought, the true spirit of English verse'.

What about Smith's responses to other traditions in his century's poetry? He would not allow the name 'poem' to be attached to Beattie's paradigmatic romantic effusion *The Minstrel*, whose organization he did not comprehend, though he recognized that a few of the 'series of verses' were 'happy.' He regarded Gray's odes as the 'standard of lyric excellence' (cf. *TMS* III.2.19), but Allan Ramsay's pastoral comedy *The Gentle Shepherd* was not much to his taste, and he preferred Virgil's *Eclogues* and Guarini's *Il Pastor Fido*, 'of which he spoke with rapture'. When Amicus pleaded for Ramsay, arguing that he was the 'single unaffected poet' the Scots have had since George Buchanan, Smith was not impressed: 'It is the duty of a poet to write like a gentleman. I dislike that homely style which some think fit to call the language of nature and simplicity'. He continued in this strain, claiming that in Percy's *Reliques of Ancient English Poetry* a 'few tolerable pieces are buried under a heap of rubbish'. He asked Amicus if he had read the ballads, 'Adam Bell', 'Clym of the Cleugh', and 'William of Cloudeslie', and being told that he did, asked: 'Well then, do you think that was worth printing?' It seems his taste had been formed by reading the neo-classical English literature, and he was not ready to widen his appreciation except that he showed some appreciation of the poetry of Ossian, and therefore of the bardic art that in time had a transforming effect on contemporary European literature (Campbell and Skinner, 1982*b*: 213; Gaskill, 1991).

Some harsh remarks and anecdotes about Goldsmith loving a 'wench and a bottle' and not being averse to lies prefaced a denunciation of the '*reviews*'. Smith declared that 'it was not easy to conceive in what contempt they were held in London'. Amicus told an improbable tale about Burke which Smith said must have come from 'some of the magazines', adding that he considered them to be lower than the reviews. He would not hear of the *Gentleman's Magazine* being excepted from his condemnation, and claimed that he 'never looked at a Review, nor even knew that names of the publishers'. This is a strange statement, since Smith knew Griffiths and Rose, the founders of the *Monthly Review*, and William Strahan had an interest in this periodical as one of the publishers. Moreover, Archibald Hamilton, founder of the *Critical Review*, edited by Smollett, was Strahan's manager (*BLJ* iii.475–6; Cochrane, 1964: 103, 121, 131).

Perhaps Smith was dismayed by what he read in the reviews about himself, but in 1776 at least he was eager to read them, as a letter to Cadell written on 27 June makes clear: 'I have yet received no letter from you in answer to my enquiries concerning the sale of my book. Send me all the criticisms you can' (Klemme, 1991: 279).

Summing up his 'present situation' in October 1780 for his Danish friend Andreas Holt, in a letter which is his one sustained autobiographical piece of writing, Smith expressed regret that the interruptions in his 'literary pursuits' caused by his Custom-house duties would hold up 'Several Works' he had projected. One of these he described to Holt as 'concerning the Imitative Arts', and he mentioned that he was employing himself in writing it in Kirkcaldy in 1776–7 after the publication of *WN* (*Corr.* No. 208). This is probably connected with the 'Philosophical History of all the different branches of Literature' still 'upon the anvil' in 1785, and is represented by the fragments preserved in *EPS*. Other works held up by the Customs duties were revised editions of *WN* and *TMS*, and the book on 'Law and Government' which had been heralded at the conclusion of *TMS* in 1759. One literary project which Smith studiously avoided in this period was overseeing the publication of the *Dialogues concerning Natural Religion*, though this project had the sanction of being Hume's deathbed wish.

Hume had begun and largely completed this composition in the 1750s, enlisting the help of Gilbert Elliot of Minto, then had returned to polish and amend it towards the end of his life. It is a skilfully conducted debate about the being and nature of God between a theist, Cleanthes; a schizoid divine, alternately fideistic and rationalistic, Demea; and a sceptic, Philo. After making Smith his literary executor with instructions to publish the *Dialogues*, and then allocating a small legacy to Smith for his pains in this matter (*Corr.* No. 157), the dying Hume came to realize that Smith balked at complying with his request. As described earlier, this caused some trouble to Hume over a matter of importance to him in his last weeks. In a codicil to his will, Hume asked Smith to undertake to publish the book within five years of his death if his nephew, David Hume the Younger, had not done so by that time (*Corr.* No. 165, 205 n. 1). Smith resisted this wish, however, and stated flatly to Strahan: 'I am resolved, for many reasons, to have no concern in the publication of those dialogues' (*Corr.* No. 172).

Now, what were those reasons that weighed so heavily with Smith? We have a clue in an unsigned draft of a letter to Strahan, written in the October following Hume's death:

I am much obliged to you for so readily agreeing to [print] the life, together with my addition separate from the Dialogues. I even flatter myself that this arrangement will contribute, not only to my quiet, but to your interest. The clamour against the dialogues, if published first, might hurt for some time the sale of the new edition of [Hume's] works and when the Clamour has a little subsided, the dialogues might hereafter occasion a quicker sale of another edition. (*Corr.* No. 177B)

Since this is only a draft, and there exists an earlier one with a version of the paragraph just quoted struck through (No. 177A), it would seem that this letter gave its writer some difficulty. Perhaps even to himself, Smith could not state in a satisfactory way why he would not see to the publication of the *Dialogues*. For some reason, Hume thought it necessary to make it clear to Smith that he considered the *Dialogues* among his best work: 'On revising them (which I have not done for these 15 years) I find that nothing can be more cautiously and more artfully written. You had certainly forgotten them' (15 Aug. 1776: *Corr.* No. 165). It is likely that Smith expressed to Hume reservations about the content of the *Dialogues*, rather than their literary merit. Indeed, he conceded to Strahan that this text was 'finely written'. Accordingly, we have to focus on Smith's perception of the content of the *Dialogues*, to establish the meaning of the reference to his 'quiet' and, to a lesser extent, his concern for Strahan's 'interest'.

In this context, the word 'quiet' could have two chief meanings. One is Smith's concern for his reputation, the peaceful enjoyment of the esteem which his reputation as a philosopher and man of letters had earned for him. He may well have read the *Dialogues* as constituting a successful attack on religion both revealed and natural (Mossner, 1977; 1978). He may have shied all the more violently away from the role of overseer of publication because there was a question of monetary gain. He had elected to live in Scotland, where religious enthusiasm was still strong, and he may have remembered that his mentor, Francis Hutcheson, and William Leechman had both clashed with the Glasgow Presbytery over holding heterodox views. Also, there was the consideration that his patron Lord Kames was excluded from the Commission of the General Assembly of the Church of Scotland for publishing such views, and could possibly have lost his judge's seat, at the time when Hume was threatened with excommunication for his alleged atheism (Ross, 1972: 156).

It is true that these events had taken place more than twenty years before. Yet the publication of Smith's supplement to Hume's *My Own Life*, in the form of a letter to Strahan detailing Hume's last illness, had aroused a storm of protest from Christians. They were infuriated because Smith had adapted as an epitaph for Hume the last sentence of the *Phaedo*: 'Upon the whole, I have always considered him, both in his lifetime and since his death, as approaching as nearly to the idea of a perfectly wise and virtuous man, as perhaps the nature of human frailty will permit' (*Corr.* No. 178). The most unchristian fury evoked in England by this linking of Hume to Socrates as truly virtuous and wise men in secular terms is well represented by *A Letter to Adam Smith, LL.D. on the Life, Death, and Philosophy of His Friend David Hume Esq. By One of the People Called Christians*, published at Oxford in 1777 by no less a personage than the President of Magdalen College, George Horne, who ended his career as Bishop of Norwich. The shock felt in Scotland by 'every sober Christian' was registered by the anecdotalist Ramsay of Ochtertyre (ed. Allardyce, 1888: i.466–7). Attacks such as Horne's led Smith to make his sardonic remark of October 1780:

A single, and as, I thought, a very harmless Sheet of paper, which I happened to Write concerning the death of our late friend Mr Hume, brought upon me ten times more abuse than the very violent attack I had made upon the whole commercial system of Great Britain. (*Corr.* No. 208)

It might be argued in view of all this that Smith wished to live quietly, without more letters appearing in print by Reverends and Right Reverends denouncing his relationship with Hume.

Nevertheless, a second chief meaning of the 'quiet' so important to Smith deserves greater consideration. This would take the word to mean his peace of mind, or intellectual repose. Involvement with the *Dialogues* may have been resisted because he had not or could not come to grips with their content. In a nutshell, if he had no answers to the sceptic Philo's demolition of the argument for a deity on the basis of the evident design of the universe, then Smith's own philosophy would be undermined. His philosophy of explanation involves final explanations, couched in terms of a purposeful nature or God, and this variety of theism is an integral party of his approach to social phenomena. He certainly distinguishes between efficient and final causes, but his stress on function centres on the attempt to show how the mechanism of efficient causation produces beneficial results intended by the utilitarian 'Author of nature' (*TMS* III.5.7). If the latter component were taken away, Smith must have felt, then his whole theoretical apparatus was seriously damaged. We may see Smith's personal moral philosophy as a form of contemplative utilitarianism or 'universal benevolence', and this is painfully undermined by the *Dialogues*. In the light of the sceptical challenge to theism in this text, some words that Smith added to the last edition of *TMS* can perhaps be taken as self-directed:

To this universal benevolence . . . the very suspicion of a fatherless world, must be the most melancholy of all reflections. . . . All the splendour of the highest prosperity can never enlighten the gloom with which so dreadful an idea must necessarily overshadow the imagination. (VI.ii.3.2)

The hasty conclusion should be rejected that Smith wished to stifle the *Dialogues* to protect his own views. As we have seen, he thought there was no doubt that Strahan would publish the book, and he offered prudential advice about the timing of the publication to quicken sales of Hume's other writings. As things turned out, Strahan refused to publish the *Dialogues*, and this task was carried out in 1779 by Hume's nephew, then 19. There was no 'Clamour', and Hugh Blair certainly considered there were no 'principles' in the book which were absent from the works published in Hume's lifetime (*HL* ii.454). It thus appears that Smith miscalculated public response to the *Dialogues*, just as he went against his own teaching about deathbed wishes in *LJ*: 'We naturally find a pleasure in remembering the last words of a friend and in executing his last injunctions, the solemnity of the occasion deeply impresses the mind' ((B) 165). In his last years Smith focused his attention on a 'practical system of Morality' (*Corr*. No. 287), which would guide the virtuous life through a balance of 'perfect prudence, of strict justice, and of proper benevolence' (*TMS* 6th edn. 6, VI.iii.1). In different circumstances, the appropriate combination of these elements of virtues is achieved through attending to the behests of the impartial spectator, a concept in its final manifestation much more connected with that of private conscience and less with that of public opinion (Raphael and Macfie, *TMS* intro. 16). On the facts of his treatment of the dying Hume's request, Smith seems to have attended more to what prudence suggested than to the advice of a supposed impartial spectator, who could be trusted to see where benevolence should override prudential considerations.

This affair has to be placed beside Smith's inaction in 1751, when he would have preferred Hume to any man as a colleague, but judged that the 'interest' of Glasgow University required deference to public opinion, which would not tolerate such an appointment (*Corr*. No. 10). Taken together, these episodes do not make Smith the 'man of prudence' he sketches in that 'practical system of Morality' added to the last edition of *TMS*. Such a man earns only 'cold esteem' for an inferior kind of self-regarding prudence exercised over health, fortune, rank, and reputation. It cannot be said, either, that Smith evinced on his best friend's behalf that superior prudence, the alliance of the 'best head' with the 'best heart' which 'constitutes very nearly the character of the . . . sage' (VI.i. 7–15). Perhaps we can settle for the view that Smith exhibited here a middling prudence, which never seems to have affected the warmth felt for him by Hume and others of his circle.

To give Smith his due, however, we must exculpate him from one tendency of the 'man of [inferior] prudence', namely, a coolness to 'those convivial societies which are distinguished for the jollity and gaiety of their conversation. Their way of life might too often interfere with the regularity of his temperance, might interrupt the steadiness of his industry, or break in upon the strictness of his frugality.' Carlyle of Inveresk is a witness to Smith's membership of the convivial clubs formed by the literati, such as the Poker, so designated by Adam Ferguson because its function was to stir up the question of a Scottish militia. Smith himself left testimony about being at a 'very jolly table' with *Dr Bonum Magnum* himself—Alexander Webster, strict Calvinist, population expert, and, as Smith put the matter, a 'very great lover and promoter . . . of mirth and jollity' (*Corr*. No. 252). Smith's own table was not abstemious, as we may surmise from one correspondent's claim that it was the scene at 2 a.m. one morning of him spouting a speech later echoed by Lord North in the House of Commons (*Corr*. No. 197). As for any renown for merrymaking, however, it was also Carlyle of Inveresk's opinion that Smith was 'ill qualifi'd to promote the Jollity of a Birthday', where he reckoned he shone himself; but at the same time he did not tax Smith with excessive prudence, rather choosing to assert roundly: 'he had the most unbounded Benevolence' (1973: 142, 213–16, 250).

Another friend of Smith's, and in this case a colleague, who sought to draw him into literary enterprise was Henry Mackenzie, whom Walter Scott saluted as the 'Scottish Addison' because of his success in reviving the art of periodical essay-writing. Smith probably met Mackenzie in the company of Hume, whose 'page' he liked to think he had been when a young man. Of Highland descent, Mackenzie grew up in Edinburgh where his father was a well-known physician, and he attended the High School, then the University, where he was influenced by Robertson and Hugh Blair. He was sent to London in 1765 to learn the procedures of the Exchequer, but returned home to practise law as a Writer to the Signet, and eventually becoming the Crown Attorney with much Customs business in Edinburgh. There he formed steady friendships with professional men, mostly lawyers but including some ministers, who continued to develop in their writings some of the leading themes of the Scottish Enlightenment, such as linking moral psychology to socioeconomic progress. Mackenzie was highly successful with his first extensive, though anonymous, publication: the novel *The Man of Feeling* (1771). This deserves a place with Richardson's *Clarissa Harlowe* (1748), Rousseau's *Julie, ou la Nouvelle Héloïse* (1761), Sterne's *Sentimental Journey* (1768), and Goethe's *The Sorrows of Young Werther* (1774) as chief contributors to the European cult of the fiction of sentiment or sensibility. Smith's theories about the emotive basis of human values have a connection, of course, with the aesthetic dimension of such novels, though his framework of Stoic ideas controls their tendencies towards emotional excess (Patey, 1984; Mullan, 1990; Boyle, 1992). Mackenzie continued a career as a novelist with *The Man of the World* (1773) and *Julia de Roubigné* (1777), which marked an advance in sensitive understanding of character. In some ways, however, Mackenzie prized as a greater accomplishment than his novels the morally didactic essays he wrote for two periodicals appearing during Smith's Edinburgh years (Mackenzie, 1927; Thompson, 1931; Dwyer, 1987: 26–7; Mullan, 1987). These were *The Mirror*, issued in 110 numbers from 23 January 1779 to 27 May 1780, and *The Lounger*, issued in 101 numbers from 5 February 1785 to 6 January 1786 (Drescher, 1971: 283).

The idea of art as the mirror of morality has a long pedigree, and is familiar to us in Hamlet's lines about acting, 'whose end both at the first, and now, was and is, to hold as 'twere the mirror up to nature, to show virtue her own feature, scorn her own image, and the very age and body of the time his form and pressure' (III.ii.17–21). Hume and Smith had given an ingenious twist to this idea by suggesting that the 'minds of men' (*Treatise* II.ii.5) and 'society' (*TMS* III.1.3) constitute the mirrors for individuals, in which they see approval and disapproval of their sentiments and learn to estimate thereby their characters and the rectitude or otherwise of their conduct. Mackenzie with like-minded friends formed a Mirror Club, itself an offshoot of another group made up of lawyers and literary men called the Feast of Tabernacles, which had formed round Henry Dundas and met at Purves's tavern in Parliament Square (Dwyer, 1987: 24; Fry, 1992: 49, 57). The general aim of these societies was the cultural development of Scotland. More specifically, the Mirror Club saw itself as a preserver and promoter of the virtue of the landowning classes of the country. The Club met to discuss moral issues of the day and agree on the essays considered fit for publication.

Mackenzie tried hard to involve Smith in providing copy for the Club's periodical, as he reveals in a retrospective account:

To Adam Smith I applied earnestly to contribute to the *Mirror* owning my Concern in it, and mentioning that I was assisted by some of his Pupils and Friends—(Lord Craig [i.e. William Craig the judge] had been a favourite Pupil of his). He half promised to comply with my request; but afterwards told me he had tried a Paper without Success. 'My Manner of Writing, said he, will not do for a Work of that Sort; it runs too much into Deduction and inference.'

Mackenzie also submitted copy for Smith's criticism and comment. For example, two days after soliciting copy, he gave Smith a text of the celebrated 'Story of La Roche', which ran in *The Mirror* in numbers 42–4. In this piece of fiction Mackenzie gives a sentimental account of a Swiss pastor and his beautiful daughter, somewhat in the tradition of Rousseau and Sterne; but of greater interest is his imaginative evocation of a historical person who is made to encounter them. This is the young Hume, 'an English [*sic*] philosopher, whose works have since been read and admired by all Europe', and who had been driven abroad 'by some disappointments in his native country'. Smith commented thus: 'My dear sir, there is not a word to which any body can object; it is an admirable Paper; but it is rather singular that with my intimate Acquaintance with Mr Hume, I have never heard the anecdote before.' Somewhat of a 'man of prudence' himself, Mackenzie did not undeceive Smith lest he offend him, acknowledging in his Book of Anecdotes that this 'was committing a falsehood by implication' (NLS MS 2537, fo. 6; Drescher, 1971: 280). Smith was also drawn into commenting on 23 May 1780 about two draft conclusions for *The Mirror* series which Mackenzie submitted to him. He expressed a decided preference for the first one as 'ten times more interesting' than the second, which he castigated as 'much flatter and colder' (*Corr.* No. 204).

Mackenzie also enlisted Smith in helping the literary career of John Logan (*Corr.* No. 215); he was a member of the Feast of Tabernacles group, and became minister of South Leith but was driven from his charge by some scandal connected with his publishing ventures, which included poetry, topical pamphlets, and historical writings. Smith did not think much of Logan's verse drama *Runnamede* (produced 1783), containing advanced views on political liberty, but he did have a high regard for 'some lectures on Universal History' which were delivered in St Mary's chapel, Edinburgh, in the course of two university sessions, 1779–81. Though presented in a fragmented form, Logan's historical thought contains important insights, to which Smith must have responded. Logan certainly felt that Smith would take his side, together with John Home and Ferguson, against 'Dr Robertson's friends', in a scheme for academic advancement at Edinburgh University (EUL MS La.II.419). The second course of lectures was published as a *Dissertation on the Government, Manners, and Spirit of Asia* (1782), and it is notable for extending the approach of Montesquieu and Ferguson's *History of Civil Society* in analysing the cultures and governments of the countries encountered by the East India Companies of Europe. In the era of the impeachment of Warren Hastings, Logan sought to understand the corrupting influence of the 'spirit of Asia', well-versed in the fears of the Roman moralists about the Asiatic influence they believed to be undermining the Roman Empire. As a basis for his system of values, Logan, in common with members of the Mirror Club, drew heavily on the moral concepts of *TMS*, and his sermons publicized Smith's teaching about sympathy and the invisible hand (Dwyer, 1987: 22–4).

On 29 September 1785 Smith described Logan to Andrew Strahan, who had taken over his father's printing and publishing company, as a 'Clergyman of uncommon learning, taste, and ingenuity; but who cannot easily submit to the puritanical spirit of this country'. He went on to recommend Logan as a reviewer of 'all Books of taste, of history, and of moral and abstract Philosophy' (*Corr.* No. 247). Before an early death hastened by alcoholism, Logan had some success in London as a man of letters, editing the *English Review*, which became a vehicle for disseminating the ideas of the Scottish Enlightenment. He had a complex character and could not resist finessing his publications, for example, *A View of Antient History* (1788–91), which he asserted to Smith was written by the master of a dissenters' academy at Uxbridge but which appears to have come from his own pen (*Corr.* No. 273). His friends included leading members of the Moderate clergy: Smith's contemporaries Blair and Carlyle, and his former pupils Thomas Somerville and Samuel Charters. There was admiration for his gifts as a poet, though controversies arose over which verses were Logan's and which those of a friend, Michael Bruce, who died as a youth, and whose poems Logan edited. Nevertheless, it can be established that he had a hand in some of the memorable paraphrases still sung in the Church of Scotland, for example, 'O God of Bethel by whose hand thy people still are fed'. This writer whom Smith befriended, likely enough at Henry Mackenzie's prompting, seems harshly treated by the historian of the Kirk's song, when dismissed as a 'shameless plagiarist, a false friend, and latterly a drunken rascal' (Patrick, 1927: 117).

The shipwreck of Logan's career, perhaps the result of ambition spreading talent too thin, and also the emotional and moral stress of moving from a Burgher family, that is, one committed to a strict Christian fundamentalism, to a role as a Moderate minister and then a professional writer for the London periodical press, contrasts with the success of the older literati whom Henry Mackenzie reviews for a correspondent named William Carmichael, some time in 1783. He considers the 'brilliant Era' to have passed with the deaths of Hume and of Kames (27 December 1782). Robertson is represented as dedicating himself to ease after publishing the *History of America* (1777). Ferguson is still active, and has just issued his *History of the Progress and Termination of the Roman Republic* (1783), but it has proved disappointing because lacking in 'those general and philosophic views of the subject which is the great distinction between Modern History, since the time of Montesquieu, and the Ancients'. Blair has finally published his *Lectures on Rhetoric and Belles Lettres* (1783), but this work is 'perhaps not so original or deep as the metaphysical enquiring turn of this age might have required', and has not had a success equal to the expectations of the booksellers or as great as that of the *Sermons* (edn. 1, 1778) now running to '9 or 10 Editions'. One figure does stand out:

Dr Smith, whom I reckon the first of our Writers, both in Point of Genius and Information, is now revising both his Theory of Moral Sentiments, and his Essay on the Wealth of Nations, in the new Editions of both which (to be published in the Spring) there will be considerable alteration and Improvement. He has lying by him several Essays, some finish'd, but the greater Part, I believe, not quite compleated, on Subjects of Criticism and Belles Lettres, which, when he chuses to given them to the World will, I am confident, nowise derogate from his former Reputation as an Author. (NLS MS 646, fos. 1–11)

In 1783 Smith was contemplating or had in hand major revisions of *TMS* and *WN*, and there were the 'two other great works' described to La Rochefoucauld as being 'on the anvil' in 1785 (*Corr.* No. 248). We can follow the fortunes of these ventures from Smith's letters. On 25 October 1780 he instructs Cadell to send copies of the second edition of *WN* (1778) to Peter Anker, Consul-General of Denmark, and his former tutor Andreas Holt, Commissioner of the Danish Board of Trade and Economy, whom he had met in Toulouse, with a further copy to go to Frants Draebye, who was Holt's successor in the Norwegian Secretariat of the Economic and Trade Department of Denmark, and who had translated the first edition of *WN* into Danish. Smith jokes to Cadell: 'I am afraid I am not only your best, but almost your only customer for this Second Edition', but he still wishes to know 'how this matter goes on' (*Corr.* No. 206). In a parallel letter to William Strahan the next day, he is in a similar self-mocking mood: 'I suspect I am now almost your only customer for my own book' (No. 207).

That same day he writes to Holt, as already mentioned, about his life since they met in France. He mentions the corrections made to *WN* for the second edition, pointing out that none of them 'affect even in the slightest degree, the general principles, or Plan of the System'. He had corrected, or took some steps to correct, matters of fact, for example, details of a tax levied from 1757 on offices with an income of more than £100 a year (v.ii.i.7); and he had improved his expression in some place or made it more idiomatic, replacing 'tear and wear', for instance, with the usual order of that phrase (IV.ix.7). In addition, he provided more information and more footnotes, as in a short passage in the account of the rise to opulence of Italian cities, dealing with the introduction into Venice of silk manufacture by families driven from Lucca by 'one of Machiavel's heroes, Castruccio Castracani' (III.iii.19). Here Smith is remembering a rhetorical exercise in the form of a biography of a famous *condottiere*, which Machiavelli wrote as a preliminary to settling down to his *History of Florence* (Skinner, 1981: 79). As his source for this episode in Venetian economic development, Smith cites Vettore Sandi's *Principi di storia civile della Repubblica di Venezia* (1755–6) which, like Machiavelli's works (1768 edn.) was in his library (Mizuta).

Smith continues his letter to Holt by describing some of the critics of *WN* and what he thought of them. One of the most acute of the early commentaries was to be found in *A Letter from Governor [Thomas] Pownall to Adam Smith*, dated 25 September 1776. The author had been Governor of Massachusetts Bay 1757–9, and was appointed to but did not assume a similar office in South Carolina in 1760. He served as an MP from 1767 to 1780, and though contemptuously dismissed by one witness as a 'little fat man [who] was given his chance to rant' in the House of Commons, he spoke sensibly about Britain's mishandling of American affairs, and urged realistic measures to end the conflict with the Americans. For example, he urged in March 1778 that independence be granted in return for a federal treaty (*HP* iii.318).

Pownall had a clear perception of Smith's system of political economy as a form of 'moral Newtonianism', and he thought that if it were corrected on the salient points he brought up, *WN* might become an institutional work on which could be based lectures 'in our Universities' (*Corr.* app. A). The chief criticisms in the *Letter* were directed at Smith's formulations concerning price, patterns of trade, restraints on importation, and the monopoly of the colony trade. Smith would have Holt believe that he obviated all Pownall's objections in the second edition of *WN*, but there is not much evidence to support this (*WN* I.ii.1 n. 3). In at least one place, however, he expanded his wording, apparently to respond to Pownall's challenge to his theory that, in the final analysis, labour constitutes the standard of value (I.v.7 and n. 15). Smith was not much surprised to find Pownall dissatisfied with his responses to the criticisms, 'as Authors are not much disposed to alter the opinions they have once published'.

Another critic whom Smith describes as being a 'man of parts and one of my acquaintance' attacked him for arguing in *WN* that a 'militia . . . in whatever manner it may be either disciplined or exercised, must always be much inferior to a well disciplined and well exercised standing army' (v.i.a.23). Smith believed this writer's name was 'Douglas'. Probably relying on the NLS catalogue, however, Halkett and Laing (1971: iii.287) ascribe the pamphlet to Carlyle of Inveresk: *A Letter from a Gentleman in Edinburgh to his Grace the Duke of Buccleugh on National Defence, with some Remarks on Dr Smith's Chapter on that Subject in his Book, entitled [WN]* (1778). Carlyle had written on the militia question and, like Smith, was a member of the Poker Club founded after the defeat of the Scotch Militia Bill in 1760 to keep the issue alive. However, this 1778 *Letter to Buccleuch* is much more heavy-handed than Carlyle's style in his well-identified piece *The Question relating to a Scotch Militia considered, in a Letter to the Lords and Gentlemen who have concerted the form of law for that establishment* (1760), ostensibly by a 'Freeholder of Ayrshire' (Carlyle, 1973: 233–4, 238–41, 257–61, 328, 331–3—list of his publications). Smith complains to Holt that the author of the *Letter to Buccleuch* has not read *WN* to the end, meaning that he had not appreciated that Smith did value militia service as a form of civic responsibility and expression of manhood, also that Smith had declared that the American militia might become a match for the British standing army, after remaining long enough in the field to acquire military discipline, the habit of 'prompt obedience', equal to that of regular troops (v.i.a.27).

Smith expresses concern that someone of his acquaintance should challenge him rudely in print and misrepresent him, but there was a more alarming context. Buccleuch, Smith's patron and the figure to whom the *Letter* was addressed, was active in the military affairs of the Scotland of the time. From his Border tenants he had personally raised a volunteer regiment, the South Fencibles, to deal with the emergencies in Scotland arising from the American war, including violent clashes over military obedience. The Duke became involved in one of these as a negotiator in September 1778 on the Crags of Arthur's Seat, when men of Lord Seaforth's Highlanders, regulars enlisted to fight in America, mutinied rather than submit to being sent to India, where the death rate from sickness was appallingly high. In the April following the Duke was ordered to send his Fencibles to Leith, to shoot down men of the Black Watch and Fraser's Highlanders who refused to be drafted into a Lowland regiment, the Royal Glasgow Volunteers, when they had been promised their distinctive culture would be preserved in the form of service in their national dress and under Gaelic-speaking officers.

Smith was living in the Canongate when the Seaforth mutineers freed comrades in the guard-house at the Tolbooth, and then marched behind the skirling of the pipes out to Arthur's Seat. He was also in the vicinity during the massacre of the Highlanders at Leith, and the transporting of the dead, wrapped in their bloody plaids, to lie in the yard of Lady Yester's kirk. In *WN* Smith had noted that when the Highland militia served under their own chieftains whom they obeyed in peace, like the militia of the Tartars and Arabs, they approached standing armies in their 'habit of ready obedience'. Unlike the Tartars and Arabs, however, the Highlanders were not nomads, and were not willing to travel far or go to war for a long period (v.i.a.26). Lord Seaforth and other chieftains of Smith's time were ready to sell their human capital to the British Government to retain their prestige and power in a changing world, and they ignored the traditions of their people. Seaforth in the end allowed his men to be sold to the East India Company, and the promise that was made to them that they would be discharged in Ross-shire was betrayed, for those asking for release at the end of the American war were abandoned on the Coast of Coromandel (Prebble, 1977: 128, 165–9, 138–40). It is to be wondered if Smith reflected on the military effect of the breaking of the attachment of the Highlanders to their chieftains, and on the use of the Border militia under Buccleuch to overwhelm the Highlanders and bring them into line with the imperial designs of England.

A final criticism of the first edition of *WN* that Smith mentions to Holt came from the agricultural expert James Anderson, whom he describes as a 'very diligent, laborious, honest Man'.[1] From his practical experience of farming and reflection on the corn laws, Anderson sought to counter Smith's objections to the bounty on corn. In the 'heat of Writing', Smith had ventured to declare that the 'nature of things has stamped upon corn a real value which no human institution can alter' (edn. 1, IV.v.a.23). In *Observations on the Means of Exciting a Spirit of National Industry* (1777), Anderson argued that Smith had acknowledged elsewhere in *WN* that 'whatever lowered the real price of manufactur'd produce, rais'd the price of rude produce, and consequently of corn' (*Corr.* No. 208). Smith accordingly changed his text for the second edition of *WN* to a form of words covering all that his argument required, stating there is a 'real value' of corn, which 'cannot be altered by merely altering its money price'. Governor Pownall had also objected to the original form of Smith's doctrine (*Corr.* app. A, pp. 361–6), and had noted that Smith shared Necker's viewpoint about the corn bounty expressed in his tract *Sur la législation et le commerce des grains* (1775).

Anderson's challenge to Smith on this issue was connected with his development of a theory of rent, which was incorporated into Ricardo's 'corn model'. This is perhaps the first example of Smith's great book giving rise to a successful extension of the analytical side of economics in which aggregate economic relationships are represented in terms of applying labour and capital to land to produce corn (O'Brien, 1975: 126).

21

Times of Hardship and Distress

In the crisis-ridden years of the ending of the American war and its immediate aftermath, Smith seems to have been struck keenly by the condition of 'something more than ordinary absurdity' in the Government's system of encouragements and restrictions applied to economic enterprises (*WN* IV.v.a.37). Because it was his duty as a Commissioner of Customs to enforce this system, he was perhaps galled all the more by the wastefulness it involved. He seems to have struck back by concentrating mostly, though not entirely, on the policy advice side of *WN* in preparing a third edition, rather than turn to the analytical side developed in James Anderson's criticism.

This third edition, it appears, was in contemplation at least from January 1779, when he wrote to an unidentified nobleman to say that he had no copies of the first two editions to give away, having retained one of each only 'in order to mark the corrections or additions which I may hereafter have occasion to make' (*Corr.* No. 198). Addressing William Eden, as we surmise, on 3 January 1780, Smith expresses strong views about bounties and prohibitions, which are reiterated in the supplementary material prepared for the new edition of *WN* of 1784, where the theme of the absurdity of the restrictions on trade with France, also of the herring fishing bounty and the corn bounty, is given prominence.

Smith had declared to Eden that the public revenues could be increased by 'three very obvious methods'. The first was by repealing 'all bounties on exportation'. Smith is scathing in his indictment of this practice: 'When we cannot find taxes to carry on a defensive war', such being the current phase of hostilities against the Americans, which had broadened into a European conflict involving France and Spain, 'our Merchants ought not to complain if we refuse to tax ourselves any longer in order to support a few feeble and languishing branches of their commerce.' The second method was repealing all prohibitions on importation. In this connection, Smith discussed the prohibition on Dutch cured herrings, which he asserts to be 'vastly superior' to the British product. He recommends placing a tax of half a guinea on the Dutch product, which will result in a price in Britain for Dutch herring off 33*s.* or 34*s.*, confining them 'altogether to the tables of the better sort of people'. British manufacturers, he confidently predicts, will try to get this high price by improving the quality of their product, and in five or six years will have achieved an improvement he despairs of seeing in the present circumstances in fifty to sixty years.

The Commissioner of Customs of two years' experience, and the realistic observer, then declares: 'Prohibitions do not prevent the importation of prohibited goods.' People go ahead and buy what they need, 'in the fair way of trade', without being aware of the restrictions. Then he tells the story of the scrape he got into by looking over the list of prohibited goods, thereafter examining his clothes, and ending up burning cravats, pocket handkerchief, and ruffles. As a third method of increasing revenue, he recommends dropping the prohibition on exporting wool and substituting a 'pretty high duty'. This will prevent the sacrifice of the grower's interest for that of the manufacturer' (*Corr.* No. 203).

These were the ideas Smith was revolving about economic matters prior to 1782, when he took four months leave in London from March to July, as already noted, seemingly to work on *WN*. On 7 December of that year he confessed to his publisher, Thomas Cadell, that he had bought many books in London, and this 'debauched me from my proper business; the preparing a new edition of the Wealth of Nations'. Sanguine in this instance about his rate of progress, he expressed the hope that in two or three months he would be able to send on the 'second Edition corrected in many places, with three or four very considerable additions; chiefly to the second volume; among the rest is a short, but I flatter myself, a compleat History of all the trading companies in G. Britain'. His intention was not only to have these additions inserted in their proper places for a third edition of *WN*, but also to have them printed separately and sold for a shilling or half a crown to the purchasers of the previous versions of the book (*Corr.* No. 222).

As described above, Smith spent some of his time in London in 1782 negotiating with the representative of the Convention of the Royal Burghs of Scotland about standardizing Customs fees and removing barriers to coastal trade. Aware that his recommendations could hurt the pockets of Customs officers, Smith nevertheless was moving policy in the direction of his free trade and natural liberty principles expressed in *WN*. It is also possible that Smith was called on for advice, or volunteered it, in connection with national affairs after North's Administration fell in March, and the Marquess of Rockingham came in as the head of one that included Burke as paymaster-general bent on reform. There was broad support for the new ministry's desire to make peace with the Americans, but a problem for Rockingham was that he led a coalition bedevilled by rivalry between his supporters, such as Burke and Charles James Fox, who served as one of the secretaries of state, and the supporters of Shelburne, the other secretary of state. The latter enjoyed more of George III's favour, because the King believed that Fox was making the Prince of Wales as dissolute as himself (Wraxall, 1904: 471).

In April 1782 Smith was in a position to inform Burke 'several times', with a view to informing Rockingham, that Henry Dundas was being courted by

Shelburne, when he had some wish to be attached to Rockingham. Through Dundas, Shelburne was likely to get the support of the Scottish MPs, thus strengthening his standing in the House of Commons considerably, while Dundas would gain control of Indian as well as Scottish affairs, and thwart Burke's drive to deal with corruption in the East India Company (Burke, *Corr.*, 1963: iv.448; Fry, 1992: 90–1). In the event, Rockingham died on 1 July, and Burke, Fox, Lord John Cavendish (Chancellor of the Exchequer), and Frederick Montagu (one of the Lords of the Treasury) all resigned rather than accept Shelburne as Prime Minister. Smith appears to have wished that Burke would rally the others to the side of Shelburne (*Corr.* No. 216), but he accepted these resignations from the ministry as carried out from principle. It is significant, surely, of Smith's recognition as a policy adviser that he deemed it necessary to call on Cavendish at this juncture to 'return him . . . most sincere thanks for his politeness and attention' (*Corr.* No. 217).

While he was in London on this visit, Smith pursued intellectual issues other than those connected with political economy, and was in the company of those prominent in society other than politicians. As usual, he lodged at 27 Suffolk Street, near Charing Cross, and thus in the vicinity of the theatres and people of fashion and culture as well as government offices. Sir Joshua Reynolds lived in Leicester Square, and not too far afield was Gerrard Street, where The Club met in the Turk's Head tavern (*BLJ* v.109, n. 5). Smith was present at several of its dinners, held once a fortnight during the sitting of Parliament. At the last of these he attended before returning to Edinburgh in July 1782, the conversation dealt with the pleasure afforded by imitation. Reynolds later reported to Bennet Langton, an absent member of The Club, that he found Smith had considered this aesthetic problem 'with attention'. The topic was resumed afterwards, and Reynolds told Smith their ideas coincided, and 'that I had wrote a great deal on detach'd bitts of Paper, which I would put together and beg him to look over, he Said he could not . . . [because he] was about finishing an Essay on that Subject' (Boswell, ed. Fifer, 1976: 126).

After he whirled north in the post chaise early in July 1782, Smith seems to have deferred further work on the imitative arts and similar topics connected with the philosophical history of the different branches of literature and expression. Thus on 17 March 1783 he writes to Buccleuch's sister, Lady Frances Scott, to thank her for returning 'his paper upon Italian and English Verse'; he promises to send a 'more perfect copy as soon as he has compleated his plan', but declares this will be some time in the future, 'as he is at present very much engaged in another business' (*Corr.* No. 225). This must be a reference to the additions and corrections to *WN*, which on completion extended to thirteen sections of the third edition of the book, making up over 24,000 words (*WN* i.62). Cadell replied to Smith's announcement this work was in progress in a letter dated 12 December 1782. He wrote that he had discussed Smith's proposal with his partner Strahan, and they would set about printing as soon as copy was received, but since there was scarcely time to publish the book during the current winter, they would postpone publication to the next one, when Parliament was in session. Cadell also wrote that he approved 'heartily' of selling the additions as a separate publication, but quite unrealistically he wished to confine the sale to those who had already bought *WN* (*Corr.* No. 223).

At this period, it was common practice for publishers to seek the greatest market for their books when London's population increased during the sitting of Parliament. Strahan, who was active as an MP, and Cadell would know, in addition, that the content of *WN* had particular appeal for those concerned with parliamentary business. Indeed, the additions undertaken by Smith dealt with highly topical and controversial issues, hotly debated in a volatile political situation, during a period characterized in this new edition of *WN* as 'times of general difficulty and distress' (IV.v.a.37).

Thus the complete history of British trading companies, mentioned to Cadell as one of the additions, focuses on the problems of the East India Company, floundering in its imperial role. Burke had wanted Rockingham to deal with those problems, and when he got back into office on the fall of the Shelburne Administration in February 1783, over the peace treaty with the Americans, he had drafted an India Bill which sought to establish a measure of parliamentary control over the Company. Smith was woefully wrong in predicting that this Bill would go through the Upper House in as triumphant a manner as it had passed the Lower one (*Corr.* No. 233). In the event, it was defeated in December 1783 in the Lords at the instigation of the King, who correctly judged that the country was opposed to terms of the Bill which handed over patronage in British India to the parliamentary majority (Cannon, 1970). The Fox–North Coalition which had sponsored the Bill was dismissed, and Pitt the Younger was asked by the King to form an Administration. He gained a majority in the House of Commons in the general election held early the next year.

Henry Mackenzie, for one, hailed the Parliament of 1784 for its legislation and initiatives that spurred national recovery in finance, diplomacy, and imperial affairs, including regulation of the East India Company. He specifically associated Smith's writings with one facet of this recovery, the move to establish profitable commercial relations between Britain and France:

Between these countries there was a war of prohibitions and high duties, which, in most articles of their mutual consumption, threw the trade into the hands of smugglers. The publications of an author, in whose mind, beyond that of any writer of his time, was genius chastened by wisdom, and wisdom enlightened by knowledge, had changed in a great measure, the opinions of mankind on the subject of commercial restrictions, and shown how much was to be gained by restoring to trade its natural freedom, by which the surplus commodities of one country could be fairly exchanged for those of another. France and England felt in a particular manner the justice of his doctrines; and it was an article in the peace of 1783, that the two countries should take measures for settling a commercial treaty between them.

Mackenzie then reported that William Eden, Smith's friend and correspondent, was sent to Paris early in 1786 to negotiate a commercial treaty with France which was concluded on 20 September of that year. He could well have backed up his claims by mentioning the fact that Smith laid the groundwork for such a move in another addition to *WN*, one dealing with the 'absurdity of restrictions on trade with France' (IV.iii.a.1, c.12–13). It is entirely possible that Pitt read Smith's thoughts on trade with France.[1] He did read Mackenzie's 'Review of the Parliament of 1784', however, or so Mackenzie claims, and more than that, Pitt 'anxiously revised and corrected' it to ensure it expressed his Government's point of view (Mackenzie, 1808: vii.257–8). Accordingly, some credence may be given to the notion that Pitt went along with the idea that Smith was successful in changing opinions about the desirability of free trade.

More about Smith's efforts in this direction is to be learned from a letter he wrote to Strahan on 22 May 1783. He begins by complaining again about the interruptions caused by the demands of his employment in the Custom-house. However, he benefited from his profession, since he was able to call on Sir Grey Cooper, by this time a lord of the Treasury in the Fox–North Administration, to provide accounts of the operation of the bounty system, that is, one favouring some manufactures and exports through cash payments from the Government. Smith describes his work as follows:

This [third edition of *WN*] will probably see me out and I should therefor chuse to leave it behind me as perfect as I can make it. The Principal additions are to the second Volume. Some new arguments against the corn bounty; against the Herring fish bounty; a new concluding Chapter upon the mercantile System; A short History and, I presume, a full exposition of the Absurdity and hurtfulness of almost all our chartered trading companies; I expect to be able to finish it in about a month after I received the treasury account which are now preparing.

Smith continues by stating that he 'must correct the press [i.e. proof-read] himself', and that Strahan should send him the sheets as they are printed, using his frank as an MP. Our author is so keen to exercise control over this third edition that he writes that he is prepared to come to London at the beginning of the next winter, and attend to the press himself. He wishes to be remembered to Cadell and to the editors of the *Monthly Review*, William Rose and Ralph Griffiths, and declares that he longs to 'have more dinners at the Packhorse', an inn or tavern frequented by London men of letters (*Corr.* No. 227).

Writing again to Strahan on 6 October, Smith states that his additions and corrections to *WN* are 'now either finished compleatly' or soon will be, but that he is still waiting for the Treasury accounts which Cooper promised him soon after Shelburne's Administration fell in the previous February. He mentions his intention of taking another four months' leave to attend to the new edition of his book, but a Welsh nephew (who has not been traced) needed £200 from him or would have to sell his Army commission. Smith came to his rescue, and writes laconically: 'This robs me of the money with which I intended to defray the expence of my expedition.' Such a report agrees with the information Dugald Stewart received that Smith did not hang on to his considerable income, and disbursed much of it in charitable acts (v.4 n.). Smith then recommends to Cadell's attention two MSS that he considered fit to be published. One was a *History of Music* (published in 1784) by Thomas Robertson, minister of Dalmeny, whose theory he found instructive, perhaps in relation to his own analysis of music for his work on the imitative arts. The other was a collection of the sermons (published in 1786) of a former pupil at Glasgow, Samuel Charters, a Moderate clergyman in Hugh Blair's circle who emphasized the cultivation of sympathy, and specialized in discourse of a melancholic and sentimental cast, matching the effusions of *Ossian* Macpherson and the fiction of Henry Mackenzie (Somerville, 1861: 50, 166–7, 195, 227; Dwyer, 1987: 14, 17, 22, 58, 60, 174). This letter to Strahan concludes with hopes for the success of the Fox–North Coalition. Smith reckons it 'comprehends the worthiest and ablest men in the nation, the heads of the two great Aristocracies', and he ventures the opinion that their previous rivalry, 'weakened the . . . Government so much as at last to occasion the dismemberment of the empire'. Far from displaying political prescience about the real state of royal and public opinion, Smith trusts that the 'usual folly and impertinence of next winter's opposition', that is, the MPs led by Pitt, 'will effectually reconcile the King to his new ministers', more than their conduct in Government has so far been able to do (*Corr.* No. 231).

By 20 November the bounty accounts have still not been sent to Smith, though Cooper promised in a letter two weeks before that he would deliver them to Strahan. Smith asks Strahan to call on Cooper a second time to get them, and he thanks his friend for the offer of hospitality in London, declaring that he will be in funds again by 6 January 1784, presumably from the quarterly payment of his salary as a Customs Commissioner, and will set out for London that day. He will take up lodgings with his old friend John Home the dramatist, but if this proves inconvenient he asks for rooms to be secured again in Suffolk Street, on the first floor and at a rent not to exceed two guineas a week. Cadell has informed Smith on the basis of some information from William Rose that the new edition of *WN* should be put into print immediately, but Smith does not himself think that a six weeks' delay matters. If Strahan believes otherwise, he will accommodate Cadell. He sees the publishing partners as being of one mind, and considers writing to Strahan or to Cadell the same thing. Do we detect some weariness of spirit—Smith was then 60, a relatively advanced age for the period—in the final comment of the postscript: 'I intend that this should be my last visit to London' (*Corr.* No. 232)?

We have no news of the Treasury accounts finally reaching Smith in Edinburgh, but he appears to have dealt with them there later on in the winter of 1783–4 or in the spring of 1784, and not to have travelled to London in January as he foretold. Perhaps Custom-house business detained him, or the illness of his mother. In April he was taken up with a visit from Burke, who came to Scotland to be installed as Lord Rector of Glasgow University, an office to which he had been elected the previous November in succession to Dundas. There were significant intellectual affinities between the two men, and Burke is said to have found Smith's manners 'particularly pleasing', while Smith has been represented as declaring that his good friend of many years' standing was the 'only man I ever knew who thinks on economic subjects exactly as I do, without any previous communications having passed between us' (Bisset, 1800: ii.429). There was tension, however, in their thinking about the poor (Himmelfarb, 1984: 66–73).

To be sure, Smith could be critical of Burke's efforts as a legislator. Thus, in the first edition of *WN* he had commented adversely on a Bill that Burke had devised to improve but essentially maintain bounties on the export of a grain, a subject still exercising him in preparing the third edition. Concerning certain features of what was enacted (13 Geo. III, c. 43, 1772), Smith wrote: 'The bounty ought certainly either to have been withdrawn at a much lower price, or exportation ought to have been allowed at a much higher. So far, therefore, this law seems to be inferior to the antient system' (IV.v.b.52–3). Burke is said to have answered this criticism of not bringing about a repeal of the corn bounty with one of those metaphorical flights for which he was famous. He neatly distinguished between Smith's role as theorist with a tendency to model his systems on geometry, as Dugald Stewart perceived, and his own role as the practical man seeking to get a law through Parliament:

it was the privilege of philosophers to conceive their diagrams in geometrical accuracy; but the engineer must often impair the symmetry as well as the simplicity of his machine, in order to overcome the irregularities of friction and resistance. (Horner, 1957: 98; Viner, 1965: 23–3)

Smith allowed the justice of this answer, and added to the second edition of *WN* (1778) a balanced comment on Burke's legislation:

With all its imperfections, however, we may perhaps say of it what was said of the laws of Solon, that, though not the best in itself, it is the best which the interests, prejudices, and temper of the times would admit of. It may perhaps in due time prepare the way for a better. (IV.v.b.53)

In the final revisions for the 1790 *TMS*, Smith included in the new section on Virtue a discussion of the 'man of system', making clear that the point Burke brought up about the corn bounty Act was germane to his own outlook:

Some general, and even systematical, idea of the perfection of policy and law, may no doubt be necessary for directing the views of the statesman [this being the drive of *WN*]. But to insist upon establishing, and upon establishing all at once, and in spite of all opposition, every thing which that idea may seem to require, must often be the highest degree of arrogance.

As in the 1778 *WN*, Smith evokes in the last edition of *TMS* the example of Solon as a legislator who, short of establishing the best system of laws, enacted the 'best the people can bear' (VI.ii.2.16, 18).

Such was the drift of the exchanges between Smith and Burke, who arrived in Edinburgh on 6 or 7 April 1784. He was entertained there by Smith together with his intimate friend Andrew Dalzel, Professor of Greek at Edinburgh, whose accurate knowledge of Greek grammar and literature attracted Smith during his last years (*Corr.* No. 229). They took Burke to the town house of Lord Maitland, heir to the Earl of Lauderdale, then a rising Whig politician, though later on a republican, then a Tory, also, in time, an original contributor to the progress of classical economic theory of growth and development (Maitland, 1804; O'Brien, 1975: 229–30). He had defended Smith against disparaging remarks by Fox, but he was not an uncritical adherent of the doctrines of *WN*, and exchanges with him on economic issues were likely to be lively and well-supported. He had taken a strong stand in favour of Fox's India Bill, and was one of the managers of the impeachment of Warren Hastings spearheaded by Burke. On Thursday 8 April the party was joined by Dugald Stewart, and they went out to Hatton, Lauderdale's Midlothian seat four miles out from East Calder and on the way to Glasgow. Built late in the seventeenth century by Charles Maitland, younger brother of the first Duke of Lauderdale, it was burned out in 1952 and largely demolished in 1955 (McWilliam, 1978: 229–30).

Stewart recorded parts of the conversation which turned on political characters: with Burke running down the Elder Pitt as 'one of the most Unprincipled Men that ever lived', and being equally scathing about the Younger Pitt, whom he likened to Blifil, the sanctimonious prig in *Tom Jones*. Fox was painted as being like the good-natured, sensualist hero of Fielding's novel. Burke is described as 'by no means a classical scholar', but getting his quotations from William Lily's Renaissance Latin grammar, still in use in the eighteenth century. However, he was well acquainted with the English poets and could repeat a 'great part of Spenser'. Burke told a number of anecdotes passed on by Lady Anne Pitt, the Elder Pitt's sister who disliked her brother 'extremely'. He regretted that he had not followed Boswell's method of writing down such materials on leaving this lady's company. After dinner Burke spoke a great deal, and very favourably, about William Dowdeswell, who was appointed Chancellor of the Exchequer in the Rockingham Administration of 1765–6. Dowdeswell was knowledgeable about financial matters, and Smith may have respected his knowledge in this area, as he was Townshend's predecessor in the Exchequer just before Smith became a policy adviser to Townshend. For a number of years, Dowdeswell was the leader of the Rockingham Whigs in the Commons, and his advocacy of moderation in American affairs must have been congenial to Smith. Burke thought that his only weakness was that he 'was always talking Atheism'.

Stewart's notes of the Hatton dialogue then conclude with one of Smith's characteristic peremptory interventions, and Burke's assessment of Smith's writings after he took his departure:

BURKE: But Dowdeswell's atheism was mere *folly*, and I trust that his Soul is now with God.
SMITH: By God, I make no doubt of it.

Smith then went to Ed[inburgh] in the Evening. Burke spoke highly of his Wealth of Nations. An excellent digest of all that is valuable in former Oeconomical writers with many valuable corrective Observations.

It was Stewart's impression that despite Burke's fulsome review in the *Annual Register* (1759), he 'spoke rather coldly of the Theory of Moral Sentiments' (EUL DC.6.III).

From Dalzel came a report that Burke was despondent over the results of the general election then in progress, when almost 160 friends of the Coalition Administration lost their seats—Fox's martyrs, they were called. Maitland was told by Burke to give up the Whigs if he wanted to assume office, but Smith entered the discussion with a prophecy that in two years there would be a change of political fortunes. Burke had been in Parliament for almost twenty years without holding office for as many months, and he quipped: 'Why I have already been in a minority nineteen, and your two years, Mr Smith, will just make me twenty-one, and it will surely be high time for me to be then in my majority' (Innes, in Dalzel, 1862: i.42). Smith's sanguine expectation of the return to power of Burke's party suggests that he continued to be loyal to the survivors of the Rockingham Whigs. As matters turned out, Pitt remained in power for twenty years. The alarmed imagination of Burke when confronting the French Revolution forced him into a conservative position, and he broke with his political friends. Maitland remained at this time a firm Foxite, and took the lead in denouncing Burke as an apostate (BL Add. MSS 32,567).

On Good Friday, Smith rejoined the Hatton party and they went on to Glasgow where they had supper that evening with Professor John Millar, who was credited with swaying Maitland to be a radical in politics. The rectorial installation was held on Saturday 10 April, when Burke gave a 'very polite and elegant speech suited to the occasion' (*Annual Register*, 1784, disputed by Rae, 1965: 389–90). Smith's former pupil Archibald Arthur, who was licensed as a minister as well as being substitute Professor of Moral Philosophy, preached in the College chapel, and then there was an academic dinner in the Hall. The next day Stewart and Dalzel went back to Edinburgh to be ready for their classes next day, but Smith and Maitland took Burke on to Loch Lomond—the finest lake in Britain according to Smith (Clayden, 1887: 92)—and then to Carron, where Smith's friend Dr John Roebuck, in partnership with Samuel Garbett of Birmingham and William Cadell, a merchant from Cockenzie, had founded a famous ironworks based on a coke-smelting process and producing guns, carronades, for the navy. Its scale of integrated operations in mining ore and coal, employing eighteen water-wheels, and preparing finished goods attracted many visitors, who were seeing the outset of industrialization and the pollution of countryside and air that came with this process (Campbell, 1961; Lenman, 1977: 98, 130; Whyte and Whyte, 1991: 216–17).

On Thursday 15 April they dined at Panmure House, Dalzel again being with them and impressed by Burke's entertaining and agreeable conversation: 'We got a vast deal of political anecdotes from him, and fine pictures of political characters both living and dead. Whether they were impartially drawn or not, that is questionable, but they were admirably drawn' (Innes, 1862: i.42).

So passed a memorable visit; but Smith remained involved with politicians, because also in the course of this general election his old and good friend Andrew Stuart, who managed the legal affairs of the Hamilton family, including their side of the celebrated Douglas Cause, unaccountably fell out with his patron, the Duke of Hamilton, and withdrew from the Lanarkshire contest. He wished his personal friends in Edinburgh, and particularly Smith, to be fully informed about the affair and sent the relevant correspondence to John Davidson to be passed on to Smith. In turn on 7 May, Smith advised showing the papers to another of their circle, the Session Court judge Lord Stonefield, a brother-in-law of the Earl of Bute, and keeping the matter firmly out of the public eye (*Corr.* No. 236). Stuart interested himself a great deal in the affairs of the East India Company, and in 1772 his name, along with that of Adam Ferguson and Smith, was mentioned in connection with membership of a commission of inquiry into the Company (*Corr.* Nos. 132, 133). Nothing came of this, but since he additionally served as a Lord of Trade under North in 1779 and was active as a behind-the-scenes negotiator in Parliament, he is one likely source of Smith's inside knowledge of parliamentary power, economic legislation, and Indian affairs.

But after the merriment and stimulation of Burke's visit, and the excitement of the general election, came a sad event for Smith, the death of his mother on 23 May. He writes of this in a letter to Strahan dated 10 June, in which he comments on receiving the proofs of the new third edition of *WN* by the cheaper conveyance of the coach, when he would have preferred the proofs of the MS 'additions', at least, to have been sent by post:

I should immediately have acknowledged the receipt of the fair sheets; but I had just then come from performing the last duty to my poor old Mother; and tho' the death of a person in her ninetieth year of her age was no doubt an event most agreable to the course of nature; and, therefore, to be foreseen and prepared for; yet I must say to you, what I have said to other people, that the final separation from a person who certainly loved me more than any other person ever did or ever will love me; and whom I certainly loved and respected more than I ever shall either love or respect any other person, I cannot help feeling, even at this hour, as a very heavy stroke upon me.

His despondency at this time was so great that Ramsay of Ochtertyre reported that the 'poor man seemed to sorrow as those without hope', presumably of any recovery of spirits, or perhaps even of reunion with the dead (1888: i.468). Smith found spirits in his correspondence, however, to express concern about Strahan's health, which was declining, and he attended to his *WN* proofs, finding that only the punctuation required correction (*Corr.* Nos. 237, 239).

Smith was perhaps still correcting proofs in July, for on the 15th of that month François Xavier Schwediauer, a well-travelled and well-connected Austrian doctor and entrepreneur, wrote from Edinburgh to his friend Jeremy Bentham in London:

> Dr Smith with whom I am intimately acquainted, is quite our man. He is busy about a new edition of his wealth of nations. We have a Club here, which consists of nothing but Philosophers, Dr Adam Smith, Cullen, Black, Mr M'Gowan etc. belong to it. Thus I spend once a week in the most enlightened, chearful and social company. (Bentham, *Corr.*, 1971: iii.294–5)

On the whole, Bentham and his circle saw Smith as an ally in their work on 'morals and legislation', deeming *WN* a major contribution in the area of political economy to their comprehensive scheme for a 'science of human nature'. In certain directions, however, Smith went too far in resisting the intrusive hand of government, according to Bentham in his *Defence of a Maximum* (Long, 1977: 191).

But on one issue Smith did not go far enough—that of controlling interest rates. Here, Bentham was defiantly radical: 'it is an old maxim of mine, that interest, as love and religion, and so many other pretty things, should be free.' In 1785 he set out for Russia, taking with him a copy of the third edition of *WN*, which had been published on 20 November the previous year. In 1787 he was writing his *Defense of Usury*, in which letter xiii, dated March, controverts Smith's arguments about maintaining a high rate of interest and restraining projectors, promoters of speculative companies and economic schemes (*WN* i.ix.5, x.b.42–3; II.iii.26; II.iv.15). Bentham sought the aid of George Wilson, a Lincoln's Inn barrister of Scottish extraction, to get his book published in London after learning that Pitt proposed to restrict rate of interest. Replying on 24 April 1787 to a letter of Bentham's on this point, Wilson encouraged his friend to complete his book, even though he personally had not heard of such a proposal by Pitt. He went on to comment on signs of progress so welcome to Bentham's circle: reform of the ecclesiastical courts, consolidation of customs, and the opening of ports to the French following the Eden Treaty. In his opinion, which seems to be in line with that of Henry Mackenzie, these changes in part could be linked to the reception of *WN*:

> Indeed, in all points of political economy, there is an evident change in public opinion within these ten years, which may be in some degree owing to the circulation of Smith's book, but still more to the events which have happened in our political and commercial connection with America, to the utter disgrace of the old thrones. (Bentham, *Corr.*, 1971: iii.533)

Wilson did see the *Defence of Usury* through the press at the end of 1787, and on 6 June 1788 he sent Bentham an appreciative notice in the *Monthly Review*

(78: 361–70), which describes the book as a 'political gem of the finest water'. In a further letter to Bentham, dated 4 December 1789, Wilson reported that Smith had acknowledged the force of the counter-arguments about limiting interest:

Did we ever tell you what Dr Adam Smith said to Mr William Adam, the Council MP, last summer in Scotland. The Doctor's expressions were that 'the *Defence of Usury* was the work of a very superior man, and that tho' he had given [Smith] some hard knocks, it was done in so handsome a way that [he] could not complain,' and seemed to admit that you were right. (quoted Rae, 1965: 423–4)

Bentham commented on this report in the 'Letter to Dr Smith' (*Corr.* 402), which he composed as a preface to the second edition of the *Defence of Usury* (1790), but he was careful to state that Smith had not himself communicated his change of mind. It is an interesting speculation that, had Smith lived beyond 1790, he might have altered his stand on reducing interest and equating projectors with prodigals.

To be sure, Bentham claims in the *Defence of Usury* that in refuting Smith's arguments about the 'policy of the laws fixing the rate of interest', he is turning his master's weapons against himself (*Corr.* 388). He means that the tendency of *WN* is to show that economic growth has been created in spite of the laws made by governments, rather than as a result of them, and that this demonstration can be extended to interest-rate controls against which the 'prudent projectors' who sustain growth have struggled with varying degrees of success (*Corr.* 391).

It is difficult not to agree with Bentham's reading of *WN* and even to see the message about the detrimental effect of most economic legislation intensified in the third edition. The 'additions' finally incorporated in it consist of the following shorter sections: an exposure of the foolishness of the motivation behind the drawback system, through review of the complicated laws regulating the carrying trade to and from the colonies and foreign countries in commodities like wine (IV.iv.3–11); analysis of the ill-advised attempt to promote the herring fishery through the bounty system (IV.v.a. 28–37 and app.); similar exposure of the bad effects of the corn bounty (IV.v.a.8–9); and comment on the absurdity of the restrictions on trade with France (IV.iii.a.1, c.12–13).

Also, there are two lengthy self-contained pieces. One is a chapter entitled 'Conclusion of the Mercantile System', which argues that the interests of consumers have been 'entirely neglected' by legislatures in contriving 'mercantile regulations', which favour producers, merchants, and manufacturers, and especially the latter, at the expense of other producers (IV.viii, particularly the last para.). The other is an article which deals with 'Publick Works and Institutions which are necessary for facilitating particular Branches of Commerce' (v.i.e). It is here that Smith examines joint-stock and regulated companies, giving most attention to those involved in foreign trade, and making a case study of the East India Company's monopoly as an example of failure in government policy, and the thwarting of forces such as competition in the market-place which would have led to economic growth in India rather than the depredations of Company tax-gatherers leading to stagnation and decline (Anderson and Tollison, 1982).

Taking into account Smith's statement in the advertisement to the fourth edition of *WN* (1786) that it included 'no alterations of any kind'—and only a few trifling ones have been found in it, and in the fifth edition of 1789—it follows that the third edition is Smith's final version of his great book. It certainly received Smith's most careful attention in the form of proof-reading and amplification. Moreover, the book was equipped with that index which his friends Hugh Blair and William Robertson had called for on its first publication (*Corr.* Nos. 151, 153). Smith acknowledged receiving 'some part of the index of his Book' on 18 November 1784, but his letter does not clarify whether he compiled the index himself, or had it done under his direction by an amanuensis, such as Alexander Gillies, or by someone else, as Edwin Cannan conjectured, who had some expertise in the matter of Scottish banking procedures (*WN* ed. Cannan, 1950: vol. i, p. xvi).

Perhaps the provision of the index was a late thought, since Smith's letter about it was dated only four days before it was published in London on 22 November 1784. As early as 10 August he was anticipating the appearance of his book, and instructing Cadell to send out presentation copies: one 'finely bound for Gilt' for a London hostess, Lady Louisa MacDonald, the daughter of the 2nd Earl Gower, who had brought a fortune to her husband, the recently appointed solicitor-general in Pitt's Administration, Sir Archibald MacDonald of Armadale Castle in Skye; and others 'in boards' to old friends, Earl Stanhope and his heir Lord Mahon; Alexander Wedderburn, created Lord Loughborough when he was made Lord Chief Justice in 1780; Lord Sheffield, Gibbon's 'best friend' and executor; and Sir Grey Cooper, who had furnished bounty accounts from Treasury records for the additions to *WN* (*Corr.* No. 241). Smith was thanked by several of these donors by 16 November, and he asked for other copies to be sent to Shelburne and members of the La Rochefoucauld circle: the young Duke, his sister the Duchess of Chabot, and the Marquis de Bombelles (*Corr.* No. 241).

Besides this circulation of the third edition of *WN* among 'the great', other contemporary readers were provided for, since Strahan doubled the print-run from that of the previous issues to 1000 copies. In our day, this edition has rightly achieved endorsement as the 'printer's copy' for the Glasgow *WN* of 1976 (i.63–4).

22

Legacy for Legislators

In what manner the natural system of perfect liberty and justice ought gradually to be restored, we must leave to the wisdom of future statesmen and legislators to determine.

In the summer before the third edition of *WN* was published, Smith was interested in the availability of his work in French. He would be aware that he could reach readers in many countries, including Spain and Italy, in that language; and soon after *WN* was published, it was translated into German and Danish. The legislators of Europe and the Americas were soon made aware of his ringing arguments against monopolies and in favour of free trade.

On 19 June 1784 he wrote to Cadell, asking him to obtain a copy of a French translation which he understood the Abbé Morellet had prepared (*Corr.* No. 239). Morellet did translate *WN*, but he never published it (1821: i.243). Perhaps this was because Blavet's version, published anonymously at The Hague in 1778–9, had also appeared in weekly instalments in the Physiocrat organ, the *Journal de l'agriculture*, from January 1779 to December 1780, and had then been issued as a book at both Yverdon in Switzerland and Paris in 1781. The translator sent his author a copy of the Paris edition with the inscription: 'À M. Smith de la part de son très humble serviteur l'abbé Blavet' (Mizuta). Smith acknowledged the gift on 23 July 1782, expressing himself as being charmed with the translation and, at least on a brief acquaintance, of the view that it was perfectly equal to the original (*Corr.* No. 218). Morellet, with an unpublished MS on his hands, understandably took a different position, and declared: 'poor Smith was traduced by Blavet rather than translated' (1821: i.244).

A third translator, undeterred by a further publication of the Blavet version in 1788, began to issue his work in 1790 based on the fourth edition of *WN* (1786). This was the poet Antoine Roucher, who had no special qualifications for dealing with Smith's book other than knowing English, a skill he had previously used in translating Thomson's *Seasons*. He was a victim of the Terror, going to the guillotine in 1794 two days before Robespierre. Smith's library contained volumes i and iii of his version (Mizuta), which promised readers that it would be followed by a volume of notes by Condorcet, another victim of the Revolution in 1794. These notes never reached print, but Daniel Diatkine (1993) has argued that we may have indication of their nature in a summary of *WN* printed in the *Bibliothèque de l'homme* (vols. iii, iv) in 1790. This publication advertised itself as offering a 'reasoned analysis of the principal French and foreign books on politics in general, jurisprudence, finance, "police" [in the sense in which Smith used this word], agriculture and trade, and on natural right and public law'. It was managed by Condorcet, by de Peyssonel, a former French consul in Smyrna, by Le Chapelier, an important politician who served as President of the National Assembly, but who also succumbed to revolutionary violence in 1794, and by 'other men of letters'.

Diatkine represents the summary as a 'patchwork' of the Roucher translation, but he also argues that its content suggests that Condorcet and others involved in producing it did not grasp the 'analytical core' of *WN*, since the summary dispatches the crucial chapters v, vi, vii, viii, and ix of book I, dealing with price, value, labour, wages, and profits, with the statement: 'We will not follow Mr Smith on these points. It is necessary to read them in the book itself, and only one reading would not suffice to go into the matter.'[1]

Condorcet was a protégé and friend of Turgot, and like him frequented the salon of Julie de Lespinasse when Smith attended it in 1766. When Turgot became Controller-General in 1774, he called on d'Alembert and Condorcet to serve on a committee directed to study the use and misuse of France's rivers, and later Condorcet was put in charge of the mint (Schama, 1989: 83; Marquet, 1989). It is likely that he saw *WN* as reinforcing the views of the Physiocrats and Turgot on such matters as capital formation and flow, and he may even have accepted as salutary Smith's attack on Quesnay's fixation that agriculture was the sole productive sector. Certainly, his view of progress included industrial application of scientific and technological advance, and like Smith he viewed education as an answer to the destruction of personality caused by the division of labour (Condorcet, 1989, drawing on *WN* v; Ando, 1993).

There is likely to have been discussion of Smith's concept of the moral personality in the Condorcet household, because his wife, Sophie de Grouchy, whose hand he had to beg in 1786 from a lover—either Smith's friend the duc de La Rochefoucauld or Lafayette—began to translate *TMS* about the time of their marriage. She completed this version, said to be the best available in her language, during the turmoil of the Revolution, and it was published in 1798 together with a translation of Smith's essay on the First Formation of Languages, also an original work, *Eight Letters on Sympathy* addressed to the Idéologue Cabanis, who was Condorcet's physician (Manuel, 1965: 57–8; Staum, 1980; Lagrave, 1989).

As perpetual secretary of the Academy of Sciences in Paris from 1776, Condorcet kept in touch with the learned world of Europe, and he forwarded to Smith a copy of his seminal work of 1785 on mathematical analysis of social groups and majority decision-making: *Essai sur l'application de l'analyse à la probabilité des décisions rendues à la pluralité des voix* (Daston, 1988; Crépel, 1989:

65–118; Baker, in Crépel, 1989: 515–24; and 1990: 165–6). This book bears the inscription: 'pour monsieur Adam Smith de la societé royale de la part de l'auteur' (Mizuta). It was joined in Smith's library by Condorcet's *Vie de Turgot*, published at London in 1786, and four pamphlets dated 1789 (Mizuta) connected with the constitutional debates of the opening stages of the French Revolution in which Condorcet took an active part, pushed on, so Mme Suard claimed, by the political drive of his wife (Manuel, 1965: 57). Smith apparently passed on these pamphlets in 1790 to someone in the Maconochie family, perhaps the Professor Allan Maconochie who lectured on public law at Edinburgh in the spirit of *LJ*.

Such professional people were keenly interested in the unfolding of the Revolution in France, as was Smith's friend Dugald Stewart, who observed the events of 1788 and 1789 during summer visits to Paris, and was criticized for his sympathetic stance towards the revolutionaries. A contemporary noted that, at Edinburgh University at this period, Andrew Dalzel spoke about liberty in ancient Greece, and Stewart, who upheld Smith's principles, spoke about liberty generally: 'anxiously were they both watched. Stewart, in particular, though too spotless and too retired to be openly denounced, was an object of great secret alarm' (Cockburn, 1856: 85).

Du Pont de Nemours, one of the revolutionary leaders at the outset and, like Condorcet, a nobleman as well as an associate of the Physiocrats and Turgot, wrote to Smith on 19 June 1788 enclosing a pamphlet which endorsed the freeing of trade covered by the Eden Treaty. His gesture was a mark of respect for *WN*, and he declared that Smith had hastened greatly the 'useful revolution' which was bringing a 'good constitution' to France, extending the principles upheld in Britain and the United States of America (*Corr.* No. 277). He associated with his tribute to Smith the esteem of his fellow *Économistes*. On the evidence of Condorcet's summary of *WN* in the *Bibliothèque de l'homme*, however, it is unlikely that Frenchmen at first appreciated the truly revolutionary nature of the teaching of *WN*: that competition and the mechanism of the market tended in certain historical conditions to improve humanity's lot, without elaborate abstract refinements in a political constitution.

Another deputy of the National Assembly deeply involved in constitution-making, Germain Garnier, who was threatened like Condorcet and Du Pont by the Terror, took refuge in Switzerland, and there in 1794 he found solace in translating *WN*. His version became the standard French text, and with his annotations and explanations, supplemented by those of J.-B. Say, Blanqui, McCulloch, Malthus, James Mill, Ricardo, and Sismondi in an edition of 1843, which explored the full range of Smith's thought, it established the leading role of *WN* in the development of European economic thought.

As for the French so for the Germans: there was an initial period of uncertainty about *WN* despite definite interest in the book, followed by a deepening response to the intellectual challenge of its principles (Waszek, 1985; 1988: ch. 2;

1993). Stages of reception were marked by translations, reviews, then popular-izations, and afterwards the fructifying of original thought about political econ-omy with application to the problems of German-speaking countries. The first translation into German and, for that matter, into any European language was made by Johann Friedrich Schiller, a cousin of the poet Friedrich Schiller, with the help of Christian August Wichmann. It was published at Leipzig, already a major centre of the German book trade, in two volumes, 1776–8. The translator Schiller names Smith as his 'friend' in the preface to the second volume; and since he was in London in the 1770s before setting up a bookshop in Mainz, it is possible he knew Smith personally when he was in London before and imme-diately after the appearance of *WN*, 1773–6 and 1777. Two copies of the first volume have survived from Smith's library (Mizuta), the one in Glasgow University bearing on its cover the monogram of George III. Perhaps the King sent this book to Smith to show that his German connections were aware of his work. Though it went through a second edition in three volumes, 1776–92, with additions and improvements, the Schiller translation was not highly regarded, and its indifferent quality may have delayed acceptance of Smith's ideas.

He was more fortunate with the second translation, that of Christian Garve, who did advance research work at the University of Leipzig on the history of philosophy, and taught there briefly, 1768–72, when it seems that, beginning with study of Ferguson's *Essay on the History of Civil Society*, he laid the foun-dation for an extensive knowledge of Scottish Enlightenment authors, including Hutcheson, Hume, Reid, Kames, and Smith. Garve gave up teaching at Leipzig apparently on the grounds of ill health, but perhaps because he wished to con-tinue a career as a philosophical writer, which had opened with admirable trans-lations of Ferguson's *Institutes of Moral Philosophy*, with a commentary, and in part Kames's *Elements of Criticism*, with notes, both publications appearing first in 1772. He settled in Breslau, and published there in three volumes, 1794–6, an excellent translation of the fourth edition of *WN*, which thus incorporated Smith's last substantial revision of 1784. Garve's reputation as a leading philoso-pher, though overshadowed eventually by that of Kant, probably won wide-spread attention to Smith's book.

A number of reviews of *WN*, both of the original and the German transla-tions, further disseminated Smith's principles. Georg Sartorius, for example, writing for the *Göttingische Anzeigen von gelehrten Sachen*, challenged the pro-fessoriate of his time to grapple with Smith's 'immortal work' (1793: 1660), and then picked up this challenge himself by producing a successful *Handbuch der Staatswirthschaft* (1796), revised as *Elemente des National-Reichthums* (1806), which offered clearly organized summaries of *WN* addressed to the general pub-lic. Another work on similar lines was August Ferdinand Lueder's *Über Nationalindustrie und Staatswirthschaft* (1800–4), which followed Smith's exam-ple in illustrating economic principles from travellers' accounts of societies at varying stages of historical development. Two popularizers of Smith's thought revealed that they were aware of the theoretical antecedents to Smith's system of political economy in the writings of Sir James Steuart and Hume: Johann Gottlieb Buhle in his *Geschichte der Theorie der Staatswirthschaft in England* (1803–4) and Christian Jacob Kraus in a translation of Hume's *Political Discourses* (1800), also in lectures at the University of Königsberg which gave rise to an intelligent recension of *WN* published as *Staatswirthschaft* (posthumous, 1808–11).

Sartorius at Göttingen and Kraus at Königsberg were the first German professors to teach political economy on Smithian principles in the 1790s, about the time that Dugald Stewart was doing the same thing in Edinburgh. Stewart attracted students from outside Scotland, including two future prime ministers of Britain, Lord Palmerston and Lord John Russell, who derived a perspective on economic affairs from Stewart's expositions of *WN*, and had a clear understanding of its policy advice reflected in their legislation during the era of reform in Britain (Semmel, 1970; Winch, 1983: 25–61). Similarly, among Sartorius' pupils these were men who made their impact on a changing Germany. Thus the Prussian statesmen Stein and Hardenberg, who had studied at Göttingen, carried out a reform programme seemingly inspired in part by Smith's thought, including the abolition of trade monopolies, emancipation of serfs, and conversion of feudal lands into freeholds. They were ably backed in putting Prussia on the road to becoming a modern industrial state by civil servants educated at Königsberg, such as von Schön and von Schrötter, who had heard Kraus lecture on *WN* (Winkel, 1988). It has been denied, of course, that the Prussian reforms were carried out by a close-knit, homogeneous group, and there is evidence that Stein and Hardenberg disliked each other intensely (Fulbrook, 1990: 99).

However, going along with practical developments in part connected with the reception of Smith's economic thought, there were theoretical advances as German scholars found ways to link *WN* with their native cameralist tradition, and achieve conceptual clarification as well as systematic comprehensiveness in formulating the chief problems to be addressed in economics. Two names to be mentioned in this connection are Karl Heinrich Rau, whose *Lehrbuch der politischen Oekonomie* (1826–37) went through many editions and nurtured most eminent nineteenth-century German economists, and Friedrich Benedict Wilhelm von Hermann, author of *Staatswirthschaftliche Untersuchungen über Vermögen, Wirthschaft, Produktivität der Arbeiter, Capital, Preis, Gewinn, Einkommen und Verbrauch* (1832), which rescued Smith's legacy from dogmatic *laissez-faire* interpretation. It has been claimed that von Hermann's own advance lay in emphasizing the role of demand in his price theory and moving towards the theory of marginal utility, but he took a modest view of his own originality, and declared: 'whoever understands something of economics has to regard himself, with respect to the chief principles of this science, as a disciple of Adam Smith' (Recktenwald, 1976: 277–87; Waszek, 1993: 170).

Smith himself never displayed towards Germany that kind of attention he gave to France, and his *Edinburgh Review* Letter of 1756 is somewhat dismissive about its intellectual achievements in 'sciences which require only plain judgment joined to labour and assiduity, without demanding a great deal of what is called either taste or genius'. Yet he put his finger on a pervasive problem for the 'learned' in Germany at the time when he wrote: that they preferred to cultivate French rather than their own language (para. 3). Frederick the Great, for example, had no time for contemporary writing in German. There is little doubt, however, that the sympathetic response in Germany to *TMS* and later *WN*, coupled with the works of other figures of the Scottish Enlightenment, and the consciousness that Smith and his fellow literati formed a distinctive philosophical school, encouraged a successful struggle to represent its thought adequately in the German language. This is surely the principal feature of the career of Garve. In turn, reflection on the work of the Scots, and Adam Smith in particular, must have stimulated German thinkers to expand their intellectual horizons, to express themselves in their own language, and to develop their own distinctive approach to political economy and other forms of the social sciences that flowered in the mighty enterprises of Hegel and Marx devoted to analysis and criticism of 'civil society'.[2]

Smith's help was sought directly by one German-speaking intellectual, the high-minded and wealthy Austrian political philosopher and publisher Count Joseph Niclas Windisch-Grätz. Prominent at Joseph II's court in youth, and given such missions as accompanying Marie-Antoinette to Paris in 1770 to wed the Dauphin who became Louis XVI, he later kept aloof from the benevolent despot Emperor because he considered his reforms ruthless (*Allgemeine Deutsche Biographie* (1898: B. 43). His cast of thought was like that of Condorcet, with whom he shared an enthusiasm for mathematical formulation of principles and arguments. Kant expressed respect for his 'philosophical talent', which he said was combined with the 'noblest attitudes of a cosmopolite' (to F. H. Jacobi, 30 Aug. 1789: Kant, 1967: 157).

On 10 May 1785 Windisch-Grätz wrote to Smith from Brussels to ask him to prevail on the Royal Society of Edinburgh to join the Academy of Sciences in Paris and a German Academy as yet to be determined in judging a competition he had devised. The object was to establish the phrasing of deeds in the clearest manner possible, so that fraud and court conflict over property transfers would be avoided, without restricting natural liberty. He had circulated a programme in Latin (*Ad Lectorem*, London, 1785: Bodleian Lib., Vet. AS d. 430) about this matter among the learned men of Europe, including Kant and Condorcet. He reported to Smith that the latter and Laplace had acceded to his request on behalf of the Paris Academy, but that he had been rebuffed by the Royal Society of London, as he was to be by the Berlin Academy. He also wrote that he preferred to approach the academies rather than universities because the solution he sought was not one of jurisprudence but should come from logic and geometry, hence the appeal to the scientific community he no doubt associated with the academies. A Paris Academy committee submitted to its parent body on 30 April a highly positive report, drafted by Condorcet, about the value of the competition, and the clever method of plural voting the judges were to use to reach a decision. When nothing was done about the proposal (or so it seems from the absence of further mention in this Academy's records), Condorcet tried to keep it alive by publishing an enthusiastic letter in the *Journal de Paris* for 9 October 1785 (pp. 1162–3). He argued that Leibniz, who had conceived the project of a universal language, would not have shared the opinion that it was impossible to solve the problem set by Windisch-Grätz, also that the word 'impossible' was itself 'hardly philosophical'. In Condorcet's view, scientific methodology could be applied to the problem; even if in the end it did prove insoluble, this was a solution, since other men would be cautioned not to take it up again (Baker, 1975: 226–7, 447). We may detect in Condorcet's efforts concerning the competition the same drive to further the project of a universal language and give mathematical rigour to the social sciences that he manifested in the publication he sent in 1785 to Smith about probability and voting.

Smith replied to Windisch-Grätz about his proposal on 27 May, agreeing on behalf of his colleagues to judge the competition (Czech Republic, Klatovy, Statni oblastni archiv, Familienarchiv Windisch-Grätz, Karton 246, No. 32). He followed this up with another letter on 4 July to say, in parallel to prevailing Paris opinion, that his private response, shared by several colleagues, was that the problem admitted of no complete solution, and not even an approximation (MS copy, Aldourie Castle, Dores, Inverness). His reasoning was threefold. First, he knew of no limit to the variety of conditions with which 'vanity and caprice' might burden the transfer of property. We all know, he wrote, the variety of ways in which the twenty-four letters of the alphabet can be combined, and 'human vanity and caprice' had long ago invented many more conditions annexable to property transference. Second, he noted that forms of conveyancing differed from country to country according to positive law, and only those skilled in the positive law of any one country could invent a set of forms acceptable there. He considered that inventing an internationally valid set of forms would be impossible. Third, he stated that every country had voluminous collections of approved forms of conveyancing, which are the product of the 'wisdom and experience of many successive generations'. No single man, he thought, and no single society could improve on these collections, called 'style books' in Scotland. Yet nobody could go to these books with a complex agreement in mind, hoping to find an appropriate form needing only blanks to be filled in with names and dates. Any such agreement required ingenuity on the part of an able lawyer to express the meaning of the parties entering into a contract.

These style books, according to Smith, were viewed as painters view Old Masters, to be imitated but not copied. He added that if Windisch-Grätz had aimed at improving the style book of his own country, in point of distinctness, simplicity, and comprehensiveness, then the competition would have resulted in a better local administration of justice. He feared that in 'aiming at a much more extensive utility' the deviser of the problem had made it useless, thus ending his counter-argument from a historical perspective against the universalism endorsed by Leibniz and Condorcet.

Smith did not believe the Royal Society of Edinburgh would want any money for assisting with the competition, since he expected it would give members little trouble to act as judges. His further opinion was that nobody living was qualified to produce a solution to the problem, and the unqualified contenders were likely to be 'some ignorant, indigent and presumptuous pretenders to literature who mean to do nothing but to impose upon you and the public and to rob you of your money'. Smith agreed to accept a French translation of the original Latin programme outlining the competition, but he thought circulation of this would suffice without newspaper advertisements. Another flash of his reserved character comes with his admission: 'I never suffer my name to appear in a newspaper when I can hinder it, which to my sorrow, I cannot always do.'

Windisch-Grätz wrote to Smith on 12 July, again from Brussels, reporting he had received Smith's letter of 27 May, summarizing letters he had written on 7 and 22 June about the French programme, and adding the name of the Royal Society of Edinburgh to the publicity about the competition. Further letters to Smith dated 2 July and 30 October 1787 have survived. They do not suggest that Windisch-Grätz was ready to accept Smith's wisdom about his problem. In the first, he mentions that two solutions have reached him and one has been sent to Condorcet, also that the Academy of Basle has agreed to judge the entries. He wants the judges to decide soon on these, so that he can propose his problem in another manner if even approximate solutions have not come in. Condorcet wants him to abandon the deadline. The second letter complains about others written from Vienna and Prague going astray, and asks for a judgement by January 1788.

Further letters from Smith to Windisch-Grätz, dated 17 January 1786 and 26 January 1788, are held in the Klatovy Archive. In the first, Smith assures his correspondent that he has circulated the programme of the competition and that, despite his private opinion about the 'practicability of the problem', nothing would make him happier than its solution. In the second Smith reports that the committee of the Royal Society of Edinburgh (consisting of himself, Henry Mackenzie, and William Craig), appointed to assess the three dissertations tendered, has decided none solves the problem, but that one is meritorious and deserves public attention. Smith begs off further correspondence: his 'numerous and burdensome occupations, joined to an advanced age and very infirm state of health' prevent him continuing it. He states that Alexander Fraser Tytler, Secretary of the RSE, will transmit to Windisch-Grätz, under cover to Condorcet, the report and final judgement of the RSE. Tytler complied on 20 February 1788, and on 11 August 1788 he wrote again to say, politely, that

the RSE declined to act in judging in any further competition to solve the problem further (Klatovy Archive; RSE *Transactions*, 1787: i.39; 1788: ii.24).

It appears that, after another deadline set for 1790 had elapsed, a dissertation
submitted by a Swedish mathematician named Törner was deemed worthy of a
prize (Raynor and Ross, forthcoming). Regrettably, however, 'vanity and caprice'
have continued to exert their sway, and lawsuits over inheritances continue
unabated.

Smith's advice had to be of a negative or at least unhelpful cast on other occasions when he was appealed to as some kind of authority in the last years of his
life. In 1782 the Chief of the Clan Mackinnon sought his help in arranging the
publication of a treatise on fortifications, and passed on a five-pound note to
cover expenses. Smith agreed with Henry Mackenzie, who also read the papers,
'that in their present condition they would not do [Mackinnon] the honour we
wish you to derive from whatever work you publish'. Smith took steps to see
that the treatise was not plagiarized, something its author feared, and returned
the fiver (*Corr.* No. 219).

That same year, the Royal Society of Edinburgh had been formed under the
presidency of the Duke of Buccleuch, as a successor to the Philosophical Society,
because the Edinburgh literati were to some degree jealous of the enterprise of
Smith's former pupil, Lord Buchan, in seeking a charter for the Society of
Antiquaries. As secretary of the Philosophical Society, Cullen wished to see
established a body modelled on the European Academies. In the event, both the
Antiquaries and the Royal Society received their charters on 29 March 1783
(according to Campbell and Skinner, 1982*b*: 21; Cant, 1981: 16, gives the date,
6 May 1781). Smith became a Fellow of the latter group because all members of
the Philosophical Society, to which he had belonged since 1752, were admitted
to it. It had a Physical class and a Literary one, of which Smith was one of the
four presidents together with his old friends Robertson, Blair, and Baron
Gordon, who kept the key of his writing desk when he was in London in 1774
(*Corr.* app. E, h.).

In preparation for the fourth meeting of the Literary class on 16 February 1784,
Smith was asked to read a Dissertation presented then, which sought to prove 'that
Troy was not taken by the Greeks'. The author, John Maclaurin, son of Colin
Maclaurin the mathematician, had apparently been reading the Eleventh Discourse
of Dio Chrysostom, a sophistic address to the Trojans denying that their city had
been captured. Blithely admitting that he was 'totally unacquainted' with
Maclaurin's source, Smith said he agreed in doubting the historicity of any fact
relating to the Trojan war, but could not go along with the claim that it was more
probable that 'Helen was an honest woman' and so forth (*Corr.* app. E, s.).

When Alexander Fraser Tytler submitted to Smith a paper on vitrified forts
in Scotland he was less sceptical but noted that it was a subject of which he was
'totally ignorant' and advised consultation with his 'Chymical friends', Drs Black
and Hutton, who had offered the opinion that vitrification was caused not by

accident, as Tytler argued, but by heaping up wood on a wall after it was built (*Corr.* No. 254).

On Monday 20 July 1789, the poet Samuel Rogers attended a meeting of the Royal Society of Edinburgh addressed by Smith's adversary on the issue of the corn bounty, James Anderson. His topic on this occasion was the revision of the laws concerning debtors, but the essay read was 'very long and dull' and Rogers reported: 'Mr Commissioner Smith fell asleep' (Clayden, 1887: 96).

Smith showed much more zeal in acquiring the Transactions of the sister Royal Society of London, to which he had been admitted in 1767. It is not clear, however, whether his interest was in their scientific content or in owning them as a book collector (Mizuta). He did draw on them for his essay on the external senses (p. 57), quoting William Cheselden's famous case history about the blind boy whose sight was restored, and who had to learn that objects familiar from touch had to be made familiar all over again as objects of sight, thus answering a query Molyneux put to Locke about sense perception (Royal Society of London, 1727–8: xxxv.447–50, 451–2).

One call upon his judgement that Smith was prepared to acknowledge was furthering the work of authors of useful publications. Thus he provided accounts of the exports and imports of Scotland, with Treasury permission, for the antiquary George Chalmers, who was compiling a socioeconomic survey for 1785 entitled *Estimate of the Comparative Strength of Britain*. Chalmers also wished to have population figures for Scotland, and Smith gave him in his letter of 10 November 1785 'what seemed an accurate account' of these for 1755, compiled by Dr Alexander Webster, a leader of the 'High-flyers' of the Church of Scotland who was developing a pension scheme for the widows and children of ministers, and had obtained statistical returns from parishes because of a prestige in church affairs that was unimpaired by his convivial habits.

Smith noted that he had used Webster's 'account' in 1775, presumably when working on *WN*, and had accepted the figure of 1,250,000 for the population of Scotland. However, he also wrote that Webster shortly before his death in 1784 told him that his estimate was too low, and that 1,500,000 would be a better figure. Smith added that this story of a revised estimate did not help to alter the low opinion he had expressed of 'Political Arithmetic' (statistics) in *WN* (IV.v.b.30), which takes away a good deal from his praise of Webster as the 'most skilful in Political Arithmetic, of all the men I have ever known' (*Corr.* No. 249). Smith continued in a critical vein in a letter to Chalmers of 22 December following, in which he attacked the 'speculations' of Dr Richard Price, the Nonconformist minister and writer on morals, politics, and economics, whom he roundly dismissed as a 'factious citizen, a most superficial Philosopher, and by no means an able calculator' (*Corr.* No. 251).

Picking up the story of Webster's final estimate of the Scottish population, Smith reported in a letter of 3 January 1786 that he had discussed this with the current collector of the pension fund and his clerk, who had been Webster's clerk, and both considered the revised figure was due to a 'sudden thought' and had not come from a serious inquiry. They had mentioned that a copy of Webster's 'account' had been made in 1779 for the use of the Prime Minister, Lord North, and that Webster had added a note pointing out that, though the 'numbers in the great trading and manufacturing towns and Villages' had increased considerably since 1755, the Highlands and Islands were greatly depopulated in these years, and even Lowland Scotland because of the 'enlargement of farms'; therefore, the aggregate population had not grown. Smith believed Chalmers could borrow Webster's population 'account' from North, and described it as a 'great curiosity', though his faith in it had been a 'little shaken' as he now supposed 'without much reason' (*Corr.* No. 252). Chalmers thought highly of Smith and drew attention to his views on foreign trade:

This subject has been amply discussed and finely illustrated by Dr Adam Smith, who merits the praise of having formerly strengthened our morals and lately enlightened our intellects. (Chalmers, 1782: 76; Mizuta)

Here is another channel for the extension of Smith's reputation as a commentator on economic policy in a book that was often reprinted. Chalmers may have thought to add Smith to his series of biographies which included Defoe, Tom Paine, and the scholar-editor Thomas Ruddiman (Duncan, 1965: 6). He collected anecdotes, already drawn upon, from David Callander, probably for biographical purposes (EUL La. II.451/2, fos. 429–34).

Smith late in life rejoiced in the renewal of one old friendship. This was with the Revd Dr James Stuart Menteath, whom he had known at Oxford and to whom he wrote on 22 February 1785 that he would be very glad to see him come to Edinburgh, to supervise the education of his son Charles at the University. He praised this institution as 'at present better provided in Professors than any other Society of the kind I ever knew', perhaps thinking of the fact that Robertson, Black, Cullen, and Robison were all still teaching there; but he did add, 'it is likely soon to be still better provided than at present' (*Corr.* No. 243). Perhaps this is a revelation of a critical attitude to Adam Ferguson, who gave up his Chair of Moral Philosophy in 1785 and was replaced by Dugald Stewart.

As matters turned, young Menteath was sent to Glasgow in 1788, most likely because John Millar was willing to board him in his house, and the father could live not too far off at the family home, Closeburn Castle in Dumfriesshire (*Corr.* No. 281). Charles Menteath had a speech impediment, it seems, and Smith interested himself in securing the help of a language teacher at Glasgow, Mr Angier, to cure him in 1789 (*Corr.* No. 284). Smith's heir, David Douglas, was attending Glasgow University at this time and had a room adjoining Menteath's in Millar's house (*Corr.* No. 289). Another young man who joined them was Henry George Herbert, heir of Smith's former pupil Henry Herbert, Lord Porchester. To the father Smith stated on 23 September 1788: 'I agree with you in preferring Glasgow to Edinburgh', so perhaps in the end, Dugald Stewart's addition to the faculty at Edinburgh did not outweigh Smith's strong feeling for his alma mater.

It was in this letter that Smith wrote movingly of his grief at the impending death of his cousin Janet Douglas, who had looked after his mother and him for so many years (*Corr.* app. E, p). Dr Menteath did his best to console Smith, sent him game from the country, and was invited to take over David Douglas's bed when in Edinburgh, which suggests the closeness of the friendship with Smith, as well as the restricted nature of accommodation at Panmure House. Menteath frequented a club with Smith, possibly the Oyster which met at a Grassmarket inn, and attended Smith's Sunday night suppers (*Corr.* Nos. 284, 288).

Concern for the advancement of family members was another characteristic of Smith's later years. In mid-December 1775, he can be found writing to Henry Dundas, recently appointed Lord Advocate by North, and was on his way to becoming 'Harry the Ninth' or the 'Satrap of Scotland'. Smith wished to secure support for the election of a cousin, Col. Robert Skene, as MP for Fife. This gentleman held the office of Inspector of Roads in the Highlands, 1767–80, and in Parliament was accepted as an authority on road bills, but Smith's recommendation of him runs thus: 'He has been one of the best Sons, Brothers, and Unkles that I have ever known; and, I am thoroughly convinced, will be an equally faithful supporter of whoever supports him' (*Corr.* No. 148). In September 1785 Smith recommended to Col. Alexander Ross, secretary to Lord Cornwallis, Governor-General of India, another cousin, Col. Patrick Ross, who was chief engineer on the Madras establishment, and he followed this up with a solicitation in December 1786 for a cousin of Edmund Burke. This was William Burke, deputy-paymaster of the forces in India: 'You never knew an honester hearted fellow; social, convivial, perfectly good natured, and quite frank and open . . .'. Smith mentioned to Col. Alexander Ross that he had met Cornwallis at the Earl of Bristol's house, presumably meaning the 2nd Earl, a diplomat and politician who died in 1775, but he did not expect to be remembered by Cornwallis (*Corr.* No. 264).

Having once violated his resolution not to trouble Cornwallis's secretary in favour of William Burke, Smith had to do so again on 13 June 1787 for a Mr Royds, who was married to the daughter of a Kirkcaldy friend, Robert White. Though Royds was unknown to him, Smith interceded for him at the behest of Alexander Wedderburn, now Lord Loughborough (*Corr.* No. 270). Smith continued his exertions on behalf of Patrick Ross, through writing to Dundas early in 1787 to have justice done to his cousin in British India. That country's affairs had been added to the Lord Advocate's portfolio. Dundas considered acting against the Court of Directors of the East India Company, but he wrote to Smith on 21 March that this might have brought ruin on Ross, so he had left it to the Commander-in-Chief of Madras, Sir Archibald Campbell, to put matters right. This letter ends with Dundas saying that he is glad that Smith is taking a vacation from the Customs Board, and that he agrees with Pitt and William

Wyndham Grenville (later 1st Baron Grenville) in the opinion that this should be spent in London. He invites Smith to stay with him in his Wimbledon villa: 'You shall have a comfortable Room and as the Business is much relaxed we shall have time to discuss all your Books with you every evening' (*Corr.* No. 267).

Smith did not attend any meetings of the Customs Board from early in January 1787 until 30 July of that year, and it is within that period that he paid his last visit to London, the smoky, malodorous, increasingly thriving 'trading city' that was also the 'constant residence of a court' (*WN* III.iii.12). Its mixed population, including chairmen who were also bricklayers, hefty coal-heavers, and beautiful though unfortunate prostitutes (I.ix.6.41), must have been approaching the 900,000 estimated in the first official census of 1801 (Schwartz, 1983: 4). Relaxation of illness as well as Dundas's flattering invitation is likely to have prompted the journey. On 6 March Smith wrote to Bishop John Douglas, fellow Snell Exhibitioner with him at Balliol, that he was in his 'Grand Climacteric', the 63rd year when tradition held that the last and most perilous of a lifetime's crises were to be expected (*Corr.* No. 266). He added that the state of his health had been a 'good deal worse than usual'. In the winter of 1786–7 William Robertson had informed Gibbon that Smith's chronic obstruction of the bowels threatened his death (Rae, 1965: 402), and this condition ultimately was responsible for his death, according to Dugald Stewart (v.7). Smith ended his letter to Douglas, however, by stating that he was 'getting better and better . . . every day', and he hoped 'with good pilotage . . . to weather this dangerous promontory of Human life'.

He was well enough to set out for London, very likely on a six-day journey by post chaise, some time before 15 April. On that day Robert Burns, who had been in Edinburgh that winter, wrote to a common friend, Mrs Dunlop of Dunlop, that 'Dr Smith was just gone to London the morning before I rec[eive]d your letter to him'. The poet never did meet this author, whose writings he had known since 1783, but it is believed that Smith suggested a place be found for Burns as a Salt Officer at £30 p.a. to provide support for him (Burns, 1931: i.83; Snyder, 1932: 232, n. 8).

Once in London, the emaciated Smith was treated for inflammation of the neck of the bladder, and cut successfully for the piles by John Hunter, the King's surgeon and brother of William, whose anatomy lectures Smith had attended with Gibbon in the 1770s (London, Royal Coll. of Surgeons, Hunter-Baillie papers, vol. i, fo. 40; Gibbon, 1956: ii.138; Brock, 1983: 78, nn. 119, 120). On 10 June, however, a friend of Gibbon's indicated that he was still worried by Smith's condition:

You will find [when you get back] near the Adelphi poor Adam Smith. I say poor because he seems very weak and not far from the end of his career; some fundamental operation has lately been performed on him by John Hunter since when he seems to pick up a little, I nevertheless fear that the machine is nearly worn out. (quoted Fay, 1956: 141)

In far-off Russia, another philosopher, Bentham, received news about London from the Scottish lawyer George Wilson, who reported on 14 July that Smith's physicians believed him to be on the mend, and that he was well enough to be of service to the Government:

He is much with the ministry; and the clerks at the public offices have orders to furnish him with all papers, and to employ additional hands, if necessary, to copy for him. I am vexed that Pitt should have done so right a thing as to consult Smith; but if any of his schemes are effectuated, I shall be much comforted. (Bentham, *Corr.*, 1971: iii.550)

At this time Pitt's ministry was deeply involved in promoting fiscal and commercial reform in a systematic way, and there is evidence that *WN* was considered as a source of relevant ideas. When Dundas invited Smith to stay with him in his Wimbledon villa, as we learned, he suggested that he and Pitt and Grenville would discuss his visitor's 'books' with him. Pitt and Grenville, who were cousins, had prepared for such an opportunity, as mentioned already, for they had read *WN* together about three years previously.

Dundas's letter to Smith referred to 'Business' being 'relaxed', but in the early months of 1787 there was a great deal of parliamentary activity connected with the commercial treaty that had been concluded with France by William Eden, also with scrutiny of taxation so that the enormous national debt arising from the American war could be steadily reduced from increasing revenue. Grenville, who served on the Boards of Trade and Control, in particular took a leading role in dealing with these issues, and among his notes there is a relevant commentary on public debts (BL Mrs O. J. Fortescue MSS, Lord Grenville, Commentaries, ch. 3: pp. 13–30). This has been described (Jupp, 1985: 56–7) as resembling closely Smith's severe criticism of the 'unfunded debt of Great Britain' (*WN* v.iii.11–13).

We noted that Smith was apparently consulted in 1766 by Charles Townshend about the creation of a sinking fund to retire the national debt (*Corr.* No. 302), but in *WN* he expressed reservations about the administration of such a Fund: 'though instituted for the payment of old debts, it facilitates very much the contracting of new debts' (*WN* v.iii.28). Pitt was attracted to this device, however, and chose a method to administer it outlined by Dr Richard Price in his *Appeal to the Public, on the Subject of the National Debt*, 1772 (Reilly, 1978: 113).

Grenville was more inclined to stick to Smith's principles, and supported a free-market policy. Thus in 1800 he opposed price regulation of grain or flour, arguing that this would lead to scarcity as it had in France. Easily caricatured because of his bulbous head and bottom, also nicknamed 'Lord Bogy' by those opposed to him, Grenville had great intellectual assurance, and he felt so strongly about maintaining Smith's free-market stand that on two occasions he gave Pitt lectures on his subject, one in connection with a bill aimed at incorporating the London Flour Company so as to control the supply and price of bread, and another to ward off parliamentary intervention during a grain shortage. Though unsuccessful in changing Pitt's mind on these occasions, Grenville's free-trade outlook made more impact later on the thought of younger Whig MPs of his time, such as Francis Horner, David Ricardo, and Sir Henry Brooke Parnell, all readers of *WN* in their own right, who in turn contributed to the Reform movement of the 1830s under Lords Grey and Melbourne. In this period, some of Adam Smith's ideas were embodied in policy at the Board of Trade and elsewhere (Jupp, 1985: 103, 281, 427, 445–7).

There was an Edinburgh tradition that on one occasion during this London visit Smith was one of the last gentlemen to come into the room in Dundas's Wimbledon villa, when Pitt, Grenville, Henry Addington, and William Wilberforce were other guests. The company rose to receive Smith, and he asked them to be seated. Pitt is represented as saying: 'No, we will stand till you are first seated, for we are all your scholars' (Kay, 1842: i.75; Rae, 1965: 405). Smith had advance notice of Pitt's good opinion of him, and had come round to valuing his ministry, despite his own adherence to the remnants of the Rockingham Whigs. Answering on 14 November 1786 a letter from the reform-minded MP Henry Beaufoy, he wrote:

I think myself much honoured by the slightest mark of Mr Pitts approbation. You may be assured that the long and strict friendship in which I have lived with some of his opponents, does not hinder me from discerning courage, activity, probity, and public spirit in the great outlines of his administration. (Piero Sraffa *Collection* B5/3, Trinity College, Cambridge)

Addington, later to be Grenville's successor as Speaker of the House of Commons, 1789–1801, and thereafter a stopgap Prime Minister until Pitt regained control of affairs in 1803, is said to have returned home after the Wimbledon meeting and composed verses to the 'author of the *Wealth of Nations*, etc.: on his visit to London and its neighbourhood in the month of June, 1787':

> I welcome you, whose wise and patriot page
> The road to wealth and peace hath well defin'd,
> Hath strove to curb and soften hostile rage,
> And to unite, with int'rest's tie, mankind:
> Dragg'd from his lonely den, and at thy feet
> The bloated fiend *Monopoly* is thrown:
> And with thy fame, its splendour to compleat,
> The pride and hope of *Britain* blends his own.
> Proceed, great soul, and error's shades disperse,
> Perfect and execute the glorious plan;
> Extend your view wide as the Universe,
> Burst every bar that sep'rates man from man,
> And ne'er may war's curst banner be unfurled,
> But commerce harmonize a jarring world!

This effusion was communicated to Smith early in 1790, and since the great man was a sound critic of poetry, Ernest Mossner once claimed it 'may well have hastened the end' (1969: 20–1).

Wilberforce tried to get some practical help from Smith, not with the anti-slavery campaign with which his name is generally associated, though Smith was vigorous in condemning slavery, but with a scheme to develop fishing villages round the coastline of the Scottish Highlands. To a director of the Society formed to execute this plan, Wilberforce reported his rebuff:

Dr Smith with a certain characteristic coolness, observed to me that he looked for no other consequence from the scheme than the entire loss of every shilling that should be expended on it, granting, however, with uncommon candour, that the public would be no great sufferer, because he believed the individuals meant to put their hands only in their own pockets. (Wilberforce, 1840: i.40)

Beaufoy's enthusiasm for the British Fisheries Society was also doused with cold water from Smith, who pointed out that fishermen in the Highlands would not be able to afford the Society's rents and repayments. He also brought up a favourite theme of his regarding such schemes, the agency problem, warning Beaufoy: 'you must lay your account with the cruellest oppression of the poor People, and the grossest frauds upon the [Society promoters], from far the greater part of your agents, overseers, and superintendants' (letter of 29 Jan. 1787). Of all the fishing stations actually built to Thomas Telford's plans, only the one at Wick, named Pulteneytown after Smith's old friend Sir William Pulteney, was successful and thus refuted Smith's scepticism (Youngson, 1973: 133).

Another philanthropist met a similarly sceptical reception. This was the Revd David Williams, who established an Academy of Sciences and Belles Lettres at Carlisle House, London, in the late 1780s, and gave lectures on the 'political principles' of Locke, Rousseau, Montesquieu, Hume, Steuart, and Smith. He published these in 1789, and dedicated his book to the Prince of Wales, whom he urged to take Smith as his tutor:

Command, from the dreary shores of Caledonia, the philosophic statesman of Britain— give the profound "Historian of the Wealth of Nations": the daily direction of half an hour of your time; contemplate with him, the venerable but disordered machine, which you may be called upon to set in motion. (Dybikowski, 1993: 165, n. 30)

Prinny's response to this idea has not been recorded, but on a philanthropic quest Williams went to a number of great men, among them Franklin, who gave him some encouragement, and Burke, who gave him a violent reception, with a proposal for a literary fund to support authors in distress. Williams believed that Smith's opinion that men of letters are unproductive labourers (*WN* II.iii.2) stood in the way of his scheme. Accordingly, he asked for an interview with Smith at the London house of General Melville, who had been at Glasgow University with Smith in 1737 and had subsequently become Governor of the West Indies. Smith heard Williams out with that 'modest diffidence, which seemed to be his character, and the appearance of which was heightened by a constitutional infirmity'. The interview then proceeded as follows in Williams' account:

When I had finished, he seemed also to have finished. After some silence I begged his permission to ask him how I could introduce my propositions if his opinion were true concerning men of letters.

He said: 'My opinion is of no consequence.'

'Allowing that for the moment to your modesty, you state it as a maxim of political economy.'

'I believe it may.'

'To invent improved methods of operation in all employments acknowledged to be productive, is it not to increase or multiply the produce?'

'Ay, that is the farmer.'

'No. Is not the claim of the man who thinks, in all such cases, as unquestionable as that of the man who executes by labour? The claim of the man who uses a spade is as unquestionable as that of the spade itself.'

He smiled.

Williams wished to continue the argument, but Smith showed signs of distress, 'from his infirmity' and the wordiness of the company who took up the topic. Before Williams left, Smith said: 'If you and I could have leisure to explain words, we might not disagree. Why don't you state your plan to the young minister [Pitt]? It seems to be a political proposition of great importance' (Williams, 1980: 43–5).

Pitt received Williams in a kind manner, though he did not take up the project. He did keep Smith firmly in mind, however, in connection with the general policy of his ministry in February 1792, when he made at that time a celebrated speech in which he reviewed Britain's economic recovery and growth since the American war (Willis, 1979; Crowley, 1990).

His arch-rival Fox may have been the first MP to mention Smith's name in a parliamentary debate, on 11 November 1783, and he and the Whigs he led twitted Pitt on occasion about not following Smith's precise prescriptions. It was Pitt, however, who paid the most generous tribute to Smith's grasp of the 'simple and obvious' principle of capital accumulation, that if public calamity is averted, and 'mistaken and mischievous policy' of government intervention is avoided, there will be natural increase:

Simple and obvious as this principle is, and felt and observed as it must have been in a greater or less degree, even from the earliest periods, I doubt whether it has ever been fully developed and sufficiently explained, but in the writings of an author of our own times, now unfortunately no more, (I mean the author of a celebrated treatise on the Wealth of Nations,) whose extensive knowledge of detail, and depth of philosophical research, will, I believe, furnish the best solution to every question connected with the history of commerce, or with the systems of political economy. (Pitt the Younger, 1817: i.358–9)

Though well aware of the 'distractions now prevailing' in France, Pitt thought fifteen years of peace might 'reasonably' be expected in Europe to advance his country's prosperity further and accelerate the sinking of the national debt. But a world war came in the wake of the French Revolution to blow up that hope. Nevertheless, Lord Grenville survived the war to lecture Lord Grey and the Whig party generally on returning to monetary orthodoxy and the comprehensive free-trade policy of the early years of the first Pitt administration, when he had the stimulation of direct contact with Smith.

One of Smith's last acts before leaving London for Edinburgh in July 1787 was to apply to Dundas to further the army career of a second cousin, Robert Douglas, a Lieutenant in the Rutlandshire Regiment (58th Foot) and elder brother of Smith's heir, David. Another younger brother, Charles, had already been promoted Captain because he had served in a recently raised regiment (MacLeod's, 73rd), but Robert was in Gibraltar during the siege and it was thought to be inappropriate to remove him from his regiment during the fighting to obtain a company for him: 'His service, therefor, has stopt his preferment, instead of promoting it.' The letter also makes mention of the army service of other brothers of Robert: William, a Colonel in the guards, and John, serving in the Engineers. Smith's knowledge of and interest in military affairs could certainly have come in part from these men. Focused on the patronage system, Smith ends his letter by suggesting to Dundas that his surgeon John Hunter should be kept in mind for the two government medical appointments held by the aged Robert Adair: 'Chelsea Hospital is the best of the two; but both would be best of all; and nothing is too good for our friend John' (*Corr.* No. 272).

November 1787 brought an honour to Smith that gave him a great deal of pleasure, his election on the 15th of that month as Lord Rector of Glasgow University. In his letter of acceptance of 20 November, he writes that 'no preferment could have given me so much real satisfaction', and that he feels a 'heartfelt joy' he cannot easily express to Principal Davidson who had communicated the news. The nomination at the outset, however, was opposed. On the view that the professors' choice should not go unchallenged, Francis Jeffrey, then a Bejant (or Bajan), later to be one of the founders and editors of the second *Edinburgh Review*, harangued some boys on Glasgow Green against voting for Smith, but this opposition was withdrawn (Cockburn, 1842: i.12–14). Smith declares to Davidson that he can come to Glasgow at any convenient time for his installation:

John Millar mentions Christmas. We have commonly at the board of Customs a vacation of five or six days at that time. But I am so regular an attendant that I think myself entitled to take the play for a week at any time. (*Corr.* No. 274)

Smith took his oath of office on 19 December 1787 and appointed as Vice-Rector his former student, William Richardson, Professor of Humanity. Both served for a second year, beginning on 27 November 1788 (GUA 26687). It does not appear that Smith gave a rectorial address on either occasion, but writing to Samuel Rose on 6 May 1788, Richardson mentions Smith's reaction to the honour paid to him, and describes a paper on the imitative arts read to the Literary

Society by the new Rector, presumably in the week before or after his first admission:

Dr Smith whom we elected Rector has been admitted. He staid a week with us. Never was honour better bestowed, for never honour made a worthy man more happy. Being a member of our Literary Society, he read us a discourse, of two hours length. The subject was the Imitative Arts: and the design was to illustrate the general principle by which they please. He treated of Statuary, Painting, and Music—and is still to treat of Poetry and Dancing. Yes dancing, for he conceives it to be an Imitative art; and I believe means to prove, that the Greek tragedy was no other than a musical Ballet. (GUL MS Gen. 520/6)

John Millar was another auditor of this paper, or knew of its delivery, and writing to Smith's heir, David Douglas, on 10 August 1790 he stated that, 'of the discourses which [Smith] intended upon the imitative arts, he read two to our Society at Glasgow, but the third was not then finished' (GUL MS Gen. 1035/178). Part iii of the discourses on the imitative arts when published in *EPS* was still a fragment, but it does have hints of the argument Smith intended to make about the role of dancing by the chorus in Greek tragedies (iii.7), though no claim is made that they constituted musical ballets.

As for other matters concerning Glasgow University, Smith reported on 16 July 1788 to Principal Davidson that he had had friendly dealings with officials of the Scottish Court of Exchequer about a legal point concerning a College lease. Concluding his letter, he commented on the death of his successor in the Chair of Logic: 'I am sorry for Clow; tho he has dyed in the fulness of years, and I dare to say, perfectly satisfyed and contented with his share of the enjoyments of human life' (*Corr.* No. 278). This is an expression of the Stoic philosophy learned in his youth, which allowed him to confront with equanimity his own approaching demise. He was secure, too, in the knowledge that his ideas about political economy had been stated to his satisfaction in the third edition of *WN*, and were receiving thoughtful attention from legislators, including the Prime Minister of his country.

23

The Precariousness of This Life

The best thing, I think, I can do is leave those works I have already published in the best and most perfect state behind me.

A measure of health had been restored to Smith as a result of the attention of his doctors in London, and Robertson wrote about this on 27 February 1788 to Gibbon: 'Our friend Mr Smith, whom we were in great danger of losing, is now almost perfectly re-established' (quoted Fay, 1956: 141). Smith devoted this health in the main to preparing the sixth edition of *TMS*: the legacy of his moral philosophy for everyone, including legislators. Smith had the modest beginning of this project in view in April 1785 when he wrote to Cadell that he was glad a fourth edition of *WN* was desired (published 1786), and added: 'If a new edition of the theory is wanted I have a few alterations to make of no consequence which I shall send to you' (*Corr.* No. 244).

One of these 'alterations' was simply dropping the reference to La Rochefoucauld in the *TMS* chapter 'Of Licentious Systems' (VII.ii.4.6). In editions 1–5 Smith had coupled the name of the author of the famous *Maxims* with that of Mandeville as devisers of 'pernicious' systems that seemed to deny there was a distinction between virtue and vice. Smith concentrated on Mandeville's system, which probably gave him more philosophical difficulty in view of his acknowledgement of the force of self-interest, and he contented himself with differentiating La Rochefoucauld's style, described as possessing 'elegance and delicate precision', from the other writer's 'lively and humorous, tho' coarse and rustic eloquence'. In a letter dated 3 March 1778, the 8th duc de La Rochefoucauld, whom Smith has met in France, remonstrated politely about the treatment of his grandfather (*Corr.* No. 194). Smith apparently promised, in a missing letter of 15 May following, that he would make an appropriate change in *TMS* (*Corr.* No. 199), but he did not do so in edition 5 (1781). He referred to his promise in a letter to the young nobleman on 1 November 1785, stating he hoped to execute it 'before the end of the ensuing winter' (*Corr.* No. 248). When Dugald Stewart went to France in May 1789, he carried a message from Smith to La Rochefoucauld expressing 'sincere regret for having introduced the name of his ancestor and that of Dr Mandeville in the same sentence', and declaring that future editions of *TMS* would be changed (Stewart, vi.256, ix.46).

Other changes to *TMS* were more complicated, and there ensued a 'long silence' which Smith broke on 15 March 1788 with another letter to Cadell about the development of his project:

The weak state of my health and my atendance at the Custom house, occupied me so much after my return to Scotland, that tho' I gave as much application to study as these circumstances would permit, yet that application was neither very great, nor very steady, so that my progress was not very great. I have now taken leave of my Colleagues for four months and I am at present giving the most intense application. My subject is *the theory of moral Sentiments* to all parts of which I am making many additions and corrections. The chief and the most important additions will be to the third part, that concerning *the sense of Duty* and to the last part concerning *the History of moral Philosophy*. . . . I consider my tenure of this life as extremely precarious, and am very uncertain whether I shall live to finish several other works which I have projected and in which I have made some progress, . . . I am a slow a very slow workman, who do and undo everything I write at least half a dozen of times before I can be tolerably pleased with it; and tho' I have now, I think, brought my work within compass, yet it will be the month of June before I shall be able to send it to you.

Smith concludes this part of the letter, so revealing about his habits of composition, by stating that he means to make Cadell a present of his additions to *TMS*, and that he does not want another edition of *TMS* to be issued meantime. He also asks to be informed about the sale of *WN* (*Corr.* No. 276), and the answer must have been satisfactory, for a fifth edition of that book came out the next year.

Marsilio Landriani, an Italian visitor travelling through Britain in 1788 to study the application of scientific inventions to industry, had been placed under Smith's care in Edinburgh, and he reported to a correspondent on 16 August that his mentor was labouring over the revisions to *TMS*, 'purging it of some expressions which, although clarified by appropriate definitions, left some confusion in the minds of readers'. Traces of a purge in the last version of *TMS* are not entirely obvious, but there is one passage dealing with divine sanctions which must have left some readers of the first five editions confused about Smith's teaching on this subject, and which he must have decided needed revision. He had pointed out that the 'different sects of ancient philosophy' upheld the maxim that the 'gods neither resent nor hurt', yet he had gone on to express himself in a Calvinist strain about the vile insect man ultimately having to appease the wrath of a justly provoked God by 'repentance, sorrow, humiliation, and contrition', and how revelation coincides here with the 'original anticipations of nature'. In edition 6 he purges the 'vile insect' discussion, and follows the statement that we think the justice of God requires the punishment in a future life of those who harm the weak with this sentence of a distinctly Humean cast:

In every religion, and in every superstition that the world has ever beheld, accordingly, there has been a Tartarus as well as an Elysium; a place provided for the punishment of the wicked, as well as one for the reward of the just. (II.ii.3.12; *TMS* app. II; 1992*a*)

Landriani's letter makes the further interesting point that he believed Smith's approach in *TMS* was based on the researches of Hutcheson and Hume on the influence of the association of ideas as giving rise to the moral sentiments (NLS MS 14,835, fos. 68–9; Pugliese, 1924; Ross and Webster, 1981).

But as matters turned out, it was a full year before Smith was ready to comment to Cadell again on the new edition of *TMS*, and he did so by way of complaining that his work on it had hurt his health to the extent that he had returned to his 'usual attendance at the Custom house . . . I may say principally for the sake of relaxation, and a much easier Business'. It is possible that his old hypochondriasis troubled him again, and the routine work of his Customs office was a form of therapy. Clearly the enterprise of revising *TMS* had grown unexpectedly bigger:

Besides the Additions and improvements I mentioned to you; I have inserted, immediately after the fifth part, a compleat new sixth part containing a practical system of Morality, under the title of the Character of Virtue. The Book now will consist of seven Parts and will make two pretty large 8vo. Volumes. After all my labours, however, I am afraid it will be Midsummer before I can get the whole Manuscript in such proper order as to send it to you. I am very much ashamed of this delay; but the subject has grown upon me. (*Corr.* No. 287)

At the beginning of May 1789 Dugald Stewart was on his way to France, where he observed developments of the French Revolution; but during a brief stay in London he called on Cadell and Andrew Strahan, William's son and heir to the printing business, to give them Smith's instructions that the new additions to *TMS* were not to be printed separately, as those for the third edition of *WN* had been. When Cadell declared himself embarrassed by this decision, Stewart had said that Smith's mind was made up, also that the nature of the new work made this arrangement impossible. Cadell then asked if this circumstance could be mentioned in the Advertisement to the new edition, but this was not done, though the extensive nature of the additions was outlined. Smith did exaggerate here, however, in stating that he had consolidated in part VII the 'greater part of the different passages concerning the Stoical Philosophy', since throughout the book many references to Stoic philosophers and teaching remain indicating how much this philosophy influenced him (*TMS* 5–6).

One new Stoic topic added is acceptance of suicide (VII.ii.1.25–35), which is extended to cover the behaviour of Indians in North America who would take their lives rather than become prisoners of war. The Glasgow *TMS* editors suggest that Smith's thought on suicide was prompted by the appearance of Hume's long-suppressed essay on this subject. Though this publication had appeared as long ago as 1777, it might have added to European interest in suicide arising from the publication of Goethe's novel *The Sorrows of Young Werther* (1774), always conceding that this work has a framework of exaggerated sensibility very different from the self-command of Stoic suicide explored by Hume and Smith

(Boyle, 1992: 171–8). The historian Simon Schama has noted that there was a growing attention to suicide as a phenomenon in the last years of Louis XVI's effective reign in France. There were also some spectacular examples, such as that of the Bishop of Grenoble in August 1788, compromised in the political struggle between the central administration and the local patriots; and that of Lamoignon, a leading minister in Loménie de Brienne's administration, in the spring of 1789. It was officially regarded as a hunting accident, but this death occurred suspiciously soon after the Government had collapsed because of a credit crisis. Brienne was himself to take his life in 1794 under threat of the Terror, as did many proscribed Girondins and, in all likelihood, Smith's acquaintance Condorcet (Schama, 1989: 171–8).

Suicide in the Stoic view is perhaps the supreme test of self-command, and it is that virtue's interaction with sensibility as part of moral formation which is a major theme of the final additions to part III of *TMS*. On the score of sensibility, Smith seems to be responsive to the focus on this in contemporary French culture.[1] Thus in a passage on 'unmerited reproach' added in edition 6, Smith turns to the Calas case brought to his attention during his stay in Toulouse to illustrate the agony felt by a father unjustly condemned to death for the murder of his son. Smith finds in the last words of the innocent man evidence of the torment of 'indignation at the injustice . . . done to him', and of the 'horror at the thoughts of the infamy which the punishment may shed on his memory'. According to Smith, Calas said to the monk who attended him after he had been broken on the wheel, and before he was thrown into the fire: 'My Father, can you yourself bring yourself to believe that I am guilty?' (*TMS* III.2.11) Elsewhere, in another passage added to part III, Smith concedes that want of sensibility for the sufferings of our family offends propriety far more than excess of such feeling. Thinking of the literature of sensibility of his century, which, as in the case of Richardson's *Clarissa Harlowe*, explores cruelty and indifference to human pain (Mullan, 1990), he cites its creators as more to be listened to than the proponents of 'stoical apathy':

The poets and romance writers, who best paint the refinements and delicacies of love and friendship, and of all other private and domestic affections, Racine and Voltaire; Richardson, Maurivaux, and Riccoboni; are, in such cases, much better instructors than Zeno, Chrysippus, or Epictetus. (III.3.14)

Nevertheless, Smith resolutely placed self-command at the centre of the struggle to live a virtuous life.

Yet another late addition argues that the 'disposition to admire the rich and the great' may be regarded as the 'most universal cause of the corruption of our moral sentiments'. Wealth and greatness are 'natural objects' of our respect, and this is conducive to securing order through 'distinction of ranks' in a society. The wealthy and great because of this may even escape criticism for their follies and vices. Disposed to admire them, and in consequence to imitate them, we follow the 'fashion' they lead, and herein lies our corruption. Our vanity drives us to acquire a reputation for fashionable vice we may inwardly condemn, and to affect to despise virtues for which we may feel veneration (I.iii.3). The issue of the moral corruption attendant upon vanity is taken up again in the entirely new part VI, as well as that of the constant dissatisfaction with which this failing and even pride are connected. The check to this, in Smith's view, is the balanced self-estimation afforded by the impartial spectator (VI.iii.37–53).

That concept receives its fullest and most sophisticated development in the revised part III of *TMS*, in which Smith distinguishes between the 'man without', operating in moral questions on the basis of what will be blamed or praised by society, and the 'man within', who judges morally on the basis of what he recognizes as admirable or reprehensible in the actions of other people. Thus, late in his life, Smith is evincing more scepticism about public opinion, as the Glasgow *TMS* editors point out (p. 16), and is seeking a standard for the application of an individual and independent conscience. He does admit, however, that the 'man within' can be 'astonished and confounded by the judgments of weak and ignorant men' (III.2.32; Raphael, 1975).

There is less chance of this moral distortion, so Smith argues, in the 'middling and inferior stations of life', where the path to virtue and that to fortune, in most cases, 'happily' tend to coincide. The argument continues that here 'real and solid professional abilities, joined to prudent, just, firm, and temperate conduct, can seldom fail of success'. In turn, such conduct depends on the good opinion of neighbours and equals, and this cannot be obtained without 'tolerably regular conduct'. This is the situation of the majority of people, 'fortunately for the good morals of society', according to Smith. When he looks at those in higher stations, he finds their success is dependent on the 'fanciful and foolish favour of ignorant, presumptuous, or proud superiors'. At this level of society, the 'solid and masculine virtues of a warrior, a statesman, a philosopher, or a legislator' will be less admired than the accomplishments of the man of fashion. Nevertheless, a man of self-command may be found, for example, the duc de Sully in the reign of Louis XIII, to rebuke the buffoons of a court and remind the sovereign of the path of virtue (I.iii.3.6).

Despite Smith's declaration on 31 March 1789 that he had 'inserted . . . a compleat new sixth part containing a practical system of Morality, under the title of the Character of Virtue', and his prediction that it would take until midsummer to get his manuscript into proper order to send to his publisher (*Corr.* No. 287), it was not until 18 November 1789 that he could write to Cadell to say that his 'Book is now at last perfectly finished to the very last sentence' (Klemme, 1991: 279). What could be the changes or additions following the March letter? It is entirely possible that in the interim he was following with some alarm the events of the French Revolution, so optimistically hailed by Dupont de Nemours on 19 June 1788 (*Corr.* No. 277) as 'much hastened' by Smith, and he wished now to offer a corrective viewpoint.

Du Pont had assisted Calonne, Controller-General of France, in preparing a constitutional and fiscal reform programme for implementation through the Assembly of Notables, which had debated it in 1787. Its members showed a knowledge of economic theory that had astonished Du Pont, but which was perhaps due to the spread of the influence of *WN* as well as the writings of the Physiocrats. This phase ended with the disgrace of Calonne and his dismissal from office on 8 April. His successor, Brienne, found that the Assembly of Notables had the bit between its teeth and would not agree to a new tax structure without guarantees of government through representation and consent, those old watchwords of the American Revolution. Brienne ended the life of the Assembly on 25 May 1787, and thereafter had to govern by forcing through the *Parlement* of Paris edicts respecting the land tax and stamp duty he had inherited from Calonne (Schama, 1990: 228–46, 254–72).

In the past Smith had been friendly with the *parlementaires* of Toulouse who had been subjected to military violence to secure the registration of edicts in 1763, and he had collected for his library an extensive pamphlet literature dealing with the struggle of the *Parlements* against Louis XV's despotism (Mizuta). The same scene was now reenacted in the capital and the twelve provincial *parlements*, but in this round the resistance to the monarchy grew frenzied, particularly over the enforced registration in the *Parlement* of Paris on 8 May 1788 of a series of edicts stripping the *parlements* of their chief jurisdictions, and thus their power to oppose the central government, but replacing all this with 'enlightened justice', a system of courts designed by Lamoignon to be impartial and accessible to most of the people. Condorcet for one approved of such a systematic reform, but there was outrage over the naked exercise of power to achieve it, and local jealousies over the regions of France were inflamed by the necessary demotion of the *parlementaire* centres.

The city of the suicidal bishop, Grenoble, proved the first flashpoint of such violent feelings on Monday 9 June 1788, the celebrated 'day of tiles', when the crowd intervened against royal troops to save the *parlementaires* from being sent into exile by *lettres de cachet*. When soldiers were ordered into the streets to control riots, in some instances by firepower, they were pelted with tiles thrown from the rooftops. In the end the royal governor withdrew his two ineffective regiments, and the crowd took over the city, pillaging the governor's residence and fêting the magistrates of the *Parlement*, who no doubt wondered where power now ultimately lay. An outcome of this confrontation was an appeal from Grenoble to the King adding to the national call for a meeting of the Estates-General last convened in 1614. The King was also asked to summon the Estates of the region, the Dauphiné, with the proviso that there should be free elections to that body, with the numbers representing the Third Estate to equal those combined of the other two orders, the clergy and the nobility. Here was anticipated the agenda of the intense constitutional debate that ensued when Brienne fell, to be succeeded by Necker; and in the face of continuing financial crisis and unrest across France, the King was prevailed upon to summon the Estates-General to meet on 1 May 1789.

In the harsh winter of 1788–9 there was hunger and therefore great anger among the poor, producing destructive riots against the game privileges of the seigneurs in the countryside, and in the towns outbursts of violence against provision dealers (Schama, 1990: 103–12, 272–83, 305–8). Smith had noticed the depressed condition of the poor in France (*WN* 1.ix.9; 'Imitative Arts' i.14), as well as the tyranny of the forced-labour requirement for road-mending (*corvée*) and the vexation of the poll-tax directed at some and property tax for others (*taille*), the exorbitancy of the salt tax, and the wastefulness and savagery against smugglers arising from the system of farming revenues: 'Those who consider the blood of the people as nothing in comparison with the revenue of the prince, may perhaps approve of this method of levying taxes.' Further, he had offered sensible ideas about reforming the French taxes, but he reckoned that privilege was so entrenched in France that nothing would be done (*WN* v.i.d.19; v.ii.k.75–7).

It seems that Smith was well aware of the tide of resentment against the social and political system of Bourbon France, which had one centre in the conservative feelings of crowds outraged by the violation of traditional rights and customs (Garrioch, 1986; Sonenscher, 1989; Farge, 1994). He also had access to the major sources of the revolutionary ideas canvassed by those who sought change and finally exploited crowd violence to this end. In 1782 he entertained the geologist Benjamin Faujas de Saint Fond, who reported that the 'best French authors occupied a distinguished place in his Library, for he was fond of our language'. One such author was the Marquis d'Argenson, whose *Considérations sur le gouvernement de la France* (1764; Mizuta) advocated a 'royal democracy', identifying the hereditary nobility as the source of his country's evils, and arguing that the remedy was a king removed from the corruption of Versailles to govern from Paris with the assistance of elected provincial assemblies and a national representative body (Schama, 1989: 112–13). Smith himself spoke to Saint Fond about Voltaire and Rousseau in terms of the highest respect, acknowledging the former's satiric strength and the latter's passion and conviction. As noted previously, he believed the *Social Contract* would avenge the persecution suffered by Rousseau (Faujas de Saint Fond, 1907: ii.246).

In preparation for the assembly of the Estates-General, Louis XVI required his subjects to gather in their orders and communities, elect deputies, and prepare *cahiers de doléances* to record their grievances and their recommendations. These documents enlarge on the theme of the oppressions of the *régime* much as Smith had perceived them, and in certain cases they achieved fame for mapping out a future of Enlightenment, one example of this being the vast production of Du Pont on behalf of the Third of Nemours. The France so envisaged, for the most part, was to be liberalized, in its Constitution, legal and status system, and economic life; and it was to be modernized in its agriculture and industry. Public finance was to be put on a sound basis, and the administration made accountable to a citizenry among whom rank and privilege were no longer to be issues. Guaranteeing the harmonious functioning of the recreated political nation, there was to be a king setting an example of selfless patriotism that aroused emulation and his enduring popularity.

Such was the view from the top down, but from the villagers and town artisans came a darker picture of the suffering caused by the modernization already in progress, the rural distress from enclosures and foreclosures dictated by rich farmers, and the urban complaints about effect of the division of labour in factories and the economic squeeze in the free labour market as well as the commodity one. The recommendations at this level ran counter to those of the liberalizing vision of minimal government, since in line with the conservative feelings of crowds alluded to previously, they called for more policing and more controls exercised by a protective and seemingly omnipresent monarchy (Hyslop, 1936; Schama, 1989: 309–22).

Familiar with France and its people, Smith must have read in the newspapers and pamphlets of the time (e.g. *Edinburgh Evening Courant*, 25 July 1789; cited in Meikle, 1912: 43, n. 1), and heard from eye-witnesses such as Dugald Stewart accounts of the events of 1789, at once thrilling and disturbing for reflective observers. In addition, Smith had a professional interest in what was happening, for had he not promised at the conclusion of the first edition of *TMS* to provide 'an account of the general principles of law and government, and of the different revolutions they have undergone in the different ages and periods of society'?

The Estates-General met on 5 May in its different orders, with the Third Estate snubbed in the matter of its reception by the King, who was also unwise enough to address the deputies about the 'much exaggerated desire for innovations' (Schama, 1989: 346). From the outset, however, the Third Estate determined that it would set about the 'common work of national restoration', so described by Sieyès, perhaps the most radical deputy, by forcing the other two orders to join it. By 17 June the clergy were doing so in increasing numbers and the Third Estate named itself the National Assembly, then accepted a motion by Mirabeau that current taxes were void unless given authority by this body. Prompted by the Queen and his youngest brother, Artois, the King rejected Necker's advice to upstage the radical deputies with a declaration that the Estates could vote in common on national issues. Instead, a *séance royale* was scheduled for the *Salle des Menus Plaisirs* in which the King was to annul the seizure of power of 17 June. Preparations for this in the *Salle* barred its use by the Assembly, and on the suggestion of Dr Guillotin, they met in a tennis court in the town of Versailles. Having already asserted that their mandate was 'to fix the constitution of the realm, effect the regeneration of public order, and maintain the true principles of the monarchy', they now swore an oath 'to God and the *Patrie* never to be separated until we have formed a solid and equitable constitution as our constituents have asked us to' (Schama, 1990: 348–59; Baker, 1990: 252–3). This was a brilliant suggestion by Mounier, one of the veterans of the Grenoble 'day of tiles'.

Undoubtedly, an inspiration was the painting of *The Oath of the Horatii*, exhibited by David in 1785. The deputies of 1789 saw themselves in the Roman mould as patriot-martyrs and gestured accordingly, right arms held just above shoulder height and finger-tips stabbing the air. In due course, David immortalized this scene as well.

The *séance royale* was held, but to no avail: the Third Estate continued on its way, gathering in more clergy and the liberal nobility headed by the King's cousin, the duc d'Orléans, whose private jurisdiction in Paris, the Palais-Royal, was a hotbed of theory about liberty and the practice of libertinism. The King agreed perforce to the uniting of the orders, and the National Assembly thereafter engaged in impassioned argument about what was meant by fixing the French constitution.

Meantime on 14 July cannon balls flew, blood was shed, and heads were exhibited on pikes in Paris on the occasion of the storming of the Bastille, that symbol of monarchic despotism whose career as a serviceable prison was virtually over. These acts were accompanied by an outburst of graphic journalism using print and pictures to inflame readers with presentations of revolutionary savagery, and justify this as a valid reaction to the horrors of *ancien régime*. On 4 August, in a paroxysm of patriotism, the National Assembly voted to abolish the feudal system and with it the privileges of the clergy and nobles. The leaders on this occasion were aristocrats who had served in America, and their intention was to calm the revolutionary violence by conspicuously embracing citizenship, making it clear that the Assembly insisted on equality before the law and the tax gatherer (Schama, 1989: 172–4, 359–67, 387–406, 419–25, 437–41, 445–7, 569–72). There was sympathy for this stand among some of Smith's friends. Young Lord Maitland went to Paris with Dugald Stewart and addressed the crowds on the theme of liberty; he also told the Duchess of Gordon he hoped soon to have the pleasure of introducing Mrs Maitland to Mrs Gordon (Rae, 1965: 390).

As to the arguments over fixing the Constitution, recent analysis has identified three chief lines that were put forward. The first was the contention that France had a constitution represented by the historical monarchy in its legislative and executive roles. But the mechanisms for securing the advice and consent of the governed had to be restored or overhauled and supplemented, with attention to a complex system of checks and balances of powers to prevent despotism. The model for this view was essentially Montesquieu's reading of the British Constitution in *De l'esprit des lois* and that of Jean Louis de Lolme's *Constitution de l'Angleterre* (1778), both books to be found in Smith's Library (Mizuta).

A second line of argument, however, repudiated the 'inconsequential Delolme'; Montesquieu, 'who could not escape the prejudices of his robe', that is, his rank as President of the *Parlement* of Bordeaux; and even John Quincy Adams, who upheld the American view of a constitution arrived at through moderate Revolution in the New World. The repudiators pressed for the creation of a new Constitution based on first principles and manifesting the sovereign general will of the people that Rousseau had conjured up in such ambiguous terms. Deputies like Jean-Baptiste Salle and the Abbé Grégoire, champion of the rights of the Jews, used abstract language of this kind, and following Rousseau they saw as a crux the problematic relationship between the practice of representation, necessary in a large country such as France, and the exercise of the general will. Their answer here was to provide for a suspensive veto entrusted to the monarch whose executive role was to be sharply divided from that of the legislative one of the Assembly.

The third line was formed by the arguments of that rigorous theorist Sieyès. He pushed Rousseau's view of the sovereignty of the people to its logical conclusion, but broke with him over the issue of representation, which he saw not as a necessary evil but as a means for expressing rationally the people's will through the discussions and votes in a single-chamber, national legislature. Sieyès formed his views about representative government, and the abandoning of hereditary privilege vested in aristocracy and a monarch through delaying powers or a veto, in the course of reflection on the ideas about social representation and progress of civil society found in the writings of the Physiocrats and Adam Smith, as well as other members of the Scottish historical school such as Hume and Robertson. He saw European societies as 'vast workshops', the majority of whose members were so preoccupied by work that they could only participate in government by electing 'representatives far more capable than they of knowing the general interest and interpreting their will in this respect'. Adam Smith's economic theory turned in a political direction is crystallized in a speech Sieyès made on 2 October 1789 asserting that representative government is mandatory, because 'division of labour pertains to political tasks as well as to all kinds of productive work' (Baker, 1990: 245–51).

The upshot of the debates, and the pressure put on the deputies from a violent newspaper campaign to declare for the Rousseauistic concept of a constitution, was twofold. First, the Assembly adopted the Declaration of the Rights of Man and Citizen on 26 August as the first part of the Constitution, arousing widespread expectations about instituting participatory democracy and immediate alleviation of the social distress of the period. Soon after taking their theoretical stand, however, the deputies began to limit the franchise and the qualifications for elected officials, with the intention of preserving the rights of property-owners, and this prompted Robespierre, as an exponent of pure democracy, to state that such measures destroyed equality (Schama, 1989: 442–5, 498; Baker, 1990: 253–71). Here was a source of further chaos and confusion for the revolutionaries.

The second upshot of the Assembly debates was that Sieyès did not persuade the deputies to adopt his strong form of representative government, and they voted on 11 September to accept the monarchy's suspensive veto. Thereafter Louis XVI only 'acceded' on his own initiative to the Declaration of the Rights of Man and the articles of the Constitution so far agreed upon. It took the social action of the women's march on Versailles and the enforced removal of the royal family to Paris on 5–6 October to secure the King's 'acceptance' of constitutional monarchy based on the manifestation of the general will. Again, formidable problems were set in train by this development. If the Constitution had been created as a fresh start on this occasion, what was to prevent it being challenged and repudiated and made over again as a further expression of the general will or national sovereignty. Also, what about the role of social action: could this not be incited again to force a change in whole or in part of the Constitution? The seeds of the Terror lay in the contentions of the highly articulate men in the Constituent Assembly and in the choices they adopted for the form of the government of their country (Baker, 1990: 271–305).

Tom Paine, for one, took a rosy view of what was accomplished in these constitutional debates, and he hoped that the people of England would follow the French example. Rejecting Burke's criticism of the National Assembly's abrogation of privileges and monopolies, Paine recalled the attack on such institutions in *WN* as part of the systematic exposition of political economy, and he declared that Burke's problem was that he lacked the ability of Smith to build a system, and therefore could not comprehend the rational organization from first principles to applications in the new French Constitution.[2] Paine could not have read the carefully thought-out analysis of political change and constitution-building which was an addition to the *TMS* being prepared for publication through 1789 and apparently as late as November.

Smith makes a contribution to contemporary debate over constitution-building in a new *TMS* chapter, which has a topic sentence at some odds with revolutionary idealism: 'The love of our country seems not to be derived from love of mankind' (VI.ii.2.4). The Glasgow editors wondered if this could be a prelude to a criticism of the content of a sermon preached by the Revd Richard Price at the Old Jewry in London on 4 November 1789 (*TMS* 229, n. 2). Entitled *A Discourse on the Love of Our Country*, its enthusiastic response to the French Revolution so enraged Burke that he responded with his *Reflections* (1790), in turn to be answered by Paine's vindication of the Revolution, *The Rights of Man*, 1791–2 (Paine, 1984; Cone, 1968: 81–97; Krammick, 1990: 58–9, 289–92; Pocock, 1989: 19–42). It is true that Smith had roundly condemned Price in a letter dated 22 December 1785 in his role both as an arouser of public opinion and as a theorist about morals and politics, also as an applied mathematician (*Corr.* No. 251), but we would have to suppose that he received word in Edinburgh of the London sermon in time to write the 'last sentence' of the revised *TMS* by 18 November, which is unlikely. Rather more latitude for last additions to the *TMS* text is provided by the fact that the printing of the sixth edition was done in January 1790.

Possibly Smith was responding to sermons preached in Scotland on 5 November 1788 commemorating the Glorious Revolution of 1688. Robertson gave one which took note of events in America and France, which presented views in accord with those of Smith (Sher, 1990). As D. D. Raphael has suggested (in a personal letter), however, sermons of other ministers might have aroused his condemnation of the 'spirit of system' manifested in revolutionary activity. The final consideration should be urged, however, that Smith saw an opportunity in dealing with the Stoic topic of love of country to articulate long-held views about political life and organization.

Nevertheless, Smith seems to join issue with the French constitutional debates, and the type of political thinking found in Price's sermon, when he gives his definition of a constitution:

Upon the manner in which any state is divided into the different orders and societies which compose it, and upon the particular distribution which has been made of their respective powers, privileges, and immunities, depends, what is called, the constitution of that particular state. (VI.ii.2.8)

Such phrasing reflects Montesquieu's viewpoint in *De l'esprit des lois*, and represents a tradition going back to Aristotle's *Politics* (Baker, 1990: 255). Smith argues that the stability of a constitution depends on the adjustment of the several orders and societies to each other, so that one does not encroach upon another. Since the paramount consideration is the preservation and prosperity of the state to which the orders and societies are subordinate, in that interest it may be necessary to restrict these powers and privileges. This is likely to arouse the resistance of those understandably partial to their own orders. In itself, this partiality has its usefulness, for it 'checks the spirit of innovation' and maintains the balance between the orders and societies. Moreover, it opposes changes in government 'which may be fashionable and popular at the time', but in so doing this partiality is helping to maintain the whole system in its stable life. This is an argument, surely, for conservatism about the privileges of aristocrats, for example, who are certainly partial to their own 'powers and immunities'. Correspondingly, Smith would expect this order to continue to furnish leaders in war and peace, thus securing the state from danger and advancing its welfare (VI.ii.2.9–10).

Smith then returns to the theme of love of country, which we might associate with the constant appeals to patriotism in first American and then French revolutionary discourse. He believes that here two principles are involved: reverence for the established constitution, and the desire to promote the welfare of our fellow-citizens. The first principle defines citizenship: respect for the law and obedience to the civil magistrate; and the second defines good citizenship: endeavouring to make a society safe and flourishing. In peaceful times, the two principles run together, but during a crisis of public discontent and extreme antagonism of the groups within a state leading to the breakdown of order, these principles clash. Even a wise person, concedes Smith, may countenance revolution, altering the 'constitution or form of government, which, in its actual condition appears plainly unable to maintain the public tranquillity'. That was exactly the situation during the French social unrest and violence of 1788–9.

It would appear, also, that Smith appreciated exactly the kind of situation that faced the French deputies to the Estates-General in the summer of 1789 as they listened to the speeches of Mounier and Lally-Tolendal, basing themselves on the one hand on the Anglo-American constitutional model, and on the other on those inspired by Rousseau, such as Salle and Grégoire, or even the brilliant Sieyès, who combined in his political theory aspects of the thought of Rousseau and the Smith of *WN*:

it often requires, perhaps, the highest effort of political wisdom to determine when a real patriot ought to support and endeavour to re-establish the authority of the old system, and when he ought to give way to the more daring, but often dangerous spirit of innovation. (VI.ii.2.11–12)

Next Smith assesses leadership during foreign wars and internal strife or, as he puts it, civil faction. The glory acquired in the former is 'more pure and splendid' than in the latter case, but the successful party leader, if he can moderate revolutionary violence, may have done much more for his country than a victor over foreigners. We might fit Washington in the American context to Smith's abstract description of the person who re-establishes a constitution, and from being a suspect leader of a faction (the Patriots) is transformed into the guarantor of enduring institutions that secure tranquillity for his fellow-citizens, thus becoming the Father of his country. Washington was perceived in this light by Smith's Scottish contemporaries, for example, Lord Buchan, who carried on a correspondence with the American general and president and regularly celebrated his birthday (Cant, 1981: 9), and Burns, who admired his fight for the freedom of his people (1968, ii.732–4).

Smith does not expand on the Washington type, however, but rather deals with the 'madness of fanaticism' that ensues when a 'certain spirit of system' mixes with the public spirit of humanitarianism during the time of revolution. He paints a picture of revolutionary leaders claiming to have a plan to alleviate immediately the social ills that have caused disorder, and to prevent their reoccurrence. This involves new-modelling the constitution, altering the government system 'under which the subjects of a great empire have enjoyed, perhaps, peace, security, and even glory, during the course of several centuries together'. The passage from discourse about citizens to mention of subjects of a country centuries old suggests that Smith is thinking about the contemporary French situation. Also, his contrast is instructive between the 'man whose public spirit is prompted altogether by humanity and benevolence', who refuses to use violence against his country, and the 'man of system' who is 'apt to be very wise in his own conceit', and who is so infatuated with the beauty of his ideal scheme that he will insist on implementing it to the last detail, no matter what interests and prejudices resist it. The French Revolution was to throw up such contrasting types of leader, not perhaps in such ideal terms for the public-spirited man, but some claims could be made that Danton on the whole was a humane and benevolent man who endeavoured to establish the best system of laws the people could bear, while his killer Robespierre certainly was a 'man of system', who wished to force the people to be free and virtuous in the insanity of the Terror which, after all, had its anticipations in 1789.[3]

At the end of this fascinating chapter, rich in political theory and application to contemporary politics, Smith's thought veers round to the 'man of system' embodied not in revolution but as the 'sovereign prince'. He concedes that a statesman must have 'some general, and even systematical, idea of the perfection of policy and law', but to insist on establishing this summarily indicates the highest degree of arrogance. In such a case, the standard of right and wrong lies in the judgement of one man who seeks to impose his system, and who believes he has a monopoly of all wisdom and worth. Because of such arrogance, Smith writes, 'of all political speculators, sovereign princes are the most dangerous' (*TMS* vi.ii.2.18). Is he thinking of James II, perhaps, whose name as that of a threatening tyrant long haunted British thought because of the Revolution of 1688–9? More likely, though, he has in mind his century's exemplars of Bourbon despotism, Louis XIV and Louis XV.

There is a history of republican sentiment behind this passage in *TMS*, and perhaps some sympathy for the attitudes of the deputies of the French National Assembly. Their memories and that of Smith retained details of the long struggle of the *parlements* against the Bourbons, and the affronts of the royal pronouncements about the location of sovereignty such that all other ranks are demeaned. Such a pronouncement was made by Louis XV at the *séance de la flagellation* in 1766, in a speech written for the King by Gilbert de Voisins, and delivered when Smith was in Paris:

As if anyone could forget that the sovereign power resides in my person only . . . that public order in its entirety emanates from me and that the rights and interests of the nation, which some dare to regard as a separate body from the monarch, are necessarily united with my rights and interests, and repose only in my hands. (Schama, 1989: 104; Baker, 1990: 225–8)

Smith saw clearly that such mad arrogance leads to violence against a country. He also saw it needs the 'highest effort of political wisdom' to handle the effects of that violence. As he finished that 'very last sentence' of the revised *TMS*, the issue in France was greatly in doubt.

Having told Cadell on 18 November 1789 that he had written that 'last sentence', Smith went on to say that his Customs Board colleague David Reid would bring his book to London and correct the proofs thus sparing him the 'expence and fatigue of a Journey to London'. Smith then reproves Cadell for offering a share in the book to the Edinburgh publisher William Creech:

I do not see that you had any business to make this offer. I intended the additions as a present to Strahan and you; and to nobody else. If the book was to be printed at Edinburgh, it is ready to go to the press to morrow. But I am intirely against this. And I must even stipulate, that at least some hundred copies be distributed in London before one single copy is sent to Edinburgh. This condition, I can assure you, from the present state of Literary faction here, may be of more consequence both to your interest and my quiet than you can well be aware of. (Klemme, 1991: 279–80)

The question naturally arises: why was Smith so opposed to printing his book in Edinburgh because of the 'state of Literary faction' there? His concern over Cadell's 'interest' and his own 'quiet' may lead to an answer. These words occur in the draft letter, already discussed, dealing with his unwillingness in 1776 to be involved in the publication of Hume's *Dialogues concerning Natural Religion*. In this text, he expressed appreciation for William Strahan's decision to publish Hume's brief autobiography, *My Own Life*, together with Smith's ostensible letter of 9 November 1776 about Hume's manner of dying, separately from the *Dialogues* (*Corr.* No. 178): 'I even flatter myself that this arrangement will contribute not only to my quiet, but to your interest' (*Corr.* No. 177A). This same draft text indicates that Smith was fearful of the 'clamour' that would be aroused by the publication of the *Dialogues*. In the event, the *Dialogues* aroused no great outcry from Christians exercised about Hume's scepticism and alleged atheism. However, the publication of Smith's letter of 9 November 1776 to Strahan did provoke outrage, represented, for example, by the Revd George Horne's effusion of 1777, already mentioned (*Corr.* No. 189). One of the sneers in this pamphlet was that Smith like Hume cared nothing for the doctrine of the immortality of the soul, 'else, it surely might have claimed a little of your care and attention . . . since it could do no harm, if it did no good, in a *Theory of Moral Sentiments*' (Horne, 1771: 1). There is good reason to think that Smith was sensitive about this kind of 'abuse' for, as he wrote in October 1780, there was ten times more of it than anything occasioned by the 'very violent attack he had made upon the whole commercial system of Great Britain' (*Corr.* No. 208).

Now, what literary faction would abuse him in Edinburgh for publishing a new edition of *TMS* already considered deficient in some quarters in point of subscription to the doctrine of the immortality of the soul, and now even more Humean in tone about the nature of an afterlife with divine rewards and punishments? The answer must surely be the writers attached to the Popular or High-flying party in the Church of Scotland, who had already shown virulence in attacking Principal Robertson for his stand on Catholic relief in 1778–9, a stand which he was forced to abandon as the strength of the Moderate party in the Church declined in the 1780s, and with it that of Smith's allies in clerical circles in Scotland. Smith must also have been conscious that the new material in *TMS* added to the existing criticism of the 'factious and party zeal of some worthless cabal' that corrupts the 'natural principles of religion' (III.5.13; cf. the new passage, III.3.43). Perhaps he counted on success in London, with his new edition blunting the force of whatever the Edinburgh press could unleash on him (Sher, 1985: 289–97; Donovan, 1987; 1990; Fry, 1992*a*: 71–6). The High-flyers would be deemed a 'Literary faction' because of their publication ventures. They tended to side with the revolutionary Patriots in the American crisis, and might be expected to side with the French revolutionaries (comment from D. D. Raphael). Smith certainly did not wish for publicity, stating quite categorically to Windisch-Grätz on 4 July 1785: 'I never suffer my name to appear in a news-paper when I can hinder it, which to my sorrow, I cannot always do' (MS copy, Aldourie Castle, Inverness).

We must not think that Smith's life was all labour over his books, worry over their reception, and refuge from concentration on chains of complex ideas in the endless ramifications of the business routine of the Customs Board. He enjoyed a stimulating social life, particularly through entertaining visitors from other countries to Edinburgh. Mention has been made of one such visitor, the geolo-gist Faujas de Saint Fond, who spent some time with Smith in October or November 1782 and recorded his views about Voltaire and Rousseau. Smith ascertained that his guest liked music and promised to take him to 'hear a kind of music of which it is impossible you can have formed any idea', adding that it would give him a great deal of pleasure to learn what impression this made. The next morning, at nine o'clock, Smith came for the Professor and took him to a concert-room filled with a large audience of ladies and gentlemen. There was a space in the middle of the room occupied by some gentlemen from the Highlands and Islands, whom Smith identified as the judges of the annual bag-pipe music competition. A prize was to be awarded for the best performance of a piece of music that was to be played by each competitor in turn.

When the folding door at the bottom of the room opened, Saint Fond was astonished to see a piper in full Highland dress emerge and march up and down, 'blowing the noisiest and most discordant sounds from an instrument which lac-erates the ear'. Smith asked the Frenchman to attend to the music carefully, and then describe afterwards the impression it had made. He was at work on his essay on the imitative arts in 1782, and he was very likely collecting further material for his discussion of instrumental music, which he considered did not really 'imi-tate' an external object or internal state, but rather created an impression ('Imitative Arts' ii.31–2). At first the visitor could make out neither 'air nor design' in the music, but was only struck with the martial appearance of the piper, the 'incredible efforts both with his body and his fingers to bring into play at once the different reeds of his instrument', emitting sounds which to Saint Fond 'made an insupportable uproar'. Gradually, he realized that the first part of the music was meant to represent the clash and din and fury of war, and the last part the wailing for the slain, at which the 'beautiful Scotch ladies' in the audience wept. The competition was followed by Highland dancing engaged in by some of the pipers while others then played 'suitable airs, which had some melody and char-acter, but the union of all these bagpipes produced an unbearable noise'.

Saint Fond's opinion was that the impression made by the music on him was so different from what it made on the audience that he could only imagine that the lively emotion of those around him was aroused not so much by the pipe music itself as by the association of ideas connecting it with historical events brought forcibly to their recollection (Faujas de Saint Fond, 1907: ii.247–52). This opinion to some extent fits in with Smith's theory.

As to what was heard on this occasion, an extract from Robert Garioch's poem 'The Big Music', dealing with a traditional piping competition, will afford a poetic 'imitation':

> Allanerlie the great Hieland pipe can mak this soun,
> this rattle of reedy noise, the owretones brattlan thegither,
> wi maybe a swirlan danger, like musardrie of maut.
> Piobaireachd adorns tragedy wi maist sensie jewels.
> Men, dour as quartz, responsive as quartz to licht,
> mak this shairp intellectual and passionat music,
> dangerous, maist dangerous, and naething moderat,
> florischan in the warld, a dauntless form of life.

> (1983: 44)

Six years later, in 1788, Smith received some Spanish gentlemen, the Rector of Valladolid University and two companions who were travelling for 'instruction and improvement', perhaps inspired by the interest shown in the Enlightenment by Carlos III. Smith did not subject them to a bagpipe competition, but sent them on to someone in his circle whom he 'considered by far the best modern linguist among us' (*Corr.* No. 282), very probably Principal Robertson, who had studied Spanish to write his histories of *Charles V* (1769) and of *America* (1777).

A visitor to Edinburgh who passed on revealing details of Smith's conversation and leisure activities in the last year of his life was the young English poet Samuel Rogers. He came recommended by Dr Price, already noted as being in Smith's black books, and Dr Kippis, the learned editor of the *Biographia Britannica*. They were friends of Rogers's father in Unitarian circles, and their word would add weight to whatever reputation came from Rogers's first publication, a slim book entitled *An Ode to Superstition and other Poems* (1786). Smith received Rogers at breakfast on Wednesday 15 July 1789 as he was eating a dish of strawberries, which he declared to be his favourite diet. He disparaged Edinburgh as a city dependent on the revenue of its courts, in keeping with his theory that the 'inferior ranks' in such a place are 'idle, dissolute, and poor', as opposed to those ranks in 'mercantile and manufacturing towns', whom he regarded as 'industrious, sober, and thriving' (*WN* ii.iii.12).

News of the fall of the Bastille had not, of course arrived, and did not until after Rogers left on 21 July; but Smith was following events in France, and denounced the British Government's refusal of grain shipments to that country, alleging that the quantity involved was trifling and would not feed Edinburgh for a day. Smith noted that in Edinburgh, as in Paris, the houses were piled high upon each other in the lands or tenements of the Old Town; but he had earlier said that this part of the city gave Edinburgh a bad name, undoubtedly because of the filth, and, as was mentioned earlier, he wished to move to the newly built George Square.

When Rogers asked Smith if he knew Dr Johnson's friend Mrs Piozzi, who was in Edinburgh at the time, he replied that he did not, but considered she had been 'spoiled by keeping company with odd people'. Oddest of these would be Dr Johnson himself, exhibited to the reading public in the three editions of Boswell's *Journal of a Tour to the Hebrides* that had appeared by 1786, and known to Smith personally in altercation:

He could, when he chose it, be the greatest sophist that ever wielded a weapon in the schools of declamation; but he indulged this only in conversation; for he owned he sometimes talked for victory; he was too conscientious to make errour permanent and pernicious, by deliberately writing it. He was conscious of his superiority. . . . His head, and sometimes also his body, shook with a kind of motion like the effect of a palsy: he appeared to be frequently disturbed by cramps, or convulsive contractions, of the nature of that distemper called St Vitus's dance. (*BLJ* v.18)

On Friday 17 July Smith invited Rogers to dine with him at the Oyster Club. The company included Black and the mathematician John Playfair, author of an encyclopaedic work on chronology and recent reporter on the astronomy of the Brahmins to the Royal Society of Edinburgh (Mizuta). On this occasion, however, the talk was monopolized by the former West India merchant Robert Bogle of Baldowie, a man of considerable information about economic subjects but one given to delivering tedious lectures.

On Sunday 19 July Rogers had breakfast with Robertson, and heard him preach in the Old Greyfriars kirk later that morning. In the afternoon he heard Blair preach in the high kirk of St Giles, and then drank coffee with Mrs Piozzi. He had gone to see Smith just before the afternoon service as the kirk bells were ringing, but found him at the door of Panmure House about to take an airing in his sedan chair. Smith invited him to return for one of his Sunday suppers, also to come again for dinner the next day to meet Henry Mackenzie. The company was much the same as that at the Oyster Club, though Bogle was absent, and the talk turned to the authorship of the *Junius Letters* (a political polemic appearing 1769–72). Smith told the story passed on to him by Gibbon that this secret had been revealed when 'Single Speech Hamilton'—the MP William Gerrard Hamilton—once informed the Duke of Richmond that a 'devilish keen letter' from Junius had appeared in that day's *Public Advertiser*. When the Duke looked in the paper, all he found was an apology for its not being there. Hamilton's name was then mentioned in connection with the *Letters*, and they ceased to appear. Modern scholarship holds that the *Letters* were most likely written by

Philip Francis, later to be Warren Hasting's enemy and proponent of his impeachment together with Burke (*HP* ii.467–8).

The talk then turned to French writers, in particular Voltaire and Turgot. It was on this occasion that Smith would not hear of some 'clever but superficial author' being called by Rogers 'a Voltaire'. Smith banged the table and declared energetically, 'Sir, there is only one Voltaire.' Regarding Turgot, he was described to Rogers by Smith as an excellent, absolutely honest, and well-intended person, who was not well versed in human nature with all its selfishness, stupidity, and prejudice. Smith mentioned that Hume had divulged to him Turgot's maxim: 'Whatever is right may be done.'

The next day, Monday 20 July, Rogers returned to Panmure House, where the chief guest was Henry Mackenzie. Other guests were a Mr Muir, described as being from Göttingen where, as already mentioned, there was considerable interest in Smith's ideas, and the antiquary and naturalist John M'Gowan, Clerk of the Signet, who was a friend and correspondent of Bishop Percy. The sprightly Mackenzie led the conversation which dealt with second sight in the Highlands, a topic that had exercised Dr Johnson on his visit to Skye in 1773 (*BLJ* v.159–60). Mackenzie told of an eccentric laird in Caithness who claimed the gift of the second sight to keep his tenants in order.

Discussion then moved to women writers. One meriting attention was Charlotte Smith, who had begun a successful career as a novelist with two publications, *Emmelinde* (1788) and *Ethelinde* (1789), making much of sentimental ladies in castles and woodlands, though outdone in the vein of the picturesque novel by Ann Radcliffe (Roper, 1978: 125–7). A second writer discussed was Hannah More, of whom Johnson averred that 'it is dangerous to say a word of poetry before her; it is talking of the art of war before Hannibal' (*BLJ* iv.149 n. 3). She was friendly with the Garricks and wrote tragedies, but renounced the stage in 1779 after the death of David Garrick, which Dr Johnson said had 'eclipsed the gaiety of nations' (*BLJ* i.82). She later turned energies to the Evangelical cause, and sought to keep the working classes free from infection by the French Revolution (Roberts, 1834; Thompson, 1968: 60–1; Gaul, 1988: 47–9). The conversation also brought in the work of the poetess Ann Home, who was the wife of Smith's surgeon, John Hunter.

Mackenzie introduced this topic, connected, perhaps, with his interests as a writer and moralizer in the *Lounger* and *Mirror* periodicals, but Smith would respond to it. As a moralist, he generally stressed the masculine virtues of self-command and prudence, but late in life he was prone to recognizing the more feminine virtue of beneficence exhibited in 'maternal tenderness' and the 'domestic affections'. It seems that he was impressed by the imaginative power of literature of sensibility to which women writers were making a notable contribution, as he reveals in the addition to the sixth edition of *TMS*, already mentioned. There he cites writers who are better teachers than the advocates of Stoicism, and he associates Mme Riccoboni with Richardson in this connection (III.3.14).

On this occasion, Smith did volunteer a judgement about Blair when Rogers expressed admiration for a passage in the sermon he had heard on 'Curiosity concerning the Affairs of Others'. In Smith's opinion, Blair was 'too puffed up', but he softened this statement by acknowledging that his friend would have been either above or below humanity if he had not been affected by the undue popularity aroused by his preaching and literary criticism.

Rogers was greatly impressed with Smith's kindness: 'he is a very friendly, agreeable man, and I should have dined and supped with him every day, if I had accepted all his invitations'. He seemed quite oblivious to the disparity in age between himself and the poet, who was then 23, and he was free with information and opinions. His manner Rogers described as 'quite familiar'; he would ask, for example: 'Who should we have to dinner?' Rogers did not see in him the absent-mindedness others stressed. Compared to Robertson, Smith seemed to Rogers far more a man of the world (BL Add. MSS 32,566; Clayden, 1887: 90, 96; Dye, 1856: 45).

24

The Great Change

But I meant to have done more.

To the end of his life, Smith interested himself in young people—perhaps they were his window on eternity. He received and was kind to a young relative, Lydia Marianna Douglas, who at 19 had married a clergyman, Richard Bingham, Fellow of New College, Oxford, on 17 November 1788, without the approval of her father, Sir Charles Douglas. She claimed she lived a miserable life with her mother when the father, an Admiral, was away on station, and her story may have aroused Smith's sympathy (*Corr.* Nos. 284, 285; Scott, 1937: 307, n. 1). Also, he was encouraging about placing the son of his former pupil Henry Herbert, now Lord Porchester, in the home of Professor George Jardine, another pupil, while attending Glasgow University, and wished to offer the young man hospitality in Edinburgh (*Corr.* app. E, r). In another letter (p) on this topic, written to Lord Porchester on 23 September 1788, he described in an affecting way the immanent passing of his cousin and housekeeper of many years, Janet Douglas:

Poor Miss Douglas is probably within a very few days, certainly within a very few weeks of her end. Some unknown disease in her Bowels which she concealed for, I believe, many years had gradually wasted her strength, reduced her to a shadow and has for some weeks past confined her to her bed where she is scarcely able to turn herself. She still, however, continues to direct the affairs of her family with her usual distinctness and attention; and waits for the great change, which she knows is very near, without any impatience, without any fear, and without much regret. Her humour and raillery are the same as usual. She will leave me one of the most destitute and helpless men in Scotland.

Smith's own conduct in the face of death was similarly Stoical, and there may have been a family tradition of this. Naming death the 'great change', of course, is a Stoic idea, and there is no great evidence that Smith put stock in an afterlife. It is true that in the discussion of the Calas case added to the sixth edition of *TMS* Smith does suggest that 'religion alone can afford any effectual comfort' to those who suffer from grave miscarriage of justice in this world, by presenting the 'view of another world; a world of more candour, humanity, and justice, than the present; where their innocence is in due time to be declared, and their virtue to be finally rewarded' (*TMS* III.2.12). However, in another added passage, Smith gives an explanation of why 'religion' presents such a picture. This is couched in the language of Hume's *Natural History of Religion*, and it should be mentioned that, in a letter to Bentham of 14 September 1784, Schwediauer had noted that Smith was an 'intimate friend of the late David Hume and has the same principles' (Bentham, *Corr.*, 1971: iii.306).

Smith's argument late in life was that we *think* (our emphasis) that the 'justice of God' requires that there should be future rewards and punishments correcting the inequalities of this life (ii.ii.3.12). Further, Smith's additions included a description of religionists reserving the 'celestial regions for monks and friars', or those resembling them in 'conduct and conversation', and condemning to the infernal ones 'all those who have invented, improved, or excelled in the arts which contribute to . . . human life'. In consequence, Smith concludes drily, the 'respectable doctrine' of the afterlife and its rewards and punishments is exposed to 'contempt and derision' (iii.2.35).

Smith anticipates that after the death of his cousin he will suffer emotional destitution, and this is an indication that she had partly filled the gap in his life left by the death of his mother, to whom he was so strongly attached. As for other ladies in his life, Dugald Stewart tells us that as a young man Smith was in love with a beautiful and accomplished young woman, but unknown circumstances prevented their marriage, and both apparently afterwards decided not to marry (*EPS* Stewart, n. K). Anecdotage reports that Smith beamed at her in company later in life, and his cousin Janet Douglas is supposed to have said: 'Don't you know, Adam, this is your ain Jeannie?' But the smile was one of general kindness rather than special favour, and nothing came of the re-encounter (Mackay, 1896: 209). In France he had sighed unavailingly for an Englishwoman named Mrs Nichol, and a French marquise pursued him without success, but he seems to have been entirely content with his existence as a bachelor.

He never enjoyed robust health, and as already noted there are indications that he had some psychosomatic disorder perhaps best described as 'hypochondriasis', which accompanied periods of intense application in his studies and writing. In the last twelve years of his life, during his residence in Edinburgh, the complaints occur more often and the pains he suffered seem more localized in the stomach (*Corr.* Nos. 214, 238, 290). On 21 January 1790 he wrote to his heir David Douglas about an 'increased shaking in my hand' which prevented writing (No. 291), and on 6 February he made his will, witnessed by his servant, James Baird, and James Dundas, clerk to David Erskine, Clerk to the Signet (SRO Warrants of register of deeds: RD13/130 Box 465, 19748/2). Its contents in due course occasioned some surprise.

On 9 February he excused himself to Robert Cullen for his absence from the funeral of Cullen's father William, his physician and friend for more than forty years. He wrote: 'A Stomach complaint has weakened me so much that I can bear no fatigue, not even that of walking from my own house to the Customhouse' (*Corr.* No. 292). He was not too weak, however, to neglect interceding with the Duke of Buccleuch to obtain from Henry Dundas a pension for Cullen's daughters. The Duke dealt with this matter immediately, and wrote to Smith on 24 February to say that Pitt and Dundas were looking after this matter. He also invited Smith to go out to Dalkeith House, where he was sure the 'Country air and gentle exercise' would be of service to him, adding some words of tender solicitude (No. 293).

Lord Buchan visited Smith in February and expressed the hope that he would see him more often the following February, when he intended to be back in Edinburgh. Smith replied that he might be alive then, but that he would not be in the same condition: 'I find the machine is breaking down, so that I shall be little better than a mummy.' Buchan wished greatly to visit Smith in his last illness, so he confessed, 'but the mummy stared me in the face and I was intimidated' (*The Bee*, 1791: 3: 166).

When the spring weather came Smith rallied sufficiently by Friday 9 April to take the Chair at the Customs Board. On this occasion he and John Henry Cochrane referred the appointment of an acting Receiver-General to the Barons of the Scottish Exchequer. They ordered the Comptroller-General to prepare accounts of the net produce of the duties of customs, excise, stamps and incidents from 5 April 1788 to the same date in 1790. Also, they cancelled the minute of 8 April dismissing a Salt Officer at Bo'ness. Then they examined and signed the establishments of officers of the Customs and Salt Duty to be sent on to the Treasury; and ordered Customs documents concerning coal bonds, certificates of foreign goods, debentures, and Isle of Man goods, prepared by the ports of Lerwick and Stornaway, to be laid before the House of Commons, with duplicates to go to George Rose, Secretary to the Treasury (SRO CE1/23: pp. 284–5). These were Smith's last official acts as a Commissioner of Customs, for he does not seem to have attended the Board's meetings again.

On 16 May he wrote to Cadell about some papers to be forwarded to him on behalf of a Mr Coope of Clapham, perhaps a would-be author, and asked that the latest volume of the Royal Society's *Transactions* be sent too. He also asked for news of the 'good or bad success of my new edition' of *TMS*, adding: 'You may safely tell me the truth as I am grown almost perfectly indifferent both as to praise and to abuse' (*Corr.* No. 294). He had a letter from Cadell on 25 May which he 'read with very great satisfaction', possibly giving an account of a good response to his book, twelve copies of which, one of them imperfect, had already reached him.

Surprisingly, we hear of a plan to visit London:

I expected by this time to have been setting out upon my Journey to London. But my progress to recovery is so very slow, and so often interrupted by violent relapses that the probability of my being able to execute that Journey becomes every day more doubtful. (*Corr.* No. 295)

Sadly, his friends came to realize that he was to set out soon on that journey from which no traveller returns. Henry Mackenzie wrote on 21 June to his brother-in-law, Sir James Grant, chief of the Clan Grant, MP, that Edinburgh had just lost its finest woman, Eliza Burnett, daughter of Lord Monboddo, and probably in a few weeks would lose its greatest man, Adam Smith: 'He is now past all hopes of recovery, with which about three weeks ago we had flattered ourselves' (quoted Rae, 1965: 432). The learned printer William Smellie confirmed this in a letter dated 27 June addressed to Patrick Clason, then in London:

Poor Smith! We must soon lose him; and the moment in which he departs will give a heart-felt pang to thousands. Mr Smith's spirits are flat; and I am afraid the exertions he sometimes makes to please his friends do him no good. His intellects, as well as his senses, are clear and distinct. He wishes to be cheerful; but nature is omnipotent. His body is extremely emaciated, because his stomach cannot admit of sufficient nourishment: But, like a man, he is perfectly patient and resigned. (Kerr, 1811: i.295)

Appreciating that Smith was on his deathbed, Adam Ferguson forthwith over-looked the quarrel between them, whatever it was about, and went to see him to resume their old friendship. He described this incident, which occurred at a time when he had become infirm himself as a result of a stroke in 1780, in a letter of 31 July 1790 to Sir John Macpherson, a kinsman of 'Ossian' Macpherson, who had become a crony of the Prince of Wales after a chequered career in India:

your old friend Smith is no more. We knew he was dying for some months, and though matters, as you know, were a little awkward when he was in health, upon that appearance I turned my face that way and went to him without further consideration, and continued my attentions to the last. (EUL MS; Rae, 1965: 433)

Ferguson must have been a remarkable sight on his way to Panmure Close, dressed for warmth despite the summer in his fur-lined cloak and felt hat, look-ing like a 'philosopher from Lapland' (Cockburn, 1856: 49). Perhaps he dis-cussed with Smith the expansion of his lectures which was published in 1792 as *Principles of Moral and Political Science*.

As his end drew near, Smith grew anxious about his literary papers; and since he did not have the strength to destroy them himself, he begged Black and Hutton many times to do so. They were named in his will as custodians of the papers. Another friend named Riddell was present on one occasion when Smith made an entreaty about the papers, and he recorded that Smith expressed regret for doing so little, adding: 'But I meant to have done more; and there are mate-rials in my papers, of which I could have made a great deal. But that is now out of the question' (Stewart, 1854–60: x.74). Smith's entreaties, which had begun before he went to London for the last time in 1787, were resisted by Black and Hutton with assurance that he could depend on their carrying out his wish. On Sunday 11 July Smith's anxiety about his papers was not removed by such a response, and he begged one of these friends to destroy the volumes of his man-uscripts immediately, and to save for possible publication only 'some detached papers'. The contents of the volumes thereupon destroyed by fire were not known to Black and Hutton or other intimate friends of Smith, but Stewart conjectures that they consisted of *LRBL* given at Edinburgh, and lectures on natural theology and *LJ* which had formed part of Smith's moral philosophy course at Glasgow (Stewart, v.8 and n.).

The 'detached papers' that were saved from the flames completed the contents of *EPS*, together with the 'History of Astronomy'. Presumably this piece was available in the 'thin folio paper book', which Smith described when he wrote on 16 April 1773 making Hume his literary executor. In this letter he gave a kind of inventory of all his 'literary papers', including those carried with him to London: the manuscript of *WN*; 'loose papers' in his desk, which we are assuming became *EPS* essays; the 'History of Astronomy'; and 'about eighteen thin paper folio books' behind the 'glass folding doors of my bureau' (*Corr.* No. 137). He did not describe what was in these latter volumes, and he asked Hume to burn them in the event of his death, 'without any examination'. We can estimate that, by 1790, there were more than eighteen volumes of manuscript writings.

As to their contents, we can go beyond Stewart's conjecture by turning to Smith's letter to La Rochefoucauld of 1 November 1785, in which he discussed his current projects. In the light of this information, it is likely that some manuscript volumes were devoted to the 'Philosophical History of all the different branches of Literature, of Philosophy, Poetry, and Eloquence', taking in *LRBL* and the lectures on the history of philosophy. Other volumes would cover the 'theory and History of Law and Government', which took in *LJ* and was intended to fulfil the promise about such a 'discourse' made at the conclusion of *TMS* and repeated in the Advertisement to the sixth edition of that work. Smith stated to La Rochefoucauld that the materials for these 'great works' were 'in a great measure collected, and some Part of both is put into tollerable good order' (*Corr.* No. 248).

Now, why was he so insistent to Hume and then to Black and Hutton as his literary executors that these volumes should be destroyed? It is clear from the history of the composition of *WN* and the last revisions for *TMS* that Smith was a slow workman, who took great pains to put what he wanted to say in the form that satisfied him. The 'great works' he planned were still 'on the anvil' and, therefore, 'not fit to see the light', as he expressed himself concerning Strahan's project to publish Hume's correspondence after his death (*Corr.* No. 181). We find Smith's prudence operating here and his concern for his literary reputation. Another point made by Stewart merits attention: that a 'higher motive' influenced Smith, a concern that important arguments about morals and politics would be impaired in unfinished work, and therefore truths of great significance to humanity would be clouded rather than clarified (v.8). Though stated generally, Stewart's idea here may have had particular relevance to the period of the French Revolution, when, as mentioned before, Stewart's teaching of liberal principles was an object of suspicion. He may have believed that Smith wished to be as circumspect as he was himself in a revolutionary era.

In any event, satisfied about the protection of his reputation or the safeguarding of moral and political truth, after the burning of his papers on that long-ago July Sunday in Panmure House, Smith felt well enough to welcome his friends in the evening with his usual equanimity. A considerable number of them came to be with him then, but he did not have strength to sit with them through supper, so he retired to bed before it. Henry Mackenzie recorded his parting words in the form: 'I love your company, gentlemen, but I believe I must leave you to go to another world' (Clayden, 1887: 168). Hutton gave Stewart some different wording: 'I believe we must adjourn this meeting to some other place' (v.8 n., p. 328). Mackenzie's version has a literary flourish, but Hutton's seems more likely. It is doubtful that Smith accepted the idea of a future life in any orthodox Christian sense, and plainly his clergymen friends, Robertson or Blair, for example, were not giving him ghostly counsel at this time. He may well have spoken of adjourning to 'some other place' in a sympathetic and imaginative way, to help his company deal with the real shock and pain of their impending loss of him. The end brought about by his 'lingering and painful' disease, which Stewart described as 'chronic obstruction of the bowels', and which he met with Stoic self-command, came on Saturday 17 July about midnight (SRO CE 1/23: p. 369). Joseph Black and James Hutton, who were medical men as well as close friends and his literary executors, were with Adam Smith when he died (Stewart v.7, 19).

He was buried on Thursday 22 July at noon in his own burial plot in the Canongate kirkyard, James Hamilton acting as undertaker (SRO Canongate Kirk Session Records, CH2/122/62, 119748). As a mark of respect to his 'Valuable Memory', his colleagues on the Customs Board had adjourned their meetings from the previous Monday when they heard of his death until after the interment. Four days later Smith's 'very worthy friend' and neighbour for ten years or more in Fife, Robert Beatson, wrote to the editor of the *Monthly Review*, Ralph Griffiths:

It is with infinite regret that I inform you that our worthy friend Dr Smith is now no more—he lingered till saturday se'night, when he expired quite worn out—he was sensible to the last, but the last two days could scarcely articulate thro' mere weakness—The world has cause to regret that some days before he died he caused burn nine or ten volumes of his Mss—he did not think them finish'd enough to give the world—and the treatment Geo[rge] Fa[u]lkner has given poor Dean Swift [in his editions of Swift's works after his death], makes many author[s] fear the same fate—two or three vols. are left—how they are to be disposed [of] I know not—his will I am afraid will be censured by many—he has left everything £400 excepted, to a young lad a grand nephew of his mothers, who has been very serviceable to him, he is bred to the law and has been under Mr Smith's tuition for some years—The £400 is to a poor relation—his faithfull servant gets by far too little, and he's too old for his brother Commissioners of the Customs to provide handsomely for him. (Oxford, Bodleian MS Add. c 890)

The will of 6 February 1790, registered as a disposition in favour of David Douglas on 22 July 'in the books of Council and Session' in Edinburgh, is certainly an austere document. Smith assigned to his heir all his property, 'heritable or moveable, real or personal', including the valuable library (described in the Introduction to Hiroshi Mizuta's *Catalogue*, forthcoming). The library, however, is not mentioned in the will as an individual item (SRO Durie vol. 251/1, fo. 195). David Douglas was to be responsible for the funeral expenses and all lawful debts, also for the legacies Smith granted. The major charge on the estate was a bequest of £400 to a 'very near relation', Rachael McGill, and her husband Hugh Cleghorn, Professor of Civil History at St Andrews. Perhaps the legacy helped to pay for Cleghorn's European travels, which were the prelude to a later career as a British secret agent, then as prime mover in the transference of Ceylon to the British empire (*Corr.* No. 283 n. 1). The remaining manuscripts and writings were to be disposed of by David Douglas with the advice of Black and Hutton, 'agreeably to such verbal or written instruction' as Smith gave. The advocate Adam Rolland, who was a Fellow of the Royal Society of Edinburgh, and the original of Paul Pleydell in Scott's novel *Guy Mannering* (1815), acted as Smith's procurator for this will.

When legal formalities were completed, with David Douglas acting as sole executor, and the will was entered in the Edinburgh Register of Testaments on 21 January 1791, there was added to the general inventory of the estate a reference to a promissory note for £650 issued by the banking firm of Sir William Forbes, James Hunter & Co. (SRO CC8/128/2, 19748/3). There is no mention in any of the forms of the will of a bequest to James Baird, Smith's servant.

Since Smith lived in a hospitable but modest way, his friends wondered at the limited nature of the bequests, though no one has been detected censuring the will, as Beatson feared. We may believe that Smith left instructions to his heir that his servant was to be looked after properly, also that he had given away generous sums from his income in secret charity, hence his slender resources at the end. The instance has been mentioned of Smith giving £200 in 1783 to a 'Welch nephew' to save him from having to sell his army commission (*Corr.* No. 231). Stewart obtained first-hand information that strengthens belief that Smith was markedly generous in an unostentatious fashion:

Some very affecting instances of Mr Smith's beneficence, in cases where he found it impossible to conceal entirely his good offices, have been mentioned to me by a near relation of his, and one of his most confidential friends, Miss Ross, daughter of the late Patrick Ross, Esq., of Innernethy. They were all on a scale much beyond what might have been expected from his fortune; and they were accompanied with circumstances equally honourable to the delicacy of his feelings and the liberality of his heart. (v.4 n., p. 326)

A range of further comment on Smith's death comes from contemporary correspondence. On 20 August J. T. Stanley, afterwards Lord Stanley of Alderly, wrote to a Dr Scott of Edinburgh:

I heard of the death of Adam Smith, a few days before I received your letter. His end was that of a good man, and he practiced to the last the philosophy he had taught. Very few men are held in so much estimation by their friends as Mr Smith was. Gentle and unassuming in the society which I so diligently attended every Friday evening at Edinburgh, and which if you remember, was called Mr Smith's club, I have heard him listened to with the greatest respect and deference whenever he delivered his sentiments on any serious subject. He never argued, indeed, I never heard any dispute on a speculative subject in that society; discussion alone took place there. Mr Smith more frequently listened than spoke; his calm composed manner when he did take a part contrasted well with Dr Hutton's vivacity, Playfair's diffidence, or Mackenzie's sprightliness of wit. (Private owner: David Christie, Europäische Schule, Kirchberg, Luxemburg)

On that same day, Samuel Romilly, then a young barrister concerned with law reform, who had been added to the group of Whig liberals surrounding Lord Shelburne, and who was an admirer of Smith's advanced ideas, wrote to a French lady in response to her request for a copy of the latest edition of *TMS*:

I have been surprised and, I own, a little indignant to observe how little impression [Smith's] death has made here. Scarce any notice has been taken of it, while for above a year together after the death of Dr Johnson [1784] nothing was to be heard but panegyrics of him,—lives, letters, and anecdotes,—and even at this moment there are two more lives of him to start into existence [possibly Boswell's, 1791; and Arthur Murphy's, 1792]. Indeed, one ought not perhaps to be very much surprised that the public does not do justice to the works of A. Smith since he did not do justice to them himself, but always considered his *TMS* a much superior work to his [*WN*]. (Romilly, 1840: i.403)

Some time after 14 July 1790, when he celebrated with 'friends of the Revolution in France' the anniversary of the fall of the Bastille the previous year, and before 4 November, when he planned to commemorate the English Revolution of 1689, Richard Price described to an unknown friend how much he had been affected by the death of Smith, whom he 'looked up to as a writer of the first abilities'. Smith had sent him a copy of the sixth edition of *TMS*, and Price noted in the Advertisement the promise to publish a treatise on the 'general principles of law and government', and the caveat that Smith's 'very advanced age' left little hope of doing this to his satisfaction:

Soon after this, death put an end to all his labours; and this must Soon happen to us all. Happy are those who at the close of life can reflect that they have lived to a valuable purpose by contributing, as he did, to enlighten mankind, and to Spread the blessings of peace and liberty and virtue. He was indeed one of the ablest writers, and his personal character was, as far as I ever knew or heard, irreproachable. We thought differently on the Subject of the origin of our Ideas of moral good and evil, but Such differences among Speculative men must always exist; and they do good by occasioning a more thorough investigation of important points, and in the end a clearer development of truth. Dr Smith had been gradually declining for more than a year before he died, nor do I know that his disorder had any particular name given it. His only publications were his Treatises on morals and on the wealth of nations; and I am told that he has left the world no room to hope for any posthumous work, except, perhaps, a few Essays. He had burnt many Volumes of Manuscripts to prevent the possibility of publishing them. Mr Dugald Stuart, the Professor of moral Philosophy at Edinburgh, is to give an account of his life in the Edinburgh Philosophical Transactions, and to attend it with some critical remarks on his books on morals and the wealth of nations. (Philadelphia, American Philosophical Soc. MS)

Romilly's indignation at the scant public response to Smith's death may well have been increased by the notices in the newspapers and periodicals. In Edinburgh the *Mercury* and the *Advertiser* provided obituaries of two small paragraphs in which a principal feature appears to have been the anecdote of gypsies abducting Smith when he was a child (Rae, 1965: 436). The *Gentleman's Magazine* for August 1790 gave an overview of Smith's life, mentioning such details as the intention of Smith's friends to send him abroad as a tutor after he returned to Kirkcaldy from Oxford in 1746, also his extreme jealousy about the 'property of his lectures', leading to outbursts, when he saw note-takers, that he 'hated scribblers' (60: 761–2). *The Times* noted the death on 24 July, and followed this up on 6 August with eleven paragraphs of mingled anecdotage and barbed comment. He is described in youth as a 'hard student', so ill-conditioned in body and mind as to be ungracious in appearance and awkward in address. His aversion to a career in the Church is put down to becoming a 'disciple of Voltaire in matters of religion'. His superiority in pronunciation of English and command of usage and in classical learning over those educated in Scotland only is assigned to his Oxford training. His intellectual formation is represented as being completed by study of the French Encyclopedists. In admiring Hume as the world's greatest philosopher, and regarding Dr Johnson as lacking in common sense, he is said to have exhibited prejudices which combined with his merit to make him a 'very fashionable Professor'. At faction-torn Glasgow University, he sided with those popular among the rich merchants. From their conversation, particularly that of John Glassford, he obtained facts 'necessary for improving his Lectures'. Teaching in a commercial town, he had 'converted the chair of Moral Philosophy into a professorship of trade and finance'. This revolution was accomplished after he published his 'ingenious but fanciful Theory of Moral Sentiments'. His absorption in his ideas is illustrated by the anecdote of a fall into a tanning pit in Glasgow, while he was discoursing to Charles Townshend on the division of labour. *WN* itself is said not to have been popular at first, but sales were raised when Fox made a banal reference to it in the House of Commons, and the 'circumstances of the country, our wars, debts, taxes etc. attracted attention to a work where such objects were treated—subjects that unfortunately have become too popular in most countries of Europe'. Smith's system of political economy is declared to be the same as that of Count Pietro Verri, two copies of whose *Meditazioni sull'economica politica* (1771) were certainly on Smith's shelves (Mizuta); of Dean Josiah Tucker; and of Hume. The illustrative material is said to have come mainly from the *Encyclopédie*. Credit, however, is given to Smith alone for the 'arrangement', and for carrying the principles to greater length, as well as strengthening their proofs more convincingly. He thus deserves the 'chief praise, or chief blame, of propagating a system which tends to confound National Wealth with National Prosperity' (quoted Fay, 1956: 33–5). A similar article appeared in *The Oracle and Public Advertiser* of London on 9 August. So much for the verdict of the national press of 1790 on the lifetime achievement of Adam Smith.

Henry Cockburn reports that older people about this time were preoccupied by the French Revolution, whereas the younger set discussed Lavoisier's 'new chemistry' and the 'economical doctrines so suitable for the country of Adam Smith'. He continues:

the middle aged seemed to me to know little about the founder of the science [first claim of this kind], except that he had recently been a Commissioner of Customs, and had written a sensible book. The young, by which I mean the liberal young of Edinburgh, lived upon him. With Hume, Robertson, Millar, Montesquieu, Ferguson, and De Lolme, he supplied them with most of their mental food. (Cockburn, 1856: 45–6)

Meanwhile Smith's circle set about creating their own memorial to him and publishing the manuscripts spared from the flames as he wished. The first news of Stewart's 'Account' of his dead friend comes in a letter of 10 August to David Douglas from John Millar, in which he welcomes the idea of publishing the posthumous essays, and states: 'It will give me the greatest pleasure to contribute any hints to Mr Stuart with regard to Mr Smiths professorial talents, or any other particular you mention, while he remained at Glasgow' (GUL MS Gen. 1035/178). Agreeable to his promise, Millar sent to Stewart in December 'some particulars about Dr Smith', and on 17 August 1792 the latter reported to Cadell as follows: 'Mr Smith's papers with the Account of his life will be ready for the press at the beginning of next winter' (NLS MS 5319, fo. 34). On 21 December Cadell offered the following terms for *EPS* to Henry Mackenzie, one of the 'privy council' advising about the publication:

the first Edition [to] be printed in Quarto and to consist of one thousand copies for which we will pay three Hundred pounds, and in case the Book should be printed again we agree to pay a further sum of two Hundred pounds. On referring back to our agreement with Mr Smith [for *TMS*] we find that we shared the profits of the Quarto Edition with the Author; that when the Book was established we paid for the property £300 for the term of 14 Years, and a further Sum of £300 in case the Author lived to assign his second term of 14 Years which you know he did. . . . We should prefer printing in London if equally agreeable to you.

Cadell added a postscript to his letter asking for a portrait of Smith: 'I much wish to add him to our list' (GUL MS Gen. 1035/177).

Stewart read his 'Account . . . of Adam Smith' at meetings of the Royal Society of Edinburgh on 21 January and 18 March 1793. Indirectly, he answers Cadell's request by stating near the conclusion that Smith never sat for a portrait, but that the medallion by James Tassie, two states of which exist, one in contemporary dress and one in the antique manner, presents an 'exact idea of his profile, and of the general expression of his countenance' (v.17).[1] Between the meetings, Stewart had written to Cadell on 13 March to say that his 'Account' was ready to send to the press 'immediately', mentioning that neither the RSE *Transactions* nor *EPS* was likely to appear 'this Season', and asking if a separate publication could be considered: 'more especially, as my papers have Swelled to Such a Size, that I suspect they must be printed in an abridged form in the Transactions' (NLS MS 5319, fos. 35–6).

The 'Account' in an unabridged form duly appeared in the third volume of the RSE *Transactions* in 1794, and it reappeared with minor changes as the first piece of *EPS* when this book was finally published in London by the firm of Cadell & Davies in 1795. Stewart once confessed: 'I hate biography', but it appears that, of the three pieces of this nature that he wrote for the Royal Society of Edinburgh, he preferred the one on Adam Smith to those on William Robertson and Thomas Reid (1854–60: vol. x, p. lxxv n. 1).

Indeed, as a member of Smith's circle, and like him a Scots Professor of Moral Philosophy, inheriting and transmitting the same intellectual tradition, Stewart was a logical choice as his friend's memorialist and must have felt some affinity for his task. He collected useful facts on Smith's life and background, and pre-served otherwise unavailable materials, such as the extract from the 1755 paper presenting key ideas dating back to the Edinburgh lectures and anticipating *WN*. He offers a shrewd commentary on that book, also on *TMS*, indicating how con-temporaries read these works. Most helpfully, he discerns their unity, finding in them a 'particular sort of inquiry' further illustrated in the essays on the History of Astronomy and the First Formation of Languages. As discussed, we find that Stewart calls this '*Theoretical* or *Conjectural* History', equating it with Hume's 'Natural History', and his comments offer true insight into Smith's intellectual approach, which involves 'tracing from the principles of human nature, or from the circumstances of society, the origins of the opinions and the institutions which he describes' (ii.52). Regarding the subject of political economy, and Smith's claim to distinction as a contributor to it, Stewart has a sufficiently extensive knowledge of its literature to assess questions of originality and con-ceptual and analytical power.

His portrait of Smith is accordingly affectionate and balanced—perhaps too genteel and too lacking in flesh-and-blood characteristics, however, to be entirely suited to modern taste. Of his principal successors, John Rae must be com-mended for providing a far more rounded account of Smith the man and the author, while W. R. Scott added greatly to our knowledge of Smith by his energy and success in recovering essential details and documents connected with his career.

EPS was naturally of great interest to Smith's friends, both from concern for his reputation and from curiosity about the fate of what they understood to be the nature of the pieces. John Millar thought that Smith's 'genius' would have been conveyed by the pieces that were burned, but they might have exhibited 'some inequality in the composition'. Writing to David Douglas on that point on

10 August 1790, he also mentioned that two of the essays on the imitative arts had been read to the Literary Society in Glasgow (we know from William Richardson's letter to Samuel Rose that this was in December 1787), but the third had not been finished at that time, and he hoped that he might now see a finished version. He continued: 'Of all Smith's writings, I have most curiosity about the metaphysical work you mention. I should like to see his powers of illustration employed upon the true old Humean philosophy' (GUL MS Gen. 1035/178).

As to what was read to the Literary Society, we might conjecture these papers were early versions of parts i and ii of the essay entitled 'Of the Nature of that Imitation which takes place in what are called The Imitative Arts'. Part iii, which deals with dancing, is very brief, and Millar may have wished for a completed version. The other brief essay, entitled 'Of the Affinity between Music, Dancing, and Poetry', was found by Black and Hutton among Smith's papers without any indication where it belonged, but since it seemed to be connected with the Imitative Arts set, they printed it after them (*EPS* 209). Stewart was of the opinion that Smith collected illustrative material for his ideas about the imitative arts during his residence in France, 1764–6, also that he had studied drama in this connection, and intended to publish his results (iii.13–15). We conjecture that Smith was at work on his 'Philosophical History' that dealt with the imitative arts in the period 1777–82, at the end of which he was considering publication (*Corr.* No. 208). Alexander Wedderburn (Lord Loughborough) was among those who saw Smith's work on the imitative arts and knew of Smith's 'alterations' to it (GUL MS Gen. 1035/179). The piece on English and Italian verses survives in a fragmentary draft in a manuscript written on paper with a watermark not known to occur before 1780; Smith wrote to Lady Frances Scott, sister of the Duke of Buccleuch, on 17 March 1783 thanking her for the return of his essay, so we know that he was giving attention to it at that time (GUL MS Gen. 1035/226; *Corr.* No. 225; *EPS* 217, n. 1). All of these pieces demonstrate that Smith is familiar with current debates about aesthetic issues and critical theory. Stewart considered that Smith came to paradoxical conclusions about literature, especially about drama, because he took too far as a 'fundamental principle' to explain our pleasure in the arts, what was called the 'difficulty of imitation' (iii.14–15). This is a hint, perhaps, of what Smith intended to expand into a system for his 'connected history of the liberal sciences and elegant arts', as Black and Hutton called the first 'great work' which Smith had in hand in his last years (*Corr.* No. 248).

As for the 'true old Humean philosophy', this is not to be found in the essay on the external senses which is influenced by Berkeley, or at least idealism, and may be in part anti-Humean (Brown, 1992: 335). In the three remaining essays, on astronomy, Ancient Physics, and Ancient Logics and Metaphysics, however, which we have associated with the Edinburgh course of lectures on the history of philosophy, subsequently given as a private course at Glasgow, there is

Humean influence. Above all, the essay on astronomy illustrates the 'principles which lead and direct philosophical enquiries', by focusing on the role of the imagination in building up the common-sense conception of the external world (Raphael, 1977). In this respect, they are contributions to that 'science of human nature' which Hume in his constructive phase strove to establish. The scepticism that is the other side to Hume's naturalism is represented by the definition of philosophy as 'that science which pretends to lay open the concealed connections that unite the various appearances of nature' ('Astronomy' iii.3). Since David Douglas lived in Millar's household as a student and was taught by him after his early education under Smith, and Millar had been Smith's pupil at Glasgow, this recognition of a Humean strain in a 'metaphysical work' by Smith is important evidence about his intellectual affinities and one source of his inspiration.

Millar's description of the lecture courses given by Smith deepens further our appreciation of his cast of mind, and Millar also provides some information about yet another work that Smith intended to write. It may have been intended as part of the 'theory and History of Law and Government', the second 'great work' mentioned to La Rochefoucauld in 1785. This additional work contemplated by Smith was a 'treatise upon the Greek and Roman republics'. In the face of Ferguson's *History of the Progress and Termination of the Roman Republic* (1783), and of Gibbon's attention to the republic in his *Decline and Fall of the Roman Empire*, Millar commented on Smith's project as follows:

And after all that has been published on that subject, I am convinced, that the observations of Mr Smith would have suggested many new and important views concerning the internal and domestic circumstances of those nations, which would have displayed their several systems of policy, in a light much less artificial than that in which they had hitherto appeared. (Stewart ii.53)

Perhaps Millar anticipated obtaining from Smith a 'natural history' of the ancient republics, delineating their rise and decay and reflecting the operation of those 'principles of human nature' used to account for systems of astronomy as well as moral philosophy and commercial society.

Posterity had to be content, however, with those vestiges of a 'connected history of the liberal sciences and elegant arts' in *EPS*. The first London edition was followed in the same year, 1795, by a Dublin one, deemed legal as long as it was not put on sale in England. A further edition was printed by James Decker at Basle in 1799, as a title in a series designated the 'Collection of English Classics'. It does not identify the original editors, Black and Hutton, but this information was available in Stewart's 'Account of . . . Smith', which formed part of the book. In 1797 there appeared in Republican Paris a French translation by Pierre Prevost, Professor of Philosophy at Geneva, and in correspondence with the Royal Society of Edinburgh. He included a translation of Smith's letter to the *Edinburgh Review*, sent to him in 1796 by Dugald Stewart, and provided annotation of some value, particularly concerning the essays on aesthetic matters (*EPS* 28–9, 218). Cadell's wish to have a portrait of Smith was realized in this edition by the inclusion of an attractive and perhaps flattering engraving, based on the Tassie contemporary dress medallion, and executed by Benois Louis Prevost.

The busts on the two Tassie medallions measure three inches from the top of the head to the bottom of the trunk, and each is dated 1787. Smith may have given the artist the brief sittings necessary at 20 Leicester Square, when he was in London that year, or Tassie may have done his modelling on a visit to Edinburgh (Holloway, 1986: 6–8). On the word of Dugald Stewart, we may take the medallion with Smith in a bag wig as the best guide to the everyday appearance of Adam Smith's profile and face (Pl. 19). The other version, 'in the antique manner' (frontispiece), suggests that Smith bore a family resemblance to his mother, at least as depicted in the portrait dated 1778. We also see that Tassie is placing Smith in the company of the 'ancient worthies' such as Seneca, Marcus Aurelius, and Cicero, whose busts were displayed in eighteenth-century libraries (Haskell and Penny, 1982: 50–1). A depiction of this kind makes exactly the right point about Smith: that first and last he was a moralist whose character bore the impress of the Roman Stoics.

As Tassie saw him, Adam Smith radiated firmness and decisiveness. Here is the man who planned and completed an exposition of the human emotions that give rise to moral judgements, then investigated the nature of wealth and how modern commercial societies acquired it. He 'struggled violently' to carry forward two other 'great works', but age and infirmity defeated him. His completed books were successful to a degree that matched his resolution in undertaking them. The Strahan printing ledgers indicate that the print-runs for *WN* rose from 500 copies of the first edition to 2,000 to the sixth one of 1791. Though he had anticipated the run for Gibbon's *Decline and Fall*, William Strahan, as we have mentioned, was surprised by the comparatively rapid sale of *WN*, since he did not think so many 'modern Readers' would understand it. Cadell offered Henry Mackenzie a contract for *EPS* covering 1,000 copies, and modelled this on the contract for *TMS*, whose sixth edition had an equal print-run. In German, French, Danish, Spanish, and Italian translations, Smith's books reached a wider audience still. Aware of something of his success on this scale, Smith appears to have remained steadfastly modest and self-deprecating.

There was another aspect to Smith, however, than the decisive man of thought portrayed by Tassie. Anecdotage loved to dwell on his absent-mindedness, even in 'large companies', wrote 'Jupiter' Carlyle; Hume accused him ruefully of 'Indolence and Love of Solitude'; and his correspondence records many instances of complaints of physical ailments, some episodes of gloomy anticipations of death, also an admission that he possessed a 'melancholy and evil boding mind' (*Corr.* No. 286), and some flashes of a 'warm' temper generally kept in tight control. One explanation of the psychosomatic disorders already pre-

Pl. 19. Adam Smith as a 'man of the world who mingled much in the society of Edinburgh and London' (Dugald Stewart), 1787. From a medallion by James Tassie (Scottish National Portrait Gallery).

sented is that Smith was a sufferer from hypochondriasis, involving chronic bouts of low spirits, anxiety about health, and listlessness, identifiable as the psychological costs of intense study and concentration on chains of abstract ideas. In the course of his life he tried various remedies to alleviate his condition: tar-water at Oxford, sea-bathing and botanizing at Kirkcaldy, and horseback riding at Dr Cullen's recommendation in 1760. In his later years he resorted to exemplary service as a Customs Commissioner, and entertaining company at his Friday Club and Sunday suppers in Panmure House.

Nature did not favour Smith in his mode of expression, it seems, for we read of his harsh voice with an almost stammering impediment, and a conversational style that amounted to lecturing (Carlyle, 1973: 141). His friends understood this, and made allowances for his disposition. According to Stewart, they 'were often led to concert little schemes, in order to engage him in the discussions most likely to interest him'. They were greatly diverted when he expatiated in his social hours in his characteristically original way on subjects relatively unfamiliar to him, or advanced extreme positions or judgements on relatively slight grounds, and then just as readily withdrew them when countervailing views were put to him. When with strangers, apparently, his manner was sometimes an embarrassed one, because he was conscious of, and perhaps on guard about, his customary absence of mind; also, he had very high speculative notions of propriety, yet an imperfect ability to live up to them. What shines through all accounts of his character and characteristics, particularly as they were displayed in his relationships with young people, was his essential kindness. Samuel Rose, grieving for the death of his father William, an old friend of Smith's from the time of his notice of *TMS* in the *Monthly Review* in 1759, wrote to a relative that 'Commissioner Smith has treated me with uncommon tenderness' (GUL MS Accession No. 4467, to Edward Foss, 19 July 1786). Somewhat in the same vein, Stewart wrote of Smith that 'in the society of those he loved, his features were often brightened with a smile of inexpressible benignity' (Stewart v.12–17).

Setting aside the idiosyncrasies of Adam Smith's character, and the hypochondriac affliction which by and large he seems to have overcome, we can affirm that he was a good man, or at least perceived as such by contemporaries in the best position to judge. We may think that he erred on the side of prudence, and in the desire to enjoy tranquillity of mind, for example, at the expense of benevolence towards Hume, in the matter of Hume's deathbed wish to have his friend oversee the publication of the *Dialogues concerning Natural Religion*.

A further question may be raised, however, about Smith's wisdom. What was the intellectual and moral legacy that he left to posterity? The *Theory of Moral Sentiments*, while held to provide important truths about the efficacy of sympathy in forming moral judgements about others, and to create in the concept of the impartial spectator an original though, in the event, unduly neglected concept available for understanding and clarifying our judgements about ourselves, is not considered a landmark in its field. The *Wealth of Nations*, to be sure, has proved to be such. Down to our time, economists of every stripe have invoked it as a foundation document of their science and, though often citing it with a high degree of selectivity and on occasion distortion, they have found it a rich mine of theory and practical illustration of the working of the market society. Together with the work of Malthus and Ricardo, the analytic part of the book largely defined the scope of 'classical economics' until the revisions of Jevons and Marshall in the nineteenth century.[2] On the policy side, successive movements for customs and tax reform, free trade, and popular education owed some impetus to Smith's book as legislators heeded its advice (Robbins, 1952; Coats, 1971; 1992: i.119–38).

Controversy has raged, of course, over Smith's stress, or apparent stress, on self-interest or self-love as the sole motive for economic transactions. In part, the difficulty arises over Smith's championship of the 'obvious and simple system of natural liberty' in the economic sphere, which historically has been interpreted as endorsement of a free-enterprise, capitalist system. Thus, parodic versions of Smith's 'invisible-hand' argument were presented to sanction the aggressive and, in some measure, unscrupulous acquisitiveness of nineteenth-century business-men. For example, in 1877 a narrowly defeated candidate for the US presidency addressed these words to a group of millionaire dinner guests:

You are, doubtless in some degree, clinging to the illusion that you are working for your-self, but it is my pleasure to claim that you are working for the public. [*Applause.*] While you are scheming for your own selfish ends, there is an overruling and wise Providence directing that the most of all you do should inure to the benefit of the people. Men of colossal fortunes are in effect, if not in fact, trustees for the public.

Thus Samuel J. Tilden, loser in the race against Rutherford B. Hayes (quoted Lux, 1990: 78–9). The stock market crash of 1929, followed by the Great Depression, put such a viewpoint under deep suspicion. And the Keynesian reformulation of economics, together with welfare state thinking and devotion to econometrics as truly scientific, seemed to push Adam Smith's philosophy of economics out of sight.

To be sure, this obscuring of Smith was never complete. In particular, schol-ars at the University of Chicago (Jacob Viner, Milton Friedman, George Stigler), from Austria (Ludwig von Mises, F. A. von Hayek), and from Scotland (W. R. Scott, Alexander Gray, A. L. Macfie) kept alive vigorous interest in Smith's eco-nomic principles and in the man himself. In the 1960s the Scottish Economic Society broached the idea of a collected edition of Smith's works to commemo-rate the 1976 bicentenary of the publication of *WN*, and this project was real-ized by an international team of editors selected by a committee at Smith's alma mater. On another front, increasing attention to the achievements of the Scottish Enlightenment inevitably threw into relief Smith's contributions to the fields which engaged his capacious mind. Further, the inquiries of John Pocock into the tradition of political discourse he identified as 'civic humanism' inevitably required attention to the writings of Smith and his problematic relationship to that tradition. This has resulted in a stimulating debate about the relative impor-tance for him of the natural-law school of thought as differentiated from 'civic humanism' (Hont and Ignatieff, 1983: p. vii). One upshot of this debate has been more precision in identifying Smith's own concept of political economy, and his legacy to successors in the field.

Further life has been granted to Smith through criticism of free-enterprise theory of economic growth as he outlined this, sometimes starting from Smith himself. In his provocative moments, Ronald Meek used to inform his students that Marx became a Communist in the 1840s through dwelling on those passages in *WN* which draw attention to the workers being exploited and oppressed by deceitful traders and manufacturers and indolent landlords (cf. I.viii.13; I.xi. p. 10; I.xi. p. 8). Meek's argument suggests that the reading of Smith reflected in Marx's *Economic and Philosophic Manuscripts of 1844* fuelled the angry denunciation of the *laissez-faire* system in *Das Kapital* (1867–94; Meek, 1977: 8–9). Marx solved his own problematic relationship to Smith's economic thought, which he respected, by discerning in it 'esoteric' (profound) elements which connected with his own system and 'exoteric' (superficial) ones which, for example, portray competition from the bourgeois standpoint (Thal, 1990).

Another approach has been to inquire into the history of Smith's argument that self-love in the economic domain gives rise to public welfare. Edwin Cannan held that this was a restatement of Mandeville's mischievous contention that private vices are public virtues (*WN*, ed. Cannan, 1950: vol. i, p. xlvi). Joan Robinson built on this interpretation to say that such a contention resulted in an 'ideology to end all ideologies, for it has abolished the moral problem. It is only necessary for each individual to act egotistically for the good of all to be attained' (1964: 53). Kenneth Lux (1990) has elaborated Robinson's point, alleging that Smith made a fundamental error in proposing that self-interest (or self-love) constituted the only motive for economic exchange, putting any appeal to benevolence out of the question. Like Robinson, in support of this criticism, Lux cites the famous passage about not expecting our dinner from the 'benevolence of the butcher, the brewer, or the baker. We address ourselves not to their humanity but to their self-love, and never talk to them of our own necessities but of their advantage' (*WN* I.ii.2). According to Lux, Smith erred again in devoting his last intellectual efforts to revisions and additions for *TMS*. He should have worked over *WN* to qualify the role of self-love, and sought to mitigate the rapacity and destructiveness which this emotion entails, when unleashed in a world of consumers and producers.

Where is the wise man of the west now, when it appears that he has turned bad into good, selfishness into mandatory economic enterprise, with pollution damage, environmental collapse, and spoliation of the underdog as necessary but unavoidable corollaries? Robinson suggested that Mandeville got under Smith's skin, and Lux endorses this view, arguing that Smith despite his disclaimers was too much impressed with the 'noise' that Mandeville made in the world (*TMS* VII.ii.4.13–14), and basically accepts the theory that man is intrinsically selfish. Lux's assessment of Smith is that he was a good man in intention and, to some extent, in deed, but the mixture of 'cynicism and naiveté' in his character led him far astray in his teaching (Lux, 1990: 86–92, 94–5, 104–7; somewhat in the same strain, McCloskey, 1990: 143).

The burden of the biography of Adam Smith now concluded is that any such reductive view of him is specious. As befitted a pupil of Hutcheson and a good friend of Hume, he was a tireless inquirer into human nature, particularly its emotional range, and thereafter into its expressive forms, scientific endeavours, and the social, economic, and political institutions it organizes, sometimes with much forethought, but sometimes seemingly with very little. With a confident intelligence, but also some elements of a 'melancholy and evil boding mind', which tempered the optimism of the Enlightenment about social advance, he addressed himself to the imagination of our race, to give an account of how people in a relatively early phase of a commercial and manufacturing society might live with justice to themselves and others. His inquiries were also directed at establishing how people, within this framework of justice, might pursue their interests to secure satisfaction of basic wants, and prudent accumulation of goods, not limited to those of a material order. He saw us as humans typically seeking to 'better our condition', and he thought that self-interest was centrally involved in the necessary transactions, but he did not by some sleight of hand convert overweening self-love into praiseworthy motivation.

The premiss of his inquiries runs thus:

how selfish soever man may be supposed, there are certainly some principles in his nature, which interest him in the fortunes of other, and render their happiness necessary to him, though he derives nothing except the pleasure of seeing it.

To obtain a coherent view of what Smith taught, we have to connect this opening sentence of *TMS* with the passage in *WN* in which he argues against misguided government intrusions in the market-place, then continues:

Every man, *as long as he does not violate the laws of justice* [*our italics*], is left perfectly free to pursue his own interest his own way, and to bring both his industry and capital into competition with those of any other man, or order of men. (IV.ix.51)

In short, Smith is saying that the happiness of others is necessary to us, and that our economic freedom, as indeed any other kind, is to be exercised with attention to justice to others. As to the exercise of that economic liberty, Smith recognized that public prejudice and private interest would always render this imperfect: 'To expect, indeed, that the freedom of trade should ever be entirely restored in Great Britain, is as absurd as to expect that an Oceana or Utopia should ever be established in it' (IV.ii.43). This surely is the voice of common sense, not doctrinaire advocacy.

Thinking of the rise of Western capitalism after Smith's own time, should we convict him of narrowness of vision, with respect to his doctrine of economic liberty? Why did he not anticipate what Marx depicts as the 'Faustian conflict between the passion for accumulation and the desire for enjoyment', forcing the capitalist to create the 'industrial reserve army', the massed ranks of unemployed or underemployed workers necessary to cope with the swings of the market? Marx's criticism is surely a perpetual challenge to the message of *WN*:

Accumulation of wealth at one pole is, therefore, at the same time accumulation of misery, agony of toil, slavery, ignorance, brutality, mental degradation, at the opposite pole, i.e., on the side of the class that produces its own product in the form of capital. (1954: i.645)

But perhaps Smith saw more deeply into commercial and manufacturing society than Marx. He was certainly aware of the mental mutilation inflicted on workers by the division of labour, and denounced this, urging that education of the people at the public charge was one answer (*WN* v.i.f.50, 61). Marx mocked the idea, claiming that this remedy was to be administered in 'homeopathic doses'(1954: i.362). Yet education in societies where there are elements of the free market has minimally prevailed, whereas Marxist revolution has generally failed, in making lives more tolerable physically and mentally.

It is also true that, while Smith did not anticipate the behaviour (in free-market societies) of manipulators of international cartels, price-rigging trusts and holding companies, and insider trading on the stock exchange, he did provide very clear warnings about the 'clamour and sophistry' as well as machinations of merchants and manufacturers. He denounced with equal vigour the drive to overwhelm and oppress that must be checked in big powers and governing classes: 'All for ourselves, and nothing for other people, seems, in every age of the world, to have been the vile maxim of the masters of mankind' (*WN* III.iv.10). Also, in facing up to a world where there is roguery and oppression, he counsels self-command, not abnegation. In all this, he strikes the candid reader as not cynical but realistic. His decision to devote his last years to moral philosophy speaks, surely, of a character that was the reverse of naïve, rather one displaying singular generosity of spirit, believing that, with wit and logic and sensitivity to our feelings, he might help us aspire to virtue rather than wealth, and so become members of a truly civil society.

Notes

1. KIRKCALDY

1. Sibbald as improving laird, medical and natural scientist, historian, and geographer, *inter alia*, who wished to lead a 'virtuous and philosophick lyfe', was a leading figure in the early stages of the Scottish Enlightenment (Emerson, 1988).
2. See the additions to *TMS* edn. 6, 1790 (III.2.35), contrasting the 'futile mortifications of a monastery' with the 'ennobling hardships and hazards of war'. Unlike Hume, however, Smith never went on a military campaign.
3. There are many references to French authors in Smith's writings, and there are many French books in his library (Mizuta), including Molière's works (1749, 1773) and Fénelon's *Télémaque* (1778), but the editions post-date the father's lifetime.
4. *LJ*(A) ii.92, *LJ*(B) 182, 335–6; *TMS* II.ii.3.11 and pp. 389–95 of this edn.
5. Cf. *LJ*(B) 295 and *WN* III.iv.3 (merchants); *WN* IV.ii.21 (farmers and gentry); and *LJ*(A) vi.62 (professional men).

2. BOYHOOD

1. GUL MS Gen. 1035/63, 20 Feb. 1723, James Oswald appointed factor to manage Hugh Smith's affairs; SRO Service of Heirs, C22/60, 29 Mar. 1724, younger Adam Smith retoured heir to his father; GUL MS Gen. 1035/71, 13 May 1735 (from London), William Smith's account rendered to executors of Adam Smith, WS, including South Sea Co. stock; Scott (1937: 21–2, 134).
2. Gifford (1988: 412–13) has details of the castle and the mansion house rebuilt by William Burn in 1824. Revd Gordon Simpson, Trinity Parish Church, Leslie, Fife, wrote to me on 18 Aug. 1993 about the local tradition concerning a mansion house dating from late in the 17th cent. On a visit in November 1993 I asked the residents of the castle and the mansion house to point out to me where they believed Adam Smith was snatched.
3. On the Stoic system of the passions, see Sandbach (1975: 59–68) and Long and Sedley (1988: 410–23); Smith responded deeply to Epictetus and the Roman Stoics, Cicero, Marcus Aurelius (whom he called Antoninus), and Seneca—see *TMS* intro.; Waszek (1984).
4. Lord Deskford wrote to James Adam as follows in 1761: 'I expect we are just going to begin a reign in Britain of Taste and Architecture in which it will give me much pleasure to see you make the greatest figure of anybody, if 'tis not my old friend Bob, who I would pardon though he were to outshine you' (Fleming, 1962: 279).

3. GLASGOW

1. *Corr.* No. 42; Smith reported on 29 Oct. 1759 that on a visit to Edinburgh he 'was often obliged either to sup or dine at places where it was improper to carry' his pupil, the Hon. Thomas Petty Fitzmaurice. To 'be sure what company he was in in a very dissolute town, [Smith] ordered a small entertainment at [their] lodgings'; cf. *LJ*(B) 204: 'In Glasgow there is not [a capital crime] in several years, but not a year passes in Edinburgh without some such disorders'; Smith attributes this state of affairs to the prevalence of servants in Edinburgh: *LJ*(A) vi.1–6; *WN* II.iii.12.
2. Recent scholarship has emphasized that members of the Kirk of Smith's generation who were divided over allegiance to 'old light' and 'new light' theology could converge in their interest in the intellectual advances of the Enlightenment: see Clark (1963), Voges (1985), McIntosh (1989), Landsman (1990; 1991); also Sher (1995).
3. Scottish economic improvement in this period, sought through reconstruction of institutions by exercise of political patronage, has been the focus of much recent research: Murdoch (1980: 30–2); Shaw (1983: chs. 5, 6); and Emerson (1992: 45–6).
4. The students' rhetoric had diverse roots in the discourse of classical republicanism (e.g. Cicero); resistance to Stuart divine right monarch (Locke); opposition to Walpole (*Cato's Letters*, 1720 on); and contemporary conflict in Ireland over English colonial control (Molesworth): see Robbins (1959), Pocock (1965; 1986: ch. ii), and Stewart (1992: 5).
5. Smith's interest in the patronage of Ilay, who became 3rd Duke of Argyll in 1743, is reflected in his *Corr.* Nos. 10, 304. Some sources dealing with Ilay's Enlightenment projects are Taylor (1966: 25, 130), Lindsay and Cosh (1973: 35–185), Berkeley and Berkeley (1974: 108–12), and Emerson (1992: 104–5).

4. THE NEVER TO BE FORGOTTEN HUTCHESON

1. Maclaurin (1748/1968: 32–3, 43–5) discusses Copernicus as the restorer of the Pythagorean system; Hutcheson's epigraph for his *Short Introduction to Moral Philosophy* (1747) is a maxim from Pythagoras; and Smith reflects admiration for Pythagorean science: 'study of the connecting principles of nature' ('Astronomy' iii.9).
2. GUL MS Murray 49, 'Notes taken by James Craig from J. Loudoun's Logic class' (1699); GUL MS Gen. 406, 'Logicae compendium dictatum', also class list, 1712; GUL MS Gen. 71, 'Robert Sheddene's compend of Logic from J. Loudoun's teaching' (1714–15); GUL MS Murray 210, 'John Hamilton's compend of Logic notes from J. Loudoun's Dictata' (1729). Logic 'dictates' are discussed by Shepherd (1975) and Moore (1990: 43–4).
3. GUL Special Collections, Bf 73.–e.34, which belonged to Patrick Erskine: *Theses Philosophicae. . . Joanne Lowdoun Praeside* (Glasgow: Robert Saunders, 1708)—32 candidates are listed, and there are references to 'Torricelli's tub', 'Boyle's machine', and 'Poiretus', i.e., Pierre Poiret, who controverted Descartes: *De Eruditione Triplici* (Amsterdam, 1707).

4. See Professor Alexander Gerrard's course at Aberdeen, described in Stewart-Robertson (1983: 35 nn. 30, 31).
5. The Simson–Stewart corr. (1741–52) deals with theorems and porisms, and reveals how Professor and student stimulated each other intellectually: GUL MS Gen. 146/1–30.

5. OXFORD

1. Carlyle of Inveresk (1973: 102) returned from Oxford in 1746 via Warwick, Lichfield, River Esk crossing at Gretna, detour by Carlisle to Annan and Dumfries to visit relatives, while a companion went on to Edinburgh via Moffat. Carlyle made a return journey from Oxford in May 1758 with John Home the poet, William Robertson the historian, and James Adam the architect, via Woodstock; Warwick; Birmingham, where they were shown the manufactures and the Baskerville Press by Samuel Garbett, a former brass worker who had prospered through 'Inventing some Stamp for Shortening Labour', and was in partnership with Dr Roebuck in managing vitriol works at Prestonpans; the homes of William Shenstone and Lord Lyttleton with their famous gardens; Chatsworth, to see the Duke of Devonshire's house; Sheffield; Wentworth Woodhouse, where the Marquis of Rockingham was highly successful in scientific farming, and coal was worked up to the shadow of the mansion; Leeds; Newcastle; and home to Scotland through Cornhill-on-Tweed (pp. 184–92).
2. Handley (1953: 181); Kitchin and Passmore (1949: 6–13); Campbell (1966: 48), arguing that Smith judged Scottish diet by 'contemporary social conventions and not by modern nutritional standards'; Gibson and Smout (1989); Mathias (1983: 175); Wilson (1971: 243–5); Dodgshon and Butlin (1978: 162–3, 243–6); Rule (1992: 10–13, 47–8, 69–71).
3. Quoted by Porter (1990: 163); this author points out (pp. 161–4) that 'many liberal families mistrusted the public school and university diet of birch, boorishness, buggery, and the bottle', and employed private tutors for their sons and also sent them on the Grand Tour; those who needed professional training went to the Dutch or Scottish universities; and Nonconformist youths went to the Dissenting academies (e.g. at Kibworth, Taunton, Daventry, Kendal, Warrington, and Mile End), some of whose teachers had excellent reputations and maintained contacts with Scottish professors.
4. Entry in Balliol College records, 1740: '*Termino Trinitatis* Iul. 4. Adamus Smith Filius unicus [*sic*] Adami Smith Generosi de Kirkaldie in Regno Scotiae admissus est Commensalis.' Charles Suttie was admitted as a Commoner on 10 July. Smith matriculated at the University of Oxford on 7 July: 'Adamus Smith e Coll. Ball., Gen. Fil. Jul. 7mo 1740', according to the extract made by Professor Thorold Rogers, quoted by Rae (1965: 19).
5. McCulloch (1855: 8); there are other versions of this anecdote, and Dr John Strang of Glasgow stated (1857: 28) that Smith used to tell this anecdote himself—see Scott (1937: 42).

6. A RESPECTABLE AUDITORY

1. Fénelon had led a movement for a New Rhetoric in France based on the 'finest precepts of Aristotle, Cicero, Quintilian, Lucian, Longinus and other famous authors', in a work known in Britain in William Stevenson's translation, *Dialogues concerning Eloquence* (1722); the case for Adam Smith's New Rhetoric is presented by Howell (1971: 536–76); there was a movement towards teaching a New Rhetoric and *belles-lettres* in the contemporary English Dissenting academies—Philip Doddridge lecturing at Northampton, 1730–51, emphasized 'plain speaking' and 'plain diverting history', but it seems there was no separate course on *belles-lettres* until Dr Andrew Kippis gave one in 1765: Peter Jones (1), 'The Polite Academy and the Presbyterians, 1720–1770', in Dwyer *et al.* (1982: 159–71).
2. In criticizing Shaftesbury's florid style, Smith is also attacking those in Scotland who seem to have imitated it, e.g. George Turnbull, David Fordyce, and the younger Thomas Blackwell at Aberdeen, William Wishart at Edinburgh, and even Hutcheson himself—this is probably what lies behind James Wodrow's resentment that Smith dared to criticize his old teacher (Ch. 9 below): see Stewart (1987*a*) and Wood (1990).
3. 'Speeches' in the Rollin tradition but composed in English by Miller's pupils in Kirkcaldy *c.*1749–50 have survived: Maruzen 1990 Bicentenary Catalogue, Adam Smith: No. 1, illus. p. 3; Smith owned a copy of Rollin's edition of the *Institutio Oratoria* by Quintilian (Mizuta).

7. HISTORY OF PHILOSOPHY AND LAW

1. Arthur, *Discourses* (1803: 409–10); another source reports that Smith's history of astronomy was mentioned in one of Arthur's 'College exercises'—anon., 'Life of Smith', prefacing *TMS* edn. 12 (Glasgow: R. Chapman, 1809): p. xxi; see also Arthur's 'Essay on the Inducements to the Study of Natural Philosophy', May 1770, entered in John Anderson's notebook: Strathclyde Univ., Anderson Lib., Anderson MSS No. 2: pp. 1–32.
2. Cf. *TMS* II.ii.3: 'Of the Utility of this Constitution of Nature'; also the *TMS* and *WN* 'invisible hand' passages and on 'extraordinary encouragements' and 'restraints' *vis-à-vis* 'natural liberty' in the market-place: *TMS* IV.i.1.10; *WN* IV.ii.9, IV.ix.49, 50; Campbell (1971: 217–20); Campbell and Ross (1981: 73–6); Haakonssen (1981: 135–6); Teichgraeber (1986: 176–7).
3. EUL La II. 451/2; Raphael and Sakamoto (1990: 274–7); text of anecdotes provided by Raphael (1992*a*: 93–103).

8. CALLED TO GLASGOW UNIVERSITY

1. Widespread 18th-cent. Scottish interest in Montesquieu, as well as Voltaire and Rousseau, is reflected in numerous editions and translations: see Howard (1959).

2. Anecdote told by Smith's student Archibald Alison to Archdeacon John Sinclair, and reported by him (1875: 9).

9. TEACHER

1. The return to Russia of Desnitsky and Tret'yakov imbued with the liberal teaching of Smith and Millar coincided with the initiative of the Economic and Agriculture Society of St Petersburg in offering a prize for a dissertation on freeing serfs. This was won by J. J. L. Graslin (1768) with a work, said to be the first book on pure economics published in Russia, that is in agreement with the theory endorsed by Smith that division of labour promotes economic growth. This theory had been explored previously by Sir William Petty, Mandeville, James Harris, and Turgot (*WN* 13–14, n. 1).

10. PUBLISHING SCHOLAR AND ADMINISTRATOR

1. The identifications of the contributors to the first *Edinburgh Review* (1755–6) come from the preface to the 1816 reprint edited by Sir James Mackintosh, who drew on seemingly reliable Edinburgh tradition: Sher (1985: 68–72).
2. The Hume marginalia are described in Sotheby's catalogue, *English Literature and History*, 15 Dec. 1987, and discussed by Stewart (1990*c*: 5–8); I examined them by kind permission of the Nagoya Maruzen Department Store Bookshop on 26 Apr. 1990— see the Maruzen 1990 Bicentenary Smith Catalogue, No. 9.
3. An account of the stimulating effect of Watt's interest in science and technology, and the activities in his University workshop, was provided by a student of Smith's for a patent case in which Watt was involved: 'Professor Robison's Narrative of Mr Watt's Invention of the improved Engine', in Robinson and Musson (1969: 23–6). Smith was a subscriber for Watt's copying machine patented in 1780 (*Corr.* No. 207).
4. Tytler (1807: i.194–5 n.); however, William Leechman wrote to Ruat on 19 Nov. 1764 that Smith had 'returned to his Students all the fees he had received from them': SRO Hope of Raehills-Johnstone Papers, Bundle 897. Also, Smith reported to a University Meeting on 10 Jan. 1764 that he had returned the fees. His last class was held between 4 and 9 Jan., and the last Meeting he attended was on 10 Jan., so he must have left Glasgow soon afterwards (*LJ* 2).

11. THE MAKING OF *TMS*

1. Hume compared Strahan to those scholarly masters of early printing Aldus, Reuchlin, and Robert Estienne (*HL* ii.259), and he had an immense business, holding the property of more than 200 books in 1771. Authors he printed, as well as Hume and Smith, included Johnson, Fielding, Thomson, Gibbon, Robertson, Kames, Reid, and Smollett.

His printing ledgers in the British Library (Add. MSS 48800–1) reveal the print-runs of books he handled: Fielding's *Tom Jones*—10,000 copies in four editions; Thomson's *Seasons*—13,240 copies in seven editions and, even more startling, the *New Universal Dictionary*—134,000 copies in three editions in 1775. Burke estimated the reading public in England in 1790 at 80,000 persons (Brack, 1968). Professors David Raphael and David Raynor have helped me establish the print-runs for Smith's books as follows:

TMS: Edn. 1, 1759: (Apr.) 1,000, 6s. each; (Sept.) 750. Edn. 2, 1761: [?750]. Edn. 3, 1767: 750. Edn. 4, 1774: [?750]. Edn. 5, 1781: 750. Edn. 6, 1790: 1,000.

WN: Edn. 1, 1776 (Mar.): [?500], £1 16s. each. Edn. 2, 1777 (Nov.): 500. Edn. 3, 1784 (Oct.): 1,000, 18s. each. Additions and corrections to edn. 2, Oct. 500. Edn. 4, 1786 (Oct.): 1,250. Edn. 5, 1789 (Feb.): 1,500. Edn. 6, 1791 (Oct.): 2,000.

EPS: Edn. 1, 1795: 1,000.

Smith seems to have received £300 from Strahan and then Thomas Cadell, Andrew Millar's partner and successor as a publisher, for assigning them the property of *TMS* for each of the two fourteen-year periods of an author's lifetime permitted by the Copyright Act. If we go by the arrangements for *WN* edn. 2, editions after the first were printed at the publishers' cost, and Smith divided the profits with them (*Corr.* Nos. 179, 180). Henry Mackenzie was promised £300 for the property of *EPS* on publication, and another £200 if the book were to be printed again (Scott, 1937: 314). Hume widened the market after Hutcheson for Scottish Enlightenment publications, but had an umpromising beginning. After concluding a 'hasty Bargain' with John Noon in 1738 for £50 for the publication of the first two books of his *Treatise* in an edition of 1,000 copies, he prevailed on Andrew Millar to take over as his chief London publisher, beginning with the *Essay* (1742). For this book, he received from Millar £150–£200, it is thought, for an edition of 1,500. Later he was given £750 in 1756 for an edition of 1,750 copies of vol. ii of the *History of England* (1757) (Mossner, 1980: 114–15, 146, 314).

2. For Joseph Butler, see Sermons 2 and 3 of *Fifteen Sermons Preached at the Rolls Chapel* (1726) on the 'principle of reflection or conscience'; and the appendix to the *Analogy of Religion* (1736) entitled 'A Dissertation upon the Nature of Virtue', for discussion of a 'moral approving and disapproving faculty' (a manner of speaking, Butler tells us, taken from Epictetus), 'whether called conscience, moral reason, moral sense, or divine reason'; and for Kames, see *Essays on the Principles of Morality and Natural Religion* (1751) referring to Butler's concept of the 'marks of authority' of conscience and arguing that they are attached to the 'moral sense' as the 'voice of God within us which commands our strictest obedience' (pp. 61–4; *TMS* 164, n. 1).

3. Smith's name among others is found on a copy of Grotius' *De jure* (1670) in GUL, which has 'Ethics Class' inscribed on an old bookplate. Smith owned a copy of Barbeyrac's edition of *De jure* published in 1735 at Amsterdam, also historical works by Grotius, and a copy of *De Veritate Religionis Christianae*, namely, Le Clerc's edition published at Glasgow in 1745 (details in Mizuta). This was the book which Hutcheson lectured on at six o'clock every Sunday (Carlyle, 1973: 36–7).

12. CRITICISM OF *TMS*

1. Dr Michael Barfoot reported to the Vancouver Smith Symposium in Sept. 1990 that he had examined Smith's copy of Cullen's treatise, *First Lines of the Practice of Physic* (1784) in EUL (Mizuta), and had found in vol. iii that the faded pink silk bookmark was placed long ago at p. 272, where exercise as a corrective to hypochondriasis is discussed. Perhaps this is an indication that six years before his death Smith was still interested in Cullen's remedy for his disease.

2. The books referred to are as follows: George, Lord Lyttleton, *History of the Life of Henry II* (1767–71); Sir James Steuart (later Steuart-Denham), *Inquiry into the Principles of Political Oeconomy* (1767); William Robertson, *History of Charles V* (1769); and Adam Ferguson, *Institutes of Moral Philosophy* (1769) or, less likely, *An Essay on the History of Civil Society* (1767); all these books were known to be forthcoming some years before reaching print. Hume wrote to Elliot and Millar in 1763 about continuing his *History of England* beyond the 1688 Revolution, taking in King William III's reign (*HL* i.382–3).

3. Walter Scott claimed in notes for *BLJ* dated 1831 to have had the 'son of a bitch' anecdote from John Millar (*BLJ* v.369, n. 5); see Middendorf (1961). The David Callander notes on Hume and Smith state: '[Hume] would not see Dr Johnson at Edin[burgh], any more than Dr Adam Smith', referring no doubt to Boswell's attempts to get the Scottish literati to meet Johnson during his northern tour (EUL Laing MSS La. 451/2).

4. AUL, Birkwood Collection, MS 2131/3/I/28: p. 6, vertically written note in right margin: see Norton and Stewart-Robertson (1980; 1984); a transcript of the quoted passage is found in (1984: 317–18); further points of Reid's criticism of Smith are detailed in *Practical Ethics*, ed. Haakonssen (1990), e.g. at pp. 376–7 n. 30, rejection of Smith's restriction of natural jurisprudence to justice, and of justice to commutative justice. Something like Reid's moral (and epistemological) realism is advocated by Subroto Roy (1991), though the pedigree advanced for this viewpoint is not traced beyond the writer's Cambridge tutor, Remford Bambrough, Wittengenstein, and G. E. Moore. The link between Reid and Moore has been noted by Keith Lehrer (1991: 6, 163). Roy's professed aim is to break the 'Spell of Hume' deluding economists into moral scepticism, but no more than Reid is he willing to examine the case that Hume and Smith, to a certain extent, should be assessed as sceptical moralists offering a non-dogmatic method for identifying moral values.

5. Information and text kindly provided by Dr Norbert Waszek, Institut für Philosophie, Universität Erlangen-Nürnberg.

6. Kant, *Gesammelte Schriften* (1900–), xv.592—*Reflexion* 1355 (reference kindly provided by Mr Heiner F. Klemme, Philipps-Universität Marburg).

7. Voltaire, *Œuvres complètes*, ed. Beaumarchais (70 vols., Kehl, 1784–9), XXI.i.71, trans. Deidre Dawson (1991: 146).

13. TRAVELLING TUTOR

1. Haut-Garonne: Archives civiles, série C, MS C.2407 (Registre): *Procès-verbaux des États de Languedoc, 1497–1789* (Toulouse), ii.645–9; Bibliothèque municipale de Montpellier 25561.39; Segoudy, 1969, drawing on Dutil, 1911, and Appolis, 1937.
2. No trace has been found so far of a diary Smith is said to have kept in France, and reported as sold in the 1920s from the bookshop of a Mr Orr, George St., Edinburgh: Scott, 1940: 273.

14. INQUIRER INTO *WN*

1. Rousseau, *Discourse on the Origin of Inequality* (1755/1963: 170), pt. i, para. 17: 'there is another very specific quality which distinguishes [men and brutes], and which will admit of no dispute. This is the faculty of self-improvement, which, by the help of circumstances, gradually develops all the rest of our faculties, and is inherent in the species as in the individual'; *Émile* (1762/1963: 173), bk. iv, para. 10: 'The origin of our passions, the root and spring of all the rest, the only one which is born with man, which never leaves him as long as he lives, is self-love'; cf. in Smith, the self-love passages: *LJ*(A) vi.46, (B) 219, ED 2.23, and *WN* I.ii.2 (the famous sentence about owing our dinners to the self-love of the butcher, brewer, and baker); also those on self-improvement or 'bettering our condition, a desire which . . . comes with us from the womb, and never leaves us till we go into the grave' (*WN* II.iii.28 etc.)—the Glasgow editors cite parallel passages from Mandeville's *Fable of the Bees* (*WN* 341–2 nn. 29, 30), but Smith linked Rousseau with Mandeville in emphasizing human 'selfishness', though he argued that Rousseau 'softened' Mandeville's views (*Edinburgh Review* Letter 11, 14); Peter France (1990) discusses comparable analysis of selfishness in Rousseau and Smith; see, also Skinner (1990*b*) for analysis of Smith's views.
2. Meek (1973*b*: p. viii) refers to Thomas Kuhn, *The Structure of Scientific Revolutions* (1970: 117, 200), but acknowledges that Kuhn himself hesitates to take his paradigm concept over from the natural to the social sciences. Imre Lakatos (1970: 91–195) sought to mediate between Kuhn's position on scientific paradigms and Karl Popper's concept of scientific methodology in a fashion that some scholars have found useful for application to economics in general, and Adam Smith in particular. See also Latsis (1976), Blaug (1992), (O'Brien, 1975: 78–84; 1976), and Brown (1988).
3. Brown (1988: 33, 46) argues that Smith's model for inquiry was language rather than Newtonian mechanics—a point he accepts in Lindgren (1969: 897–915); Raphael (1988: 45) cautions us that Smith thought of scientific systems as 'imaginary machines', and was not arguing the economic order was sustained by 'quasi-gravitational forces'.
4. For an estimate of the reception given to Steuart and Smith by contemporary reviewers, see Rashid (1982: 70–9; 1990: 1–24; 1992: 129–52); on Smith confuting Steuart, see Anderson and Tollison (1984: 464–7); for a balanced view of Steuart's alleged 'mercantilism', see Skinner (1981: 20–42; 1988: 117–44). Comparing and contrasting Steuart and Smith as economists has interested Japanese scholars, including Nobaru Kobayashi, who has completed a systematic analysis of Steuart's *Principles*; see also

Kunohiro Watanabe and Shigeshi Wada in Tanaka (1990). On the relationship of Smith to Steuart and a historical survey of Smith's predecessors, see Hutchison (1988).

15. THE AMERICAN CRISIS AND *WN*

1. St Andrews obtained the endowment of the Chandos Chair of Medicine and Anatomy in 1721, but the University and the city were far too small in the 18th cent. to support medical teaching. The Chair was exploited, however, to sell medical degrees, albeit in some cases to notable people: Robert Whytt, Andrew Duncan, and John Brown (leaders of the Edinburgh medical school), Edward Jenner (pioneer of vaccination), and, in 1775, Jean-Paul Marat (French revolutionary): Cant (1992: 105, n. 2).
2. *HP* i.73–8, 334; ii.148–50, 457; but see Colley (1989: 80–1) for qualification of Namier's argument that the American crisis was not a concern in many constituencies—Colley cites Newcastle, where a local issue was linked to the Government's designs against the American colonists.

16. *EUGE! BELLE!* DEAR MR SMITH

1. Following normal 18th-cent. practice, dictated by the volume of books to be handled, the reviews present summaries of *WN*, incorporating extracts and, to the disappointment of modern scholars, adding rather little in the way of evaluative comment: Burke is said to have been responsible (according to Rae, 1965: 286) for the *Annual Register*'s notice (1776: 241–3), which mainly consists of Smith's Introduction and Plan of the Work; William Enfield was responsible for choosing and linking the *Monthly Review*'s serialized extracts (Jan.–June 1776: 299–308, 455–65; July: 16–27, 81–93); see, similarly, *Critical Review* (Mar. 1776: 193–200; Apr.: 258–64; May: 361–9; June: 425–33); cf. also *London Magazine*, *Scots Magazine*, *Edinburgh Weekly Magazine*, and *Hibernian Magazine* for the same period. Further details and analysis of these reviews are to be found in Rashid (1982: 64–85); and Teichgraeber (1987: 337–66)—Dr Teichgraeber kindly made available to me a typescript paper (1988) entitled, 'WN and Tradition: Adam Smith before Malthus', which deals with the reviewing of *WN* in the context of contemporary print culture.
2. The Newtonian organization of Smith's economic model is discerned by Governor Pownall in his Letter of 1776: 'you have . . . endeavoured to investigate *analytically* those principles, by which nature first moves and then conducts the operations of man in the individual, and in community: And then, next, by application of these principles to fact, experience, and institutions of men, you have endeavoured to deduce *synthetically*, by the most precise and measured steps of demonstration, those important doctrines of practice, which your very scientifick and learned book offers to the world of business' (*Corr.* app. A: p. 337).
3. Smith wrote that he had Turgot's 'friendship' and 'esteem', but they did not correspond, except for Turgot sending him a copy of his *Procès-verbal* of 1776 (*Corr.* 248);

his library did contain runs of the *Éphémérides du citoyen* (1766–9, 42 nos. in 15 vols.; Mizuta), which have the first two parts, at least, of the *Réflexions*; see Viner (1965: 128–32) and Groenewegen (1969: 271–87). Hume wrote to Turgot in Sept. 1766 about the 'very opulent Body' of merchants and shopkeepers and master-tradesmen, 'who employ their Stocks in Commerce' (*HL* ii.94), so the passage of hints about capital formation might have been from Hume to Turgot to Smith or more directly from Hume to Smith; see Perrot (1992: 238–55) on the economic thought of Turgot and the stimulus from Hume.

4. Hutchison (1976: 517; 1988: 362–75); there is a vast and ever-growing secondary literature on Smith's economics thought: the outline presented here owes much to O'Brien (1975: 29–37); Skinner (1979: 104–29, 151–83); Teichgraeber (1986: ch. 4); helpful but more technical commentary is to be found in Hollander (1973); Skinner and Wilson (1975: pt. ii—see esp. Adolph Lowe, 'Adam Smith's System of Equilibrium Growth' (pp. 415–54), and Nathan Rosenberg, 'Adam Smith on Profits: Paradox Lost and Regained' (pp. 377–89), as well as this scholar's excellent articles 'Some Institutional Aspects of *WN*' (1960: 557–70) and 'Adam Smith and the Stock of Moral Capital' (1990: 1–17); John Cunningham Wood (1983–4: ii and iii) brings together many important articles; Muller (1993) synthesizes recent scholarship on Smith, focusing on the relationship between moral philosophy and social science in his work, and offering an incisive review of the relevant intellectual history for understanding *WN*.

5. For commentary on the 'invisible hand' concept, see Macfie (1967: ch. 6), Viner (1972), Cropsey (1979: 165–76), Friedman and Friedman (1980), Friedman (1981), McMahon (1981), Ingrao and Israel (1990), Macleod (1990), Perrot (1992: 333–41), and Muller (1993: 86–92).

6. The colonists raised and trained the Continental army on the European (largely Prussian) model, and this force won crucial battles up to the British surrender at Yorktown in October 1781. Washington complained about the supporting patriot militia's indiscipline and cowardice in action, but its presence and growth eventually sapped British strength and morale, while the loyalist militia never remained effective for long: Shy in Kurtz and Hutson (1973: 141–2, 148–53). Without accurate information about the distinction of types of force in action in America, Smith correctly appreciated that militia remaining under arms over a considerable period of time could win a war against regulars.

17. DIALOGUE WITH A DYING MAN

1. This anecdote is alluded to in Thomas Tickell's elegy on the death of Addison, printed as part of a brief biography that prefaces his edition of Addison's works; Smith possessed a 1761 issue (Mizuta).

18. SETTLEMENT IN EDINBURGH

1. For a useful statistical and conceptual analysis of Customs Board functions with relevant data, see Anderson *et al.* (1985: 740–59); these writers did not understand, however, that there were differences between the Scottish and English systems; they did not investigate relevant Customs papers in the PRO, Kew; and the picture they paint of Smith as a 'hard-nosed regulator' and 'enforcer' of the mercantile system on the Board is incomplete.

19. COMMISSIONER OF CUSTOMS

1. The fight at Westminster for Irish free trade is recorded in the *Journals of the British House of Commons*, 37: 532; for the Irish side of the story, see O'Connell (1965: 129–67); on Dundas's role, see Fry (1992*a*: 63–4).
2. Mathias (1983: 91, 269), citing James Mill (East India Co.), James Deacon Hume (Customs Service and Board of Trade), and John McGregor (Board of Trade); account of abolition of the Navigation Acts in 1849 (p. 275); Rule (1992: 316).
3. A prominent tobacco merchant who spent five years in Virginia in the 1760s, and was the victualling agent in 1776 for shipping contracted to take troops to America; founder of the Glasgow Chamber of Commerce; and later a reformer and police magistrate in London: Devine (1975: 132, 179).

20. LITERARY PURSUITS

1. Besides marrying twice and raising a family of thirteen children, farming successfully in the Lothians and Aberdeenshire, writing voluminously on scientific agriculture, and other subjects such as chimneys and solar heat, editing and producing periodicals (including *The Bee*), and resisting the imposition of a poor's rate, Dr James Anderson interested himself in the American crisis and carried on a correspondence with Washington (Anderson, 1863: i.26–9).

21. TIMES OF HARDSHIP AND DISTRESS

1. Pitt's colleague, Lord Grenville, recorded in a letter to the Prime Minister dated 24 Oct. 1800 that about 1784, he and Pitt read *WN* together and 'became equally convinced of its arguments on political economy': Jupp (1985: 47–8), based on PRO, W. D. Adams MSS, 30/58/3/85.

22. LEGACY FOR LEGISLATORS

1. Relying on Jérôme de Lalande, 'Notice historique sur la vie et les ouvrages de Condorcet', *Mercure français*, 20 Jan. 1796: p. 156, Faccarello (1989) cautions that Condorcet may have let his name be used by Le Chapelier and de Peyssonel in connection with the *WN* summary in the *Bibliothèque de l'homme public*, but the wording was still Roucher's; Lluch (1989) deals with the translation by Carlos Martinez de Iruja of the alleged Condorcet summary (*Compendio de la obra intitulada Riqueza de las Naciones, hecho por el Marqués de Condorcet*, 1792, 1803, 1814), pointing out that Smith's name is not attached to it, perhaps because under his name *WN* was denounced in 1791 to the Holy Tribunal in Spain and banned the next year, while Condorcet's name as that of a marquis was acceptable despite his political leanings. The Spanish translator knew *WN* in English, and felt free to advise that the invisible hand had to be the 'hand of Government' in Spain, because there was no market mechanism driven by the profit motive to adjust supply and demand. The Spanish summary was more successful in presenting Smith's ideas than the incomplete translation of the whole book, shorn of its attacks on the Catholic church, published by Alonso Ortiz at Valladolid in 1794: see Lasarte (1976: 17–127); for additional details of *WN*'s Spanish and Latin American connection, see Smith (1957). Smith's economic ideas were known in Italy at first through articles in enlightened journals (e.g. Vicenza's *Giornale enciclopedico*) and debates in the Academies, then an Italian translation of the Blavet version of *WN* appeared in 1790, but the French original was most widely circulated: Gioli (1993: 225–49). See generally on this topic, Palyi (1928/1966: 180–233); Simon Schama traces the Dutch early reception and selective use of Smith's economic policy ideas, especially by the Grand Pensionary, Rutger Jan Schimmelpenninck, and the Finance Minister, Isaac Jan Alexander Gogel (1992: 258–61, 385–7, 500–3).

2. Hegel (1942; 1991); some regard *The Philosophy of Right* as the apotheosis of Stein's Prussian state, but in it Hegel explores the actuality of freedom in the family and political community, also in civil society where he sees competition and labour organization in a commercial phase resulting in the oppression of workers (paras. 243–8, echoing accounts in Ferguson and Smith of the devastating effects of division of labour). Hegel also adapts his 'cunning of Reason' concept from the arguments of Smith and Ferguson about unintended outcomes and spontaneous order arising from 'natural' human activities. In 1843 Marx began his great programme of social thought with a critique of Hegelian philosophy and, influenced by Feuerbach, he rejected the concept, promoted by the Scottish Enlightenment, of the 'general development of the human mind' as an explanation of legal relations and the forms of the state, choosing to focus on the 'material conditions of life, the sum total of which Hegel, following the example of the Englishmen and Frenchmen of the eighteenth century, combines under the name of "civil society" '. His next point reveals why he had to study Adam Smith, and why his treatment of alienation has Smithian as well as Hegelian overtones: the 'anatomy of civil society is to be sought in political economy' (Preface to *Critique of Political Economy*, 1859), quoted in McLellan (1972: 140); see also pp. 209–65, covering *inter alia* references to Smith in the 1844 Paris Manuscripts and the theme of alienation there—it is in these papers that Marx quotes with approval the aphorism of Engels that Smith is the 'Luther of economics'.

23. THE PRECARIOUSNESS OF THIS LIFE

1. Schama (1989: 149–62) illustrates the meaning of *sensibilité* as 'intuitive capacity for intense feeling', and the possession of '*un cœur sensible*' as the 'precondition for morality', principally by discussing the cultural importance of Rousseau's writings, *Émile* and *La Nouvelle Héloïse*; see also Kennedy (1989: 105–39), who explores sensibility in drama, music, and the visual arts of the period as well as its writing.
2. Paine (1984: 157: *Rights of Man*, pt. i); in 1796 S. A. Joersson issued a book entitled *Adam Smith Author of an Inquiry into the Wealth of Nations and Thomas Paine Author of the Decline and Fall of the English System of Finance*, allegedly published in Germany but more likely in France, devoted to the thesis that Smith's theories are to be found in a corrupt form in Paine's works. This book is perhaps the first extended criticism of *WN*.
3. Perhaps Rousseau got his revenge on the French, as Smith predicted, through the impact of *The Social Contract* on Robespierre, who took it with utter seriousness, including the chilling words: 'since every wrongdoer attacks the society's law, he becomes by his deed a rebel and a traitor to the country; by violating its law, he ceases to be a member of it; indeed, he makes war against it. And in this case, the preservation of the state is incompatible with *his* preservation; one or the other must perish; and when the guilty man is put to death, it is less as a citizen than as an enemy' (bk. ii, ch. 5); see Blum (1986) and Cobban (1973). Danton's humanity and Robespierre's inhumanity are stressed in Norman Hampson's biography (1978), also in Georg Büchner's play, *Dantons Tod* (1835), and Andrzej Wajda's film, *Danton* (1982). The Robespierre/Danton conflict, of course, is a theme in European drama: Howarth (1989).

24. THE GREAT CHANGE

1. The Scottish National Portrait Gallery has a canvas by an unknown artist (Muir-Romanes portrait), said to date back to *c*.1800; and there is one in the Scottish Museum of Antiquities from the same date, signed 'Ty. [= Tyron] Collopy', perhaps based on the Tassie medallions: Fay (1956: 162–5, app. by A. L. Macfie). Macfie thought the Muir portrait (illustration prefacing Fay's book) displayed Smith's 'essential qualities, strength and sweetness', absent from the Collopy one, which he characterized as a 'humourless treatment' of a 'precise, rather dandified old gentleman'. He also provides information about 19th-cent. busts and a statue of Smith.
2. See the accounts of Jevons and Marshall in Keynes (1963); also assessments of Smith in Winch (1971; 1978; 1993) and Blaug (1992).

Bibliography

I. MANUSCRIPTS

A. Britain

1. ABERDEEN

AUL, Birkwood Papers (Thomas Reid), 2131.3(III)(9), (10), (19), (20), (21), (25); 3.I.28—comments on TMS; 2131.4.II—inaugural lecture, Glasgow, 10 Oct. 1764; 2131.4.III—moral philosophy lecture.

City Archives: Burgh Register of Sasines, B1/1/62, AS's sale of tenement of foreland, Castlegate.

2. DORES, Inverness: Aldourie Castle (Col. A. E. Cameron), Count Windisch-Grätz to AS, 10 May, 12 July 1785; 2 July, 30 Oct. 1787.

3. EDINBURGH

City Chambers, Town Council Minutes, 6 June 1770: AS made burgess.

EUL:
Corr. of Allan Maconochie, Lord Meadowbanks, A-C, letter from Patrick Clason, 29 Mar. 1772.
Customs Board printed letter, 2 Sept. 1784, co-signed AS.
MS letter Adam Ferguson/Sir John Macpherson, 31 July 1790.
MS Dc.1.42, Nos. 5, 25, dialogues by Adam Ferguson.
MS Dc.5.126, Membership of Poker Club.
MS Dc.5.126* Poker Club Attendance.
MS Dc.6.III, Dugald Stewart's memorial about a jaunt with Burke and AS, 1784.
MS La.II.99⁷, Alexander Ross/Robert Simson, 5 Feb. 1745.
La.II.419, No. 2, John Logan/Alexander Carlyle, 25 Jan. 1780.
La.II.451/2, fos. 429–34, David Callander's anecdotes about AS.

NLS:
MS 646, fos. 1–11, Letter (copy) from ?Henry Mackenzie to Mr Carmichael, 1781.
MS 1005, fos. 14–16, John Home/Col. James Edmonstoune, 18 Feb. 1772.
MS 2537, Henry Mackenzie's Book of Anecdotes.
MS Acc. 4811, Minute Book of Kirkcaldy Kirk session, 1736–47.
MS 5319, fo. 34, Dugald Stewart/Thomas Cadell, 17 Aug. 1792; fos. 35–6, 13 Mar. 1793.
MS 11,009, 9 letters Gilbert Elliot of Minto/David Hume, from c.1761 to 11 July 1768.
MS 14,835, fos. 68 ff., Marsilio Landriani/Giacomo Melzi, 16 Aug. 1788, and Aug. 1788 to Marchese Longo.
MS 16,577, fo. 221, Alexander Dunlop/Charles Mackie, 15 Feb. 1739.
MS 16,696:74, John Home (the poet)/Lord Milton, Aug. 1756.

Hume MSS (old nos.) iii.35, Isaac Barré/DH, 4 Sept. 1765 iv.34–7, from Abbé Colbert du Seignelay de Castlehill: 4 Mar., 22 Apr. 1764; 26 Feb., 10 Apr. 1765. vi.36, Andrew Millar/DH, 22 Nov. 1766; 38, John Millar/DH, [1776]. vii.67, William Strahan/DH, 12 Apr. 1776.

Saltoun MSS, Andrew Fletcher/Lord Milton, 9 Jan. 1752.

SRO:

Service of Heirs, C22/60, AS retoured heir of father, 29 Mar. 1724; Register of Deeds, DUR vol. 251/1, fo. 195, registered disposition by AS in favour of cousin, David Douglas, 11 July 1790; Canongate Kirk Session Records, CH2/122/62, burial of AS, 22 July 1790; Edinburgh Register of Testaments, CC8/128/2, registered testament of AS.

Board of Customs:

Minute Books 1778–91, CE1/15–23.

Letter Books, CE56/2/5A-F (Dunbar outport), CE53/2/1–2 (Montrose), CE62/2/1–2 (Inverness), CE62/2/3–63/4/1 (Kirkcaldy).

Buccleuch Muniments, GD224/47/2, Mr Townshend's History of the Funds, AS's calculations.

Burn-Callander Papers, Preston Hall, Lothian: Corr. of John Callander, 7 July 1773 on.

Clerk of Penicuik MSS, John Clerk of Eldin's life of Robert Adam.

Hope of Raehills-Johnstone Papers, Bundle 269, Robert Dundas/Lord Hopetoun, 13 Feb. 1759; Hopetoun/Lord Findlater, 17 May 1759; William Ruat/Hopetoun, ?25, 26 May 1759; Bundle 897, William Leechman/Ruat, 19 Nov. 1764.

NRA:

(S) 631, Bute (Loudoun Papers), Bundle A/1319, letter from father AS, 6 Sept. 1720. 1454, Blair Adam Papers (Mr Keith Adam), Section 4/Bundle 3, William Adam/ brother John, 23 Jan. 1775; 4/3/20, William Adam/?, 1775.

4. GLASGOW

GUA:

26640, 26642, 26643, 26645, 26649, 26650, 26757, 26687: Minutes of University Meetings, 1751–64, 1787, and related documents.

GUL:

MS Bf. 73.-e.34, *Theses Philosophicae . . . Joanne Lowdoun Praeside*, Glasguae: Robert Saunders, 1708.

Buchan MSS, Isabella, Lady Buchan/Lord Buchan, 8 Mar. 1763.

Cullen MSS III:3, William Cullen's address on Dr John Clerk, Edinburgh Royal Infirmary, 24 June 1752.

MS Murray 49, 210, 225: John Loudoun's dictates on Logic, 1690s.

MS Gen. 71, 406, Compends of Logic from Loudoun's teaching, 1710s.

MS Gen. 146/1–30, Corr. Robert Simson/Matthew Stewart.

MS Gen. 451, AS's burgess ticket, Glasgow, 3 May 1762, signed by Provost Andrew Cochrane.

MS Gen. 520/6, William Richardson/Samuel Rose, 6 May 1788.

MS Gen. 1018/5, 12, Letters from Francis Hutcheson to Thomas Drennan.

MS Gen. 1035/2, Father AS's journal of voyage from Leith to Bordeaux.

MS Gen. 1035/21, 22, 31, Corr. of father AS, 1710s.

MS Gen. 1035/23, William Smith/father AS, 4 Apr. 1712.

MS Gen. 1035/33, father AS/Lilias Drummond Smith, 11 Apr. 1713.

MS Gen. 1035/43, 47, Dispositions, father AS to son, Hugh Smith, 30 Aug. 1718, 13 Nov. 1722.

MS Gen. 1035/44, 48, 50, 124, 125, father AS's accounts, 1713–22.

MS Gen. 1035/51, Marriage contract, father AS/Lilias Drummond, 13 Nov. 1710.

MS Gen. 1035/55, 56, Dr John Clerk/James Oswald, 24, 28 Jan. 1723.

MS Gen. 1035/61, 62, Inventories of father AS's books, and furniture, 20 Feb. 1723.

MS Gen. 1035/ 63, 69, 70, Corr. anent Hugh Smith, 1724.

MS Gen. 1035/71, Account: executors of father AS, 13 May 1735.

MS Gen. 1035/115, 119, 120 (sentinel), 123, Papers anent courts martial in Scotland, 1704–16.

MS Gen. 1035/152 (y), Walter S. Laurie, Camp on Charles Town Heights, 23 June 1775, and Characters of the Boston Patriots.

MS Gen. 1035/177, Thomas Cadell/Henry Mackenzie, 21 Dec. 1792.

MS Gen. 1035/178, John Millar/David Douglas, 10 Aug. 1790.

MS Gen. 1035/179, Alexander Wedderburn, Lord Loughborough/David Douglas, 14 Aug. 1790.

MS Gen. 1035/218, AS's deed of sale of Aberdeen property.

MS Gen. 1035/219, AS's Quaestor's accounts for books bought for GUL, 1758–60.

MS Gen. 1035/221, État des habit linge et effet appartenant à Monsieur Smith.

MS Gen. 1035/222, AS's burgess ticket, Musselburgh, 26 Sept. 1767.

MS Gen. 1035/228, Prices of corn, cattle, etc. in Scotland from the earliest accounts to the death of James V.

MS Gen. 1035/231, Observations sur les Revenues et les dépences de la Républiques de Gênes [Genoa].

MS Gen. 1097/11, Funeral expenses of father AS.

MS Access. 4467, Samuel Rose/Edward Foss, 17 July 1786.

MITCHELL LIBRARY, Buchan MSS, Baillie 32225, fos. 47–51, James Wodrow/Lord Buchan, June 1808; fos. 53–7, Samuel Kenrick/Wodrow, 27 Apr. 1808.

STRATHCLYDE UNIVERSITY, Anderson Library, Anderson MSS, John Anderson/ Gilbert Lang, 27 Dec. 1750.

MS 35.1, pp. 368–292, John Anderson's Commonplace Book, extracts from student's notes of early version of *LJ*.

Anderson MSS No. 2, pp. 1–32, Archibald Arthur, Essay on the Inducements to the Study of Natural Philosophy, May 1770.

5. KIRKCALDY

Town House, Kirkcaldy Council Records, 1/1/3, 1718–46; Town Council Minutes, 1/1/7, 1769–93; Burgh Court Book, 1/6/14, 1725–45; 1/6/17, 1766–92.

6. LONDON

BL:

Add. MSS 32,566, anecdotal material about Samuel Rogers.

32,567, about Lord Maitland.

32,574, Notebooks of Revd John Mitford, Vo. XVI, report of the finding of AS's fragment on justice.

48800; 48802A,B; 48803; 48806; 48809; 48810; 48815: William Strahan's Printing Ledgers, 1738–91.

Bentham MSS, Corr., George Wilson/Bentham, 4 Dec. 1789.

Egerton MS 2181, fo. 6, John Douglas's 'Remembrance' of his Balliol tutor, George Drake.

Mrs O. J. Fortescue MSS, Lord Grenville's 'Commentaries' on *WN*, ch. 3, pp. 13–30.

Dr Williams's Library, MS 24.157, Corr. Samuel Kenrick/James Wodrow, Nos. 14 (20 Dec. 1751), 16 (21 Jan. 1752), 60 (16 Mar. 1778), 92 (22 Feb. 1785).

HLRO, Journals of the House of Lords:

xxxi.535b (23 Mar. 1767), Act to enable the Duke of Buccleuch as minor to make a marriage settlement.

xxxv.445b (4 Apr. 1778) tax on servants.

xxxv.767b (1 June 1779) tax on houses given up.

xxxvi.23–5 (21–23 Dec. 1779) Irish Trade Bill.

xxxvii.156–170 (13–19 Aug. 1784) Act for the more effective prevention of Smuggling.

London University, Goldsmiths' Library of Economic Literature, MS, État actuel des finances, with AS's bookplate.

Royal College of Surgeons, Hunter Baillie Papers, vol. i, fo. 40, Gibbon/William Hunter.

PRO:

Chatham Papers, 30/48, vol. 31, fo. 11, Alexander Dalrymple/Lord Shelburne, 24 Nov. 1760.

Treasury, T1/589, CAPS 29555, Report on memorial anent warehousing, co-signed by AS, 18 June 1783.

Treasury, T1/589, xiv/0173, Report from Commissioners of Excise concerning smuggling, 4 Dec. 1783.

Treasury, T1/619, CAPS 29555, Letter from Scottish Board of Customs concerning smuggling, co-signed by AS, 7 Apr. 1785.

W. D. Adams MSS 30/58/3/84, Lord Grenville/Pitt, 24 Oct. 1800, recollecting they read *WN* together *c*.1784.

7. MANCHESTER

John Rylands Library, Benson Coll., William Leechman/George Benson, 9 Mar. 1743/4.

8. OXFORD

Balliol College:

Admissions: 4 July 1740, AS admitted as Commoner.

Battel Books, 1740–6.

MS Certificate of AS's election as Snell Exhibitioner, 11 Mar. 1740. Consent to admission, 4 July 1740.

MSS, College Lists, College Minutes, 1739–68.

Bodleian Library:
MS Add. c890, Robert Beatson/Ralph Griffiths, 26 July 1790.
Vet. AS d.430, *Ad Lectorem*, London, 1785—concerning Windisch-Grätz's competition for a universally applicable and foolproof property transfer deed.

Queen's College MSS 442 (1), 475, fos. 93 ff.: questions for completion of Oxford degrees compiled by Provost Joseph Smith.

University Matriculation Records: AS matriculated 7 July 1740.

B. Czech Republic

Klatovy, Statni oblastni archiv, Familienarchiv Windisch-Grätz, Karton 245, Nos. 1, 2: Alexander Fraser Tytler/W-G, 20 Feb. 1788, 11 Aug. 1788.

C. France

Montpellier:
Archives départmentales de l'Hérault, Archives Civiles: Série D. 199, Articles C4.668–C6.890.
Bibliothèque Municipale, MS 25561.39: Jean Segoudy, 'Histoire de Montpellier' (typescript 1969).

Paris: Bibliothèque Nationale, Fond Français MS 6680, S. P. Hardy (libraire parisien), 'Mes loisirs, ou Journal des évènements tels qu'ils parviennent à ma connaissance [1764–89]'.

Toulouse:
Archives départementales, Haut-Garonne, Archives Civiles, Série C, MS C.2407 (Registre): *Procès-verbaux des États de Languedoc, 1497–1789* (Toulouse) ii.645–9, 1764–5.
Bibliothèque Municipale, Annales des Capitoules.

D. Luxemburg

Kirchberg, Europäische Schule (Mr David Christie), J. T. Stanley, later Lord Stanley/Dr Scott of Edinburgh, 20 August 1790.

E. Switzerland

Berne, Bürgerbibliothek MSS, Letters from Lord Kames to Daniel Fellenberg: 1 Feb. 1763, 20 Apr. 1773.
Coppet, Château de, Necker Papers.
Geneva, University Bibliothèque, Bonnet MSS:

Charles Bonnet/H. B. Merian, 2 Sept. 1785—AS's relationship with Hume.

Patrick Clason/Bonnet, 9 July 1787—account of AS in London, successfully cut for haemorrhoids *à un point effrayant* by John Hunter. Pitt the Younger is seeing AS often and Clason suspects he will keep AS in London to be his mentor.

F. USA

Ann Arbor, University of Michigan, William L. Clements Library, Buccleuch MSS, GD224/296/1, 11 letters Charles Townshend/3rd Duke of Buccleuch, 1761–7.

New Haven, Yale University Library, Boswell Papers, Lord Hailes/Boswell, 13 Feb. 1763.

New York, Pierpont Library, Pulteney Corr. v. 6, Adam Ferguson/William Pulteney.

San Marino, Calif., Huntington Library:
Loudoun Papers, LO 9409–12, 9047, Corr. of father AS.
Montagu Corr., MO 480, 489: James Beattie/Elizabeth Montagu, 23 Apr. 1776, Hugh Blair/Montagu, 8 June 1776.

Philadelphia, American Philosophical Society, Benjamin Vaughan/Lord Shelburne, 23 Jan. 1781; B P93, Richard Price/?, 1790.

II. EIGHTEENTH-CENTURY NEWSPAPERS AND PERIODICALS

Allgemeine Literatur-Zeitung.
L'Année littéraire.
Annual Register.
The Bee.
Bibliothek der schönen Wissenschaften und der freyen Künste.
Bibliothèque de l'homme public.
Bibliothèque des sciences et des beaux arts.
Caledonian Mercury.
Critical Review.
Edinburgh Advertiser.
Edinburgh Courant.
Edinburgh Mercury.
Edinburgh Review.
Edinburgh Weekly Magazine.
English Review.
Éphémérides du citoyen.
European Magazine and London Review.
Frankfurter Gelehrte Anzeigen.
Gentleman's Magazine.
Giornale enciclopedico.
Glasgow Courier.

Glasgow Journal.
Glasgow Mercury.
Göttingische Anzeigen von gelehrten Sachen.
Hibernian Magazine.
Journal de l'agriculture.
Journal encyclopédique.
Journal littéraire.
Journal de Paris.
Journal des Savants.
London Chronicle.
London Magazine.
London Oracle and Public Advertiser.
The Lounger.
Mémoires de l'Academie des Belles Lettres.
Mercure Français.
The Mirror.
Monthly Review.
Münchner Gelehrte Anzeigen.
New Evening Post.
Philological Miscellany.
Scots Magazine.
Teutsche Merkur.
The Times.

III. WRITINGS OF ADAM SMITH

1. Manuscripts

a. Corr. (found after 2nd edn. published, 1987)

AS/William Cullen, Aug. 1773: GUL Cullen MS 242.

/Thomas Cadell, 27 June 1776, 18 Nov. 1789: Staatsbibliothek, Preussischer Kulturbesitz, Berlin, Sig. Sammlung Darmstädter 2g 1776 (1).

/Lord Stanhope, 15 Apr. 1777: Far Eastern Books, Tokyo (28 Feb. 1995).

/Count Windisch-Grätz, 27 May 1785, 17 Jan. 1786, 26 Jan. 1788: Klatovy, Czech Republic, Statni oblastni archiv—Familienarchiv Windisch-Grätz, Karton 246.

4 July 1785: Aldourie Castle, Dores, Inverness (Col. A. E. Cameron).

/Henry Beaufoy, 14 Nov. 1786, 29 Jan. 1787: Piero Sraffa *Collection* B5/3, 4, Trinity College, Cambridge.

b. Documents

Smith's Thoughts on the State of the Contest with America, Feb., 1778: Ann Arbor, Mich., William L. Clements Library, Rosslyn MSS.

Report to the Lords of Treasury on uniform table of Customs fees, etc., 24 May 1782: PRO, Kew, Treasury T1/570 CAPS 29552.

Will, 6 Feb. 1790: SRO, Warrants of Register of Deeds: RD13/130 Box 464.

c. Texts

Fragment of lecture on justice (pre-1759): GUL MS Gen. 1035/227.

ED of *WN* (pre-April 1763): SRO, Duke of Buccleuch's Muniments, GD224/33/4.

Fragments (FA, FB) of *WN* (1760s): GUL MS Gen. 1035/229.

LJ(A), 1762–3: GUL MS Gen. 94/1–6.

LRBL, 1762–3: GUL MS Gen. 95/1, 2.

LJ(B), 1763–4/1766: GUL MS Gen. 109.

'Of the Affinity between certain English and Italian Verses', 1783: GUL MS Gen. 1035/226.

d. Missing

Paper enumerating Smith's leading principles, both political and literary, 1755: Stewart, iv.25.

Diary kept by Adam Smith in France, 1764–6: sold by Mr Orr, Bookseller, George St., Edinburgh, *c.*1920–5 (Scott, 1940: p. 273).

e. Doubtful

Thoughts Concerning Banks, and the Paper Currency of Scotland (Edinburgh, Nov. 1763); *Scots Magazine* (Dec. 1763) (Gherity, 1993).

2. Printed Books and Articles

1748, 2 Dec. Preface to *Poems on Several Occasions*, by William Hamilton. Glasgow: Robert & Andrew Foulis; (repr. 1758), with a dedication by Smith to 'Mr. William Craufurd, Merchant in Glasgow'.

1755, 1 Jan.–July. Review, 'A Dictionary of the English Language by Samuel Johnson', *Edinburgh Review* No. 1.

1755, July–1756, Jan. 'A Letter to the Authors of the Edinburgh Review', No. 2.

1759. *The Theory of Moral Sentiments.* London: A. Millar; Edinburgh: A. Kincaid & J. Bell.

   1761. 2nd edn., rev.

   1767. 3rd edn., enlarged as *TMS. To which is added A Dissertation on the Origin of Languages.*

   1774. 4th edn., retitled *TMS; or, An Essay towards an Analysis of the Principles by which Men naturally judge concerning the conduct and Character, first of their Neighbours, and afterwards of themselves.*

   1781. 5th edn.

1791. 6th edn., considerably enlarged and corrected, 2 vols.

1809. 12th edn., *TMS Enriched with a Portrait and Life of the Author*. Glasgow: R. Chapman.

1761. *Considerations concerning the first formation of Languages, and the different genius of original and compounded Languages*, in *Philological Miscellany*. London: printed for the Editor [William Rose] and sold by T. Beckett & P. A. Dehondt. i.440–79.

1776. *An Inquiry into the Nature and Causes of the Wealth of Nations*, 2 vols. London: W. Strahan & T. Cadell.

1778. 2nd edn. rev.

1784. 3rd edn. with 'Additions and Corrections' and index, 3 vols.

1786. 4th edn.

1789. 5th edn.

1791. 6th edn.

1795. *Essays on Philosophical Subjects . . . To Which is prefixed An Account of the Life and Writings of the Author, by Dugald Stewart*, ed. Joseph Black and James Hutton. London: T. Cadell Jun. & W. Davies; Edinburgh: W. Creech.

1896. *Lectures on Justice, Police, Revenue and Arms, Delivered in the University of Glasgow by Adam Smith, Reported by a Student in 1763*, ed. Edwin Cannan. Oxford: Clarendon Press.

1950. *The Wealth of Nations*, ed. Edwin Cannan, 6th edn., 2 vols. 1904. London: Methuen, pb.

1963. *Lectures on Rhetoric and Belles Lettres delivered in the University of Glasgow by Adam Smith, Reported by a Student in 1762–63*, ed. John M. Lothian. London: Nelson.

3. Works

1811–12. *The Works of Adam Smith. With an Account of his Life and Writings by Dugald Stewart*. 5 vols. London: T. Cadell & W. Davies; Edinburgh: W. Creech.

1976–87. *The Glasgow Edition of the Works and Correspondence of Adam Smith*. Oxford: Clarendon Press. (Citations from this edition are given in the biography according to the scheme in the Abbreviations, prelims above.)

4. Translations

i. French

TMS

1764. *Métaphysique de l'âme: ou théorie des sentiments moraux*. Traduite de l'angloise de M. Adam Smith . . . par M.[Marc-Antoine Eidous] 2 vols. Paris: Briasson.

1774–7. *Théorie des sentiments moraux*; traduction nouvelle de l'anglois de M. Smith, ancien professeur de philosophie à Glasgow; avec une table raisonnée des matières contenues dans l'ouvrage, par M. l'abbé Blavet. Paris: Valade.

1798. *Théorie des sentiments moraux*; traduite de l'édition 7ième [1792] par Sophie de Grouchy, Marquise de Condorcet, avec *Considérations sur la première formation des langues*, et un appendice, '[Huit] Lettres à Cabanis sur la sympathie'. Paris: F. Buisson.

WN

1781. *Recherches sur la nature et les causes de la richesse des nations*. Traduit de l'anglois par M. l'abbé Bl[avet]. 3 vols. Paris.

1786. *Recherches sur la nature et les causes de la richesse des Nations*. Traduit de l'anglois de M. Smith [par l'abbé J.-L. Blavet]. London and Paris: Poinçot.

1790. *Recherches sur la nature et les causes de la richesse des nations*, traduites de l'anglois de M. Smith, sur la quatrième édition [1786], par M. Roucher; et suivies d'un volume de notes [*which never appeared*] par M. le marquis de Condorcet, de l'Académie Françoise, et secrétaire perpétuel de l'Académie des Sciences. Paris: Buisson.

1802. *Recherches sur la nature et les cause de la richesse des nations*. Traduction nouvelle, avec des notes et observations, par G. Garnier. 5 vols. Paris: Agasse. Avec portrait en buste.

1843. *Recherches sur la nature et les causes de la richesse des nations*. French translation by the Comte Germain Garnier, completely revised and corrected and prefixed with a biographical notice by Blanqui. With commentaries by Buchanan, G. Garnier, McCulloch, Malthus, J. Mill, Ricardo, Sismondi; to which is added notes by Jean-Baptiste Say and historical explanations by Blanqui. 2 vols. Paris.

EPS

1797. *Essais philosophiques*, par Adam Smith, Docteur en droit, de la Société Royale de Londres, de celle d'Edimbourg, etc. etc. Précédés d'un précis de sa vie et de ses écrits; par Dugald Stewart, de la Société Royale d'Edimbourg. Traduits de l'anglais par P. Prevost, professeur de philosophie à Genève de l'Académie de Berlin, de la Société des Curieux de la Nature, et de la Société d'Edimbourg. Première partie. Paris: Agasse. (Avec portrait en buste, B.L. Prevost, *sculp.*)

Languages

1796. *Considérations sur la première formation des langues, et le différent génie des langues originales et composées*. Traduit par A. M. H. B[oulard]. Paris.

ii. German

TMS

1770. *Theorie der moralischen Empfindungen*, übers. d. 3. A. [1767] v. Christian Günther Rautenberg. Braunschweig.

1791. *Theorie der sittlichen Gefühle*, übers. v. Ludwig Theobul Kosegarten. 2 vols. (vol. ii containing the additions to edn. 6 1790 and an account of Kant's moral philosophy). Leipzig.

1926. *Theorie der ethischen Gefühle*, übers. v. Walther Eckstein [from ed. 6 but including variants in earlier edns.]. 2 vols. Leipzig.

WN

1776–8. *Untersuchungen der Natur und Ursachen von Nationalreichthümern*. Aus dem Englischen, übers. v. J. F. Schiller u. C. A. Wichmann. 2 vols. Leipzig: Weidmanns Erben u. Reich.

1794–6. *Untersuchung über die Natur und die Ursachen des Nationalreichthums.* Aus dem Engl. d. 4. A. [from 4th edn. 1786], neu übers. von Christian Garve, 4 in 2 vols. Breslau: W. G. Korn.

IV. SECONDARY SOURCES

Aarsleff, Hans (1982). *From Locke to Saussure: Essays on the Study of Language and Intellectual History.* London: Athlone Press.

Adam, William (1980). *Vitruvius Scoticus,* 1812, fac. edn., intro. James Simpson. London: Paul Harris.

Adams, Walter, and Brock, James W. (1993). *Adam Smith Goes to Moscow: A Dialogue on Radical Reform.* Princeton, NJ: Princeton Univ. Press.

Addison, W. Innes (1901). *The Snell Exhibiutions from the University of Glasgow to Balliol College, Oxford.* Glasgow: J. Maclehose.

—— (1913). *The Matriculation Albums of the University of Glasgow, 1728–1858.* Glasgow: J. Maclehose.

Alekseyev, Mikhail P. (1937). 'Adam Smith and His Russian Admirers of the Eighteenth Century', in Scott (1937: app. vii).

Alexander, Gregory S., and Skąpska, Grażyna (eds.) (1994). *A Fourth Way? Privatization, Property, and the Emergence of New Market Economies.* New York: Routledge.

Allais, Maurice (1992). 'The General Theory of Surpluses as a Formalization of the Underlying Theoretical Thought of Adam Smith, His Predecessors and His Contemporaries', in Michael Fry (ed.), *Adam Smith's Legacy.* London: Routledge.

Allen, Revd Dr (1750). *An Account of the Behaviour of Mr James Maclaine, from the Time of his Condemnation to the Day of Execution, October 3, 1750.* London: J. Noon & A. Millar.

Allgemeine Deutsche Biographie (1875–1912). 56 vols.

Anderson, Gary M. (1988). 'Mr Smith and the Preachers: The Economics of Religion in WN', *Journal of Political Economy,* 96: 1066–88.

—— Shughart, William F., II, and Tollison, Robert D. (1985). 'Adam Smith in the Customhouse', *Journal of Political Economy,* 93: 740–59.

—— and Tollison, Robert D. (1982). 'Adam Smith's Analysis of Joint Stock Companies', *Journal of Political Economy,* 90: 1237–55.

—— —— (1984). 'Sir James Steuart as the Apotheosis of Mercantilism and His Relation to Adam Smith', *Southern Economic Journal,* 51: 464–7.

Anderson, R. G. W. (1986). 'Joseph Black', in Daiches *et al.* (1986: 93–114).

Anderson, Robert D., and Khosla, S. Dev (1994). *Competition Policy as a Dimension of Economic Policy: A Comparative Perspepctive.* Ottawa: Bureau of Competition Policy, Industry Canada.

Anderson, William (1863). *The Scottish Nation.* 2 vols. Edinburgh: Fullarton.

Ando, Takaho (1993). 'The Introduction of Adam Smith's Moral Philosophy to French Thought', in Mizuta and Sugiyama (1993: 207–9).

Anikin, Andrei (1988). *Russian Thinkers: Essays on Socio-Economic Thought in the 18th and 19th Centuries,* trans. Cynthia Carlile. Moscow: Progress Publishers.

—— (1990). *Der Weise aus Schottland: Adam Smith*, trans. Günther Wermusch. Berlin: Verlag der Wirtschaft.

Anon. (1658). *The Whole Duty of Man.*

Anon. (1809). Life of Smith, prefacing *TMS* 12th edn. Glasgow: R. Chapman.

Appleby, Joyce Oldham (1980). *Economic Thought and Ideology in Seventeenth-Century England*. Princeton, NJ: Princeton Univ. Press.

Appolis, Émile (1937). *Les États de Languedoc au XVIIIᵉ siècle.*

Arnot, Hugh (1788). *The History of Edinburgh*, 2nd edn. Edinburgh.

Bagehot, Walter (1899). 'Adam Smith as a Person', in Richard Holt Hutton (ed.), *Biographical Studies*. London: Longmans, Green.

Bailyn, Bernard (1973). 'The Central Themes of the American Revolution: An Interpretation', in Kurtz and Hutson (1973: 9–13).

—— (1992). *The Ideological Origins of the American Revolution*. Cambridge, Mass.: Harvard Univ. Press.

Baker, Keith (1975). *Condorcet: From Natural Philosophy to Social Mathematics*. Chicago: Univ. of Chicago Press.

—— (1989). 'L'Unité de la pensée de Condorcet', in Crépel *et al.* (1989: 515–24).

—— (1990). *Inventing the French Revolution: Essays on French Political Culture in the Eighteenth Century*. Cambridge: Cambridge Univ. Press.

Bakhtin, Mikhail Mikhailovich (1975/1981). *The Dialogic Imagination: Four Essays*, ed. Michael Holquist, trans. Caryl Emerson and Michael Holquist. Austin: Univ. of Texas Press.

Banke, Niels (1955). 'Om Adam Smiths Forbindelse med Norge og Danmark', *Nationaløkonomisk Tidsskrift* (trans. Mogens Kay-Larsen, 1967): 170–8.

Barfoot, Michael (1990). 'Hume and the Culture of Science in the Early Eighteenth Century', in Stewart (1990c: 151–90).

—— (1991). 'Dr William Cullen and Mr Adam Smith: A Case of Hypochondriasis?', *Proceedings of the Royal College of Physicians of Edinburgh*, 21: 204–14.

Barker-Benfield, G. J. (1992). *The Culture of Sensibility: Sex and Society in Eighteenth-Century Britain*. Chicago: Univ. of Chicago Press.

Barthes, Roland (1968/1986). 'The Death of the Author', in *The Rustle of Language*, trans. Richard Howard. New York: Farrar, Straus & Giroux.

Barton, J. L. (1986). 'Legal Studies', in Sutherland and Mitchell (1986: 593–605).

Bazerman, Charles (1993). 'Money Talks: The Rhetorical Project of the *Wealth of Nations*' in Henderson *et al.* (1993: 173–99).

Beaglehole, J. C. (1968). *The Exploration of the Pacific*, 3rd edn. Stanford, Calif.: Stanford Univ. Press.

—— (1974). *The Life of James Cook*. Stanford, Calif.: Stanford Univ. Press.

Beard, Geoffrey (1981). *Robert Adam's Country Houses*. Edinburgh: John Bartholemew.

Beattie, James (1770). *An Essay on the Nature and Immutability of Truth, in Opposition to Sophistry and Skepticism*. Edinburgh: A. Kincaid & J. Bell.

—— (1771, 1774). *The Minstrel*. London. E. & C. Dilly.

Becker, Carl L. (1964). 'Benjamin Franklin', in *The American Plutarch*, ed. Edward T. James, intro. Howard Mumford Jones. New York: Scribner's.

Bejaoui, René (1994). *Voltaire avocat: Calas, Sirven et autres affaires*. Paris: Tallandier.

Bentham, Jeremy (1968–89). *Correspondence*, ed. Timothy L. S. Sprigge *et al.* 9 vols. London: Athlone Press; Oxford: Clarendon Press.

Berkeley, Edmund, and Berkeley, Dorothea S. (1974). *Dr John Mitchell*. Durham, NC: Univ. of N. Carolina Press.

Berkeley, George (1901). *Works*, ed. Alexander Campbell Fraser. 4 vols. Oxford: Clarendon Press.

Bien, David (1962). *The Calas Affair: Persecution, Toleration, and Heresy in Eighteenth-Century Toulouse*. Princeton, NJ: Princeton Univ. Press.

Bisset, Robert (1800). *Life of Burke*, 2nd edn. London: George Cawthorn.

Black, R. D. Collison (ed.) (1986). *Ideas in Economics. Proceedings of Section F (Economics) of the British Association for the Advancement of Science, Strathclyde, 1985*. London: Macmillan.

Blaicher, Günther, and Glaser, Brigitte (eds.) (1994). *Anglistentag 1993 Eichstätt*. Tübingen: Niemeyer.

Blair, Hugh (1765). *A Critical Dissertation on the Poems of Ossian, the Son of Fingal*, 2nd edn. London: T. Beckett & P. A. de Hondt.

—— (1781–94). *Sermons*. 4 vols. London: W. Strahan.

—— (1812). *Lectures on Rhetoric and Belles Lettres*, 12th edn. 2 vols. London: T. Cadell *et al.*

Blaug, Mark (ed.) (1991). *François Quesnay* (Pioneers in Economics, 1.). Cheltenham: Edward Elgar.

—— (1992). *The Methodology of Economics, or How Economists Explain*, 2nd edn. Cambridge: Cambridge Univ. Press.

Blum, Carol (1986). *Jean-Jacques Rousseau and the Republic of Virtue*. Ithaca, NY: Cornell Univ. Press.

Bolgar, R. R. (1977). *The Classical Heritage and Its Beneficiaries*. Cambridge: Cambridge Univ. Press.

Bonar, James (1932). *A Catalogue of the Library of Adam Smith*, 2nd edn. London: Macmillan.

Bond, R. C. (1984). 'Scottish Agricultural Improvement Societies, 1723–1835', *Review of Scottish Culture*, 1: 70–90.

Bongie, L. L. (1958). 'David Hume and the Official Censorship of the "Ancient Régime" ', *French Studies*, 12: 234–46.

—— (1965). *David Hume: Prophet of Counter-Revolution*. Oxford: Clarendon Press.

Bonnefous, Raymonde *et al.* (eds.) (1964). *Guide littéraire de la France*. Paris: Hachette.

Book of the Old Edinburgh Club (1924).

Boswell, James (1950–). Yale Editions of the Private Papers and Correspondence:

    (*a*) Trade Edition of Journals, ed. F. A. Pottle *et al.*: (1950) *London Journal, 1762–3*. (1952) *Boswell in Holland, 1763–4*. (1952) *Portraits*, by Sir Joshua Reynolds. (1953) *Boswell on the Grand Tour: Germany and Switzerland, 1764*. (1955) *Boswell on the Grand Tour: Italy, Corsica, and France, 1765–6*. (1957) *Boswell in Search of a Wife, 1766–9*. (1960) *Boswell for the Defence, 1769–74*. (1961) *Boswell's Journal of a Tour to the Hebrides with Samuel Johnson, LL.D.* (1963) *Boswell: The Ominous Years, 1774–6*. (1970) *Boswell in Extremes, 1776–82*. (1977) *Boswell, Laird of Auchinleck, 1778–82*. (1981) *Boswell: The Applause of the Jury, 1782–5*. (1986) *Boswell: The English Experiment, 1785–9*. (1989) *Boswell: The Great Biographer, 1789–95*. New York: McGraw-Hill; London: Heinemann (some different dates).

    (*b*) Research Edition of Boswell's Corr.: (1966) *Corr. of JB and John Johnson of Grange*, ed. R. S. Walker. (1969) *Corr. and Other Papers Relating to the Making of the 'Life of Johnson'*, ed. Marshall Waingrow. (1976) *Corr. of JB with Certain Members of The Club*, ed. C. N. Fifer. (1986) *Corr. of JB with David Garrick, Edmund Burke, and Edmond Malone*, ed. P. S. Baker *et al.* New York: McGraw-Hill. General Editor: Claude Rawson: (1993) *General Corr. of JB 1766-9*, ed. R. C. Cole *et al.* (forthcoming) *Boswell's Estate Corr. 1762-95*, ed. N. P. Hankins and John Strawthorn. (forthcoming) *Corr. between JB and William Johnson Temple*, ed. Thomas Crawford.

   (*c*) Research Edition of Papers: (forthcoming) *An Edition of the Original Manuscript of Boswell's 'Life of Johnson'*, ed. Marshall Waingrow. Edinburgh: Edinburgh Univ. Press/New Haven, Conn.: Yale Univ. Press.

—— (1992). *The Journals of JB 1762-95*, sel. and intro. John Wain. London: Mandarin.

Bouguer, Pierre (1749). *La Figure de la terre determinée par les observations de MM. Bouguer et de la Condamine, avec une relation abrégée de ce voyage par P. Bouguer.* Paris: Jombert.

Bouwsma, William J. (1988). *John Calvin: A Sixteenth-Century Portrait.* New York: Oxford Univ. Press.

Boyle, Nicholas (1992). *Goethe: The Poet and the Age*, i: *The Poetry of Desire: 1749-1790.* Oxford: Oxford Univ. Press.

Braudel, Fernand (1982). *The Wheels of Commerce*, trans. Siân Reynolds. London: Fontana.

—— (1988). *The Identity of France*, i: *History and Environment*, trans. Siân Reynolds. New York: Harper & Row.

—— (1991). *The Identity of France*, ii: *People and Production*, trans. Siân Reynolds. London: Fontana.

Brewer, John, and Porter, Roy (eds.) (1993). *Consumption and the World of Goods.* London: Routledge.

Brock, C. H. (ed.) (1983). *William Hunter, 1718-1783: A Memoir by Samuel Foart Simmons and John Hunter.* Glasgow: Glasgow Univ. Press.

Brock, William R. (1982). *Scotus Americanus: A Survey of the Sources for Links between Scotland and America in the 18th Century.* Edinburgh: Edinburgh Univ. Press.

Brown, A. H. (1974). 'S. E. Desnitsky, Adam Smith, and the Nakaz of Catherine II', *Oxford Slavonic Papers*, n.s., 7: 42-59.

—— (1975). 'Adam Smith's First Russian Followers', in Skinner and Wilson (1975: 247-73).

Brown, I. A. (1987). 'Modern Rome and Ancient Caledonia: The Union and the Politics of Scottish Culture', in Hook (1987).

Brown, Iain Gordon (1989). *Building for Books: The Architectural Evolution of the Advocates' Library, 1689-1925.* Aberdeen: Aberdeen Univ. Press.

Brown, Kevin L. (1992). 'Dating Adam Smith's Essay "Of the External Senses" ', *Journal of the History of Ideas*, 53: 333-7.

Brown, Maurice (1988). *Adam Smith's Economics: Its Place in the Development of Economic Thought.* London: Croom Helm.

Brown, Richard Maxwell (1973). 'Violence and the American Revolution', in Kurtz and Hutson (1973: 81-120).

Brown, Vivienne (1993). 'Decanonizing Discourses: Textual Analysis and the History of Economic Thought', in Henderson *et al.* (1993: 64-84).

—— (1994). *Adam Smith's Discourse: Canonicity, Commerce, and Conscience.* London: Routledge.

Brühlmeier, Daniel (1988). *Die Rechts- und Staatslehre von Adam Smith und die Interessentheorie der Verfassung*. Berlin: Duncker & Humblot.

Bryant, Christopher G. A. (1993). 'Social Self-Organisation, Civility and Sociology: A Comment on Kumar's "Civil Society" [1993]', *British Journal of Sociology*, 44: 397–401.

Buchanan, David (1975). *The Treasure of Auchinleck*. London: Heinemann.

Burke, Edmund (1958–70). *Correspondence*, ed. Thomas W. Copeland *et al.* 9 vols. Cambridge: Cambridge Univ. Press; Chicago: Univ. of Chicago Press.

Burns, Robert (1931). *Letters*, ed. J. De Lancey Ferguson. 2 vols. Oxford: Clarendon Press.

—— (1968). *The Poems and Songs of Robert Burns*, ed. James Kinsley. Oxford: Clarendon Press.

Burt, Edward (1815). *Letters from a Gentleman in the North of Scotland* [*c*.1730]. 2 vols. London: Gale, Curtis, & Fenner. Repr. Edinburgh: Donald, 1974.

Burton, John Hill (ed.) (1849). *Letters of Eminent Persons Addressed to David Hume*. Edinburgh & London: William Blackwood.

Butler, Joseph (1726). *Fifteen Sermons Preached at the Rolls Chapel*. London: J. & J. Knapton.

—— (1736). *Analogy of Religion*. London: J. & P. Knapton.

Cadell, Patrick, and Matheson, Ann (1989). *For the Encouragement of Learning: Scotland's National Library, 1689–1989*. Edinburgh: HMSO.

Cairns, John W. (1992). 'The Influence of Smith's Jurisprudence on Legal Education in Scotland', in Jones and Skinner (1992: 168–89).

Campbell, R. H. (1961). *Carron Company*. Edinburgh: Oliver & Boyd.

—— (1966). 'Diet in Scotland: An Example of Regional Variation', in T. C. Barker *et al.* (eds.), *Our Changing Fare*. London: MacGibbon & Kee.

—— (1990). 'Scotland's Neglected Enlightenment', *History Today*, 40: 22–8.

—— (1992). *Scotland since 1707: The Rise of an Industrial Society*. Edinburgh: Donald.

—— and Skinner, Andrew S. (eds.) (1982*a*). *The Origins and Nature of the Scottish Enlightenment*. Edinburgh: Donald.

—— —— (1982*b*). *Adam Smith*. London: Croom Helm.

Campbell, T. D. (1971). *Adam Smith's Science of Morals*. London: Allen & Unwin.

—— and Ross, I. S. (1981). 'The Utilitarianism of Adam Smith's Policy Advice', *Journal of the History of Ideas*, 42: 73–92.

—— —— (1982). 'The Theory and Practice of the Wise and Virtuous Man: Reflections on Adam Smith's Response to Hume's Deathbed Wish', *Studies in Eighteenth-Century Culture*, 11: 65–75.

Cant, R. G. (1992). *The University of St Andrews: A Short History*, 3rd edn. St Andrews Univ. Library.

Cant, Ronald G. (1981). 'David Stewart Erskine, 11th Earl of Buchan: Founder of the Society of Antiquaries of Scotland', *The Scottish Antiquarian Tradition*, ed. A. S. Bell. Edinburgh: John Donald.

Carlyle of Inversek, Alexander (1760). *The Question Relating to a Scots Militia Considered*. Edinburgh: G. Hamilton & J. Balfour. Repr. in Mizuta (1977: 28–54).

—— (1910). *The Autobiography of Dr Alexander Carlyle of Inveresk*, ed. John Hill Burton. London: T. N. Foulis.

—— (1973). *Anecdotes and Characters of the Times*, ed. James Kinsley. London: Oxford Unv. Press.

Carlyle, Thomas (1881). *Reminiscences*, ed. J. A. Froude. 2 vols. London: Longmans.

Chalmers, George (1782). *An Estimate of the Comparative Strength of Britain . . . To which is added an essay on population, by the Lord Chief Justice Hale*. London: C. Dilly *et al.*

Chamberlayne, John (1737/1741). *Magnae Britanniae Notitia; or, The Present State of Great Britain*. London: D. Midwinter *et al.*

Chambers, Robert (1912/1967). *Traditions of Edinburgh*. Edinburgh: Chambers.

Charlevoix, Pierre-François Xavier de (1744). *Histoire et description générale de la nouvelle France*. Paris: Rollin.

Charvat, William (1936/1961). *The Origins of American Critical Thought 1810–1835*. New York: Barnes.

Checkland, S. G. (1975). 'Adam Smith and the Bankers', in Skinner and Wilson (1975: 504–23).

Cheselden, William (1727–8). 'Case of a Blind Boy', Royal Society of London, *Philosophical Transactions* 35: 447–52.

Chitnis, A. C. (1982). 'Provost Drummond and the Origins of Edinburgh Medicine', in Campbell and Skinner (1982a: 86–97).

Christie, John R. R. (1987). 'Adam Smith's Metaphysics of Language', in A. E. Benjamin, G. N. Cantor, and J. R. R. Christie (eds.), *The Figural and the Literal*. Manchester: Manchester Univ. Press.

Clark, Ian D. L. (1963). 'Moderates and the Moderate Party in the Church of Scotland 1752–1805', Ph.D. thesis, Univ. of Cambridge.

Clarkson, Thomas (1808). *History of the Abolition of the Slave Trade*. 2 vols. London: Longman.

Clayden, P. W. (1887). *Early Life of Samuel Rogers*. London: Smith, Elder.

Coase, R. H. (1988). *The Firm, the Market and the Law*. Chicago: Univ. of Chicago Press.

Coats, A. W. Bob (ed.) (1971). *The Classical Economists and Economic Policy*. London: Methuen.

—— (1992). *On the History of Economic Thought*; i: *British and American Economic Essays*; ii: *Sociology and Professionalization of Economics*; iii: *Historiography and Methodology of Economics*. London: Routledge.

Cobban, Alfred (1973). *Aspects of the French Revolution*. St Albans: Paladin.

Cobbett, William (1806–12) and Hansard, T. C. (1812–20) (eds.). *The Parliamentary History of England*, 1066–1803. London.

Cochrane, J. A. (1964). *Dr Johnson's Printer: The Life of William Strahan*. London: Routledge & Kegan Paul.

Cockburn, Henry, Lord (1842). *Life of Lord Jeffrey*. 2 vols. Edinburgh: Adam & Charles Black.

—— (1856). *Memorials of His Time*. Edinburgh: Adam & Charles Black.

Coke, Lady Mary (1889–96). *The Letters and Journals*. 4 vols. Edinburgh; privately printed.

Colden, Cadwallader (1972). *The History of the Five Indian Nations*, fac. edn. Toronto: Coles.

Coleman, D. C. (1988). 'Adam Smith, Businessmen, and the Mercantile System in England', *History of European Ideas*, 9: 161–70.

Colley, Linda (1989). *Lewis Namier*. London: Weidenfeld & Nicolson.

—— (1992). *Britons: Forging the Nation 1707–1837*. New Haven, Conn.: Yale Univ. Press.

Collini, Stefan, *et al.* (eds.) (1983). *That Noble Science of Politics: A Study in Nineteenth-Century Intellectual History*. Cambridge: Cambridge Univ. Press.

Condorcet, Marquis de (1989). *Cinq mémoires sur l'instruction publique* [1791], intro. and notes by C. Coutel and C. Kintzler. Paris: Edilig.

Cone, Carl B. (1968). *The English Jacobins: Reformers in Late 18th Century England*. New York: Scribner's.

Confession of Faith, and the Larger and Shorter Catechism, First agreed upon by the Assembly of Divines at Westminster (1671). Edinburgh.

Connon, R. W. (1977). 'The Textual and Philosophical Significance of Hume's MS Alterations to *Treatise* III', in G. P. Morice (ed.), *David Hume: Bicentenary Papers*. Edinburgh: Edinburgh Univ. Press.

Corbett, Edward P. J. (1965). *Classical Rhetoric for the Modern Student*. New York: Oxford Univ. Press.

Coseriu, Eugenio (1970). 'Adam Smith und die Anfänge der Sprachtypologie', *Tübinger Beiträge zur Linguistik*, 3: 15–25.

Coutts, James (1909). *A History of the University of Glasgow from Its Foundation in 1451 to 1909*. Glasgow: James Maclehose.

Cowen, D. L. (1969). 'Liberty, laissez-faire and licensure in nineteenth-century Britain', *Bulletin of the History of Medicine*, 43: 30–40.

Craig, John (1806). 'Account of the Life and Writings of the Author', prefixed to John Millar, *The Origin of the Distinction of Ranks*, 4th edn. Edinburgh: Blackwood; London: Longmans.

Craveri, B. (1987). *Mme Du Deffand et son monde*. Paris: Seuil.

Crawford, Robert (1992). *Devolving English Literature*. Oxford: Clarendon Press.

Cregeen, Eric (1970). 'The Changing Role of the House of Argyll in the Scottish Highlands', in N. T. Phillipson and Rosalind Mitchison (eds.), *Scotland in the Age of Improvement*. Edinburgh: Edinburgh Univ. Press.

Crépel, Pierre *et al.* (eds.) (1989). *Condorcet: mathématicien, économiste, philosophe, homme politique*. Paris: Minerve.

Cropsey, Joseph (1957). *Polity and Economy: An Interpretation of the Principles of Adam Smith*. The Hague: Martinus Nijhoff.

—— (1979). 'The Invisible Hand: Moral and Political Consideration', in Gerald P. O'Driscoll, Jr. (ed.), *Adam Smith and Modern Political Economy*. Iowa City: Iowa State Univ. Press.

Cross, A. G. (1980). *Russians in Eighteenth-Century Britain*. Newtonville, Mass.: Oriental Research Partners.

Crowley, John E. (1990). 'Neo-Mercantilism and WN: British Commercial Policy after the American Revolution', *Historical Journal*, 33: 339–60.

Cullen, William (1784). *First Lines of the Practice of Physic*, 4th edn. 4 vols. Edinburgh: Elliot & Cadell.

Culpeper, Nicholas (1671). *A Directory for Midwives; or, A Guide for Women in their Conception, Bearing, and Suckling their Children*. London: George Sawbridge.

Currie, J. D. (1932). *History of Scottish Medicine*, 2nd edn. London: Bailliere, Tindale & Cox.

Currie, James (1831). *Memoir*. 2 vols. London: Longman.

Daiches, David (1969). *Scotch Whisky: Its Past and Present*. London: André Deutsch.

—— Jones, Peter, and Jones, Jean (eds.) (1986). *A Hotbed of Genius: The Scottish Enlightenment 1730–1790*. Edinburgh: Edinburgh Univ. Press.

Dalzel, Andrew (1794). 'Account of John Drysdale', *RSE Transactions*, 3, app. ii, pp. 37–53.

—— (1862). *History of the University of Edinburgh*. 2 vols. Edinburgh: Edmonston & Douglas.

Darnton, Robert (1979). *The Business of the Enlightenment: A Publishing History of the Encyclopédie, 1775–1800*. Cambridge, Mass.: Bellnap Press.

Daston, Lorraine (1988). *Classical Probability in the Enlightenment*. Princeton, NJ: Princeton Univ. Press.

Davie, George Elder (1961). *The Democratic Intellect: Scotland and Her Universities in the Nineteenth Century*. Edinburgh: Edinburgh Univ. Press.

—— (1965). 'Berkeley's Impact on Scottish Philosophers', *Philsophy*, 40: 222–34.

Davis, H. W. (1963). *A History of Balliol College*, rev. R. H. C. Davis and Richard Hunt, supplemented by Harold Hartley *et al*. Oxford: Blackwell.

Dawson, Deidre (1991). 'Is Sympathy so Surprising? Adam Smith and French Fictions of Sympathy', *Eighteenth-Century Life*, 15: 147–62.

—— (1991–2). 'Teaching Sensibility: Adam Smith, Rousseau, and the Formation of the Moral Spectator', *Études Écossaises Colloquium Proc*. TS, Grenoble.

Defoe, Daniel (1927). *A Tour Thro' the Whole Island of Great Britain (1724–7)*, ed. G. D. H. Cole. 2 vols. London: Peter Davies.

Derrida, Jacques (1967*a*/1976). *Of Grammatology*, trans. Gayatri Spivak. Baltimore: Johns Hopkins Univ. Press.

—— (1967*b*/1978). *Writing and Difference*, trans. Alan Bass. Chicago: Univ. of Chicago Press.

Devine, T. M. (1975). *The Tobacco Lords: A Study of the Tobacco Merchants of Glasgow and Their Trading Activities c. 1740–90*. Edinburgh: Donald.

—— (ed.) (1978). *Lairds and Improvement in the Scotland of the Enlightenment*. Glasgow Univ., Dept. of Scottish History.

—— (1985). 'The Union of 1707 and Scottish Development', *Scottish Economic and Social History*, 5: 23–40.

—— (ed.) (1989). *Improvement and Enlightenment*. Edinburgh: Donald.

—— and Jackson, Gordon (eds.) (1995). *Glasgow*, i: *Beginnings to 1830*. Manchester: Manchester Univ. Press.

Devlin-Thorp, Sheila (ed.) (1981). *Scotland's Cultural Heritage*, ii: *The Royal Society of Edinburgh: Literary Fellows Elected 1783–1812*. Univ. of Edinburgh, History of Science and Medicine Unit.

Di Folco, John (1978). 'The Hopes of Craighall and Land Investment in the Seventeenth Century', in Devine (1978: 1–10).

Diatkine, Daniel (1993). 'A French Reading of WN in 1790', in Mizuta and Sugiyama (1993: 213–23).

Dickinson, P. C. M. (1967). *The Financial Revolution in England: A Study in the Development of Public Credit*. London: Macmillan.

Dodgshon, R.A. (1980). 'The Origins of the Traditional Field Systems', in M. A. Parry and T. R. Slater (eds.), *The Making of the Scottish Countryside*. London: Croom Helm; Montreal: McGill-Queen's Univ. Press.

Dodgshon, R.A. and Butlin, R. A. (eds.) (1978). *An Historical Geography of England and Wales*. London: Academic Press.

Doig, Andrew (1982). 'Dr Black, a Remarkable Physician', in A. D. C. Simpson (ed.), *Joseph Black: A Commemorative Symposium*. Edinburgh: Royal Scottish Museum.

Donovan, A. L. (1975). *Philosophical Chemistry in the Scottish Enlightenment*. Edinburgh: Edinburgh Univ. Press.

Donovan, Robert Kent (1987). *No Popery and Radicalism: Opposition to Roman Catholic Relief in Scotland 1778–1782*. New York: Garland.

—— (1990). 'The Church of Scotland and the American Revolution', in Sher and Smitten (1990: 81–99).

Dorward, David (1979). *Scotland's Place Names*. Edinburgh: Blackwood.

Dougall, J. (1937). 'James Stirling', *Journal of the Glasgow Mathematical Association*, I.

Douglas, Sir Robert (1813). *The Peerage of Scotland*, rev. J. P. Wood, 2nd edn. Edinburgh: G. Ramsay.

Drescher, Horst W. (1971). *Themen und Formen des periodischen Essays in späten 18. Jahrhundert: Untersuchungen zu den schottischen Wochenschriften The Mirror und The Lounger*. Frankfurt am Main: Athenäum.

[Duclos, R.] (1802). *Dictionnaire Bibliographique, historique et critique des livres rares*. 3 vols. Paris: Delalain; Gênes: Fantin, Gravier.

Dull, Jonathan R. (1985). *A Diplomatic History of the American Revolution*. New Haven, Conn.: Yale Univ. Press.

Duncan, Douglas (1965). *Thomas Ruddiman: A Study in Scottish Scholarship in the Early Eighteenth Century*. Edinburgh: Oliver & Boyd.

Duncan, W. J. (1831). *Notes and Documents Illustrative of the Literary History of Glasgow*. Glasgow: Maitland Club.

Du Pont de Nemours, Pierre-Samuel (1782). *Mémoires sur la vie et les ouvrages de M. Turgot, Ministre d'État*. [Paris:] Philadelphia.

—— (1787). *Œuvres posthumes de M. Turgot, ou Mémoires de M. Turgot sur les administrations provinciales, mis en parallèle avec celui de M. Necker, suivi d'une lettre sur ce plan [par Dupont de Nemours], et des observations d'un républicain . . . [par J.-P. Brissot]*. Lausanne.

—— (1788). *Lettre à la Chambre de Commerce de Normandie; sur la Mémoire qu'elle a publié relativement au Traité de Commerce avec Angleterre*. Rouen/Paris: Moutard.

Durie, A. J. (1978). 'Lairds, Improvement, Banking and Industry in Eighteenth-Century Scotland: Capital and Development in a Backward Country—A Case Study', in Devine (1978: 21–30).

Durkan, John, and Kirk, James (1977). *The University of Glasgow 1451–1577*. Glasgow: Univ. of Glasgow Press.

Dutil, Leon (1911). 'L'État économique de Languedoc à la fin de l'ancien régime (1750–1789)', thèse de doctorat-ès-lettres. Paris.

Dwyer, J. *et al.* (eds.) (1982). *New Perspectives on the Politics and Culture of Early Modern Scotland*. Edinburgh: Donald.

Dwyer, John (1987). *Virtuous Discourse: Sensibility and Community in Late Eighteenth-Century Scotland*. Edinburgh: Donald.

—— and Sher, Richard B. (eds.) (1991). 'Sociability and Society in Eighteenth-Century Scotland', *Eighteenth Century Life*, 15: 194–209.

Dybikowski, James (1993). *On Burning Ground: An Examination of the Ideas, Projects and Life of David Williams.* Oxford: Voltaire Foundation.

Dyce, Alexander (ed.) (1856). *Recollections of the Table-Talk of Samuel Rogers.* New York: Appleton.

Egret, Jean (1975). *Necker: Ministre de Louis XVI.* Paris: Champion.

Ehrman, John (1969). *The Younger Pitt.* 2 vols. London: Constable.

Emerson, Roger L. (1973). 'The Social Composition of Enlightened Scotland: The Select Society of Edinburgh, 1754–1764', *Studies on Voltaire and the Eighteenth Century*, 114: 291–321.

—— (1979a). 'The Philosophical Society of Edinburgh, 1737–1747', *British Journal for the History of Science*, 12: 154–91.

—— (1979b). 'American Indians, Frenchmen, and Scots Philosophers', *Studies in Eighteenth-Century Culture*, 9: 211–36.

—— (1981). 'The Philosophical Society of Edinburgh, 1748–1768', *British Journal for the History of Science*, 14: 133–76.

—— (1984). 'Conjectural History and Scottish Philosophers', *Historical Papers/ Communications historiques*, 63–90.

—— (1986). 'Natural Philosophy and the Problem of the Scottish Enlightenment', *Studies on Voltaire and the Eighteenth Century*, 242: 243–91.

—— (1988). 'Sir Robert Sibbald, Kt., the Royal Society of Scotland and the Origins of the Scottish Enlightenment', *Annals of Science*, 45: 41–72.

—— (1990). 'Science and Moral Philosophy in the Scottish Enlightenment', in Stewart (1990c: 11–36).

—— (1992). *Professors, Patronage and Politics: The Aberdeen University in the Eighteenth Century.* Aberdeen: Aberdeen Univ. Press.

Endres, A. M. (1991). 'Adam Smith's Rhetoric of Economics: An Illustration Using "Smithian" Compositional Rules', *Scottish Journal of Political Economy*, 38: 76–95.

Erskine, Patrick (1708). *Theses Philosophicae . . . Joanne Lowdoun Praeside.* Glasgow: Robert Saunders.

Etzioni, Amitai (1994). *The Spirit of Community: Thoughts, Responsibilities, and the Communitarian Agenda.* New York: Crown.

Evans, H., and Evans, M. (1973). *John Kay of Edinburgh: Barber, Miniaturist and Social Commentator, 1742–1826.* Aberdeen: Aberdeen Univ. Press.

Eyre-Todd, George (1934). *History of Glasgow, iii: From the Revolution to the Passing of the Reform Acts 1832–33.* Glasgow: Jackson, Wylie.

Faccarello, Gilbert (1989). 'Présentation, économie', in Crépel *et al.* (1989: 121–49).

Falconer, William (1789). *A Universal Dictionary of the Marine.* London: T. Cadell.

Fallows, James (1994). *Looking at the Sun: The Rise of the New East Asian Economic and Political Systems.* New York: Pantheon.

Farge, Arlette (1994). *Fragile Lives: Violence, Power and Solidarity in Eighteenth-Century Paris*, trans. Carol Shelton. Oxford: Polity.

Faujas de Saint Fond, Barthélemy (1907). *Travels in England, Scotland, and the Hebrides [1784]*, ed., rev., trans. by Sir Archibald Geikie. 2 vols. Glasgow: Hugh Hopkins.

Fay, C. R. (1956). *Adam Smith and the Scotland of His Day.* Cambridge: Cambridge Univ. Press.

Fénelon, François (1722). *Dialogues concerning Eloquence*, trans. William Stevenson. London.

Ferguson, Adam (1756). *Reflections Previous to the Establishment of a Militia*. London: R. & J. Dodsley. Repr. in Mizuta (1977: 1–27).

—— (1767/1966). *An Essay on the History of Civil Society*, ed. and intro. Duncan Forbes. Edinburgh: Edinburgh Univ. Press.

—— (1773). *Institutes of Moral Philosophy*, 2nd rev. edn. London: W. Strahan.

—— (1776). *Remarks on a Pamphlet Lately Published by Dr Price . . . in a Letter from a Gentleman in the Country* [Adam Ferguson]. London: T. Cadell.

—— (1783). *The History of the Progress and Termination of the Roman Republic*. 3 vols. London: W. Strahan & T. Cadell; Edinburgh: W. Creech.

—— (1792). *Principles of Moral and Political Science*. 2 vols. London: A. Strahan & T. Cadell; Edinburgh: W. Creech.

Ferguson, William (1968). *Scotland 1689 to the Present*. Edinburgh and London: Oliver & Boyd.

Fetter, Frank W., (ed.) (1957). *The Economic Writings of Francis Horner in the Edinburgh Review*. London: London School of Economics and Political Science.

Findlay, J. T. (1928). *Wolfe in Scotland*. London: Longmans.

Fish, Stanley (1980). *Is There a Text in This Class?* Cambridge, Mass.: Harvard Univ. Press.

—— (1989). *Doing What Comes Naturally: Change, Rhetoric, and the Practice of Theory in Literary and Legal Studies*. Oxford: Clarendon Press.

Fleischacker, Samuel (1991). 'Philosophy in Moral Practice: Kant and Adam Smith', *Kant-Studien*, 82: 249–69.

Fleming, John (1962). *Robert Adam and His Circle in Edinburgh and Rome*. London: John Murray.

—— and Honour, Hugh (1977). *The Penguin Dictionary of the Decorative Arts*. London.

Fleming, Revd Thomas (1791). 'Parish of Kirkcaldy', *[Old] Statistical Account of Scotland*, ed. Sir John Sinclair. Edinburgh.

Fletcher of Saltoun, Andrew (1749). *The Political Works*. Glasgow: Printed by Robert Urie for G. Hamilton & J. Balfour, Edinburgh.

Flinn, Michael (ed.) (1977). *Scottish Population History from the 17th Century to the 1930s*. Cambridge: Cambridge Univ. Press.

Fontana, Biancamaria (1985). *Rethinking the Politics of Commercial Society: The Edinburgh Review 1802–1832*. Cambridge: Cambridge Univ. Press.

Fontenelle, Bernard Le Bovyer de (1728). *A Week's Conversation on the Plurality of Worlds*, trans. William Gardiner, 2nd edn. London: A. Bettesworth.

Foucault, Michel (1966/1973). *The Order of Things: An Archaeology of the Human Sciences*, trans. A. Sheridan. New York: Random House; repr. Vintage.

—— (1969/1977). 'What Is an Author?', in *Language, Counter-memory, Practice*, ed. D. Bouchard. Ithaca, NY: Cornell Univ. Press.

Forbes, Duncan (1982). 'Natural Law and the Scottish Enlightenment', in Campbell and Skinner (1982*a*: 186–204).

Fox-Genovese, Elizabeth (1976). *The Origins of Physiocracy: Economic Revolution and Social Order in Eighteenth-Century France*. Ithaca, NY: Cornell Univ. Press.

France, Peter (1990). 'The Commerce of the Self', *Comparative Criticism: A Yearbook*, 12: 39–56.

Fraser, Antonia (1970). *Mary Queen of Scots*. London: Panther.

Frêche, Georges (1974). *Toulouse et la région Midi-Pyrénées au siècle des lumières (vers 1670–1789)*. Paris: Cujas.

Freeholder of Ayrshire, A (1760). *The Question relating to a Scotch Militia considered, in a Letter to the Lords and Gentlemen who have concerted the form of law for that establishment*. Edinburgh and London: J. Tower.

Friedman, Milton (1974). 'Schools at Chicago', *University of Chicago Magazine*.

—— (1981). *The Invisible Hand in Economics and Politics*. Singapore: Institute of Southeast Asian Studies.

—— and Friedman, Rose (1980). *Free to Choose*. New York: Harcourt Brace Jovanovich.

Fry, Howard T. (1970). *Alexander Dalrymple (1737–1808) and the Expansion of British Trade*. Toronto: Univ. of Toronto Press.

Fry, Michael (1992a). *The Dundas Despotism*. Edinburgh: Edinburgh Univ. Press.

—— (ed.) (1992b). *Adam Smith's Legacy: His Place in the Development of Modern Economics*. London: Routledge.

Fulbrook, Mary (1990). *A Concise History of Germany*. Cambridge: Cambridge Univ. Press.

Garioch, Robert (1983). *Complete Poems*, ed. Robin Fultin. Edinburgh: Macdonald.

Garrioch, David (1986). *Neighbourhood and Community in Paris 1740–1790*. Cambridge: Cambridge Univ. Press.

Garrison, James W. (1987). 'Mathematics and Natural Philosophy', *Journal of the History of Ideas*, 48: 609–27.

Gaskell, Philip (1964). *A Bibliography of the Foulis Press*. London: Hart-Davis.

Gaskill, Howard (ed.) (1991). *Ossian Revisited*. Edinburgh: Edinburgh Univ. Press.

Gaul, Marilyn (1988). *English Romanticism: The Human Context*. New York: Norton.

Gellner, Ernst (1994). *Conditions of Liberty: Civil Society and Its Rivals*. London: Hamish Hamilton.

George III (1927). *Correspondence . . . from 1760 to 1783*, ed. Sir John Fortescue, ii. London: Macmillan.

Gherity, James A. (1993). 'An Early Publication by Adam Smith', *History of Political Economy*, 25: 241–82.

Gibbon, Edward (n.d.). *The Decline and Fall of the Roman Empire*. Based on Everyman edn., ed. Oliphant Seaton. 3 vols. New York: Random House.

—— (1950). *Autobiography*. Oxford: Oxford Univ. Press.

—— (1956). *Letters*, ed. J. E. Norton. 3 vols. London: Cassell.

Gibson, A., and Smout, T. C. (1989). 'Scottish Food and Scottish History', in R. A. Houston and I. D. Whyte (eds.), *Scottish Society 1500–1800*. Cambridge: Cambridge Univ. Press.

Gibson, John (1777). *The History of Glasgow*. Glasgow: R. Chapman & A. Duncan.

Gifford, John (1988). *Fife: The Buildings of Scotland*. Harmondsworth: Penguin.

—— (1989). *William Adam 1689–1748*. Edinburgh: Mainstream.

—— McWilliam, Colin, Walker, David, and Wilson, Christopher (1988). *Edinburgh: The Buildings of Scotland*. Harmondsworth: Penguin.

Gioli, Gabriella (1993). 'The Diffusion of the Economic Thought of Adam Smith in Italy, 1776–1876', in Mizuta and Sugiyama (1993: 225–49).

Godechot, J., and Tollon, B. (1974). 'Ombres et lumières sur Toulouse (1715–1789)', in Philippe Wolff (ed.), *Histoire de Toulouse*. Toulouse: Édouard Privat.

Godley, A. D. (1908). *Oxford in the Eighteenth Century*. London: Methuen.

Goethe, J. W. von (1774/1962 pk.). *The Sorrows of Young Werther*, trans. Catherine Hutter. New York: Signet.

Graham, Henry Gray (1899). *Social Life of Scotland in the Eighteenth Century*. 2 vols. London: Adam & Charles Black.

—— (1908). *Scottish Men of Letters in the Eighteenth Century*. London: Adam & Charles Black.

Grant, James (1876). *History of the Burgh Schools of Scotland*. London: Collins.

Gray, John M. (ed.) (1892). 'Memoirs of the Life of Sir John Clerk of Penicuik . . . From His Own Journals, 1676–1755', in John M. Gray (ed.), *Publications of the Scottish History Society*, xiii. Edinburgh: Constable.

Griswold, Charles (1991). 'Rhetoric and Ethics: Adam Smith on Theorizing about Moral Sentiments', *Philosophy and Rhetoric*, 24: 213–37.

Groenewegen, P. D. (1969). 'Turgot and Adam Smith', *Scottish Journal of Political Economy*, 16: 271–87.

Grotius, Hugo (1670). *De jure belli ac pacis*. Amsterdam: J. Blau.

—— (1735). *De jure belli ac pacis*, ed. J. Barbeyrac. Amsterdam: Jansson-Waesberg.

—— (1745). *De veritate religionis Christianae*, ed. J. Le Clerc. Glasgow: R. Ure.

Gutting, Gary (1991). *Michel Foucault's Archaeology of Scientific Reason*. Cambridge: Cambridge Univ. Press.

Guttmacher, M. S. (1930). 'The Views of Adam Smith on Medical Education', *Johns Hopkins Hospital Bulletin*, 47: 164–75.

Haakonssen, Knud (1981). *The Science of a Legislator: The Natural Jurisprudence of David Hume and Adam Smith*. Cambridge: Cambridge Univ. Press.

—— (ed.) (1988). *Traditions of Liberalism*. Sydney: Centre for Independent Studies.

—— (1990). 'Natural Law and Moral Realism: The Scottish Synthesis', in Stewart (1990c: 61–85).

Hailes, Sir David Dalrymple, Lord (1776). *Annals of Scotland*. 2 vols. in 1. Edinburgh.

Haldane, A. R. B. (1952). *The Drove Roads of Scotland*. Edinburgh: Nelson.

—— (1970). 'The Society of Writers to Her Majesty's Signet', *Journal of the Law Society of Scotland*, 15.

Halévy, Elie (1955). *The Growth of Philosophical Radicalism*, trans. Mary Morris. Boston: Beacon Press.

Halkett, Samuel and Laing, John (1971). *Dictionary of Anonymous and Pseudonymous Publications*, ed. J. Kennedy *et al.* 8 vols. New York: Haskell House.

Hall, A. Rupert (1980). *Philosophers at War: The Quarrel Between Newton and Leibniz*. Cambridge: Cambridge Univ. Press.

—— and Trilling, L. (1976). *The Correspondence of Isaac Newton*. Cambridge: Cambridge Univ. Press.

Hamilton, Henry (1963). *An Economic History of Scotland in the Eighteenth Century*. Oxford: Clarendon Press.

Hamilton, Sir William (1853). *Discussions on Philosophy and Literature, Education and University Reform* (chiefly from the *Edinburgh Review*), 2nd edn. London: Longman.

Hampson, Norman (1978). *Danton*. London: Duckworth.

Handley, James E. (1953). *Scottish Farming in the Eighteenth Century*. London: Faber & Faber.

Hann, C. M. (ed.) (1990). *Market Economy and Civil Society in Hungary*. London.

Harris, R. D. (1979). *Necker, Reform Statesman of the Old Regime.* Berkeley, Calif.: Univ. of California Press.

Haskell, Francis, and Penny, Nicholas (1982). *Taste and the Antique: The Lure of Classical Sculpture 1500–1900.* New Haven, Conn.: Yale Univ. Press.

Haskell, Thomas L., and Teichgraeber, Richard F., III (eds.) (1993). *The Culture of the Market: Historical Essays.* Cambridge: Cambridge Univ. Press.

Hay, Douglas *et al.* (eds.) (1977). *Albion's Fatal Tree: Crime and Society in Eighteenth-Century England.* Harmondsworth: Penguin.

Haym, Niccola Francesco (1803). *Biblioteca italiana: ossia notizia de libri rari italiani.* 2 vols. Milan: Giovanni Silvestri.

Hatch, Gary Layne (1994). 'Adam Smith's Accusation of Plagiarism Against Hugh Blair', *Eighteenth-Century Scotland,* 8: 7–10.

Hazen, Allen T. (1969). *A Catalogue of Horace Walpole's Library, with Horace Walpole's Library by W. S. Lewis.* 4 vols. London: Oxford Univ. Press.

Heath, Sir Thomas L. (1955). Intro. to *Euclid's Elements,* ed. Isaac Todhunter. London: Dent.

Hegel, Georg Wilhelm Friedrich (1942). *Philosophy of Right,* trans. with notes, T. M. Knox. Oxford: Clarendon Press.

—— (1991). *Elements of the Philosophy of Right,* ed. Allen W. Wood, trans. H. B. Nisbet. Cambridge: Cambridge Univ. Press.

Heirwegh, Jean-Jacques, and Mortier, Roland (1983). 'Les duchés de Luxembourg et de Bouillon', in Hervé Hasquin (ed.), *La Vie culturelle dans nos provinces (Pays-Bas autrichiens, principauté de Liège et duché de Bouillon) au XVIIIe siècle.* Brussels: Crédit Communal de Belgique.

Henderson, Willie *et al.* (eds.) (1993). *Economics and Language.* London: Routledge.

Herbener, Jeffrey M. (ed.) (1993). *The Meaning of Ludwig von Mises: Contributions in Economics, Sociology, Epistemology, and Political Philosophy.* Auburn, Ala.: Ludwig von Mises Institute.

Henderson, Willie, Dudley-Evans, Tony, and Backhouse, Roger (eds.) (1993). *Economics and Language.* London: Routledge.

Hetherington, Sir Hector *et al.* (1985). *The University of Glasgow Through Five Centuries.* 1951. Glasgow Univ.

Hill, John (1807). *An Account of the Life and Writings of Hugh Blair.* London: T. Cadell & W. Davie; Edinburgh: J. Balfour.

Himmelfarb, Gertrude (1984). *The Idea of Poverty: England in the Early Industrial Age.* New York: Knopf.

Hirschman, Albert O. (1977). *The Passions and the Interests: Political Arguments for Capitalism Before Its Triumph.* Princeton, NJ: Princeton Univ. Press.

Holdsworth, Sir William (1966). *A History of English Law,* xii: *The Eighteenth Century: The Professional Development of the Law.* London: Methuen/Sweet & Maxwell.

Hollander, Samuel (1973). *The Economics of Adam Smith.* Univ. of Toronto Press.

Holloway, James (1986). *James Tassie 1735–1799.* Edinburgh: National Galleries of Scotland Trustees.

Home, John (1822). *Works.* With an account of his Life and Writings by Henry Mackenzie, 3 vols. London: Hurst, Robinson; Edinburgh: A. Constable.

Hont, Istvan, and Ignatieff, Michael (eds.) (1983). *Wealth and Virtue: The Shaping of Political Economy in the Scottish Enlightenment.* Cambridge: Cambridge Univ. Press.

Hook, Andrew (ed.) (1987). *The History of Scottish Literature*, ii: *1660–1800*. Aberdeen: Aberdeen Univ. Press.

—— and Sher, Richard B. (eds.) (1995). *The Glasgow Enlightenment*. Edinburgh: Canongate Academic.

Hope, Vincent (1989). *Virtue by Consensus: The Moral Philosophy of Hutcheson, Hume, and Adam Smith*. Oxford: Clarendon Press.

Horn, D. B. (1967). *A Short History of the University of Edinburgh, 1556–1889*. Edinburgh Univ. Press.

Horne, Revd George (1777). *A Letter to Adam Smith, LLD. on the Life, Death, and Philosophy of his Friend David Hume, Esq. By One of the People Called Christians*. Oxford.

Horner, Francis (1957). *Economic Writing*, ed. Frank W. Fetter. London: London School of Economics and Political Science.

House, Jack (1965). *The Heart of Glasgow*. London: Hutchinson.

—— (1975). *The Lang Toun*. Kirkcaldy: Kirkcaldy Town Council.

Houston, R. A. (1985). *Scottish Literacy and the Scottish Identity*. Cambridge: Cambridge Univ. Press.

—— (1989). 'Scottish Education and Literacy, 1600–1800: An International Perspective', in Devine (1989: 43–61).

—— (1994). *Social Change in the Age of the Enlightenment: Edinburgh, 1660–1760*. Oxford; Clarendon Press.

Howard, Alison K. (1959). 'Montesquieu, Voltaire and Rousseau in Eighteenth Century Scotland: A Check List of Editions and Translations of Their Works Published in Scotland before 1801', *The Bibliotheck*, 2: 40–63.

Howarth, W. D. (1989). 'The Danton/Robespierre Theme in European Drama', in Mason and Doyle (1989: 21–34).

Howell, William Samuel (1971). *Eighteenth-Century British Logic and Rhetoric*. Princeton, NJ: Princeton Univ. Press.

Hudson, Nicholas (1988). *Samuel Johnson and Eighteenth-Century Thought*. Oxford: Clarendon Press.

—— (1992). 'Dialogue and the Origins of Language: Linguistic and Social Evolution in Maudeville, Condillac, and Rousseau', in Kevin Cope (ed.), *Compendious Conversations*. Frankfurt am Main: Peter Lang.

Hume, David (1766). *Exposé succinct de la contestation . . . entre M. Hume et M. Rousseau, avec pièces justicatives*, trans. J.-B. A. Suard [ed. Jean Le Rond d'Alembert]. Paris.

Hutcheson, Francis (1969). *Collected Works*, fac., ed. Bernhard Fabian. Hildesheim: Georg Olms.

Hutchison, Terence (1976). 'Adam Smith and WN', *Journal of Law and Economics*, 19: 507–28.

—— (1988). *Before Adam Smith: The Emergence of Political Economy, 1662–1776*. Oxford: Blackwell.

Hyslop, Beatrice (1936). *Guide to the General Cahiers of 1789*. New York: Columbia Univ. Press.

Ignatieff, Michael (1986). 'Smith, Rousseau and the Republic of Needs', in T. C. Smout (ed.), *Scotland and Europe 1200–1850*. Edinburgh: Donald.

Ingrao, Bruno, and Israel, Giorgio (1990). *The Invisible Hand*, trans. Ian McGilvray. Cambridge, Mass.: MIT Press.

Innes, Cosmo (1862). 'Memoir of Dalzel', in Dalzel (1862).

—— (1872). *Lectures on Scotch Legal Antiquities*. Edinburgh: Edmonston & Douglas.

Iser, Wolfgang (1972/1974). *The Implied Reader*, trans. David Henry Wilson. Baltimore: Johns Hopkins Univ. Press.

Jacob, Margaret C. (1991). *Living the Enlightenment: Freemasonry and Politics in Eighteenth-Century Europe*. New York: Oxford Univ. Press.

Jacobs, Jane (1984). *Cities and the Wealth of Nations: Principles of Economic Life*. Harmondsworth: Penguin.

Jammes, Paul (1976). *Dix-huitième siècle; Catalogue 227*. Paris: Librairie Paul Jammes.

Jardine, Nicholas (1987). 'Scepticism in Renaissance Astronomy: A Preliminary Study', in R. H. Popkins and Charles B. Schmitt (eds.), *Scepticism from the Renaissance to the Enlightenment*. Wiesbaden: Otto Harrosswitz.

Joersson, S. A. (1796). *Adam Smith Author of an Inquiry into the Wealth of Nations and Thomas Paine Author of the Decline and Fall of the English System of Finance*. Germany. 2nd edn. London: repr. for D. I. Eaton.

Jogland, Herta H. (1959). *Ursprünge und Grundlagen der Soziologie bei Adam Ferguson*. Berlin: Duncker & Humblot.

Johnson, Samuel (1810–11). *Works*. New edn. with an Essay on his Life and Genius by Arthur Murphy. 14 vols. London: J. Nichols *et al.*

—— (1985). *A Journey to the Western Isles of Scotland* (1775), ed. David Fleeman. Oxford: Clarendon Press.

Jones, Jean (1986). 'James Hutton', in Daiches *et al.* (1986: 116–36).

—— (1990). *Morals, Motives & Markets: Adam Smith 1723–90: A Bicentenary Exhibition Catalogue*. Edinburgh: Royal Museum of Scotland/Adam Smith Bicentenary Committee.

Jones, John (1988). *Balliol College: A History 1263–1939*. Oxford Univ. Press.

Jones, Peter (1) (1982). 'The Polite Academy and the Presbyterians, 1720–1770', in Dwyer *et al.* (1982: 156–78).

Jones, Peter (2) (ed.) (1988). *Philosophy and Science in the Scottish Enlightenment*. Edinburgh: Donald.

—— (ed.) (1989). *The 'Science of Man' in the Scottish Enlightenment: Hume, Reid and Their Contemporaries*. Edinburgh: Edinburgh Univ. Press.

—— (1992). 'The Aesthetics of Adam Smith', in Jones and Skinner (1992: 56–78).

—— and Skinner, Andrew S. (eds.) (1992): *Adam Smith Reviewed*. Edinburgh: Edinburgh Univ. Press.

Jupp, Peter (1985). *Lord Grenville: 1759–1834*. Oxford: Clarendon Press.

Kames, Henry Home, Lord (1747). *Essays upon Several Subjects concerning British Antiquities*. Edinburgh: A. Kincaid.

—— (1751). *Essays on the Principles of Morality and Natural Religion*. Edinburgh: A. Kincaid & A. Donaldson. (1779) 3rd edn. London: J. Murray; Edinburgh: J. Bell.

—— (1758). *Historical Law-Tracts*. London: A. Millar; Edinburgh: A. Kincaid & J. Bell.

—— (1760). *Principles of Equity*. London: A. Millar; Edinburgh: A. Kincaid & J. Bell.

—— (1762). *Elements of Criticism*. 2 vols. Edinburgh: A. Kincaid & J. Bell.

—— (1774). *Sketches of the History of Man*. 2 vols. London: W. Strahan & T. Cadell; Edinburgh: W. Creech.

—— (1776). *The Gentleman Farmer*. Edinburgh: W. Creech.

Kant, Immanuel (1900–). *Gesammelte Schriften*, ed. Königlichen Preußischen [later Deutschen] Akademie der Wissenschaften. Berlin: Georg Reimer [later Walter de Gruyter].

—— (1967). *Philosophical Correspondence*, ed. and trans. A. Zweig. Chicago: Chicago Univ. Press.

Kay, John (1842). *A Series of Original Portraits and Character Etchings*. 2 vols. Edinburgh: Hugh Paton.

Keane, John (ed.) (1988). *Civil Society and the State: New European Perspectives*. London: Verso.

Kemp, Peter (ed.) (1979). *Oxford Companion to Ships and the Sea*. London: Oxford Univ. Press.

Kennedy, Emmet (1989). *A Cultural History of the French Revolution*. New Haven, Conn.: Yale Univ. Press.

Kenyon, J. P. (ed. and intro.) (1969). *Halifax: The Complete Works*. Harmondsworth: Penguin.

Kerr, Robert (1811). *Memoirs of the Life, Writing, and Correspondence of William Smellie*. 2 vols. Edinburgh: John Anderson.

Keynes, John Maynard (1963). *Essays in Biography*. New York: Norton.

Kidd, Colin (1993). *Subverting Scotland's Past*. Cambridge: Cambridge Univ. Press.

Kitchin, A. H., and Passmore, R. (1949). *The Scotsman's Food: An Historical Introduction to Modern Food Administration*. Edinburgh: Livingstone.

Klein, Lawrence E. (1994). *Shaftesbury and the Culture of Politeness: Moral Discourse and Cultural Politics in Early Eighteenth-Century England*. Cambridge: Cambridge Univ. Press.

Klemme, Heiner (1991). 'Adam Smith an Thomas Cadell: Zwei neue Briefe', *Archiv für Geschichte der Philosophie*, 73: 277–80.

Knapp, Lewis Mansfield (1949). *Tobias Smollett: Doctor of Men and Manner*. Princeton, NJ: Princeton Univ. Press.

Kobayashi, Noburu (1967). 'James Stewart, Adam Smith and Friedrich List', Science Council of Japan, Division of Economics, Commerce and Business Administration, Economics Series No. 40.

Krammick, Isaac (1990). *Republicanism and Bourgeois Radicalism*. Ithaca, NY: Cornell Univ. Press.

Kuhn, Thomas (1970). *The Structure of Scientific Revolutions*, 2nd edn. Chicago: Univ. of Chicago Press.

Kumar, Krishnan (1993). 'Civil Society: An Inquiry into the Usefulness of an Historical Term', *British Journal of Sociology*, 44: 375–95.

Kurtz, Stephen G., and Hutson, James H. (eds.) (1973). *Essays on the American Revolution*. New York: Norton.

Lafitau, Joseph-François (1977). *Customs of the American Indians Compared with the Customs of Primitive Times*, ed. and trans. William N. Fenton and Elizabeth L. Moore. Toronto: Champlain Society.

Lagrave, Jean-Paul de (1989). 'L'Influence de Sophie de Grouchy sur la pensée de Condorcet', in Crépel *et al.* (1989: 434–42).

Lakatos, Imre (1970). 'Falsification and the Methodology of Scientific Research Programmes', in I. Lakatos and A. Musgrove (eds.), *Criticism and the Growth of Knowledge*. Cambridge: Cambridge Univ. Press.

Landsman, Ned C. (1990). 'Witherspoon and the Problem of Provincial Identity in Scottish Enlightenment Culture', in Sher and Smitten (1990: 29–45).

—— (1991). 'Presbyterians and Provincial Society: The Evangelical Enlightenment in the West of Scotland, 1740–1775', in Dwyer and Sher (1991: 194–209).

Lane, Robert E. (1991). *The Market Experience*. Cambridge: Cambridge Univ. Press.

Lasarte, Javier (1976). *Economica y hacienda al final del antiquo regimen: dos estudios*. Madrid.

Latsis, S. J. (1976). 'A Research Programme in Economics', in Latsis (ed.), *Method and Appraisal in Economics*. Cambridge: Cambridge Univ. Press.

Laugier, Lucien (1979). *Turgot ou le mythe des réformes*. Paris: Albatros.

Law, Alexander (1965). *Education in Edinburgh in the Eighteenth Century*. London: Athlone Press.

—— (1984). 'Scottish Schoolbooks of the Eighteenth and Nineteenth Centuries', pt. ii, *Studies in Scottish Literature*, 19: 56–71.

Lecky, W. E. H. (1878). *A History of England in the Eighteenth Century*. New York: Appleton.

Lee-Warner, E. (1901). *The Life of John Warner, Bishop of Rochester 1637–1666*. London: Mitchell & Hughes.

Leechman, William (1755). Preface to Francis Hutcheson, *A System of Moral Philosophy*. Repr. in *Works* (1969).

Lehrer, Keith (1991). *Thomas Reid*. London: Routledge.

Lenman, Bruce (1977). *An Economic History of Modern Scotland 1660–1976*. London: Batsford.

—— (1980). *The Jacobite Risings in Britain: 1689–1746*. London: Eyre Methuen.

Lescure, A.-M. de (1869–71). *Nouveaux mémoires du maréchal duc de Richelieu 1696–1788*. 4 vols. Paris: Dentu.

Leslie, Charles Robert, and Taylor, Tom (1865). *Life and Times of Sir Joshua Reynolds*. London: John Murray.

Lindgren, J. R. (1969). 'Adam Smith's Theory of Inquiry', *Journal of Political Economy*, 77: 897–915.

Lindsay, Ian G., and Cosh, Mary (1973). *Inverary and the Dukes of Argyll*. Edinburgh: Edinburgh Univ. Press.

Lluch, Ernest (1989). 'Condorcet et la diffusion de la *Richesse des nations* en Espagne', in Crépel *et al.* (1989: 188–95).

Lobel, Mary D., and Crossley, Alan (1969). *A History of the County of Oxford*, ix: Bloxham Hundred. (The Victoria History of the Counties of England.) Oxford: Oxford Univ. Press for the Institute of Historical Research.

Lochhead, Marion (1948). *The Scots Household in the Eighteenth Century*. Edinburgh: Moray Press.

Long, A. A., and Sedley, D. N. (1988) *The Hellenistic Philosophers*, i: *Translation of Principal Sources with Philosophical Commentary*. Cambridge: Cambridge Univ. Press.

Long, Douglas G. (1977). *Bentham on Liberty*. Toronto: Univ. of Toronto Press.

Lowe, Adolph (1975). 'Adam Smith's System of Equilibrium Growth', in Skinner and Wilson (1975: 415–54).

Lux, Kenneth (1990). *Adam Smith's Mistake: How a Moral Philosopher Invented Economics and Ended Morality*. Boston: Shambala.

Lynch, Michael (1994). *Scotland: A New History*. London: Pimlico.

McCloskey, Donald N. (1990). *If You're So Smart: The Narrative of Economic Expertise*. Chicago: Univ. of Chicago Press.

—— (1993). *Knowledge and Persuasion in Economics*. New York: Cambridge Univ. Press.

McCulloch, J. R. (1855). *Sketch of Life and Writings of Adam Smith, LL.D*. Edinburgh: privately printed by Murray & Gibb.

McDonald, A. H. (1978). 'Eutropius', *The Oxford Classical Dictionary*, 2nd edn. Oxford: Oxford Univ. Press.

MacDonald, Alexander (1751). *Ais-eiridh na sean chanoin Albannaich* [*The Resurrection of the Ancient Scottish Tongue*]. Edinburgh.

Macfie, A. L. (1961). Review of C. R. Fay, *The World of Adam Smith* (1960), *Economic Journal*, 61: 151.

—— (1967). *The Individual in Society: Papers on Adam Smith*. London: Allen & Unwin.

—— (1971). 'The Invisible Hand of Jupiter', *Journal of the History of Ideas*, 32: 595–9.

McIntosh, J. R. (1989). 'The Popular Party in the Church of Scotland', Ph.D. thesis, Univ. of Glasgow.

Mack, Mary P. (1962). *Jeremy Bentham: An Odyssey of Ideas 1748–1792*. London: Heinemann Educational.

Mackay, A. J. G. (1896). *A History of Fife and Kinross*. Edinburgh: Blackwood.

McKean, Charles, and Walker, David (1982). *Edinburgh: An Illustrated Architectural Guide*. Edinburgh: RIAS Publications.

MacKechnie, Hector (ed.) (1936). *An Introductory Survey of the Sources and Literature of Scots Law*. Edinburgh: Stair Society.

Mackenzie, Henry (1808). *A Review of the Principal Proceedings of the Parliament of 1784*, in *Works*, vii. Edinburgh: Archibald Constable & Co./William Creech *et al.*

—— (1927). *Anecdotes and Egotisms, 1745–1831*, ed. Harold W. Thompson. London: Oxford Univ. Press.

Mackie, J. D. (1948). 'The Professors and Their Critics', *Proceedings of the Royal Philosophical Society of Glasgow*, 72: 37–58.

—— (1954). *The University of Glasgow 1451 to 1951*. Glasgow: Jackson.

McKindrick, Neil, Brewer, John, and Plumb, J. H. (eds.) (1982). *The Birth of a Consumer Society: The Commercialization of Eighteenth-Century England*. Bloomington, Ind.: Univ. of Indiana Press.

Maclaurin, Colin (1968). *An Account of Sir Isaac Newton's Philosophical Discoveries (1748)*, 1st edn. fac., intro. by L. L. Laudan. New York: Johnson Reprint.

McLellan, David (1972). *Marx before Marxism*. Harmondsworth: Pelican.

Macleod, Alistair M. (1990). 'The Invisible Hand: Milton Friedman and Adam Smith', TS, Vancouver Smith Symposium, 1990.

McLynn, Frank (1991). *Charles Edward Stuart: A Tragedy in Many Acts*. Oxford: Oxford Univ. Press.

McMahon, Christopher (1981). 'Morality and the Invisible Hand', *Philosophy and Public Affairs*, 10: 247–77.

Macpherson, James (trans.) (1765). *The Works of Ossian*. 2 vols. London.

Macpherson, John (ed.) (1980). *The Minute Book of the Faculty of Advocates*, ii: 1713–1750.

M'Ure, John (1736). *A View of the City of Glasgow*. Glasgow.

McWilliam, Colin (1978). *Lothian except Edinburgh: The Buildings of Scotland.* Harmondsworth: Penguin.

Maitland, James, 8th Earl of Lauderdale (1804). *Inquiry into the Nature and Origin of Public Wealth.* Edinburgh: Constable.

Manuel, Frank E. (1965 pk.). *The Prophets of Paris: Turgot, Condorcet, Saint-Simon, Fourier, Comte.* New York: Harper.

Marchak, M. Patricia (1991). *The Integrated Circus: The New Right and the Global Economy.* Montreal/Kingston: McGill-Queen's University Press.

Marquet, Louis (1989). 'Condorcet et la création du système métrique décimal', in Crépel *et al.* (1989: 52–62).

Marshall, David (1984). 'Adam Smith and the Theatricality of Moral Sentiments', *Critical Inquiry*, 10: 592–613.

Marshall, Gordon (1980). *Presbyteries and Profits: Calvinism and the Development of Capitalism in Scotland, 1560–1707.* Oxford: Clarendon Press.

Marshall, P. J. (ed.) (1981). *The Writings and Speeches of Edmund Burke*, v: *India, Madras and Bengal 1774–1785.* Oxford: Clarendon Press.

Marshall, Rosalind Kay (1973). *The Days of Duchess Anne.* London: Collins.

Martinez de Iruja, Carlos (marques de Casa) (1792/1803/1814). *Compendio de la obra intitulada Riqueza de las Naciones, hecho por el Marqués de Condorcet.* Madrid: Imprim. Real.

Maruzen (1990). *Bicentenary Adam Smith Catalogue.* Tokyo.

Marx, Jacques (1976). *Charles Bonnet contre les lumières, 1738–1850.* 2 vols. Oxford: Oxford Univ. Press.

Marx, Karl (1859). Preface to *Critique of Political Economy*, in Marx and F. Engels, *Selected Works.* Moscow: Foreign Languages Publishing House, 1935.

—— (1954). *Capital: A Critical Analysis of Capitalist Production*, trans. from 3rd German edn. by Samuel Moore and Edward Aveling, ed. Frederick Engels. 2 vols. Moscow: Foreign Languages Publishing House.

Mason, H. T., and Doyle, W. (eds.) (1989). *The Impact of the French Revolution on European Consciousness.* Gloucester, UK/Wolfeboro, NH: Allan Sutton.

Mathias, Peter (1983). *The First Industrial Nation: An Economic History of Britain 1700–1914*, 2nd edn. London: Methuen.

Matthew, W. M. (1966). 'The Origin and Occupations of Glasgow Students, 1740–1839', *Past and Present*, 33: 74–94.

Maupertuis, M. (1738). *The figure of the earth, determined from observations made by order of the French King, at the polar circle.* London: T. Cox, A. Millar *et al.*

May, Henry E. (1978). *The Enlightenment in America.* New York: Oxford Univ. Press.

Meek, Donald E. (1990). 'The Gaelic Ballads of Scotland: Creativity and Adaptation', in Howard Gaskill (ed.), *Ossian Revisited.* Edinburgh: Edinburgh Univ. Press.

Meek, Ronald L. (1962). *The Economics of Physiocracy.* London: Allen & Unwin.

—— and Skinner, Andrew S. (1973). 'The Development of Adam Smith's Ideas on the Division of Labour', *Economic Journal*, 83: 1094–1116.

—— (1973a). *Turgot on Progress, Sociology and Economics.* Cambridge: Cambridge Univ. Press.

—— (ed.) (1973b). *Precursors of Adam Smith.* London: Dent.

—— (1976). *Social Science and the Ignoble Savage.* Cambridge: Cambridge Univ. Press.

Meek, Ronald L. (1977). *Smith, Marx, and After: Ten Essays in the Development of Economic Thought*. London: Chapman & Hall.

—— and Kuczynski, Marguerite (eds.) (1972). Quesnay's *Tableau économique*. London: Macmillan.

Meikle, Henry W. (1912). *Scotland and the French Revolution*. Glasgow: Maclehose.

Mémoire et consultation sur une question du droit des gens (1763). Paris: P. Simon.

Middendorf, John (1961). 'Dr Johnson and Adam Smith', *Philological Quarterly*, 40: 281–96.

Millar, John (1779). *Origin of the Distinction of Ranks*, 3rd edn. London: J. Murray.

—— (1796). *Letters of Crito*. Edinburgh (serially published in *Scots Chronicle*, May–Sept.).

—— (1803). *An Historical View of the English Government: From the Settlement of the Saxons in Britain to the Revolution in 1688; to which are Subjoined some Dissertations Connected with the History of Government from the Revolution to the Present Time*, ed. John Craig and James Mylne, 3rd edn. 4 vols. London: Mawman.

Minowitz, Peter (1994). *Profits, Priests, and Princes: Adam Smith's Emancipation of Economics from Politics and Religion*. Cambridge: Cambridge Univ. Press.

Minto, Countess of (1868). *A Memoir of the Rt. Hon. Hugh Elliot*. Edinburgh: Edmonston & Douglas.

Mitchell, Harvey (1987). 'The "Mysterious Veil of Self-Delusion" in Adam Smith's TMS', *Eighteenth-Century Studies*, 20: 405–21.

Mizuta, Hiroshi (ed.) (1977). *Scottish Militia Tracts*. With Intro. Nagoya Reprints of the Scottish Enlightenment, No. 3.

—— (forthcoming). *Adam Smith's Library: A Catalogue*. Oxford: Clarendon Press.

—— and Sugiyama, Chuhei (eds.) (1993). *Adam Smith: International Perspectives*. London: Macmillan.

Momigliano, Arnaldo (1990). *The Classical Foundations of Modern Historiography*. Berkeley, Calif.: Univ. of California Press.

Monboddo, James Burnett (1774–1792). *Of the Origin and Progress of Language*. 6 vols. Edinburgh: A. Kincaid & W. Creech.

—— (1779–1799). *Antient Metaphysics*. 6 vols. Edinburgh: J. Balfour.

[Monro, Alexander, and Hume, David (eds.)] (1754). *Essays and Observations, Physical and Literary*. Edinburgh: G. Hamilton & J. Balfour.

Moore, James (1990). 'The Two Systems of Francis Hutcheson: On the Origins of the Scottish Enlightenment', in Stewart (1990c: 37–59).

—— and Silverthorne, Michael (1983). 'Gershom Carmichael and the Natural Jurisprudence Tradition in Eighteenth-Century Scotland', in eds. Hont and Ignatieff (1983: 73–87).

Morellet, Abbé A. (1821). *Mémoires*, ed. Pierre-Édouard Lémontey. 2 vols. Paris: Ladvocat.

Morison, Samuel Eliot (1964). *John Paul Jones: A Sailor's Biography*. New York: Time.

Mossner, Ernest Campbell (1960). ' "Of the Principle of Moral Estimation: A Discourse between David Hume, Robert Clerk, and Adam Smith": An Unpublished MS by Adam Ferguson', *Journal of the History of Ideas*, 21: 222–32.

—— (1963). 'Adam Ferguson's "Dialogue on a Highland Jaunt" with Robert Adam, William Clerghorn, David Hume, and William Wilkie', in Carroll Camden (ed.), *Restoration and Eighteenth-Century Literature: Essays in Honour of Alan D. McKillop*. Chicago: Univ. of Chicago Press.

—— (1965). Review of John M. Lothian (ed.), *Adam Smith, LRBL* (1963), *Studies in Scottish Literature*, 2: 203–4.

—— (1969). *Adam Smith: The Biographical Approach*. Univ. of Glasgow: David Murray Lecture Series.

—— (1977). 'Hume and the Legacy of the *Dialogues*', in G. P. Morice (ed.), *David Hume: Bicentenary Papers*. Edinburgh: Edinburgh Univ. Press.

—— (1978). 'The Religion of David Hume', *Journal of the History of Ideas*, 39: 653–64.

—— (1980). *The Life of David Hume*, 2nd edn. Oxford: Clarendon Press.

Mullan, John (1987). 'The Language of Sentiment: Hume, Smith, and Henry Mackenzie', *History of Scottish Literature*, 2: 273–89.

—— (1990). *Sentiment and Society: The Language of Feeling in the Eighteenth Century*. Oxford: Clarendon Press.

Muller, Jerry Z. (1993). *Adam Smith in His Time and Ours: Designing the Decent Society*. New York: Free Press/Macmillan.

Murdoch, Alexander (1980). *'The People Above': Politics and Administration in Mid-Eighteenth-Century Scotland*. Edinburgh: Donald.

Mure, William (ed.) (1883). *Selections from the Mure Family Papers Preserved at Caldwell*, 2/i. Glasgow: Maitland Club.

Murison, David (1982). *The Scottish Year*. Edinburgh: Mercat Press.

Murray, David (1924). *Early Burgh Organization in Scotland*. Glasgow: Maclehose, Jackson.

—— (1927). *Memories of the Old College of Glasgow*. Glasgow: Jackson, Wylie.

Myers, M. L. (1976). 'Adam Smith's Concept of Equilibrium', *Journal of Economic Issues*, 10: 560–75.

Namier, Sir Lewis, and Brooke, John (1964). *Charles Townshend*. London: Macmillan.

New Statistical Account of Scotland (1845). Edinburgh: Blackwood.

Nicholls, James C. (ed.) (1976). 'Mme Riccoboni's Letters to David Hume, David Garrick, and Sir Robert Liston, 1764–1783', *SVEC* 149.

Nicolaisen, W. F. H. (1976). *Scottish Place-Names: Their Study and Significance*. London: Batsford.

Nietzsche, Friedrich (1882/1961). *The Gay Science*, extract trans. R. J. Hollingdale in intro. to *Thus Spoke Zarathustra*. Harmondsworth: Penguin.

Nissen, Walter (1989). *Kulturelle Beziehungen zwischen den Universitätsstäden Halle/Wittenberg und Göttingen im Zeitalter der Aufklärung*. Göttingen: Sparkasse Göttingen.

Norton, David Fate (1992). 'Salus populi suprema lex', in Smyth (1992: 14–17).

Norton, David Fate (1976). 'Francis Hutcheson in America', *Studies on Voltaire and the Eighteenth Century*, 154: 1547–68.

—— and Stewart-Robertson, J. C. (1980; 1984). 'Thomas Reid on Adam Smith's Theory of Morals', *Journal of the History of Ideas*, 41: 381–98; 45: 309–21.

O'Brien, D. P. (1975). *The Classical Economists*. Oxford: Clarendon Press.

—— (1976). 'The Longevity of Adam Smith's Vision: Paradigms, Research Programmes and Falsifiability in the History of Economic Thought', *Scottish Journal of Political Economy*, 23: 133–51.

O'Brien, Patrick (1988). *Joseph Banks: A Life*. London: Collins Harvills.

O'Connell, Maurice R. (1965). *Irish Politics and Social Conflict in the Age of the American Revolution*. Philadelphia: Univ. of Pennsylvania Press.

Oncken, August (1897). 'The Consistency of Adam Smith', *Economic Journal*, 7: 443–50.

Pagden, Anthony (ed.) (1990) *The Languages of Political Theory in Early Modern Europe*. Cambridge: Cambridge Univ. Press.

Paine, Tom (1984) *Common Sense, The Rights of Man, and Other Essential Writings*, intro. Sidney Hook. New York: Meridian.

Palyi, M. (1928/1966). 'The Introduction of Adam Smith on the Continent', in John M. Clarke *et al.* (eds.), *Adam Smith, 1776–1926*. New York: Kelley.

Patey, Douglas Lane (1984). *Probability and English Literary Form: Philosophic Theory and Literary Practice in the Augustan Age*. Cambridge: Cambridge Univ. Press.

Patrick, Millar (1927). *The Story of the Church's Song*. Edinburgh: Scottish Churches Joint Committee on Youth.

Paul, Sir James Balfour (ed.) (1922). *Diary of George Ridpath, Minister of Stichel, 1755–61*. Edinburgh: Scottish History Society.

Penchko, N. A. (ed.) (1962). *Dokumenty i materialy po istorii Moskovskogo Universiteta vtoroy poloviny* [Documents and Materials for the History of Moscow University] XVIII *veka*, ii. 1765–6.

Perrot, Jean-Claude (1992). *Une histoire intellectuelle de l'économie politique XVIIe–XVIIIe siècles*. Paris: Édition de l'École des Hautes Études en Sciences Sociales.

Persky, Joseph (1989). 'Adam Smith's Invisible Hands', *Journal of Economic Perspectives*, 3: 195–201.

Phillips, Mark (1993). 'Adam Smith and the Narrative of Private Life', Hume Society/Eighteenth-Century Scottish Studies Society Conference paper TS, Ottawa.

Pitt, William (the Younger) (1817). *Speeches . . . in the House of Commons*, ed. W. S. Hathaway, 3rd edn. 3 vols. London: Longman, Hurst, Rees, Orme, & Brown.

Plank, Frans (1987). 'The Smith–Schlegel Connection in Linguistic Typology: Forgotten Fact or Fiction?', *Zeitschrift für Phonetik, Sprachwissenschaft und Kommunikationsforschung*, 40: 198–216.

—— (1992). 'Adam Smith: Grammatical Economist', in Jones and Skinner (1992: 23–38).

Pocock, J. G. A. (1965). 'Machiavelli, Harrington, and English Political Ideologies in the Eighteenth Century', *William and Mary Quarterly*, 3rd ser., 22: 549–83.

—— (1986). 'The Varieties of Whiggism from Exclusion to Reform', in *Virtue, Commerce, and History*. Cambridge: Cambridge Univ. Press.

—— (1989). 'Edmund Burke and the Redefinition of Enthusiasm', in *The French Revolution and the Creation of Modern Political Culture*, iii: *The Transformation of Political Culture*, ed. François Furet and Mona Ozouf. Oxford: Pergamon Press.

Poiret, Pierre (1707). *De Eruditione Triplici*. Amsterdam: Westen.

Polanyi, Karl (1957). *The Great Transformation*. Boston: Beacon Press.

Porquerol, Élisabeth (ed.) (1954). *Véritable vie privée du maréchal de Richelieu, contenant ses amours et intrigues*. Paris: Le Club de Meilleur Livre.

Porter, Michael (1990). *The Comparative Advantage of Nations*. New York: Free Press.

Porter, Roy (1990). *English Society in the Eighteenth Century*, rev. edn. Harmondsworth: Penguin.

Pottle, F. A. (1965). 'Boswell's University Education', in *Johnson, Boswell and Their Circle: Essays Presented to L. F. Powell*. Oxford: Oxford Univ. Press.

—— (1966). *James Boswell: The Earlier Years 1740–1769*. New York: McGraw-Hill.

—— (1981). *Pride and Negligence*. New York: McGraw-Hill.

Pratt, Samuel Jackson (1777). *Supplement to the Life of David Hume, Esq.* London.

Prebble, John (1977). *Mutiny: Highland Regiments in Revolt 1743–1804.* Harmondsworth: Penguin.

Preble, G. H., Lt. USN (1859). 'Gen. Robert Melville', *Notes and Queries,* 1st ser., 11: 247–8.

Precipitation and Fall of Messrs Douglas, Heron and Company, late Bankers in Air with the Causes of their Distress and Ruin investigated and considered by a Committee of Inquiry appointed by the Proprietors (1778). Edinburgh.

Prevost, Pierre (1805). *Notice de la vie et des écrits de George-Louis Le Sage de Genève.* Geneva: J. J. Paschoud.

Priestley, Joseph (1774). *Examination of Dr Reid's Inquiry into the Human Mind on the Principles of Common Sense, Dr Beattie's Essay on the Nature and Immutability of Truth, and Dr Oswald's Appeal to Common Sense in behalf of Religion.* London: J. Johnson.

Prior, Sir James (1853). *Life of Burke,* 5th edn. London: Bohn.

Pufendorf, Samuel (1724). *De Officio Hominis* . . . supplemented by G. Carmichael. Edinburgh.

Pugliese, S. (1924). 'I viaggi di Marsilio Landriani', *Archivio storico lombardo,* ser. 6, 1: 145–85.

Quarrie, P. (1986). 'The Christ Church Collection Books', in Sutherland and Mitchell (1986: 493–506).

Rae, John (1895/1965). *Life of Adam Smith.* London: Macmillan. Repr. New York: Augustus M. Kelley.

Ramsay of Ochtertyre, John (1888). *Scotland and Scotsmen in the Eighteenth Century,* ed. A. Allardyce. 2 vols. Edinburgh and London: William Blackwood.

Raphael, D. D. (1972–3). 'Hume and Adam Smith on Justice and Utility', *Proceedings of the Aristotelian Society.*

—— (1975). 'The Impartial Spectator', in A. S. Skinner and T. Wilson (eds.), *Essays on Adam Smith.* Oxford: Clarendon Press.

—— (1976). 'Adam Smith as a Professor', TS paper, Edinburgh IPSA Congress.

—— (1977). ' "The True Old Humean philosophy" and its Influence on Adam Smith', in G. P. Morice (ed.), *David Hume Bicentenary Papers.* Edinburgh: Edinburgh Univ. Press.

—— (1980). *Justice and Liberty.* 2 vols. London: Athlone Press.

—— (1985). *Adam Smith.* Oxford: Oxford Univ. Press.

—— (1988). 'Newton and Adam Smith', *Queen's Quarterly,* 95: 36–49.

—— (1990). 'Adam Smith's Moral Philosophy', Nagoya Smith Symposium 1990, lecture TS.

Raphael, D. D. (1992*a*). 'Adam Smith 1790: The Man Recalled; The Philosopher Revived', in Peter Jones and A. S. Skinner (eds.), *Adam Smith Reviewed.* Edinburgh: Edinburgh Univ. Press.

—— (1992*b*). 'A New Light', in Smyth (1992: 2–3).

—— (1994). 'Adam Ferguson's Tutorship of Lord Chesterfield', *SVEC* 323: 209–23.

—— Raynor, D. R., and Ross, I. S. (1990). ' "This Very Awkward Affair": An Entanglement of Scottish Professors with English Lords', *SVEC* 278: 419–63.

—— and Sakamoto, Tatsuya (1990). 'Anonymous Writings of David Hume', *Journal of the History of Philosophy,* 28: 271–81.

Rashid, Salim (1982). 'Adam Smith's Rise to Fame: A Reexamination of the Evidence', *The Eighteenth Century: Theory and Interpretation,* 23: 70–9.

Rashid, Salim (1990). 'Adam Smith's Acknowledgements, Neo-Plagiarism and WN', *Journal of Libertarian Studies*, 9: 1–24.

—— (1992). 'Adam Smith and the Market Mechanism', *History of Political Economy*, 21: 129–52.

Raynal, Jean (1759). *Histoire de la ville de Toulouse*.

Raynor, David R. (1978). 'On Hume's Corrections to *Treatise* III', *Philosophical Quarterly*, 28: 265–8.

—— (1982*a*). 'Hume's Critique of Helvétius' *De l'esprit*', *Studies on Voltaire and the Eighteenth Century*, 215: 223–9.

—— (ed.) (1982*b*). *Sister Peg: a pamphlet hitherto unknown by David Hume*. Cambridge: Cambridge Univ. Press.

—— (1984). 'Hume's Abstract of Adam Smith's TMS', *Journal of the History of Philosophy*, 22: 51–79.

—— (1987*a*). 'Hume and Robertson's *History of Scotland*', *British Journal for Eighteenth-Century Studies*, 10: 59–63.

—— (1987*b*). 'Hutcheson's Defence Against a Charge of Plagiarism', *Eighteenth-Century Ireland*, 2: 177–81.

—— (forthcoming). 'Adam Smith: Two Letters to Henry Beaufoy, MP'. *Scottish Journal of Political Economy*.

—— and Skinner, Andrew S. (1994). 'Sir James Steuart: Nine Letters on the American Conflict, 1775–1778', *William and Mary Quarterly*, 3rd ser., 51: 755–76.

—— and Ross, I. S. (forthcoming). 'Adam Smith and Count Windisch-Grätz: New Letters'.

Recktenwald, Horst Claus (1976). *Adam Smith: Sein Leben und sein Werk*. Munich: C. H. Beck.

Reder, Melvin (1982). 'Chicago Economics: Permanence and Change', *Journal of Economic Literature*, 20: 1–38.

Reid, John (1683). *The Scots Gard'ner*. Edinburgh.

Reid, Thomas (1967). *Philosophical Works*. 2 vols. Hildesheim: Georg Olms.

—— (1990). *Practical Ethics, Being Lectures and Papers on Natural Religion, Self-Government, Natural Jurisprudence, and the Law of Nations*, ed. with intro. and commentary by Knud Haakonssen. Princeton, NJ: Princeton Univ. Press.

Reilly, Robin (1978). *Pitt the Younger 1759–1806*. London: Cassell.

Ricardo, David (1821/1929). *The Principles of Political Economy and Taxation*, 3rd edn. London: Dent.

Richardson, J. S., and Beveridge, James (1973). *Linlithgow Palace*, 2nd edn. Edinburgh: HMSO.

Richardson, William (1803). 'Account of . . . [Archibald Arthur]', in *Discourses on Theological and Literary Subjects. By the late Rev. Archibald Arthur, M.A., Professor of Moral Philosophy in the University of Glasgow*. Glasgow: Glasgow Univ. Press.

Ridpath, George (1922). *Diary*, ed. and intro. Sir James Balfour Paul. Edinburgh: Constable.

Riley, P. W. J. (1964). *The English Ministers and Scotland 1707–1727*. London: Athlone Press.

Robbins, Caroline (1959). *The Eighteenth-Century Commonwealthman*. Cambridge, Mass.: Harvard Univ. Press.

Robbins, Lionel (1952). *The Theory of Economic Policy in English Classical Political Economy*. London: Macmillan.

Roberts, William (1834). *Memoirs of . . . Mrs Hanna More*, 2nd edn. 4 vols. London: Thomas Ditton.

Robertson, John (1983). 'The Scottish Enlightenment at the Limits of Civic Tradition', in Hont and Ignatieff (1983: 141–51).

—— (1985). *The Scottish Enlightenment and the Militia Issue*. Edinburgh: John Donald.

—— (1990). 'The Legacy of Adam Smith: Government and Economic Development in WN', in *Victorian Liberalism: Nineteenth-Century Political Thought and Practice*, ed. Richard Bellamy. London: Routledge.

Robertson, William (1818). *Works*. With an account of his Life and Writings by the Revd. Alex Stewart. 12 vols. Edinburgh: Peter Hill *et al.*

Robinson, Joan (1964). *Economic Philosophy*. Harmondsworth: Pelican.

Robison, John (1969). 'Narrative (1796) of Mr Watt's Invention of the improved Engine', in Eric Robinson and A. E. Musson, *James Watt and the Steam Revolution: A Documentary History*. London: Adams & Dart.

Roche, Daniel (1978). *Le Siècle des lumières en province: académies et académiciens provinçiaux 1680–1789*. Paris: Mouton.

Rollin, Charles (1759). *The Method of Teaching and Studying the Belles Lettres*, 4 vols. Edinburgh: A. Kincaid *et al.*

Romilly, Sir Samuel (1840). *Memoirs*. 2 vols. London: Murray.

Roper, Derek (1978). *Reviewing before the Edinburgh, 1788–1802*. London: Methuen.

Rorty, Richard (1984). 'The Historiography of Philosophy: Four Genres', in R. Rorty, J. B. Schneewind, and Q. Skinner (eds.), *Philosophy in History*. Cambridge: Cambridge Univ. Press.

Rosenberg, Nathan (1960). 'Some Institutional Aspects of WN', *Journal of Political Economy*, 18: 557–70.

—— (1975). 'Adam Smith on Profits: Paradox Lost and Regained', in A. S. Skinner and Thomas Wilson (eds.) (1975: 377–89).

—— (1990). 'Adam Smith and the Stock of Moral Capital', *History of Political Economy*, 22: 1–17.

—— (1994). *Exploring the Black Box: Technology, Economics, and History*. Cambridge: Cambridge Univ. Press.

Ross, I. S. (1964). 'Hutcheson on Hume's *Treatise*: An Unnoticed Letter', *Journal of the History of Philosophy*, 4: 69–72.

—— (1965). 'A Bluestocking Over the Border: Mrs Elizabeth Montagu's Aesthetic Adventures in Scotland, 1766', *Huntington Library Quarterly*, 28: 213–33.

—— (1972). *Lord Kames and the Scotland of His Day*. Oxford: Clarendon Press.

—— (1974). 'Educating an Eighteenth-Century Duke', in G. W. S. Barrow (ed.), *The Scottish Tradition: Essays in Honour of R. G. Cant*. Edinburgh: Scottish Academic Press.

—— (1984a). 'The Physiocrats and Adam Smith', *British Journal of Eighteenth-Century Studies*, 7: 177–89.

—— (1984b). 'Adam Smith as Rhetorician', *Man and Nature: Proceedings of the Canadian Society for Eighteenth-Century Studies*, 2: 61–73.

—— (1984c). 'Adam Smith and Education', *Studies in Eighteenth-Century Culture*, 13: 173–87.

—— (1987). 'Aesthetic Philosophy: Hutcheson and Hume to Alison', in Andrew Hook (ed.), *The History of Scottish Literature*, ii: 1660–1800. Aberdeen: Aberdeen Univ. Press, 248–51.

Ross, I. S. and Webster, A. M. (1981). 'Adam Smith: Two Letters', *Scottish Journal of Political Economy*, 28: 206–9.

Ross, W. D. (1959). *Aristotle: A Complete Exposition of His Work and Thought*. New York: Meridian.

Rothbard, Murray N. (1988). *Ludwig von Mises: Scholar, Creator, Hero*. Auburn, Ala.: Ludwig von Mises Institute.

—— (1993). 'Mises and the Role of the Economist in Public Policy', in Herbener (1993: 193–208).

Roughead, William (ed.) (1909). *Trial of Captain Porteous*. Glasgow: William Hodge.

Rousseau, Jean-Jacques (1959). *Œuvres complètes*, i: *Les Confessions; Rousseau juge de Jean-Jacques; et autres textes autobiographiques*, ed. Bernard Gagnebin, Marcel Raymond, and Robert Osmont. Paris: Gallimard.

—— (1963a). *Discourse on the Origin of Inequality* [1755], trans. G. D. H. Cole. Everyman edn. London: Dent.

—— (1963b). *Émile* [1762], trans. Barbara Foxley. London: Dent.

Rowse, A. L. (1975). *Oxford in the History of England*. New York: Putnam's.

Roy, Subroto (1991). *Philosophy of Economics: On the Scope of Reason in Economic Inquiry*. London: Routledge.

Royal Commission on Historical Monuments in England (1939). *An Inventory of the Historical Monuments in the City of Oxford*. London: HMSO.

Royal Society of Edinburgh (1787, 1788). *Transactions*, i, ii.

Rule, John (1992). *The Vital Century: England's Developing Economy 1714–1815*. London: Longman.

Ruwet, Joseph, *et al.* (eds.) (1976). *Lettres de Turgot à la duchesse d'Enville (1764–75 et 1777–80)*. Louvain: Bibliothèque de l'Université.

Sacke, G. (1938). 'Die Moskauer Nachschrift der Vorlesungen von Adam Smith', *Zeitschrift für Nationalökonomie*, 9: 351–6.

Saint Clair, Rex E. (1964). *Doctors Monro: A Medical Saga*. London: Wellcome Historical Medical Library.

Samuels, Warren J. (ed.) (1976). *The Chicago School of Political Economy*. East Lansing: Michigan State Univ. Graduate School of Business Administration.

Sandbach, F. H. (1975). *The Stoics*. London: Chatto & Windus.

Saunders, Margaret H. B. (1992). *Robert Adam and Scotland*. Edinburgh: HMSO.

Sauvy, Alfred, *et al.* (eds.) (1958). *François Quesnay et la physiocratie*. 2 vols. Paris: Institut National d'Études Démographiques.

Savile, Sir George (1762). *Argument Concerning the Militia*. London.

Say, Jean-Baptiste (1840). *Cours complet d'économie politique pratique*, 2nd edn. 2 vols. Paris: Guillaumin.

Schama, Simon (1989). *Citizens: A Chronicle of the French Revolution*. Toronto: Vintage Books.

—— (1992). *Patriots and Liberators: Revolution in the Netherlands 1780–1813*, 2nd edn. London: Fontana.

Schroeder, Paul W. (1994). *The Transformation of European Politics 1763–1848*. Oxford: Clarendon Press.

Schumpeter, Joseph (1954). *History of Economic Analysis*. New York: Oxford Univ. Press.

Schwartz, Richard B. (1983). *Daily Life in Johnson's London*. Madison: Univ. of Wisconsin Press.

Scotland, James (1969). *The History of Scottish Education*, 2 vols. London: Athlone Press.

Scott, P. H. (ed.) (1979). *1707: The Union of Scotland and England*. Edinburgh: Chambers.

Scott, Sir Walter (n.d.). Review [1824] of *The Works of John Home*, in *Essays on Chivalry, Romance and the Drama*. London: Frederick Warne.

Scott, W. R. (1900). *Francis Hutcheson: His Life, Teaching and Position in the History of Philosophy*. Cambridge: Cambridge Univ. Press.

—— (1935–6). 'Adam Smith at Downing Street, 1766–7', *Economic History Review*, 6: 79–89.

—— (1937). *Adam Smith as Student and Professor*. Glasgow: Jackson.

—— (1940). 'Studies Relating to Adam Smith during the Last Fifty Years', ed. A. L. Macfie, *Proceedings of the British Academy*.

Segoudy, Jean (1969). 'Histoire de Montpellier', TS, pt. iii: 'Montpellier ville royale, sous la dynastie des Bourbons.'

Semmel, Bernard (1970). *The Rise of Free Trade Imperialism*. Cambridge: Cambridge Univ. Press.

Seward, William (1797). *Anecdotes of Some Distinguished Persons*. London: T. Cadell & W. Davies.

Shackleton, Robert (1972). 'The Greatest Happiness of the Greatest Number: The History of Bentham's Phrase', *Studies on Voltaire and the Eighteenth Century*, 90: 1461–82.

Sharp, L. W. (1962). 'Charles Mackie: The First Professor of History at Edinburgh University', *Scottish Historical Review*, 41, 23–45.

Shaw, John Stuart (1983). *The Management of Scottish Society 1707–1764: Power, Nobles, Lawyers, Edinburgh Agents and English Influences*. Edinburgh: Donald.

Shelton, George (1981). *Dean Tucker and Eighteenth-Century Economic and Political Thought*. London: Macmillan.

Shepherd, Christine M. (1975). 'Philosophy and Science in the Arts Curriculum of the Scottish Universities', Ph.D., Univ. of Edinburgh.

—— (1990). 'The Arts Curriculum at Glasgow University, 1680–1725', Eighteenth-Century Scottish Studies Conference paper, Univ. of Strathclyde.

Sher, Richard B. (1982). 'Moderates, Managers and Popular Politics in Mid-Eighteenth-Century Edinburgh: The Drysdale "Bustle" of the 1760s', in Dwyer *et al.* (1982: 179–209).

—— (1985). *Church and University in the Scottish Enlightenment: The Moderate Literati of Edinburgh*. Princeton, NJ: Princeton Univ. Press.

—— (1990). '1688 and 1788: William Robertson on Revolution in Britain and France', in Paul Dukes and John Dunkley (eds.), *Culture and Revolution*. London: Pinter.

Sher, Richard B. (1995). 'Commerce, Religion in the Enlightenment in Eighteenth-Century Glasgow', in Devine and Marshall (1995: 312–59).

—— and Smitten, Jeffrey R. (eds.) (1990). *Scotland and America in the Age of Enlightenment*. Princeton, NJ: Princeton Univ. Press.

Sherbo, Arthur (1992). 'Some Early Readers in the British Museum', *Transactions of the Cambridge Bibliographical Society*, 6.

Shy, John (1973). 'The American Revolution: The Military Conflict Considered as a Revolutionary War', in Kurtz and Hutson (eds.) (1973: 121–56).

Sibbald, Sir Robert (1803). *The History . . . of Fife and Kinross*, ed. R. Tullis. Cupar: Tullis.

Simpson, John (1990). 'Some Eighteenth-Century Intellectual Contacts between Scotland and Scandinavia', in Grant G. Simpson (ed.), *Scotland and Scandinavia*. Edinburgh: Donald.

Simpson, M. C. T. (1979). 'Books Belonging to Adam Smith in EUL', *The Bibliotheck* 9: 187–199.

Sinclair, Archdeacon John (1875). *Sketches of Old Times and Distant Places*. London: John Murray.

Sinclair, Sir John (1831). *Correspondence*. 2 vols. London: H. Colburn & R. Bentley.

Skinner, Andrew S. (1979). *A System of Social Science: Papers Relating to Adam Smith*. Oxford: Clarendon Press. [2nd edn. forthcoming]

—— (1981). 'Sir James Steuart: Author of a System', *Scottish Journal of Political Economy*, 28: 20–42.

—— (1983). 'Adam Smith: Rhetoric and the Communication of Ideas', in A. W. Coats (ed.), *Methodological Controversy in Economics: Historical Essays in Honour of T. W. Hutchison*. London: JAI Press Inc.

—— (1986). 'Adam Smith: Then and Now', in Black (1986: 16–42).

—— (1988). 'Sir James Steuart: Economic Theory and Policy', in Peter Jones (ed.), *Philosophy and Science in the Scottish Enlightenment*. Edinburgh: Donald.

—— (1990a). 'The Shaping of Political Economy in the Enlightenment', *Scottish Journal of Political Economy*, 37: 145–65.

—— (1990b). 'Adam Smith and America: The Political Economy of Conflict', in Sher and Smitten (1990: 148–62).

—— (1992a). 'Smith and Physiocracy: The Development of a System', TS revision of ch. 4, *A System of Social Science* (1979).

—— (1992b). 'Adam Smith: Ethics and Self-Love', in Jones and Skinner (1992: 142–67).

—— (1993). 'The Shaping of Political Economy in the Enlightenment', in Mizuta and Sugiyama (1993: 113–39).

—— and Wilson, Thomas (eds.) (1975). *Essays on Adam Smith*. Oxford: Clarendon Press.

Skinner, Quentin (1981). *Machiavelli*. Oxford: Oxford Univ. Press.

—— (1988). 'A Reply to My Critics', in James Tully (ed.), *Meaning and Context: Quentin Skinner and his Critics*. Cambridge: Polity Press.

Smart, Alastair (1992). *Allan Ramsay: Painter, Essayist and Man of the Enlightenment*. New Haven, Conn.: Yale Univ. Press.

Smellie, William (1800). *Literary and Characteristical Lives of J. Gregory, Home of Kames, Hume and Smith*. Edinburgh.

Smelser, Neil J., and Swedberg, Richard (eds.) (1994). *The Handbook of Economic Sociology*. Princeton, NJ: Princeton Univ. Press.

[Smith, John] Anon. (1722). *A Short Account of the Late Treatment of the Students of the University of G——w*. Dublin.

Smith, R. S. (1957). 'WN in Spain and Hispanic America, 1780–1830', *Journal of Political Economy*, 65: 104–25.

Smitten, Jeffery R. (1990). 'Moderation and History: William Robertson's Unfinished History of British America', in Sher and Smitten (1990: 163–79).

Smout, T. C. (ed.) (1978). 'Journal of Kalmeter's Travels in Scotland 1719–20', in R. H. Campbell (ed.), *Scottish Industrial History: A Miscellany*. Edinburgh: Scottish History Society.

—— (1983). 'Where Had the Scottish Economy Got to by the Third Quarter of the Eighteenth Century?', in Hont and Ignatieff (1983: 45–72).

—— and Fenton, A. (1965). 'Scottish Agriculture before the Improvers: An Exploration', *Agricultural History Review*, 13: 73–95.

Smyth, Damian (ed.) (1992). *Francis Hutcheson. Fortnight*, 308, supplement.

Snyder, F. B. (1932). *The Life of Robert Burns*. New York: Macmillan.

Somerville, Thomas (1861). *My Own Life and Times, 1741–1814*, ed. W. L. Edinburgh: Edmonston & Black.

Sonenscher, Michael (1989). *Work and Wages: Natural Law, Politics, and the Eighteenth-Century Trades*. Cambridge: Cambridge Univ. Press.

Sotheby's Catalogue (15 Dec. 1987). *English Literature and History*. London.

Speeches Delivered at the Official Meetings of the Imperial Moscow University by the Russian Professors thereof, Containing Their Short Curriculum Vitae (1819). Moscow: Association of the Lovers of Russian Letters.

Spengler, J. J. (1978). 'Smith versus Hobbes: Economy versus Polity', in F. R. Glahe (ed.), *Adam Smith and WN: 1776–1976 Bicentennial Essays*. Boulder: Colorado Associated Univ. Press.

Spink, J. S. (1982). 'Lévesque de Pouilly et David Hume', *Revue de littérature comparée*, 56: 157–75.

Sprat, Thomas (1667/1958). *History of the Royal Society*, ed. Jackson I. Cope and Harold W. Jones. St Louis: Washington Univ.

Staum, Martin S. (1980). *Cabanis: Enlightenment and Medical Philosophy in the French Revolution*. Princeton, NJ: Princeton Univ. Press.

Steele, Peter (1845). 'Parish of Dalkeith', *New Statistical Account of Scotland*, i. 490. Edinburgh and London: W. Blackwood.

Steuart, Sir James (1767/1966). *An Inquiry into the Principles of Political Œconomy: Being an Essay on the Science of Domestic Policy in Free Nations*, ed. and intro. Andrew S. Skinner. 2 vols. Edinburgh: Oliver & Boyd.

—— (1805/1967). *The Works: Political, Metaphysical and Chronological*, ed. Sir James Steuart, Bart. 6 vols. London: T. Cadell and W. Davies. Repr. New York: Augustus M. Kelley.

Stevenson, David (1988). *The Origins of Freemasonry: Scotland's Century, 1590–1710*. Cambridge: Cambridge Univ. Press.

Stevenson, J. B. (1985). *The Clyde Estuary and Central Region*. Edinburgh: HMSO.

Stewart, Dugald (1854–60). *Collected Works*, ed. Sir William Hamilton. 11 vols. Edinburgh: Blackwood.

Stewart, M. A. (1985). 'Berkeley and the Rankenian Club', *Hermathena*, 139: 25–45.

Stewart, M. A. (1987a). 'George Turnbull and Educational Reform', in Jennifer Carter and Joan Pittock (eds.), *Aberdeen and the Enlightenment*. Aberdeen: Aberdeen Univ. Press.

—— (1987b). 'John Smith and the Molesworth Circle', *Eighteenth-Century Ireland*, 2: 89–102.

—— (1990a). 'James Moor and the Classical Revival', TS, Eighteenth-Century Scottish Studies Society Conference, Univ. of Strathclyde.

—— (1990b). 'The Origins of the Scottish Greek Chairs', in E. M. Craik (ed.), *'Owls to Athens': Essays . . . Presented to Sir Kenneth Dover*. Oxford: Clarendon Press.

Stewart, M. A. (ed.) (1990c). *Studies in the Philosophy of the Scottish Enlightenment*. Oxford: Clarendon Press.

474 *Bibliography*

—— (1991). 'The Stoic Legacy in the Early Scottish Enlightenment', in M. J. Osler (ed.), *Atoms, Pneuma, and Tranquility*. Cambridge: Cambridge Univ. Press.

—— (1992). 'Abating Bigotry and Hot Zeal', in Smyth (1992: 4–6).

—— and Wright, John P. (eds.) (1995). *Hume and Hume's Connexions*. Edinburgh: Edinburgh Univ. Press.

Stewart, Mary Margaret (1970). 'Adam Smith and the Comtesse de Boufflers', *Studies in Scottish Literature*, 7: 184–7.

Stewart-Robertson, J. C. (1983). 'Cicero Among the Shadows: Scottish Prelections of Virtue and Duty', *Rivista critica di storia della filosofia*, 1: 25–49.

Stigler, George J. (1977). 'The Successes and Failures of Professor Smith', in M. J. Artis and A. R. Nobay (eds.), *Studies in Modern Economic Analysis*. Oxford: Blackwell.

Stimson, Shannon C. (1989). 'Republicanism and the Recovery of the Political in Adam Smith', in Murray Milgate and Cheryl B. Welch (eds.), *Critical Issues in Social Thought*. London: Academic Press.

Stones, L. (1984). 'The Life and Career of John Snell (c. 1629–1679)', *Stair Society Miscellany*, 2: 148–85.

Strang, John (1857). *Glasgow and Its Clubs*, 2nd edn. London and Glasgow: R. Griffin.

Streminger, Gerhard (1989). *Adam Smith*. Reinbek bei Hamburg: Rowohlt.

—— (1994). *David Hume: sein Leben und sein Werk*. Paderborn: Ferdinand Schönigh.

Sudo, Yoshiaki (1995). 'An Unpublished Lecture of Hugh Blair on the Poems of Ossian'. *Hiyoshi Review of English Studies*, Keio Univ., Yokohama: 160–94.

Sutherland, L. S., and Mitchell, L. G. (eds.) (1986). *The History of the University of Oxford*. v: *The Eighteenth Century*. Oxford: Clarendon Press.

Swedberg, Richard (1994). 'Markets as Social Structures', in Smelser and Swedberg (1994: 255–82).

Szenberg, Michael (ed.) (1993). *Eminent Economists: Their Life Philosophies*. Cambridge: Cambridge Univ. Press.

Tanaka, Hideo (1993). 'Lord Kames as Economist: Hume–Tucker Controversy and the Economic Thought of Kames', *Kyoto University Economic Review*, 63: 33–50.

Tanaka, Toshihiro (ed.) (1989). *The Scottish Enlightenment and Economic Thought in the Making: Studies of Classical Political Economy*, i [In Japanese.] Tokyo: Nihon Keizai Hyoronsha.

—— (ed.) (1990). *The Formation and Development of Classical Political Economy: Studies of Political Economy*, iii [In Japanese.] Tokyo: Nihon Keizai Hyoronsha.

—— (1992). *David Hume and the Scottish Enlightenment: A Study in the History of Eighteenth-Century British Economic Thought* (in Japanese). Kyoto: Koyoh Shobo.

Taylor, Eva G. R. (1966). *Mathematical Practitioners of Hanoverian England*. Cambridge: Cambridge Univ. Press.

Taylor, John (1832). *Records of My Life*. 2 vols. London: Bull.

Taylor, Norman W. (1967). 'Adam Smith's First Russian Disciple', *Slavonic Review*, 45: 425–38.

Teichgraeber, R. F., III (1986). *'Free Trade' and Moral Philosophy*. Durham, NC: Duke Univ. Press.

—— (1987). ' "Less Abused than I Had Reason to Expect": The Reception of WN in Britain, 1776–90', *Historical Journal*, 30: 337–66.

—— (1988). 'WN and Tradition: Adam Smith before Malthus', TS, ASECS Meeting, Knoxville, Tenn.

Terry, Charles Sanford (ed.) (1922). *The Forty-Five: A Narrative of the Last Jacobite Rising by Several Contemporary Hands*. Cambridge: Cambridge Univ. Press.

Thal, Peter (1990). 'Esoteric and Exoteric Elements in Adam Smith's Economic Thinking: Consequences for the Reception of His Theories Today', Vancouver Smith Symposium 1990, lecture TS.

Thirkell, Alison (n.d.). *Auld Anster*. Anstruther: Buckie House Gallery.

Thom, William (1764). *Motives which have determined the University of Glasgow to desert the Blackfriars Church and betake themselves to a Chapel*.

Thompson, E. P. (1968). *The Making of the English Working Class*. Harmondsworth: Pelican.

—— (1993). *Customs in Common: Studies in Traditional Popular Culture*. New York: The New Press.

Thompson, Harold W. (1931). *A Scottish Man of Feeling: Some Account of Henry Mackenzie . . . and of the Golden Age of Burns and Scott*. London: Oxford Univ. Press.

Thomson, Derick S. (1952). *The Gaelic Sources of Macpherson's Ossian*. Edinburgh: Oliver & Boyd.

—— (1963). ' "Ossian", Macpherson and the Gaelic World of the Eighteenth Century', *Aberdeen University Review*, 40.

—— (1974). *An Introduction to Gaelic Poetry*. London: Gollancz.

—— (1979). Foreword to repr. of Macpherson's *Fragments*, 2nd edn. Dundee.

—— (1983). *The Companion to Gaelic Culture*. Oxford: Blackwell.

Thomson, John (1832). *Life, Lectures and Writings of William Cullen*. 2 vols. Edinburgh: Blackwood.

Todd, William B. (1974). 'David Hume: A Preliminary Bibliography', in Todd (ed.), *Hume and the Enlightenment: Essays Presented to Ernest Campbell Mossner*. Edinburgh: Edinburgh Univ. Press; Austin: Univ. of Texas Humanities Research Center.

Todhunter, Isaac (ed.) (1955). *Euclid's Elements*, intro. by Sir T. L. Heath. London: J. M. Dent.

Tomasson, Katherine (1958). *The Jacobite General*. Edinburgh: Blackwood.

Tribe, Keith (1988). *Governing Economy: The Reformation of German Economic Discourse 1750–1840*. Cambridge: Cambridge Univ. Press.

Tucker, Thomas (1656/1881). 'Report upon the Settlement of the Revenues of Excise and Customs in Scotland', in J. D. Marwick (ed.), *Miscellany of the Scottish Burgh Records Society*. Edinburgh.

Tully, James (1991). Intro. to Samuel Pufendorf, *On the Duty of Man and Citizen*. Cambridge: Cambridge Univ. Press.

Turnbull, Gordon (1994). 'Boswell in Glasgow: Adam Smith, Moral Sentiments and the Sympathy of Biography', in Hook and Sher (1995).

Turner, G. L. E. (1986). 'The Physical Sciences', in Sutherland and Mitchell (1986: 672 ff.).

Turnock, David (1982). *The Historical Geography of Scotland since 1707*. Cambridge: Cambridge Univ. Press.

Tweedie, C. (1922). *James Stirling*. Oxford: Clarendon Press.

Tytler, A. F., Lord Woodhouselee (1807). *Memoirs of the Life and Writings of the Honourable Henry Home of Kames*, 1st edn. Edinburgh: William Creech.

Veitch, John (1869). *Memoir of Sir William Hamilton, Bart*. Edinburgh and London: Blackwood.

Vicenza, Gloria (1984). *Adam Smith e la cultura classica*. Pisa.

Vickers, Brian (1971). Review of Howell (1971), *TLS*, 5 Aug.

——— (1985). 'The Royal Society and English Prose Style: A Reassessment', in Vickers (ed.), *Rhetoric and the Pursuit of Truth: Language Change in the Seventeenth and Eighteenth Centuries*. Univ. of California, Los Angeles: William Andrews Clark Memorial Library.

Viner, Jacob (1958). *The Long View and the Short*. Glencoe, Ill.: Free Press.

——— (1960). 'The Intellectual History of Laissez Faire', *Journal of Law and Economics*, 3: 45–69.

——— (1965). 'Introductory Guide' to Rae (1965).

——— (1966). 'Adam Smith and Laissez Faire', in *Adam Smith, 1776–1926*, fac. of 1928 edn. New York: Augustus M. Kelley.

——— (1972) *The Role of Providence in the Social Order: An Essay in Intellectual History*. Princeton, NJ: Princeton Univ. Press.

Viroli, Maurizio (1990). 'The Concept of *Ordre* and the Language of Classical Republicanism in Jean-Jacques Rousseau', in Pagden (1990: 159–78).

Voges, Friedhelm (1985). 'Moderate and Evangelical Theology in the Later Eighteenth Century: Differences and Shared Attitudes', *Records of the Scottish Church History Society*, 32: 141–57.

Voltaire (1748). 'Dissertation on Ancient and Modern Tragedy', preceding *Sémiramis*.

——— (1784–89). *Œuvres complètes*, ed. Beaumarchais. 70 vols. Paris: Kehl.

Wada, Shigeshi (1990). 'Steuart and Smith with Respect to the Formation of Political Economy', in Tanaka (1990).

Walker, Bruce, and Ritchie, Graham (1989). *Exploring Scotland's Heritage: Fife and Tayside*. Edinburgh: HMSO.

Wallis, Helen, *et al.* (1975). *The American War of Independence 1775–1783: A Commemorative Exhibition*. London: British Museum Publications.

Walmsley, Peter (1990). *The Rhetoric of Berkeley's Philosophy*. Cambridge: Cambridge Univ. Press.

Walpole, Horace (1937–83). *Correspondence*, ed. W. S. Lewis *et al.* 48 vols. New Haven, Conn., Yale Univ. Press.

Waszek, Norbert (1984). 'Two Concepts of Morality: Adam Smith's Ethics and its Stoic Origin', *Journal of the History of Ideas*, 45: 591–606.

——— (1985). 'Bibliography of the Scottish Enlightenment in German', *SVEC* 230: 283–303.

——— (1988). *The Scottish Enlightenment and Hegel's Account of Civil Society*. Dordrecht: Kluwer Academic.

——— (1993). 'Adam Smith in Germany, 1776–1832', in Mizuta and Sugiyama (1993: 163–80).

Watanabe, Kunohiro (1990). 'Steuart's Response to the Current Forth–Clyde Canal Problem', in Tanaka (1990).

Watson, J. Steven (1960). *The Reign of George III, 1760–1815*. Oxford: Clarendon Press.

Watson, Mark (1990). *Jute and Flax Mills in Dundee*. Tayport: Hutton Press.

Webster, Alison (1988). 'Adam Smith's Students', *Scotia: American-Canadian Journal of Scottish Studies*, 12: 13–26.

Weinbrot, Howard D. (1993). *Britannia's Issue: The Rise of British Literature from Dryden to Ossian*. Cambridge: Cambridge Univ. Press.

Werhane, Patricia H. (1991). *Adam Smith and His Legacy for Modern Capitalism*. New York: Oxford Univ. Press.

West, E. G. (1976). *Adam Smith: The Man and His Works*. Indianapolis: Liberty Press.

Weulersse, G. (1910/1968). *Le Mouvement physiocratique en France de 1756 à 1770*. New York: Johnson Reprint.

Whatley, C. A. (1984). *'That Important and Necessary Article': The Salt Industry and Its Trade in Fife and Tayside c.1570–1850*. Dundee: Abertay Historical Society.

—— (1986). 'Sales of Scottish Marine Salt', *Scottish Economic and Social History*, 6: 4–17.

Whitrow, G. J. (1988). *Time in History: The Evolution of Our General Awareness of Time and Temporal Perspective*. Oxford: Oxford Univ. Press.

Whittington, G., and Whyte, Ian D. (eds.) (1983). *A Historical Geography of Scotland*. London: Academic Press.

Whyte, Ian, and Whyte, Kathleen (1991). *The Changing Scottish Landscape 1500–1800*. London: Routledge.

Whyte, Ian D. (1979). *Agriculture and Society in Seventeenth Century Scotland*. Edinburgh: Donald.

Wilberforce, Robert Isaac, and Wilberforce, Samuel (eds.) (1840). *The Correspondence of William Wilberforce*, London: John Murray.

Wilkinson, J. (1988). 'The Last Illness of David Hume', *Proceedings of the Royal College of Physicians of Edinburgh*, 18: 72–9.

Williams, David (1980). *Incidents in My Own Life*, ed. with an account of his published writings by Peter France. Falmer: Univ. of Sussex Library.

Williams, Neville (1959). *Contraband Cargoes: Seven Centuries of Smuggling*. London: Longmans, Green.

Williamson, Elizabeth, Riches, Anne, and Higgs, Malcolm (1990). *Glasgow: The Buildings of Scotland*. London: Penguin.

Willis, Kirk (1979). 'The Role in Parliament of the Economic Ideas of Adam Smith, 1776–1860', *History of Political Economy*, 11: 505–44.

Wilson, Charles (1971). *England's Apprenticeship 1603–1763*. London: Longman.

Winch, Donald (1969). *Economics and Policy: A Historical Study*. London: Hodder and Stoughton.

—— (1971). *The Emergence of Economics as a Science*. London: Collins.

—— (1978). *Adam Smith's Politics*. Cambridge: Cambridge Univ. Press.

—— (1983). 'The System of the North: Dugald Stewart and His Pupils', in Collini *et al.* (1983: 25–61).

—— (1988). 'Adam Smith and the Liberal Tradition', in Haakonssen (1988: 83–104).

—— (1993). 'Adam Smith: Scottish Moral Philosopher as Political Economist', in Mizuta and Sugiyama (1993: 85–112).

Windham, William (1866). *Diary*, ed. Mrs H. Baring. London.

Winkel, Harald (1988). 'Zur Entwicklung der Nationalökonomie an der Universität Königsberg', in Norbert Waszek (ed.), *Die Institutionalisierung der Nationalökonomie an deutschen Universitäten*. St Katharinen: Scripta Mercaturae.

Winslow, Carl (1977). 'Sussex Smugglers', in Hay *et al.* (1977: 119–66).

Wodrow, Robert (1843). *Analecta, or Materials for a History of Remarkable Providences, 1701–31*, ed. M. Leischman. 4 vols. Edinburgh: Maitland Club.

Wood, John Cunningham (ed.) (1983–4). *Adam Smith: Critical Accounts*. 4 vols. London: Croom Helm.

Wood, Paul B. (1984). 'Thomas Reid, Natural Philosopher: A Study of Science and Philosophy in the Scottish Enlightenment', Ph.D. diss., Univ. of Leeds.

—— (1990). 'Science and the Pursuit of Virtue in the Aberdeen Enlightenment', in Stewart (1990*c*: 127–49).

Wood, Paul B. —— (1993). *The Aberdeen Enlightenment: The Arts Curriculum in the Eighteenth Century*. Aberdeen: Aberdeen Univ. Press.

Woolley, A. R. (1972). *The Clarendon Guide to Oxford*, 2nd edn. Oxford: Oxford Univ. Press.

Wootton, David (1990). 'Hume's "Of Miracles": Probability and Irreligion', in Stewart (1990*c*: 191–229).

Wraxall, Sir N. William (1904). *Historical Memoirs of My Own Time*. London: Kegan Paul, Trench, Trubner.

Wright Saint Clair, Rex E. (1964). *Doctors Monro: A Medical Saga*. London: Wellcome Historical Medical Library.

Yolton, John (1986). 'Schoolmen, Logic and Philosophy', in Sutherland and Mitchell (1986: 565–91).

Youngson, A. J. (1966). *The Making of Classical Edinburgh*. Edinburgh: Edinburgh Univ. Press.

—— (1973). *After the Forty-Five: The Economic Impact on the Scottish Highlands*. Edinburgh: Edinburgh Univ. Press.

Index

Explanatory Note

Smiths and Douglases from Adam Smith's family appearing in this index are identified by their relationship to him. He is referred to throughout as AS, and his good friend David Hume appears as DH. AS's works are mentioned without naming the author, and are cited by the acronyms and short titles listed in References and Abbreviations in the preliminaries.

The entry for AS is long and subdivided thus: (1) childhood and family background, (2) early socio-economic context, (3) health, (4) education, (5) religion, (6) relations with women, (7) friendships, principal, (8) as rhetorician, (9) as critic, (10) as theorist and system-builder, (11) as historian, (12) as jurist, (13) as moral philosopher, (14) as political economist, (15) as political theorist, (16) as instructor of youth, (17) students, (18) as university administrator, (19) as Commissioner of Customs, (20) finances, (21) journeys and travels, (22) anecdotes, (23) physical appearance, (24) estimates of (a) himself, (b) others, (25) degrees, honours, and soubriquets, (26) sayings and maxims, (27) works, in general, (28) short pieces, (29) *TMS*, (30) *WN*, (31) *EPS*, (32) projected works, (33) missing works, (34) doubtful work, (35) policy documents, (36) students' reports, (37) will.

Anonymous publications are listed alphabetically by short title, and other books are indexed by author. Dates of first editions are given where known. Entries from notes cite page, note number/chapter number.

Abbot, John, Fellow of Balliol, 71
Abercromby, George, Prof. of Public Law at Edinburgh, 151
Aberdeen: AS's property in, 87; grammar school curriculum, 20; universities, 3, 29, 39
Adam: father William (architect), 10, 13, 26–7, 82, 84, 147; sons (architects), Robert, 1, 22, 27–8, 84, 189, 228, 253, 265, 302, 315, James, 228, 421n. 4/2, John, 232; son, William (London merchant), 262, 264–5
Adam, William, MP, 264, 265, 360
Adams, John, 2nd President of USA, 267–8
Adams, John Quincy, 6th President of USA, 390
Adams, Samuel, Clerk to the Massachusetts House of Representatives, 268
Addington, Henry, MP (later Prime Minister), 376
Addison, Joseph, and Steele, Sir Richard, 16, 50, 86, 430n. 1/17; *Spectator*, 15, and *TMS*, 165
Aldrych, Henry: *Artes Logicae Compendium* (1691), 74
d'Alembert, Jean le Rond, 1, 250, 289, 363
Alison, Archibald, the elder, Lord Provost of Edinburgh, 127
America, 252, 255, 258, 261–2, 267, 293–6, 325; and free market theory, xxiv, 250, 281; constitution, xxvii; AS on, 248, 327, concept of an Atlantic union, 268–9, 281
Amerindians: song of death, 169
Anacreon (poet), 96
Anderson, Adam: *Origin of Commerce* (1764), 227
Anderson, James (agricultural improver), 348, 371, 431n. 1/20
Anderson, John, Prof. of Natural Philosophy at Glasgow, 109, 148; records early *LJ*, 121–2

Andrews, Gerard, Fellow of Balliol, 71
Angier, Mr (language teacher at Glasgow Univ.), 372
Anker, Peter and Karsten, 202, 345
Annual Register, 357; Burke's review of *TMS* (1759), 181
Anson, Capt. George, RN, 224
Apollonius of Perga (*c*.250 BC, geometer), 45
Argathelians (supporters of Argyll leadership), 36, 37
d'Argenson, Marquis: *Considérations sur le gouvernement de la France* (1764), 387
Argyll, John Campbell, 2nd Duke of, 4, 5, 36, 82, 210
Argyll, 3rd Duke of, *see under* Ilay, Archibald Campbell
Aristotle: *De anima*, 43, 73–4; *Poetics*, 86; AS contrasts his method with Newton's, 93; First Cause, 102; AS's edition of works, 119; *Metaphysics*, 172; *Politics*, 392
Army, 83, 141–2
Arnauld, Antoine, and Lancelot, Claude: *Grammaire générale et raisonnée* (1703), 15; —— and Nicole, Pierre, *Art of Thinking* (1662), 42
Arniston House, Lothian, 27
Arnot, Archibald (surgeon, AS's guardian), 12, 17
Arthur, Archibald, Prof. of Moral Philosophy at Glasgow, 96–7, 131, 357
d'Artois, Charles Philippe, comte (later Charles X), 388
Atterbury, Francis, Bishop of Rochester, 67
Ayr Bank, 242–3

Bach, Johann Sebastian (composer), 1
Bacon, Mathew: *New Abridgment of the [English] Law* (1739–59, 1766), 147